Deviance

DEVIANCE

Social Constructions and Blurred Boundaries

Leon Anderson

UNIVERSITY OF CALIFORNIA PRESS

University of California Press, one of the most distinguished university presses in the United States, enriches lives around the world by advancing scholarship in the humanities, social sciences, and natural sciences. Its activities are supported by the UC Press Foundation and by philanthropic contributions from individuals and institutions. For more information, visit www.ucpress.edu.

University of California Press
Oakland, California

Library of Congress Cataloging-in-Publication Data
Names: Anderson, Leon, 1950- author.
Title: Deviance : social constructions and blurred boundaries / Leon Anderson.
Description: Oakland, California : University of California Press, [2017] | Includes bibliographical references and index.
Identifiers: LCCN 2017003648 (print) | LCCN 2017006809 (ebook) | ISBN 9780520292376 (pbk. : alk. paper) | ISBN 9780520965935 (ebook)
Subjects: LCSH: Deviant behavior. | Criminal behavior. | Mental illness. | Social interaction. | Social ethics.
Classification: LCC HM811 .A57 2017 (print) | LCC HM811 (ebook) | DDC 302.5/42—dc23
LC record available at https://lccn.loc.gov/2017003648

26 25 24 23 22 21 20 19 18 17
10 9 8 7 6 5 4 3 2 1

Contents

Preface

This book embraces a vision of deviance as a set of social processes involving a wide range of social dynamics and influences, including the multiple influences on human behavior emphasized by many positivistic theories of deviant behavior. The overarching approach of the book, however, is fully grounded in symbolic interactionism. Among the analytic approaches to deviance, only symbolic interactionism (or social construction, as some prefer) moves beyond the limited question of "what causes deviant behavior?" As valuable as the answers to that question can be, focusing solely on the causes of deviant behavior can give the inaccurate impression that what is defined as deviant behavior is always and everywhere the same. But while all human cultures have made distinctions between good and bad acts, what has been considered good or bad has varied widely. Definitions of deviance are far from universal, even within most societies at any given point in time. Focusing exclusively on the causes of deviant behavior misses more of the deviance process than it captures.

THE DEVIANCE PROCESS

Symbolic interactionism has been critical to the study of deviance since the early 1960s, but in the 1970s popular interpretations of interactionist contributions to the study of deviance focused overwhelmingly on labeling theory. The core insight of labeling theory was the idea that being identified and treated as deviant often leads to increased deviant behavior and role engulfment in a deviant identity. The social contexts in which that insight holds remains an important empirical question, but it is only a piece of what symbolic interaction has to offer to the study of deviance. This book provides instructors and students with a broader interactionist/constructionist analysis of the deviance process, focused on (1) activities of moral entrepreneurs who seek to define certain behaviors and statuses as deviant, (2) thoughts and actions of rule-breakers who knowingly or unknowingly violate the rules, (3) social control efforts focused on identifying and sanctioning or treating rule-breakers, and (4) the responses of rule-breakers to the formal and informal social control efforts directed at them.

Moral Entrepreneurship

The term "moral entrepreneur" was created by Howard Becker in his 1963 study of the Federal Bureau of Narcotics campaign to define marijuana as harmful and its users as evil. Scholars have found the concept useful for examining the social construction of what Stanley Cohen (1973) terms "moral panics" related to a wide range of deviance categories. Analysis focused on the creation and dissemination of "atrocity tales" (Bromley et al. 1979) has provided an additional vantage point to assess the narrative similarities underlying the creation of moral panics related to a wide range of deviance categories. Finally, David Snow and colleagues'

(Snow et al. 1986a; Snow and Benford 1988) studies of "framing processes" have provided additional concepts for analyzing deviance that link moral entrepreneurship to social movements, medical discourse, and popular culture.

Rule-Breaking

Rule-breaking has always been a central focus of deviance studies, both from positivistic and interpretive perspectives. While positivistic theories seek explanations for rule-breaking that are external to, or at least largely beyond the control of, those who violate social norms, symbolic interactionism gives voice to the experiences and identities of those who are defined as deviant. Ethnographic research can be valuable in all fields of sociological inquiry, but it is especially critical when seeking to understand the experiences of those who consciously violate social norms. This contribution of symbolic interactionism and ethnographic research is a staple of deviance textbooks. This book continues the tradition of drawing on deviance ethnographies to share "deviants'" voices in their own words. But rather than relying mostly on classic past studies, I have mined the wealth of recent ethnographies for up-to-date descriptions of deviants' experiences and voices.

Social Control

The interactionist/constructionist approach to the deviance process recognizes that normative violations are embedded in broader social contexts that gain particular salience when individuals are identified and treated as rule-breakers. At that point, people who are identified as "deviants" find themselves subject to formal and informal sanctions and treatment. Often, they are pulled into organizational processing through the criminal justice system or medicalized treatment programs. The societal responses to those identified as specific types of deviants change over time, typically in tandem with changing definitions of the causes and consequences of deviant behavior. But both labeling and treating of "deviants" can vary enormously based on race, class, and gender. This book draws upon both quantitative and qualitative research to discuss current societal responses and biases in punishment and treatment of different kinds of deviants.

Stigma Management and Resistance

Those identified as deviant seldom passively accept stigmatizing labels and the punitive treatment directed toward them. Instead, they engage in a range of stigma management activities: passing as nondeviant, seeking to minimize the perception of their deviance, embracing recovery, and even at times turning the alleged deviance into a source of pride and power. The options available for resistance and stigma management vary across deviance categories and over time, frequently with race, class, and gender differences.

The deviance process is multifaceted and seldom static for long. What was acceptable and/or legal at one point in time (regular opiate use or prostitution) becomes unacceptable and illegal. What was illegal (use of contraceptives) or considered mental illness (homosexuality) becomes widely accepted. As of this writing, "pot" is (or soon will be) legally sold for recreational use in eight states, while in many adjacent states and at the federal level selling marijuana is a felony. Prison populations soar, leading even conservative politicians to question mandatory sentencing practices. And the Internet provides venues for both moral entrepreneurship and resistance. The symbolic interactionist/constructionist perspective outlined above provides an analytic framework for understanding deviance as a continually recursive process.

ORGANIZATION

This book is divided into four sections. Section 1 introduces students to the field of deviance studies, comparing empirical sociological study of deviance to popular cultural conceptions of deviant behavior as rooted in evil, illness, or relativistic cultural differences. Chapter 2 highlights sociology's commitment to empirical research, with particular emphasis on the value of ethnographic research for studying deviance. Chapter 3 examines positivistic theories of deviant behavior and Chapter 4 presents the symbolic interactionist perspective that will be used in each of the substantive chapters. The following three sections of the book focus on specific common deviance categories.

Section 2 provides an analysis of several kinds of criminal deviance that involve unwilling victims: murder, rape, street-level property crime, and white-collar crime. These forms of deviance (or at least the first three) represent types of deviance characterized by high public consensus and formal legal sanctions. Virtually all societies consider certain kinds of killing, sexual coercion, and property crime as reprehensible acts. And yet, what counts as murder, rape, or robbery varies significantly from one culture to another and even within the United States over time.

Section 3 examines three types of what is often termed "lifestyle deviance." These deviance categories are characterized by significantly less public consensus concerning their harmfulness to individuals and society as well as greatly increased subcultural proliferation. Participants often justify these kinds of deviance by assertions of legitimate lifestyle choice—of individual rights and the lack of a victim—claims that moral entrepreneurs strongly contest.

Section 4 examines a set of deviance categories often referred to as "status deviance." People in these categories are considered deviant by virtue of negatively evaluated and largely involuntary statuses, conditions, or identities that they have (e.g., illnesses, physical defects, alternative sexual orientations and gender identities, etc.). While status deviance categories involve the same social processes as other deviance categories, they exhibit more deviant identity transformation and collective action associated with positive conceptions of those associated with the deviance category.

The chapters in Sections 2 through 4 follow a uniform organization in order to provide students with consistency across chapters and reinforcement of key concepts and issues.

PEDAGOGICAL FEATURES

Three pedagogical features of this book warrant brief discussion. First, each chapter includes two *Blurred Boundary* sections, one at the start of the chapter and the other at chapter end. The term Blurred Boundaries is used throughout this book to refer to (1) the often hazy distinctions between what is considered moral versus immoral, or good as opposed to bad, (2) the confusion that results from conflicting and often overlapping explanations that are given to explain why people engage in deviant behavior, and (3) the challenges of developing social policies to address social harm while respecting human rights. The Blurred Boundaries theme is integrated throughout the text, challenging students to move beyond black-and-white, knee-jerk reactions and to engage in thoughtful assessments of deviance categories and social policies.

Second, each chapter includes an optional mini-research project titled *Pushing Your Boundaries* that asks students to collect and/or briefly analyze some "data" that are relevant to specific course topics. These assignments, which have been field-tested in several classes, help students see connections between the course and the world beyond the classroom and reinforce the importance of empirical research.

Third, all chapters (except the introduction) include a short *Claims-Maker Profile* of an individual (or couple) who has been a notable advocate for particular claims—either in defining deviance or responding to it. Chapters in the first section of the book profile exemplary deviance scholars, while chapters in the rest of the book profile people who have played significant roles in social policy or social action related to the chapter's topic. The profiles connect personal faces and memorable stories to chapter topics, illustrating the importance of engaged social action.

SUPPLEMENTAL MATERIALS

The *Instructor's Manual* includes chapter outlines; Power Point lectures; a test bank with essay, short-answer, and multiple-choice questions; and suggested video and Internet resources for each chapter. The *Instructor's Manual* also provides suggested student Blackboard/WebCT discussion group topics and exercises for instructors who want to use web-based pedagogy.

ACKNOWLEDGMENTS

This book has been a long time in coming. I want to thank Chris Caldeira and Thomas Vander Ven for their early enthusiasm and support for the project. Seth Dobrin and Nic Albert at the University of California Press have given me critical guidance for bringing the book to completion. Matthew Austin provided teaching assistance the first time I taught the course using these materials at Ohio University. Stephen Van Geem at Utah State University took the plunge early and taught with previous versions of the manuscript, providing feedback along the way. Kenny Chumbley provided excellent support with graphics and permissions. Over a dozen anonymous reviewers have read versions of the manuscript and given sage advice on how it could be improved. My gratitude to you all.

This project has been bookended by a sabbatical at Ohio University where I began the book and a sabbatical at Utah State University where I have completed it.

I want to thank my wife, Kate, especially, for her consistent encouragement and for never losing faith in the project—or my ability to pull it off.

Finally, this textbook is only possible because countless scholars in the social sciences and humanities have found the interactionist/constructionist approach valuable in their research. I am indebted to all whose work I draw upon. This is a collective effort and I hope I have done your work close to the justice it deserves.

SECTION 1

THEORIES AND METHODS IN DEVIANCE STUDIES

CHAPTER

1 Views of Deviance

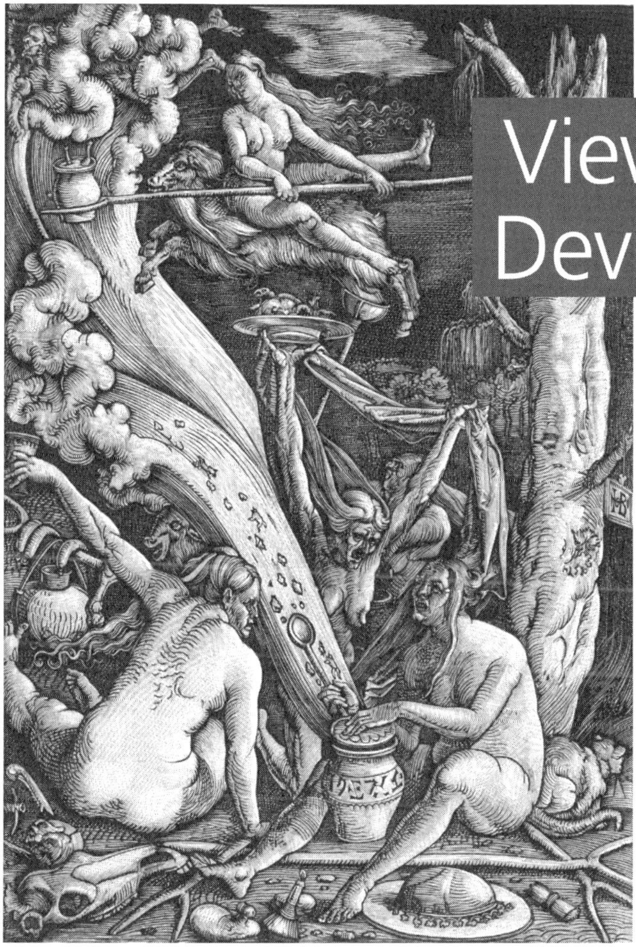

Witches' Sabbath, woodcut by German artist Hans Baldung "Grien" (1510, Ivy Close Images/Alamy Stock Photo).

CONTENTS

LEARNING OBJECTIVES

After reading this chapter, you will be able to:

- Define deviance in sociological terms
- Recognize "blurred boundaries" as a key feature of deviance
- Describe three "popular" explanations of deviance
- Explain the sociological approach to studying deviance
- Summarize the importance of a sociological understanding of deviance

INTRODUCTION

Virtually all humans make distinctions between right and wrong, good and bad, normal and weird. It is hard to imagine that we could be human—or survive as a species—without making such distinctions. The sociology of *deviance* is devoted to studying the "bad," "wrong," and "weird" side of these divisions: what people consider immoral, criminal, strange, and disgusting. Deviance includes the broadest possible scope of such activities—not just criminal acts, but also any actions, thoughts, feelings, or social statuses that members of a social group judge to be a violation of their values or rules. This book provides a sociological understanding of deviance, as well as examines many of the major categories of deviance in contemporary American society.

Few things in life touch such sensitive nerves as seeing or hearing about things we consider deviant. Our blood rises, our tempers flare, we are flooded with disgust, and we often find ourselves struggling to understand how anyone could do something so immoral or obscene. Even so, unless we have lived the most sheltered of lives, we also recognize that not everyone sees things the way we do. Some people approve of behaviors that we personally find reprehensible, and some acts that we personally enjoy or participate in may be considered reprehensible by others. Even when almost all of us agree that someone is deviant or has engaged in deviant behavior, we may find ourselves disagreeing about the reasons for their deviance. We may believe the person is evil, sick, inconsiderate, or just does not know better than to behave that way.

One of the key features of deviance is its *blurred boundaries*, the often hazy distinctions between what is considered good or bad, right or wrong, and the confusion that we face when we try to explain why. We can start our journey with a few examples that give a sense of the range of things that fall under the deviance umbrella. At first blush, each of the following cases is likely to seem crystal clear as a case of deviance. However, as we probe deeper, a disquieting realization that the boundaries that separate these acts and conditions from what some may consider acceptable becomes cloudier. Further, each case may be explained in radically different ways.

BLURRED BOUNDARIES: THE DRAMA OF DEVIANCE

First, consider the case of calculated, cold-blooded murder as related by a professional "hit man" explaining his "craft" compared to murders that occur in the heat of the moment. "There are people who will go ape for one minute and shoot," he says, "but there are very few people who are capable of thinking about, planning, and then doing it." He continues:

> There are three things you need to kill a man: the gun, the bullets, and the balls. A lot of people will point a gun at you, but they haven't got the courage to pull the trigger. It's as simple as that. It may be that some are born with "heart," while others acquire it. But you can't let feelings get in the way. Take my last hit: The victim began to beg. He went so far as to tell us where he had stashed his money. Finally, he realized there was absolutely nothing he could do. He sat there quietly. Then, he started crying. I didn't feel a thing for him.
>
> —Joey (1973 p.56)

The second case involves a form of child sex abuse that, hidden for decades, has become well documented in recent years: sexual relations between some Catholic priests and children, as illustrated by one young man's experience:

> Ed's abuse began as a condition of absolution. The youth confessed to impure thoughts and to the sin of pride. Father Terrence directed him to learn self-control. The lesson was simple, Ed alleges: the priest would masturbate him, or lie on top of him rubbing their groins together, but would stop just shy of Ed's ejaculation. "Desensitization," Father Terrance called this. . .Ed remembers Father Terrance telling him, "You are special. You are pleasing to God. But you have this corruptible side you must learn to control."
>
> —Burkett and Bruni (1993, p.76)

Our third case comes from the world of professional baseball. During the 1998 season, a great sports rivalry unfolded as the Saint Louis Cardinals' Mark McGwire raced with the Chicago Cubs' Sammy Sosa to break the record for most home runs in a single season. Baseball audiences were electrified as they watched Sosa and McGwire exchange the lead. As they closed in on the new record, both players' accomplishments were undermined by revelations that they were using performance-enhancing drugs:

> In late August 1998, Steve Wilstein, an Associated Press reporter, peered inside McGwire's locker and noticed a bottle of androstenedione, a pill that produced male hormone for the intended purpose of building muscle mass. Andro, as it was called, was a dietary supplement whose creation was designed to mimic a steroid. Confronted about the substance, McGwire admitted to using it. The news swept baseball like a prairie fire. Suddenly the home run chase was embroiled in scandal. The *New York Times* blared: "The News is Out: Popeye is Spiking His Spinach."
>
> —Bryant (2005, p.134)

While these examples of deviance involve illegal or illicit actions, the field of deviance also includes a variety of socially unacceptable or stigmatized conditions or statuses. One commonly stigmatized condition in American culture is obesity. While many of us may feel that it is unfair to look down on those who are considered "fat," we are all aware of the self-consciousness that many heavy people feel and of shameful behaviors toward them, such as that captured in the following young woman's experience:

> I was fat on this Saturday. I know how fat. I would let a torturer use pliers to pull teeth from the tender gums in the back of my head before I would say what I weigh

> when I'm fat. What I weigh seems like a secret that must be hid carefully. But what happened that Saturday was that a white Chrysler convertible, top down, sped south, toward me. Four boys were in the convertible, college boys is what they looked like. . .A grin spread across the face of the boy in the front passenger seat and I knew what was coming. "Oink, oink, oink," he squealed. His companions joined him, "Oink, oink, oink." And a two-fingered high-pitched whistle and "Sooey, sooey, pig!" Then they were gone in the stream of traffic and I looked straight ahead and just kept walking. This was not the first time in my life that someone had called out to me, "Sooey, sooey, pig." I was used to being called names.
>
> —Moore (2005, p.32)

Each of these examples illustrates part of the drama of deviance. Why do people engage in behaviors that are disapproved of and often punished? And why do they allow themselves to have a status that is widely looked down upon? Before we look at deviance from a sociological perspective, it is useful to consider some of the common ways deviance has been explained in human societies. Three popular explanations in particular provide useful comparisons. We can refer to these explanations of deviance as "the demonic," "the psychotic," and "the exotic."

Each of these views points to a different cause of deviant behavior. The demonic view argues that "the devil made him do it." The psychotic view proposes, "She did it because she was crazy." And the exotic view explains, "That kind of thing is okay where they come from."

How is it possible for things that we see as so clearly bad to be viewed in such different ways? This is one of the central questions of deviance at the blurred boundaries.

DEVIANCE AS DEMONIC

In the Bible, Eve (and then Adam) committed the first act of transgression against God by eating fruit from the tree of the knowledge of good and evil. Here, early in Jewish and Christian scriptures, we see an example of perhaps the oldest explanation for deviance. Why did Eve deviate from the sacred rule of God? She did so because a demon, Satan in the form of a serpent, tempted her. Deviance, according to this view, is caused by *demonic* possession.

While other societies may have much different stories of creation and images of God or gods, many societies have held beliefs that evil acts and objectionable conditions are caused by malevolent, evil forces. Thus we find Loki, the Norse god of guile and deception; Eris, the Greek goddess of strife; and Native American myths of Trickster Coyote who seduced women—and men—and caused general discord as he conned his way across the countryside. Indeed, belief in evil spirits has been remarkably widespread. Some of the earliest known writings, those of Sumerian culture nearly 6,000 years ago, refer to demons called *gid-dim*—demons believed to cause mental problems and disordered behavior. Zoroastrianism (a Middle Eastern religion in the millennium before the Christian era) proclaimed that the evil god, Angra Mainyu, ensnared humans in sinful lust through his witchcraft. And numerous more localized folk beliefs have attributed individuals' bad and unusual behaviors to becoming possessed by malevolent spirits that inhabited the woodlands, marshes, and animals in their worlds.

The most extreme beliefs in demonic possession occurred in Europe in the Middle Ages, where from the early decades of the fifteenth century through the 1650s, an estimated 200,000 to half a million people, most of them women, were burned at the stake, hung, or otherwise executed for being witches (Goode and Ben-Yehuda 2009, p.144). In 1487, two Dominican priests published what was to become the key text for witch hunting for the next two centuries. Their book, *Malleus Maleficarum* ("The Witch's Hammer"), claimed that Europe was experiencing an epidemic of women conspiring with Satan against God. When women lost their virginity, the priests argued, they became obsessed with sexual desires, thus making it easy for the Devil, in the form of an incubus (a demon in human form), to seduce them. Once seduced by Satan, women became witches and turned to sorcery (rituals to cause supernatural effects) and heresy—devil worshipping and antireligious practices such as the "Black Sabbath" or inverted Mass (portrayed in the sixteenth-century wood engraving at the start of this chapter, titled *Witches' Sabbath*, by German artist Hans Baldung Grien). In the American colonies, on a smaller scale, the Salem Witch Trials of 1692 dramatically played out the belief in the demonic possession of witches, culminating in the imprisonment of nearly 200 Salem residents and the hanging of 20 of them.

Beliefs about the paths by which people become possessed by demons vary from culture to culture. In some, individuals who are out after dark are thought to fall prey to evil-spirited night animals such as owls or cats. In Europe during the Middle Ages, as we have seen, women were believed to be sexually seduced into conspiring with the devil. In the early twentieth century in the United States, popular Protestant evangelist Billy Sunday preached that men, not women, were the most vulnerable to the devil's wiles, and that liquor, not sex, was the means by which he ensnared them. In his famous sermon, "The Devil's Boomerangs," Sunday proclaimed:

> Listen! Seventy-five per cent of our idiots come from intemperate parents, 80 per cent of the paupers, 82 per cent of the crime is committed by men under the influence of liquor, 90 per cent of the adult criminals are whiskey made. The saloon is the sum of all villainies. It is worse than war or pestilence. It is the crime of crimes. It is parent of crimes and the mother of sins. It is the appalling source of misery and crime in the land and the principal cause of crime. The devil doesn't let a man stop to think what he is doing, that in every added indulgence in a drink he grows weaker.
>
> —Sunday (1920)

As we will see later, Billy Sunday's sermon's on "demon rum" struck a responsive chord in the era leading to Prohibition, winning him many followers—as well as many enemies. But even many who did not accept Sunday's message were enthralled by his preaching style—a dramatic and compelling fight with the devil that has yet to be matched by even the most dramatic televangelists.

It is easy, perhaps, for most of us to discount beliefs in demonic causes of deviance when they come from cultures far from our own. In fact, many Americans today discount belief in demons and Satanic forces entirely, preferring more secular explanations for deviance. Of course, many other Americans continue to believe that the devil is a real force in the world today. Whatever your personal beliefs, it is clear to see how demonic explanations could provide one kind of answer to the question of why people engage in deviance. Consider each of the cases with which we started the chapter.

The professional hit man's willingness to kill for money, his affiliation with an underworld of crime and corruption, and his stone cold heart as he pulls the trigger to end another person's life all seem to locate him squarely in the devil's dominion. Similarly, a priest who takes advantage of his sacred authority to trick a child into sexually gratifying him can be seen as having fallen prey to the devil's "temptations of the flesh." In comparison to the hit man and the pedophile priest, a professional athlete's willingness to cheat by using illicit performance-enhancing drugs may seem relatively mild. But greed for fame and personal gain has long been associated with the devil. One of the most enduring legends in American folk culture tells of the great blues singer, Robert Johnson, selling his soul to the Devil in exchange for a superb ability to play guitar. The parallel to Mark McGwire's and Sammy Sosa's use of illicit drugs to excel in professional baseball is obvious.

Finally, we have the case of the overweight young woman. At first glance, it might seem difficult to conceive of her deviance as inspired by demonic forces. And yet, gluttony, or the sin of overindulgence, was considered one of the seven cardinal, or deadly, sins of early Christianity. Like sexual desire and greed, it was one of Satan's temptations, to be resisted by those seeking God's salvation. In his letters to the Philippians, Paul counsels against the sin of overeating, writing of those who overindulge that "their destiny is destruction, their god is their stomach, and their glory is in their shame" (Philippians 3:19). Even today, the language of sin and temptation permeates our talk about food, as "sinfully delicious" and "temptingly tasty." And, as we will see later in this book, "fat" people are often stereotyped as weak willed and lacking moral discipline.

DEVIANCE AS PSYCHOTIC

The belief that evil forces or demons cause deviance has persisted over thousands of years, making it the longest-lasting explanation of deviance in human history. But today, in America, evil is a less pervasive explanation of deviance than in the past. In the US and other modern western cultures, the most common explanation for many forms of deviance is illness—specifically, mental illness of one kind or another. In popular terms (as opposed to precise medical definitions), we can refer to this view of deviance as *psychotic*.

Medical explanations for objectionable behaviors and conditions are not new, but they expanded enormously in their influence during the twentieth century, in tandem with the rise of medical science in general, and psychiatry in particular. Psychology courses titled "Abnormal Psychology" exemplify this kind of explanation. Broadly speaking, abnormal psychology scholars explain mental disorders and deviance as caused by either biological defects or problematic psychological development. Behavioral genetics, for instance, is widely discussed among psychologists and psychiatrists as a cause of "such diverse disorders as schizophrenia, depression, criminality, and mental retardation" (Sarason and Sarason 2005, p.53). Alternatively, psychological theories of abnormality may focus on problematic psychological development resulting from traumatic experiences or unresolved psychological conflicts. In each of these explanations, whether due to defective genetics or unhealthy psychological development, deviant behavior is a sign of sickness.

The American Psychiatric Association's (APA) diagnostic manual provides the most comprehensive list of mental and behavioral disorders in the United States. According to the APA, there are hundreds of mental illnesses, ranging from classic cognitive and emotional disorders such as schizophrenia and depression to illnesses revealed primarily in behavior, such as drug addiction, paraphilias (abnormal sexual attraction), and childhood conduct disorders. Many behaviors that had previously been classified as "sin" came to be defined and treated as illnesses during the twentieth century. This shift in explaining deviant behaviors has been so common that sociologists have given it a name: the *medicalization of deviance* (Conrad and Schneider 1992).

But the notion of deviance being caused by mental illness is not just a medical phenomenon. It also shows up regularly in everyday language, particularly when we refer to those who do objectionable things as "psycho," "sick," or "perverted." The idea that mental illness causes deviance is also a staple of popular culture and the American movie industry, reflected time and again in psychological horror movies. In *Psycho* (1960), the most famous psychological thriller of all time, we witness two grisly murders in an out-of-the-way motel, and watch with horror as the murderer is revealed to be the deranged young hotel proprietor who lives with a split personality—half his own and half that of his dead mother, who he murdered and has preserved in the motel basement. Many more recent movies play on similar themes of mental illness causing violent and bizarre behavior. The movie, *One Hour Photo* (2002), for instance, portrays the disturbing life of Sy Parrish, a desperately lonely photo technician (played by Robin Williams) at a one-hour photo service. Sy becomes obsessed with a family that brings their photos to him to develop. As the story unfolds, Sy stalks the father, who is having an affair, and ultimately forces him to pose with his illicit lover for pornographic photos. In the movie's final scene, as Sy is being interrogated by the police who have arrested him, he reveals that his father made him do "sick, disgusting things that no kid should ever have to do." The cause of his obsessive behavior is thus traced back to childhood trauma.

As the foregoing discussion shows, the notion that deviant individuals are psychologically sick is common in psychiatric medicine and in popular culture. Each of the examples of deviance at the beginning of this chapter could be explained as caused by psychological sickness. The mafia hit man who claims to feel nothing for those he murders might well be explained as exhibiting Antisocial Personality Disorder, an illness characterized by a pervasive pattern of disregard for and violation of the rights of others. Similarly, the sexually abusive priest's behavior can be explained psychiatrically as pedophilia, a sexual disorder involving attraction primarily or exclusively to prepubescent children. And while steroids are clearly used by athletes in hopes of improving athletic performance, the National Institute of Drug Abuse reports that steroids are often used by male—and female—body builders who suffer from a behavioral syndrome called body dysmorphic disorder, which causes them to have a distorted image of their bodies. Finally, the overweight young woman quoted at the start of this chapter might well be considered a victim of Binge Eating Disorder, a mental illness characterized by recurrent and obsessive binge eating without purging (itself a symptom of another deviant eating pattern called bulimia).

DEVIANCE AS EXOTIC

Where the two preceding popular explanations for deviance are centered on the deviant individual—say, a young woman with an eating disorder or a priest misled by Satan—the final popular explanation of deviance looks at the broader cultural environment in which deviance occurs. This explanation argues that different cultures often have very dissimilar beliefs regarding right and wrong, normal and weird, and that much of deviance is simply a matter of cultural variation. Just as plants that seem exotic to us grow in natural environments different from our own, so do human behaviors that seem exotic to us develop in social environments that are distant from ours.

The view of deviance as *exotic* is cosmopolitan in its scope, looking far beyond our own localized experiences to acknowledge and appreciate the diversity of human behavior across the globe. The person who did the most to popularize this explanation was one of the great world travelers of all time: Robert Ripley, the founder of "Ripley's Believe It or Not!" For over 30 years, Ripley traveled the world in search of mind-boggling oddities to bring to readers of his syndicated comic panel, which continues to run in newspapers even today. While some of his "discoveries" were biological oddities, like two-headed animals and human "giants," many of the tales that Ripley reported in his illustrated newspaper panels were stories of unusual human customs from distant parts of the world. One of the most famous human rituals that Ripley reported was the "headshrinking" practices once common among some indigenous Ecuadorians. As the Ripley's website explains:

> The practice of shrinking heads was once common amongst the Jivaro Indians of Ecuador. It was a ritual that had been handed down through generations. The heads of slain warriors were valued as trophies or symbols of bravery. When a fighter killed his enemy, the victim's head was removed. The skin was then peeled away from the skull and hot stones and sand were poured into the cavity. The head was sewn shut and boiled in herbs until it had shrunk to the size of a fist.
>
> —Ripley's (2006)

Today, more than 60 years after Ripley's death, Ripley Entertainment, Inc. continues to publish their famous cartoons, along with books, blogs, and videos. In its nearly 30 museums worldwide, aptly dubbed "odditoriums," it offers visitors a tour through a wealth of exotic oddities, including many that most of us would classify as deviance. If you visit the Ripley's Odditorium in Orlando, for instance, you will see displays that illustrate various forms of ritual cannibalism around the world and such striking body modification practices as Padaung women in Burma who used brass rings to elongate their necks and natives from the Chad in Africa who inserted wooden plates in their lips to stretch them to as much as eight inches in diameter.

In addition to illustrating the notion of deviance as exotic, the tremendous success of Ripley's *Believe It or Not!* demonstrates how our interests are often piqued by the bizarre and deviant. Indeed, travelers' tales of strange doings in distant lands—from Marco Polo's account of "the Orient" to modern anthropologists' reports on "primitive societies"—have long fascinated listeners. Even *National Geographic*, a source that many of us turn to for nonsensationalized reporting from around the world, has found an audience for its television series *Taboo*, which recounts stories of deviations in human behavior in different cultures around the globe.

The notion of deviance as exotic challenges our belief that we can easily distinguish good from bad or normal from strange. While it does not necessarily challenge the correctness of our beliefs regarding right and wrong in our own culture, it clearly suggests that beliefs regarding what is appropriate can only be made within a specific cultural context. Still, it is important to recognize that the exotic behaviors reported by Ripley and *National Geographic* are considered normal, not deviant, within their own cultures—although they were often misunderstood by early travelers. According to Ripley, it simply was not deviant for the Jivaro Indians of Ecuador to engage in activities that we have come to describe as "headshrinking." Nor was it deviant for members of

Yanomamo society in Brazil to eat parts of their deceased relatives' bodies. On the other hand, serial killer Jeffrey Dahmer did violate the norms of American culture and engaged in deviant behavior when he killed, dismembered, and at times ate parts of his victims.

As the preceding examples illustrate, the view of deviance as exotic behavior sensitizes us to the variability of social norms, illustrating that what is deviant in one context may not be in another. This is a valuable insight, revealing that our ways of looking at things are not the only ways of looking at things. Such an approach can be taken in regard to the cases of deviance with which we started the chapter—arguing, that is, that behaviors and conditions similar to them have been viewed as acceptable and appropriate in cultures other than our own. So, for instance, while we look with disgust and horror at the mafia hit man's cold-blooded killing, in other societies professional classes of killers—like the Samurai in the Tokugawa period in Japan—were revered as powerful and honorable men (Ikegami 1995). Similarly, while most Americans strongly disapprove of adult males engaging in sex with adolescent boys, in classical Greek culture homoerotic activities between men and boys were accepted as part of older males' affection for the young men they were responsible for educating and introducing to political life (Herdt 1997, p.69). Nor is it difficult to find examples of cultures in which performance-enhancing drugs have been widely accepted. The leaves of the coca plant (from which cocaine is derived) have long been used by llama herders on the high plateaus of the Andes mountains to increase their strength, endurance, and resistance to the cold (Plowman 1986). And amphetamines were widely used to enhance European and Japanese soldiers' alertness and performance in World War II, as illustrated by the headline of a major British newspaper in 1941 that proclaimed, "Methedrine Wins the Battle of London" (Escohotado 1999, p.93). Finally, many heavier women whose bodies are stigmatized in America today would have been viewed as highly sensual and beautiful in seventeenth-century Holland where the attraction of full-figured voluptuous women was provocatively captured in the paintings of Peter Paul Rubens.

DEVIANCE AS SYMBOLIC INTERACTION: A SOCIOLOGICAL APPROACH

Each of the preceding explanations for deviance provides a way of looking at the world and explaining what seems otherwise inexplicable: why people act in ways that violate our sense of right and wrong. This book provides a fourth kind of approach: a sociological view of deviance.

Sociology is the study of human societies and social interactions. It is directed toward gaining a better understanding of the organizational patterns and social processes through which people enact social life and create and sustain societies. For the moment, we can consider two basic characteristics of the sociological approach, especially as compared to the preceding explanations of deviance. First, sociology is focused on human *social acts*. Second, sociologists seek to test and refine their understanding of social life through close *examination of observable human behaviors*.

Social Acts

The sociological focus on social acts refers to all human actions that take others' behaviors, feelings, and ideas into account and are influenced by them. Social acts are the building blocks of society, linking individuals with other individuals and with social groups. Social institutions, from families to schools to international corporations, are created through human beings fitting their behaviors together with other people. This is not to suggest that all social acts are cooperative or consensual—far from it. The use of force, trickery, and violence is as much social acts (i.e., needing to take into account others' behaviors) as are acts of love, compassion, and sharing. A burglar sneaking into a home while the family sleeps must be closely attuned to the potential behaviors of his victims. Social acts cover a wide range of human behavior, from a quick greeting between two people passing on the sidewalk to a courtroom trial, and even your reading of this book. Sociologists seek to understand different kinds of social acts, how they are organized, and what their consequences are for individuals, social groups, and societies. In terms of understanding deviance, a focus on social acts directs us toward (1) the ways in which people come to define certain behaviors or conditions as deviant, (2) the processes through which some individuals are identified and treated as deviants, and (3) the ways in which "deviant" individuals and groups respond to their treatment.

When we look at deviance from a sociological angle, we can see important aspects of human behavior that are not seen as clearly (if at all) by the other kinds of explanations we have discussed. At the same time, a sociological understanding of deviance does not address some of the central issues focused on by these other explanations. The difference between sociological and demonic explanations of deviance is obvious. From the demonic perspective, deviance is caused by the evil influence of supernatural beings. While the demonic view may call for a social response to deviants (e.g., punishing them or praying for them), deviance itself is not, in essence, seen as a matter of social interaction. The sociological perspective, on the other hand, does not address the "reality" of spiritual beliefs that are central to a demonic explanation of deviance. Sociology certainly considers the important influence of religions in human societies, but as a social science it does not presume to address whether or not any particular set of religious beliefs are justified.

The sociological approach to deviance can also be distinguished from the view of deviance as psychotic. From the psychotic perspective, deviance is a matter of individual sickness, caused by such things as defective chromosomes and traumatic psychological experiences. The focus on biological aspects of deviant behavior in the field of abnormal psychology (discussed more in Chapter 3) clearly directs attention away from the social acts that interest sociologists. Social developmental theories of abnormal behavior, on the other hand, at times overlap with the sociological approach to deviance since they focus on the impact of various kinds of problematic social interaction (e.g., unresolved familial conflicts or social trauma). But insofar as a psychotic view locates deviance as a problem within the individual, attention is directed toward the individual's psychological experience and away from social interaction.

The exotic view of deviance seems at first glance to share more similarity with a sociological approach to deviance than the other two kinds of explanations. It is true that the view of deviance as exotic acknowledges the role of culture in defining behaviors and conditions as deviant. But few treatments of deviance as exotic attempt to provide any significant analysis of how and why social acts we treat as deviant in our society are considered normal and honorable in other cultures. Robert Ripley, for instance, built his reputation and fortune by condensing the exotic practices of other peoples into comic strip *Believe It or Not!* factoids that reported the existence of strange behaviors, but never explained them in any detail. In contrast, the goal of sociology is not simply to describe deviance, but also to provide an explanation of the social processes through which deviance is constructed.

Focus on Observable Behavior

The way in which sociologists develop their explanations of deviance (as well as other kinds of social acts) also distinguishes the sociological approach. Sociological theories are developed and refined (or rejected) through a close *examination of observable human behavior.* In the next chapter, we will consider the challenges and techniques of sociological research, but for the moment it is sufficient to consider simply the sociological commitment to evaluating ideas about human behavior by looking closely at observable human acts. Like other sciences (both natural sciences and behavioral sciences), sociology is based on the belief that rigorous examination of observable phenomena (in this case, human acts and artifacts) can provide insights that help us understand patterns of activity in the world around us. As a mode of inquiry, sociology emphasizes the tentativeness of our understandings of social life and the importance of challenging our beliefs about how people act by comparing those beliefs with observable behavior. This emphasis on trying to observe things that could contradict or challenge our beliefs clearly distinguishes a sociological approach from a religious approach to deviance. Religious traditions encourage faith as "the assurance of [things] hoped for, the conviction of things not seen" (New American Standard Bible, Hebrews 1:1). In contrast, sociology is limited to observable human behaviors—people's talk, actions, interactions, and artifacts.

The limitation of sociology is also one of its greatest strengths because these observations, or *empirical data*, provide sociologists with a way to test and refine their ideas. To understand why this is a strength, consider for a moment our common everyday approach to life. We live our daily lives with a multitude of assumptions about how the world works. We take it for granted that a grocery store clerk will sell us what we take to the checkout stand, that our doctors will give us good health advice, and that our friends will not rob us. We seldom question these assumptions because they "work," which is to say that they enable us to achieve our goals, from taking care of our physical needs to maintaining harmonious relationships with our families and friends. Typically, the only time we question our assumptions is when they no longer help us achieve our goals. So, for instance, we are likely to question our assumptions about a romantic partner when he or she consistently fails to return our phone calls. In such circumstances, we often seek out new information that can help us modify our assumptions—say, to confirm that our romantic partner has unexpectedly had to leave town for an emergency or that they have lost interest in us. Guided by new information, our new assumptions are likely to enable us to better achieve, or revise, our goals.

In our daily lives, we would find it extremely hard to live if we continuously questioned our assumptions, but a skeptical attitude and a focus on empirical data have big advantages for developing sociological theories. By comparing our ideas about social life with the actual behavior of human beings, sociologists are able to better comprehend whether or not their beliefs and assumptions accurately represent the social acts that they seek to understand. Further, as social scientists share and compare their observations to those of other scholars, they are able to work together to deepen our knowledge of social life. This book is an attempt to organize and present a sociological understanding of deviance that is based on observations by hundreds of sociologists across a diverse range of deviant topics.

However, just because sociologists focus on observable behavior does not mean that they all see exactly the same things or that they all agree on why people act in the ways they do. Different fundamental beliefs about the nature of social life and human behavior direct attention to different aspects of our complex and multifaceted social world. Various sociological theories or paradigms provide powerful insights into a certain range of social acts (e.g., social class conflicts, or the integrative functions of social structures), but they often fail to acknowledge other social dynamics and processes.

Symbolic Interaction

Among *sociological paradigms*, the theoretical perspective of *symbolic interaction* stands out as especially multifaceted in its approach to human behavior. Symbolic interaction offers both an analytic perspective on social life and guidelines for how best to study it. It is also the sociological paradigm that is drawn upon most consistently in this book. You will learn much more about symbolic interaction in the following chapters, but for now it will be sufficient to understand a few of the basic principles. Perhaps the most succinct and widely quoted explanation of symbolic interaction's principles was provided by one of its most important founders, Herbert Blumer, who laid out three basic premises of this perspective:

> The first premise is that human beings act toward things on the basis of the meanings those things have for them. . .The second premise is that the meaning of such things is derived from, or arises out of, the social interaction that one has with one's fellows. The third premise is that these meanings are handled in, and modified through, an interpretive process used by the person in dealing with the things he [or she] encounters.
>
> —Blumer (1969, p.2)

Blumer's three premises have major implications for understanding social life in general, and certainly for explaining deviance. To begin with, Blumer argues that in order to understand human behavior we must know how people define things. Deviance, according to this view, does not inhere in specific kinds of behaviors, but in the meanings that people attach to those behaviors. Second, our understanding of the meanings of things develops through social interaction. Even the languages that we use to think about our world and communicate with others are learned through social interaction. While humans clearly have a unique biological ability to use symbols in complex ways, children who are deprived of social interaction fail to develop that ability in anything more than rudimentary ways.

A further important implication of Blumer's premises is that people are active interpreters and responders to the world around them. We do not blindly and robotically react to stimuli in our environments. Rather, we endeavor to make sense of occurrences and respond to them according to the meaning we attach to them. Think back to the example of the romantic partner who does not return your phone call. Your response to their silence will depend on how you define it. If you know that they have a seriously ill relative, you are likely to feel concern for them and leave a comforting message on their phone. On the other hand, if you have worries that they have been dating someone else behind your back, your next phone message—if you even leave another one—may well be antagonistic and condemning. In each case, the stimulus (their failure to return your call) is the same, while your interpretation of it makes all the difference for your response.

Finally, Blumer's basic principles of symbolic interaction clearly suggest that the most valuable research for sociologists will be closely attuned to the meanings people give to things and the processes through which those meanings are created and sustained in human interaction. The importance of this point for the study of deviance is enormous since deviance exists at the intersection of conflicting beliefs regarding right and wrong, good and bad, acceptable and reprehensible. In order to understand deviance, we must grasp the meanings that guide the actions of and interactions among different people, including, most prominently, (1) those who seek to ban, punish, or otherwise control deviance and (2) those who become identified and treated as deviant. Among the research methods used by sociologists, two are particularly well suited for the task of investigating meaning: participant-observation and in-depth interviews. Taken together, these two methods are often referred to as *ethnography*, or the detailed description of people acting and interacting in social worlds.

This book is designed to provide you with an analysis of deviance that is grounded in symbolic interactionist sociology and ethnography. Given our emphasis on symbolic interactionism, we will focus on understanding the *social constructions*, or meanings, that people create to define what is deviant and what should be done about it. We will examine in close detail the roles of social groups and social selves in creating the meanings of deviance, both for those who are identified as deviants and for those who label them. In the process, we will come to see that the line between moral and immoral behavior is much more of a blurred boundary—a hazy and shifting distinction—than we often recognize in our daily lives. This does not mean that the boundaries between good and bad are any less important—far from it. Humans would not be fully human without a sense of right and wrong. But the boundaries of deviance and morality are fluid, shifting, and at times confusing. In order to understand deviance, it is not enough to simply feel confident in our own values, expectations, and behaviors. We must find ways to understand the values, expectations, and behavior of others as well.

THE SOCIOLOGICAL PROMISE

Today, topics related to deviance pervade public debates and private lives. Indeed, as Adler and Adler (2006, p.129) have observed:

> The field of deviance offers unparalleled insight into society, particularly in current times. Deviance thrives in America, from the underbelly of hidden life worlds to the new frontiers of discovery and social change. There can be no mistake that the empirical world around us is filled with deviance and deviance makers. We live in what we might call a "deviance society."

The sheer pervasiveness of deviance in our society offers one good reason to take a course on it. Issues related to deviance are likely to touch many aspects of your life in the years ahead. At the personal level, you and/or family members and friends may experience deviance firsthand, whether as victims of criminal behaviors or as people who are stigmatized as deviants yourselves. You may also find yourself called upon to handle issues related to deviance in your professional life. Today in many—perhaps most—kinds of work, from teaching and law enforcement to medical services and business, professionals find themselves confronting client groups who are classified in various deviance categories, or being called upon to develop policies that define what is deviant in their workplaces. And at the public level, informed citizenship in the twenty-first century demands an understanding of both the general processes through which deviance is constructed and the history of debates and human struggles surrounding various deviance categories.

If you take this course seriously, you will gain a deeper understanding of many critical issues in contemporary social life. That is the sociological promise. The knowledge and analytic tools that you will be called upon to develop in this course will prepare you to confront issues related to deviance in an informed and more effective manner. Taking full advantage of this opportunity, however, requires discipline, hard work, and—perhaps most importantly—a willingness to move beyond your personal comfort zone. In the study of deviance, we are all forced to examine some of our most deeply held assumptions about right and wrong and about why people act in the ways they do. Hopefully you will find the hard work in the course more than offset by the interesting nature of the topics we will cover and the compelling stories that sociologists have gathered in their studies of deviance.

SUMMARY

- All societies distinguish some behaviors and conditions as objectionable. Sociologists seek to understand the activities of both those who define behaviors and conditions as objectionable and those who become identified as deviants.
- All societies have beliefs about the causes of deviant behavior.
- The "demonic" explanation views deviant behavior as caused by evil forces that compel people to engage in immoral acts.
- The "psychotic" view of deviance asserts that mental illness causes deviance.
- The view of deviance as "exotic" explains what appears to be deviance as a product of living in a culture with different beliefs and values about good and bad, normal and strange.
- The sociological approach to deviance focuses on analyzing social acts and the close examination of observable behavior.

- Within the field of sociology, the symbolic interactionist perspective focuses on the meanings that people attach to their and others' behaviors. The definitions that people create for what is right and what is wrong may shift over time and across cultures.
- The sociological study of deviance promises to help us broaden our understanding of social life today in the "deviance society."
- A sociological understanding of deviance offers valuable insights for personal life, professional careers, and informed citizenship.

KEYWORDS

blurred boundaries: A term used throughout this book to refer to (1) the often hazy distinctions between what is considered moral versus immoral, or normal as opposed to abnormal and (2) the confusion that results from conflicting and often overlapping explanations for why people engage in deviance.

deviance: The processes through which social groups (1) define certain actions or conditions as bad or immoral, (2) identify some people as engaging in these actions or conditions, and (3) treat the people they have identified as deviant.

demonic (view of deviance): A belief that deviance is caused by supernatural possession by evil spirits.

empirical data: The information collected by social and natural scientists from systematic observation and used to develop theoretical understanding.

ethnography: A research method that uses participant-observation and in-depth interviews to investigate the meanings people give to things and the processes through which those meanings are created and sustained in human interaction.

exotic (view of deviance): A belief that deviance is simply behaviors that are based on cultural norms or ways of life that are different from our own.

medicalization of deviance: The defining of various kinds of deviance as medical problems and dealing with them through medical treatment.

psychotic (view of deviance): A popular culture belief that deviance is caused by mental illness.

social constructions: The beliefs that people create and maintain through human interaction and communication about the nature of events and objects in the world around them, including beliefs about their own subjective feelings and being.

social norms: Cultural expectations about what is appropriate and inappropriate behavior. Violation of social norms may lead to individuals being labeled as deviant.

sociological paradigm: A sociological theory or perspective that provides a broad framework for explaining social behavior and methods for studying social life.

symbolic interaction: A sociological paradigm based on the principle that people act on the basis of the meanings that they apply to things in their environment. Such meanings arise in the course of social interaction as people actively seek to understand and respond to the world around them.

CHAPTER

2

Getting Close to Deviance

Ethnographic researcher Philippe Bourgois in homeless camp (Jeffrey Schonberg).

CONTENTS

LEARNING OBJECTIVES

After reading this chapter, you will be able to:

- Describe the primary kinds of data and research methods used to study deviance
- Appraise the value of official statistics and surveys
- Analyze the limitations of official statistics and surveys
- Outline the goals of ethnographic research
- Explain the challenges and practice of deviance ethnography

BLURRED BOUNDARIES I: GETTING CLOSE TO DEVIANCE

For 15 years, the television series *CSI: Crime Scene Investigation* captured the imagination of the American public. With its suspenseful drama of an elite team of forensic investigators who solve disturbing crimes, a big part of the show's appeal lies in the way it gave the viewer a chance to get inside the crime itself, to get a glimpse of the criminal's thoughts and actions. With visions of *CSI* and shows like it fresh in their minds, some students arrive at college with plans of becoming crime scene investigators. Many talk about a desire to develop a special understanding of crime and criminals by studying forensic anthropology, chemistry, and psychology. Yet, without diminishing the knowledge and skills of forensic scientists, the case can be made that some sociologists investigating deviance get closer to the actual contexts of criminal acts than do most forensic researchers. And when they do, they can find themselves confronting blurred boundaries where it is hard to decide what is right and what is wrong—for them as much as for those they study. Consider, for instance, the three following cases.

To learn about burglary from the inside, Richard Wright and Scott Decker (1994) asked 70 active burglars to take them to the scenes of recent burglaries and explain how they did them. At times, getting this close to the action placed them in dangerous situations. One day, for instance, they sat in front of a house as two burglars described how they recently broke into the place and stole cash, drugs, and weapons. As they talked, four males came out of the house and walked toward the car. One of the burglars shouted, "Get out of here. They're gonna shoot us!" They will never know if he was right or not; Wright and Decker took his warning and sped off without delay.

In her research with prostitutes in an urban "sauna parlor," Teela Sanders (2005) became accustomed to spending much of her fieldwork among semi-naked women waiting for male clients to show up. She was not prepared, however, when her prostitute companions encouraged her to watch them perform sex with their clients—in order to "see what it's really like." Their request forced Sanders to think hard about where to draw the line between acceptable and unacceptable fieldwork practices.

Finally, few sociologists have been as forthright as Erich Goode in admitting that they have had sexual relations with those they have studied. In an essay on sex and fieldwork, Goode acknowledges sleeping with informants during his participant observation with the National Association to Advance Fat Acceptance (NAAFA). During this study, he attended conventions, parties, and dances with men and women NAAFA members. Goode, who was attracted to heavy women, felt that he would not be seen as a full-fledged member of the organization unless he dated and showed a sexual interest in the women members. Further, he argues, "in the NAAFA study, sex and romance were more or less what [the research] was about. Ignoring my own sexual experiences during the course of the study seems inconceivable" (1999, p.314).

These sociologists put themselves close to the experiences of people engaged in criminal behavior or with stigmatized social statuses. The researchers put themselves up close because they believe that knowledge based on firsthand experience and understanding provides unique insight into human behavior. While not all sociologists studying deviance go into the field to look at deviance from the inside, those who do draw on a rich tradition of deviance ethnography. But getting close to deviance can place researchers in uncharted territory, forcing them to improvise and make quick decisions in the field.

In this chapter, we will explore a range of methods and data that sociologists use to study deviance, with most of our attention focused on the research strategies and challenges of deviance ethnographers. Some of the examples of deviance ethnography may strike you as extreme—at times even foolhardy or absurd. At other times, the research may strike you as exciting and even courageous. As Erich Goode has noted, "Risky though research on deviance is, few areas of study have as much potential for action, thrills, adventure, and personal satisfaction" (2005, p.111).

While sociological research can at times be thrilling and personally satisfying, the core purpose of research is intellectual. The deviance ethnographer is not there primarily for the adventure (however, intriguing it might sometimes be), but to better understand the social world under investigation. Up close to deviance, the researcher must confront the blurred boundaries of deciding how close is close enough, and how close is "too close"—a question we will return to at the end of this chapter.

SOCIOLOGY AS A MODE OF INQUIRY

When people think of sociology, they tend to think of the topics of sociology courses (e.g., family, religion, social inequality) and the theories (e.g., functionalism, conflict theory, symbolic interaction) that sociologists use to explain the dynamics of social life. Often we give short shrift to perhaps the deepest, most fundamental characteristic of sociology: its commitment to learning. At its heart, sociology is a mode of inquiry. It is based on the belief that we can improve our understanding of human behavior and social life if we take the time to systematically examine what people think and do. As a social science, sociology demands openness to learning from observation. This is why research is so important. The observations we collect in research can challenge our present ideas and call us to rethink how best to explain things.

As we noted briefly in the first chapter, many approaches to social life are oriented to sustaining previously held beliefs rather than modifying or changing them. Most of our daily life is spent taking things for granted. We take for granted that people (from the grocery store checkout clerk to our parents) are who they say they are and that they will act in ways that are consistent with their stereotypical identities. Yet, the stereotypes that we take for granted can be misleading, and sometimes we are forced to reexamine our beliefs. In personal life, we may have a grandparent who begins to suffer from Alzheimer's and who seems no longer able to function in the role we have expected of them. Or a close friend may confide that she is pregnant as a result of an unplanned sexual encounter and is struggling with what to do next. Such personal experiences may force us to change our ideas and our beliefs. The grandparent who looked after us may now need to be looked after. And it isn't only "bad girls" who want to get abortions. In facing challenges to our beliefs, we expand our ways of understanding the possibilities in the world around us.

The most fundamental difference between everyday life and sociology is that sociology requires a commitment to consistently looking at the social world around us as a potential "learning experience." But sociological learning today does not occur in a historical vacuum. It grows in large part out of the learning experiences of scholars who have gone before us, mapping out ideas about the dynamics of social life that we continue to explore.

In this chapter, we examine the methods by which sociologists gather data about deviance. We will see that sociologists often seek data that allow them to gain a deeper understanding of two broad sets of questions. The first set of questions focuses on rates and causes of deviant behavior. That is, how many (and what proportion of) people engage in a certain kind of deviance (e.g., drug abuse or white-collar crime) and why do they do it? The second set of questions involves the meanings and processes through which deviant behavior is enacted. These questions focus more on social psychological aspects of deviance (e.g., what is the meaning of the behavior for the individual?) and the practical issues of how they go about doing it (e.g., how do a prostitute and a "john" find each other?).

In the following pages we will examine several sociological methods for studying deviance. We begin with official statistics and researcher-designed surveys—primarily used to address questions regarding the rates and causes of crime and deviance. Then we look at deviance ethnography with its emphasis on data that can address more contextually oriented questions regarding cultural meanings and social processes. Each of the different methods and kinds of data discussed in this chapter can provide insights into the social organization of deviance, but it is critical that we come to grip with the limitations of our data as well. If the data do not measure or represent what we think they do, they will lead us to mistaken conclusions. With this fundamental issue in mind, we turn now to an examination of the kinds of data sociologists collect and analyze in order to understand the deviance process.

COUNTING DEVIANTS

Let's begin by considering one of the basic challenges of studying deviance. Many behaviors classified as deviant are statistically rare and geographically dispersed. Relatively few Americans, for instance, commit murder or sexually abuse children. Still, in the United States overall, it is estimated that, in recent years, around 15,000 people have been murdered and 90,000 children have been sexually abused annually (Federal Bureau of Investigation [FBI] 2015a). It is hard to imagine that any sociologist would be able to personally collect enough data from across the country to examine these phenomena. Fortunately, several governmental agencies have taken on the task of collecting data on these and many other types of crime and deviant behavior. Sociologists studying deviance—especially criminal deviance—often turn to official statistics as a major source of data. However, while official statistics are an indispensible tool in analyzing some aspects and some kinds of deviance, we must be clear about what they are and what they are not.

Value of Surveys and Official Statistics

There are a wide variety of national, state, and city agencies that collect data related to many kinds of deviance. Crime data, for instance, are gathered by city police officers and county sheriffs, by various state agencies from the highway patrol to the department of corrections, and at the national level by the FBI and other US Department of Justice agencies. Similarly, many governmental agencies collect information about health-related deviance, including mental illness, alcoholism, and obesity. The term "official statistics" refers specifically to information that has been collected by government agencies or international public organizations (such as the World Health Organization). Such statistics may include data about behaviors (e.g., rates of smoking, criminal arrest rates) and attitudes and beliefs (e.g., about gay marriage or birth control). In addition to official agency statistics, many social scientists collect data on various kinds of crime and noncriminal deviance.

Official statistics and survey data collected by other social science researchers are particularly attractive to sociologists and criminologists because they provide information about large numbers of people. The *Uniform Crime Reports* (UCRs), published by the FBI, are compilations of crime reports and arrests from law enforcement agencies throughout the US. Surveys and official statistics are often used to establish the *rates* of particular kinds of deviance, that is, what proportion of the population engages in or is victimized by specific kinds of deviant behavior. Looking at the rates of different kinds of deviance among different social groups or settings enables sociologists and criminologists to examine two other issues: correlation and causation. *Correlation* refers to a pattern of things that tend to be found together. For instance, violent crime is correlated with age, as far more violent crime occurs among teens and young adults than among those over 35 years old. *Causation* refers to a special kind of correlation in which one specifiable condition leads to another, as in the case of cigarette smoking being a major cause of lung cancer. As sociologists are quick to point out, just because two things are correlated does not mean that one caused the other. Lung cancer is correlated to gender; more men than women get it. Does that mean that being male causes lung cancer? Obviously not. Rather, males are more likely than females to smoke and it is smoking, not gender, that leads to the high rates of lung cancer among men. To make the argument that one thing caused another, you must be able to demonstrate not only that (1) the causal factor occurred first, but also that (2) no other factors intervened to influence or produce the behavior you are seeking to explain. The issue of causation is clouded by the fact that there are often multiple potential causes for the same outcome. While smoking is a major cause of lung cancer, many people who smoke do not get lung cancer and many people who do get lung cancer never smoked. The issue of what causes deviant behavior is very controversial.

Such controversy notwithstanding, most sociologists find it useful to get some sense of how common specific categories of deviance are, as well as the kinds of things that are frequently associated with those behaviors, conditions, or statuses. Official statistics and other large-scale surveys offer valuable resources for examining these issues. But these kinds of data can also mislead us unless we clearly understand how they are created and what their limitations are.

Limitations of Official Statistics

Every year the FBI gathers data from local law enforcement agencies across the United States and compiles summaries of arrests and crimes in the *UCRs*. The primary *UCR* statistics focus on violent and property crimes called index crimes. These are crimes that we are most aware of as serious crimes and that are most likely to be reported to the police, including murder, robbery, forcible rape, aggravated assault, burglary, and motor vehicle theft. The *UCR* statistics on index crimes represent an enormous effort to collect large-scale data, but, even so, it is widely acknowledged that the reports are not a completely accurate reflection of serious crime across the country. Most obviously, these data only list crimes that get reported to law enforcement agencies. That is not a serious problem for some crimes, such as murder, where nearly all cases are reported. But for other crimes, many cases may not be reported.

How common is it for victims of crimes to not report them? Perhaps as many as half of all crimes never get reported to law enforcement agencies. In an attempt to get more accurate statistics on crime than those from law enforcement agencies, the US Bureau of Justice Statistics conducts a *National Crime Victimization Survey* (usually referred to as the NCVS) that is administered to over 75,000 households around the United States each year. This extensive survey explains different kinds of crimes and asks individuals if anyone in their home has been the victim of such a crime in the last 12 months. The reports of crime victimization in NCVS data show that most property crimes are never reported, but even some violent crimes are widely unreported.

Counting Rape and Sexual Assault

Consider the crime of rape. Most of us believe we know what rape is and that we could recognize it when it occurred. We also agree that it is a serious crime and that those who commit it should be prosecuted. In attempting to understand rape, we might well turn to official statistics for a sense of how often it occurs and what the social characteristics are of the perpetrators and the victims. But official statistics on rape are far from an accurate account of rape in American society, and an even less accurate picture of sexual assault more broadly. We can think of the relationship between rape and official statistics on rape in terms of a pyramid, as shown in the rape reporting graphic below.

At the apex of the pyramid, we have the cases of rape that result in convictions. While it is possible that some convicted rapists are innocent—as we see in some notable cases of men who have been released from prison after DNA evidence exonerated them of the crimes—most who are convicted have likely engaged in sexual assault that we would consider rape. But there are far more rape arrests than there are convictions for the crime. Only about half of rape arrests end in convictions. And even when we look at rape arrests rates, we are still toward the tip of the pyramid that would include all cases of the crime. Out of every 10 rapes that are reported to law enforcement officials, an average of only four leads to arrest. That means that 60 per cent of reported rapes are never "cleared" by the criminal justice system. If we were to rely simply on the FBI's UCRs, that would be where our count of rapes ended. The data would provide us with a picture of females who have reported being raped and we would have a profile of men who have been arrested and convicted of rape. But what is left out of these data? First and most obviously missing are the cases of women (and girls) who have been raped but have not reported it. Why might someone not report being raped? Some of these cases involve women who are too embarrassed to report their rapes or who are afraid of how they will be treated by the criminal justice system. Following the trauma of being raped, many women withdraw into themselves and keep their experiences secret, or reveal them only to a few close family members or friends. Yet other women and girls do not report rape because of their relationships with those who have raped them, such as family members and close friends. In order to learn more about crimes that

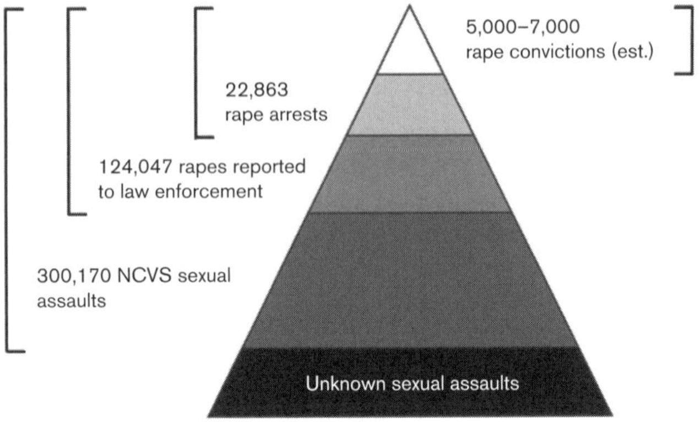

Figure 2.1 Rape and sexual assault reporting pyramid (drawing by Kenny Chumbley).

have not been reported, the US Department of Justice instructs the NCVS to gather information from households about crime victimization, including crimes that did not get reported to law enforcement officials. The NCVS data on rape are considerably higher—around 40 per cent higher—than the rates of rape reported in the UCRs, adding another tier to the total of rapes in figure 2.1.

Even yet, we have not included all incidents of rape in our society. What cases of rape might we still have failed to capture? What about women and girls who either don't know or are unsure of whether they have been raped? If a female is under the influence of drugs or alcohol, she may lack clear recall and be confused about whether or not she willingly engaged in sex. Or what about a prostitute who is a victim of sexual attack? Can drunk women and prostitutes be raped? While most of us would agree that they can be victims of rape, we also understand why they would be unlikely to go to the police or even report their experiences to survey researchers.

Finally, we need to consider how our beliefs regarding what rape is will make certain kinds of aggressive sexual acts visible as crime to us, while obscuring our view of other possibilities. For example, can a married woman be raped by her husband? "Marital rape" is a relatively new addition to the definition of rape in the United States, with the state of South Dakota being the first to make it a crime—in 1975. Or what about the rape of males? As you might have noticed, all of this discussion of rape has focused on sexual assault against women. That has not been accidental. In many venues, including UCR data, sexual assault against a male has not been included in rape data until very recently.

As the rape reporting pyramid shows, the counting of rape is a difficult challenge with multiple layers. But the points that we need to grasp now are (1) official statistics capture only a segment of the actual cases and (2) to understand official statistics, we must know how they have been created, and especially the

PUSHING YOUR BOUNDARIES

Unreported Crime Interviews

Official statistics capture only the officially identified cases of criminal behavior. In response to this problem, the National Crime Victimization Survey (NCVS) seeks to gather information on unreported crime. The survey finds that most victims of crimes do not report them. But why? What are the reasons that people give for not reporting crimes?

In this project, you are asked to conduct short interviews with two of your friends who have been victims of crimes that they have not reported. In your search to find two friends who have been victims of unreported crimes, keep track of how many people you had to ask before you found two who met this criterion. Begin your interview by telling them that you would like them to answer a few questions about their experience and that you will be taking notes, but that you will not include their name in anything you write. Then, ask them the following questions.

- Tell me about the crime (or crimes) that you were a victim of, but did not report. What was the crime? Describe what happened.
- Tell me about how you handled the incident. Can you explain to me why you didn't report it to the police?
- When you look back at what happened to you, do you wish that you would have reported the crime to the police? And tell me why you feel that way.

After the interviews, write up summaries of what the interviewees told you. Did they report similar or different types of crimes? How about their explanation for why they didn't go to the police? Finally, consider what you think you would have done in similar circumstances? Do you think you would have reported the crime or not?

criteria and procedures for counting an individual or event as a case. Statistics on crime and deviance do not represent pure counts of objective instances of deviance. Humans construct them through their thoughts and actions. As John Kitsuse and Aaron Cicourel put it, "Official statistics are compiled by specifiable organizations, and those statistics must be explained in terms of the deviant-processing activities of those organizations" (1963, pp.136–137).

Official Statistics as Organizational Processes

When we look at official and other agency statistics as organizational processes of defining some kinds of acts as deviant and developing routines for identifying and handling people who become labeled as deviants, we see things in a new light. Instead of reifying official statistics (looking at them as objective reality), we can focus our attention on better understanding of what they capture—and what they miss. In later chapters on specific categories of deviance we will take a closer look at how statistics and rates for each category are created. For now we will emphasize just two basic points.

First, the amount of human behavior we count as deviant depends on how we define things. Second, it depends on how we react to things. All too often these issues are missed. Newspaper reports with such dramatic titles as "Downtown Prostitution Doubles in Last Six Months" or "Teenage Meth Use on the Rise" are often based on increased arrest rates that reflect greater police attention to the activity rather than an actual increase in the activity itself. Similarly, in the early 1990s, the rate of diagnosis of Attention Deficit Disorder (ADD) rose exponentially in the United States. But that increase was not a result of a sudden dramatic rise in the number of children suffering from the disorder. Rather, the rise was connected to the marketing of medications to treat the disorder and to the enactment of the Individuals with Disabilities Educational Act—a law that provided new educational resources for children diagnosed with ADD.

Nor do decreases in official rates necessarily mean that the number of people engaging in a behavior is declining. As sociologists Harold Garfinkel and Egon Bittner (1967) noted many years ago, there are often "good reasons for bad organizational records." Social service and criminal justice agencies that deal with many forms of deviance face constant pressures to maintain or increase their resources on the one hand, and to avoid trouble on the other. The agency routines and records reflect these interests. The court system provides an excellent example. While the courts are officially in place to prosecute crime, the actual processing of criminal cases may depend on the interests and resources of prosecutors, the costs associated with cases, and how busy the courts are at a particular point in time. Criminal prosecutors usually have considerable discretionary power in deciding how to proceed with a given case. Depending on how heavy their caseloads are at a given point in time, prosecutors may decide to take a case to trial, or they may choose an alternative course of action. They may decide that even though the case has some merits, it lacks sufficient evidence to take to court. Or the prosecutor may agree to reduce the criminal charges as part of a plea bargain—say, lowering felony charges of burglary to misdemeanor charges of breaking and entering. While the defendant's behavior has not changed, the definition and consequences of it change dramatically under these different scenarios.

Not only are official statistics in significant part a result of organizational processes. They are also potentially subject to several different kinds of social biases. Crime and deviance-processing organizations, like many other organizations, often treat people differently based on who they are. Self-report surveys that ask people to tell whether or not they have committed certain crimes or deviant behaviors consistently find more "deviants" than are reported in official crime statistics. Self-reports also show that, for many types of crime, the differences between lower-class and middle-class individuals, or members of different racial or ethnic groups, are far less than what arrest rates would suggest. In a classic study of juvenile delinquency, William Chambliss (1973) found that middle-class and lower-class male high school students reported engaging in roughly equivalent amounts of delinquent behavior. But lower-class boys were far more likely to be formally charged and punished. And numerous studies have shown that law enforcement personnel tend to watch and react more severely to African-American males than to white males—leading to higher rates of arrest. From a different angle, gender stereotypes can also play a significant role in the labeling of people as deviant. Women going to physicians to report physical symptoms suggesting heart problems are frequently sent away with prescriptions for antidepressants in the (often mistaken) medical opinion that their problem was psychological rather than physical (CNN 2007). Men reporting the same symptoms are far more commonly diagnosed as suffering from heart disease.

These kinds of issues force us to recognize that official statistics—or any statistics, for that matter—should not be taken simply at face value. We need to know how the statistics have been created in order to understand (a) what they are counting and (b) how well they can be compared to other statistics about the same topic or condition.

Summing Up the Numbers

We can wrap up our discussion of official statistics and surveys by emphasizing four points. First, counting crime and deviance is a daunting task, plagued with blind spots and inaccuracies. The relative rarity of many kinds of deviant behavior, the stigma and secrecy that often surround it, the biases that often come into play in identifying and processing deviants—all of these present roadblocks to getting a clear and accurate count of the number of people involved in various types of crime and deviance. Official statistics and surveys cannot provide a completely accurate snapshot of the numbers of deviants or their behaviors, but—and this is our second point—even flawed as they are, official statistics and surveys have valuable uses.

Official statistics often provide the only extensive counts of certain kinds of behaviors, especially crime. Even if the data don't capture every case, it is useful to know whether there were 20 or 200 reported murders last year in a given city. Large-scale statistics offer opportunities to make at least rough comparisons of rates of crime and deviance according to individual and geographical demographics and other variables. We can document different rates of violent crimes, such as murder and assault, in different age groups and according to community size. While it is important to avoid mistaking correlation with causation, the fact of correlation can sensitize us to look for the meaning of such relationships.

The third point is that official statistics are a good measure of the *official processing* of those who become labeled and treated as criminals or deviants. Official statistics do capture the way we treat certain categories of people identified with deviant behavior at a given point in time. Looking at changes in official statistics can sensitize us to how official definitions and treatments of deviants are transformed over time. Official data from the Bureau of Justice Statistics show a huge increase in the number of incarcerated criminals in America from 1980 to 2000. Statistics from the National Institute of Mental Health show a massive decrease in the number of hospitalized mentally ill persons from the 1950s to the 1990s. Does this mean that we have more criminals and fewer mentally ill people in the United States today? Not at all. But it does mean that we define and treat people who are labeled as criminals or as mentally ill differently today than we did in the past.

Finally, while well-conducted surveys can help us improve the quality of our data, there are many issues that sociologists researching deviance cannot effectively use official statistics and surveys to study. Many deviant activities are hidden from officials and survey researchers going door-to-door or emailing people to ask them questions. Perhaps the most critical issues that deviance scholars must address is the meaning of activities that are labeled deviant for those on the inside—the so-called "deviants" themselves. If we take seriously Blumer's proposition (discussed in Chapter 1) that "people act toward things on the basis of the meaning that those things have for them," then before we do anything else, we need to investigate the meanings that individuals and groups construct. We must get close enough to deviance to understand it from the inside. When we try to do this we find that we must conduct research not just to know the answers to our questions, but also to know what questions to ask in the first place. Only then will we see the view up close.

CHALLENGES OF DEVIANCE ETHNOGRAPHY

Sociologists who approach deviance from the symbolic interactionist perspective argue that in order to understand deviance we must investigate how the meanings of the behavior or condition are socially constructed. Nothing in and of itself is universally evil, bad, or wrong, they contend. Our notions of right and wrong are social constructs that we talk into being. In order to understand deviance from this point of view, we need to grasp the meanings that members of relevant groups have created for objects, relationships, and events in their social world. For answers to these kinds of questions, we must turn to what sociologists refer to as ethnographic research methods.

Ethnographic research involves spending time with people, observing their actions, and talking with them. As Jack Douglas, a leading deviance scholar in the 1970s, explained, "We know quite clearly that official information is not only an unreliable source for studying deviance but also that it is systematically biased in line with the needs and desires of officials and important segments of the public, so that it provides a systematically distorted picture of deviance" (1972, p.4). The only real alternative, Douglas argued, was to "become involved in the everyday lives of the individuals we wish to study so that we can come to share enough of the commonsense meanings of those activities to the individuals doing them to be able to understand what those meanings are" (1972, p.4).

The ethnographic interest in *direct* observation and apprehension of the social world reflects a certain *epistemology*, or theory of knowledge. The central tenet of this theory is that face-to-face interaction is the fullest condition for achieving intimate familiarity with the actions and orientations of other human beings. Rather than trying to learn about crime and deviance from agency records, official statistics, and surveys, ethnographers believe they will learn far more by watching and talking to people as they go about their daily lives. Deviance ethnographers creatively, and at times even courageously, confront the challenges of directly studying deviance. They do so primarily because they believe that there is no practical alternative. In the process, they often find that the hard work of deviance research is filled with its own unique rewards.

Focus of Deviance Ethnography

The first thing that we need to clarify as we turn our attention to deviance ethnography is that it involves more than just studying particular groups of people who have been labeled deviant. Deviance ethnographers who work in the symbolic interactionist and social constructionist tradition of sociology are interested first and foremost with the creation of meaning and alignment of individual and group activities in social interaction.

The social constructionist approach to deviance takes a broad view of three different, but interrelated, aspects of the deviance process: rule-making, rule-breaking, and rule-enforcing. *Rule-making* involves those individuals, groups, and activities that focus on defining certain acts or conditions as deviant and on banning them from the society. The group Mothers Against Drunk Drivers is an excellent example, as are groups that seek to ban public smoking or pornographic bookstores. *Rule-breaking* refers to the activities of individuals or groups who violate expectations and rules that rule-makers seek to impose. Finally, *rule-enforcing* includes the range of activities by such people as police officers, county prosecutors, and drug counselors to identify those who are breaking rules and punish or treat them in ways designed to control their misbehavior. Of these three groups, it is the rule-breakers—those labeled as criminals and deviants—who have received the bulk of ethnographic research attention.

While some scholars have lamented the disproportionate attention that those who have been labeled as deviant receive in comparison to those who make the rules and those who enforce them, there are good reasons why deviance ethnographers have paid so much attention to them. First, those who are labeled as deviants and rule-breakers are the focus of the attention of the other players in the deviance drama. Rule-makers and rule-enforcers make claims about who the deviants are, why they engage in deviant behaviors, and what should be done about them. But the claims that rule-makers and rule-enforcers make about deviants tend to be made with little if any attempt to learn about deviants by talking directly to them or directly observing their activities. Deviance ethnographers serve a vital function in providing more accurate understandings of these individuals and groups, since they are among the few people who endeavor to understand their experiences and points of view. Not surprisingly, the research of deviance ethnographers often challenges the popular images of deviants promoted by rule-makers and rule-enforcers. By virtue of their interest in learning and sharing the insider views of those they study, ethnographers provide opportunities for those who are labeled deviant to have their voices heard.

This book pulls together the research from deviance ethnographers who have studied all three groups: rule-makers, rule-breakers, and rule-enforcers. It is impossible to understand the deviance process without looking at each of these kinds of groups and activities and the interconnections among them. But, in keeping with the work of deviance ethnographers themselves, we will draw especially deeply upon ethnographic work that has looked at the social worlds and experiences of those who become labeled as deviants.

Gaining Access

The first task in conducting deviance ethnography is gaining access, which involves locating where the people and activities you want to study are and then negotiating with formal and informal gatekeepers who influence access to the setting or groups. Both present their own challenges.

Think for a minute about trying to locate members of a particular group of deviants or rule-breakers. Some are obvious because we cross their paths in the course of our daily lives. We may see a group of homeless people regularly hanging out in the park, or a group of antiabortion protestors picketing the local Planned Parenthood clinic. We may have driven past (perhaps even stopped at) adult bookstores and strip clubs, and we are likely to have seen (from inside or out) the police headquarters and city jail. In short, we know where to find some of the subjects and settings relevant to deviance ethnography. But many of the activities and groups we might want to study are concealed from public view and more difficult to find. Those who are at risk of being labeled as deviant or criminal often have spots that are hidden from the public eye where they congregate and interact. At times, their settings may be camouflaged. What appears to be a pizza parlor or video arcade may in fact be a front for selling drugs. In other cases, back alleys and hidden alcoves of public settings may be appropriated for the purposes of deviant transactions, sometimes strewn with tell-tale signs like hypodermic needles, condoms, or empty bottles.

When we are interested in studying particularly sophisticated and privileged groups, whether they are rule-breakers or rule-enforcers, we often find that they are especially secretive and protected from our view. White-collar crime is conducted largely behind the corporate doors of banks and businesses—places much harder to penetrate than low-level drug dealing out of an abandoned building. And secretive law enforcement agencies set up clandestine operations in places like Guantanamo, or even on ships at sea, where they can escape public scrutiny.

Finally, what about the Internet? Today a huge amount of social interaction occurs on the web. Twitter, YouTube, and Facebook are just a few of the best-known sites, used by millions of people on a daily basis. Not surprisingly, as the technologies and popularity of the web have grown, it has become a major nexus for deviance-related communication and interaction. The rise of Internet communication has led to the emergence of a new variation of ethnography, often referred to as virtual ethnography (e.g., Hine 2000), or netnography, that is devoted to studying online interaction and subcultures. In terms of deviance, the Internet is undoubtedly most recognized as a venue for pornography and sex. When Dennis Waskul and his co-researchers investigated online sexual interactions, they found that, "At any given time (but particularly at night), hundreds of [easily identified] channels intended for the purpose of cybersexual encounters can be accessed" (Waskul et al. 2000, p.378). But what about other kinds or aspects of deviance? Clearly a huge number of relevant sites exist on the Internet, but they may be far more difficult to locate than pornography. So, for instance, many pro-eating disorder websites, dubbed "pro-ana" (anorexic) and "pro-mia" (bulimia) websites are short-lived, as some major web hosts like Yahoo remove any sites that are identified with this activity (Gailey 2009). Yet, other websites, including many associated with various kinds of deviance and illegal activities, are hidden from public view on what is called the Dark Net, an anonymous Internet network that cannot be accessed by search engines like Google and Yahoo. By virtue of the anonymity it provides users, the Dark Net facilitates communication and exchange for a wide range of illegal behavior, such as the drug website, Silk Road, that sold more than a billion dollars of illegal drugs before it was shut down in late 2013 (Bartlett 2015). Still other deviance-related activity, such as law enforcement officials pretending to be children in order to discover sexual predators, goes on without our being able to identify it without inside knowledge.

Like investigative reporters, deviance ethnographers must often go out and nose around for contacts and clues to see what they can find. When ethnographers have found appropriate settings and groups, they have taken the first step in their research. The next step is to negotiate the approval from official and unofficial *gatekeepers*—those who may open or block opportunities to engage in research. For academic social scientists today, one important requirement is to submit one's research for approval by the university's *Institutional Review Board* (or IRB, as they are typically called). IRB committees are composed of faculty members and administrators responsible for reviewing research projects to certify that they meet standards for the ethical treatment of human subjects. In order to receive IRB approval, researchers must provide: (1) an assessment of the potential risks and benefits associated with the research, (2) an explanation of *informed consent*, or how those they are studying will be informed of the research and asked to consent to be part of it, and (3) a statement of how the identities of research subjects and potentially sensitive information about them will be protected.

Often there is a second set of gatekeepers in the setting itself. These gatekeepers may include officials such as prison wardens, mental hospital directors, police chiefs, or even business owners without whose endorsement the researcher will be unable to get into a particular facility or meet with participants. Informal settings may have gatekeepers as well. Illegal operations such as crack houses or brothels often require some kind of special endorsement in order to get in—especially if one is interested in conducting interviews rather than buying drugs or sex. Fieldworkers may also find it useful, even necessary, to build relationships with individuals from the settings who are willing to serve as guides in the field, helping researchers find their way and make contacts once they are allowed in.

Getting People to Open Up

While getting into a setting is crucial, the researcher must also find ways to get participants to open up to them. People engaged in stigmatized and potentially illegal activities have plenty of reasons to be wary of strangers. They may fear being looked down on or not being understood. They may not want their secrets revealed to the public, and they may worry about being turned over to authorities. On the other hand, law enforcement officers may be cautious about opening up to researchers, fearing that their investigative tactics might be revealed or that their ethics might be challenged. Given how many reasons there are to keep quiet, the most pertinent question is: what possible reason would someone have to let researchers learn about their lives? What do they stand to gain?

We can begin with what they don't do it for: money. While there are occasional cases where deviance researchers pay their informants, it is an extremely uncommon practice. Typically, deviance ethnographers work with very tight budgets, often funding their research out of their own pockets. When they do have money to pay their informants, it is seldom more than a token amount. When Richard Wright and his colleagues interviewed active burglars at the scenes of recent crimes, they offered each burglar 50 dollars. While none of the men refused the money, it was not the cash that motivated most of them to share their stories. Indeed, just to prove that he did not need the money, one of the burglars pulled out his wallet at the interview and showed the researchers that it was stuffed with thousands of dollars. So what motivated the burglars to consent to be interviewed? Perhaps the most common reason, Wright and his co-researchers argue, was that it gave the offenders a chance to share their stories. "The secrecy inherent in criminal work," they write, "means that offenders have few opportunities to discuss their activities with anyone besides associates—which many of them find frustrating. As one informant put it, 'What's the point of scoring if nobody knows about it?'" (Wright et al. 1992, p.154)

Just as this burglar was attracted to the opportunity to share his exploits, others often appreciate attention—so long as they feel safe in sharing their stories. Members of stigmatized groups that are marginalized and ignored, such as the homeless, may be especially pleased when researchers take an interest in them. Even respected professionals, such as law enforcement officers or rehabilitation counselors, often appreciate a chance to share their expertise and knowledge. Frequently, those who share their lives and stories with ethnographers do so in part out of a desire to correct what they feel are mistaken impressions that other people have about them. As one undercover narcotics agent bluntly told ethnographer Bruce Jacobs, "Maybe I can clear you up some" (1992, p.202). Similarly, one of the homeless women who Elliot Liebow (1993) spent time with during his research voiced her hope that he would "tell them who I am"—a request that he took to heart so seriously that he made it the title of his book on homeless women.

Finally, given the amount of time that ethnographers spend talking and sharing in the daily activities of those they study, they may become close friends with their informants. And just as with other friends, they may become confidantes and sources of material and social support. In their research with drug dealers, for instance, Patricia and Peter Adler provided small loans, babysat kids, and even took one of their informants into their home when he had no place else to stay. In situations such as this, rapport, good will, and openness develop in the course of daily life together.

Fieldwork Roles

Another common challenge of ethnographic research lies in finding or creating a social role that provides a reason (beyond just the research itself) for being in the setting. Social roles provide others with a sense of who we are and what they can expect from us. Establishing a social role or identity in interactions with those one is studying enables them to see the researcher as someone who is not a complete outsider—someone who can be trusted. Finding a viable fieldwork role is a key task of ethnographic research and a crucial test of one's ability to fit into the group or setting.

Sometimes deviance ethnographers try to bypass open fieldwork roles by pretending to be members of a group. The practice of *covert research*, or *disguised observation*, is controversial among sociologists and occurs far less commonly today than in the past. In a classic 1973 study of the experiences of mental hospital patients, David Rosenhan (1973) and his fellow researchers faked symptoms of mental illness and were admitted to mental hospitals. While they quit faking any signs of mental illness as soon as they were admitted, they found that the medical staff continued to view them as mentally ill (although other patients sometimes suspected they were faking). In defense of their disguised observation, deviance ethnographers—again, mostly in the past—have argued that it would have been impossible to gain access to the people and activities they observed if they had not hidden their research identities.

The use of covert research is far less common today than in the past, in large part because IRBs require that those being studied will be informed of, and consent to, being part of the research. Still, it is often the case that many people who are present in settings studied by deviance ethnographers are either not informed at all, or only minimally aware, that they are being observed. It is simply impractical and inappropriate, for instance, to try to announce one's self as a researcher to a large gathering or to everyone in a public setting. Covert research is more common among researchers who are accessing information and interaction online. In her extensive research on prostitution, Teela Sanders has not hidden her research role from the women she has met face-to-face. But on the Internet, she has acted differently. "Mostly," she writes, "I adopted the role of a lurker, covertly observing online interactions between buyers and sellers in chat rooms and bulletin boards" (2005, p.27). Since publicly accessible space on the Internet is available to everyone, and since the true identities of those who interact online are often hidden, this kind of covert observation has not drawn the disapproval associated with covert face-to-face research.

Some deviance ethnographers have no reason to engage in covert research because they are or have been members of the groups they study. These ethnographers engage in what has been termed *autoethnography*, drawing on their own personal experiences as they analyze the meanings and social processes associated with a particular kind of deviance. Carol Rambo Ronai (1998, 1999) used her personal experience as a strip club table dancer to develop an analysis of interactional dynamics associated with erotic dancing. Monique Watford (2008) has developed insights into bereavement following a spouse's suicide by examining her own experience as a spousal suicide survivor. Other ethnographers have used their personal experiences with various kinds of deviance to hone their analyses and to build connections to others with similar experiences. Peter Hennen's (2005) interest in gay "bear" subculture grew out of his experience as a middle-aged, large gay man looking for similar companions. David Karp (1996, 2006) has been motivated to study the experiences of people struggling with depression in large part because he himself has suffered from depression throughout his adult life. The use of personal experience and autoethnography in social science research has sparked lively debate, even among ethnographers (e.g., Atkinson 1997; Coffey 1999), but the value of rigorous autoethnographic inquiry (e.g., Anderson 2006) to gain an insider's view of many deviance topics is undeniable.

Most deviance ethnographers do not go into the field with personal experiences as members of the groups that they are studying. Nor do they go in as covert observers. Most often they find or create roles that combine their research interests with other activities and connections with the groups and settings they are studying. One common role is that of the *buddy researcher*, a blending of the roles of researcher and friend. The fieldworker makes it clear that she or he is keeping notes and writing up observations as a researcher, but much of their interaction with those they are studying is focused on everyday activities. In contrast to the informal buddy researcher role, many deviance ethnographers find it useful to have more specific roles in their research settings. In his research with hospitalized mental patients, Erving Goffman (1961) took on the role of assistant to the recreation director on one of the hospital wards. While the recreation assistant role gave him an official reason to be in the psychiatric ward, it left plenty of room for him to spend time talking with and observing the patients. In preparation for ethnographic research on street life and AIDS in San Francisco in the late 1980s, Robert Broadhead and Kathryn Fox (1990) became certified as community health outreach workers before going onto the streets to spend time with homeless youth, drug users, and sex workers whose lives were being devastated by the disease.

Getting Along in the Field

Deviance ethnographers feel a sense of accomplishment when they locate appropriate settings and find a role that will make their presence acceptable. But fieldwork is an ongoing process filled with continuing challenges. Once the researcher is in the setting, she must build relationships and trust with those from whom she seeks to learn. Human relationships, including those in the field, are not static. They are created and recreated through social interaction over time, and marked by shifting patterns of intimacy, closeness, distance, and conflict. The relationships that deviance ethnographers develop with those they study are made more difficult than most relationships by the contexts of stigma, illegal behavior, and distrust in which they are embedded. These researchers must find ways not only to "get in," but also to "get along," to manage the daily challenges involved with interpersonal relations with those they are studying. Three such challenges illustrate this point: ethnographers' handling of presumptions about who they "really are," avoiding participation in activities without damaging relationships, and deciding when there is no option but to back out.

Many social settings of interest to deviance ethnographers include several different kinds of people and activities. A strip club for instance often includes dancers, their audience, bartenders and cocktail waitresses, bouncers, and possibly undercover vice officers. Even a fieldworker who has worked hard to explain their research interests to some key people in the setting will find it impossible and inappropriate to try to explain to everyone. Not surprisingly, misunderstandings can arise. Teela Sanders' experience one night while doing research at Foxy's, a prostitution sauna house, provides an example.

> About 10 o'clock, one of Emma's regulars arrived. I could tell he was a regular by the casual nature of the greeting. The man came into the lounge and sat opposite me on the sofa and proceeded to talk about the weather. This all seemed normal until I noted that both Emma and Belinda had gone out of the room . . . After a long silence he confided that he always 'tried out' the new girls, even though Emma was his regular, and if I was free, would I mind seeing him in the Jacuzzi room.
>
> —Sanders (2005, pp.28–29)

Sanders goes on to explain that, a few minutes later, as she sputtered awkward excuses, Emma came to rescue her and took the client to a room. What Sanders learned as an ethnographer from that experience is critical. People often make assumptions about who the researcher is and why they are there. Deviance ethnographers must recognize others often read things into their presence that they may not even be aware of, and managing field relationships requires handling such presumed identities and interests in a way that does not damage rapport. In their research on transsexuals and cross-dressers, Richard Tewksbury and Patricia Gagne experienced several instances where their informants indicated that they "knew" (mistakenly) the researchers were cross-dressers. "Such challenges must be handled carefully," Tewksbury and Gagne explain, "because the misrepresentation must be corrected without appearing to distance ourselves from the stigma" (2006, pp.61–62).

Most of the time the presumptions made about the researcher involve attempts to make sense of why they are in the setting or interested in the activities. Typically people are presumed to be personally involved in settings and activities that they are seen in. It is not surprising that Sanders was thought to be a prostitute. Nor is it surprising when ethnographers in drug settings are presumed to be drug users—or for that matter, suspected of being undercover narcotics agents. In suspicious contexts, suspicion is understandable. Deviance ethnographers must be sensitive to how they may be perceived and prepared for appropriate action. Terry Williams, a seasoned ethnographer in the New York drug scene, has developed the following technique for avoiding misinterpretation of his presence:

> Initially I prefer to be taken into a crack house or dealing location by someone who is known there. They vouch that I'm OK and no cop. . . . I may explain that I'm writing a book on crack houses (or another topic). I usually have a copy of a book I've written to show people. This approach goes a long way toward convincing skeptical persons that I'm an author.
>
> —Williams et al. (1992, p.351)

By anticipating and planning ways to manage the assumptions that others are likely to make about them, fieldworkers can nip some problems in the bud. Yet, fieldwork decisions and interactions cannot be completely scripted in advance. Deviance ethnographers frequently experience pressures to engage in activities that they prefer to avoid. In such situations they face the dilemma of not fully participating while at the same time not alienating those they are studying. Researchers may find themselves in such predicaments as being pressured to use illegal drugs, to convert to deviant spiritual beliefs, or to become romantic or sexual partners with members of the group. In each case, refusing might hurt their relationships with those they are studying.

At times, some ethnographers have decided to embrace the overtures and expectations of their research subjects. Some have converted to new religious beliefs and practices, developed romantic relationships, or used drugs with their informants. But most deviance ethnographers have steered clear of such involvements. In order to minimize problems associated with such decisions, ethnographers may plan in advance for confronting situations. Female ethnographers—even unattached ones—may wear wedding rings as visible announcements that they are not romantically available, or to show as their reason for turning down a request for a date. Deviance ethnographers also frequently rely on evasive finessing, or finding ways to avoid doing things without looking like they are completely unwilling to participate. Terry Williams found that cocaine users themselves sometimes turned down an offer to use some by explaining, "my nose is coked out," an account that he found useful at times for explaining why he wasn't snorting coke with his informants. As Williams' example demonstrates, finessing strategies tend to be spontaneous and highly contextualized, representing "a consummate test of the fieldworker's grasp of local culture" (Emerson and Pollner 2001, pp.251–252).

Collecting Data

In addition to talking and interacting with people associated with various aspects of the deviance enterprise being studied, deviance ethnographers must also record their observations and interviews in order to analyze and draw conclusions from them later. This means that when deviance ethnographers engage in participant observation, they participate with a different mindset than do others in the setting. While others are focused almost exclusively on the immediate tasks at hand (e.g., buying drugs, selling sex, making—or avoiding—arrests), the deviance ethnographer must also attend to issues of how to record what they are witnessing.

Ethnographers, in general, and deviance ethnographers, in particular, often find it difficult, if not impossible, to take notes openly while participating in relevant activities. In order to avoid disrupting interactions, ethnographers frequently make jotted notes in the field and write up more detailed field notes later. Even when they write short jotted notes to themselves in the field, ethnographers often take pains to do so in ways that don't draw attention to their writing. One common strategy is to withdraw to the privacy of a bathroom to hurriedly jot down key words and phrases that will spur their memories later—thus giving rise to the joke that ethnographers suffer from a professional tendency toward weak bladders.

Even when they openly conduct interviews, ethnographers often find that they must adapt to the special circumstances of the people and settings they are studying. While the ideal interview involves a focused and sustained discussion (preferably recorded for optimal recall), Judith Porter and Louis Bonilla found that their interviews with women in the sex industry were made up of "broken snippets of information filtered through their working schedules" (2010, p.167). In her research on drug-using street prostitutes in Brooklyn, Lisa Maher (1997) had to adapt her interviews to short time frames since many heroin users nodded out at repeated intervals or became fidgety and unable to focus due to withdrawal symptoms. In situations where interviews are conducted in odd moments and places, it may be nearly impossible to record the conversation.

As these examples illustrate, deviance ethnography requires the researcher to juggle several activities at once and to improvise according to the dictates of the situation. Whether engaged in participant observation or interviewing, the researcher must be ready to roll with the punches and adapt to the situation. For those involved in participant observation, in particular, it can be a challenge to avoid being so caught up in the action that there is little time or energy left to record it. Unlike other participants in the setting, the fieldworker does not walk away from the activity or event once it is over. Instead, they must replay the interactions and conversations they have just witnessed and write out detailed descriptions of the day's (or night's) activities. No matter how rich and interesting the researchers' experiences in the setting are, they are only useful for sociological analysis if they are written out in enough detail that the ethnographer can revisit the events later in order to gain new insights and ideas into the people and activities they are investigating.

Narrative Analysis

Those who are labeled as deviants are only one, however important, group in the deviance process. Deviance researchers must situate deviants' activities within the broader society in which they are labeled as bad, sick, or morally inferior. Some deviance ethnographers study deviance claims-makers, or individuals and groups who seek to define a kind of behavior or status as deviant. Others focus their research on rule-creators such as legislative officials, or rule-enforcers such as police and prison staff. Typically such ethnographers find themselves using similar methods and facing many of the same challenges as those who study "deviants" themselves.

As deviance researchers collect and analyze data, they may also engage in various types of narrative or content analysis to examine the stories told about deviants—and by deviants themselves. Narrative analysis includes a range of analytic strategies as well as a variety of possible kinds of narrative or discourse. Deviance scholars turn to narrative analysis to understand the ways in which deviance categories are constructed and change over time. As Donileen Loseke (2007) observes, stories exist at every level of social life. At the broadest level they are reflected in popular culture portrayals, including those of deviants, in public discourse and the media. At an institutional level, narratives are embedded in laws and social policies, presenting images of deviants and ways to manage or control them. Deviance-processing organizations, such as law enforcement agencies and therapeutic treatment programs, have manuals and guides describing the "presenting problems" and appropriate responses to deviants under their jurisdiction. Finally, deviants themselves invoke narratives to characterize who they are and how they are treated.

Social constructionist scholars analyze the narratives used to create and define deviants and how to treat them. Researchers seek to identify key themes and metaphors used in deviance claims-making and track changes in narratives over time. So, for instance, Craig Reinarman (2009) has examined the typical ways in which drug scares are constructed in the media, Abigail Saguy (2013) has analyzed how major newspapers and magazines have portrayed obesity and eating disorders, and Philip Jenkins (1998) has studied changes in sex offender statutes over the twentieth century. Given the wide variety of venues in which narratives are constructed, narrative analysis takes many creative turns, as in Joshua Gamson's (1998) analysis of the framing of LGBT issues on television talk shows and Karen Dias' (2003) examination of the narrative self-portrayals of anorexic and bulimic young women on "pro-ana" websites. Valuable findings and insights provided by narrative analysis are drawn upon in chapters throughout this book.

Understanding Social Worlds Different from Our Own

Deviance ethnography requires a special attitude toward new and potentially unsettling situations and people. Both intellectually and emotionally, deviance ethnographers must work to keep themselves open to seeing the world through the eyes of those they study. While they do not necessarily need to agree with

RESEARCHER PROFILE

Deviance Ethnographer Philippe Bourgois

Over the past 30 years, Philippe Bourgois has conducted ethnographic research with drug users in desperate inner city neighborhoods across the United States. In the late 1980s, Bourgois lived with his wife and young son in an East Harlem tenement house while crack emerged as the "fastest growing equal opportunity employer of men in Harlem." Bourgois focused on the meaning of the drug economy and drug use among those he studied. The title of his 1995 book, *In Search of Respect*, captures his insight that selling drugs was one of the few ways the men he studied could find a sense of personal importance and respect. Bourgois also saw the personal and social costs—violence, incarceration, the loss of family—that the men experienced as they pursued respect in the drug economy. Living in the "barrio," Bourgois at times would be out with his young son, Emiliano, who had been diagnosed with cerebral palsy. Looking back, he recalls how Emiliano "melted everyone's heart while proudly learning to use his walker over broken sidewalks littered with crack vials" (1995, p.xi).

After his research in East Harlem, Bourgois took a position at San Francisco State University and began 10 years of research with graduate student and professional photographer, Jeff Schonberg, on a group of San Francisco heroin and crack users. Bourgois and Schonberg spent time with members of the group, observing and documenting their struggles to survive on the streets. When they published *Righteous Dopefiend* in 2009, Bourgois and Schonberg were criticized by some for including photographs they had taken in the field. In response to one such challenge, Bourgois shared what one addict had told him: "If you can't see the face, you can't see the misery" (Shea 2009).

Since 2011, Bourgois has been doing research in the Puerto Rican neighborhood of North Philadelphia and leading research projects on poverty, incarceration, and racism at UCLA's (University of California, Los Angeles) Center for Social Medicine. Reflecting on his experiences conducting ethnographic research, he observes:

> It's always surprising to me, but when one treats with respect people who have been treated as pariahs, they become real human beings. You can become friends with them. That's part of what the magic of ethnography is: to bring out the humanness of the "Other."
>
> Shea (2009)

the meanings that guide others' actions, they have to be able to understand from inside the perspective of those they study. And they must do so not only with an open mind, but also with an open heart—a willingness to see the humanity in us all. This can be particularly difficult when you are studying groups whose activities and ideas strike you as strange or even repugnant. But unless deviance ethnographers are genuinely open to learning from others about their experiences, they will fail to achieve their most fundamental research goals.

Of course, ethnographic research on deviance varies widely in terms of the groups and activities that are studied. Often deviance researchers study groups that they are particularly sympathetic to (as in David Karp's studies of people suffering from depression) or find especially interesting (as Leila Rupp and Verta Taylor's [2003] ethnography of drag queen performers). In these situations the researcher is already receptive to the insiders' perspective. But many other groups studied by researchers evince less positive initial reactions, and deviance ethnographers must fight against the urge to hold themselves at arm's length and failing to look at their world from their point of view. This was certainly the case for Douglas Pryor in his research for *Unspeakable Acts*, a study of men who had sexually abused children. As Pryor explains:

> The mere mention [of men who sexually abuse children] can stir intense emotions, including anger, contempt, shock, and disgust. I know. I have experienced these and other feelings across the course [of my research], and have experienced them particularly strongly because I myself am the father of two young daughters.
>
> —Pryor (1996, p.1)

But despite his emotional reaction, Pryor recognized the value of learning from abusers, in their experiences and their words, how involvement in sexual offending unfolded. "However repulsed one might feel about the issue," he writes, "such feelings do not diminish the importance of trying to understand how and why sexual situations between adults and children occur" (1996, p.2). Deviance ethnographers do not need to approve of the behaviors or agree with the beliefs of those they study; their goal is to understand the meanings that guide their informants' actions.

GETTING THE BIG PICTURE: SOCIOHISTORICAL COMPARISON

Deviance ethnographers develop their understanding of different groups and aspects of the deviance process through up-close study. By virtue of the detailed attention they give to the settings and groups they study, few deviance ethnographies attempt to present a complete picture of the deviance process. Most ethnographies focus on one particular social group or deviance category, such as street prostitutes in a given city or recreational drug users on a specific college campus. Caught in the local details of a particular group or setting, it is easy to lose sight of the bigger picture: the actions and interactions of rule-makers, rule-breakers, and rule-enforcers that comprise the overarching context of a particular kind of deviance, in a particular local setting, at a specific point in time.

A crucial element of understanding any kind of deviance lies in awareness of the broader social context in which it occurs. In order to get the bigger picture, we must be able to grasp the perspectives of different groups and their interactions, both among themselves (e.g., interactions between law enforcement and those who break the law) and with other groups in the broader society. Further, in order to get a more balanced understanding, we need to have a sense of how similar categories of deviance have—or have not—been present in other cultures and other times. Therefore, we will not focus solely on deviants themselves at one particular point in time, but will also examine the constructions of different kinds of deviance both cross-culturally and historically in the United States.

BLURRED BOUNDARIES II: HOW CLOSE IS TOO CLOSE?

In pursuing a richer understanding of the deviance process, ethnographers must put their minds and bodies in closer proximity to deviance than is required of other kinds of research. But how close is close enough? And how close is too close? Look at the following cases. Do you feel they represent legitimate research decisions, or do you feel that some (or all) of these researchers discussed below have crossed the line?

Anthropologist Sue Estroff (1981) used ethnographic methods to study the lives and experiences of seriously mentally ill individuals who were treated in the community rather than in mental hospitals. Recognizing that virtually all of the people she was studying were prescribed psychiatric medication—and that many complained about the effects the drugs had on them—Estroff decided that, in order to better understand their experiences, she should take Prolixin, the antipsychotic medication that many of them were prescribed. While her friends and family strongly warned her against taking the medication, Estroff found a doctor who was willing to prescribe it to her. For six weeks, she took daily doses of the drug and chronicled its impact on her thoughts and feelings in her "Prolixin Diary." Reflecting on her experience of irritability, physical discomfort, and shakiness while on the drug, as well as anxiety and suicidal thoughts during withdrawal, Estroff found that her experience provided a very personal and instructive means of learning about psychiatric medication.

Patricia Adler and her husband, Peter, became close friends with several drug dealers during their research for *Wheeling and Dealing* (Adler 1993)—a book that explores the experiences of upper-level drug dealers in Southern California. When one of the dealers got out of prison, he showed up broke on their doorstep. They let him live with them for several months—even, for a while, as he sold drugs out of their home. While they never sold drugs themselves, they did use them with their informants. As Adler explains, "It would have been impossible for a nonuser to have access to this group . . . This was the minimum involvement necessary to maintain even the courtesy membership we achieved" (1993, p.24).

Criminologist Kenneth Tunnell has spent decades studying criminal activity. Along the way, he has travelled to criminals' homes to interview them. He has become privy to crimes he has never reported, and has shared alcohol and drugs with some of his informants in an effort to build rapport and collect richer data. Recounting one such occasion, he writes:

> There I was, in the living room of a twice-convicted felon, an ex-con, surrounded by electronic and decorative items collected from previous burglaries, smoking dope, and being made privy to his recent crimes . . . I came away with some excellent data made possible by a connection established through methods other than those promulgated by hard science, objectivity, and researcher neutrality—a connection lubricated by weed and drink.
>
> —Tunnell (1998, p.207)

There are a number of arguments both for and against different levels of getting close to deviance. Where is it appropriate to draw the line, both legally and morally? How close is close enough? How close is too close? These kinds of concerns will surface time and again in the following chapters, forcing us to confront the fact that researching deviance, like deviance itself, involves blurred boundaries, judgment calls, and tough decisions. What criteria do you feel are most important for deciding what is acceptable versus unacceptable in research? Why? Given the criteria you identify, how would you evaluate the acceptability of the research activities described here? Explain how your criteria are relevant to these research examples.

SUMMARY

- Sociology is an empirical mode of inquiry focused on rigorous study of human behavior and social life.
- Official statistics are extremely important in the study of crime and deviance, especially for providing information about large numbers of people across the country.
- Official statistics are also limited in several ways.
    - They only capture cases that are reported.
    - They rely on current official definitions of deviance.
    - They reflect the priorities and structure of the agencies that collect the data.
- Deviance ethnographers study rule-makers, rule-breakers, and rule-enforcers to understand deviance from their specific points of view.
- Ethnographers must gain access to settings in which the different aspects of deviance are enacted and get those who are active in these settings to open up to them about their views and experiences.

- In developing fieldwork roles that enable them to fit into deviance-related settings and develop rapport with those they study, ethnographers must make decisions about how close they can get to those they study without violating professional ethics and losing objectivity.

KEYWORDS

autoethnography: Ethnographic research in which the researcher is a complete member of the social group she or he is studying.

buddy researcher: An ethnographic fieldwork role involving being a regular companion to a member or members of a social group while also being clear that one is also engaged in observation and research.

causation: A statistical correlation in which one sociological variable can be demonstrated to occur prior to, and produce changes in, another variable.

correlation: A pattern in which two or more sociological variables tend to be found together.

covert participant observation: A controversial research strategy in which a fieldworker seeks to pass as a member of the setting under study and does not reveal that she or he is engaged in research. Also commonly referred to as "disguised observation."

deviance ethnography: The use of ethnographic methods (e.g., participant-observation and in-depth interviews) to study different aspects of deviance, including, most prominently, the meanings that members of the group (or groups) under study attach to relevant objects and activities.

gatekeepers: Individuals, groups, or organizations that guard access to people and settings that researchers may want to study.

informed consent: A research subject or informants' (written or verbal) consent to be observed or interviewed for a research project based on their having been informed of the nature and purpose of the study.

National Crime Victimization Survey (NCVS): A national survey conducted by the Bureau of Justice Statistics that asks a sample of Americans if they have been victims of certain kinds of crime during the past year.

rates (of deviant behavior): Statistics that measure the proportion of a specific population that share a characteristic or engage in a particular kind of behavior.

Uniform Crime Reports (UCRs): An annual report compiled by the Federal Bureau of Investigation (FBI) that includes crime report and arrest data from law enforcement agencies throughout the United States.

victimless crime: An act that is defined as a crime by law but that involves only consenting adults who do not believe they are being harmed and do not complain to law enforcement.

CHAPTER 3

Positivistic Theories of Deviant Behavior

Broken windows: a sign of urban disorganization (Jonathan Weiss/Alamy Stock Photo).

CONTENTS

LEARNING OBJECTIVES

After reading this chapter, you will be able to:

- Identify and describe the four main positivistic approaches to deviance
- Discuss contributions and limitations of each of the positivistic approach
- Describe new or current directions in the theory
- Explain how the theories would address a case of young adult deviance

BLURRED BOUNDARIES I: WHY IS MIKE IN JAIL?

Mike is a stocky, red-haired young man who has just turned 18—the youngest person in the holding cell in the Cincinnati jail. Late last night, he slipped behind the counter at a convenience store to grab a carton of cigarettes and some lottery tickets while the cashier was stocking the cooler. When the cashier caught him, Mike pulled a handgun out and demanded the money from the till. He was arrested a few hours later when he showed up at another convenience store and tried to cash in two of the lottery tickets he had stolen.

This isn't Mike's first trouble with the law. He has been in and out of juvenile facilities and group homes for disturbed kids ever since he dropped out of high school in his sophomore year. He has been arrested for shoplifting, selling drugs, and beating up a homeless man in a city park. The scars on his face and hands have been earned in a dozen street fights, one of which landed him in the hospital. As his social worker puts it, "Mike has been around the block. Several times."

The question that the theories discussed in this chapter ask is, "Why?" Why does Mike break the law? What causes him to persist in violent and predatory behavior? Or, more broadly, why does anyone engage in deviant behavior?

A psychiatrist who has examined Mike believes she knows the answer. Mike's problems, she says, are the result of his mother's alcohol and drug addiction while she was pregnant with him. The drugs and alcohol led to his low birth weight and childhood illnesses, but, even more critically, they damaged his central nervous system and have resulted in attention deficits and impulsive behavior. The psychiatrist has seen this tragedy many times. She hopes that, with proper medication and counseling, Mike may be able to overcome his problems and live a more stable life.

The social worker who has handled Mike's case for the past five years has also witnessed such stories all too many times. While he agrees that it is a tragic waste of a young man's life, he disagrees with the psychiatrist about the causes of Mike's behavior. He has seen many boys and girls from the neighborhood end up in trouble with the law. Mike seems no different from the rest. "The kids in this neighborhood barely stand a chance," he says, pointing to the run-down apartment complexes butting up against freeway aqueducts. The schools and streets, he explains, are filled with violence and drugs. Few kids graduate, except for those who go on to get a GED in prison. It is not medical problems that have led to Mike's deviant behavior. Rather, it is the experience of living in a disorganized and brutal environment.

Both the psychiatrist and the social worker are knowledgeable experts with years of experience working with troubled kids. But who is right? Which of them can best explain Mike's delinquent and criminal acts? Can they each be partly right? Or are they both wrong? Is there another, better explanation for Mike's behavior?

In this chapter, we will examine a wide range of theories about the causes of deviant behavior. Each of their explanations can seem simple and obvious on the surface. But things become more complicated when we delve into the depths of real-life cases. As Mike's case illustrates, good arguments can be made on many sides. So, how can sociological theories help us understand deviance at the blurred boundaries of social life? Hopefully this chapter will provide some answers.

INTRODUCTION TO POSITIVISTIC THEORIES

Sociologists who direct their attention to understanding the causes of deviant behavior usually work within what is called a *positivistic* social science orientation. The term "positivism" derives from the writings of August Comte, a nineteenth-century French social philosopher and one of the founders of the field of sociology. Comte believed people could achieve understanding of social life by moving away from unquestioned beliefs and taking a scientific approach. The positivist method that Comte proposed is distinctly "this worldly" in its orientation, based on the belief that we can learn about human societies and social life through close empirical observation—by the evidence we can obtain from our senses. As it developed, positivistic social science came to be characterized by several more key features.

Three particular features characterize positivistic theories of deviance. First, positivistic theories are directed almost exclusively to *causal explanations* of deviant behavior. Rather than asking why and how some behaviors come to be defined as deviant while others do not, positivistic theories accept existing social norms and definitions of deviance. Taking current criminal law and social norms for granted, positivistic theorists seek to understand why individuals break the law or engage in other forms of norm violation. Second, positivistic theories invoke a *deterministic* approach to behavior, assuming that deviant behavior is determined by forces over which individuals have little conscious control. A third feature of positivistic theories involves the nature of theoretical claims regarding deviant behavior. Positivistic theories seek to provide a general theory, or universal explanation for deviant behavior. As we will see in this chapter, each positivistic theory proposes one or just a few basic factors as a general explanation for why individuals engage in deviant behavior.

In short, positivistic theories endeavor to identify the specific cause or causes of deviant behavior. This chapter discusses four kinds of positivistic theories of deviant behavior: (1) biological explanations, (2) social structural theories, (3) theories of socialization and social learning, and (4) theories focused on social control. We will examine the basic arguments of these theories, as well as their strengths and limitations. As we will see, positivistic theories of deviance can make important contributions (but not universal explanations) to our understanding of deviance by highlighting a range of factors that play significant roles in the deviance process.

Before we discuss positivistic theories of deviance, we need to briefly consider the dominant view of crime and criminal justice that preceded the development of scientific approaches to deviance.

What today is referred to as *classical criminology* is a philosophy regarding crime and punishment that emerged in the late eighteenth century, particularly in the writings of two influential philosophers, the Italian Cesare Beccaria (1963 [1764]) and his British disciple, Jeremy Bentham (1948 [1780]). A full description of classical criminology is beyond the scope of this book, but a few key features of Beccaria and Bentham's philosophy can help us understand the context within which the biological positivists of the Italian school of criminology brought forth their view of crime and deviance.

Beccaria and Bentham criticized the existing criminal justice policies of their day, arguing that they were based on faulty notions of both why people commit crimes and what should be done to people who commit them. In contrast to traditional, religiously based ideas about crime, Beccaria proposed that human beings exercise free will and choose among different courses of action based on a calculation of pleasure versus pain. The potential for pleasure-seeking deviant, antisocial behavior—what Beccaria referred to as the "despotic spirit"—is in all humans. The key to preventing criminal behavior, Beccaria asserted, was to make people aware that punishment would be swift and certain. The severity of punishment should be in proportion to the severity of the crime—just a little more pain than the pleasure afforded by the crime, but enough to make people unwilling to make the trade.

Further, Beccaria argued, out of a sense of equality among all people, society should "treat the crime, not the criminal." This stood in stark contrast to the situation across Europe at the time, where (as is still common today in the United States) one's social class and status strongly influenced the punishment one received for committing a crime. In contrast, Beccaria wrote, the specific punishments for crimes should be written directly into the law. The courts and judges should only be responsible for determining a defendant's innocence or guilt. That way, the pain involved in deviance and crime would be obvious to all, and citizens, in their desire to maximize their pleasure and minimize their pain, would see that deviance was not in their best interest.

Beccaria and Bentham believed that the policies they proposed would bring order and consistency to the criminal justice system and, through reducing crime in the most rational way, ultimately contribute to "the greatest happiness for the greatest number of people"—a central principle of the Utilitarian philosophy Bentham founded. They were motivated by concerns of social justice, as demonstrated in their advocacy of a level playing field for all. Further, they believed that the underlying motivation for deviant behavior was the same for everyone. Regardless of their social class and personal attributes, all human beings, Bentham and Beccaria argued, had the ability to choose how to act based on their perception of the pain or pleasure associated with their actions.

BIOLOGICAL THEORIES OF DEVIANCE

The concepts of free will and rational choice, so central to classical criminology, were key features of the intellectual era in Western Europe known as the Enlightenment, an era that challenged established beliefs and religious doctrines by asserting that human beings could understand the world through scientific observation and rational thought. Beccaria and Bentham proposed that all people shared the ability to make free will decisions based on their calculation of pleasure and pain. The rise of science as a way of looking at the world, however, led others to the belief that human behavior was determined by biology rather than free choice.

Lombroso's Italian School of Positivist Criminology

Cesare Lombroso was a nineteenth-century Italian physician who is often credited as being the "father of modern criminology." While his specific beliefs about the causes of crime are widely discredited today, Lombroso was one of the first researchers in the field of crime to attempt to use empirical data to develop and refine his theoretical ideas. In his role as a prison and mental hospital physician, Lombroso examined the bodies of thousands of living and dead individuals in asylums and prisons. In his influential book, *Criminal Man*, published in 1876, Lombroso wrote that criminals were physiologically different from law-abiding people. Adapting Darwin's evolutionary theory to his own purposes, Lombroso argued that while most humans in civilized societies are born with the traits of civilized men, some are atavistic or genetic throwbacks to earlier stages of evolution. Lacking the intellectual and emotional capacities of civilized men, these degenerates were born criminals, no more capable than violent animals of living moral and peaceable lives.

Lombroso admitted that at times normal people commit crimes, but these crimes, he argued, tended to be crimes of passion—momentary and fleeting criminal acts in an otherwise civilized and law abiding life. In contrast, born criminals were destined to lives of crime by virtue of their physical and moral constitution. Lombroso believed that personality and moral character were revealed in people's bodies, so that it was possible for those educated in criminal anthropology to identify born criminals even before they had committed a crime. According to Lombroso, born criminals were revealed by *atavistic stigmata*, or physical defects characteristic of the criminal population.

Lombroso claimed to have turned the study of crime into a science that drew its conclusions from empirical data and case studies. But his method of investigating born criminality involved little more than compiling an extensive list of physical anomalies observed among those who were incarcerated. Among the many criminal stigmata that Lombroso and his colleagues compiled, most were related to the head and face: small heads, thin necks, sloping foreheads, high cheekbones, bushy eyebrows, flat noses, strong jaws, fleshy lips, and—the most commonly identified mark of criminal man—protruding ears. Other common criminal stigmata included long arms, stubby fingers and toes, oversized genitalia, and insensitivity to pain.

Many scholars have noted that Lombroso's practice of scientific method was deeply flawed by biased assumptions, unexamined claims, and a failure to recognize disconfirming evidence. As Stephen Jay Gould has observed, "Lombroso constructed virtually all of his arguments in a manner that precluded their defeat, thus making them scientifically vacuous. He cited copious numerical data to lend an air of objectivity to his work, but whenever he encountered a contrary fact, he performed some mental gymnastic to incorporate it within his system" (1981, pp.125–126). In the end, the Italian criminal anthropologists produced, as David Garland puts it, "a rag-bag amalgam of differences and stigmata" by which they claimed to be able to identify criminals (1985, p.124).

While criminal anthropologists were motivated by "a genuinely humane hope of preventing the harm of crime and [where possible] improving the character of offenders," Garland writes, more often their theory led to the "continued repression of disadvantaged sectors of the population than it did to the liberation of society from the problem of crime" (1985, p.110). One example of the repressive nature of Lombroso's theory is his assertion that stooping shoulders and poorly developed rib cages represented stigmata frequently found among habitual criminals. While Lombroso considered these features to be innate signs of criminal degeneracy, they were commonly the result of poor environment, meager diet, and the prevalence of tuberculosis among members of the lower classes. Criminal anthropology deflected attention from the impoverished living conditions that contributed to the stunted growth, deformities, and sickly physical appearance of most imprisoned criminals, focusing instead on their bodies as the cause of their offenses.

Biological Theories in Twentieth-Century America

During the early 1900s, Lombroso's ideas were influential in the United States, where interest in the biological underpinnings of crime and deviance found a receptive audience. Over the course of the twentieth century, other theories of the biological causes of crime and deviance also gained widespread attention in the United States. In the late 1940s, psychologist William Sheldon (1949) developed a theory of juvenile delinquency based on bodily physique. Different body builds, he argued, indicated different temperaments and predispositions to delinquency. Young men with strong athletic builds were especially predisposed to physical aggression and criminality. Like Lombroso, Sheldon linked his theory to notions of evolution and physical degeneracy, but his research also suggested that "hypermasculinity," or an excess of masculine characteristics, caused deviance and crime.

Two decades later, in the 1960s, another theory of crime and deviance asserted that biological hypermasculinity led to criminal behavior. This theory, often referred to as the *XYY syndrome*, argued that males who were born with an extra Y chromosome—a rare occurrence, including approximately one in 1,000–2,000 males (Curran and Renzetti 1994)—evinced heightened aggressive and criminal tendencies. The XYY syndrome exploded into the public limelight when the attorneys for Richard Speck, murderer of eight student nurses in Chicago, claimed that he was XYY—a claim that was, in fact, untrue. As Stephen Jay Gould has observed:

> The link between XYY and aggressive criminality never had much going for it beyond the singularly simplistic notion that since males are more aggressive than females and possess a Y that females lack, Y must be the seat of aggression and a double dose spells double-trouble.
>
> —Gould (1981, p.144)

Nonetheless the XYY syndrome argument seemed to researchers at the time to represent a link between genetics and social traits for which criminal anthropologists and psychologists have long been searching.

As the foregoing examples demonstrate, biological approaches to the study of deviance have been plagued by many false starts and a lack of scientific rigor. The research on which these theories were based has been widely criticized for inappropriately generalizing from small and selective samples, and for making universal and deterministic claims regarding biological causes of deviant and criminal behavior. But just because much of the earlier research and theorizing about biological causes of crime was done poorly does not mean that this field of investigation has nothing to offer in helping us understand crime and deviance.

Critique and Further Directions

Contemporary biological explanations of deviance and criminality tend to focus little attention on the external bodies of deviants. Rather, drawing upon new technologies and medical advances, they focus most of their attention on the internal structures and functioning of the body. Two particularly high profile and interrelated lines of investigation into biology and deviant behavior today are genetic research and research on hormones and neurotransmitters.

Technological advances in recent years have enabled researchers in behavioral genetics to identify specific genes or chromosomal regions that appear to be correlated to specific kinds of behaviors. Since the late 1980s, the media have been quick to report the "discovery" of genes for a host of deviant behaviors, including a "gay gene" (Petit 1993), a "schizophrenic gene" (Maugh 1988), and an "alcoholic gene" (Altman 1990), among others. Yet, early research findings have often been disconfirmed by later studies, leading journalist Robert Cooke to observe that "A critical lesson from the race to uncover important genes is that it pays to keep an eraser handy" (1990, p.6).

Some of the public confusion related to behavioral genetics has come from enthusiastic genetics researchers making broader claims than their research actually supports, but as Rick Weiss (2006) has noted, the news media often overstate and simplistically report on research findings. Researchers usually conclude that materials associated with specific genes may predispose individuals to certain kinds of perceptions and behaviors, rather than asserting that a specific chromosome causes a specific behavior. The subtlety of such claims is often lost when new genetic findings are reported in the popular press.

Another aspect of biological explanations focuses on hormones and neurotransmitters as the chemical pathways through which genetics influence the brain and individuals' behaviors. Deviant behavior as viewed by biochemical researchers is a result of abnormalities in individual's levels of specific hormones and neurotransmitters, which may be caused by genetics or other influences on the body, such as injury or disease. Researchers have paid particular attention to the effects of sex hormones, such as the influence of the male hormone testosterone on aggression and of the female hormone progesterone on premenstrual symptoms like irritability and depression. Even more research in recent years has focused on major neurotransmitters such as serotonin and norepinephrine that are viewed as key influences on moods, cognitions, and behaviors. Biomedical researchers argue that abnormally low or high levels of hormones and neurotransmitters lead to various kinds of antisocial or maladaptive behaviors, including aggression, impulsiveness, and a need for sensory stimulation.

One limitation of biological approaches to deviance is that they cannot cover the entire spectrum of deviance categories. Biological explanations can be applied much more easily to some types of deviance than to others. Schizophrenics may be relatively good candidates for biological explanations, while tax evaders would seem to be less likely candidates. Further, even in the more obviously antisocial and severe kinds of deviance, not all who come to be identified as committing deviant acts exhibit the genetic, hormonal, or neurochemical anomalies. A second limitation is that biological theories do not address the definitional issues of why some behaviors and not others come to be labeled as deviant, nor why different societies (and even a single society over time) vary in the kinds of behavior viewed as deviant.

Given the limitations and false starts of biological approaches to crime and deviance, it could be tempting, from a sociological vantage point, to completely discount such explanations. But it would be foolish to do so. While biological theories cannot provide universal explanations of deviant behavior, it is obvious that genetics, brain chemistry, and hormones play significant roles in human behavior across the board. The most complete and realistic sociological approach to understanding deviance must acknowledge the importance of human physiology even while it focuses its primary attention on the social dynamics involved in the deviance process.

The next set of theories that we examine offers a very different angle of vision from biological explanations, shifting attention to the roles that the social environment plays in generating deviant behavior. These theories are referred to as "structural" theories of deviance because they focus on how the social structure of communities and societies contributes to deviant and criminal behavior.

SOCIAL STRUCTURAL THEORIES

Like biological theories of deviance, social structural theories argue that deviant behavior is caused by a kind of sickness or deficiency. But while biological theories focus on physiological problems, social structural theories focus on societal deficiencies or dysfunctions. The two most dominant social structural approaches to deviance are social disorganization theory and anomie theory, each of which proposes a particular kind of societal sickness or dysfunction that leads to deviant behavior.

Social Disorganization Theory

When the University of Chicago was founded in 1892, it opened the first sociology department in the United States and became the nation's center for sociological ideas and research. At the time, Chicago was a hotbed of social life. A rough and tumble city, it emerged from being nothing more than a small log fort in 1833 to a major US city just 60 years later. At the same time, waves of immigrants surged into the city to work in the steel industry, meat packing plants, and railroads that became the sites of many of America's most infamous labor union battles. Soon the city would also become a notorious home for organized crime.

One of the leading influences in the development of Chicago sociology was Robert Park, a former journalist, world traveler, and social activist, who played a major role in developing social disorganization theory. With fellow sociologist Ernest Burgess, Park proposed that cities develop geographic zones in which certain kinds of activities and populations become localized (Park and Burgess 1925). The innermost central zone was the home of commerce and industry. Just beyond it was a "transitional zone" where the poor and new immigrants tended to live, followed by a working-class residential zone, a zone of affluent residents, and a zone of less affluent workers who commuted into the city.

Park and Burgess believed that urban environments in general produced more deviance than rural settings, but they saw deviance as particularly a problem for the transitional zone in which poorer groups, and especially new migrants to the city, were concentrated. To understand their theory, we must consider the broader social transformation within which they saw modern social life as evolving. From the 1780s through the 1800s, Western Europe experienced the Industrial Revolution, moving from an economy of locally based, labor-intensive production of goods to an economy dominated by factory and machine production. As factories grew (along with new legislation that dramatically reduced peasants' rights to use rural lands), massive numbers of peasants moved from the countryside into industrializing urban centers, a process referred to as *urbanization*. The combination of *industrialization* and urbanization produced a very different social environment in cities than that which had characterized rural village life.

Rural life, Park and Burgess believed, had been characterized by stable social relationships and social values across people's lives and over the village's generations. In small communities, virtually everyone knew everyone else and interacted with them across a wide range of activities, forging strong primary relationships (e.g., extended family) and facilitating uniform community values. In such circumstances, social norms were relatively easy to inculcate and monitor through informal social control (e.g., gossip and social disapproval), resulting in low levels of deviance. In contrast, many of the traditional social supports for harmonious and deviance-free communities were absent in urban life. In an influential article titled "Urbanism as a Way of Life," Louis Wirth, a colleague of Park and Burgess, described life in the city as characterized by "a substitution of secondary for primary contacts, the weakening of bonds of kinship, the declining social significance of the family, the disappearance of neighbourhood and the undermining of traditional basis of social solidarity" (1938, p.8). In short, urban life broke down the established functional organization of society and produced social disorganization that was the root cause of many of the problems of modern life, including deviance.

But while modern urban life in general was viewed as less stable and more conflictual than earlier community life, Park and Burgess argued that the transitional zone in particular was prone to a high degree of social disorganization and deviance. The transitional zone tended to be the first stop for migrants (e.g., African-Americans from the southern states) and immigrants (e.g., eastern Europeans) who needed the cheap housing when they arrived, but who moved out of it and into more desirable neighborhoods as soon as they could. Unlike other, more stable and homogeneous residential areas in the city, the transitional zone was characterized by high population density, a mix of different ethnic groups, and rapid turnover of residents. The mix of ethnic groups, many of them new immigrants who brought their Old World languages and customs with them, produced an environment marked by conflicting social norms and values, as well as tensions and conflict. Given the demoralizing and anonymous conditions of life in the transitional zone, those who lived there felt overwhelmed and had little emotional attachment to the community and little interest in helping to make it a more livable environment. Such conditions, Park and Burgess argued, provided fertile ground for deviant behavior to thrive.

Among the many young scholars who built upon Park and Burgess' ideas was Clifford Shaw, who became the first director of the Chicago Area Project, a community-based and research-guided program to develop and test delinquency prevention techniques. Shaw and his colleague, Henry McKay, tested social disorganization theory by collecting police and court data on delinquent youths and then mapping the youths' residences in the city. Comparing the maps, Shaw and McKay (1942) found that the pattern of delinquency rates corresponded to Park and Burgess' concentric zone model. Delinquency rates were stable over time in the impoverished neighborhoods, even as different ethnic groups moved into and out of them. The implication was clear: the youth's deviant behavior was not located in their biological constitutions, but rather in the social environment in which they lived.

Shaw and McKay spent their professional lives refining the social disorganization approach to crime and deviant behavior. In addition to using police and court records, they advocated collecting life histories, or what they often referred to as the boys' "own stories" that provided more detailed and sensitive understanding of delinquents' personal lives. Shaw and McKay (1938) expanded social disorganization theory by describing a social transmission model of how young people in impoverished transitional zones became involved in deviant and criminal activities. Over time, they argued, deviant or delinquent subcultures develop in such communities and provide social bonds, norms, and values to which many young people become committed—a topic that was to be explored in much more detail in the socialization theories that we will discuss later in this chapter.

Critique and Further Directions

Despite considerable evidence supporting the basic thrust of social disorganization theory, its popularity among social scientists diminished in the 1960s and 1970s. During these years of civil rights and Vietnam War protests, many sociologists turned their attention toward issues of social conflict and power relations. Further, while social disorganization theory seemed well suited for helping to explain certain kinds of deviance, especially juvenile delinquency, it had far less relevance for many other kinds of deviance, such as those associated with the "sexual revolution" that began to draw more sociological interest in the 1960s. By 1982, deviance scholars Jack Douglas and Frances Waksler wrote, "Social disorganization is no longer an important sociological concept" (1982, p.74), even while they noted that some key variables of social disorganization remained significant in explanations of deviance.

Yet, social disorganization theory had barely been declared defunct by some scholars before others began to revive it. Rodney Stark (1987) published an article titled "Deviant Places" that sought to pull together the main ideas in social disorganization literature by more clearly specifying the characteristics of high deviance neighborhoods and the deviance-producing conditions to which they give rise. According to Stark, high deviance neighborhoods in cities tend to be characterized by five features, including poverty, high population density, mixed use, transience, and dilapidation. The combination of these conditions, he proposed, leads to cynicism among residents, increased opportunities and motivation for deviance, and diminished social control. Other scholars have also endeavored to refine social disorganization theory conceptually. Robert Sampson and Byron Groves (1989) have argued that a community with strong social organization involves residents who are connected through extensive friendship and kinship ties and who participate broadly in community social life. This, they argue, results in social relationships and organizational activities that enhance supervision of community youths and, by virtue of increased supervision, reduce deviance.

The focus on enhanced supervision and external control is also highlighted in *routine activities theory*, an approach—primarily to predatory crime—that reflects some basic elements of social disorganization theory. Routine activities theory argues that criminal activities occur when there is a conjunction of three factors: a motivated offender, a suitable target, and the absence of a capable guardian (Felson 2002, 2006). While the theory stipulates that a "motivated offender" must be present for a crime to occur, sociologists working with this approach seldom focus much attention on motivated offenders, but rather attend almost exclusively to the other two factors. Indeed, routine activities theory can be simply summarized as: given a constant supply of motivated offenders, the rate of criminal behavior will vary based on the availability of suitable targets and the presence or absence of capable guardians. In essence, like Sampson and Groves, routine activities scholars focus on the impact of a lack of external controls on deviant behavior. It is easy to see how such approaches can help explain higher levels of deviant behavior in poor and interstitial neighborhoods. However, such a narrow focus misses perhaps as much as it captures in its explanation of deviant behavior. For one thing, this approach, with its specification of "offender," "target," and "guardian," limits itself to the study of predatory crime—admittedly an important topic, but only one piece of the deviance pie.

In conclusion, it is important to recognize both the strengths and limitations of social disorganization theory. At its most basic level, social disorganization theory was directly intended to refute biological and psychological theories that only people with hereditary defects and abnormal personalities engaged in deviant behavior. Based on over 70 years of research, social disorganization theory has provided compelling evidence for this argument, sensitizing us to the consequences of a lack of social support and guidance.

Nonetheless, the perspective also has its limitations. In particular, the theory is limited by its narrow focus on disorganization and deficiency. Adopting a view of social norms and values as based on widespread consensus, social disorganization theory fails to recognize that many deviant groups are actually organized—but organized in terms of a different set of values and norms. Ironically, the early Chicago School ethnographies that were used to develop social disorganization theory, including Shaw and McKay's work on social transmission of deviant subcultural values, offered rich potential insights into just this issue. In this respect, Douglas and Waksler have observed that "the data of the Chicago theorists were far superior to their general social disorganization theory. The many insights gathered in their detailed research studies serve as elements in [more] current theories about deviance" (1982, p.75).

Anomie Theory

American sociologists were by no means alone among early social scientists in asserting that social factors played an important role in causing crime and deviant behavior. 20 years before Park and Burgess published their ideas, the French sociologist, Emile Durkheim, wrote a book titled *Suicide* (1966 [1897]) in which he presented an analysis of deviance that shared similarities with Park and Burgess later work. Like them, Durkheim was concerned with the societal changes brought about by industrialization and urbanization. He believed that the health of a society was largely the result of social integration, or interpersonal connections. Unlike Lombroso, Durkheim was not as interested in why particular individuals deviate as he was concerned with why rates of deviance differ so dramatically in different societies and among different groups in a single society.

Durkheim's "Anomie"

Drawing upon suicide statistics that showed significantly different rates of suicide among Catholics and Protestants, and variation during times of economic stability as opposed to economic upheaval, Durkheim asserted that even such a personal act as suicide was heavily influenced by social rather than purely personal forces. Durkheim used the term *anomie* to refer to a social condition of normlessness in which people lost their moral bearings, and were thus more likely to engage in deviant behavior. Durkheim's concept of anomie influenced American sociologist Robert K. Merton, who adapted the concept to his analysis of deviance more generally in American society. In 1938, Merton published his ideas in an article titled "Social Structure and Anomie" that was to become one of the most widely cited and influential sociology articles ever published.

Merton's "Social Structure and Anomie"

Like Durkheim and the social disorganization theorists, Merton sought to counter the claims of those who explained criminality as a result of biological predispositions. Durkheim and Merton both believed that deviance was caused by a lack of social guidance toward appropriate behavior, but Merton took a somewhat different approach from Durkheim to analyzing the nature of that lack of guidance. Merton distinguished between two aspects of the social structure that he believed were important to understanding deviant behavior. On one hand, he argued, societies are characterized by cultural goals that provide individuals with a set of aspirations toward which to strive. On the other hand, societies provide normative expectations regarding the acceptable institutionalized means for achieving those goals. A balanced and healthy society, Merton argued, is one in which the cultural goals and institutionalized ways of achieving them are well synchronized, providing most of the members of the society with acceptable ways to reap societal rewards. However, when there is a mismatch between cultural values and the means for achieving them, individuals may feel pressure to adapt to the situation in less acceptable ways. Looking at American society at the height of the Great Depression, Merton could see that not everyone had an equal opportunity to achieve the American Dream of financial success. And analysis of the pursuit of the American Dream served as the illustrative centerpiece of his theory of deviance.

Merton's ideas about the relationship between cultural goals and legitimate means for achieving them are often represented in a table like figure 3.1. This figure illustrates possible variation in the presence of cultural goals and legitimate means. As noted above, in a well-balanced society, Merton believed that most individuals are socialized to cultural goals that they may achieve through legitimate ways. So, for instance, in terms of the American Dream, a young person will be socialized to value financial success, and will pursue that goal through the hard work of getting education and pursuing a good career. Merton refers to this kind of behavior as *conformity*, arguing that, to the extent that a society is stable, conformity is the most common relationship between goals and means.

However, even a quick glance at the world around us reveals that not all members of society have the same level of legitimate opportunities for achieving the dream of financial success. While a child from a wealthy family in a suburb with well-funded schools may be nicely positioned to pursue the dream through legitimate channels, a child from an impoverished rural area will find it far more difficult to build the social and educational capital needed to reach

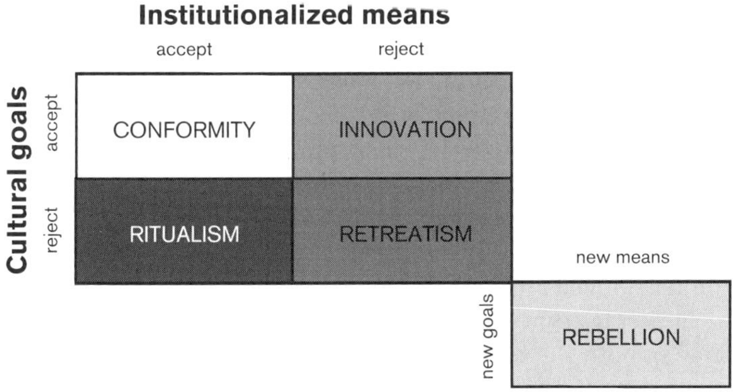

Figure 3.1 Merton's deviance typology (Merton 1938).

this cultural goal through similar means. The combination of cultural emphasis on particular goals with a lack of structural opportunities for legitimately achieving them, Merton argued, led to *innovation*, or the use of illegitimate means to achieve one's goals. Merton applied his idea of innovative deviance to what was commonly reported about the poor in urban slums—that they used various forms of vice to pursue financial success. Merton argued that innovation is most common among members of the lower class because they face the strongest pressures for some semblance of financial success while experiencing the fewest legitimate means for achieving it. In other societies, such as those with rigid caste systems, the goal of wealth and financial success has been considered appropriate for only a few members of the society and not held out as a goal toward which all should aspire. In America, by contrast, "the culture makes incompatible demands of those located in the lower reaches of the social structure" (Merton 1968, p.199). As a result, Merton observed ironically, "a cardinal American virtue, 'ambition,' thus promotes a cardinal American vice, 'deviant behavior'" (1968, p.200).

While Merton focused on innovation as the primary form of deviant behavior in his analysis, he also noted that there were other possible modes of adaptation to imbalances between social goals and the means for achieving them. In some cases individuals may abandon their attachment to socially valued goals—say, by letting go of the American Dream of financial success—while still going through the motions of adhering to societal expectations in terms of their behavior. This mode of adaptation, which Merton termed *ritualism*, is captured in such clichés as, "Don't aim high and you won't be disappointed" (1968, p.198). Such an individual might, for instance, take a modest-paying job in a large organization and never seek to advance beyond it. Alternatively, Merton argued, some individuals withdraw from the pressures of social life by rejecting both cultural goals and institutional means of achieving them.

Merton believed such escapist behavior, which he termed *retreatism*, was less common than innovation, but in a sense more drastic. "Sociologically," he wrote, "retreatists constitute the true aliens" (1968, p.205). Although they are in society, such individuals are no longer truly a part of it. Among those who have often been considered retreatists are the mentally ill, drug addicts, alcoholics, and the homeless. By giving up totally, Merton explained, "Their escape is complete, the conflict is eliminated and the individual is asocialized" (1968, p.206).

Finally, Merton recognized an adaptation that fell outside the categories in the table above. This final type of adaptation, which he termed *rebellion*, involved a rejection of both the society's goals and means of achieving them. But in contrast to retreatists, the rebels' rejection of society is matched with a call for action rather than withdrawal. "When the institutional system itself is regarded as the barrier to legitimate goals," Merton writes, "the stage is set for rebellion . . . not tinkering with the system, but a complete overhaul" (1968, p.210). Political rebels, like the American socialist labor organizers of the early 1900s or Latin American socialists like Che Guevera and Fidel Castro, exemplify the rebellion mode of adaptation.

Merton's anomie theory has been one of the most influential theories of deviance. His analysis of social structure, anomie, and deviance has been examined, extended, tested, and criticized by thousands of social scientists, who have applied the theory to an extensive list of deviant behaviors.

Critique and Further Directions

Merton's approach has often been referred to as a "strain theory" of deviant behavior, since it asserts that stresses and discrepancies in a society's structure produce the impetus for individuals to engage in deviance. As valuable as this insight is, however, anomie theory as it was presented by Merton has some major limitations as a theory of deviant behavior.

One big problem with anomie theory is that it is largely irrelevant to most kinds of deviant behavior. The theory is at its best in providing insights into "money crimes" and other types of deviance where people use illegitimate means to achieve culturally valued goals. But many kinds of deviance do not fit this kind of model. For example, most murders, assaults, and rapes cannot be well understood as innovative attempts to achieve socially valued goals. Further, Merton's other categories of adaptation have proven less useful than his category of innovation as accurate descriptions of the social dynamics in deviance. Many sociologists (e.g., Clinard and Meier 2008) have particularly questioned the accuracy of Merton's concept of retreatism, arguing that it does not realistically reflect the dynamics and behaviors associated with the kinds of deviance he included in this category, such as mental illness, drug and alcohol addiction, and homelessness.

A second critique that is frequently made of Merton's anomie theory is that it has a "class bias," or prejudice against lower social classes. Merton's analysis certainly deserves some critique on this point, since he states that innovative deviance is most widespread among members of the lower class. In focusing his attention on the lower class, Merton played a role in directing social scientists' attention toward gang activities and other forms of lower-class vice rather than toward deviance among social elites. Fortunately, the implications of anomie theory for white-collar crime have been pursued by other social scientists (e.g., Messner and Rosenfeld 2007) whose work we will examine in Chapter 8.

Finally, anomie theory has been criticized for presenting an oversimplified explanation of deviance. It is true that Merton's treatment of anomie theory skimmed the surface and left many issues unaddressed. Merton recognized that he was sketching only the broad outline of anomie theory, and he welcomed efforts by others to test and refine the theory. Over time, scholars have enriched the theory by addressing several topics that Merton did not cover. Three particular topics that have helped to flesh out anomie theory and make it more sophisticated include (1) extending anomie theory to acknowledge differing levels of opportunity to engage in deviant behavior, (2) expanding analysis of the various kinds of strain that can influence one's participation in deviance, and (3) analyzing the socialization processes through which deviant behavior is learned.

The issue of differing levels of opportunity to engage in deviant behavior was highlighted by Richard Cloward and Lloyd Ohlin in their book *Delinquency and Opportunity* (1960), in which they used the example of juvenile gangs to argue that not all potential delinquents have opportunities to become part of a criminal subculture. Their insight that opportunities for deviance and crime are not evenly distributed is a valuable addition to anomie theory, sensitizing us to the need to examine not only limited legitimate opportunities, but also the presence of certain kinds of illegitimate opportunities when seeking to understand why some individuals (as opposed to others) participate in certain kinds of deviant behavior.

The relationship between social strain and deviance has also been clarified and developed beyond Merton's original formulation. Most significantly, Robert Agnew (2001) has suggested that other kinds of strain may also influence the likelihood that an individual will turn to deviant behavior. Agnew focuses specifically on negative strains, such as the loss of positive aspects of one's daily life (e.g., loss of a friend or a job) or the strain of negative experiences (e.g., unpleasant school experiences or parental abuse), arguing that such negative stressors increase tendencies toward deviance and delinquency—a claim that has received support from empirical studies (e.g., Mazerolle 1998).

The last limitation of Merton's anomie theory is that it did not explore the social processes through which cultural values and normative expectations are communicated, shared, and learned. Yet, as Merton wrote, he had "largely

PROFILE

Strain Theory Scholar Robert Agnew

Robert Agnew was raised in Atlantic City, New Jersey, in the 1950s and 1960s when it was a struggling resort city that had not yet turned to gambling tourism to boost its economy. The city was home to a large lower working-class population. "I grew up in a working class neighborhood that slowly declined during my time there," he told fellow criminologist, Timothy Brezina, in a 2014 interview. "There was a lot of class division, race and ethnic division." As a teenager, Agnew worked in the summer selling hot dogs on the boardwalk, where he was exposed to a lot of different people. He also took a high school economics class that introduced him to sociology. "The impact of that class and growing up in Atlantic City more generally really increased my interest in social questions and especially the impact of the social environment on the individual."

Agnew pursued a PhD in Sociology at the University of North Carolina—Chapel Hill. In spite of having no formal training in graduate school in criminology, he wrote a dissertation on delinquency and was hired as a criminologist at Emory University. In the following years, he devoted himself to studying criminology research and theory, continuously revising and strengthening his theoretical approach which came t o be known as general strain theory. The theory argues that individuals who experience various types of strain are more likely to turn to criminal behavior. The importance of Agnew's work in criminology led to his being selected for the 2015 Edwin H. Sutherland lifetime achievement award by the American Society of Criminology. In recent years, Dr. Agnew has turned his attention to the potential impact of climate change on crime. "Climate change will increase exposure to strains," he explains, "including extreme weather events (such as heat waves, flooding, droughts), food and freshwater shortages, the loss of livelihood, health problems, forced migration, poverty and inequality. We are already starting to see . . . that these strains will increase the likelihood of crime" (Hunt 2016).

neglected but not denied the relevance of [such] social psychological processes" (1968, p.209). The next set of theories in this chapter is focused specifically on just such issues.

SOCIALIZATION THEORIES

The social structural theories of deviance provide broad insights that help us understand how different social environments influence the rates of certain kinds of deviance, but those theories only shed light on the big picture. They do not explain in any detail the actual processes through which individuals are influenced to participate in deviant behaviors. Social structural theories are frequently criticized for failing to explain why some individuals in disorganized or strained social contexts engage in deviant behavior while others do not. This is important since even in the most impoverished neighborhoods not everyone engages in crime or deviance. Why do some individuals embrace deviant behavior while others in similar social circumstances continue to conform to societal expectations? It is just this question that is addressed by socialization theories such as differential association theory and social learning theory.

Differential Association Theory

Differential association theory was developed in the writings of Edwin Sutherland, one of the early sociologists trained at the University of Chicago. Through his training and research in Chicago, Sutherland was well versed in the ideas of social disorganization theory. He was particularly influenced by Shaw and McKay's ideas regarding social transmission of deviant values and behaviors. He was also deeply familiar with and impressed by criminologist Thorstein Sellin's (1938) explanation of crime as a result of culture conflict among different cultural groups, such as immigrants who brought cultural values at odds with American values with them from their home countries. Sutherland used Sellin's idea of conflicting cultures to revise his own conception of social disorganization to what he termed "differential social organization." It was not, he argued, that communities were disorganized, but rather that they were characterized by different social groups with different values and norms.

Sutherland was sharply critical of biological explanations of criminal behavior. In contrast, the differential association theory that he developed asserted as its central tenet that criminal behavior—and law-abiding behavior—is learned through social interaction. Criminal and deviant behaviors, he argued, were learned through association with individuals and groups that engaged in and supported such behaviors. Sutherland's sensitivity to the role that learning plays in deviant behaviors came in part from his research into the life of a colorful and accomplished Chicago thief, whom he called "Chic Conwell," and whose story he told in *The Professional Thief* (1937). Rejecting Lombroso's argument that "criminals are born, not made," Sutherland explained the importance of learning in reference to Conwell and other skilled thieves:

> A person can become a professional thief only if he is trained by those who are already professionals. It is ridiculous to imagine an amateur deciding to become a pickpocket, con man, penny-weighter (jewelry thief), or shake man (extortionist) without professional guidance. He knows nothing of the racket, its techniques or operations, and he can't learn these things out of books.
>
> —Sutherland (1937, p.21)

While it is easy to see that one needs to learn criminal behavior in order to enter the ranks of accomplished professional thieves, Sutherland believed that learning was at the heart of virtually all deviant behavior.

Sutherland's Key Principles

In systematizing his ideas, Sutherland developed nine basic principles (Sutherland et al. 1992), the most significant of which are listed below.

1. Criminal and deviant behavior is learned through social interaction, particularly in the context of personal face-to-face encounters.
2. Criminal/deviant behavior is learned through acquiring the techniques of committing deviant acts and the specific motives, rationalizations, and attitudes that make the behavior attractive or acceptable.
3. Person turns to deviant/criminal behavior as a result of an excess of definitions favorable to violation of law over definitions unfavorable to it.
4. Differential associations may vary in frequency, duration, priority, and intensity. Commitment to deviant behavior is stronger when deviant associations occur earlier in one's life, more frequently, over a longer period of time, and with greater positive emotional intensity.
5. The process of learning criminal behavior involves all of the mechanisms that are involved in any other learning.

Several of these principles of differential association theory are deceptively simple and warrant further discussion. To begin with, the first principle's highlighting of face-to-face interaction suggests that impersonal and secondhand sources of learning are less effective in transmitting knowledge, interest, and commitment to deviant behavior. Sutherland believed that few people learn deviant behavior through exposure in the media (e.g., in newspapers, movies, television—or, today, on the Internet), and he paid virtually no attention to the possibility that individuals might discover techniques for accomplishing deviant behavior on their own.

Sutherland's second principle stresses not only the learning of specific techniques associated with committing deviant acts (e.g., how to pick pockets or how to smoke marijuana), but also the acquiring of motives and attitudes—or social definitions—that provide the mind-set within which a particular kind of deviant behavior is viewed as acceptable and enticing. One learns, that is, not only behaviors, but also the meanings of those behaviors.

The third principle listed above has proven to be one of the more problematic features of Sutherland's theory. Quite simply, it states that individuals will engage in deviant behavior when they have acquired more favorable than unfavorable "definitions" or attitudes and beliefs regarding a behavior. While this statement seems generally reasonable, it has been criticized (e.g., Cressey 1960) as so vague that it offers little guidance for research.

The fourth principle is actually a list of several different variables that Sutherland argued were associated with the learning of deviant and nondeviant behaviors alike. Three of the variables—priority, frequency, and duration—are potentially measurable, although, as Sutherland and Cressey acknowledged, it is almost impossible for most people to remember who they first learned about different kinds of deviant behavior from and for how long. The "intensity" variable presents even greater challenges to systematic and rigorous observation.

Finally, Sutherland's fifth principle asserts that there are no exceptional social dynamics through which individuals learn deviant as opposed to nondeviant ways of behaving. The same basic socialization processes unfold in one person's learning to be a dentist as in another's learning to be a professional thief. The differences lie not in the learning process itself, but in what one learns and from whom.

A good example of the application of differential association theory can be provided by considering adolescent cigarette smoking. According to this theory, we would expect smoking to be more common among adolescents who spend time with other smokers. While there are images of smokers in the movies, magazines, and other media, differential association theory argues that adolescents who decide to take up smoking are influenced primarily by face-to-face interaction with their friends. If a teenager's peers smoke cigarettes and see it as a positive activity, they can provide opportunities for smoking as well as motives and attitudes that embrace the activity. Further, the more frequently an adolescent interacts with friends who smoke, the more positive experiences and definitions they are likely to develop toward smoking. According to differential association theory, the learning process through which the teenager becomes a smoker is the same as the process through which he or she learns other, nondelinquent behaviors, such as participating in sports or becoming a member of the school debate team. The only difference is in those with whom one associates.

Critique and Further Directions

Like other positivistic theories, differential association cannot provide an all-inclusive explanation of deviant behavior. Sutherland's theory is strongest when examining kinds of deviance that require significant learning and socialization. It is not accidental that Sutherland developed many of his ideas while studying a skilled professional thief. In contrast, a child (or adult) who engages in petty shoplifting does not need to learn much, or to associate with other shoplifters. Similarly, differential association cannot adequately explain crimes of passion, such as impulsive violence and murder. The principles of differential association, then, must be viewed as issues to be examined in specific cases rather than as automatically applicable to all deviant behavior.

Scholars have also criticized Sutherland for assuming that the learning of deviant behavior is largely restricted to face-to-face interaction. Sutherland et al.'s assertion that "impersonal agencies of communication, such as movies and newspapers, play a relatively unimportant part in the genesis of criminal behavior" (1992, p.88) has been criticized for failing to acknowledge the role that the media may play in socialization to deviance. Additionally, the rise of the Internet as an avenue for social interaction has provided new and extensive possibilities for association that Sutherland and his colleagues could not have anticipated. The role of Internet communication as a medium for learning and reinforcing deviant behavior has weakened arguments for the dominance of face-to-face interaction in learning deviance.

Social Learning Theory

Ronald Akers' writings have served as a major positivistic and psychologically oriented revision of Sutherland's differential association theory. In an influential critique, coauthored with Robert Burgess, Akers acknowledged two key insights in Sutherland's theory: that deviance is learned behavior and that such learning is principally based in social interaction (Burgess and Akers 1966). However, Burgess and Akers felt that Sutherland's theory was underdeveloped because it did not explain the psychological process through which learning occurred. They revised Sutherland's principles of differential association to make them consistent with the principles of learning in psychological *reinforcement theory.*

Reinforcement theory is based on the simple premise that humans—as well as other animals, from pigeons to dolphins—tend to persist in behaviors for which they are rewarded, and to discontinue behaviors for which they have been punished. The difference between those who engage in deviance and those who do not, from this perspective, is the result of "differential reinforcement" based on associating with different people. Akers' later writings, especially *Deviant Behavior: A Social Learning Approach* (1985), have deepened and extended his and Burgess' approach. The basic principles of social learning theory, which have remained consistent throughout Akers' work, are succinctly summarized in the following sentence:

> Whether individuals will refrain from or initiate, continue committing, or desist from criminal and deviant acts depends on the relative frequency, amount, and probability of past, present, and anticipated rewards and punishments perceived to be attached to the behavior.
>
> —Akers (1998, p.66)

For Akers, rewards and punishments are the key to understanding how individuals learn and become committed to deviant behavior. Differential association is important in his theory because differential reinforcement takes place for the most part in contexts of social interaction. Associating with different people exposes us to different behaviors and patterns of reward and punishment. Akers argues that individuals are reinforced not only through direct experience, but also vicariously as they witness the consequences of others' behavior. An observer will tend to imitate others—particularly others whom they like, respect, or admire—if they see their behavior rewarded, while avoiding similar behavior if it is punished.

As with other positivistic approaches, social learning theory claims to be a general theory of deviant behavior, with all the problems associated with any general theory of deviance. In general, social learning theory certainly has a strong foundation in the assumption that most forms of deviant—and nondeviant—behavior are dependent on some degree of learning from and with other people and on feeling some positive benefits associated with the behavior. Further, Akers has broadened the range of important influences on behavior beyond Sutherland's emphasis on primary groups and close associates to also include the positive and negative reinforcements experienced in less intimate settings, such as schools and workplaces, and in such media as magazines, television, and the movies.

Critical Evaluation

Still, Akers' use of reinforcement theory moves away from Sutherland's broader emphasis on the meaning of behavior for those who engage in it. For Akers, meaning is reduced to positive and negative rewards. Further, since social learning theory is open to incorporating any and all potential reinforcing factors that go into human behavior, from hedonistic gratification to respect or status in the eyes of other people, the theory is "so vague as to be tautological—true by definition" (Goode 2008, p.54).

Social learning theory also shares with other positivistic theories an inability to speak to issues of how and why different societies define deviant behavior in different ways and react to them in the ways that they do. As Akers acknowledges, "The theory is . . . incapable of accounting for why anyone or anything is socially defined as undesirable" (1985, p.43).

Further, as Curran and Renzetti have observed, social learning theory "overlooks the differential access of certain groups to a society's resources and rewards, as well as their differential power to escape punishment, to punish others, and to label others criminal or deviant" (1994, p.197). Ultimately, then, social learning theory is inadequate to the goal of providing a general theory of deviance, but it does provide another set of insights regarding the causes of deviant behavior.

SOCIAL CONTROL THEORIES

The final set of positivistic theories that we cover, social control theories, takes a different approach from the theories we have examined so far. Social control

PUSHING YOUR BOUNDARIES

A wide variety of crimes are regularly reported in the media. Identify two recent crimes in the news. Based on what is reported about the crimes, answer the following questions with short descriptions and brief quotes (such as an illustrative sentence or two) from the articles to show what you found.

- Is there anything in the reporting to suggest that some biological issue or chemical imbalance played a role in the person's committing the crime?
- Is there anything in the stories to suggest that some social structural dynamics (such as poverty, unsafe neighborhood, or social stress) played a role in the crime?
- Is there anything in the stories to suggest that peer relationships or socialization played a role in the crime?
- What about social control? Is there anything to suggest that the individual was especially impulsive or lacking in normal control of their behavior when they committed the crime?

Based just on what you found in the news articles, which of the major positivistic theories of crime and deviance was most supported? Come to class prepared to discuss your findings and compare them with other students.

theorists begin with the assumption that, at its core, human behavior is directed toward gratification of individual needs and desires. Thus, it is argued, human nature is in essence antisocial, impulsive, and self-centered. People commit crimes and other deviant acts because it is in their nature to do so. The question that really needs to be answered is not why some people commit deviant acts, but rather why most people do not commit them.

The roots of social control theory hark back the writings of the early British political philosopher, Thomas Hobbes, who argued that without control over individual human impulses and ambitions, life for people would be reduced to a war of all against all in which life was "solitary, poor, nasty, brutish, and short" (1991 [1651], p.xiii). In order to live stable and prosperous lives, Hobbes argued, individuals must submit to an authority that establishes and enforces social order and has the ability to control otherwise destructive human nature. While Durkheim was more focused on culture than on the authority of the state, he too believed that a stable and well-functioning society was one in which largely unbounded human urges and ambitions were controlled—in his case, by social norms and relationships. The central idea in all control theories is that the social environment functions to encourage, monitor, and enforce conformity. When social environments are weak or unstable, they fail to fulfill those functions and individuals' natural tendencies toward deviant behavior are free to be expressed in action.

Social Bond Theory

The most broadly influential versions of control theory have been associated with the writings of Travis Hirschi who developed two different variants of control theory during his career. Hirschi's first version of control theory, social bond theory (1969), was directed primarily toward explaining juvenile delinquency. Hirschi argued that adolescents who had weak conventional social bonds had few "stakes in conformity" and were thus susceptible to natural human urges to engage in deviant and criminal behavior. Hirschi cited the family as the social group that provides individuals with the most effective and enduring social bonds, while other secondary associations including schools, peers, and religious institutions play significant but less dominant roles. He contended that if social bonds were sufficiently strong they would inhibit the effectiveness of peer pressure to engage in delinquent acts. Social bond theory specified four interrelated elements of the social bond that connected adolescents (and the rest of us) to conventional society.

The first element of the social bond is what Hirschi refers to as "attachment," which involves individuals forming affective relationships with conventional others (e.g., parents, teachers, etc.). When such attachments are strong, individuals are sensitive to the opinions and expectations of others and tend to behave accordingly. Secondly, there is the element of "commitment," which refers to an individual's investment in conventional kinds of behavior. Those who have invested considerable time and energy in conventional lines of action such as pursuing an education or building a good employment record have developed a "stake in conformity." The third aspect of the social bond discussed by Hirschi is "involvement," which refers to mental and physical involvement in conventional activities. Those who are engaged in conventional activities are likely to be too busy to become involved in deviant behavior. The fourth element is "belief," by which Hirschi refers to an individual's belief that they should obey the rules of conventional society. Unlike differential association and social learning theorists who see different social groups holding different values and beliefs, Hirschi argues that individuals with weak social bonds simply do not feel compelled to follow rules.

Social bond theory has been positively received by many social scientists, especially those doing research on adolescent delinquency. However, many scholars have questioned the theory's potential for explaining crime and deviance more generally. Ross Matsueda, for instance, has argued that social bond theory is best-suited for analyzing only "trivial impulsive deviant acts, such as status offenses . . . rather than serious offenses, such as crimes against persons" (1989, p.432). Further, the theory's assumption that societies have central value systems that are recognized by virtually all members of the society is inconsistent with the reality of complex modern and postmodern societies that are characterized by a variety of cultural and subcultural groups with often conflicting values and social expectations.

By 1990 Hirschi had turned away from social bonding theory, although it remains popular today among some sociologists. Hirschi's motivation for abandoning the theory, however, had nothing to do with his acceptance of others' critiques of the theory, but rather was due to his own rethinking of basic control theory and tenets of classical criminology.

Self-Control Theory

Michael Gottfredson and Hirschi (1990) proposed what they term a "general theory of crime." Harking back to Beccaria and Bentham's belief that criminal behavior is based on individual calculations of pleasure and pain associated with different lines of action, Gottfredson and Hirschi proposed that "the common element in crime, deviant behavior, sin, and accident is low self-control," or the inability of some people "to avoid acts whose long-term costs exceed their momentary advantages" (1990, p.3). Crime and other antisocial behavior, they argue, are the result of impulsive pursuit of pleasure with minimal consideration of long-term consequences. "In sum," they explain, "people who lack self-control will tend to be impulsive, insensitive, physical (as opposed to mental), risk-taking, short-sighted, and nonverbal, and they will tend therefore to engage in criminal and analogous acts" (1990, p.90). Further, Gottfredson and Hirschi argue that "The major 'cause' of low self-control appears to be ineffective child-rearing" (1990, p.97).

Turning their attention away from the elements of social bonds and toward self-control, Gottfredson and Hirschi downplay the significance of external social factors and focus on individual personality characteristics. The family, they argue, is virtually the only major influence on a child's development of self-control. Further, once children reach adolescence, they will either have acquired or not acquired self-control as a stable personality trait. Once such personality patterns are set, they tend to persist over the life course. "In our view," they write, "the origins of criminality and low self-control are to be found in the first six to eight years of life, during which time the child remains under the control and supervision of the family or a familial institution" (1990, pp.272).

In order for children to adequately develop self-control, Gottfredson and Hirschi contend, parents must closely monitor their behavior, recognize deviant behavior when it occurs, and punish it. Only through such stern socialization will children develop the internal patterns of self-control that are critical to becoming law-abiding adults. "Self-control is highly efficient," they argue, "precisely because it is effective in a variety of settings, many of which lack social or legal surveillance" (1990, p.4).

Gottfredson and Hirschi see self-control theory as returning to the roots of classical criminology with its emphasis on individuals as calculators of pleasure and pain. The difference between law-abiding individuals and criminals or deviants, they argue, is that those who engage in antisocial behavior have not been trained to be capable of calculating the long-term consequences of different kinds of actions. As a result, they fall into the trap of pursuing short-term impulsive pleasures at the cost of more enduring satisfactions. Further, such individuals are not only incapable of taking a long-range view of their actions, but are also insensitive to the needs and desires of others. In essence, they are unsocialized humans in their natural state. This assumption of self-control theory leads Gottfredson and Hirschi to reject theories that suggest criminal behavior is socially transmitted or learned. Rather, they say, criminal behavior is primal, impulsive, and asocial. Not surprisingly, they suggest that routine activities theory (discussed earlier in the section on social disorganization theory) provides the only practical approach to crime prevention (outside of changing family dynamics) since it focuses on how routine daily activities and environments may either impede or increase immediate opportunities for criminal activity.

Critical Evaluation

It does not take much examination of the research literature, or even of cases reported in the media, to recognize that impulsiveness and lack of long-range thinking play a significant role in many kinds of crime and deviant behavior. Much, if not most, juvenile delinquency involves little conscious thought about the consequences of behavior. Many adult criminals are equally oblivious to potential negative results of their activities. But such findings do not support the assertion that low self-control is the cause of *all* crime and deviance. Gottfredson and Hirschi overstate the ability of their theory to provide a general theory of crime and deviance. Many kinds of deviance cannot be explained as simply a matter of low self-control due to poor parenting. Mental illness, for instance, may in some instances be influenced by family dynamics and relations, but by no means can it be reduced to them. And other forms of what we will refer to as status deviance later in the book, such as lesbian and gay identities and sexual orientations, would be distorted far more than clarified by explaining them a result of low self-control. Further, the belief that virtually all deviant behavior can be reduced to low self-control ignores the critical role of social power in constraining human behavior. Young Thai girls who are sold by family members to work in the Bangkok sex tourism industry have virtually no opportunity to resist their participation in deviant behavior. In short, self-control theory offers some insight for understanding a limited range of deviant behavior, but leads us far astray from understanding deviance in many other contexts.

Hirschi and Gottfredson's self-control theory is highly suspect in its assertion that there is some natural unsocialized state of human cognition and emotion that is inherently self-seeking and harmful to others. While hurtful and self-seeking behavior are certainly common in social life, there is no convincing evidence to suggest that dark and evil impulses are more core to human nature than are more sociable and cooperative feelings. The very notion that large numbers of humans go through life as largely unsocialized beings—and that these individuals alone are society's criminals and deviants—is a caricature, or distortion that exaggerates certain aspects of social life at the expense of a richer and more multifaceted understanding.

BLURRED BOUNDARIES II: "INFLUENCES" VERSUS "CAUSES"

In this chapter, we have discussed a bewildering array of explanations for deviant behavior: biological predisposition, social disorganization, poverty, lack of legitimate opportunities, associating with delinquent friends, poor parenting, and lack of self-control. Each theory has emphasized one or a few of the foregoing factors. So which theory is the right one? Which theory can explain Mike, the young man with whom we started the chapter? And what about all the other kinds of deviant behavior, from murder to alcohol abuse to obesity? Is there a single theory that can explain what causes all these different kinds of deviance? By now you should recognize that no theory can provide a universal explanation of the causes of deviant behavior.

But just because a theory fails to provide a universal explanation does not mean that we should abandon it. While none of the theories we have examined can explain all deviance, most of them can be useful at least some of the time—especially if we consider them as potential influences, rather than as determinative causes of deviance. Influences are not complete explanations in and of themselves. Their impact varies. Sometimes influences are stronger, sometimes weaker. Sometimes they do not exist at all. The theories discussed in this chapter alert us to the importance of many potential influences on deviant behavior—influences that can even overlap. Being influenced by one factor does not preclude being influenced by others.

So, how should we use the theories discussed in this chapter to understand Mike, the young man whose story started this chapter? The answer, from the interactionist perspective, is that before we can use them, we need to learn more about Mike's life. Using the research methods discussed in Chapter 2, we should seek to gain a deeper familiarity with his life experiences and contexts while keeping an eye open for the kinds of influences we have discussed in this chapter. As we learn about Mike's life in more detail, influences that have played a part will become more apparent. But they are also likely to shift in significance over time. To reach an understanding of how Mike ended up in jail today does not mean that we will reach some final explanation of who he is or what he can become. While causes are concrete determining forces, influences

Table 3.1 Positivistic Theories of Deviant Behavior

Theory	Cause of Deviant Behavior	Remedy for Deviance
Biological Theories		
Criminal anthropology	Biological defects, atavism	Confinement, limit reproduction
Current biological theories	Genetic defects Neurochemical abnormalities	Medical treatment (e.g., medications)
Social Structural Theories		
Social disorganization	Bad environment (poverty, overcrowding, lack of guidance)	Community development Improved socialization
Anomie theory	Imbalance between cultural values	More legitimate opportunities to achieve cultural goals
Socialization Theories		
Differential association	Associating and learning from deviant peers	Increased association with conventional peers
Social learning theory	Social and behavioral	More reinforcement toward approved behavior
Social Control Theories		
Social bond theory	Weak social bonds	Improved socialization and positive social involvement
Self-control theory	Lack of self-control and poor parenting	Stronger socialization and disciplining of children

have less weight. They are, at least in part, what we make them. When we reframe the theories discussed in this chapter as influences rather than causes, their impact becomes less grand and definitive, but more consistent with the blurred boundaries of real life.

Looking at the positivistic theories in table 3.1, can you see how the explanations described in more than one of the theories could be an influence on why Mike has ended up in jail?

SUMMARY

- Positivistic theories of deviance seek to explain the causes of deviant behavior.
- Biological theories emphasize the physiological causes of deviant behavior. Early biological theories focused on deviants' external bodies, while contemporary biological approaches look at hormonal and genetic causes of deviance.

- Social structural theories make the case that deviant behavior is the result of dysfunctional social features in a society.
  - Social disorganization theory states that deviance is caused by a lack of effective formal and informal social control.
  - Anomie theory asserts that lack of social integration and clear moral norms leads to deviant behavior.
- Socialization theories argue that both deviant and nondeviant behaviors are learned in social interaction with individuals and groups that support such behavior.
- Social control theories posit that antisocial and self-centered impulses are inevitable unless controlled by pro-social relationships and effective socialization in childhood.
- Positivistic theories seek to provide an explanation for the causes of all forms of deviant behavior, but each theory falls short of such broad ambitions.
- A more realistic approach to explaining deviant behavior acknowledges the variable influence of the different kinds of causal dynamics proposed by positivistic theories in specific cases of deviant behavior.

KEYWORDS

anomie: A term used by Emile Durkheim to refer to social conditions in which social norms and values are weak or absent. Durkheim believed this state of normlessness led to increased rates of suicide and other forms of deviant behavior.

anomie theory: Robert Merton's adaptation of the concept of anomie in his social structural theory of deviant behavior. The theory states that deviance is caused by discrepancies between culturally valued goals and the availability of legitimate institutionalized means for attaining them.

atavism: An evolutionary throwback to a more primitive form of life.

causal explanation: An explanation of deviant behavior that focuses specifically on underlying individual or social environmental factors that produce the behavior.

Chicago School (of sociology): The sociological approach developed at the University of Chicago through the 1920s and 1930s focusing on urban sociology and ethnographic fieldwork.

classical criminology: An influential theory of criminal justice developed by Cesare Beccaria and Jeremy Bentham in the eighteenth century. Based on the belief that human behavior is a response to pleasure and pain, the theory advocated swift and certain punishment to fit the crime.

concentric zone model (of deviant behavior): A theory developed by Chicago School sociologists that as cities develop, they form into specialized zones of activity. According to social disorganization theory, deviance is most common in the inner city area termed the zone of transitional zone.

conformity: Robert Merton's term in his anomie theory of deviance for conforming or nondeviant behavior in which individuals pursue socially valued goals through legitimate institutional means.

deterministic (theories): Sociological theories that view behavior as determined by factors outside personal control.

differential association theory: Edwin Sutherland's socialization theory of crime and deviance as caused by the learning of techniques, motives, and definitions of deviant acts through interaction with other deviants.

industrialization: The transformation of European societies in the late 1700s and 1800s from rural labor-intensive locally based economies to nationally and internationally marketed factory and machine production.

innovation: The term used in Robert Merton's anomie theory for deviant behavior in which individuals pursue a society's cultural goals through illegitimate or noninstitutional means.

Italian school of criminology: The biological approach to crime and deviance associated with the work of Cesare Lombroso and his associates in which deviance is believed to result from biological devolution and to be revealed by bodily abnormalities or atavistic stigmata.

positivistic (theories of deviant behavior): Theories of deviant behavior that emphasize the objective reality and deterministic causes of deviance.

rebellion: The term used in Robert Merton's anomie theory for deviant behavior in which individuals rebel against a society's cultural values and the institutionalized means for attaining them.

reinforcement theory: A psychological theory that individual behavior is determined by the experience of rewards and punishments. The theory serves as the basic component of Ronald Aker's social learning theory of deviant behavior.

retreatism: The term used in Robert Merton's anomie theory for deviant behavior in which individuals reject a society's cultural values and the institutionalized means for attaining them, withdrawing from participation in the society (e.g., through becoming alcoholics or drug addicts).

ritualism: The term used in Robert Merton's anomie theory for deviant behavior in which individuals reject a society's cultural values, but persist in ritualistically enacting the institutionalized means for attaining them.

routine activities theory (of predatory deviance): A theory of criminal activity developed by Marcus Felson that focuses on environmental aspects of criminal activity. Predatory crime is viewed as a consequence of three factors: vulnerable targets, motivated offenders, and the absence of capable guardians.

self-control theory: A theory of deviance proposed by Michael Gottfredson and Travis Hirschi, arguing that those who engage in deviant behavior are impulsive, insensitive individuals who, largely because of poor childhood socialization, lack the ability to evaluate the long-term consequences of their acts.

social bond theory: A social control theory of deviance proposed by Travis Hirschi that views deviance as a result of weak or attenuated social bonds. Hirschi has since rejected the theory and embraced self-control theory.

social learning theory: A socialization theory of deviance developed by Ronald Akers that views deviant behavior as learned through personally or vicariously experiencing rewards and punishments for the behavior.

urbanization: The massive shift of human populations over the past several centuries from predominantly rural settings into cities.

XYY syndrome: A genetic syndrome proposed in the 1960s in which males who are born with an extra Y chromosome are believed to be highly aggressive and prone to criminal behavior.

CHAPTER

4

Symbolic Interactionist/Social Constructionist Perspective

Medical marijuana protest march (Gina Kelly/Alamy Stock Photo).

CONTENTS

LEARNING OBJECTIVES

After reading this chapter you will be able to:

- Explain the social constructionist approach to deviance
- Outline the history of the roots of symbolic interactionism/social constructionism
- Discuss four aspects of the deviance process: the social construction of deviance categories, initial rule-breaking and primary deviance, processing deviants, and stigmatization and resistance
- Challenge popular beliefs about deviance, including the belief that deviance is a black-and-white affair, and that it is a quality of individuals

BLURRED BOUNDARIES I: CONSENSUS AND CONFLICT IN CONSTRUCTING DEVIANTS

Paul Lowe, a 43-year-old insurance executive, committed suicide after his wife walked in on him having sex with their 12-year-old daughter. Mr. Lowe drove away from their home while his wife called the police. Later, as the police reported, he was found, in a shopping mall parking lot, dead from a self-inflicted gunshot. On the car seat beside his body was a note that read, "I am so ashamed and so sorry. What I have done can never be forgiven."

Mr. Lowe committed an act that virtually all of us agree is wrong. While we know that incest and child sexual assault do sometimes occur, virtually none of us would suggest that such acts be legalized and accepted. The very idea strikes us as abhorrent. Even Mr. Lowe was so ashamed that he felt suicide was his only option.

In the world of deviance, we can find cases where we all agree that an act is immoral. But often things are not so clear. Consider the case of Jaime Vega. Jaime was arrested as he left a San Antonio restaurant where he worked 60 hours a week as a dishwasher. His crime was working illegally in the United States. Four months earlier, Jaime slipped across the Mexico–Texas border and made his way to San Antonio where friends had a job waiting for him. Since then, he worked almost every day and sent nearly 3,000 dollars home to his family. Should Jaime and the over 11 million other individuals illegally in the United States (Pew 2015) be considered criminals and deviants? Some say yes, and some say no.

The group, Americans for Legal Immigration (2014), says that "illegal aliens" are outlaws that show a disregard for American values. They drain the US economy by taking government handouts, and are a major conduit for bringing drugs and gangs into the United States. They are a scourge that should be removed from our society.

Many other US citizens disagree, arguing that those who slip across the border are mostly hardworking people willing to risk almost everything for the chance to improve their lives and those of their children. Undocumented workers, they say, make significant contributions to the economy by taking jobs no one else wants—and paying taxes that fund services they never themselves receive. In short the United States gains far more than it loses from the labors of undocumented workers.

The interactionist approach to deviance views our attitudes about both incest and illegal immigrants as "social constructions," or beliefs that we have developed through conversations and interactions. It is easier to see the socially constructed nature of our beliefs when we disagree among ourselves, but even our most deeply held beliefs emerge in the context of social interaction and communication. What does it mean to say that we socially construct our ideas of good and bad, right and wrong? How do we create deviants? And how do those who are labeled as deviants respond?

In this chapter, we explore these questions by glimpsing behind the curtain of the taken-for-granted world to look at how social constructions of deviance are created, enforced, and resisted or changed.

The Roots of Symbolic Interaction: The Social Self

Our discussion of symbolic interactionist and social constructionist approaches to deviance will benefit from a short consideration of the roots of the symbolic interaction perspective in the conception of the *social self* and the social origins of human minds.

The early twentieth-century sociologist, Charles Horton Cooley, is often credited as one of the first social scientists to articulate a conception of the social origins of the self. In contrast to spiritual traditions that viewed the self as a soul given to individuals by God, and in contrast to biological views of the self as physiologically preordained set of instincts and predispositions, Cooley argued that an individual's sense of self emerged in the process of socialization. Cooley said it is impossible to separate the individual and society. "There is no sense of 'I'," he wrote, "without its correlative sense of you, or he, or they" (1902, p.182). Cooley captured the social nature of the self in his term the "looking glass self." People's self-feelings, he explained, are comprised of three elements: (1) how we imagine we appear to others, (2) our imagination of how others judge our appearance, and (3) a resulting self-feeling. In imagining others' judgments of us, we develop feelings about ourselves, such as a sense of pride, shame, or embarrassment.

Cooley's ideas of the looking glass self were extended by George Herbert Mead, a philosopher whose book *Mind, Self, and Society* (1934) was critical to the development of the symbolic interactionist perspective. Mead argued that the development of the self occurs as a child becomes able to "take the role of the other." This ability to see things from someone else's point of view is possible because humans have the capacity to communicate through the use of complex symbol systems—most notably language. In providing us with a set of symbols that call forth similar ideas in us as they do in others, language enables us to interpret others' thoughts and behaviors and to coordinate our interactions with them. The ability to take the role of the other enables us to see ourselves from their perspectives and to orient our behavior accordingly.

Further, language enables us to create "symbolic universes" that provide maps for seeing and understanding the world around us. And inside us: for Mead, the concept of "mind" referred not simply to physiological brain functions or to some mysterious entity separate from the body, but rather to the incorporation of linguistic symbols and the social process of communication within the individual. Mind is an active and ongoing affair. Because people possess minds, they are able to create, discover, and communicate new realities. They are active, self-conscious agents who can express meanings and plan their actions, thus asserting some control over their environments. The importance of the social self, language, and mind for the study of deviance will become apparent in the following discussion of labeling theory.

LABELING THEORY AND SOCIAL CONSTRUCTION

Labeling theory emerged as a set of ideas about the role that labeling deviant behavior can play in increasing and solidifying deviance rather than decreasing it. Labeling theory is identified with the work of sociologists who applied symbolic interactionism to deviance in the 1950s and 1960s, but similar ideas had been discussed by earlier social scientists. Durkheim, whose ideas about anomie and deviance we examined in the previous chapter, recognized the importance of labeling when he discussed the "dramatization of deviance." When we identify and punish deviants, Durkheim argued, we clarify our collective moral boundaries—indicating through our reaction that certain kinds of behavior are unacceptable to us and that bad consequences follow engaging in such acts. In the process of mobilizing our feelings against a common enemy, we also reaffirm our own moral identity. Durkheim believed that moral boundaries are so critical to the functioning of a healthy society, that a world without "taboo behavior" is impossible. In one of his most famous quotes, Durkheim asserted:

> Imagine a society of saints, a perfect cloister of exemplary individuals. Crimes, properly so called, will be there unknown; but faults which appear venial to the layman will create there the same scandal that the ordinary offense does in ordinary consciousness. If then, this society has the power to judge and punish, it will define these acts as criminal and will treat them as such.
>
> —Durkheim (1938, p.68)

The behaviors that are considered deviant, according to Durkheim, will vary according to social contexts. "What confers this [deviant] character upon acts," he writes, "is not the intrinsic quality of a given act but that definition which the collective conscience lends them" (1938, p.69).

Political scientist Frank Tannenbaum also anticipated central components of the labeling perspective. Based on his field study of delinquent gang activity in a Mexican village, Tannenbaum (1938) argued that the apprehension and labeling of members of the gang moved them more deeply into criminal behavior, rather than serving as a way to break them of their youthful deviance. What began as annoying, childish adventures of breaking windows, running around porches, stealing from pushcarts, and playing truant turned sinister as some boys were singled out as the "real" culprits for the gang's misdeeds. Once a boy was singled out, Tannenbaum argued, the community's perceptions changed. "There is a shift from the definition of the specific acts as evil to a definition of the individual as evil, so that all his acts come to be looked upon with suspicion" (1938, p.37). The boy becomes viewed as a "bad boy" and it becomes routine to look for the worst in him and use any further misdeeds as evidence of his evil character. Processing the young man through the criminal justice system and exposing him to more seasoned miscreants in detention facilities increases his knowledge of crime and his personal identification of himself as a criminal. What began as little more than youthful exuberance is transformed by community labeling and processing of some boys into full-fledged criminal behavior and identity. In essence we have witnessed an example of what Robert Merton (1968) termed the self-fulfilling prophecy, or the power of labeling to create behavior that is consistent with the label.

The insights of Durkheim and Tannenbaum, as well as the implications of symbolic interaction more generally, lead sociological analysis of deviance in a radically different direction from the positivistic approaches we examined in Chapter 3. If, as Durkheim contends, deviance is not an intrinsic quality of a given act, but rather the "definition which the collective conscience lends them," then our understanding of deviance should start by examining how definitions of deviance are created. Taking deviance categories for granted and talking only about the causes of deviance is like jumping into the river halfway downstream and thinking we can talk knowledgeably about its source. This is not to say that we do not need to study those who become identified as deviants, but it does suggest that it is at least as important to look at how societies create the categories of deviance. As Howard Becker, one of the leading early labeling theorists, observed, "It is an interesting fact that most scientific research and speculation on deviance concerns itself with the people who break rules rather than with those who make and enforce them. If we are to achieve a full understanding of deviant behavior, we must get these two possible foci of inquiry into balance" (1963, p.248).

Similarly, John Kitsuse called for a shift in "the focus of theory and research from the forms of deviant behavior to the processes by which persons come to be defined as deviant" (1962, p.248). Kitsuse identified three distinct aspects of the social construction of deviance: (1) the process of defining certain kinds of behaviors, lifestyles, or conditions as deviant, (2) the identifying of certain people as examples of those kinds of deviance, and (3) the formal and informal social reactions to individuals who become labeled as deviants. Such an approach provides a useful vantage point from which to examine social, political, and historical shifts in public moral discourse. In revealing the often conflicted and contingent nature of social conceptions of deviance, as well as in demonstrating the critical role of social power in defining official reality, the social constructionist approach to deviance makes sense of many aspects of the deviance landscape that cannot be addressed via theories that focus only on deviance causation.

But a focus on moral claims-making and the social construction of deviance categories provides only part of the picture. As we noted in Chapter 2, the meanings that "deviants" themselves apply to their contexts and behaviors may vary significantly from official or stereotypical images developed by other people. Since those who are labeled deviant must live within the contexts of others' constructions of "people like them," we must also consider the interplay between individuals, their deviant peers, and the broader society. In order to pull together the wealth of symbolic interactionist and social constructionist insights, we will divide the discussion that follows into four broad parts of the deviance process. First, we examine the social construction of deviance categories. Next, we consider the social process through which individuals first engage in disapproved behavior. We then explore the ways people tend to respond to those who are labeled as deviant. Finally, we look at the ways in which deviants themselves respond to the treatment that is accorded them.

SOCIAL CONSTRUCTION OF DEVIANCE CATEGORIES

Research on the social construction of deviance seeks, as Kitsuse and Spector (1975, p.586) have explained, "to provide a description and explanation of the definitional process in which morally objectionable conditions or [deviant] behaviors are asserted to exist, and the collective activities that become organized around those assertions." Sociologists who focus on this kind of analysis have made extensive use of Becker's (1963) discussion of the deviance-making enterprise. Using a business metaphor, Becker argues that publicly recognized kinds of deviant behavior are created and sustained through the active and concerted efforts of *moral entrepreneurs*. Just as people in other lines of business create and promote their products, moral entrepreneurs create and promote views of immoral behavior and deviant people. The term "moral entrepreneurs" includes two somewhat different but overlapping kinds of activities: creating rules and enforcing them. In this section of the chapter, we focus on rule-creators.

In complex societies there are many different social groups with varying values and norms, thus leading to potential conflict among them. We can consider the deviance-making enterprise as beginning when an individual or group comes to feel that a certain behavior (e.g., drinking and driving) or condition (e.g., obesity) is a threat to them and to the broader society. Public concern about many kinds of deviance wax and wane, gaining prominence at times and then receding, only to reemerge later as either new or rediscovered problems. At other times, novel circumstances (e.g., technological changes like the Internet) give rise to concerns about new problems that have not been seen before.

Frequently we see deviance entrepreneurs or rule-creators who are motivated by personal experiences that make them especially sensitive to a particular problem, and who come to view the problem as a broader public issue. An example of a moral entrepreneur whose deviance-making career started with a personal trouble is provided by Candace Lightner, who founded Mothers Against Drunk Driving after her 13-year-old daughter was killed by an intoxicated driver. Another example is provided by the parents of Jeanne Clery, a Lehigh University student who was raped and murdered in her residence hall. Angered that students and parents had not been informed about other violent crimes on or near the university's campus in recent years, Clery's parents turned their attention to the national level, playing a major role in the federal 1990 Campus Security Act that requires colleges and universities to keep and disclose information about crime on and near their campuses.

Deviance rule-creators are moral crusaders. Whether they are on the right or the left of the political spectrum, whether they are religiously or secularly oriented in their beliefs, moral entrepreneurs seek to publicize the issues that worry them. They believe that they know how to solve the problems they have uncovered, and they seek to enlist the support of others in promoting these solutions, which may include such remedies as new laws, increased policing, new medical treatments, or campaigns to promote religious conversion.

It is important to recognize that awareness of a problem and the mounting of a moral campaign against it does not require that the problem be an objectively validated one in terms of meeting the canons of scientific evidence. The success or failure of a deviance-making campaign depends on the support it receives from influential audiences to whom the problem is communicated. What matters from the practical standpoint of deviance entrepreneurs is that they succeed in convincing enough people of the reality of the problem so that the remedy can be implemented.

Rule-creators, then, are in the business of changing people's perceptions, converting them to believing in the existence of a particular problem and the necessity of the proposed solution. However, as Hilgartner and Bosk (1988) have noted, there are many potential evils in the world and only a limited amount of public interest and attention span. Moral entrepreneurs thus find themselves in competition with each other for the attention and support of the public in general and other groups with more specialized interests.

Resource Mobilization and Deviance Framing

In their efforts to promote their causes, deviance entrepreneurs face the same kinds of problems as those experienced by other social problems *claims-makers* (Spector and Kitsuse 1977; Best 1987) and social movement advocates. Most importantly, they all face the interrelated tasks of securing resources to pursue their causes and framing their concerns in ways that will attract supporters. Social movement theorists have devoted considerable attention to analyzing social movement activities directed toward these goals.

Resource Mobilization

Within the field of social movement research, *resource mobilization* theory (e.g., Edwards and McCarthy 2004) has shown that social movements' opportunities for success are enhanced when they have critical resources, including financial support, human labor, and media access. Deviance entrepreneurs, like other social movement activists, are most effective when they can draw in resources, mobilize supporters, and forge alliances. Such alliances form the backbone of effective deviance enterprises. The support and endorsement of one's cause by influential individuals and/or groups of legislators, law enforcement officials, school administrators, physicians, or attorneys can dramatically improve the chances of getting laws passed to control disapproved behaviors and conditions. Indeed, deviance entrepreneurs often fail to achieve their goals in large part because material and political conditions at the time are not favorable to building alliances and securing the resources needed to move their cause forward. But support for any deviance enterprise, just as for other social problems, depends on the skill and commitment of moral entrepreneurs as they communicate their causes.

Deviance Framing

Taking seriously the symbolic interactionist principle that "people act toward things on the basis of the meaning things have for them," David Snow and his colleagues (e.g., Snow et al. 1986b; Benford and Snow 2000) have developed a perspective for research and analysis of social movements that focuses on how social problems are defined or "framed" and how those framings may draw diverse people together in pursuit of common goals. The analysis of social movement framing processes advanced by Snow and his colleagues dovetails with Joel Best's work on social problems claims-making. Both demonstrate the dynamics involved in the framing of problems and the importance of those framings in building support for one's cause.

Moral entrepreneurs engage in three basic kinds of framing (Snow and Benford 1988). *Diagnostic framing* involves identifying or naming a particular problem, providing an explanation of what it is and how it came about. For instance, different moral entrepreneurs provided very different diagnostic framings of AIDS during its early years. Some entrepreneurs framed the HIV tragedy as a plague visited by an angry God on homosexuals for their immoral behavior (Parsons et al. 2006). In contrast, medical professionals argued that AIDS was caused by a sexually transmitted virus. According to this diagnostic framing, gay men were being victimized by a deadly disease, not punished for their sins. Yet, other claims-makers, particularly Africans from devastated nations, claimed that the epidemic was an American plot to wipe out African peoples (Krouse 1999). Finally, in addition to naming problems and identifying their causes, diagnostic framings of deviance indicate the kinds of emotional reactions—whether anger and outrage or sympathy and compassion—that are appropriate, and toward whom these emotions should be directed.

While diagnostic framing names a problem, *prognostic framing* proposes a solution to it. Typically, as Benford and Snow note, "the identification of specific problems and causes tends to constrain the range of possible 'reasonable' solutions" (2000, p.616). So, for instance, advocating for "safe" gay sex is not an appropriate solution to AIDS if the disease is defined as God's punishment for gay men's sinful behavior. In a similar vein, framing cigarette smoking as an addiction suggests that preventing people from ever starting, and providing medical help (e.g., nicotine patches) for those seeking to quit may be valuable solutions. On the other hand, framing cigarette smoking as a matter of smokers victimizing innocent bystanders with secondhand smoke implies that restricting places where people can legally smoke is the most appropriate response.

The third type of framing, *motivational framing*, provides a "call to arms," making the case for why people should become involved in addressing the problem. Motivational framings frequently express deviance entrepreneurs' concerns regarding the severity of the problem and the urgent need to respond. Statistics may be invoked to portray problems as widespread and seriously harmful, documenting the number of lives touched and the depth of harm. Arguments regarding the urgency to act may focus on the need to limit harm as quickly as possible, or they may make the case for unique opportunities that must be seized at just this moment. In any case, motivational framing provides a call to arms to act now and help take control of a dangerous situation.

Credibility

The power of moral entrepreneurs to mobilize others to their cause depends in large part on the perceived credibility of their claims as well as on the credibility of the claims-makers themselves. Respected leaders, individuals with relevant professional credentials (e.g., academic, medical, or military), and those with experiential credentials (e.g., reformed deviants or social workers) are often perceived as particularly credible and featured prominently as spokespeople. Those who have been victimized by deviance (e.g., victims of child abuse) are also often seen as being able to speak with special veracity by virtue of having "lived through the experience" or as having a moral right to have their views honored.

The credibility of the claims made by deviance entrepreneurs is critical to building support from the general public or more specific groups. Given the prevalence of statistics as a basic form of evidence for claims in American society, deviance entrepreneurs often present statistical data to support their claims. But the statistics upon which they draw tend to be fitted to their interests and concerns. This does not mean that deviance entrepreneurs deliberately create misleading statistics (although such deception may occur). More frequently, as Joel Best explains, they simply:

> Start with their own interests or concerns, which leads them to run across, or perhaps actively uncover, relevant statistical information. When these figures support what they already believe—or hope, or fear—to be true, it is very easy for them to adopt the numbers, to overlook or minimize their limitations, to find the figures first arresting, then compelling, and finally authoritative.
>
> —Best (2004, p.xv)

Atrocity Tales

There are clear advantages of depicting a problem as being as large—and as scary—as possible. Selective use of statistics can provide compelling evidence. But even more valuable than statistics, oftentimes, are shocking stories that illustrate the problem. Deviance entrepreneurs tend to select extreme and disturbing examples in order to get media attention and create public support.

The media are often receptive to shocking and melodramatic claims that typify social problems in terms of "victims who are exploited by villains and who must be rescued by heroes" (Best 1995, p.15).

Consider the treatment of child abuse in the media. As John Johnson (1995, p.23) has noted, the most common cases of child abuse are not particularly dramatic, involving "a nonserious injury to a child under three, committed by a young person (usually the mother), who is under much stress while having few resources to manage the circumstances." Such typical cases, however, are seldom focused on by deviance entrepreneurs or covered in any detail in the news. Rather, the stories recounted by deviance entrepreneurs and the media tend to be more shocking, as in a newspaper story that reports: "A forty year-old man has been charged with assaulting his fifteen year-old daughter by hanging her upside down by her toes and then beating her" (Johnson 1995, p.23). The details of such outrageous stories capture public attention and linger in people's memories, eliciting strong negative emotions, thus making them a valuable resource for moral entrepreneurs.

Horror stories of sensational deviant behavior, or *atrocity tales* as they are often called, are key features of the social construction of deviance. By associating deviant individuals and groups with violations of basic human decency, atrocity tales provide visceral evidence for negative labels that justify efforts to outlaw or otherwise control harmful behaviors or conditions. In vividly portraying the horrors associated with deviance, atrocity tales also emphasize the urgency of dealing with the problem as swiftly as possible.

While there is no doubt that horrifying examples of many kinds of deviance do take place, the use of atrocity tales by moral entrepreneurs is intended to "recraft worst cases into typical cases and the episodic into the epidemic" (Reinarman 2009, p.144). So, for instance, moral entrepreneurs seeking to ban marijuana often tell stories that portray marijuana as a "gateway drug" to hard drug use. The examples they present suggest that the path from "smoking grass" to "shooting up heroin" is a common pattern for marijuana users. The most disturbing stories are used to mobilize public sympathy for the cause.

Cultural Resonance

The claims of deviance entrepreneurs do not have to be universally accepted in order to be influential, but they do have to garner support from at least some groups in the society. The chances of gaining support are enhanced when claims resonate with other concerns and beliefs. In large, complex societies, many cultural issues are of considerable salience to some groups, but of little concern to others. Deviance claims may resonate with some groups, while gaining little support elsewhere, depending on how consistent the claims are with a group's prior beliefs. So, for instance, claims of a US medical conspiracy to infect African nations with the AIDS virus were far more likely to be considered plausible among African immigrants and African-Americans than among white Americans (Krouse 1999; Lemelle 2003).

Often the deviant behavior is described by moral entrepreneurs as connected to stigmatized social groups, especially racial minorities. The ethnocentric linkage of deviant behaviors or conditions to already stigmatized classes of people may gain resonance among members of some groups by bundling newly perceived "bad acts" with long-standing prejudices regarding some minority groups as "bad people." A good set of examples are provided by successive waves of US "drug scares" associated with different minorities including:

- The late 1800s campaign against the "Mongolian vice" of opium smoking associated with the "Yellow Peril" of Chinese immigrants (Baumohl 1992).
- Widespread claims in the early 1900s that cocaine use spurred African-American men to rape white women (Musto 1999).
- The crusade by the Federal Narcotics Bureau against "killer weed" (marijuana) that was claimed to be responsible for violent behavior among Mexican-Americans (Dickson 1968).

In cases like these, the claims of deviance entrepreneurs gain momentum because they act as surrogates for other kinds of conflicts, such as those related to race, ethnicity, and social class.

Deviance entrepreneurs may also gain support from various professional groups or social organizations that see themselves as benefiting from the creation of new deviance categories or the expansion of existing categories. Law enforcement agencies may rally behind the claims of deviance entrepreneurs in part because they hope to increase the resources available to them in the process—as Becker (1963) argues was the case in the Federal Narcotics Bureau campaign against marijuana in the 1930s. Similarly, drug companies may find it appealing to support the creation of new categories of mental illness for which they have recently patented new medications (Healy 2002; Horwitz 2002). Prominent deviance entrepreneurs often come from organizations that stand to gain from the activities associated with policing and control of deviant populations. This does not necessarily imply that such individuals or groups are motivated only by vested interests. Most are likely to be strong believers in the deviance constructions that they promote. But the dovetailing of material interests with moral conviction can produce particularly strong and self-reinforcing commitment to the cause.

Ultimately, the creation of deviance is a political process in which moral entrepreneurs seek to publicly define certain behaviors or conditions as immoral and to establish new methods of social control. The development of new categories of deviance and new forms of social control serves instrumental functions in outlawing or medicalizing certain behaviors or conditions. It also has a symbolic effect, giving legitimacy to some interest groups and denying it to others. In this regard, the enactment of laws banning deviance (e.g., the Prohibition ban on alcoholic beverages) is a mark of visible success for the moral entrepreneurs associated with a particular cause at a particular point in time. While the political victory of enacting laws stands as a mark of success, however, the moral entrepreneur's battles are not over, but simply shifted to a new set of issues regarding how to implement and enforce the law.

We will turn our attention to the issue of implementing and enforcing policies directed against deviants later in this chapter. But first, we need to discuss what labeling theory has to say about the social processes and contexts in which individuals initially engage in deviant or rule-breaking activities.

INITIAL RULE-BREAKING AND PRIMARY DEVIANCE

Labeling theory begins with a distinction between initial or episodic rule-breaking, on the one hand, and more long-term and visible identification as a "rule-breaker" on the other. According to Edwin Lemert (1951), one of the first advocates of the labeling approach, the decision to engage in rule-breaking or deviant behavior is *polygenetic*, meaning that it may be influenced by a wide variety of "causes." A person may engage in a bout of excessive drinking for a range of subjective reasons or situational circumstances, including (among many other possibilities) to unwind after a stressful week, to enjoy a party with friends, or in response to the death of a loved one. The cause or causes of such deviance, Lemert argues, are less significant than are the potential social reactions. If a community is open to or tolerant of certain kinds of behaviors—in this case, heavy consumption of alcoholic beverages—that kind of behavior may not even cross the threshold of being considered deviant. But, even when acts or conditions are broadly considered deviant within a culture, not every case of rule-breaking will be identified and condemned. Labeling theorists argue that there is a world of difference between incidental unlabeled deviant behavior on the one hand, and behavior that has been publicly identified and condemned on the other.

Primary versus Secondary Deviance

Lemert uses the terms *primary deviance* and *secondary deviance* to refer to the difference between incidental, unlabeled deviance and kinds that are publicly identified and condemned. Primary deviance occurs when individuals engage in deviant or rule-breaking acts, but when those acts do not become the basis for an individual's identification as a deviant. In many cases people are not identified because they are secret deviants who hide their disapproved activities from others, as in the case of bulimic young women who hide their purging behaviors from family and friends. In other cases, the rule-breaking activities are so fleeting or irregular that even though others observe them, they do not see them as central features of the individual's personality or identity. For instance, an adolescent may drink an occasional beer or smoke a few cigarettes, but not necessarily be viewed by self or others as a problem drinker or smoker. In contrast, secondary deviance involves being socially labeled as a specific kind of deviant and having organized one's life in large part around activities associated with that deviant identity. We will examine the issue of secondary deviance later in this chapter. For the present, however, we continue our focus on the first steps of participation in rule-breaking behavior.

Biography and Effective Environment

Symbolic interactionists believe that most people, most of the time, exert some degree of volition, or conscious control over their actions, as opposed to having their behaviors determined by their biology or their environment. But just because humans exert some control over their actions does not imply a completely free will to do whatever we might wish. As David Matza (1969) notes, the idea of "free will" takes the notion of "will" out of context, making it an abstraction that is of little use for understanding flesh-and-blood real people. It is true that we make decisions on which we act, but those decisions are made by specific individuals with specific biographical experiences in specific situational contexts.

An individual's *biography* provides the framework within which we define ourselves and make sense of our lives. Our biographies, symbolic interactionists observe, are not just a set of objective facts. Rather, they are a mix of fragmented memories of experiences and conditions that we weave together in a story about our lives. Biographies develop out of our experiences and the meanings that we impute to them. Further, we create our current biographies from our present standpoints, and, as we add new experiences to our lives, the meanings of our past experiences—our biographies—may be redefined and reevaluated. Biographies, then, provide a significant part of our sense of who we are and who we might become. By virtue of our specific biographical experiences, we find ourselves open (or closed) to considering different kinds of behaviors.

Our openness to engaging in different kinds of behaviors also emerges within specific social contexts, or what interactionists refer to as an *effective environment.* Just as they view biography as imbued with meaning—an interpretation of highlighted experiences in our lives—symbolic interactionists use the term effective environment to emphasize the subjective meaning of our social situation and surroundings. The effective environment is the environment as we define and experience it. Such an approach builds upon Mead's (1938) insight that perception is a "collapsed act," by which he meant that our perception of things in our environment is based on the way we anticipate ourselves interacting with them. So, for instance, an open door on a plane filled with passengers may be viewed as an extreme danger from which we pull back in fear, but for a group of skydivers it is a sign that they have reached "jump altitude" and may safely exit the plane. Similarly, a knife may be perceived as a tool

PUSHING YOUR BOUNDARIES

Reflections on the Meaning of "Skipping Class"

Going to college presents students with new opportunities, social situations, and even new biographies, or a changing sense of who they are and of what their activities mean about them. Consider the experience of skipping classes. In most high schools, student attendance is tightly monitored, but in college, especially in large classes, it is often hard for professors to be sure if particular students are showing up or not. Even beyond not getting caught for skipping class, students may find that the meaning of skipping class is different for them in college from what it was in high school.

Look back on your experience of skipping classes in high school compared to college. First describe how often—and why—you skipped class in high school. What were the consequences for skipping? How did skipping class fit into your biography, or your sense of who you were at that time in your life? Now describe how often—and why—you skip college classes. What circumstances are ones in which you would consider skipping classes today? How is this "effective environment"—the college environment as you define and experience it—different from your experience in high school? Does "skipping class" mean something different for you as a college student from what it meant in high school? How does skipping class fit into your personal biography, your perception of who you are? Does it mean you are less committed to school than you were in high school? Does it mean you are more committed and identified with other aspects of your life?

This simple exercise illustrates how our openness to new experiences and to breaking social norms is connected to our biographies and effective environments. Come to class prepared to share your reflections with other students.

for preparing a family meal, or, under different circumstances, as a weapon for attacking an abusive spouse.

The combination of biography and effective environment produces an openness in us to different kinds of activities, including potentially deviant ones. They do not, however, *cause* us to engage in deviant behavior. Rather, they open us to what Matza (1969, p.112) refers to as the "invitational edge" of deviance, to seeing oneself as "the kind of person who might possibly do the thing." So, for example, spending time in the jazz music scene of the early 1960s provided both biographical experiences and an effective environment that led many aspiring musicians in Becker's (1963) study to view themselves as the kind of person who would try smoking marijuana. Similarly, many new college students find that life as a university student provides both new biographical experiences and an effective environment that opens them to the "invitational edge" of seriously considering underage drinking.

Still, flirting with the idea of doing something and actually doing it are two very different things. One may be open, but hesitant, stopping short of actually smoking a joint or cheating on an exam. Often the potential rule-breaker recognizes that the act they are considering is socially disapproved. While feeling drawn to the activity, they have trouble with seeing themselves in the bad light that it would imply about them. And unless they are able to neutralize these concerns, at least for the moment, they may be unwilling to take the final step.

Techniques of Neutralization

Faced with the problem of overcoming the view of an act as wrong, and therefore of themselves as "bad people" if they participate in it, how do people proceed? Symbolic interactionists have found a variety of ways in which those at the invitational edge of deviance neutralize moral constraints, accepting the rules in general, but defining their own acts as "not really deviant."

Sometimes individuals come up with ways to neutralize or justify potential acts on their own. In his classic study of embezzlers, Donald Cressey (1953) found that those who took illegal advantage of their access to other people's money typically justified their behavior at first by telling themselves they were "only borrowing the money" and that they would pay back the funds as soon as their finances improved. In other cases, where a deviant subculture exists, deviant peers provide rationalizations that free participants from the negative implications of their behaviors.

Gresham Sykes and David Matza (1957) used the term *techniques of neutralization* to refer to the kinds of arguments that people invoke to make the case that their potentially deviant acts should not be considered deviant or immoral. Among the many techniques of neutralization they identified are:

- Denial of responsibility: alleging that one had no control over one's behavior at the time.
- Denial of injury: the assertion that no one was hurt by the activity.
- Denial of victim: the argument that the victim "had it coming."
- Condemnation of the condemners: presenting rule-breaking as acceptable since those who condemn it are themselves immoral.
- Appeal to higher loyalties: stating that one's rule-breaking is in the service of a higher good.

Techniques of neutralization provide rationalizations that enable an individual to violate social norms while at the same time believing that it is important to obey them—except in their particular circumstances. These kinds of verbalizations are also used frequently to explain one's misdeeds after the fact (a matter that we will address later in this chapter). But in the early stages of flirting with the possibility of committing a deviant act, such mental maneuvers can give one the green light to proceed.

The Roles of Others

Symbolic interactionists agree with differential association and social learning theorists that other people—especially other "deviants"—often play influential roles in our decisions to engage in deviant behaviors. In addition to offering verbal rationales for why it is okay to engage in deviant acts, friends and other associates also provide an individual with behavioral role models, demonstrating how to engage in deviant behaviors. Peers are also useful, especially in the early stages of a deviant career, in providing the social contacts, such as sex clients, or facilitating substances, such as drugs, that are necessary for various kinds of deviant acts. Finally, one's fellow deviants may offer significant social support in managing the stigma of deviance.

Turning On

When we participate in any new kind of activity, our experiences influence whether or not we will be drawn to engage in the behavior again. We may be "turned on" by an experience, finding it exciting, physically pleasurable, or otherwise personally gratifying. We may feel that our personal horizons and interpersonal relationships are expanded, as some people claim after first using mind-altering drugs or having a satisfying new sexual experience. In the face of such positive experiences and self-evaluations, we are likely to remain open to participating in similar behaviors in the future.

On the other hand, we may find that engaging in the act was not the positive experience we anticipated. A recreational drug may make us violently ill; a new sex act may make us feel disgusted with ourselves; or cheating on an exam may make us feel cheap and unworthy of our grade. These negative experiences and self-evaluations are likely to reduce our future openness to similar activities.

It is important to recognize that our biographies continue to evolve over time. As our experiences and environments change, our openness to various kinds of activities and relationships may change too. Based on our sense of ourselves and the meanings that different activities have for us, we may decide to discontinue our participation in them. Or, on the basis of new experiences and new self-attitudes, we may become willing to consider engaging in activities that we once looked upon with loathing and disdain. Unlike social control theorists who view the personality as largely imprinted and unchangeable after childhood, symbolic interactionists view the social self as a lifelong process of becoming. And in that process our openness to different kinds of deviance may change over time.

Limits of Voluntary Choice

The foregoing discussion focuses on the contexts within which personal decisions are made to engage in rule-breaking activity. The symbolic interactionist approach to deviance emphasizes personal choice based on the meaning an activity has for the individual. But while such an approach has advantages for understanding deviant or rule-breaking behavior in general, it is clear that there are circumstances in which people do not voluntarily choose deviant behavior. Most significantly, there are cases where childhood socialization and biological influences play critical roles in individuals' involvement in deviance. A good example of circumstances in which early socialization may lead to participation in deviant behavior is provided by Patricia and Peter Adler's (1978) study of "tiny-dopers"—children who are socialized to use marijuana from a very young (even toddler) age. Raised by parents who are regular marijuana users, these children are allowed to watch and imitate adults' behavior, and they may learn to smoke marijuana and enjoy its effects by the time they are only four or five years old. These youngsters' exposure to marijuana occurs at such an early age that it makes no sense to view them as more than passive recipients of intergenerational values and behaviors. Indeed, these children are raised in families in which it is normative to smoke marijuana, and in this sense they are not even aware of engaging in deviant behavior until they reach an age (typically around seven years old) at which they become cognizant of the broader societal norms regarding marijuana.

There are also cases in which human biology may play an important role in behaviors and conditions that come to be classified as deviant. For instance, many researchers have presented evidence to suggest that individuals' primary sexual orientations originate before birth and are linked to genetic or hormonal traits (Hamer and Copeland 1994; Roper 1996). Such findings do not mean that all homosexual acts are biologically determined, nor that all who adopt a gay lifestyle or identity do so as a result of biological predisposition, but they do illustrate that factors other than "free choice" may play a critical role in the development of gender and sexual identities.

The foregoing cases demonstrate the limits to a completely voluntaristic approach to deviant behavior. Nonetheless, symbolic interactionists emphasize that while factors other than social cognition may influence the predisposition to some kinds of acts, identities, or conditions, the meanings of those acts and identities is still socially constructed. And even in situations where early socialization and/or biological influences play significant roles in deviant behaviors and conditions, those who are identified as deviant will be subjected to various social control processes. We turn, therefore, to the subject of social control.

PROCESSING DEVIANTS

The development of deviance categories as we discussed earlier in this chapter entails the social construction of deviance as objectively real. But it is in the actual identifying of "deviants" and responding to them that moral entrepreneurs' social constructions become embodied. Symbolic interactionists are particularly concerned with the contexts and processes of social interaction through which deviance—and deviants—are brought into being.

Stereotyping and Master Statuses

A key feature of creating deviants is the development of stereotypes—simple images by which we identify and characterize different kinds of people. In large urban societies like the contemporary United States, we find ourselves surrounded by what Lyn Lofland has termed "a world of strangers." "To live in a city," Lofland writes, "is, among other things, to live surrounded by large numbers of persons whom one does not know" (1973, p.ix). Stereotypes reduce the complexity of a world of strangers, giving us a sense that we know about certain kinds of people with whom we have little personal experience. But the oversimplified knowledge that stereotypes provide is distorted in two ways. First, it misses much of the detail and complexity of real-life people, focusing on just a few selected features that come to stand for the whole. Second, the picture we get from stereotypes is overly broad, giving the impression that all cases of a given kind of person (whether they be "grandmothers" or "drug addicts") are basically the same.

We tend to use and accept stereotypes to inform our understanding of people from whom we are socially distant. In contrast, people with whom we are familiar often seem more complex and multifaceted to us than stereotypes of people "like them" would suggest. This is particularly the case in terms of stereotypes of deviants, which tend to be laced with assertions of sickness or immorality.

Everett Hughes (1945) provides a valuable way to understand certain kinds of stereotypes in his analysis of what he termed *master status* and *auxiliary characteristics*. A master status, Hughes says, is a particularly visible and powerful social status that tends to be associated with a set of "auxiliary characteristics which come to be expected of its incumbents" (1945, p.353). So powerful are our stereotypes regarding master statuses that if we identify a person in terms of such a status, it "tends to overpower, in most crucial situations, any other characteristics which might run counter to it" (Hughes 1945, p.357). The master status of "a physician," for instance, has tended to be associated with such auxiliary traits as middle age, white, male, reserved, and serious demeanor. While the auxiliary characteristics associated with the master status of physician have been undergoing some change in recent years (as more women and minorities have entered medical schools and pursued medical careers), a youthful, nonwhite, or female physician—particularly one with an easy, joking demeanor—may still seem odd or unusual, not "really what a doctor should be."

While the foregoing example is of a highly respected master status, Howard Becker extends Hughes' analysis to the field of deviance. Once one has been labeled with the status of "deviant," Becker argues, "the identification proves to be more important than most others. One will be identified as a deviant first, before other identifications are made" (1963, p.33). A deviant master status implies a set of morally negative characteristics, suggesting that deviance is a defining feature of who they are. It is easy to understand the appeal of stereotypes of deviants, but in real life such images are often inaccurate. While in popular perception we tend to categorize people in mutually exclusive terms (deviant versus normal), in lived experience, deviance and normality often coexist. Pimps and strippers may be conventionally oriented family members or romantic partners (e.g., Milner and Milner 1973; Bradley 2007), individuals struggling with mental illnesses may be competent and reliable members of the workforce (Karp 1996), and professional thieves may find ways to integrate their illicit pursuits with legal business activities (Klockars 1974). Time and again, ethnographic research documents that being deviant in some aspects of one's life is often compatible with conventional behavior more generally.

However, if an individual comes to be recognized and identified primarily in terms of a deviant master status, the social reactions of others will tend to be based on beliefs regarding the moral character and social traits associated with that status, rather than on more specific personal characteristics of the individual.

Institutionalizing Deviance

When people become publicly labeled as deviant, they often find themselves forced to interact with various kinds of organizations that have the authority and responsibility for processing those who have been identified as specific kinds of deviants. The institutionalization of deviance refers to the creation of social structures and processes that are used to identify and respond to deviants. It involves creating typologies or classification systems for identifying deviants, developing methods of social control for those identified as deviant, and establishing the personnel and bureaucratic lines of authority necessary for achieving these goals. Many kinds of deviance are responded to primarily by the criminal justice system. The dominant responses to other kinds of deviance are more connected to medical institutions, such as mental health agencies or eating disorder clinics. Yet, other kinds of deviance may be handled largely through social service agencies, such as welfare agencies that deal with child abuse or shelters that deal with the homeless. In addition, some deviance categories are characterized by peer-support networks, including a wide variety of Twelve Step programs designed to assist individuals in gaining control over their deviant behavior. Often several different kinds of organizations coalesce around the management of a particular deviance category. Responses to alcohol abuse may draw simultaneously upon the criminal justice system, mental health programs, and Twelve Step groups. The particular mix of institutionalized responses tends to change over time as the definitions of different kinds of deviance are transformed. Yet, it is the particular mix at a given point in time that serves to practically define deviance categories and the experiences of those who become labeled as deviant.

The organizations that are responsible for identifying and responding to deviance tend to reflect and reinforce prevalent cultural assumptions about different deviance categories. This is not to say that they reflect cultural consensus about deviance. Indeed, many deviance categories are better characterized by cultural conflict than consensus. But, the development of publicly sanctioned organizations for dealing with deviants requires a significant degree of support from some sectors of the society. And, insofar as they are perceived as successful in managing the problems associated with deviance, agencies in turn provide evidence and justification not only for their own programs and policies, but also for broader cultural assumptions.

Typifications and Recipe Knowledge

Agencies that are charged with the social control of deviants must develop routines for identifying, admitting, and processing their clients. One key element in organizational routines for dealing with deviants is the creation of *typifications*, or standardized categories to define the agency's clients. Typifications enable agencies to deal with their clients not as individually unique people, but rather as cases of a particular "type of person," thus allowing agencies to manage "the messiness of lived reality within organizationally imposed limitations" (Loseke 1992, p.5). Agency typifications tend to be more general and less detailed than the classification systems in scholarly books and medical articles. They are working categories that are often learned on the job to manage clients in particular settings (Shover 1984). Typifications serve agency needs for standardizing the treatment of deviants, but they are often a source of conflict with clients who tend to resist being placed in cookie-cutter categories.

A second, closely related process is the creation of what Alfred Schutz (1962) termed *recipe knowledge*. At a general level, recipe knowledge refers to the knowledge that people develop for standardized or routine ways of—or "recipes for"—doing things. In the context of agencies that work with deviants, recipe knowledge involves a working understanding of agency routines and the "way things are done around here." It includes the "tricks of the trade," or practical techniques and shortcuts that make it possible to manage common difficulties associated with the processing of deviants through the organization. David Sudnow (1965) has described how short-staffed public defenders and district attorneys offices respond to the need to avoid taking most cases to trial by developing "a set of unstated recipes" for reducing original charges to lesser

PROFILE

Symbolic Interactionist Howie Becker

"Howie" Becker ("only my mother," he says, "ever called me Howard") fell in love with playing piano at the age of 12. Since many adult piano players were off fighting in World War II, as a teenager in the 1940s, Becker found opportunities to play boogie-woogie piano at Chicago strip clubs. "I always wanted to be a piano player," he recounts. But knowing that his father, a first-generation Jewish immigrant, would be appalled if his son spent his life playing piano in saloons, Becker enrolled at the University of Chicago where he could pursue an education during the day while playing piano jazz at night. When he read *Black Metropolis: A Study of Negro Life in a Northern City*, an anthropological study of Black life in Chicago, Howie saw a way to connect his love of jazz with his education. "I thought, 'Wow! If I just wrote down what I was doing at night, just what everyone said and what I observed, then those were field notes'" (Gopnik 2015). Becker went on to get a PhD at the University of Chicago. Even in graduate school, Becker thought he might continue his musical career. "It was only after I finished the PhD," he says, "that I more or less realized that my choice now was to be the most educated piano player on Sixty-Third Street or start taking sociology more seriously."

Drawing on his experiences with other Chicago jazz musicians, Becker became one of the first sociologists to look at deviance through the eyes of those who are labeled as deviant. In 1953, he published an article, "Becoming a Marihuana User," that described the process through which jazz musicians learned to use and enjoy marijuana. In later work, Becker explored the history of the Federal Narcotics Bureau's fight to define marijuana use as a major social problem that required new laws and policing efforts. He created the term "moral entrepreneur" to refer to individuals and organizations that are in the business of persuading the public and officials that certain kinds of behavior are harmful and that specific policies must be enacted to protect society. Becker's work continues to inspire deviance research today.

In 2015, Howie Becker received his most recent honorary doctorate, from Goldsmith's University of London where he was described as "the piano playing sociologist who changed the way we think about deviance."

offenses for which defendants would be willing to enter a guilty plea. A "normal burglary," for example, would be reduced to "petty theft." According to Sudnow, the recipe knowledge for such plea bargains is essential to effective work as a public defender. Similarly, Lisa Frohmann (1991) has documented how deputy district attorneys' decisions to prosecute sexual assault cases are based in large part on recipe knowledge about what constitutes a case that is likely to lead to conviction. Prosecutors pay close attention to such details as the alleged victim's demeanor, personal history, and to discrepancies in the victim's account. Only those cases that appear likely to lead to conviction tend to be filed. As Sudnow's and Frohmann's studies demonstrate, recipe knowledge enables criminal justice workers (and others who deal with deviants) to handle cases in an effective manner.

The use of typifications and recipe knowledge enables those who work in agencies that are responsible for processing deviants to handle the flow of inmates, patients, and clients through their organizations. In addition to providing "appropriate treatment" for their deviant clientele, organizations that work with deviants must also keep an eye on other concerns—especially on managing their resources and maintaining good public relations. As deviance-processing agencies respond to internal and external pressures and challenges over time, their workers—police officers, judges, psychologists, social workers, and others—develop new typifications and recipe knowledge to enable their work with deviants to proceed as smoothly as possible in the face of emergent challenges, such as cuts in funding or changes in public priorities. Meanwhile, at any given time, a deviance-processing organization will tend to define and treat its clients in a particular way. As Goffman has observed, the definition of the situation in such organizations "automatically begins to operate as soon as the inmate enters, the staff having the notion that entrance is *prima facie* evidence that one must be the kind of person the institution was set up to handle" (1961, p.380).

STIGMATIZATION AND RESISTANCE

While public perceptions of deviants vary widely depending on the deviance category with which they are associated, virtually all deviants face at least potential stigmatization, or being viewed as abnormal, inferior, or defective human beings. People who are stigmatized confront a social world in which they are looked down upon, in which they have, as Goffman put it, a "spoiled identity." But stigmatized individuals and groups do not simply accept the external judgments of those who look down on them. Those who are labeled as deviant react in a variety of ways to the stigma they confront. Some accept and internalize the negative images of themselves. Others turn the negative images upside down and claim them as a source of pride. And still others, perhaps most deviants, pursue a middle road of trying to minimize the impact of their stigma while refusing to internalize the negative perceptions that others have of them. The reactions of stigmatized deviants do not occur in a social vacuum. Many, although by no means all, of the deviance categories covered in this book are associated with subcultures or groups that provide social (and sometimes material) support for their members. Whether they go it alone or in the company of their peers, deviant actors must chart a path through the experience of stigmatization.

Stigmatization and Role Engulfment

Being labeled as a deviant often means that one is treated as a less than a "normal" person in interaction with many other people. In less severe cases, stigmatization may involve little more than subtle exclusion, disapproving glances, and gossip. At the more extreme end of the spectrum, a person labeled as deviant may find herself or himself arrested, imprisoned, or hospitalized. They may lose their jobs, be rejected by friends and family, and become targets of humiliation and even violence.

One potential way in which individuals may respond to such demeaning experiences is to make apologies and amends and seek to return to "normal," nondeviant life. Many people take getting caught in deviant behavior as a "wake-up call," and renounce their actions. Labeling theorists acknowledge that many people quit participating in deviant behavior when they are caught, publicly labeled, and treated, whether in the criminal justice system, the mental health system, or other venues of social control. But labeling theorists also propose another, more disturbing, and seemingly contradictory possibility: being labeled and treated as a deviant may lead to more, rather than less, participation in deviant behavior. As Tannenbaum explains, the labeling and stigmatizing process can inadvertently "become a way of stimulating, suggesting, emphasizing and evoking the very traits that are complained of" (1938, p.20). Sociologists refer to this as the process of *deviance amplification.*

Deviance amplification occurs when "rule breakers become entrenched in deviant roles because they are labeled deviant by others and excluded from continuing in normal roles in the community" (Mankoff 1971, p.207). One long-cited example is that of an illicit drug user who, by virtue of a drug conviction, finds it difficult to secure regular employment and turns to illegitimate kinds of activities, such as robbery or theft, to survive and support his habit (e.g., Becker 1963). Those who are labeled deviant may find themselves not only excluded from normal roles and relationships, but also thrust into new situations and relationships around which their lives become organized, as in the case of an adolescent lawbreaker who is sent to a juvenile detention facility and is befriended by other delinquents who encourage yet more lawbreaking. The result is secondary deviance in which the deviant's life becomes substantially organized around their identification as deviant.

Along with deviance amplification, a person who is labeled as deviant may develop a subjective identity and self-attitudes consistent with the moral judgments expressed by others. The term *role engulfment* refers to a person being caught up in the deviant role by virtue of others relating to them largely in terms of their spoiled identity (Schur 1971). Many agencies that work with various kinds of deviants encourage their clients to adopt a particular image of themselves, often one that places them in a position of dependency on the kinds of services provided by the agency.

Yet, not everyone who is labeled deviant becomes enmeshed in deviance amplification and role engulfment. For one thing, deviant behaviors vary in terms of just how negatively they are viewed. The minor shoplifter has far less serious a stigma to overcome than does a convicted rapist. Second, those who have little or no commitment to or investment in the behavior for which they have been chastised are likely to find it relatively easy to discontinue the activity, as Cameron (1964) reported was the case with middle-class shoplifters. Third, individuals with higher social status often find it easier to overcome stigmatizing labels than do people with lower social status, as William Chambliss (1973) found in his study of two groups of adolescent delinquents. While both groups of boys engaged in similar amounts of deviant behavior, Chambliss found that the lower-class boys were more stigmatized for their delinquent acts than were their middle-class peers. Yet, a fourth influential factor in deviance amplification and role engulfment involves just how publicly the deviant label is applied. Those who are officially and publicly labeled and processed are more likely to experience role engulfment, in part because the consequences of labeling are more extensive than they are for those whose deviance remains hidden to a greater degree. Based on just such concerns, the US medical community has developed special programs to treat physicians who are at a higher risk than the general population of abusing pharmaceutical opiates and tranquilizers (Hughes et al. 1992). Rather than publicly prosecuting doctors who self-prescribe or otherwise illicitly become heavy users of sedatives and painkillers, medical associations often keep the abuses confidential and work with physicians to get treatment without public disclosure of their abuse (O'Connor and Spickard 1997).

In summary, those with higher social status, engaged in less serious forms of deviance, to which they have less attachment, and who are dealt with in a more private manner tend to exhibit less deviance amplification and role engulfment. Such a broad generalization, however, masks considerable diversity. Further, as Mankoff (1971) observed, labeling and stigma are at best only partial explanations for deviance amplification. Many people become habitual rulebreakers or become involved in deviant careers without having been publicly labeled and stigmatized. While they are potentially vulnerable to labeling and stigma, these people have avoided detection, at least for the time being.

Stigma Management and Resistance

As we have discussed, people who experience stigma face embarrassment, humiliation, and social rejection. The degree of disapproval and rejection that they face derives in part from the prevailing societal attitudes toward their particular type of stigma or deviance. But symbolic interactionists are quick to point out that those who confront stigmatization can be very creative in finding ways to challenge stigmatized labels of them or to reduce the stigma's impact. In fact, deviants' efforts to manage stigma typically begin even before they have been publicly labeled.

Stigma Management among the Discreditable

We begin our discussion of stigma management with Goffman's (1963) distinction between those who are "discreditable" and those who are "discredited." A discreditable individual is one whose deviant activities or condition are not known to those who would be likely to stigmatize them. They are engaged in what Becker (1963) terms "secret deviance." Examples of secret deviance abound: a physician who surreptitiously steals the painkiller OxyContin from his clinic, a stranger rapist who has not been identified, and a "closeted" bisexual man who hides his sexual encounters with other men. In contrast, the discredited are those whose deviance is known to others and who, by virtue of that, are labeled with a stigmatized identity. At first glance it might seem that discreditable secret deviants do not have to concern themselves with stigmatization, but in fact it is very common for them to spend considerable time and energy hiding their deviance in order to avoid its consequences. Secret deviants rely on tight information control over their potentially discrediting acts or attributes. They attempt, often successfully, to "pass" as nondeviant individuals. In order to pass as "normal," secret deviants often pay special attention to avoiding stigma symbols, or signs that might call attention to one's deviant status. In addition to avoiding items that might betray their deviant status, secret deviants may use "disidentifiers," or symbols that imply that they are clearly not the kind of deviant that they fear being revealed to be. One example is provided in Carrier's (1976) study of covert homosexual men in a Mexican city who made a point of publicly whistling at female passersby and of periodically having sex with female prostitutes in order to give the impression that they were heterosexual.

Secret deviants may also develop deceptive explanations for potential signs of deviant activity, as in the case of a married woman interviewed in Bradley's research with exotic dancers. "Sometimes I'll sneak out and work at the club," the woman explained to Bradley. "But my husband hates it and doesn't want me to do it. So, when I work I lie and tell him I won the money at bingo" (2007, p.395). Further, since many kinds of deviant activities require participation with other people, secret deviants may find themselves leading double lives in which they need to keep one set of associates separate or hidden from the other.

Stigma Management among the Discredited

While the discreditable deviant faces the challenge of keeping his or her stigma from being discovered, the discredited deviant must find ways to minimize the relevance of a stigmatized status that has already been applied to them. Persons who are ready to admit possession of a stigma (in many cases because it is known about or immediately apparent) may nonetheless make a great effort to keep the stigma from looming large. The stigma management strategies of destigmatization and deviance avowal illustrate the variety, creativity, and often hard work of stigma management.

Destigmatization involves an effort to expunge a deviant identity and replace it with a positive one. Two common types of destigmatization are purification and transcendence.

Purification involves efforts to replace the deviant self with a morally purified self, transforming "from a sinner to a saint." Often this transformation is achieved by those who go through a religious conversion, as exemplified in the biography of Malcom X, who transformed from being a thief, drug dealer, and pimp to becoming an abstinent, educated, and devoted black Muslim. As Malcom X's life illustrates, destigmatization frequently has an inspirational quality to it, as one-time deviants overcome seemingly insurmountable obstacles to become models of moral virtue and discipline. While purification is frequently associated with religious conversion, there are also more secular means for turning one's life around. One of the most common today in the United States is through Twelve Step programs like Alcoholics Anonymous (AA), in which an alcoholic commits to living in accordance with the principles of AA in order to change their life.

Transcendence offers a different avenue for expunging a deviant identity based on rising above a deviant status or condition. Transcendence is a common stigma management strategy among those who rise above physical stigmas or disabilities by engaging in activities that are not ordinarily available to, or achieved by, people like them—as in the case of a blind former British soldier who became an international celebrity after setting a world speed skiing record (*USA Today* 2007).

While destigmatization emphasizes removing stigma through moral purification or remarkable achievement, another form of stigma management, *deviance avowal* (Turner 1972), involves admitting a deviant act, but arguing that it was an exception to the rule. Two common strategies, noted by Scott and Lyman (1968), are excuses and justifications. Similar to techniques of neutralization, excuses and justifications are intended to neutralize the wrongfulness of actions by explaining things in a way that will make others view you less harshly. Excuses revolve around claims that one has no control over the act or condition in question, as when a person suffering from depression explains to a friend that they have a "medical condition." In contrast, justifications are based on the argument that while one had control over the deviant act, in this case their decision to do it was justified by the circumstances. In her study of college students' accounts for missing class, for instance, Kathy Kalab (1987) found that they frequently justified missing class by explaining that they needed to take care of a sick relative or attend a family funeral. In providing such justifications, students acknowledge the importance of attending class, while arguing that in their particular circumstances, other activities had to take precedence.

Another common deviance avowal strategy used to reduce the impact of stigma is *distancing.* In distancing, individuals seek to separate themselves from the stigmatized acts or conditions with which they fear they are associated. One distancing strategy, termed "role distancing," involves emphasizing the difference between oneself and others who fall into a particular deviant category, as in the case of a newly homeless man who explained to Snow and Anderson, "If you want to know about street people, I can tell you about them, but you can't really learn about street people from studying me, because I'm different" (1993, p.215). Alternatively, an individual can seek to define their deviant behavior as unusual and different from what is typical for "that kind of deviant." Thorne observed this kind of distancing among several people who had declared bankruptcy, including a woman who explained, "What I was filing bankruptcy on was NOT credit cards. . . . It was NOT a credit card bankruptcy. We've never did that. . . . And even our attorney said, 'This is not a normal bankruptcy. Normally you see a lot of credit card debt'" (Thorne and Anderson 2006, p.89).

In-Group Stigma Management

The foregoing discussion focuses on stigma management by individuals with others who do not share their deviant status. But stigmatized individuals also engage in a considerable amount of stigma management with their deviant peers. In-group members who share an individual's stigma are often more likely to accept one as a full-fledged person rather than as defective. Participation with in-group peers can provide opportunities to commiserate with fellow sufferers, to be oneself and not have to worry about interacting with others who look down on you.

The nature and extent of in-group stigma management varies widely across different deviance categories. In some categories, such as criminal deviance like murder, there is relatively little contact among those who have engaged in the behaviors (at least outside of prison settings). On the other hand, some types of deviance associated with lifestyle and identity politics, such as recreational drug use, or gay and lesbian activities and identities, are characterized by rich subcultures and interpersonal connections. In-group deviant subcultures provide fertile soil for the development of alternative value systems and ideologies that find pride in the very attributes or activities that are stigmatized in mainstream culture. They can even provide a base for publicly and legally challenging prevailing social constructions of deviance.

Over the past several decades, members of many stigmatized groups in the United States have turned to protest and collective action to advance their interests and challenge perceptions of them as deviants. Building in significant part on the model of the civil right's movement, these groups have moved beyond trying to manage stigma within the confines of negative stereotypes to openly advocating for the lives they live and the values those lives express. Kitsuse, who was among the first sociologists to comment on collective action among members of deviant groups, developed the term *tertiary deviance* to refer to "the deviant's confrontation, assessment, and rejection of the negative identity embedded in secondary deviation, and the transformation of that identity into a positive and viable self-conception" (1980, p.11). In the process, he writes, "guilt is turned into moral indignation, and the victim into an activist" (p.11). At this point we come full circle in the social construction of deviance, with those "who have been culturally defined and categorized, stigmatized, and morally degraded now declaring their presence openly and without apology to claim the rights of citizenship" (Kitsuse 1980, p.7). Formerly cast as deviants, members of these groups seek to redefine morality and frame their stigmatization as an act of oppression and a social problem that itself demands redress.

BLURRED BOUNDARIES II: FRAMING SURPRISING ALLIANCES

Using the symbolic interactionist/social constructionist perspective, we have seen that deviance involves far more than just individual abnormality or deviation. What a society—or more accurately, what different groups within a society—consider deviant depends on what moral entrepreneurs can convince others to outlaw or condemn. In order to gain support for their definitions of deviant behavior and how to deal with it, moral entrepreneurs must build alliances with various other constituencies. Often such alliances seem to be based on obvious values and interests that different groups have in common. We are not surprised to find drug companies reaching out to families with difficult children in order to build support for medical treatment of hyperactivity. Similarly, we expect alliances between feminist groups like the National Organization of Women and social workers seeking stronger laws against domestic violence. But at other times we can be startled to find supportive alliances between what would seem to be the most unlikely of partners.

In the spring of 2007, residents of Prince William County in Virginia debated the passage of aggressive new measures to crack down on illegal immigrants. The county's Board of Supervisors argued that an influx of undocumented workers was causing economic hardship and lawlessness and that they had to do something since the US Congress has failed to enforce immigration laws. The new policy would demand that anyone using city services, such as emergency medical facilities, the city pool, or the library, be required to provide proof of citizenship—a good way, the Board argued, to catch "illegals." To no one's surprise, civil rights groups associated with undocumented workers protested the new law, saying it was racist and unconstitutional. But the story caught the eye of National Public Radio (2007) when, as they put it,

"Amazingly, the strongest opposition came from longtime police chief, Charlie Dean." In a tense and packed town hall meeting, the police chief protested that it would be extremely unwise to use new measures to identify illegal immigrants and enforce the law. Chief Dean explained, "I'm concerned that crime rates among our youth will rise. If immigrant children are not allowed access to recreational facilities, or if health clinics deny, or cause a chilling effect, sufficient to keep sick women, children, or the elderly away, there will be harsh unintended consequences" (National Public Radio 2007). In short, the chief of police was arguing, against the Board of Supervisors, for lax law enforcement. And yet, the way he framed his argument had a clear logic and drew supporters to his way of viewing the issue.

As you think about how different kinds of deviance and policies to deal with them can be framed, it will be useful to "think outside the box" of conventional wisdom. While we might not agree with alternative ways of framing deviance-related policies, we can all benefit from at least understanding different arguments and approaches. As we conclude this chapter, take a few minutes to see if you can think of ways to frame the following issues that would support the surprising alliance suggested.

First, consider the case of colleges across the United States that struggle to find ways to handle student alcohol abuse. High rates of underage and binge drinking among college students have been the focus of many studies and university policies. Some university presidents and deans of students argue that the problem of student alcohol abuse could be reduced (but by no means eliminated) if we were to lower the drinking age. How can they make such a seemingly counterintuitive argument? How do you imagine they frame the problem of student alcohol abuse and policies to deal with it that makes their argument make sense?

The second case involves human rights groups and the issue of violence against women. Human Rights Watch and Amnesty International have been major voices in promoting women's rights to live free of violence and oppression. In recent years, both of these international organizations have come out in support of decriminalizing prostitution. Many, probably even most Americans, see prostitution as degrading to women and putting them at risk of violence and abuse. How can these major human rights groups make a case that decriminalizing prostitution can promote women's well-being and reduce violence against them?

Hopefully, thinking outside the box on these two examples can help us see that conceptions of deviant behavior and social policy are not simply black-and-white affairs. Deviance does not exist in the act, the condition, or the person. It is a social process in which individuals and groups collectively define, and often argue over, what is right and what is wrong, who is good and who is bad. The surprising alliances that may at times emerge among different people and groups bear witness to the challenges of building moral consensus at the blurred boundaries of social life.

SUMMARY

- The interactionist/constructionist approach views human beings as active agents in their own lives.
- Deviance is a social process involving deviance claims-makers, individuals who break rules or violate social norms, and those who enforce rules and norms.
- Moral entrepreneurs frame the problems that concern them in ways that draw support from other individuals and groups. In this process, they engage in:
    - Diagnostic framing that identifies the problem.
    - Prognostic framing that proposes solutions.
    - Motivational framing that compels others to support their cause.
- Successful moral entrepreneurs mobilize important resources, such as people, money, and the media.
- Atrocity tales portray deviance in especially horrific cases.
- Primary deviance involves deviant acts or statuses that are not publicly identified as deviance.
- Secondary deviance occurs when deviant acts or statuses become publicly labeled and acted upon.
- People's decisions to engage in deviance emerge in the context of their personal biographies and effective environments.
- Those who break rules often use techniques of neutralization that help them rationalize why their acts are okay.
- Various kinds of rule enforcers identify and process deviants.
- Deviance-processing agencies develop typifications and recipe knowledge for identifying and processing their clients.
- Deviants face potential stigmatization, criminalization, and punishment.
- Many people who face being labeled as deviant hide their deviant acts or conditions, passing as "normals" through secrecy and deception.
- Those who are publicly labeled as deviant frequently use stigma management techniques such as destigmatization and deviance avowal to mitigate stigmatization that is directed toward them.
- Some people associated with several kinds of deviance find pride and value in their behaviors and conditions and pursue collective action to challenge negative stereotypes and social policies directed against them.

KEYWORDS

appeal to higher loyalties: A technique of neutralization in which a rule-breaker asserts that they engaged in rule-breaking in order to meet higher or more important responsibilities or obligations.

atrocity tales: Extreme and dramatic stories of harm and tragedy told about deviants, often as part of an effort by moral entrepreneurs to mobilize public attitudes against them.

auxiliary characteristics: A set of secondary social or personality traits associated with a person who occupies a specific master status.

biography (symbolic interaction definition): The subjective story of one's life as told from the present point of view, developed out of fragmented memories of our past experiences and the meanings we impute to them.

claims-makers: Individuals or groups that are engaged in making public claims about the nature, causes, and potential solutions for activities or conditions that they define as social problems (including deviance).

condemnation of condemners: A technique of neutralization in which a rule-breaker justifies violating rules by arguing that the people who would condemn him or her actually engage in behaviors that are worse than what they condemn.

denial of injury: A technique of neutralization in which a rule-breaker justifies violating the rules by asserting that no real harm was done.

denial of responsibility: A technique of neutralization in which a rule-breaker asserts that forces beyond their control caused them to break the rule, and, therefore, they have no responsibility for having done so.

denial of victim: A technique of neutralization in which a rule-breaker justifies harm to another person by arguing that the person deserved to be harmed and therefore was not really a victim.

destigmatization: A technique of stigma management in which a "deviant" seeks to expunge a deviant identity and replace it with a positive one.

deviance amplification: An increase in the amount or intensity of deviance in which an individual is involved, typically associated with increased identification with a deviant identity.

deviance avowal: A technique of stigma management in which a stigmatized person acknowledges their abnormal condition but seeks at the same time to present a positive social identity and status.

diagnostic framing (of deviance): Moral entrepreneurs' arguments or statements that name a particular kind of deviance and provide an explanation of what causes it.

effective environment: An individual's environment (i.e., social situation and surroundings) as she or he defines and experiences it. The term emphasizes the meaning of the environment for the person.

labeling theory: A set of ideas developed by symbolic interactionists in the 1950s and 1960s emphasizing that labeling people as deviant can at times increase their participation in and identification with deviance.

looking glass self: A term coined by Charles Horton Cooley to refer to the feelings about oneself that result from how we think other people see us.

master status: A particularly visible and definitive social status that is associated with a set of secondary traits (or auxiliary characteristics) expected of those with such a status.

moral entrepreneurs: People who are actively involved in creating and promoting the belief that some kinds of behaviors or conditions are immoral and should be outlawed, punished, or otherwise controlled.

motivational framing (of deviance): Moral entrepreneurs' arguments or statements that provide a "call to arms," making the case for why people should become involved in the fight against a particular kind of deviance.

polygenetic (causes of deviant behavior): The potential for rule-breaking behavior to be caused by a wide variety of reasons, as illustrated by the many different kinds of reasons that might lead a person to engage in a bout of excessive drinking.

primary deviance: Deviance that occurs when individuals engage in deviant or rule-breaking acts, but when those acts do not become the basis for the person becoming identified as a deviant.

prognostic framing (of deviance): Moral entrepreneurs' arguments or statements that propose a solution (e.g., new law or medical treatments) to the kind of deviance that they seek to eliminate or control.

recipe knowledge: The standardized or routine ways that people develop for doing things, including the standardized routines of workers in agencies that deal with various kinds of "deviants."

resource mobilization: The activities of moral entrepreneurs that are directed toward building alliances and securing the resources needed to move their cause forward.

role engulfment: A process in which a person becomes identified with and committed to a deviant role by virtue of others relating to them largely in terms of a deviant master status.

secondary deviance: Deviant or rule-breaking behavior associated with being socially labeled as a specific kind of deviant and having one's life organized in large part around activities associated with that deviant identity.

social self: The symbolic interactionist conception of the self as self-awareness that arises through social interaction and learning to view oneself from the perspectives of other people.

stigma management: Activities by stigmatized individuals and groups to control information about their negative statuses and to negotiate interactions in ways that minimize the impact of their stigma.

tertiary deviance: The transformation of a deviant identity into a positive one.

typifications (of deviants): Stereotypical images that workers in deviant-processing agencies use to define the "type of person" with which the agency works and the kinds of treatment that are appropriate for them.

SECTION

2

HIGH CONSENSUS CRIMINAL DEVIANCE

CHAPTER

5

Murder

Father remembers murdered son (Enigma/Alamy Stock Photo).

CONTENTS

LEARNING OBJECTIVES

After reading this chapter, you will be able to:

- Describe the most common categories of murder in the United States today
- Explain the challenges of, and strategies for, studying homicide
- Identify different historical definitions and causal explanations for murder
- Explain the social capital analysis of different homicide rates across communities
- Analyze the interactional contexts in which expressive and instrumental homicide most often occur
- Describe the stigma management strategies frequently used by convicted murderers
- Assess arguments for and against treating physician-assisted suicide as murder

BLURRED BOUNDARIES I: TWO CONVICTED MURDERERS

On April 15, 1967, 24-year-old drifter, Richard Speck, was convicted of murdering eight student nurses in their Chicago apartment. Late one night the previous July, Speck entered the apartment to burglarize it, but took the young women hostage when he found them home. Armed with a knife and high on a mix of alcohol and drugs, Speck tied them up in a bedroom. During the night, he took them, one by one, into another room, where he strangled and stabbed them to death, raping the last of his victims before strangling her with a piece of bedsheet.

In the heat of his brutal violence, Speck had lost track of one of the young women who hid under a bed all night. In the light of early morning when Speck had gone, she crawled out a window onto a ledge where she began screaming to neighbors, "They are all dead!"

Two days later, Speck, who was on the run as a suspect in the deaths of seven other women in the Midwest as well, slit his wrists and ended up in the Cook County Hospital emergency room. There, a physician who had seen news reports recognized a tattoo on Speck's arm that read "Born to Raise Hell."

Based on the testimony of the only woman who survived the assault, Speck's jury deliberated for less than an hour before pronouncing him guilty of eight counts of first degree murder. Initially given the death penalty, Speck's sentence was commuted to 400 to 1,200 years in prison when the US Supreme Court declared capital punishment unconstitutional. At the time, Speck claimed not to remember murdering the women, but later he was caught on a prison video telling fellow inmates, "It just wasn't their night . . . If you're asking me if I felt sorry, no."

Today Richard Speck is remembered as a deranged killer, one of the most reviled criminals in our nation's history. We are sickened by his lethal violence.

And yet others who have been convicted of murder may strike us as sympathetic—even heroic figures. Consider the case of convicted murderer, Dr. Jack Kevorkian.

On April 13, 1999, Jack Kevorkian was convicted of murder in the death of 52-year-old Thomas Youk. It was not the first time that Kevorkian had been in front of a jury. Known in the United States and throughout the world, as "Dr. Death," Kevorkian had been charged several times with assisting in the deaths of terminally ill people who wanted to end their lives. By his own count he had assisted in over 100 deaths, including Youk, to whom he administered a lethal injection—with Youk's full consent and documented on video that was shown later on CBS *Sixty Minutes*. Youk, who was suffering from the final stages of the degenerative nerve disease ALS, had pleaded with Kevorkian for his assistance. Youk's wife not only accepted her husband's wish to die, but publicly thanked Kevorkian for his role in her husband's death. "I was so grateful," she told *Sixty Minutes* host, Mike Wallace, "to know that someone would relieve him of his suffering."

The Michigan criminal justice system was not so understanding or forgiving, sentencing the 70-year-old Kevorkian to 10–25 years in prison. He served eight years before being paroled on good behavior. After his release from prison Kevorkian turned away from assisting in the deaths of terminally ill people, but continued to speak out for decriminalizing physician-assisted suicide. While his cause and actions were highly controversial, Kevorkian was widely respected around the world. In 2006, he was awarded the Gleitsman Foundation Citizen Activist Award at Harvard University where he was praised as a "selfless believer in death with dignity" who "has sacrificed his medical license and his own freedom toward that cause." The same year, he was paid a $50,000 honorarium to present his views to a packed house at the University of Florida.

Richard Speck and Jack Kevorkian are both convicted murderers, even though they could hardly be less similar. Indeed, many people would argue that what Kevorkian has done should not even be called murder. While we often think of murder as a straightforward criminal act that we would know when we see it, cases like Kevorkian's force us to face the fact that murder in real life is at times less clear-cut than the evil portrayed in novels and movies.

CURRENT CONSTRUCTIONS OF MURDER IN THE UNITED STATES

Murder is one of the most basic taboos in human cultures. Virtually all societies outlaw it, and if there is any form of deviance that we would consider objective and obvious when it happens, murder would be it—an act that leaves one or more people dead in its wake. But even murder is a social construction. To understand this, we need to grasp the difference between the words "kill" and "murder." While these words are often used as synonyms, their meanings are different. As Erich Goode has noted, "to kill is objective and descriptive. It simply refers to the taking of human life, regardless of motive or circumstances"

(2015, p.112). In contrast, he notes, "murder" represents a judgment that "a specific killing belongs to a certain category . . . a *criminal* form of killing" (2015, p.112). Several of the most commonly discussed types of murder today include serial murder, mass murder, stranger murder, and acquaintance murder.

Types of Murder

The term *serial killer* was first used in the early 1980s to refer to murderers who kill strangers over an extended period of time. Of course, serial murders did not suddenly begin in the 1980s. A century earlier, the most famous serial killer, Jack the Ripper, appears to have murdered at least seven London prostitutes, often mutilating their bodies. While Jack the Ripper was never caught, the first well-known American serial killer, Herbert Mudgett, was convicted and hanged in 1896 for a series of grisly murders. In keeping with the sensationalism of the era's newspapers—and presaging the media popularity of serial killers in the years to come, Mudgett was paid $7,500 by Hearst Newspaper for a written confession in which he described having killed 27 people, many of whom he said he had buried in his Chicago castle. While serial killers are a regular staple of movies and television, they are extremely rare in reality. Sociologists James Fox and Jack Levin have observed that "there may actually be more scholars studying serial murder than there are offenders committing it" (1999, p.166).

The image of *mass murder* is most commonly associated with shootings in schools and public settings, such as the 2012 movie theater shooting in Aurora, Colorado, and the deadly attack at an Orlando nightclub in 2016. While serial killing and mass murder may haze into each other at the edges, the term "mass murder" commonly refers to one-time murderous events. Further, while the most common victims of serial killers are prostitutes, the victims of mass murder tend to be students, teachers, random members of the public, or members of a group despised by the shooter. By virtue of the large numbers of victims and shocking unexpectedness of mass murder, it receives widespread media attention. Yet, while mass murder presents more threat to the general population than does serial murder, both of these kinds of killings are very uncommon, representing at most 2 per cent of all American homicides (Jenkins 1994, p.46).

Yet, another common image of homicide is that of *stranger murder* in either a "senseless" act of violence, such as a non-targeted drive by shooting, or in the process of committing some other crime, such as robbery, burglary, or rape. Many Americans consider stranger killings the most prevalent type of murder in the United States, but while stranger murders are far more common than serial and mass murders, they are still relatively uncommon. Less than one out of four males murdered in the United States dies at the hands of a stranger. And for women the proportion is even smaller—approximately one out of eight.

By far the most common type of murder in the United States is *intimate and acquaintance murder* that take place between family members, friends, and acquaintances. In the United States today, nearly 90 per cent of female murder victims and 75 per cent of male victims are killed by people they know, including nearly two-thirds of female victims who are murdered by family members or intimate partners (Catalano et al. 2009). Romantic and familial relationships are often the most intense personal connections we have, leading to strong emotions—both positive and negative. Intimate relationships and friendships can become the contexts not only for love and support, but also for distrust, jealousy, and anger, in ways that less close relations do not. As Erich Goode has observed, "The more intimate the relationship, the greater the likelihood that one person will kill another" (2015, p.147). However, women are twice as likely as men to be victims of intimate murder (Catalano et al. 2009), while men are more likely to be killed by a male friend or acquaintance.

Statistical Snapshot

Murder is the most closely documented form of deviance in our society—and most other societies as well. As historian Roger Lane explains, "murder is the easiest of crimes to trace through time: always taken seriously, almost always subject to law, never common enough to be completely tolerated or overlooked" (1997, p.5). Since the 1930s, murder statistics in the United States have been reported to the FBI and compiled in the *Uniform Crime Reports* (UCRs). Murder is the most likely crime to be reported when it occurs and the most likely crime to lead to arrest. Over 60 per cent of murders and negligent manslaughters reported to the police were cleared by arrest in 2014 as compared to 40 per cent of rapes and only 29 per cent of robberies (FBI 2015b).

In recent years, the number of murders in the United States has hovered around a rate of 4.5 to 4.8 per 100,000 people (FBI 2015a), down significantly from a rate of 8 to 10 per 100,000 in the early 1990s. Clear patterns can be seen in the FBI's national statistics on murder. Among the most visible are the patterns related to age, sex, and race of murder victims. As table 5.1 shows, males account for nearly four out of five murder victims in the United States. Most victims of murder are late adolescents to middle-aged, with about six out of 10 murders occurring among people 17 to 39 years of age. The risk of murder for African-Americans far exceeds that of white Americans. In 2014, the homicide rate for blacks was nearly six times higher than the rate for whites. The age, sex, and race of offenders closely parallel those of victims, as murderers themselves are predominantly young adults, mostly males, with African-Americans greatly overrepresented in comparison to their proportion of the population.

Table 5.1 Murder Victims by Age, Sex, and Race, 2014

		Sex		Race		
Age	**Total**	Known Male	Known Female	White	Black	Hispanic
Total	11,961	9,246	2,861	5,397	6,095	1,871
Percent distribution		77.3%	22.4%	45.1%	51%	17.7%
Under 18	1,095	692	388	492	545	203
18 and over	10.773	8,493	2,268	4,866	5,517	1,658
17–19	861	733	127	294	549	167
20–29	3,941	3,349	591	1,349	2,482	654
30–39	2,461	1,967	491	1,078	1,284	433
40–49	1,583	1,162	417	841	666	234
50–59	1,183	847	335	705	424	143
60–69	531	388	142	340	169	47
70 and over	419	216	202	328	76	19

SOURCE: FBI (2015a).

CHALLENGES IN RESEARCHING MURDER

Homicide researchers face two kinds of challenges: identifying and counting murder events and understanding the contexts and motivations of offenders and victims. At first glance, nothing looks easier than counting murder. Most of the time it leaves a dead body in its wake. By virtue of the seriousness with which we treat murder, most homicides are officially recorded. Studying murder across historical periods and cultures presents some difficulties, but the difficulties of getting close to murder experiences are a greater challenge.

Counting Murder

One major reason why it can be difficult to compare murder rates over time is that what is defined—and/or prosecuted—as murder can vary from one place and time to another. While today we consider infanticide (the killing of newborn and young children) a form of murder, historically it has been an acceptable practice in many cultures. Not only do laws and official policies change, but informal social practices change too—and not always consistently with changes in the law. While legal statutes outlawing infanticide were officially on the books in Medieval England, the general population did not support the statutes and the law was very seldom enforced (Hanawalt 1979). Similarly, during the era of slavery in the

United States, none of the colonies or early states officially approved the murder of slaves, but it was extremely rare for such killings to be prosecuted.

The connection between violence and murder has also changed over time. Murder rates in the United States in the late 1800s were significantly higher than they are today, but part of the explanation is that those who were seriously injured in fights in the late 1800s had a far greater chance of dying from their injuries. As emergency transportation and medical care improved over the years, many who would otherwise have died from "murder" became able to survive their assaults.

But perhaps the biggest problem in counting murders is that they are so rare that it can be difficult to get a bigger perspective than just a few cases—say, those reported by one city's or county's Coroner's Office. In order to get an understanding of patterns of homicide, it is valuable to collect data across entire states, or even nationally. The FBI's *UCRs* provide just such a set of statistics. Only when we can see this bigger picture are we able to systematically identify certain important patterns and trends in murder, such as the age, race, and gender patterns noted above.

Getting Close

Sociologists who want to understand deviance from an insider's perspective must find ways to get access to insiders' views. Perhaps the most informative data in this regard would come from personal observation of the activities in their naturally occurring settings. This is seldom possible in cases of serious criminal deviance. It is virtually impossible to get firsthand observational access to murder. Most murders tend to be spur-of-the-moment affairs, often in private homes. Not only is there no practical way to locate murderous situations before the fact and plan to witness them, but it would be beyond the realm of ethical behavior to take such an objective approach to watching a murder take place. If we could foretell the time and place of murders, we would want to prevent them, not observe them. The ethnographic researcher seeking to understand murder from the inside must take an alternative approach. Almost all symbolic interactionist studies of murder involve interviewing those who were present at the time of the lethal encounter, including murderers, witnesses, and attempted murder victims who survive.

Prison interviews with convicted murderers present numerous challenges. Researchers must gain approval from the prison administration and the prisoners themselves. While researchers seek to protect all informants against negative consequences from participating in the research, ethnographers studying convicted murderers must be particularly careful since they are interviewing prisoners about the very crimes that led to their incarceration. Prison ethnographers are expected to keep their data protected from authorities. To fail to do so would put research informants at risk and jeopardize the possibility of future research with such groups. But perhaps the most convincing reason to guarantee confidentiality to those convicted of serious crimes is that without some guarantee of protection they would be unwilling to honestly discuss their experiences.

Typically, prison ethnographers keep their interviews in locked, secure files, and delete names and other identifiers when the interviews are transcribed. In some cases, even more precautions are needed. In one especially interesting case, Ken Levi was conducting research with convicted murderers in a Michigan prison when one of the men he was interviewing expressed shame for the sloppiness of a bar room murder he had committed and indicated he would like to reveal more. Sensing the import of the man's overture, Levi stopped his tape recorder and asked the prisoner if he had been a professional hit man. When the man replied that he had, Levi arranged for several further interview sessions.

This prisoner had already received a guarantee of anonymity in the research, but now, as Levi recalled, "As a further guarantee, we agreed to talk about him in the third person, as a fictitious character named Pete, so that none of his statements would sound like a personal confession" (1981, p.52). Levi was well aware that some people might question the ethics of researching a self-confessed hit man and granting him anonymity. However, he felt the decision was justified because this was such an unusual opportunity and presented no imminent danger since the killer was behind bars. Further, Levi reasoned, "Hit men are hard to come by. Unlike [most] murderers, the hit man (usually) takes infinite care to conceal his identity" (1981, p.53). In such a situation, Levi believed, the chance to gain insight into a seldom-revealed aspect of crime and deviance warranted the guarantee of anonymity.

But why would a person who has been convicted of murder, and in this case, committed murders for which he had not been convicted, be willing to be interviewed about their criminal acts? Part of Pete's motive for wanting to be interviewed, Levi believed, was "his desire to set the record straight concerning what he deemed an illustrious career, now that he had arrived at the end of it" (1981, p.54). Pete felt proud of his career as a hit man. Throughout his interviews, he emphasized the skills necessary for the professional killer and the work he put into developing those skills. Of course, most murderers are not professional hit men who have honed the skills of killing. Most people who are convicted of murder are one-time amateurs, many of whom had no intention of committing the act until they were caught up in the heat of the moment. Yet, even one-time murderers may feel a need to set the record straight. Some are certainly appalled by the acts they have committed and find an interview a good opportunity for expressing their regret. But more commonly, convicted murderers seem motivated by simply having the opportunity to tell their side of the story.

CROSS-CULTURAL CONSTRUCTIONS OF MURDER

The meaning of murderous acts, as well as the responses to those acts, depends largely on the surrounding culture and one's place in it. Murder stretches back into prehistory and shows several enduring patterns across time, but there are also important variations—in rates of lethal violence, in the kinds of killing that are considered murder, and in the ways in which those who commit murder are treated.

Different Definitions

Erich Goode's distinction between "killing" and "murder" is critical for understanding different definitions of murder across time and cultures. Today in the United States we view some killings as "accidental" and therefore not murder, including killings that we classify as *manslaughter*. Many cultures have made no such distinction. English records did not differentiate between murder and manslaughter prior to the sixteenth century (Beeghley 2003) and, among Native Americans, the Cherokee made no distinction between murder and accidental killings (Lane 1997). For the Cherokee, any killing was considered murder and supposed to be avenged. By contrast, many cultures have approved some forms of killing that we consider murder today. The killing of newborn children and infants, especially girls, has been an accepted form of family planning in many societies across history (Milner 2000) and in numerous cultures the killing of unfaithful wives by their husbands has been approved as "honor killing" rather than murder (LaFree 1999; Baron 2006).

Human sacrifice associated with religious rituals was fairly widely practiced among Mesoamerican cultures (Besom 2013) as well as the Vikings and some precolonial African societies (Milner 2000). Wives, concubines, and servants were killed and buried with pharaohs and other Egyptian nobility to attend to them in the afterlife. And gladiators were pitted against each other in fight-to-the-death battles for entertainment of the masses in ancient Rome (Auguet 1994). In short, many kinds of killing that we would consider murderous have been approved and even celebrated in other times and cultures.

Different "Causes"

Just as definitions of murder have changed over time, so have beliefs about why people kill and what should be done about it. In many religions, murderous behavior has been attributed to demonic possession. In Scandinavian mythology, the trickster god, Loki, secretly arranged for the killing of his foster brother, Baldur, the god of Innocence. Through the Middle Ages in Europe, murder was often attributed to witches under Satan's spell.

In contrast, the first murder recounted in the Bible, the slaying of Abel by Cain in the book of Genesis, lays the responsibility not on the devil, but on Cain himself and his jealous rage when God praised his younger brother's sacrificial offering. While the moral of this Biblical story extends beyond the issue of controlling one's emotions, the belief that strong emotions can push individuals to murderous acts has a long and enduring history. Many cultural legends describe lethal emotions aroused by insults to one's dignity, as in the story of Oedipus, who murdered his (unknown) father, King Laius, for trying to force him off the road on a journey to Thebes. Even more commonly, romantic or sexual jealousy had been viewed as propelling men (and sometimes women) to murder. In some countries, such as eighteenth-century France, *crime passionnel* (or "crime of passion" brought on by jealous rage) was considered a valid defense against prosecution for murder.

Hate, too, has been considered an emotional motive for murder, as in "bias crimes" against members of certain racial, religious, or stigmatized groups. Frequently such hatred is fostered by atrocity tales that vilify and dehumanize members of the group. While hatred as a motive for murder is by no means new, it has become more prominent in recent years since the FBI developed a specific category called "hate crimes" that includes murders motivated by bias against racial groups, homosexuals, and the mentally ill.

Yet, another commonly cited reason for murder is intoxication. As we saw in Chapter 1, Billy Sunday preached that the devil used demon rum to take hold of those who could not resist temptation, often with tragic consequences. But alcohol in and of itself has often been believed to lower inhibitions and lead to immoral behavior, including murder. In Greek mythology wine is celebrated widely, but it is also said that "wine makes the coward bold." This is exemplified in the story of the murder of Orpheus at the hands of the women of Thrace who resented Orpheus taking their husbands with him on his wanderings. The women did not have the courage to kill him until they became drunk on wine. According to mythology, seeing how the wine had emboldened their wives, the men of Thrace thereafter braced themselves in war by getting drunk before they marched into battle.

In each of the causes of murder discussed above—emotional rage, demonic possession, and intoxication—there is a sense that individuals have lost control of their actions and the ability to act rationally and morally. The notion of insanity or mental illness as the cause of murder takes this line of reasoning to its logical conclusion. Variations of the "insanity defense" have been used in many countries to judge a murderer "not guilty by reason of insanity." While the insanity defense is seldom invoked—and not often successful when it is—it does point to beliefs that some murderers pursue their acts because they are mentally deranged. A diagnosed paranoid schizophrenic who has stopped taking medication and kills his child while believing that she is Satan is likely to be hospitalized in a mental institution rather than being sentenced to prison for murder.

Each of the foregoing views of the causes of murder focuses at the individual level, but many other explanations are directed toward social and environmental influences. Several of these explanations hark back to social disorganization theory. Overcrowding, inner city poverty, lack of adequate policing, and the many stresses of urban life are often invoked as underlying causes of high murder rates in large American cities. Other explanations focus on exposure to cultural contexts in which violence is viewed as an acceptable means for achieving goals and resolving conflicts. Many scholars have argued that the high rates of deadly violence among Irish immigrants in the late 1800s, southern white males in the early 1900s, and urban gang members today have been encouraged by *subcultures of violence* where the demonstration of masculinity is associated with courage and skill in violent encounters (Lee 2011).

Finally, one other widespread belief about the underlying reason for high murder rates in the United States must be addressed: guns. It is no accident, some argue, that the United States has the highest number of guns per capita of any nation in the world and also leads industrial nations in its murder rate. Many countries tightly restrict the ownership and use of firearms in the belief that a society with fewer guns is a safer society. In contrast, today in the United States there are over 350 million guns in circulation owned by about one-third of US households (Ingraham 2016). The fact that 70 per cent of murders in the United States result from gunshot wounds would seem to support the notion that more guns make society a more dangerous place. However, critics of this view, such as the four million-member National Rifle Association (NRA), argue that an armed citizenry enables individual citizens to protect themselves and others. This argument fails to explain why a country with such liberal gun laws as the United States would have such high murder rates relative to other countries. Nonetheless, the issue of gun rights has little impact on many countries around the world, but continues to be highly charged politically in the United States, with all 50 states and Washington, DC, now allowing adult citizens to carry concealed weapons.

Different Responses

Societal responses to murder have varied dramatically. At one extreme, murder may simply be ignored, as in the case of late nineteenth-century unprosecuted lynchings in the Southern United States. In such cases the victim is often portrayed as deserving of their fate and the authorities turn a blind eye. In other cases, what we would consider murder is ignored because the act is not defined as murder in the cultural context in which it occurred.

In many societies with weak or nonexistent law enforcement, it fell to the family of the victim to retaliate. Vendettas, or blood feuds, were common among the Anglo-Saxon and Germanic tribes that once populated much of Europe. Also known as revenge murders, vendettas were carried out in the belief that retaliation should be "an eye for an eye"—or a life for a life. Frequently, the result was a cycle of violence as members of extended family repaid vengeance on each other time and again. But in time the "eye for an eye" retaliation gave way in many societies to a practice of repayment in *blood money* or "wergild" to compensate for the loss. The actual amount of compensation was often based on specific monetary values placed on people of different social positions, from members of the nobility, to farmers, to serfs and slaves.

Virtually all countries today have criminal court systems where accused murderers are put on trial. The objectivity of courts and the protections afforded accused murderers in criminal justice systems have varied significantly. In Medieval Europe torture was used to extract confessions. In England during those years, a trial was conducted with a jury of 12–24 men who lived in the vicinity and likely knew the murderer and victim. These men of the jury were often witnesses of the crime itself. Trials provided little new testimony and the jury was supposed to arrive at a unanimous verdict swiftly, often in a matter of minutes, with punishment for those who were convicted handed down almost immediately.

The punishments for convicted murders have included banishment or exile, imprisonment, torture, execution, and psychiatric treatment. While we often see movies or hear stories about demonically creative and brutal murderers, societies have devised at least as creative and brutal a range of ways to punish those convicted of murder. In the Roman Empire, murderers were often crucified—nailed or hung on a pole or cross in public view to die of blood loss, infection, and dehydration. In Medieval Europe, male murderers and other criminals were at times boiled in scalding oil. More often they were disemboweled and castrated while still alive and their entrails and genitals burned in front them, after which they were beheaded. Women convicted of murder and various other crimes were often burned at the stake. Stoning and hanging have also been traditional forms of capital punishment, while firing squads, electric chairs, gas chambers, and lethal injection are more recent inventions. Often executions have been public events, drawing large and sometimes unruly crowds. The last public execution in the United States took place in Kentucky in 1936. Today about half of the nations in the world do not allow capital punishment and 18 US states prohibit it, including Michigan, where it has been banned since 1846.

HISTORY OF MURDER IN THE UNITED STATES

In the relatively short course of American history, there have been some dramatic shifts in terms of what is considered murder as opposed to other kinds of killing. Over time, there have also been changes in the most common types of murder in the United States, as well as transformations in how we respond to those who commit it.

Early America

In order to understand the history of murder in the United States, it is vital to consider race relations in colonial North America. The British colonies were a place where three races from three continents were entangled in ways that provoked the continuous threat of violence. The nature, contexts, and consequences of murder in the colonies, and later the United States, have been deeply influenced by these different race relations.

Whites and Native Americans

The relationship between the first colonists and Native Americans was a mixture of respect and distrust. At least some early relations with Native Americans demonstrated openness to interracial alliances. When the early European settlers arrived they did not have a significant military advantage. Their muskets were not that superior to Native Americans' bows and arrows. And conflicts and killings took place on both sides—Indians killing colonists and colonists killing Indians, mostly in the contexts of armed conflicts, or wars. Outside the context of wars, when interracial murder occurred, both whites and Native Americans were expected to take responsibility for policing their own members. But as the colonies grew and settlement continued west, and as many Native American tribes were decimated by war and disease, a different pattern emerged in which Indians accused of murdering whites were usually turned over to be tried in white courts, but whites accused of murdering tribal Indians were never surrendered to Indian justice (Lane 1997, p.39).

Whites and Slaves

Slavery in North America developed largely in tandem with the emergence of tobacco as a major export product from colonies like Virginia. Early tobacco planters continually moved from one piece of swampy land to another to grow their crop. These farmers were independent, armed, and constantly in need of laborers for the backbreaking labor of growing tobacco. Many of the laborers they used at first were indentured servants imported from England's poorhouses. While they were supposed to be treated much like their master's children and eventually released from servitude, most of the time they were subjected to overwork, malnutrition, and ill-treatment—with appalling effects. The death rate for indentured servants in Virginia was as high as 80 per cent per year (Lane 1997, p.42).

The first Africans taken prisoner and brought to the colonies were officially indentured servants (like their British counterparts) rather than slaves. English law (and these were British colonies) prohibited lifelong slavery. But slavery served a purpose and the king—or any kind of law enforcement—was far away. It was easy to cheat kidnapped slaves who were in a foreign land, knew no English, and had no idea of when, if ever, their terms of servitude should be over. In 1664, the legislature of Maryland decreed not only that all "negroes" were to be slaves for life, but that the children of all female slaves were also to be slaves, ensuring that those with known African ancestry were doomed to serve forever.

As slavery spread, the need to control black slaves became a fact of life in the South and sometimes in the North as well. The most basic need was to deal with daily confrontations and acts of defiance. In 1669, Virginia declared that the master's rule had the force of law and that anything he did, short of murder, was acceptable. In actuality, even murder of slaves was condoned. So long as the intention was "correction," the master could not be prosecuted even if a slave died of violent means.

Over the nearly two centuries of US slavery, blacks occasionally found ways to lash out violently against whites as well. The most deadly episode carried out by slaves was the 1831 rebellion organized by the preacher slave, Nat Turner. Turner and a loose band of supporters spent two days moving across Virginia, gathering other slaves as they went, and murdering a total of 60 white men, women, and children before being subdued. The slave rebellion orchestrated by Turner was the most violent uprising of slaves in American history and produced a panic among whites that was incommensurate with the actual level of violence they faced from slave and free blacks. In reality, far more blacks were murdered by whites during this era than vice versa.

White-on-White Murder

In contrast to the tolerance for white violence against Native Americans and black slaves, in colonial outposts, villages, and towns, white-on-white murder was rare, and when it occurred it was treated swiftly and harshly—although seldom by execution. Murder and manslaughter typically involved quarrelsome servants, laborers, or small farmers. Capital punishment would deprive the colony and master of workers, so a common sentence was to impose more years of servitude—which for many, in effect, was a life sentence. But, perhaps due largely to the widespread abundance and economic growth that white men experienced in this era, male white-on-white murder rates were strikingly low.

Civil War to World War I

The years leading up to and following the Civil War saw changes in the landscape of murder in the United States. One change during these years was the creation of the handgun. When the Second Amendment was passed in 1789, and for nearly 50 years after that, there was nothing that could accurately be called a handgun. But in the 1840s, revolvers began to be manufactured, and Henry Derringer's pocket-sized pistol (the kind of gun used to assassinate Abraham Lincoln) was widely sold by the 1850s. As handguns became commonly available, they gradually became the weapon of choice in most murders. In contrast to fists, clubs, and even knives that had been the most common murder weapons in the past, guns proved extremely quick and efficient killing tools, leading to death in many altercations that would never have turned deadly if participants had to rely on more primitive means such as fists and knives.

After the Civil War, many young men migrated to the cattle plains and mining towns of the western states and territories. Most of the images we have of murder during this era come from Hollywood westerns, but in reality mining towns were more murderous than the cattle plains. On the gold rush frontier, overwhelmingly the killings resulted not from attempted robberies or fights over women, but rather from the escalation of trivial arguments between young, single, heavy drinking, and armed males. Yet, other murders in the west reflected deep racial tensions between whites and Native Americans, Mexicans, and the Chinese who were brought to serve as laborers in mining camps and on the railroads.

Racially charged murder in the tension-ridden and "lawless" West paled in comparison to the white murder of blacks in the South following the Civil War. In the Reconstruction era following the repeal of slavery, murder was often used by whites as a vigilante means of social control. In the late 1800s, white-on-black killings in the South reached their notorious peak, including acts of violence that Lane has described as among "the most barbaric episodes in the history of American homicide" (1997, p.92). The vigilante "justice" of lynching was often a public event, with entire families at times in attendance as black men accused of crimes—most frequently and falsely of rape or assault of white women—were brutally beaten and hanged without the right to a trial.

By World War I the murder rate in the United States had declined—and dropped further as the war took large numbers of young men out of the country. But during the early 1900s several changes in the United States occurred that would lead to a marked shift in murder styles and policing. One kind of murder that emerged at this time was urban armed bank robbery. While armed robberies of banks and railroads had been common earlier on the Western frontier where police presence was spotty at best, it was not until the Automobile Age that bank robbery gained a foothold in US cities. Cars provided what Lane has called "mobile striking units" that allowed quick get away from the crime. As bank robbery became more common, so did news of related murders by such notorious bank robbers as John Dillinger, Baby Face Nelson, Pretty Boy Floyd, and Bonnie and Clyde. These criminals were popular with the media, due in part to their daring exploits, and to the way in which FBI director J. Edgar Hoover dramatized their pursuit by labeling many of them as "Public Enemy Number One."

The enactment of Prohibition in 1919 also created a climate in which the enormous profits from illegal gains led to conflicts between law enforcement and criminals involved in the vice trades and to intense battles among rival gangs. In Chicago alone during the "Lawless Decade," there were hundreds of gangland murders, most unsolved, with the killers speeding away in Buicks or dumping bodies in the river. Along the way, gangster movies captured the public imagination and became standard Hollywood fare. The distinction between facts and movies became blurred as Hoover arranged to be caught on film as he personally arrested Alvin "Creepy" Karpis and Louis "Lepke" Buchalter, the head of a loosely organized group of killers who called themselves "Murder, Inc."

The images of gangsters and bank robbers that dominated 1920s and 1930s news stories of murder represented only the most sensational cases of murder at the time. They failed to capture the majority of murders, characterized by dreary, often impoverished lives, and one-time offenders. But at the same time that Hoover played to the media with sensationalistic cases, the FBI was working toward the creation of a national system for collecting statistics on murder and other crimes in what would become the *UCRs*.

Post-World War II

When the United States entered World War II the nation's murder rate went down, just as it had in World War I. That was not surprising since millions of young males, the group most likely to commit murder, had been sent off to fight in other countries. But when they returned from the War, something surprising did happen: the murder rate continued to decline. By 1957, in the early years of prosperity following the War, the murder rate in the country dropped to 4.0 per 100,000 people, the lowest murder rate in the United States since good records had been created.

The most common types of murder also had changed, as revealed in sociologist Marvin Wolfgang's study, *Patterns in Criminal Homicide* (1958). While murder continued to be committed primarily by young adult males, mostly within racial lines, there had been a shift away from stranger murders and murders in public places, such as drinking establishments, toward murders in the home—what Lane has called the *domestication of murder.* Saying that murder had become domesticated does not mean that it became less violent. Often murderous attacks are more brutal in intimate relationships. But from a law enforcement perspective, domestic murder had one major advantage. It is often easy to identify the perpetrator. Frequently the offender, himself or herself, notifies the police of the murder and remains with the body until they arrive.

A second change in murder rates following World War II was a shift in racial patterns. While murder rates among blacks in urban settings had long been higher than those of whites, and while over 90 per cent of murders were intraracial, in the early 1950s for the first time in American history, the number of whites killed by blacks was higher than blacks killed by white assailants. Still, the actual number of interracial murders remained relatively low, and blacks continued to be far more at risk of being both victims and perpetrators of murder than did their white counterparts—a pattern that continues to the present day.

Landscape of Murder in the New Millennium

After reaching a low point of 4.0 murders per 100,000 US citizens in 1957, murder rates began to slowly rise again, more than doubling by the 1970s and reaching a postwar high of 10.2 per 100,000 people in 1980. After that, murder rates gradually declined again. Since the start of the twenty-first century, the rate has remained stable at 4.5–5 per 100,000—a significant reduction from their 1980s highs. Further, there have been some shifts in patterns of murder over the past decade. Perhaps most notable is the higher proportion of stranger killings than in the past. The higher proportion of stranger killings, however, is not the result of increased number of such murders, but due to a decrease in domestic and acquaintance murders. Second, the percentage of murders that are cleared by arrest today is lower than it was in the 1960s and 1970s. This too is directly related to the decrease in familial and acquaintance killings, which have always been easier to solve.

Violent crimes of murder and assault are relatively low in the United States today, although the fear of victimization remains high (Ledbetter 2014). But even with our relatively low historical rates of murder, we continue to have the highest rate in developed societies—and an especially sobering rate of murder among African-American males.

SOCIAL CAPITAL AND HOMICIDE

When positivistic social scientists focus attention on murder they seek to uncover its causes. But while it is usually easy to identify murder when it occurs, it is far more difficult to clearly specify what causes it. Assertions about the cause or causes of murder involve decisions about where to place the blame for deadly violence. Many lethal conflicts would not have ended in murder if a gun had not been available to the offender and quicker police or ambulance response could have saved many victims' lives. But the violent encounters that lead to murder are not specifically caused by guns or by a lack of medical response. Positivistic social scientists often seek to explain varying rates of

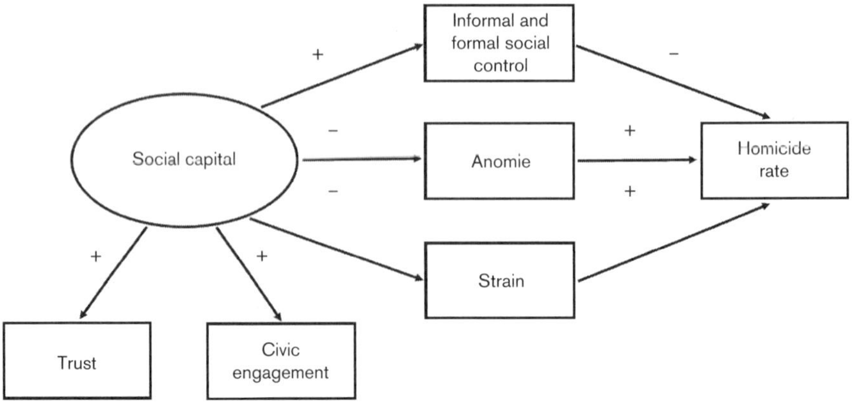

Figure 5.1 Social capital and homicide (Rosenfeld et al. 2001).

deviant behavior in different societies or social contexts rather than focus on the cause of individual acts themselves. Building on social disorganization theory and Merton's anomie theory, criminologist Richard Rosenfeld et al. (2001) argue that homicide rates vary based on community levels of *social capital*, or the degree to which communities provide social networks, norms, and trust that foster cooperation. Social capital includes formal institutions like schools, churches, and law enforcement agencies—insofar as they are viewed as trustworthy by citizens—as well as informal social capital like goodwill among neighbors and shared expectations of mutual support in neighborhood social control. Communities or neighborhoods that are rich in social capital also exhibit what has been called "collective efficacy," or the ability to achieve common goals. A social capital analysis of homicide is diagrammed in figure 5.1. Social capital includes "trust," in the sense of being able to trust that others will follow social norms, while "civic engagement" refers to citizens' participation in collective social life. When social trust and civic engagement are high, Rosenfeld et al. argue, both formal and informal social control are high as well. In such contexts, the police are trusted and responsive to calls for assistance while community members also feel connected and look out for each other's well-being. Anomie and social strain in such settings is minimal since social norms are clear and lead to predictable outcomes. Rosenfeld and his colleagues' research shows that homicide rates are lower in communities with higher levels of social trust and civic engagement.

In contrast, some communities have particularly low social capital. Loïc Wacquant suggests that many impoverished minority neighborhoods are characterized not just by low levels of social capital, but often by "negative social capital," where public organizations such as law enforcement and schools have become "instruments of surveillance, suspicion, and exclusion rather than

PUSHING YOUR BOUNDARIES

Murder in the Media

Find news reports (on television, radio, Internet news sites, or print media) about four recent murders. Look for reports that provide at least some statements about why the murder happened. For each of the reported murders, answer the following questions:

- What kind of murder (e.g., serial, mass, stranger, or intimate murder) is reported?
- Does the news report discuss any possible explanations for why the murder occurred? If so, list them?
- Write a paragraph describing the variables you found in the news reports you examined. If you had to develop an explanation of the cause(s) of murder based just on these reports, what would you say? Do you feel there are other important variables that could have been raised but were not?
- Come to class prepared to share what you have found.

vehicles of social integration and trust-building" (1998, p.26). The lack of formal social capital, along with the erosion of wage-labor jobs, undermines the creation of informal social capital as well, creating what Douglas Massey describes as a "segregated ecological niche characterized by a high risk of physical injury, violent death, and criminal victimization" (1995, p.1217). While Wacquant's and Massey's observations are nearly 20 years old, recent research (e.g., Sharkey 2013) finds that residential patterns in urban America remain highly segregated, with minority communities continuing to experience low levels of social capital. Within these contexts it is disturbing, but sadly not surprising, to see great differences in murder rates for white and black Americans. For young African-American males the difference is especially appalling. Black young men between the ages of 18 and 24 have almost eight times as great a risk of being victims of murder as do their white counterparts (Cooper and Smith 2011).

A social capital analysis of murder rates provides insight into the social contexts in which murder is more common, but it does not delve into the actual situations in which murders take place. For such an up-close analysis we turn to qualitative homicide research.

INTERACTIONAL CONTEXTS AND ETHNOGRAPHIC VOICES

Researchers seeking to understand the situations in which murders occur often distinguish between instrumental and expressive motives for lethal violence.

Instrumental murders involve killing as a means to achieve a material goal, such as murder in a robbery or killing a family member in hopes of inheriting their money. In contrast, *expressive murders* occur when emotionally charged interactions take a deadly turn, as in quarrels at a bar or domestic disputes that result in murder. In an extensive analysis of murder reports, Terance Miethe and Wendy Regoeczi (2004) found that most homicides in the United States fall into one of three situational patterns: instrumental felony murders, expressive murders involving interpersonal disputes, or expressive domestic violence.

Felony murder is the term used to refer to murder that is committed while in the act of another felony crime (e.g., rape, robbery, auto theft, or burglary). Killings during robberies are the most prevalent type of instrumental homicide situations (Miethe and Regoeczi 2004, p.121). Most muggers do not intend in advance to kill their victims. They often threaten force in the hope of achieving their goals without serious physical violence, but the potential for injury and death is still very present. While robbery-related murders involve some planning ahead of time, the majority of such murders are perpetrated by young men who have engaged in very limited planning—and even more seldom, any planning to kill the victim. A considerable number of these murders occur while attempting to rob other young men who are selling drugs (Miethe and Regoeczi 2004).

Expressive murders involving interpersonal disputes are far more common than instrumental murders. Men are much more likely than women to commit expressive murders of family members or intimate partners as well as less close acquaintances. But women are more likely than men to be the victims. Over 40 per cent of female murder victims die in the course of a dispute with an intimate partner, as compared to only 7 per cent of males (Cooper and Smith 2011). In contrast, nearly 60 per cent of male murder victims are killed by an acquaintance, and over one in four by a stranger (Cooper and Smith 2011). Compared to men, women more frequently kill intimates and kill in situations in which their victim initiated the physical aggression (Jurik and Winn 1990).

The common view of murder is that it is done by one malicious person on an unwitting innocent victim. But most murders involve some degree of social interaction between the killer and their victim. In at least a quarter of reported murder cases, the slayer was attacked first by the ultimate victim, a phenomenon referred to as "*victim-precipitated homicide*" (e.g., Felson and Steadman 1983). While, as Lonnie Athens (2005) has pointed out, we should resist blaming most victims for their murder, it is important to recognize that many murders occur in heated interactional encounters where both parties have engaged in insults and aggression.

Character Contests: Six Stages

The most well-known analysis of murderous encounters has been developed by David Luckenbill (1977) based on his study of official documents including police, psychiatric, and witness reports, offender interviews, victim statements, and court testimony. Luckenbill found that murderous encounters typically involved a *character contest* in which two individuals, often in the presence of an audience, become embroiled in insulting interaction that ultimately ends in one of them being killed. Luckenbill identifies six stages in which character contests escalate to deadly violence. Several other scholars have modified or expanded his analysis of the sequenced stages of deadly interactions.

Stage One: Personal Offense

Most cases of personal murder begin with an individual engaging in some offensive behavior toward another person. The offending behavior may be verbal, such as calling someone a name, or an action, such as cutting a driver off in traffic. Lonnie Athens (2005) describes the initial stage of a murderous encounter as involving a dominance claim in which one person asserts through words or actions that they are superior to the other person. But the offending behavior or dominance claim does not necessarily need to be intentional. Luckenbill gives the example of a five-week-old baby crying and not responding to his father's order to stop. The child clearly was not continuing to cry in resistance to his father's command, despite his father's perceptions.

Stage Two: Assessment

In the second stage of an escalating murderous encounter, the eventual murderer assesses the behavior of the other person. Was it a joke? An accident? Was it meant to be offensive? In several cases, Luckenbill found, the soon-to-be murderer was initially confused about what was going on and whether or not they should perceive the act as an insult. At other times, however, the future victim "teases, dares, defies, or pursues the killer" (Katz 1988, p.20), making their disrespectful motives crystal clear. Ultimately, the deciding factor in escalating the encounter is how the person comes to define the situation. If the individual believes that they have been disrespected, humiliated, or treated unfairly, they may feel moved to take further action.

Stage Three: Retaliation

When the offended person acts to salvage their status by refusing to walk away or accept the dominance claims of the other party, they reject the role that the other person has placed them in. Emotions run high, and the soon-to-be killer is flooded with feelings of injustice and contempt for the other person. As Katz explains, the killer becomes consumed with rage:

> Humiliation and rage are holistic feelings, experienced as transcending bodily limitations. In humiliation, the person is overcome with an intolerable discomfort . . .

> Like humiliation, rage draws the whole body into its service . . . Humiliation threatens to be endless and diffuse, while rage searches for a target to extinguish itself.
>
> —Katz (1988, p.25)

Caught up in the moment of rage, Katz argues, the soon-to-be killer is "blinded to the practical future implications of the moment" (p.31). Humiliated and filled with contempt, they feel a sense of "righteous slaughter" and lash out with verbal and/or physical attacks that their opponent may respond to in kind, leading to the next stage of lethal encounters.

Stage Four: Working Agreement

By this point, both participants in the interaction have come to define the situation as one that will be resolved through aggressive action. The participants engage in verbal and physical "role sparring" (Athens 2005) in which each tries to claim a dominant position. Frequently they are encouraged toward physical violence by bystanders—especially in the case of young males in the presence of their peers (Polk 1994). At this stage, violence is imminent even if its outcome is unclear.

Stage Five: Battle

In the next—and lethal—stage of murderous encounters "at least one [if not both] of the two disputants must decide to use physical force to settle the issue" (Athens 2005, p.659). They have now placed their character on the line and expressed their commitment to a violent course of action. At this stage of the encounter, the dominance of one of the opponents will be determined—by the violent subjugation of the other. Yet, often deadly violence leaves even the "victor" with a stunned sense of surprise. Indeed, murder is often a chance or precarious outcome of violent encounters. As Katz explains:

> Whether an event ends in a criminal homicide or an aggravated assault depends on such chance factors as the distance to the hospital; the quality of medical services available; whether a gun was used and, if so, what caliber; whether a head reeling from a punch strikes a rail or a concrete floor; or whether the knife chanced to hit a vital organ.
>
> —Katz (1988, p.32)

Stage Six: Resolution

In the aftermath of the murder, the killer must decide what to do next. In about 60 per cent of the cases studied by Luckenbill, the killer fled the scene. But another 30 per cent stayed voluntarily at the site of the murder until the police arrived. The remaining 10 per cent were forced to stay by others at the scene. The decision to leave or stay was influenced by the relationship between the offender and the victim and whether or not an audience was present. In cases where there was no audience, when the killer and victim were intimately related, the killer typically notified the police and stayed at the scene. But when the killer did not know their victim, they usually fled the scene, often attempting to dispose of their victims and incriminating evidence before they left.

Most murders occur in the presence of an audience, and in such cases Luckenbill found about one-third of the audiences apprehended the killer, assisted the victim, and immediately notified the police. In about half as many cases, bystanders stood by stunned as the victim died and the murderer left the scene. In the other 50 per cent of cases, the audience was supportive of the killer, rendering assistance in his escape, destroying incriminating evidence, and initially maintaining ignorance of the event when questioned by the police.

The portrait of murderous events provided by Luckenbill and other scholars provides a valuable corrective to media portrayals of serial killers and hit men. Focusing on more typical murders, Luckenbill found that "Personal murder is not a one-sided transaction with an unwitting target playing a passive, noncontributory role. Rather, it is an outcome of a dynamic interchange between offender, target, and the bystanders" (Best and Luckenbill 1994, p.149).

CONTEMPORARY RESPONSES TO MURDER

The crime of murder is considered among the most serious of deviant acts. Frequently it has been repaid in kind, through kin-based vendettas or through state-based executions. Police forces in modern societies have only seriously taken on the role of murder investigation in the last century or so. In contrast to earlier eras' relative neglect of murder investigation, today most large police departments have professional detectives and even homicide units. At the national level, the FBI devotes substantial manpower to specific kinds of murder, such as those associated with serial killers and terrorism. The development of forensic specialists and DNA analysis has further professionalized the field of murder investigation. Yet, many murders require little in terms of investigation. From the homicide detective's vantage point, many murders are "walk-throughs," or cases in which the perpetrator is easily identified—and often apprehended (Terry and Luckenbill 1976). Many murders occur in front of an audience that willingly identifies the murderer, and those who kill friends and family members often report the crime and stay with the body until the police arrive. "Whodunit" cases in which police detectives must investigate who the killer is represent a smaller, if still significant, number of murder cases. Taken over all, the majority of murders are solved; homicide is more likely to result in arrest of an individual who is charged with the crime than any other index crime.

In recent years, over 60 per cent of homicides reported to the police have been cleared by an arrest or some "exceptional" means (e.g., suspect commits suicide or flees the country), as compared to only 40 per cent of rapes and just 13 per cent of burglaries. Still, the percentage of US murders cleared by arrest has dropped significantly since 1960 when law enforcement officials cleared 92 per cent of homicides—a number that is close to the 95 per cent clearance rate today in Japan (Riedel 2008). What can help explain the drop in clearance rates in the United States over the past 50 years as well as the dramatic difference between the United States and Japan today? While it is impossible to unravel the entire picture, one important factor is that murder patterns have shifted over the years. The rate of murder committed by family members and romantic partners has declined, while the rate of stranger murder has remained more stable. Since stranger murders are typically more difficult to solve than intimate killings, as the proportion of stranger murders has increased, so has the proportion of murders that remain uncleared. In contrast, in Japan (where the murder rate is only one-tenth of that in the United States) a far greater proportion of murders continue to be among family members. Further, most murders in Japan are committed with weapons other than firearms, such as knives and fists. The use of weapons other than firearms contributes to higher clearances, since guns can be used at a greater distance from the victim and typically leave less forensic evidence for investigators. Nonetheless, with a clearance rate of over 60 per cent, murder has the highest rate of arrest of any serious crime in the United States. Further, seven out of 10 people who are arrested for murder are convicted of the crime, either through pleading guilty or by being convicted in a court trial.

Punitive Responses

The criminal justice system response to homicide focuses primarily on the punishment of convicted murderers. From a criminal justice perspective, the two most commonly offered rationales for long prison sentences or execution are that the murderer will be unable to kill (at least members of the general population) again, and that the presence of severe penalties for killing will deter people who might otherwise commit murder. The actual deterrent effect of harsh punishment for murder is a matter of considerable debate. This is particularly true for the death penalty. While at first glance it might seem reasonable that the threat of capital punishment would keep people from committing murder, we should consider the actual circumstances in which most murders occur. Most homicides involve heated emotional arguments, often between acquaintances, family members, or romantic partners. As Katz notes, in such encounters, those who end up committing murder typically report having been overcome with intolerable feelings of humiliation and rage. Often they are intoxicated at the time of the murder and frequently they feel threatened by the person they end up killing. These are not conditions under which individuals are likely to spend much time calculating the potential long-term consequences of their behavior. Caught up in feelings of humiliation and/or fear, they tend to react to the immediate situation. And often they are stunned by the outcome.

According to a recent survey by the Pew Research Center (2015a), over 60 per cent of Americans do not believe capital punishment deters murder, but nearly the same percentage support the death penalty. Public support for the death penalty, however, has declined over the past two decades, dropping from a high of 78 per cent in 1996 to 56 per cent in 2015. Perhaps even more significantly, the use of capital punishment in the United States has dropped dramatically in recent years, with only 15 executions nationwide in 2015. Currently about 2,950 convicted murderers sit on "death row," challenging or awaiting execution (Death Penalty Information Center 2016). If current criminal justice trends continue, the overwhelming majority of these cases will eventually be converted to life sentences.

But whether the punishment is incarceration or execution, the criminal justice system is designed to react to murder after the fact. In contrast, the contextual responses to which we turn next approach violent crime in terms of broader situational and social dynamics, considering the circumstances in which deadly violence occurs and seeking to manage that environment in ways that may preempt deadly outcomes—before they occur rather than dealing with their aftermath.

Contextual Responses

The most commonly discussed contextual approach to reducing murder and other injuries due to violence is controlling access to guns. The argument for gun control is simple. Since 70 per cent of murders, as well as a large percentage of other violent crimes, involve guns, restrictions on who can own and carry guns and where, it is argued, will give us safer homes, schools, and streets. The most common gun control policies include (1) background checks and restrictions against gun purchases by individuals believed to represent a high threat of danger, (2) restrictions on the kinds of guns often associated with violent crime, especially lethal weapons that serve no sport or recreational purpose, and (3) restrictions on where guns can be carried.

Gun rights advocates who fight against gun control policies argue that the ownership of guns is a constitutional right guaranteed by the Second Amendment and that denying people access to guns leaves them more vulnerable to being victims of violent crimes. In his book, *More Guns, Less Crime*, the gun rights scholar, John Lott, Jr., has gone so far as to claim that "the carrying of concealed handguns appears to be the most cost-effective method for reducing crime" (2010, p.20). Lott proclaims that concealed weapons deter crime

CLAIMS-MAKER PROFILE

Jim and Sarah Brady Campaign to Prevent Gun Violence

On March 30, 1981, White House Press Secretary Jim Brady was the first member of President Ronal Reagan's entourage to be shot in an assassination attempt by 25-year-old John Hinckley. President Reagan and two bodyguards were also shot, but recovered quickly. Brady was less fortunate. The bullet in his head left him with slurred speech and confined to a wheelchair for the rest of his life. As information on Hinckley was uncovered, it became clear that he had a delusional obsession with actress Jodie Foster and had planned the assassination of President Reagan as a way to impress her.

Four years later, the Brady's young son grabbed what he thought was a toy gun on a friend's car seat and began pointing it. Brady's wife, Sarah, recognized the gun as very much like the one that had shot her husband. Angered by the careless lack of gun safety that had enabled her son to pick up a loaded handgun, Sarah decided to become involved in promoting gun safety. Between her public relations expertise, including four years as Coordinator of Field Services for the Republican National Committee, and her husband's high profile story as a victim of gun violence, Sarah and Jim Brady became the most effective advocates of gun control in the country.

Their efforts led to the 1993 passage of the Brady Handgun Violence Prevention Act that mandated federal background checks on firearm purchasers. The Brady Act drew strong opposition from gun rights advocates, including the NRA, which funded lawsuits in several states to strike it down. In 1997, the US Supreme Court ruled that the federal government could not require state law enforcement officials to perform the background checks. Most states, however, continue to do so, using the FBI's National Instant Criminal Background Check System.

Today, the Brady Campaign organization continues to advocate for "gun laws, regulations, and public policies through grassroots activism, electing public officials who support gun laws, and increasing public awareness of gun violence" (Brady Campaign 2016).

Jim Brady passed away in 2014. The medical examiner ruled his death a homicide resulting from his gunshot wound 33 years earlier.

because, "When guns are concealed, criminals are unable to tell whether the victim is armed before striking, which raises the risk to criminals of committing many types of crimes" (2010, p.5).

The federal government and all states have at least some laws restricting who may own or purchase certain kinds of guns and where they are allowed to carry them. The majority of American adults consistently support measures to regulate guns (Pew Research Center 2015b), but it has proven extremely difficult to enact expanded gun control legislation. Criminologists have come to refer to this discrepancy between public attitudes and laws as the *gun control paradox* (Schuman and Presser 2013). The paradox is exemplified in an experiment in which the Gallup polling agency (2011) asked people whether they would vote for a law expanding background checks. Over 80 per cent of respondents said yes. But when the question was changed to whether or not "the U.S. Senate should pass such a law," the positive responses drop by 20 per cent (Cook and Goss 2014, p.179). The American public, it seems, is supportive of restricting gun access in principle, but more ambivalent about enacting specific regulations.

American resistance to new gun laws is also due in part to the political power of the NRA which refers to itself as "the nation's oldest civil rights organization," emphasizing the protection of the Second Amendment and the promotion of firearm ownership rights. According to *Fortune* magazine, the NRA is regularly ranked as "the nation's most powerful political lobbying organization by lawmakers and congressional staffers" (Time Warner 2009). The NRA has demonstrated the ability to mobilize resources, including its current annual budget of about $250 million, and, even more significantly, the devotion of its members in support of political action (Surowlecki 2015). In contrast, gun control advocates have not mobilized nearly as extensively or successfully (Goss 2006)—although current gun control advocates are showing greater organizational and political sophistication than in the past (Surowlecki 2015). The future contexts in which violent crimes and murder occur will depend in part on the outcome of these debates.

STIGMA MANAGEMENT AND RESISTANCE

To be a "murderer" is to be labeled as one of the most despicable and dangerous kinds of people. While a few violent criminals pride themselves on their reputations for cold-blooded violence, the overwhelming majority of people who are charged with or convicted of murder feel a need to justify their actions to others and to themselves. Most obviously, in murder trials, those charged with homicide typically seek to make the case that the circumstances in which the killing took place should absolve them from the murder charges. Even when they admit that they did kill another person or persons, they are likely to argue that they were acting in self-defense or that the killing was accidental.

In one notable study, Melvin Ray and Ronald Simons (1987) asked 25 convicted murderers to recount the deadly encounters. While the men admitted killing, they offered excuses, such as intoxication and emotional stress, and justifications, such as deserved retaliation, to explain their violent behavior.

Mark Progrebin et al. (2006) found similar accounts among violent gun offenders who were incarcerated in the Colorado Department of Corrections.

When asked to explain their violent encounters, the offenders told stories that either indicated that the victim got what he or she deserved or they explained that they did not have control of their actions at the time. In the case of "denial of victim," violent offenders spoke of situations in which the person they murdered had provoked them by physically attacking, humiliating, or otherwise harming them before they took their violent action. One man explained that he and his boss had been arguing:

> Then he fired me on the spot. I was very upset. The money I was making at the apartment complex was to help my family in Colombia. The guy had to pay for what he did. I wanted to explode you know. I had a .38 caliber gun in my car. When I grabbed the weapon I knew I was ready. When I approached him the other maintenance man said, "Robert, watch out!"
>
> When he said that, "Boom." I shot him. I sat down and waited for the police. It was a relief for me.
>
> —Progrebin et al. (2006, p.487)

In cases like this, the offender presented a scenario in which the killing was ostensibly justified and the murdered individual got what they deserved. Yet, others provided excuses for their violent acts, explaining how romantic partner or friends had pressured them to engage in violence. Many explained that they had been carried away by their emotions and would never have committed murder if they had been in control. Indeed, both justifications and excuses were at times woven into the same narrative, as in the case of a young man who explained:

> My stepfather would break my mom's ribs, break her jaw, break her nose. . . . I was 18, living on my own and I went to visit my mom. She had a black eye so I told my stepdad, "You hit her again and I'm coming after you." He said, "If I hit her again, I'll kill her and I'll end up killing you too."
>
> [Later] the person with me [a friend] kept egging me on, having me go through every time I'd seen my stepdad hit my mom and every time he hit me. Every time I started to cool down he would start in again. He kept me so pumped up, I was totally disconnected from myself. [It felt like] I saw somebody I didn't know shooting my stepdad. Once the act was over, I was back to myself, total rush, dizziness, everything was blurry. I just freaked out.
>
> —Progrebin et al. (2006, p.497)

In these accounts, we see how people who have engaged in murder define the situation in ways that absolve them of responsibility or make their behaviors more understandable. As Progrebin et al. conclude, "The gun users we interviewed sought to dispel the view that their deviation was a defining characteristic of who they really were" (2006, p.498).

Although it is clear that the accounts offered by convicted murderers involve attempts to present themselves in a more positive light, we must be careful not to see their comments as merely face-saving endeavors. Many of these violent offenders are giving accurate accounts—of their own experience of the murderous events. Indeed, it seems that many individuals who commit murder feel justified in their violence (if not necessarily, its deadly outcome) at the time.

BLURRED BOUNDARIES II: IS ASSISTED SUICIDE MURDER?

We began this chapter with an observation that murder involves not just killing, but "criminal killing" of another person. What is considered criminal killing can vary from one society to another over time. There are even cases in which we may disagree among ourselves about what should be considered murder today. What separates murder—criminal killing—from acceptable killing? Two key criteria that we usually consider are that murder is intentional, perhaps even planned in advance, and that it is motivated by malice, or the desire to do harm. But there are some situations where these criteria may not provide enough guidance for distinguishing between acceptable killing and murder.

The beginning of this chapter described Jack Kevorkian, the US physician called "Dr. Death." Kevorkian, who died in 2011, was implicated in over 130 deaths by his own count. After four previous trials in which he was acquitted, in 1999 he was convicted of second degree murder for having administered a lethal injection to 52-year-old terminally ill Thomas Youk at the man's and his wife's request. Kevorkian, who was released from prison at the age of 77 after serving eight years of a 10–25-year sentence, is considered by many people to have been a hero rather than a criminal.

Should helping a person kill himself or herself be considered an act of murder? Under many circumstances, most of us would say yes. But what about situations in which the person seeking to commit suicide is suffering from a painful and disabling terminal illness, as in the cases of people Kevorkian assisted? Six states in the United States currently allow physicians to assist some terminally ill patients in hastening their death, while doing so in other states may be classified as manslaughter or murder.

Should a doctor who is asked by a terminally ill patient to help her end her life be charged with murder for doing what she asks? If the answer is "yes," then there are thousands of uncharged murderers practicing medicine in the United States today. According to a study reported in the *New England Journal of Medicine*, during a one-year period in the late 1990s, 12 per cent of physicians surveyed reported that they had been asked to assist one or more patients in suicide—and that they had honored about one in four of those requests, in spite of the fact that it was illegal to do so (Back et al. 1996). In another national study reported in the *Journal of the American Medical Association*, almost 20 per cent of physicians said they had received request, and over 16 per cent of those who had received requests had at times provided help (Meier et al. 1998). The implication of these findings is that there are likely thousands of US physicians who have played a conscious role in patients' deaths.

When we consider physician-assisted suicides, we face a dark sea of unknown, largely unprosecuted, and hardly ever discussed intentional killings. Why are many of us unwilling to call them murder? The answer, in large part, is that many of us feel that the contexts of these killings make them different. Physicians who help patients commit suicide are motivated out of a sense of compassion for people who are struggling with pain, disability, and a loss of dignity. And they are acting on the expressed wishes of those they kill—often at considerable risk to themselves. In cases such as these, many people do not believe that intentionally planning to terminate another person's life should be considered murder.

There is no avoiding the fact that murder is what we define it to be—and that what we define as murder plays a part in defining the character of the society in which we live. As a member of our society, where would you draw the line in regard to assisted suicide? Do you believe it should be defined as murder? What role do premeditation and the intent to do harm play in your assessment? Are there other concerns that you feel should be considered as well?

SUMMARY

- Murder is a social construction that classifies certain kinds of killing as unjustifiable and criminal.
- Serial killers and mass murderers are common in entertainment media, but rare in reality.
- Stranger murders of all kinds are less common than acquaintance murders and intimate murders at the hands of friends and family members.
- The US murder rate is far lower today than it was 30 years ago, but the United States has the highest murder rate of any developed country in the world.
- The FBI's *UCRs* are a valuable source for statistics on patterns and trends in murder rates.
- Researchers seeking up-close understanding of murder frequently rely on prison interviews with convicted murderers.
- The most common beliefs about the causes of murder in human cultures include demonic possession, mental illness, and subcultures of violence.
- Prior to the creation of nation-states and police forces, families often avenged their relatives' killings through vendettas or demanding blood money.
- Race relations have played a critical role in defining and reacting to murder in America, with Native Americans and black slaves at high risk of unprosecuted deaths.
- White-on-black murder by lynching rose in the years following the Civil War.
- Following World War II, in the 1950s the US murder rate dropped to its lowest recorded rate.
- Social disorganization theory and anomie theory suggest that communities with high levels of social capital have relatively low homicide rates.

- The concepts of instrumental and expressive motives for murder distinguish homicide in pursuit of personal gain from murder that occurs in the heat of interpersonal conflict. Expressive murders are far more common.
- Luckenbill identifies six stages in which social interactions escalate to expressive murder. Such murders are the result of conflictual interaction between the offender, the victim, and, frequently, an audience that encourages the conflict.
- Convicted murderers in the United States typically face long prison sentences, and, in rare cases, capital punishment.
- Social policy analysts suggest that laws restricting access to guns could reduce the number of murders, but it has proven extremely hard to craft gun control legislation that can garner enough political support to be enacted.
- Individuals who are charged with committing murder frequently argue that they were justified or that they were not wholly responsible for their actions. Such accounts enable murderers to manage their stigma and present themselves in a more positive light.
- Many physicians violate the law each year by helping suffering patients end their lives. Some of us see them as acting with compassion outside of the law, while others see them as committing murder.

KEYWORDS

acquaintance murder: The murder of an individual known by the person committing the murder.

blood money: A historical practice in which money, livestock, or goods were paid by a murderer or his family to the family or kin group of the murder victim to compensate them for their loss.

character contest: A social interaction in which an individual feels he or she has been humiliated and must respond in order to save face.

domestication of murder: A shift in murder trends in the 1950s in which more murder occurred among family members and in the home.

expressive homicide: Murder that occurs in the context of an emotional conflict such as a marital dispute or an argument between friends or acquaintances.

felony murder: Murder that is committed while in the act of another felony crime (e.g., rape, robbery, auto theft, or burglary).

gun control paradox: A term used to describe the discrepancy between high levels of public opinion in favor of gun control, on the one hand, and the lack of sustained gun control legislation on the other.

instrumental homicide: Murder that is committed in the pursuit of personal gain, such as a murder committed in the act of robbery or burglary.

intimate murder: Murder of romantic partners, such as spouses, boyfriends, or girlfriends.

manslaughter: A legal term for circumstances in which an individual unintentionally, or through negligence, caused the death of another person.

mass murder: One-time murderous events involving multiple victims.

second amendment: The second amendment to the US Constitution, which states that "the right of the People to keep and bear arms shall not be infringed." Used extensively by gun rights advocates to challenge the constitutionality of gun control laws.

serial killer: Term often used for a murderer who kills strangers over an extended period of time.

social capital: Social resources that provide social networks, norms, and values that foster interpersonal cooperation, social support, and both formal and informal social control.

stranger murder: Homicide in which the offender does not know their victim or victims.

subcultures of violence: Subcultural settings or groups in which violence is considered an appropriate and honorable way to resolve conflicts and express masculine identity.

CHAPTER

Rape 6

Antirape protest (Janine Wiedel Photolibrary/Alamy Stock Photo).

CONTENTS

LEARNING OBJECTIVES

After reading this chapter, you will be able to:

- Describe the most common types of rape recognized in the United States today
- Explain the challenges of, and strategies for, studying rape
- Identify different historical definitions of, and causal explanations for, rape
- Apply rape proclivity theory and routine activity theory to sexual assault
- Analyze the interactional contexts in which stranger rape and party rape most often occur
- Explain the "second rape" description of the criminal justice processing of rape cases
- Assess complexities in establishing policies regarding "affirmative consent" in situations where drinking is involved

BLURRED BOUNDARIES I: TWO SEXUAL ASSAULTS

The warm May evening began as a celebration at a popular bar near the university. 22-year-old Deena Hatcher laughed and danced with her friends as they toasted to their coming graduation. But around midnight when Deena headed to the restroom things turned serious. Seeing a line out the door of the women's restroom, she headed back to a smaller, less used commode down a hallway. As a young man walked out of the restroom, Deena stepped in and pulled the door behind her—only to feel it yanked back, as the man stepped back in and locked the door. By the time she realized the situation, there was little she could do. As the dance music blared in the bar, the man pushed Deena to the floor, knocking her half unconscious on the toilet bowl and reaching under her skirt. The rest was a blur of fighting back, but lacking the strength to get away.

Caught up in dancing, Deena's friends did not realize she had been gone for nearly half an hour until the police arrived to care for her and transport her to a nearby hospital where she filed a rape report, had a physical exam, and was treated for a concussion. The next day, the local newspaper reported Deena's rape, although not her name, and as much description of the rapist as she could give. In response to the rape, the bar owner added more security and closed off the restroom with the locking door.

Cases like Deena's come to mind when we think of sexual assault. Virtually all of us would agree that her assailant committed rape. But while we recognize rape is a serious crime, there are cases where charges of rape or sexual assault may strike many of us as inappropriate. Consider, for example, the case of 17-year-old Genarlow Wilson's arrest and conviction for sexual assault.

On New Year's Eve, 2003, Genarlow Wilson attended a hotel room party with a bunch of other teenagers. The partiers drank, smoked marijuana, and had sex, some of which was captured on camera, including video that showed Wilson receiving oral sex from a 15-year-old girl. Police who investigated the party found the video and arrested several young men, including Wilson. Although the girl in the video said she had consented to oral sex with him, Wilson was charged with sexual assault of a minor. While Georgia had a law that treated sex between minors differently from sex between a minor and an adult, that law covered only sexual intercourse. Oral sex was a felony with a mandatory prison sentence. Genarlow Wilson was convicted as a sex offender and sentenced to ten years in prison.

Several of the jurors who convicted him expressed dismay at his sentence. Members of the NAACP, including prominent religious leaders and the girl's mother, protested the conviction and punishment of the former high school honor student. The *New York Times* condemned the Court's decision, arguing that Wilson was not a sexual predator and that his behavior would have only been a misdemeanor if he had intercourse with the girl instead of oral sex. The law under which Wilson was convicted was changed after his conviction, but since it was not retroactive, Wilson's sentence stood until late 2007 when the Georgia Supreme Court ruled Wilson's punishment "cruel and unusual" and ordered his release from prison (Tuck 2013).

While we would all agree that Deena Hatcher's assailant committed rape, many of us would question the reasonableness of calling Genarlow Wilson's act a sexual assault. Indeed, many states have "*Romeo and Juliet laws*" to avoid treating sex between consenting teenagers as a crime.

As with other kinds of deviance, what is considered sexual assault can vary dramatically across time and space, and among members of different social groups. Such an observation by no means implies that sexual violence does not really occur. Acts that we and others recognize as rape or sexual assault have occurred throughout human history. But answers to the questions "what counts as rape?" and "how should rape be dealt with?" have depended on cultural beliefs about sexuality, as well as gender, property, race, and the nature of childhood. The lines we draw around what counts as sexual assault are clear in some places, blurred in others, and subject to erasure and re-drawing over time. In this chapter, we examine contemporary, cross-cultural, and historical constructions of sexual assault as a form of deviance, the challenges in researching sexual violence, and the interactional contexts in which rape occurs in the United States today.

CURRENT CONSTRUCTIONS OF RAPE IN THE UNITED STATES

Sexual assault and rape are legal terms and socially constructed definitions of specific kinds of acts. Sexual assault is a broader term, in contrast to rape which has often been defined specifically as forcible and unwanted penetration by the penis of the vagina. Under such a definition, long used in the FBI's *Uniform Crime Reports* (UCRs), sexual assault of males was not classified as rape, nor was sex that was not physically resisted by the victim. The FBI (2015c) revised and broadened the definition of rape to include "any penetration of the vagina or anus and oral penetration by a sex organ of another person without the consent of the victim." This definition is broadly consistent with what most Americans consider rape.

Types of Rape

Rape, rapists, and rape victims have been classified in a variety of ways. Among the most commonly discussed kinds of rape include stranger rape, acquaintance rape, party rape, marital rape, and prison rape.

Stranger rape involves sexual assault by an assailant that the victim does not know. In stranger rape, the victim may be assaulted in a public place or they may be victimized in their own homes. While stranger rape is the most common image people have of sexual assault, only one in five cases of reported rape involve assault by a person unknown to the victim.

Far more common than stranger rape is *acquaintance rape* in which a victim is assaulted by someone they know, such as a friend, intimate, or relative. According to recent research, most female rape victims are assaulted by someone they know (Bureau of Justice Statistics 2016a). Two types of acquaintance rape are especially common among university students, including *date rape* and *party rape*, both of which often take place in drinking and partying contexts.

Marital rape is rape committed by one spouse against another. This type of rape has historically been controversial because of the assumption that marriage takes away spouses' rights to refuse sex. Until 1976, rape laws in all 50 states contained a Marital Rape Exemption to prevent husbands who had forced sex with their wives from being charged with a crime. Today, all states have laws against marital rape, although 33 states consider marital rape a lesser crime than other types of rape.

Prison rape refers to the rape of inmates in prison by other inmates or prison staff. While accurate statistics on prison rape are unavailable, it is clear that rape is a real and present danger in prison settings and that, like rape in the broader society, prison rape goes largely unreported. Based on self-report data collected by the Bureau of Justice Statistics (2014a), about 4 per cent of prison inmates and 3 per cent of jail inmates nationwide experience sexual victimization annually in recent years.

Statistical Snapshot

In contrast to murder, where almost all cases are reported, the majority of rapes are not reported to the police, making it difficult to estimate how many rapes occur. But, the picture that emerges from the data that we do have provides some sense of rape and sexual assault in the United States today.

In 2013, the FBI changed its 80-year-old legal definition of rape to one that includes a wider variety of sexually assaultive acts, including sexual assault of males. By virtue of the changed official definition of rape, the number of reported rapes added nearly 32,000 cases of sexual assault that would not have previously been included. The total number of rapes reported in 2013 under the new definition was over 113,000, with about one in four reports resulting in an arrest (FBI 2014). Keeping in mind that UCR rape data are limited to cases that have been reported to law enforcement, it is not surprising that estimates of total sexual assault in the United States are far higher. In 2013, the National Crime Victimization Survey (NCVS) reported slightly over 300,000 sexual assault incidents—nearly three times the number of rapes reported to law enforcement agencies (Bureau of Justice Statistics 2014b). The overwhelming majority of sexual assaults nationally involve males assaulting females, although male on male sexual assault (previously ignored or not officially considered rape) is acknowledged today, particularly in prison settings. Nonetheless, more than 90 per cent of rape victims are female. While a woman (or man) of any age can be raped, victims of rape are predominantly young, with rates of rape and sexual assault more than twice as high for women aged 16–24 as for any other age group (Bureau of Justice Statistics 2014b). Further, the majority of rapes and sexual assaults are committed by individuals known to the victim. In 2013, for instance, the NCVS data suggested that three-quarters of all rapes and sexual assaults occurred at the hands of a friend or acquaintance (38 per cent), romantic partner or intimate (28 per cent), or family member (7 per cent). Given that most sexual assaults involve a perpetrator known to the victim, it is not surprising that nearly half of sexual assaults occur at home or in the home of a relative or friend. The rate of reported rape in the United States has decreased over the past two decades. In the early 1990s, the rate of reported rape hovered around 40 per 100,000, cresting at a total number of over 109,000 reported rapes in 1992. In contrast, comparable data show about 82,000 reported rapes in 2013 (under the old definition of rape)—or a rate of under 24 per 100,000. This 40 percent decline in rates of reported rape is particularly notable since the rate of victims reporting rape appears to have increased over this time as well. Yet, despite a significant decline in reported rape over the past two decades, the US rate of 24 per 100,000 is still high when compared to many other developed countries, such as the United Kingdom (20), Germany (9.4), and Japan (1.7) (United Nations 2012).

CHALLENGES IN RESEARCHING RAPE

Like murder researchers, those who study rape face a variety of challenges—some of them even more difficult than challenges faced by homicide researchers. For one thing, while almost all murders are reported to law enforcement, the majority of rapes go unreported. Getting good estimates of the rates of sexual assault and understanding the interactional contexts in which it occurs present unique research problems.

Counting Rape

Rape statistics miss more cases than they record. While murder is the most reported of major crimes, rape is the most underreported. Why is the crime of rape so underreported? And how can social scientists strive to get a more accurate count of the number of rapes that occur?

Rape victims may not report a rape for many reasons, such as fear, embarrassment, not clearly understanding the legal definition of the term, not wanting to define someone they know as a rapist, or because they worry that others might blame them for the assault. The NCVS provides an opportunity for rape victims to anonymously report sexual assault, thus avoiding much of the potential resistance associated with public disclosure. But even NCVS data do not catch all cases. Even in the relatively safe context of the NCVS survey, some people still hide sexual assault out of embarrassment, confusion, or simply a lack of recognition that what happened to them could be classified as sexual assault. A Department of Justice study of sexual assault among college women (Fisher et al. 2000) clearly illustrates this. In contrast to NCVS survey questions that asked simply if an individual had been the victim of a rape or sexual assault, Fisher and her colleagues used more descriptive questions to better assure that respondents understood what they were asking, as in the following question:

> Since school began this year, has anyone made you have oral sex by force or threat of harm? By oral sex, I mean someone's mouth or tongue making contact with your vagina or anus or your mouth or tongue making contact with someone else's genitals or anus.
>
> —Fisher et al. (2000)

When asked in such a descriptive way about sexually assaultive behavior, an astonishing ten times as many women reported that they had been rape victims in the past year. Based on their data, Fisher et al. estimate that nearly 5 per cent of college women are victimized in any given calendar year—and that over the course of a college career between one-fifth and one-quarter of women are likely to be victims of completed or attempted rape (2000, p.10).

Fisher and her colleagues also found a striking difference between the way they, as researchers, defined rape and the interpretations of the women they surveyed. Nearly half of the women who were categorized by researchers as having been raped did not personally define their experience as rape even after answering yes to explicit questions about forced sexual encounters. This finding clearly suggests that it is not only perpetrators who may not define aggressive, forced sexual encounters as rape or assault. Victims themselves are often unclear on the matter.

Getting Close

Given the importance of social context and cultural beliefs for what is understood by individuals and the public as rape, it is critical for researchers to get close enough to sexual assault to understand it from the perspectives of those who are involved in it, including those who perpetrate the crime, those who are victims of it, and those, such as law enforcement and medical personnel, who are charged with responding to it.

Researchers seeking to get close to the experience of sexual assault face a variety of challenges. First, they must find ways to identify and locate those they wish to study. Some are much easier to locate than others. Those who report their rapes to law enforcement are easier to locate since they are identified in court proceedings and often in the public press. On the other hand, it is harder to identify and locate sexual assault victims who have not reported their assaults. Similarly, while it is possible for researchers to identify those alleged rapists who have been arrested, it is much harder to locate perpetrators of sexual assaults who have not been arraigned in the criminal justice system, whether because the police were unable to find them or because their crimes were never reported in the first place.

Even when it is possible to identify those involved in sexual assault, there is no guarantee researchers will be able to get them to talk about their experiences. Victims of sexual abuse are often embarrassed and traumatized. As Patricia Yancey Martin explains:

> Rape is an emotional firestorm. Rape victims experience intense, evening debilitating emotions that they have trouble managing. . . In particular, skepticism and lack of support from family, friends, community service providers, and "society" prompt rape victims to blame themselves, "stuff" their anger, and engage in self-destructive behavior.
>
> —Martin (2005, p.186)

Researchers seeking to get close to rape victims must create an interview context in which victims can share their experiences and feelings without fear of judgment. When sexual assault victims feel respected and understood by those who interview them, the interview can become a setting in which they feel encouraged and supported to "tell my story"—sometimes for the first time.

While it is easy to understand and sympathize with sexual assault victims' needs for a safe environment to feel free to share their experiences, it may be more difficult to understand that those who have committed sexual assaults also must be provided some sense of safety if they are going to open up about their experiences. Of course, it would be unethical and criminal to provide safety to individuals who are carrying on sexual assault activities. But those who have been convicted and imprisoned for sexual assault must be provided with some sense of safety before they will discuss their experiences. As Diana Scully (1990) noted, the convicted rapists she studied had reason to fear potential further prosecution if they openly discussed their violent criminal behavior with her. Scully used several strategies to provide a sense of security to the convicted rapists she interviewed in prisons. For instance, she kept only hand written notes during her interviews with the men since by state law tape-recorded interviews could be used against the men in court, while interviews based on her notes and recollections would be considered inadmissible hearsay evidence.

In addition to providing a sense of safety to those they study, researchers also face the challenge of achieving sympathetic understanding of the views and experiences of their informants. This does not mean that researchers need to personally agree with those they study, but they need to be able to understand the meanings that informants—whether victims, perpetrators, or legal prosecutors of sexual assault—attach to their experiences and actions.

Again, Scully's research with convicted rapists provides a valuable example. She was often confronted with startling and repugnant statements by the men she interviewed, especially as they offered accounts through which they sought to reduce the severity of their crimes, as in common statements that "nice girls don't get raped" and that many of their victims eventually relaxed and enjoyed the sex. While well aware that these statements were seriously flawed as objective accounts of rape situations, Scully listened closely and sought to understand the ways in which these men themselves made sense of their experiences.

Those who endeavor to get close to the stories and experiences of rape victims face challenges from a different angle. One rape crisis counselor interviewed by Patricia Yancey Martin explained, "You hear horrifying stories of abuse, see women who are injured and broken inside; there is no way this cannot affect you" (2005, p.202). Listening closely to the stories of rape survivors can take a personal toll, as Rebecca Campbell recounts in her study of the emotional impact of researching rape:

> Shocked and surprised by what we were hearing from survivors, each one of us on the research team was jolted from the safety of thinking about rape. A case, then cases, got under our skin. It became personal, and no amount of abstract thinking could soothe the emotional violation.
>
> —Campbell (2002, pp.38–39)

Based on her experience with rape research, Campbell counsels researchers to recognize the emotional impact and create a supportive environment for managing it through developing supportive colleagues, relationships and self-care, as well as keeping in mind the ultimate goals of the research to improve women's lives. In the end, Campbell argues, the toll of conducting research on rape is a price that must be paid. "The emotionally engaged researcher," she writes, "bears witness to the pain, suffering, humiliation, and indignity of others over and over again" (2002, p.150). Without bearing witness to that pain scholars would be unable to truly grasp the meaning of sexual assault for those who experience it.

CROSS-CULTURAL CONSTRUCTIONS OF RAPE

In addition to gaining an understanding of the experience of rape in our culture today from the perspective of those who are intimately involved, a well-rounded view of the topic of rape requires us to take a broader look at sexual assault across history and different cultures. And, as with other forms of deviance, such a view demonstrates striking variation in the perception of rape from one culture and time to another.

Different Definitions

The defining issue in rape and sexual assault is the use of force to get sex. In the United States today, the forcing of sex on unwilling participants is considered a violation of human rights and a crime. However, in many societies across human history, certain high-status individuals or social groups have been viewed as having the right to use force on members of lower-status groups. In cultures where force is legitimized in human relationships, the very concept of rape as deviant, criminal, or evil may make little sense. The use of force to get sex was seen as a prerogative of the powerful in some ancient cultures. In Greek mythology, the most powerful god, Zeus, raped numerous women as well as the young male prince, Ganymede. And while Greek culture is viewed as the birthplace of democracy, the *demos* was restricted to Athenian males, many of whom owned slaves who they could use for their own sexual pleasure and force into prostitution.

Similarly, in times of war, dominating armies have often taken physical and sexual possession of the girls and women they conquered. At times, such acts of force have been based in part on a desire to father children by the women. In the book of *Judges* in the Old Testament, we read of the Israelite's attack on the city of Jabesh-Gilead, in which 400 virgins were spared slaughter and given to the men of the tribe of Benjamin as wives. At times rape has even been portrayed as a heroic act, as in the tale of the Roman warriors' rape of the Sabine women. Unable to obtain wives peacefully, it is written, the Romans invited the neighboring Sabines to a festival and, at a signal from their leader, each man violently seized a Sabine woman and took her for his wife. The violent abduction of the Sabine women was portrayed as an act that was fundamental to the founding of the Roman Empire and valorized in Renaissance paintings that glorified sexual violence as what Diane Wolfthal (1999) has termed "heroic rape."

The Latin term *raptus*, from which our modern word rape derives, carried a different meaning than its modern counterpart. From ancient Rome to medieval England, the term raptus described the use of force to "carry off" a woman against her will. The notion was not necessarily one of harm, but rather of taking possession, often with the assumption that a girl would come to identify with her abductor over time. As the notion of "carrying off" implies, the focus of *raptus* was on theft rather than sexual assault. It is impossible to understand the definition of rape and responses to it in medieval and Renaissance Europe—as well as many other cultures—unless we recognize that women were considered property of their fathers and husbands, rather than as people with rights of their own. Damage done by rape was perceived as harm to the father and family and only secondarily to the victim. As social historian Roy Porter explains, "From Old Testament Jewish codes up to feudalism, rape was treated primarily as theft, as a property offence perpetuated against men. The crime was principally that of stealing a woman from her rightful proprietors, normally her father or husband" (1986, p.217).

In medieval and Renaissance Europe, a married woman could not accuse rape without her husband's authorization. One legal scholar of the period wrote, "The wrong done to the wife is regarded as done to the husband" (Vigarello 2001, p.46). As a result, judges did not focus on violence against women. In one notable case, for instance, of the brutal rape of a nun, legal authorities proclaimed, "It is God her husband who is primarily injured" (2001, p.253). In actuality, rape was seldom reported to authorities. Through the sixteenth and seventeenth centuries in Paris, charges of rape were extremely rare—less than a half a dozen per decade—and those few that were prosecuted were brutal rapes of young children whose cases drew public sympathy.

In the late 1700s, however, new sensibilities regarding sexual violence began to emerge in the context of the political and intellectual transformations associated with the Enlightenment. Three changes in social thought had a dramatic impact on Enlightenment jurisprudence. First, the Enlightenment's focus on reason and science involved a shift away from religious authority, away from a focus on sin to a focus on social harm and personal injury. Second, Enlightenment thought involved the assertion of individual human rights. As the French *Declaration of the Rights of Man* proclaimed, "Every man is the sole owner of his person." While the place of women within this new view was at times ambiguous, this shift opened the possibility of perceiving rape less as a crime of theft and more as violent harm against the victim of the assault. Finally, this period of European history was marked by a new sensitivity toward interpersonal violence and suffering, as exemplified in Louis XVI's 1780 edict outlawing the use of torture to extract confessions. The new attitude toward violence, along with a focus on human rights, led to a deeper concern about the suffering of rape victims. This was combined with widespread public outrage in relation to several high-profile cases of brutal sexual violence by members of the "libertine" French nobility—such as the infamous Marquis de Sade—against poor and unprotected women. Yet, it would be another 100 years and more before our modern understanding of rape as serious violence would become widespread in popular consciousness and the law.

Different "Causes"

Just as the definition of what rape is has varied across time, so have beliefs about what causes a person to force himself or herself on another person. Theories about the "causes of rape" have included "demonic," "psychotic," and even "exotic" explanations. Demonic explanations have focused on rape as caused by sinful desire for physical gratification. From this perspective the thirteenth-century theologian, St. Thomas Aquinas, writes in the *Summa Theologiae*, "Rape is a species of lust that takes a person away from their relationship with God." Writing in an era prior to modern conceptions of rape, Aquinas focused on rape as a spiritual issue, as well as a crime of theft, rather than a violent crime against the raped victim.

In contrast to demonic explanations of rape, the exotic perspective would view rape as a kind of behavior that is acceptable in some societies. As discussed earlier, societies that allow the use of force by some people against others often accept sexual imposition as a right of the powerful. In this sense, there are many societies that have permitted acts that we would consider rape, but only by the powerful. In contrast, the use of force by a member of a lower social class against those of higher classes brought swift and violent punishment.

In societies such as ours, where the use of force to gain sex is proscribed and illegal, men who engage in sexual assault have often been viewed as sick. Throughout much of the twentieth century, rapists were viewed by psychiatrists and many criminal justice practitioners as being emotionally disturbed. In the 1950s and 1960s, "the disease model became the popularly accepted explanation for why men rape" (Scully 1990, p.37). At the core of the disease model are two assumptions: that rape is the result of a mental illness, and that it often includes an uncontrollable impulse. Frequently in psychoanalytic literature it was argued that men with hidden homosexual urges and those with hostility toward their mothers were particularly likely to act out their mental disorders through rape. One prominent psychiatrist in the 1960s wrote that mothers were often to blame for their sons becoming rapists by virtue of having been "seductive but rejecting" of their boys. Rape, he explained, was "an act of hostility toward a mother figure, an attempt to force her into submission" (Abrahamsen 1960, p.163).

In contrast to views of rape as caused by psychological illness, evolutionary psychologists and sociobiologists have argued that rape is an evolutionary reproductive strategy for men to maximize their potential offspring. Two proponents of this explanation, Randy Thornhill and Craig Palmer argue,

> Owing to the difficulty of gaining sexual access to choosy females throughout evolutionary history, there would have been strong selection pressures favoring traits in males that increased their access to mates. . . . Getting chosen is not the only way to gain sexual access. In rape, the male circumvents the female's choice."
> —Thornhill and Palmer (2000, p.53)

Thornhill and Palmer do not argue in support of rape. Rather, they suggest that throughout evolutionary history natural selection has provided reproductive advantages to aggressive males. It is, they assert, natural for males to use sexual force against unwilling females. They are just doing what has worked for men through the course of human evolution. This argument, not surprisingly, has produced strong reactions from scholars who criticize both the scientific evidence on which Thornhill and Palmer build their case (e.g., Tobach and Reed 2003) and the assumption that rape increases males' reproductive success.

Symbolic interactionists and cultural anthropologists argue that rape is not a natural phenomenon—that is, an objective phenomenon in nature. Rather, they contend, rape and sexual assault emerge within a set of cultural norms, values, and beliefs held by members of a given society or social group. Anthropologist Peggy Reeves Sanday (1981) studied ethnographic materials from 95 small tribal societies, finding a significant number in which rape was extremely uncommon or unknown, while in a few societies rape was much more likely. She termed these *rape-free* and *rape-prone cultures*. The rape-free societies discouraged sexual aggression and encouraged sexual equality, while rape-prone societies encouraged sexual aggression and male dominance.

Different Responses

Societal reactions to rape have varied dramatically as well. On one end of the continuum, sexual assault may be ignored because the act of forced sex is not defined as wrong in the culture in which it occurred—as in the case of sexual imposition by a husband against his wife prior to the creation of marital rape laws in the United States.

In societies where rape has been conceived as a property crime, the perpetrator has often been required to make a financial payment to the father or the family of the woman who has been "stolen." Additionally, in some cultures, men have been required to marry the woman they raped. For instance, in the Old Testament it is decreed that, "If a man is caught in the act of raping a young woman who is not engaged, he must pay fifty pieces of silver to her father. Then he must marry the young woman because he violated her, and he will never be allowed to divorce her" (*Deuteronomy* 22:28–29). While it strikes us today as outrageous that a victim of rape should be required to marry the person who assaulted them, we must remember that the conceptions of rape, and marriage for that matter, were vastly different in these times. In societies where women have had little choice as to marriage partners and where a woman's virginity was in essence her father's property, a woman who had lost her virginity outside marriage faced dire social prospects, and marriage provided her with at least some support.

In many societies rape has been punishable by death. Two categories of rape in particular have been treated as capital offenses by virtue of the seriousness with which they have been viewed. One category involves the rape of young children. In 1285 in England, statutory rape (then defined as girl under 12, but reduced to the age of 10 in 1576) was made a capital offense (Cocca 2004). The torture and killing of child rapists was common across Europe in the Middle Ages, and even in the United States it was not until 2008 that the US Supreme Court declared capital punishment unconstitutional for the crime of raping a child. Rape has also often led to execution when it has involved a member of a lower status group raping a member of a higher status group. Indeed, after the Civil War, the mere accusation of a black man raping a white woman resulted in many lynchings in the US South. Today imprisonment and supervised parole or probation are the most common punishments for sexual assault in developed societies.

Castration has been another common punishment for sexual assault, often with the goal of making the perpetrator impotent as well as punishing him. Today there are medications, such as Depo-Provera, that reduce testosterone production, and that are used as a form of *chemical castration* of some sex offenders. Nine states in the United States authorize the use of either chemical or physical castration, although the effectiveness and ethics of such practices are highly controversial (Daley 2008).

Finally, in the last 20 years sexual assault prevention programs have focused on training women in strategies for reducing vulnerability to rape and on making law enforcement for more effective in responding to it. Sexual assault prevention programs draw heavily on routine activities theory to reduce the availability of easy targets for predatory crime and insure the nearby presence of capable guardians. Schools, law enforcement agencies, and even the US military today offer sexual assault prevention programs.

HISTORY OF RAPE IN THE UNITED STATES

Definitions of what counts as sexual assault and what should be done about it have varied across human societies, depending on beliefs regarding social equality across races and between men and women. The history of rape in the Unites States illustrates how dramatic changes in race and gender relations have influenced what is defined as sexual assault and how perpetrators are treated.

Early America

Historian Sharon Block writes that "rape in early America was both pervasive and invisible" (2006, p.1). While preachers and the founding fathers railed against it as a heinous act, forced sex was a fact of life for some sectors of the population. Many women had no recourse to the law and had to suffer their sexual abuse in silence. Race, class, and gender played major roles in the understanding of, and responses to, sexual assault in colonial America.

Like St. Thomas Aquinas 500 years earlier, colonial American culture saw little separation of rape from other forms of immoral sexuality, such as bestiality, sodomy, and adultery. Force in the act of sex was not a major concern for colonial American men. Along with their European counterparts, they viewed forced sex as at most an unfortunate result of sexual desire. Sexual interaction was not viewed as an equal relationship, but rather women were viewed as useful receptacles for male-centered sexual practices. As Ben Franklin proclaimed, women "were designed to gratify our [men's] Passions" (Block 2006, p.20). Men seemed to assume that they could sexually overpower a woman as a matter of course. And women were expected to resist, and to need overpowering. As one southern planter who often wrote in his diary of sexual encounters he had and observed noted, the women "struggle just enough to make the Admirer more eager." Females were expected to show some resistance to sexual advances, but only for appearance sake—an early American version of the argument that when women say no, they mean yes. A song in a 1750 novel by a Maryland author included the lines:

> Coy maidens swear, if you're rude they will bawl
> But they whisper so low,
> By which you may know,
> 'Tis artifice, artifice, all.

While women in general were disadvantaged in relation to men, white women had a significant advantage over women of color (especially African-American slaves and Native Americans) in warding off sexual coercion. Patriarchy held out the possibility of protection for white women, especially if they were of relatively high social standing. Nonwhite women did not have powerful male protectors—or, in the case of female slaves, were under the authority of male patriarchs who could abuse them with impunity. In colonial Virginia, "African women could not, in law, be raped: no such crime was defined or prosecuted" (Lane 1997, p.63). A slave who defended herself against the attack of her white master was often subject to cruel beatings. And if she became pregnant at the hands of her master, her child was born into lifelong slavery and potential forced sexual relations as well.

Race and culture also played a significant role in sexual assaults among white men and Native Americans. While white soldiers, traders, and settlers were often reported to take advantage of "Indian" girls and women, few reports exist of Native Americans raping white women, even those taken as captives. It was not that the Indians were incapable of violence toward their enemies. They were recorded as murdering husbands, slashing children's throats, and scalping, but almost never of rape. The reason appears to be that many Native American cultures had strong cultural norms rejecting sexual coercion, especially with captives taken in battle. A report to the Secretary of War from an observer in the early 1800s recounted, "If a young man were . . . to indulge himself with a captive taken in war, he would incur indelible disgrace" (Block 2006, p.224). The difference between Native American warriors and their British and US counterparts was conveniently turned against the "Indians" by many white commentators who reasoned that Native American men raped less because they were undersexed, "not so lascivious as Europeans" (Block 2006, p.31). In short, Native American males were not real men.

Post-Civil War Era

Following the Civil War, during the period of Reconstruction, rape laws became less discriminatory toward blacks and took away significant white male power. States that had allowed execution of black males convicted of rape, but not of convicted whites, were forced (at least temporarily) to eliminate capital punishment for black rapists. Further, white men could now be jailed for rape of a black female. Just as important, new laws allowed nonwhites to testify in court against whites. The right of African-Americans to testify against white defendants removed a major obstacle for black rape victims seeking justice.

These changes in rape laws, however, did not eliminate race as a factor in public perception of rape. Many white citizens reacted to the dismantling of slavery with intense anger and hostility exemplified in the creation of the *black beast rape myth*—a myth that portrayed black men as oversexed monsters intent on raping white women. The late 1800s witnessed a moral panic over the threat of black men, portrayed as seething with anger over slavery and under the sway of uncivilized, oversexed impulses. Atrocity tales of brutal black male rapes of white women were chronicled in novels written by white southern authors, painting freed black men as lustful savages lurking in the shadows. Such novels typically "featured inflammatory black-on-white rape scenes as tragic denouements that justified the 'birth of a nation,' the Ku Klux Klan, and its deadly tactics" (Sommerville 2004, p.177). Lynchings of black men—almost always on allegations of their having raped a white woman—rose sharply in the 1870s and 1880s, peaking in the 1890s, when they averaged about 100 per year.

A number of prominent African-Americans spoke out strongly against the sham of the black beast rapist. In 1894, Frederic Douglass offered a "colored man's view" of the myth, noting that the charge of assaults by Negroes upon white women had never been raised in the time of slavery, "but now, whether true or false, is certain to raise a mob and to subject the accused to immediate torture and death" (1950, p.493). Ida Wells-Barnett, an outspoken black journalist, argued that while slavery had made black men powerless, southern whites now used the myth of the black rapist to try to exert their control over the black population.

While charges of rape by black men—and their subsequent lynchings—represented one way in which whites tried to exert control over the black population, yet another form of domination occurred in relation to black women. African-American women faced vulnerability to sexual assault after emancipation as white men began to use rape as a *weapon of terror* to intimidate black women and their families. As Sommerville concludes, "It is quite clear that the white rape of freedwomen during Reconstruction was used as an instrument of terror to intimidate and exercise control over the entire black community" (2004, p.148.).

Feminist Era: 1960s–Present

Only one other period in US history has seen such extensive social change in relation to our cultural understandings and legal practices surrounding sexual assault. That period was the 1960s and 1970s, the era in which feminism emerged as a social movement. While issues of race and social class continued to be important factors in determining who was likely to report, be charged with, or convicted of sexual assault, feminists focused attention primarily on the ways in which law and the criminal justice system discouraged women from seeking redress for sexual assault. Well into the 1970s, many states required raped women to pass a polygraph test to show they were not lying, prove they "resisted to the utmost," report their rape immediately, and provide physical evidence that the assailant's penis had penetrated their vagina (Konradi 2007, p.8).

In the late 1960s and 1970s, feminists organized to bring the issue of sexual assault into broader public consciousness and to increase the number of women who reported rape and successfully prosecuted it. Activists publicized violence against women through marches, like the now widespread Take Back the Night marches. They turned to public and governmental support to create rape hotlines and rape crisis centers, and they worked with law enforcement agencies to develop new procedures for dealing with rape victims. Specialized training was developed for rape responders, including Sexual Assault Response Teams and Sexual Assault Nurse Examiners. Lobbying groups like the National Organization for Women critiqued existing laws, proposed new legislation, and built coalitions to push new laws through the criminal justice system.

Feminists were successful in getting state laws changed to eliminate the requirement that a woman immediately report rape to police and that her testimony be corroborated by physical evidence. Survivors' reports of rape to anyone became legally acceptable evidence of "prompt disclosure." Further, the symptoms of *rape trauma syndrome* (a form of posttraumatic stress disorder that psychiatrists commonly attribute to rape survivors) became evidence of victimization in many states. Feminist antirape advocates also successfully lobbied to limit the kinds of information that could be brought into court to discredit a victim. *Rape shield laws* were created to protect rape survivors during trials by not allowing the victim's past sexual history to be used against them.

One notable change in rape law in the 1970s was the elimination of the spousal exemption. Rape had traditionally been defined in the United States as "sexual intercourse by a man with a female not his wife without her consent" (Barshis, 1983, p.383). Feminists argued that this definition provided husbands with a "license to rape." By 1993, all states had laws recognizing *marital rape* as a crime (although definitions of the crime vary from state to state).

The widespread reform of rape laws and policies has removed many statutory obstacles to prosecution and sent a symbolic message that rape is a crime of violence. The more supportive understanding of rape as a serious crime, as well as recognition that rape can occur between intimates and acquaintances, has emboldened many women to report rapes that they would not have reported in the past. Yet, even with these changes rape remains the most underreported of violent crimes and rape victims often face serious challenges in seeking redress for their assaults and managing the stigma and shame they all too commonly experience.

RAPE PROCLIVITY AND ROUTINE ACTIVITY THEORIES

Positivistic social scientists focus on both the micro and macro "causes" of rape. At the micro-level, they seek an explanation of characteristics of individuals who are more likely to commit rape than others. At the macro level, they look for the characteristics of social settings and cultures where rates of sex crimes are high in comparison to cultures and settings where sexual assault is less common.

Psychologist Neil Malamuth et al. (1992) have developed *rape proclivity theory* to identify a set of characteristics that they argue must converge in a man to motivate him to engage in rape. These characteristics include (1) becoming aroused by sexual assault, (2) feelings of hostility toward women, (3) attitudes that support violence toward women, and (4) participating in promiscuous sex. If a man who ranks high in terms of these four characteristics is presented with the opportunity to force a woman into sex, Malamuth and his colleagues argue, the man is more likely than other males to engage in sexual assault.

Other sexual assault researchers use *routine activities theory* to explain the contexts in which rape is more likely to occur. Routine activity theory proposes

CLAIMS-MAKER PROFILE

Connie and Howard Clery

When Connie and Howard Clery visited Lehigh University with their daughter, Jeanne, they found an idyllic 1,600 acre college campus on the top of a hill above Bethlehem, Pennsylvania. The school and its setting seemed safe and serene and the couple felt fortunate that their daughter decided to enroll in a college that was little more than an hour drive from their home. But in the spring of her freshman year, a male student broke into Jeanne Clery's dorm and brutally raped and murdered her. During the investigation that followed, Connie and Howard Clery learned that there had been 38 violent crimes—including rapes, robberies, and assaults—on the Lehigh campus in the three years before their daughter's death. Had they known that, they would have counseled their daughter not to go there.

The Clerys were stunned to learn that colleges had no responsibility to publish information regarding crime on their campuses or their efforts to provide student security. The couple filed a lawsuit against the university and received a multimillion dollar settlement, which they used to found the Clery Center for Security on Campus. They lobbied state legislatures and Congress to require colleges to report campus crimes. In 1990, three years after the Clery Center was founded, the US Congress approved the Crime Awareness and Campus Security Act, later renamed the Jeanne Clery Act.

The Clery Act requires colleges and universities to publish annual crime reports and to disclose their security policies. The law also requires support for victims of campus sexual assaults and requires the US Department of Education to disseminate campus crime statistics.

"This law has honored Jeannie in such a wonderful way by knowing that she is saving lives all over the country," Connie Clery has said. "How much more can I ask for?" (O'Dell and Ryman 2016).

that victimization occurs in places where individuals are (1) vulnerable as targets, (2) in the presence of motivated offenders, and (3) in the absence of capable guardians. Such locations, they argue, tend to be hot spots for criminal victimization. Using this approach, David Maume (1989) found that rates of rape are high in communities where there are wide discrepancies in income, large numbers of single and divorced women, unemployed men, and high residential turnover. Maume explains that such communities have high numbers of potential offenders (e.g., men with uncommitted time on their hands) and vulnerable targets (e.g., women who are alone), as well as a low level of guardianship. He concludes that one of the prices of inequality is that many low-income women are constrained to live in risk-prone neighborhoods.

Researchers have found that routine activities theory helps explain high rates of rape in another, more affluent population—white female college students—as well. The National Institute of Justice estimates that between one-fifth and one-quarter of women are the victims of completed or attempted rape while in college, placing them at a higher risk for rape than other women their age (Fisher et al. 2000). Rape scholars (e.g., Mustaine and Tewksbury 2002; Weiss and Dilks 2016) argue that this is largely because college bars and fraternities are hot spots for sexual victimization. Dimly lit, loud, and crowded college bars filled with often inebriated young women, as well as intoxicated young men looking for sexual opportunities, present nearly ideal conditions for sexual predation. College frat parties are often designed to give even less protection to female partiers, as women are plied with alcohol and may be escorted to unsupervised settings where they are easily assaulted. Researchers find that female students are especially vulnerable during the fall semester of their first year at college, a period often termed the "red zone" of sexual assault when new students are least aware of the risks of unsupervised partying and the most vulnerable as targets of sexual coercion (Kimble et al. 2008).

INTERACTIONAL CONTEXTS AND ETHNOGRAPHIC VOICES

All sexual assault involves forced sexual encounters, but the nature of the interaction between the victim and the perpetrator varies significantly depending on their relationship and the contexts of the assault. In the following discussion, we examine two different interactional contexts of rape. First, we consider typical stranger rape situations. Next, we explore party rape among college students. In both cases we will focus on the social interactions between victims and those who sexually abuse them, seeking to understand the social contexts in which these different kinds of sexual assault occur.

Stranger Rape

Similar to Luckenbill's analysis of the stages of homicidal encounters discussed in Chapter 5, Diana Scully's research with incarcerated stranger rapists provides insights into "phases" in which stranger rapes occur. In an analysis of Scully's interview data with stranger rapists, Brian Monahan et al. (2005) identified five phases of stranger rapes.

Phase One: Preexisting Life Tensions

Stranger rapists interviewed by Scully described personal lives that were filled with problems and tensions. More than half had come from abusive and broken homes, and their adult lives were characterized by marital and financial difficulties, psychological problems, and conflicts with their wives and girlfriends. Further, the daily problems they experienced seemed to become particularly intense in the period right before the assault. They became overwhelmed, sleepless, desperate, and often felt especially angry toward their wives or girlfriends.

In addition to feeling desperate and angry, those who would soon become rapists also held *misogynistic*, hostile, and demeaning attitudes toward women. The majority of the men regarded force as an appropriate means for men to control sexual relationships and nearly half of them said they believed that "some women like to be hit because it is a sign of caring" (2005, p.294).

However, the mere presence of these factors did not make rape inevitable. Faced with tension and trouble in their lives, these rapists did not confront the source of their troubles, but rather sought to redress their grievances by displacing their aggression. In the context of troubled lives in which they felt overwhelmed, stranger rapists generally depicted their assaults as attempts to restore control in their lives.

Phase Two: Transformation of Motivation into Action

The combination of personal tensions, violent proclivities, misogynistic attitudes, and perceived victimization created an openness among the men toward a violent solution in which women were the targets. Their decisions to rape women they did not know developed along two different paths. Many of the men reached a point where they decided they were going to rape a woman and explicitly went out looking for a vulnerable target. For others, though, the decision to commit rape was situationally emergent, as in the case of a man who offered assistance to a woman whose car had broken down. When he was unable to repair the car, he offered her a ride home and then, with her in his car, decided he wanted to have sex with her. When she refused, he raped her.

Whether the men chose to rape before going in search of a victim or whether they found themselves taking advantage of an emergent situation, they selected victims on basis of anger, a desire for revenge, sexual attraction, and, most importantly, the women's availability. The single most common characteristic of women who were raped was that they were in situations, such as unlit city streets or home alone, where there was no one they could turn to for help.

Phase Three: Perpetrator–Victim Confrontation

When a potential rapist commits rape, he has to directly confront the victim. Most often stranger rapists use a combination of verbal persuasion and display of force and intimidation. At this point the encounter between the victim and the perpetrator becomes defined as an act of force for the rapists and as an assault for the victim. Suddenly the woman finds her safety and well-being unexpectedly threatened. The rapist faces the immediate problem of gaining control over his victim. Often rapists use violence to reduce resistance, as reflected in one rapist's comment that, "I grabbed her and hit her a couple of times to get her to cooperate" (p.301). Many of the men also brandished weapons to show their victims that they could be seriously harmed. Not having expected to be violently attacked, victims have little opportunity to formulate a plan for resistance. They may plead with their assailants and some physically resist, often leading to further violent reactions.

Phase Four: Situation Management

After the initial moments of the attack and establishing dominance over their victims, rapists must continue to manage their victim's compliance and their own strong emotions. Many rapists reported having to overcome their own nervousness: "I was not really in control, totally confused and frightened. I didn't take any clothes off. I was too scared. I kept questioning myself during the act" (p.304). When a victim quits physically resisting, as a victim who fears being beaten or killed may well do, the victim's calmness may reduce the rapist's nervousness. "Seeing her laying there helpless," one rapist explained, "gave me confidence I could do it" (p.305). But other men became emotionally caught up in brutal coercion, as explained by another rapist who recounted, "Once I got into the rape, I didn't think about precautions . . . I had made up my mind that this rape was what I was going to do" (p.305).

While it is difficult for most of us to understand, many rapists who do not rely simply on brutal physical assault redefine the rape as "normal" consensual sex. It was common for stranger rapists in this study to assert that they believed their victim enjoyed the sexual encounter. As one rapist explained, "I treated her as if it was normal and tried to get her as high as me . . . I was trying to please her . . . We did it like normal sex, with foreplay" (p.306). Yet, another rapist recounted, "I always asked, Does it feel good? Want more? And when they said 'good,' I believed it, even though I know it was crazy to do so" (p.307).

Phase Five: Disengagement

In the final phase of the rape, rapists must disengage from the assaultive interaction. Most rapists had no plan for how to leave, but just made a hasty retreat after telling the victim not to move or scream until they were gone. Those rapists who did develop disengagement plans tended to use "sealing actions" to keep the victim from reporting the assault. One type of sealing action was to apologize and negotiate with the victim. Men who sought to negotiate with the women they had raped at times believed their rapes would not be reported because they had created the illusion that the sexual encounter had been largely consensual. In cases of more violent rapes, rapists seldom harbored such illusions and some killed their victims in order to silence them. Others contemplated murder, but found that they could not face the prospect of killing someone despite having raped them.

Party Rape

While stranger rape is typically a spur-of-the-moment crime, party rape is a more predictable occurrence, particularly at colleges and universities with strong party school reputations. In contrast to stranger rape, party rape involves a victim who knows some or all of her assailants and may have consented to sex with one of them. Typically intoxicated and in a party environment, the young woman finds herself trapped in a situation where she is coerced into sex with one or more young men, often being raped when she is too drunk to put up any resistance.

The partying scene of drinking and flirtatious socializing is a big draw for many young people when they go to college. Partying with their peers offers a way to feel a part of college life, to fit in, and to find friends. Residential college campuses with strong fraternity presence and off-campus housing offer students opportunities to party with minimal, if any, supervision—creating a situation ripe for underage and heavy drinking. At fraternity parties, women's access to the party and the attention they receive is heavily based on their perceived sexual attractiveness. And as guests at the parties, they cede control of the setting, transportation to and from the house, and access to liquor.

Having fun at parties involves throwing oneself into the flow of the event, drinking, playfully interacting, and trusting the other participants. But fun situations can shift, gradually or quite suddenly, into dangerous circumstances. Many college men attend parties looking for casual sex and some use deception and pressure to get it. The contexts of party rape and those who commit it are quite different from stranger rape. As Michael Messner explains, the party rapist:

> is not the stereotypical rapist who jumps out of bushes. He's the guy who eyes you seductively when you walk into a party, dances with you flirtatiously, and seems so solicitously chivalrous in making sure your drink is always refilled.
>
> —Messner (2015)

Rather than using guns or fists to force sex, party rapists get women drunk enough that they have trouble "saying no," or remembering later that they did. Fraternity brothers who control access to alcohol may promise more or better liquor to women as a way to lure them into private spaces of the fraternities. They may also make it hard for women to leave by blocking doors or refusing transportation.

While routine activities theory explains much of the context of party rape by focusing attention of vulnerable targets and a lack of guardians, the issue of "motivated offenders" is not as simple. Not all men are attracted to forcing sex on their partners, nor are all cultural settings equally supportive of sexual coercion. Peggy Reeves Sanday uses the term "rape-prone culture" to refer to societies, subcultures, and settings that provide conducive environments and beliefs for sexual assault. A key component of rape-prone settings is the belief in *rape myths*, such as the belief that men are naturally sexually aggressive and that women often need to be pushed into having sex. In such settings men may feel that tricking women into sex is a way to show their masculinity. And their sexual exploits may be supported and even admired by other men.

Nonetheless, most sexual encounters at parties are fun and consensual. Given the social role of the party lifestyle and the identities it creates for many students, partiers tend to discount the possibility of rape. When claims of rape do occur, both male and female partiers tend to blame the victim for what happened, arguing that smart careful women will be safe. Further, the manipulative strategies of party rapists, including encouraging their targets to get drunk, make it hard for victims to convince others—or even themselves—that they were victims of sexual assault (Armstrong et al. 2006).

CONTEMPORARY RESPONSES TO RAPE

The antirape movement of the 1970s has been referred to as a "textbook case of legal mobilization," or the use of legal concepts and the law to address a social problem (Corrigan 2013, p.1). But while laws in state after state were changed to provide more scope and sensitivity to sexual assault, cultural attitudes and law enforcement practices have often failed to keep step with changes in the law. Today, as in the past, many rape victims feel stigmatized in their interactions with the criminal justice system.

Identifying and Processing Rapists

Social reactions to rape depend on victims reporting their assaults. But, as we have seen, the proportion of sexual assaults that come to the attention of law enforcement is lower than for any other major crime. Victims fail to report sexual assaults for a variety of reasons. They may be afraid of their attacker; they may be too traumatized to go to the police; or they may not feel clear in their own minds that they have, in fact, been sexually assaulted.

Often, victims of sexual assault turn first to family, friends, and trusted others to discuss their experiences. They are far more likely to move forward with reporting sexual assault when family members or coworkers encourage them to define what happened as a "rape" and to go to the police. When sexual assaults are discounted by victims' confidantes, they are less likely to report assaults.

There are many times when a sexual assault, especially a stranger rape that closely fits our cultural stereotypes of "real" rape, is defined at the moment it occurs as a violent criminal act. This kind of sexual assault is very likely to be reported to the police, often within a matter of minutes after the rapist has completed the assault. Many women interviewed by Amanda Konradi (2007) in her study of rape "survivors" said that while they were being raped they already knew they would report it—and that their decision influenced their behavior during the attacks. These women struggled in the midst of being raped to clearly remember information that they would want to report.

But even when sexual assault is reported, prosecution is not guaranteed. When police report a rape to district attorneys (who are responsible for deciding which cases come to trial), the attorneys must decide which cases are worth taking to court. District attorneys are concerned not only about the case, but also their own reputations and careers. For a district attorney to get promoted, they must have a strong rate of convictions for the cases they bring to court. They have an organizational and career stake in bringing to trial only cases that they feel are most likely to get guilty verdicts. Prosecuting attorneys often fall back on stereotypes of what "clear rape cases" and "good witnesses" should look like. The women who are strong cases for rape charges, from the DA's perspective, should demonstrate upstanding character and be consistent in their accounts of what happened to them (Frohmann 1991), regardless of the fact that a victim of a rape may be confused about the event. Despite legal changes to improve sensitivity to rape victims, Cassia Spohn and David Holleran (2001) report that the perceptions of the victim's character remain critical factors in prosecutors' decisions to file charges. In cases of acquaintance rape, prosecutors hesitate to file charges when the victim was known to be sexually active or involved in sexually oriented work, such as stripping. In cases of stranger rape, prosecutors were far more likely to file charges if a weapon such as a gun or knife was used in the assault. In short, Spohn and Holleran find that prosecuting attorneys are still influenced by assumptions about what constitutes "real rape" and who are "real victims."

Treatment of Rape in the Courts

Approximately four out of 10 reported rapes result in an arrest. And about one-quarter of arrests result in convictions. Of those who are convicted, about three out of four are convicted when the assailant pleads guilty—although not necessarily to charges of felony rape. Prosecuting attorneys often wish to avoid an expensive and time-consuming court case and, in order to do so, they may be willing to settle cases by offering the defendant the possibility of pleading guilty to a lesser crime than what they would be brought to court on. For example, a defendant being prosecuted for felony rape may be offered the opportunity to plead guilty to charges of misdemeanor statutory rape—thus potentially avoiding jail time (Konradi 2007, p.144). The decision to offer a plea bargain is made by the district attorney, not the victim, sometimes leaving the victim feeling that the seriousness of the assault against them has been watered down in the process.

Many victims of rape feel abused by the criminal justice system when their cases go to court. Lee Madigan and Nancy Gamble (1991) refer to rape victims' experiences of feeling betrayed and put on trial themselves as a *"second rape."* The adversarial nature of the criminal justice system forces women who are seeking to prosecute their assailants into being subjected to medical and legal procedures in which they may come to feel objectified and distrusted (Martin and Powell 1994). Victims often feel mistreated when they are subjected to cross-examination by defense attorneys who seek to discredit their accounts and who may find ways around rape shield laws in order to present embarrassing information about the victim's sexual history.

But not all experiences that sexual assault victims have in the criminal justice system are so negative and demoralizing. Konradi's (2007) research counters the image of the rape victims as uniformly traumatized participants in rape trials. Based on detailed interviews with nearly 50 female rape victims, Konradi found that many women actively involved themselves in the prosecution process. Like Konradi, who was herself a victim of rape, the women she interviewed worked at preparing their own testimony, striving to present themselves as credible witnesses to the assaults against them. They consciously planned how to present a personal appearance in court that would avoid any negative stereotypes. They often rehearsed their testimony with prosecuting attorneys, friends, or relatives, to make sure their words were convincing and clear and that their display of emotion was not one that would undermine their case.

Rape victims' concerns that they convey an acceptable appearance and credibility seem justified in the face of the previously discussed findings about how prosecutors determine whether or not to file charges. Konradi found that the courtroom experiences of sexual assault survivors vary dramatically for women who have been raped by strangers as opposed to those who have suffered acquaintance rape. Women who were raped by strangers were typically treated with trust and respect by legal personnel, making them feel like important contributors to the prosecution. In contrast, women who were raped by known assailants were often treated with distrust, asked time and again to give accounts of their rape and to establish their credibility in other ways. What we see here is the continuing impact of stereotypical beliefs about "real rape" that disadvantages victims of acquaintance rape. Further, Rodney Kingsworth et al. (1999) have found that even if rape cases result in guilty verdicts, punishment is often far less severe if the victim is perceived as having negative characteristics (e.g., being homeless or a substance abuser) or exhibiting potentially contributory behavior (e.g., hitchhiking or being alone in a bar).

PUSHING YOUR BOUNDARIES

Analyzing Narrative of a Second Rape

On March 30, 2016, 19-year Stanford student athlete, Brock Turner, was convicted of three counts of sexual assault against a 22-year-old woman known in court as "Emily Doe." Doe had gone to a party with her younger sister in January 2015. After drinking heavily she left for home without her sister. Turner claimed in court that he and Doe left together and that she consented to have sex with him beside a dumpster. Two international students riding bikes by the dumpster saw a man on top of a woman who looked unconscious. When they stopped to investigate, Turner ran away from the scene. One of the international students went to check the woman, while the other ran Turner down and, with the help of other passersby, held him until the police arrived.

Turner pled not guilty to all charges, but was convicted of assault with intent to rape, and sexual penetration of an intoxicated and unconscious person with a foreign object (his fingers). At his sentencing hearing, Emily Doe read a letter describing the impact of the assault and trial on her life. The letter was published online by Buzzfeed.com and read by millions of people. While the prosecutor argued for a six-year prison sentence, the judge (himself a Stanford alum and star college athlete) sentenced Turner to six months in county jail and three years of probation. He was released after three months in jail despite widespread public protest.

Find Emily Doe's victim impact letter online (at Buzzfeed.com or another online source) and read it to identify statements that illustrate the concept of the trial as a "second rape." How did the trial of the man accused of sexually assaulting her turn into a proceeding that made her feel judged and on trial herself? Is it inevitable that rape trials must grill accusers in ways that challenge and demean their morals and behavior? Or are there ways that rape trials could be changed to better protect accusers without undermining the rights of the accused?

STIGMA MANAGEMENT AND RESISTANCE

Almost all people who find themselves cast in deviant identities use some stigma management strategies to present themselves as more acceptable than their stigmatized identity would suggest. Diane Scully's study of convicted rapists provides an excellent example of just such processes.

Scully distinguished between two different groups of convicted rapists: *admitters* and *deniers*. Admitters told essentially the same account of their crimes as police and victims did. That is, they admitted to having committed rape. Deniers, on the other hand, stated that they had not really committed rape. Both admitters and deniers explained the crimes they had been convicted of in ways that served to reduce the severity of what they had done to some degree. But the arguments they used to exonerate themselves differed.

Deniers argued that they had not committed rape and that their victims were willing participants. One denier, for instance, who had been convicted of rape at knife-point and accompanying crimes of burglary, sodomy, and abduction, admitted to the breaking and entry, but argued that when the victim discovered him, he had tried to leave but she asked him to stay. After telling him that she cheated on her husband, he said, the woman had voluntarily removed her clothes and seduced him. Two-thirds of deniers claimed that the women they had raped had agreed to have sex with them. The other one-third of deniers admitted that their victim had resisted, but went on to justify their behavior by arguing that either the victim had not resisted enough or that her "no" had really meant "yes." Many said that women like to be overpowered before sex, so they themselves had simply done what was natural in sexual encounters. As one of the men put it, "A man's body is like a Coke bottle, shake it up, put your thumb over the opening and feel the tension. When you take a woman out, woo her, then she says 'no, I'm a nice girl,' you have to use force" (Scully 1990, p.104).

Some admitters said they believed during the rape that the victim was willing. Only later did these rapists redefine their acts as rape. For example, an admitter, who used a bayonet to threaten an employee of the store he had been robbing, stated, "At the time I didn't think it was rape. I just asked her nicely and she didn't resist" (p.104). Demonstrating a similar lack of awareness of their victim's perspective, many deniers justified their behavior by claiming not only that the victim was willing, but also that she enjoyed herself. A denier who had broken into his victim's house, but who insisted the victim let him in voluntarily, declared, "She felt good, kept kissing me and wanted me to stay the night. She felt proud after sex with me" (p.106).

Deniers also tended to argue that "nice girls don't get raped" and that their victims' bad reputations were largely responsible for their sexual encounters. For example, a denier who claimed he had picked up a woman he knew while she was hitchhiking said, "To be honest, we [his family] knew she was a damn whore and whether she screwed one or fifty guys didn't matter" (p.108). Additionally, deniers often tried to deflect attention from the rapes they had been convicted of by claiming that they had been guilty of a minor wrongdoing, but not a serious sexual assault, as in the case of a denier who claimed he picked up his underage victim at a party and that she voluntarily went with him to a motel. According to presentence reports, the victim had been abducted at knife point from a party. In an attempt to present himself in a more acceptable light, the offender explained:

> After I paid for a motel, she would have to have sex but I wouldn't use a weapon. I would have explained. I spent money and, if she still said no, I would have forced her. If it had happened that way, it would have been rape to some people but not to my way of thinking. I've done that kind of thing before. I'm guilty of sex and contributing to the delinquency of a minor, but not rape.
>
> —Scully (1990, pp.110–111)

In sum, deniers argued that, while their behavior may not have been completely proper, it should not have been considered rape. In contrast, admitters regarded their behavior as morally wrong and beyond justification. They blamed themselves rather than the victim, although some continued to believe that the victim had contributed to the crime.

Admitters used excuses that explained their acts as caused by forces outside their control. One frequent excuse was that they had been high on alcohol and/or drugs when they committed the offense. An admitter who estimated he had drunk eight beers and taken four "hits of acid" reported, "Straight, I don't have the guts to rape . . . To say, 'I'm going to do it to a woman,' knowing it will scare and hurt her, takes guts or you have to be sick" (p.124).

Consistent with the previous admitter's comment, many admitters argued that they engaged in raped because of emotional problems. But while admitters often used psychological explanations to portray themselves as having been temporarily sick at the time of the rape, they argued that they had now recovered. So, for instance, a multiple rapist asserted that his "problem" was due to "something buried in my subconscious" that was triggered when his girlfriend broke up with him. "I was a rapist," he stated, "but not now. I've grown up, had to live with it. I've hit the bottom of the well and it can't get worse. I feel born again to deal with my problems" (p.127).

Admitters also often tried to downplay the seriousness of their crimes by relating stories that presented them as nice guys in spite of what they had done. As one man who had participated in a rape–murder, but who insisted his partner did the murder, confided, "I wish there was something I could do besides saying I'm sorry. I live with it 24 hours a day and, sometimes, I wake up crying in the middle of the night because of it" (p.125). Yet, others presented themselves as nice guys not by virtue of remorse for their actions, but by pointing to how their crimes could have been much worse if they had not been concerned about their victims' well-being. One admitter claimed to have been especially gentle with his victim after she told him she had just had a baby. Another admitter, a multiple rapist, whose pattern was to break in and attack sleeping victims in their homes, tried to repair his self-image by explaining, "I never beat any of my victims and I told them I wouldn't hurt them if they cooperated. I'm a professional thief. But I never robbed the women I raped because I felt so bad about what I had already done to them" (p.130).

BLURRED BOUNDARIES II: WHAT IS TOO DRUNK TO SAY YES?

College campuses have become major sites for trying to forge new antirape policies and culture. At many colleges and universities today there is a policy requiring "*affirmative consent*," or clear permission to engage in sex. But as Robin Wilson has observed, many students are not sure what that means. "Gauging sexual interest can be tricky for anyone. How to give and get consent . . . is something college students are still trying to figure out" (Wilson 2016, p.A10). One challenging question is the issue of consent when a woman is intoxicated. Should it be considered rape if a male at a party has sex with a woman he hooked up with who has been drinking? In one ethnography of college partying and sexual assault, Ayres Boswell and Joan Spade (1996) found that college students had differing opinions on the matter. One first-year woman told them, "If a girl is drunk and the guy knows it and the girl says, 'Yes, I want to have sex,' and they do, that is still rape because the girl can't make a conscious, rational decision under the influence of alcohol." But other women disagreed. Another first-year woman stated, "I don't think it is fair that the guy gets blamed when both people involved are drunk" (1996, p.142).

In many jurisdictions, sex with a person who is drunk can be categorized as rape since an intoxicated person is considered mentally impaired. But whether they were aware of the legal definitions of rape or not, most men in Boswell and Spade's study rejected the idea that a woman who is intoxicated is unable to consent to sex. One fraternity brother said, "Men should not be responsible for women's drunkenness." A first-year male student commented, "If that is the legal definition of rape, then it happens all the time on this campus." A fraternity senior argued, "I don't care whether alcohol is involved or not; that is not rape. Rapists are people that have something seriously wrong with them." And another first-year male student claimed that when women get drunk, they invite sex. He said, "Girls get so drunk here and then come on to us. What are we supposed to do? We are only human" (1996, p.142).

The mixing of drinking and sex is pervasive on college campuses across the United States. Obviously not all sex involving drinking is rape, but where and how should we draw the line between intoxication and consensual sex on the one hand, and sexual assault on the other? Virtually all of us would agree that a woman who has passed out drunk cannot consent to sex. But just how intoxicated is too drunk to consent? One suggested standard has been that anyone who is too inebriated to legally drive a car is too drunk to consent to sex. Many students and university officials, however, argue that a person with that level of intoxication can consent and that establishing such a standard is unrealistic.

If you were asked to contribute to developing a university policy regarding drinking and sexual consent, what would you consider as important issues and circumstances for setting the line that should not be crossed at the blurred boundary of drinking and sexual consent?

SUMMARY

- The most commonly recognized kinds of rape in the United States today include stranger rape, acquaintance rape, marital rape, prison rape, and statutory rape.
- Rape has the lowest rate of reporting to police of any major crime.
- Most sexual assaults are committed by individuals known to the victim.
- Since the 1990s, there has been a decline in reported rapes in the United States, even though the percentage of victims reporting rape appears to have increased.
- Getting an accurate count of sexual assaults is difficult since many victims are ashamed or afraid to report it.
- Researchers must create interview contexts in which victims can share their experiences without feeling judged.
- In many cultures rape of girls and women has been seen as a form of property theft from the father or husband.
- In colonial America, race played a major role in defining what counted as rape and what did not. Native American women and black slaves were at high risk of sexual coercion at the hands of white men.
- During the period of Reconstruction, most public discussions of rape focused on the myth of black men as "black beast rapists" attacking white women.
- In the 1960s, feminists brought sexual assault to broader public consciousness. Laws were enacted to recognize marital rape as a crime and rape shield laws were created to limit the use of victims' sexual histories in court.
- Rape proclivity theory argues that men who engage in rape hold hostile feelings toward women, are aroused by violent sexual images, and espouse rape myths that coercion is a natural part of sexual conduct.
- Routine activity theorists find that rape is more common in settings with high numbers of potential offenders, vulnerable targets, and a low level of guardianship.
- The interaction between rape victims and the perpetrators varies depending on the contexts of the assault.
- Stranger rapists use verbal persuasion and physical force to intimidate their victims into compliance.
- Party rape typically involves an intoxicated victim who knows her assailant(s). The victim is often raped when she or he is too drunk to resist.
- Rape victims are more likely to move forward with reporting sexual assault when friends and family define what happened as a rape and urge them to go to the police.

- When police report a rape to district attorneys, the attorneys invoke stereotypes of what clear rape cases and good witnesses should look like before deciding to take a case to trial.
- Many rape victims feel mistreated by the criminal justice system, but today more women actively participate in the prosecution process than in the past.
- Those who are charged and/or convicted of rape often use stigma management strategies to deny that their acts constituted rape or to claim that they were not fully responsible for their behavior.
- University officials and college students today are trying to more clearly define how consent to engage in sex should be established, especially with a potential partner who is intoxicated.

KEYWORDS

acquaintance rape: Rape that involves an offender the victim knows, such as a friend, romantic partner, or family member.
admitters: Convicted rapists in Diane Scully's research who admitted that they had committed the sexual assault for which they were convicted.
affirmative consent: A voluntary and mutual permission (by words or actions) to engage in sexual activity.
age of consent: The age at which a person is legally considered capable of giving consent to engage in sexual activity. Based on state laws, the age of consent varies.
black beast rape myth: An atrocity tale that circulated in the US South in the later part of the 1800s that portrayed black men as sexual savages intent on brutally raping white women.
chemical castration: The administration of medication designed to reduce testosterone production in male sex offenders with the intent of reducing their libido and of preventing them from repeating their crimes. Used in nine states in the United States.
Clery Act: A federal law enacted in 1990 that requires colleges and universities that participate in federal financial aid programs to report information about crime on and near their respective campuses. Originally known as the Crime Awareness and Campus Security Act.
date rape: A term used to refer to some kinds of acquaintance rape, particularly those involving rape occurring on a date or in a party setting.
deniers: Convicted rapists in Diane Scully's research who denied that they had committed the sexual assault for which they were convicted.
marital rape: Rape that occurs between martial partners. Also known as "spousal rape" and sometimes used to refer to rape that occurs in any committed relationship.
misogynistic: The hatred of women as a sexually defined group.
party rape: Rape that occurs in the context of drinking and partying, particularly among students at "party school" universities.
prison rape: Sexual abuse in prison settings.
rape myths: Inaccurate beliefs about women and sexual assault that legitimate and rationalize forced sex as natural and acceptable.
rape proclivity theory: A theory that men who are more likely to rape have feelings of hostility toward women and become sexually aroused by sexual assault.

rape prone culture: A culture or subculture that has beliefs and practices that condone or support sexual violence.

rape trauma syndrome: A psychiatric diagnosis of a form of posttraumatic stress disorder that mental health practitioners and counselors believe is commonly experienced by rape victims.

rape shield laws: Legislation that limits defense attorneys' ability to present a rape victim's previous sexual history in order to discredit claims of rape.

Romeo and Juliet laws: Statutes that are designed to avoid harsh penalties for statutory rape committed by teenage romantic partners that are near the same age.

second rape: A term used to refer to the experience of rape victims in the criminal justice system, where they may feel abused and degraded in interactions with police, medical personnel, and the court system.

sexual assault: The blanket term for all types of sexual offenses that involve touching or penetration of an intimate part of a person's body without consent, including rape, forced oral or anal sex, and any form of undesired sexually related touching.

stranger rape: Rape that is committed by a person who is not known to the victim.

weapon of terror (rape as): Rape that is committed as an act of humiliation and to instill fear in the victim and others in his/her community, especially in civil war settings and other arenas of ethnic conflict.

CHAPTER

7

Financially Motivated Crime in the Streets

Convenience store robbery (MIXA/Alamy Stock Photo).

CONTENTS

LEARNING OBJECTIVES

After reading this chapter, you will be able to:

- Describe the most common types of street-level property crime
- Explain the challenges to, and strategies for, studying street crime
- Identify different historical definitions of and explanations for street-level property crime
- Apply Merton's anomie theory to street crime
- Analyze the interactional contexts in which street-level thieves commit crimes
- Explain the extent and costs of incarcerating street-level offenders today
- Frame an argument for or against providing educational opportunities for incarcerated offenders

BLURRED BOUNDARIES I: TWO THIEVES

In contrast to the physical and sexual violence discussed in the previous two chapters, Chapters 7 and 8 examine criminal deviance focused primarily on property or financial gain. While violence and physical injury may occur in many financially motivated crimes, the primary purpose of the crime is to take other people's money or belongings. There are many different types of financially motivated crime. Our focus in this chapter is primarily on what are called *street crimes*, such as robbery and burglary. In the next chapter, we will examine elite financially motivated crimes committed by business professionals. Although they are different in many ways, both street crime and *white-collar crime*, as business-oriented property crime is often called, are motivated by a desire to acquire other people's money or goods by illegal means. Before we begin, consider two "street-level" thieves, Terry Johnson and Mimi Wilson.

26-year-old African-American Terry Johnson expected to get a harsh sentence when he was arrested and charged with armed robbery outside a convenience store off the Pomona Freeway in East Los Angeles. Perhaps he would never have been caught if he had not tried to use the credit cards in the wallet of the man he had robbed. But when he tried to purchase a television with one of the credit cards the day after the robbery, he was apprehended by the police.

It didn't help his case that, when he was arrested, he was on parole for robbery and burglary charges three years earlier. In a two-day court trial, he was convicted of armed robbery, credit card fraud, and possession of an unregistered handgun. Under California's *three-strikes law*, which mandates longer prison sentences for offenders who are convicted of three or more serious criminal offenses, Johnson was sentenced to life in prison with possible parole after 25 years.

The prosecutor praised the sentence, telling reporters that "there is only one way to keep this hoodlum from stealing, and that is to incarcerate him." Johnson's recent victim agreed. "I want to thank the police and the judge," he said, "for making this neighborhood safer by putting that man behind bars."

But not all of the testimony at the trial painted the young man as a "career criminal." Several family members pleaded with the judge for mercy in Johnson's case, saying he grew up without a father and that his mother was addicted to drugs. Family members told the judge and jury that Terry had been a good student and a talented athlete in high school before he became involved with an east side gang and drugs.

The prosecuting attorney disagreed, pointing out that Johnson had been on community supervision before while attending a drug rehabilitation program. "I hate to say it," he told the jury, "Terry Johnson may be a product of the streets, but he has become an unfixable problem."

When we talk about property thieves, we think of crimes like burglary, car theft, and armed robbery. And the image that most commonly comes to mind is that of a lower-class minority young man like Terry Johnson, typically from a broken home, with a history of violence, drug and alcohol abuse, and trouble with the law. Indeed, jails and prisons across the United States are filled with such young men. Today, more than one in three African-American males spends time incarcerated during their lifetime (Lyons and Pettit 2011).

In contrast, 75-year-old nursing home resident Mimi Wilson hardly looks the stereotypical part of a thief, but that did not prevent Atlanta police officers from arresting her for $100 worth of unpaid-for cosmetics as she walked out of a shopping mall. When security guards confronted her, Mrs. Wilson claimed not to have known that lotions and perfumes from Macy's and Dillard's were in her purse. Later, the county prosecutor learned that Mrs. Wilson had been convicted for shoplifting 10 years earlier in Florida. Like California, Georgia has one of the most severe three-strikes law in the country, and under that law, Mrs. Wilson could have been sentenced to life in prison for her shoplifting offense if she had been charged and convicted of shoplifting from both Macy's and Dillard's.

The case against Mrs. Wilson became complicated, though, when a niece testified that her aunt had been showing signs of Alzheimer's disease in recent months—a claim that Mrs. Wilson herself rejected, but that the judge found disturbing. Without clear medical evidence of the illness, the prosecutor charged Mrs. Wilson, but with just one charge of shoplifting. The judge sentenced her to only six months in the county jail. Yet, even this sentence was hailed by many in the community—and across the country once the story hit the Internet—as outrageous.

"What are we doing putting grandma in jail?" one blogger wrote.

Others took a different view. "Grandma did the crime, let her do the time," one post read. And another blogger argued, "An example like this sends a message: we're tired of paying more for goods to pay for pilferers—no matter how old or crazy they are!"

Still others focused less on Mrs. Wilson's age and possible Alzheimer's than on the value of the goods in comparison to the sentence she received. "Six months for $100?" wrote one blogger. "That's less than a buck a day. Even grandma's time is worth more than that." Another responded, "It costs us more to keep her in jail than if we just paid Macy's for the shirts and sent her back to the old folks home."

Finally, another commenter complained, "Macy's should be doing time for the prices they charge on the junk that they sell. FREE GRANDMA."

These two cases—and the punishments for them—illustrate several issues that most of us see as important in judging property crimes. First, we are likely to weigh property crimes more seriously if they are accompanied by violence or the threat of violence, especially when the threat of deadly force is used. Second, we tend to focus on the worth of what is stolen, as reflected in the distinction between "petty theft" (in many states classified as theft worth no more than $1,000) and "grand theft." Third, we may consider the characteristics of the offender. Is the person accused of stealing a sympathetic figure, say an abused child or a mentally troubled senior citizen? In short, we are likely to weigh several issues in deciding whether a given act of theft should be counted as a serious crime. Most of us would characterize Terry Johnson as a repeat offender of serious crime meriting serious penalty, although many of us would argue that life in prison is too extreme. But most of us would be less certain about Mrs. Wilson, her crime, and her punishment.

CURRENT CONSTRUCTIONS OF STREET-LEVEL PROPERTY CRIMES IN THE UNITED STATES

When we think of financially motivated crimes, the images that come most readily to mind are crimes such as robbery, car theft, and burglary. Each of these crimes entails not only stealing from another person, but also the possibility of face-to-face confrontation and personal violence. These crimes are often referred to as street crimes because many of them occur on the streets or in public places. Street crime is commonly associated in the media and public consciousness with lower-income social groups and disadvantaged minorities. Several kinds of economic crimes are clearly defined by state and federal laws and enforced by local, state, and federal law enforcement. The FBI's *Uniform Crime Reports* (UCRs) include annual arrest statistics on key kinds of "street-level" economic crimes.

Types of Street-Level Property Crime

One type of economic crime in particular—the crime of robbery—stands as the most stereotypical image of street crime. *Robbery*, as legally defined, represents the illegal taking of another person's property in their presence and by the use of violence or intimidation. The threat of violence is what distinguishes robbery from other kinds of property crimes. Whether the robber brandishes a weapon or simply engages in strong-arm tactics of threatening a beating, robbery carries the message that the victim will be injured if he or she does not comply. While the motivation for robbery is primarily economic, the fact that it is based on the threat of violence has led the FBI to include it in the UCR as a crime of violence.

In contrast to robbery, the property offenses of burglary, larceny-theft, and motor vehicle theft do not involve the threat of force or violence against the victim. *Burglary*, as officially defined by the UCR, is focused on unlawful entry into a building (e.g., home or business) with the intent to commit a theft. The act of *larceny-theft* involves the unlawful taking of property from another's possession in situations where no threat of force or unlawful entry occurs, including crimes like shoplifting, purse-snatching, and bicycle theft. Legal statutes, varying from state to state, recognize different degrees of larceny-theft, ranging from small *misdemeanor* offenses (such as shoplifting of less than $250, typically considered sixth-degree larceny) to large *felony* offenses (such as first-degree felony thefts of property valued at more than $10,000). Finally, *motor vehicle theft* is listed as a separate category of offense in the UCRs. While motor vehicle theft includes stealing of any motorized vehicle, such as cars, motorcycles, and powerboats, the overwhelming majority of motor vehicle thefts involve automobiles. Car theft runs the gamut from antics of short-term adolescent joyriders to planned thefts by professional auto thieves who steal cars to sell, either whole or in parts.

Statistical Snapshot

With the exception of shoplifting, which is almost equally common among males and females and by no means restricted to poorer segments of the population, the majority of financially motivated street crimes are committed by individuals of low socioeconomic status, and frequently minority young men. These crimes tend, by and large, to be perpetrated on victims who share similar attributes to the offender—that is, they are predominantly of the same race and social class. It is estimated that 10–15 per cent of US citizens are victims of street-level property crimes each year (Siegel 2007, p.368). By far the largest number of property crimes involve larceny-theft (including shoplifting), which account for nearly 70 per cent of all property crimes. Burglary accounts for almost 20 per cent of reported property crimes, and motor vehicle theft about 8 per cent. Robbery is by far the least common of these crimes, representing only 4 per cent of financially motivated street crimes in 2014 (FBI 2015a).

As shown in *table 7.1* below, according to UCR data, the numbers and rates of street-level property crime have declined dramatically in recent years. In fact, the total number of these crimes reported in 2014 was nearly 20 per cent lower than the number reported in 2000—and 37 per cent lower than the number in 1990, in spite of substantial growth in the US population during this same period. The bottom line is clear: Americans overall are dramatically less at risk of street crimes today than they were 25 years ago.

Nonetheless, the fear of victimization remains high in the United States, fueled in significant part by constant media attention to street crime, both in

Table 7.1 Financially Motivated Street Crime Statistics

	Robbery		Burglary		Larceny-Theft		Vehicle Theft		
UCR	Total In Millions	Rate Per 100K	Total	Rate	Total	Rate	Total	Rate	**Total**
1990	0.64m	256	3.2m	1,232	7.9m	3,185	1.6m	656	13.64m
1995	0.58m	221	2.6m	987	8m	3,043	1.5m	560	12.68m
2000	0.41m	145	2.1m	728	7m	2,477	1.2m	412	10.71m
2005	0.42m	141	2.2m	727	6.8m	2,288	1.23m	417	10.65m
2010	0.37m	119	2.2m	716	6.3m	2,060	0.79m	259	9.66m
2014	0.33m	102	1.7m	542	5.9m	1,837	0.69m	216	8.62m

SOURCE: FBI (2016).

the news and in prime-time entertainment (e.g., Altheide 2014). And, while burglary, larceny-theft, and motor vehicle theft are not considered violent crimes, like robbery, the possibility of accidentally being caught up in a physical confrontation always looms as a potential problem in burglaries, shoplifting, and car theft. Like robbery, each of these ways of stealing involves the thief's physically absconding with another's property. And by virtue of having to be physically present in the theft, the thief faces the possibility of direct face-to-face confrontation.

CHALLENGES IN RESEARCHING STREET-LEVEL PROPERTY CRIMES

While the number of street-level property crimes has dropped over the last 25 years, there are still well over eight million reported robberies and thefts per year in the United States. Researchers who study the contexts and extent of street-level property crime have many good resources available to them, but they also face challenges in collecting their data.

Counting Street-Level Property Crime

In the United States, many governmental agencies take on the task of collecting data on street crime. Most notably, the FBI's *UCR* pulls together the reports of crime and arrests from law enforcement agencies across the country. As we have seen in earlier chapters, there is often a discrepancy between the number of crimes actually committed and those that are reported to officials. Overall, the proportion of crime reported is relatively high for property offenses—not

PUSHING YOUR BOUNDARIES

The FBI's Uniform Crime Reporting (UCR) Program publishes data on crimes in the United States every year. You can find the UCR Crime Reports online at https://ucr.fbi.gov/ucr-publications.

Table 1 in annual reports UCR data shows the number of crimes and the rate per 100,000 people for the last 20 years. Table 5 shows similar data for the most recent year state by state. Go to the FBI's UCR website and examine these tables to answer the following questions:

From Table 1:

- What was the number of crimes reported in the most recent year for robbery (defined in the UCR as a violent crime), total property crimes, burglary, larceny-theft, and motor vehicle theft.
- What was the rate per 100,000 people for each of these types of crime?
- What year shows the highest rate of each of these types of crime?
- How do the rates for the most recent year compare to the high years?

From Table 5:

- What is the most recent year's rate for these crimes in the state where you live?
- How does the rate for your state compare to the national rate?

Come to class prepared to discuss what you have found. Do the findings surprise you or reinforce what you already thought about street-level property crime in the United States?

as high as the rate of reporting for murder, but considerably higher than for sexual assault. However, rates of reporting for different types of property crimes vary dramatically. According to the National Crime Victimization Survey (NCVS 2014), in 2013 about 75 per cent of motor vehicle thefts and 68 per cent of robberies were reported, while only 30 per cent of larceny-thefts were taken to the police. In comparison to other types of crime, the data we have on street crimes—despite some limitations—are among the most reliable and accurate statistics we have on any type of deviance. We tend to know it when we see it, report it (for the most part) when we are victims of it, and law enforcement officials are ready and waiting to respond when we report it.

Getting Close

A deep sociological understanding of financially motivated crimes requires getting close to the experiences of those who commit them and being able to grasp the meaning of their acts from the offender's point of view. This presents a challenge since, given the penalties for being discovered, property criminals have many reasons to avoid publicity or attention. Most of the detailed accounts that deviance ethnographers have collected of street crime have come from interviewing incarcerated offenders who have been tried and convicted. Experienced crime researchers, such as Neal Shover and Andy Hochstetler, have demonstrated that offering offenders an opportunity to tell their side of the story once they have been caught can yield valuable insights into their thinking and behavior.

Still, as with other kinds of criminal deviance, researchers need to be cautious in accepting the recollections and statements of those who have been convicted. For one thing, interviews with incarcerated offenders occur long after the offenses were committed and after the offenders have had time to potentially forget or revise their memories of what happened. Second, even though researchers typically go to great lengths to maintain the confidentiality of those they interview, imprisoned offenders may fear that being honest could get them into more trouble with the law. As criminologists Richard Wright and Scott Decker have noted, "Assurances of confidentiality notwithstanding, many prisoners remain convinced that what they say will affect their chances of being released and, therefore, they portray themselves in the best possible light" (1994, p.5).

In contrast to criminologists conducting prison interviews, some criminologists have engaged in research with active robbers and burglars. In Chapter 2, we briefly discussed Richard Wright and Scott Decker's (1994) research with burglars who they asked to take them to the scene of recent burglaries and explain how they did them. Similarly, Paul Cromwell and James Olsen conducted an 18-month ethnographic fieldstudy of "skilled burglars"—burglars who had demonstrated an ability to make a living and avoid being caught while committing their crimes. While lots of convicted criminals know how to "talk a good crime," Cromwell and Olsen argue, "Only when the researcher actually goes in to the field—into the social and physical environment of the subjects being studied—must the informant actually demonstrate any skills" (2004, p.5). Being in the social and physical environment of skilled burglars, however, presents practical and ethical challenges. Cromwell and Olsen felt a need to draw a line between past crimes and anticipated future burglaries:

> We did not participate in planning or in discussing crimes to be committed in the future by our informants. We advised them orally and in writing that the promise of confidentiality would not extend to new crimes. . . . We justified this procedure on the basis that the crimes we studied had already been committed and that we had no involvement in them whatsoever . . . No one (including the victim) was damaged further for our having knowledge of the identity of the guilty party. On the other hand, if the knowledge we gained allowed us to suggest more effective crime prevention strategies, society benefitted.
>
> —Cromwell and Olsen (2004, p.8)

In short, criminologists have a wealth of data on street-level property crime. The NCVS finds that most of those who are victims of such crimes report them, thus giving us confidence in the *UCR* statistics about the extent of property crime. Many property crime offenders are caught and spend significant time in jails and prisons where researchers are able to find and interview them. And some tenacious researchers have even managed to get on the inside of this kind of criminal activity. As a result, sociologists have a fairly detailed understanding of property crime. But before looking more closely at street-level property crime today, we can take a broader look at such crime across cultures and over time.

CROSS-CULTURAL CONSTRUCTIONS OF STREET-LEVEL PROPERTY CRIME

Property crime extends back in history as far as human cultures have conceived of the notion of property itself, and especially of private property that could be owned by individuals. Most historical codes of law across cultures specify some property rights, at least for some individuals, and by virtue of this also identify some kinds of taking of physical goods or money as a form of theft. In modern western societies the rights of property are different from many past societies. We extend the right to own property to virtually every citizen, not just certain classes of people. In earlier tribal societies it was often acceptable, at times even praiseworthy, to take things from members of another tribe or clan. As nation-states developed, however, members of different clans or ethnic groups became united under common laws and norms regarding property rights. Today in most nations, even noncitizens, such as tourists from other countries, are afforded some property rights and protected, at least officially, by laws against stealing from them. While most societies have had formal and informal norms consistent with the Biblical eighth commandment that "thou shalt not steal," what counts as stealing and who can be treated as a thief has varied depending on cultural beliefs and the power of different social groups. Conceptions of theft depend on what is considered property and what is considered an appropriate way to obtain it. "Stealing" fruit from a tree can only occur if we define the tree as belonging to someone who has the sole right to its fruit.

Different Definitions

Definitions of what counts as property crime and the kinds of property crimes that are considered most serious and punished most harshly have varied across cultures and time. The biggest differences in defining property crimes have revolved around whose property was stolen—and how. In societies where the rich and powerful have dominated, they have often created laws that justified their taking what they wanted from others in tribute or taxes, thus at least officially defining their appropriation of property and goods—even by force, if necessary—as acceptable. In most cultures, the perceived seriousness of property crimes has depended on the value of what was stolen and whether or not thieves confronted their victims with force and threat of injury. In the Ottoman Empire of the Middle East during the 1700s and 1800s Islamic law distinguished between *sarika* (similar to simple theft) which required restitution, and *ghasb*, which involved the use of force and was considered a more serious crime, punishable by amputation of the thief's right hand (Zarinebaf 2010). Islamic law also considered stealing from private homes as more serious than theft from public places and shops.

In Renaissance Europe, beggars were often viewed as inveterate thieves and con men. As large numbers of desperately poor families and individuals flocked to the cities when displaced from village lands, the number of people who resorted to crime to meet their daily needs rose significantly. Perceptions of crime among the lower classes were promoted by the emergence of the printing press and mass-produced tracts and novels. Literate citizens of the era were almost exclusively members of the clergy or social elite, and the popular published materials of the period catered to their interests. Among the most popular literatures of the early printers were purported exposés and insider stories of con men and an "underworld" of criminals. As early as 1509, Martin Luther—the founder of the Protestant Reformation—published a tract by the title of *Liber Vagatorum* that claimed to be the confession of a wandering thief, revealing the many forms of trickery he engaged in to dupe his victims. Over the next century the stories of wayfaring thieves became a staple of printing presses across Europe. In Spain, the publication of *Lazarillo de Tormes* in 1554 marked the rise of the picaresque novel, stories of con men and rogues who managed to survive in a harsh world by using their wits. The picaresque novels of the era ranked with religious writings and stories of knights and chivalry as among the most popular literature of the period. Elite European society was both appalled and fascinated with the stories of thieves and con men who stole from more well-to-do citizens. The term "cony-catchers" was often used to refer to thieves who preyed on citizens who were seen as innocent and vulnerable, like rabbits (often then called conies) waiting to be caught (Salgado 1972). Such cony-catchers, wrote pamphleteer Robert Green in 1591, "putrify with their infections this flourishing estate of England" (Beier 1985, p.7). The literature on thieves in Europe in this period, like much of the crime reporting in the news media, television, and movies today, looked to more extreme and sensationalized cases and often portrayed underclass property crime as far more organized and specialized than was the case. The literature described an organized underworld of vagrant thieves who specialized in such narrow crimes, such as "till friskers," who robbed shop owners' cash tills, "sawney hunters," who specialized in stealing bacon, "noisy-racket men," who stole glassware from china shops, and "snow gatherers," who pilfered clothes that were set outside to dry (Mayhew 1861). The literary portrayal of underworld thieves was taken by many as literal truth and popularized by innumerable writers of the period. Any respectable European gentleman's library contained a wealth of such stories, cautioning against trusting the poor (McCall 2004).

Different "Causes"

Just as definitions of what constitutes property crime have varied across time and cultures, so have beliefs about what causes a person to steal another's belongings. Demonic explanations have focused on property crime as caused by greed, a sinful desire for material goods. Frequently in Christian literature, greed is personified as a false god or demon called Mammon, who St. Thomas Aquinas described metaphorically as "carried up from Hell by a wolf, coming to inflame the human heart with Greed" (Stockhammer 1965, p.134). But while the view of sinful temptation as the cause of property crime can be seen in religion today as well as in the past, psychological and sociological views have become far more common explanations.

Some psychological explanations of the cause of property crime share similarities to the Biblical view in their assumption that those who commit such crimes fail to see their acts in the bigger social (or cosmic) picture. Rather than focusing on sin and temptation, social psychological theories tend to focus on immaturity or a lack of moral development. Gottfredson and Hirschi's general theory of crime, for example, views property crime (as well as virtually all other forms of crime and deviance) as caused by the inability of some people "to avoid acts whose long-term costs exceed their momentary advantages" (1990, p.3). Individuals who lack self-control, they argue, cannot resist immediate gratification, despite the longer-term cost or the expense to other people. In short, they lack the good judgment of those who have developed self-discipline. Yet others have argued that some forms of property crime are caused by mental illness, such as the mental disorder of kleptomania that is viewed by some in the psychiatric field as a cause of shoplifting (e.g., Sarasalo et al. 1997).

Another explanation of a cause of property crime that also focuses on poor judgment is the belief that people lose their ability to make good decisions when they are under the influence of alcohol and drugs. In the 1700s and 1800s in Europe and the Middle East, as urban crimes of robbery and theft increased, officials and journalists widely attributed the increases to a lack of social restraint and civility brought on by the rise of distilled spirits (Collinson 1967; Zarinebaf 2010). Similar explanations are raised today in the media and by some social scientists who present data that document high rates of drug and alcohol use among street criminals.

An alternative view of the relationship between drug use and property crime has to do with the pressing financial needs that are associated with addictive illegal drugs. Given their constant need for money to support their illicit habits, drug addicts may turn to street crimes, such as prostitution and theft to secure quick cash or goods to exchange for drugs. The belief that desperation and lack of alternatives may lead people to engage in property crimes is also reflected in arguments that are sometimes made to explain high rates of property crimes such as shoplifting and petty theft among the poor and homeless (e.g., Snow et al. 1989).

The foregoing views of the causes of property crime as rooted in sinful temptation, poor socialization, mental illness, substance abuse, and poverty are all based on a deficit explanation of property crime. That is, they are all focused on something the thief lacks—such as moral character, mental capacity, or financial wherewithal—that motivates him or her to steal. While these have been the most common explanations for property crimes, another explanation focuses on the emotional thrill of what Stephen Lyng (1990) refers to as "edgework." Theft and robbery are acts that can provide those who engage in them with a rush of adrenaline and a feeling of at least momentary empowerment. The thrill of risky action is often a powerful component of the experience of stealing, whether that of an underclass young man enacting tough-guy masculinity by robbing a pedestrian at gunpoint (Katz 1988) or that of a middle-class housewife experiencing the sneaky thrill of shoplifting at Macy's (Shteir 2011).

Finally, we should note that popular culture in film and novels often embraces the view of some property thieves as folk heroes, portraying them as either seeking revenge for the wrongs of the rich and powerful, like Robin Hood robbing from the rich and giving to the poor, or pursuing daring heists that are a staple of Hollywood movies. Key to such folk hero stories is their thrilling edgework and the assertion that no innocent people were killed or harmed by their actions. Part of the popular culture allure of such heroes lies in their ability to beat the rich and powerful at their own game. Such heroes often emerge in popular culture at times when the general population feels a sense of powerlessness and exploitation—as with the rise of such legendary heroes during the Great Depression.

It is important to recognize that any one explanation of any kind of deviance is inadequate to explain all cases. Further, there is no reason to assume that any given individual is motivated to engage in property crime by only one of the causes discussed above. Desperation, greed, a lack of good judgment, a sense of excitement, and an urge for revenge may all play important parts in decisions to commit street-level property crimes.

Different Responses

Societal reactions to property crimes have varied widely. On one end of the continuum, there is a history of harsh reaction to property crimes, focused on punishment or *retribution*. In many cultures thieves have been subjected to *corporal punishment*, including such physical punishments as whippings, torture, branding, and amputation of body parts. In the Ottoman Empire, theft was viewed as a crime against God and the law imposed punishment by flogging and amputation of the thief's right hand for the first offense and left foot for the second—although often the most severe punishments were not imposed (Zarinebaf, 2010, p.74). In Medieval and Elizabethan England, death, whippings, and confinement in stocks were common, as property thieves were subjected to public punishment and humiliation—which also served as a warning to other would-be criminals. Even relatively minor theft could be punished by death, as exemplified in the Shoplifting Act passed by the English Parliament in 1699 that made shoplifting of items worth more than five shillings a hanging offense (Shteir 2011).

It has also been common for the crown, the state, or other powerful interests, to fit the punishment of thieves to their own interests. In the era of oceanic exploration and colonial expansion from the sixteenth to the eighteenth centuries, convicted thieves across Europe and the Ottoman Empire were often sent to row in the galleys of commercial and military ships (Zarinebaf 2010), or sentenced to indentured servitude in the colonies (Beier 1985).

In contrast to punishment and retribution, many societies have focused primarily on *restitution* for property crimes, requiring thieves to repay their victims for what they have stolen. In early societies where extended family groups sought justice for wrongdoing, it was common for them to seek compensation for property crimes rather than the punishment of thieves. Restitutional approaches to property crime date back thousands of years. Both ancient Jewish and Roman laws specified repayment for property crimes. Today, many US courts seek both punishment and restitution for property crimes.

Yet, a third broad kind of social response to property crime has involved pursuing *reform* and moral transformation of the heart and mind of the criminal. Across Europe, beginning in the sixteenth century, prisons and workhouses were created with the explicit goal of reforming thieves and other criminals and turning them into disciplined and productive workers (Beier 1985). While incarceration in jail or prison is often seen by most of us as a form of punishment, much of the nineteenth century official rationale for incarceration in America focused on placing the criminal in an environment where he or she would learn habits of good discipline, be removed from bad influences, and have an opportunity to reflect on their misdeeds and seek moral redemption. Zebulon Brockway, the leader of the American Prison Association, explained in 1877, "The supreme aim of prison discipline is the reformation of criminals, not the infliction of vindictive suffering" (Colvin 1997, p.157). Most of the efforts to reform criminals in Brockway's time grew out of Protestant women's movements, such as the Social Purity crusade, that focused on moral and spiritual reform of poor immigrant women, who comprised nearly 40 per cent of incarcerated prisoners in some northern states during the middle of the nineteenth century (Freedman 1981, p.14). By the twentieth century, however, efforts to reform street criminals focused far more on psychological and therapeutic approaches, typically involving individual or group counseling. Today, US policy-makers continue to debate the use of punishment, restitution, and reform with those convicted of property crimes.

HISTORY OF STREET-LEVEL PROPERTY CRIME IN THE UNITED STATES

Property crime has always been a fact of life in American society, although the nature of property crime has varied significantly across time and space, reflecting the broader contours and forces in Anglo-American culture, including race and ethnic relations, class relations, the technologies of property management, and patterns of financial exchange. In the colonies and the early years of the United States, North America offered an open expanse of land and opportunity for many European immigrant groups. In colonial days, robbery was a felony punishable by death. But what counted as robbery was defined significantly by race. Land and goods, such as valuable furs, were taken from Native Americans by force and fraud, often involving guns and alcohol, but such acts were seldom defined as crime—and even less often prosecuted. Meanwhile, the legal enslavement of kidnapped and imported Africans and their descendants defined a whole set of people as property, the taking of whom from their "owners" could be defined as a property crime. Most property crime in early America was much more a matter of stealing goods—from clothing and food to horses and chickens—than it was of stealing money, since money was far less widespread in use. Larger scale robberies were focused on main avenues of moving people and goods to North America and across it, particularly the major waterways. Few highway robbers existed in America before the nineteenth century. More common were river pirates who roamed the Ohio and Mississippi Rivers to prey on commercial and passenger traffic.

By the late nineteenth century, as business expanded, more money and gold were being transported across the country and new criminal opportunities arose. In 1869, the railroad magnate Leland Stanford drove the "golden spike" connecting the first transcontinental rail line across the United States, which was followed over the next several decades by dramatic increases in railroad lines and traffic. From the late 1800s through the early 1930s, the transportation of money and gold by train offered opportunities of big takes to daring thieves like Jesse James, Butch Cassidy, and the "Sundance Kid," and was partly responsible for the meteoric rise of the Pinkerton Detective Agency, whose well-armed detectives often protected money and gold in transit on the trains. As banks proliferated across the country, they too became common marks for the most daring and high-profile thieves, especially from the early 1900s through the 1930s. While most property crime of that era was far less dramatic and violent, bank robbery captured the public imagination and several of the most publicized bank robbers became popular folk heroes. The exploits of Bonnie Parker and Clyde Barrow, a couple in their early twenties, were front page news across the country from 1931 until their deaths at the hands of law enforcement in 1934. Another of the era's famous bank robbers, Charles "Pretty Boy" Floyd, was cast as a Robin Hood hero in Woody Guthrie's song, "Pretty Boy Floyd." In the era of the Great Depression, with widespread unemployment, bank foreclosures on people's homes, and anger at the abuses of big business, the tales of daring underdog thieves with their guns and fast getaway cars provided a satisfying fantasy for the public, especially when tied to the Robin Hood theme of robbing from the rich and giving to the poor. It was this theme that featured prominently in Guthrie's tale of Pretty Boy Floyd when he sang:

> Many a starving farmer
> The same old story told
> How the outlaw paid their mortgage
> And saved their little homes.
> Others tell you 'bout a stranger
> That come to beg a meal,
> And underneath his napkin
> Left a thousand dollar bill.

The realities of the crimes and lives of such heroic bank robbers were far less romantic than their media portrayals. Many of them came from hardscrabble lives of poverty and abuse and most of them died violent deaths at an early age. But the era of the Great Depression stoked popular frustrations with big business and the government, while the newspapers and emerging film industry fitted the stories to dramatic public interest. Bonnie and Clyde took pictures of themselves and J. Edgar Hoover orchestrated high profile arrests with the media. It was an era infatuated with property crime, with bank robbery standing as the iconic property crime in American culture.

During World War II, media attention shifted away from sensational crimes to the drama of patriotic war themes. The rates of property crime across the United States were relatively low following the war until the late 1960s when street-level property and violent crime rose significantly. The number of reported burglaries in the United States more than doubled from 1960 to 1970. Rates of robbery nearly tripled during the same time period. American's fear of crime shot up during those years and played a significant role in national politics as President Richard Nixon was elected on a platform emphasizing the need to reduce crime in the streets. Nixon's policies did little to cut rates of street-level property crime, which continued to rise until the early 1980s. Then beginning in the early 1980s, most types of street-level property and violent crime began to drop. Today, as we saw in table 7.1, property crime rates in the United States are less than half of what they were 40 years ago.

MERTON'S SOCIAL STRUCTURE AND ANOMIE

As discussed in Chapter 3, Robert Merton proposed anomie theory to explain how cultural norms and values can motivate individuals to engage in criminal behavior. According to Merton, American society strongly values material success and individual achievement, seeing these goals as something everyone should strive to achieve. But access to legitimate opportunities to pursue these goals is not equally available to everyone. Those who lack socially approved and legitimate means for pursuing material success may turn to other ways to get ahead. The combination of cultural emphasis on particular goals with a lack of structural opportunities for legitimately achieving them, Merton argued, led to *innovation*, or the use of illegitimate means to achieve one's goals. Merton applied his idea of innovative deviance to what was commonly reported about the poor in urban slums—that they used various forms of crime, including theft and other property crimes, to pursue financial success where only such deviant means would allow them to be successful.

Terry Johnson, the young man featured in the opening section of this chapter, provides a good application of Merton's concept of innovation. Growing up without parental guidance and support in a poor neighborhood with substandard schools, Terry had few opportunities to build the kinds of skills and connections that would enable him to become financially successful through societally acceptable means. Lacking those opportunities, Merton would argue, many young people in Terry's situation turn to street crimes such as shoplifting, burglary, and robbery in an attempt to achieve material success—even though such success is often short-lived.

It is easy for many of us to see how Merton's concept of innovation may help explain why some poor and relatively powerless individuals turn to street crime. But while this broad explanation is critical to understanding property crime, it addresses only the macro level of such criminal behavior. It does not provide deeper insight into the interactional contexts in which property crimes are committed and criminals are caught and punished. For an understanding of these issues, we must turn to qualitative research into the lives of those who engage in property crimes.

INTERACTIONAL CONTEXTS AND ETHNOGRAPHIC VOICES

All financial crimes involve some action or set of actions through which money or belongings are illegally taken from one or more people. In this section, we examine the social dynamics of street thieves' decisions to commit crimes and the activities involved in committing them.

Crime novels and movies are filled with plots of elaborate thefts by mastermind (even though usually apprehended) burglars and robbers. But such dramatic and intricately planned heists are less common in real-life street crimes. While there is some planning involved in street crime such as burglary and robbery, it is typically short-term planning mostly done at a time when the potential thief feels an immediate need for money. As such, there is little time—or inclination—on the part of the offender to do more than find a vulnerable target and commit the crime.

Burglary presents a greater need for planning than do other forms of street-level thievery like shoplifting and robbery. Burglars must identify locations with valuables to be stolen, determine when a home or business is likely to be unoccupied, and figure out how to gain entry to it. In research for their book, *Breaking and Entering: Burglars on Burglary*, Paul Cromwell and James Olsen describe three typical patterns used by burglars to select their targets. First, a burglar can happen by chance to see a potential burglary site at an opportune moment when the occupants are clearly gone and the residence is especially vulnerable—as with a garage door or window unintentionally left open. Such an open site is available for immediate theft. Second, a burglar may cruise a neighborhood in search of promising targets to break into later. Third, and most commonly, burglars come across a site during a legitimate occasion when they are a guest, delivery person, or worker in the home, business, or neighborhood. One of Cromwell and Olsen's informants explained:

> One time I was working on this roofing job in this real nice area. I got to know the schedules of almost everybody on the block. I knew when they left in the morning and came home at night, and who stayed home during the day. About two weeks after the job was done I came back and did [burglarized] almost every house on that block.
>
> —Cromwell and Olsen (2004, p.23)

As Joel Best and David Luckenbill (1994) have noted, burglars are drawn to targets that they believe hold valuable goods and where they can gain access without a high risk of being caught. Once a target has been selected, burglars must manage to enter the business or home without arousing suspicion, frequently by either posing as a person who should be on the premises (such as a janitor or maintenance person) or by sneaking in during the night when no one is watching. Burglars frequently find that the risk and secrecy of breaking and entering produces an excitement and thrill that becomes part of the motivation for engaging in the activity. The edgework thrill of breaking and entering was mentioned by almost every one of Cromwell and Olsen's 60 informants, and particularly central to the experience of young burglars. Gerald, a 20-year-old burglar, told them, "I used to love that adrenaline rush you get when you first go in the window. It's as good as coke. Heart starts thumping and you get shaky and feel super alive. When I was fifteen, sixteen years old, I lived for that feeling. I still get scared and get the rush, but now I do it for money" (2004, p.17). Similarly, another informant explained, "There's no feeling like it. It's fear and sex and danger and every other exciting feeling you ever had all rolled into one. I'd do crime just for that rush. I *do* crime just for that rush. Sometimes" (2004, p.17).

But if burglary provides a seductive edgework thrill, it avoids the heftier potential risks associated with stealing in the act of robbery. Burglary does not involve face-to-face interaction between victims and offenders except when things go wrong. By far the majority of street-level property criminals seek to avoid face-to-face interaction with their victims. Property crimes that do not require face-to-face interaction, including burglary and simple larceny (nonviolent taking of another's possessions—like bike theft and shoplifting), are far more common than robbery. As shown earlier in table 7.1, in 2014 there were 333,000 robberies reported to US law enforcement officials in comparison to 1.7 million reported burglaries and nearly six million cases of larceny-theft. This means that there were over 20 times as many burglaries and simple thefts (including shoplifting) in the United States as there were robberies. One reason for this is that most property offenders prefer to steal property without having to engage in direct confrontation. Many thieves fear confrontation with potential victims far more than being caught by the police. As a car thief in Hochstetler and Copes study of property criminals succinctly put it, "The police take ya to jail, but the owner'll kill ya" (2006, p.103).

In contrast to burglary, robbery involves face-to-face intimidation and the threat of force. Like burglary, robbery typically involves only a modest amount of planning. The offender who decides to commit a robbery usually chooses a victim with certain characteristics, including appearing to have what the offender wants (e.g., money) and being vulnerable to attack. Strangers are often preferred since they are less likely to be able to identify the offender later. But in Richard Wright and Scott Decker's study of active robbers, they found that many robbers "preyed on individuals who themselves were involved in lawbreaking" (1997, p.62). Most commonly, they preferred to rob drug dealers, especially young street level dealers. The appeal of robbing drug dealers for them was twofold. First, drug dealers typically use cash for their transactions, so they tend to carry a lot of money on them. Second, by virtue of their own illicit activities, drug dealers are unlikely to go to the police for assistance if they have been robbed. Yet, another common target for robbery is a married man, especially an intoxicated one, in search of a prostitute—again an ideal victim by virtue of the likelihood that he is carrying cash and that he will not report the robbery for fear of his illicit activities becoming public.

Both burglars and robbers must overcome fear of what may happen in their criminal acts. While burglars expect to avoid confrontation with their victims, they realize that they may unexpectedly be caught in the act. Robbers know that confrontation is part of the action they are about to engage in. Whether intentionally (to blunt their fear) or by unintentional circumstance, a significant proportion of property thieves are under the influence of alcohol or drugs when they commit their crimes. "When I am drinking," a convicted thief told

Hochstetler and Copes, "I ain't too scared. It kills my nerves. That alcohol have me pumped up, you know" (2006, p.104). Additionally, property thieves often talk themselves up and mentally build their confidence to act. "Much like the athlete who enters a competitive event with a mindset that they can and will win," Hochstetler and Copes explain, "offenders enter the crime 'knowing' that they will be successful" (2006, p.109). Much of this confidence, especially for young men who are new to such criminal activity, involves projecting a masculine bravado when challenged by peers:

> I was worrying about what they going to say, that I ain't got the balls enough to do this. I said, man I got to do this or they going to look down upon me. I said the hell with it, I'm just going ahead and doing it. I had to or they would clown [make fun of] me.
>
> —Copes and Hochstetler (2003, p.293)

For some more experienced thieves, the criminal act can be an opportunity to enact "badass" masculinity, demonstrating their tough-guy character and coolness under pressure (Katz 1988).

Robbers typically look for a way to get close to their victims without being detected, such as by pretending to be a customer in a store or a fellow pedestrian on the street. As one of Wright and Decker's informants described his technique, "I just come up on you. You could be going to your car. . . . I want to be on your blind side . . . where I can get up on you without you noticing me and grab you and say, 'This is a robbery, motherfucker, don't make it no murder!' I kind of like shake you. That's my approach" (1997, p.97).

Announcing the stick up is the moment in which the robber makes clear to victims that they are in danger. Most robbers open their robberies by stating their intentions and by demanding that the would-be victim stop and listen to them. The threat of violence in robbery "sets in motion an interactive chain of events in which neither party can know for sure what will happen next" (Wright and Decker 1997, p.96). One goal of the robber is to exact immediate compliance from the victim. They must threaten would-be victims enough to compel compliance without either paralyzing them with fear or emboldening them to resist. Typically robbers show a weapon or announce the threat of force (like "don't make it no murder!"), occasionally backed up by a bit of "roughing up" to get the victim to turn over their belongings. Those who resist may be beaten or shot, although robbers relatively rarely resort to killing their victims.

Resisting or taunting robbers is a risky game. They tend to like the power and control that having a weapon confers. For some, the feeling of control in the stick-up encounter is one of the main appeals of this type of crime, offering them a chance to engage in "a thrilling demonstration of personal competence" (Katz 1991). Armed robbers often embrace a street machismo that can quickly turn to violence. As Wright and Decker observed, "The armed robbers we spoke with typically displayed far more anger and hostility than the active residential burglars who took part in our earlier study. Even in casual conversations, their strong propensity for sudden violence seemed to lurk just below the surface" (1997, p.56).

After taking a victim's money or goods, a robber must manage to make an escape. Typically, the robber prefers to be the one to leave the setting. Often they threaten victims to stay where they are for a while on fear of being beaten or shot if they disobey. Sometimes victims are tied up to keep them from running to the police. And robbers who target men involved in illicit sexual activities will often take the men's clothes and leave them naked, too vulnerable and embarrassed to offer chase (Wright and Decker 1997, p.117).

While burglars and robbers run a high risk of getting caught, convicted, and punished for their crimes, they seldom think about those possibilities before or during the commission of their crimes. In Kenneth Tunnell's interview study of repeat property crime offenders, he reports that "All sixty respondents reported that they (and nearly every thief they knew) simply do not think about the possible legal consequences of their criminal actions before committing crimes" (1992, p.87). This finding is repeated time and again in research literature that documents the cavalier attitude toward getting caught that characterizes property crime offenders, as captured in the words of an offender interviewed by Neal Shover and David Honaker (1992):

INTERVIEWER: Did you think about getting caught?
OFFENDER: No.
INTERVIEWER: How did you manage to put that out of your mind?
OFFENDER: It never did come into it.
INTERVIEWER: Never did come into it?
OFFENDER: Never did, you know. It didn't bother me.

How, we may ask, can this be? While we might be able to understand how those who commit murder can do so in the heat of a moment—once, but seldom more, without thinking of the consequences—how can property criminals persistently engage in their high-risk criminal behaviors and not find themselves worrying about getting caught? The answer, crime researchers find, lies in mindset and lifestyle experiences of persistent thieves. As Neal Shover (1996) explains, persistent thieves spend many of their leisure hours partying and enjoying good times, albeit in a frenetic and always precarious way. They tend to live in the moment, partying and not thinking about committing a theft until the need strikes. Their decisions to go out on "jobs" are governed largely by the amount of money in their pockets. One of Wright and Decker's informants told them, "A burglary will get me over the rough spot until I can get my shit straightened out. Once I get it straightened out, I just go with the flow until I hit that rough spot where I need the money again. . . . The only time I would go and commit a burglary is if I needed the money at that point in time" (1997, p.37).

One reason for this spontaneity in their decisions to commit crimes lies in the context and dynamics of street life and hustling. To understand the choices made by street criminals, especially persistent ones, it is important to look at the social worlds in which they spend their time. In *Great Pretenders* (1996), Neal Shover provides a glimpse into the daily lives of persistent thieves and the contexts in which they pursue their criminal careers. The center of their lifestyle, Shover argues, is the experience of "life as party," focused on enjoying good times, lubricated with drugs and alcohol, and with little concern for other commitments. Life as party is pursued in the company of others. In bars and lounges, on street corners, or cruising in automobiles, partiers celebrate their spontaneity and freedom along with their resourcefulness in finding ways to cover their expenses, especially drugs. Given the large expenses involved, life as party requires lots of cash. No single "score" brings in enough money to last more than a few days. When the money runs low, pressure builds to find a quick way to get more.

Planning for a theft is seldom much more than a spur-of-the-moment decision, often with companions one hardly knows. After a few hours together drinking and doing drugs, men who barely know one another may come to feel they are best friends and be ready to do nearly anything to make sure that the fun does not end. The combination of intoxication and social bonding promotes a feeling of "serendipitous optimism" (Hochstetler 2002, p.45) in which they talk up the opportunity with little sense of vulnerability. As one thief recounted to Shover:

> [After a day of partying], I got to talking about making some money, because I didn't have no money. This guy that we were riding with had all the money . . . So me and him and my nephew, we get together, talking about making some money. This guy tells me, 'man, I know where there's a good place."
>
> Q: Okay, so you suggested you all go somewhere and rob?
> A: Yeah, 'make some'—well, we called it 'making money.'
> Q: So you and this fellow met up in the bar . . . Tell me about the conversation.
> A: Well, there wasn't much of a conversation to it, really . . . I asked him if he was ready to go, if he wanted to go do something. And he knew what I meant. He wanted to go make some money somehow, any way it took.
>
> —Shover (1996, p.72)

Keeping the party going requires continuing to engage in risky offenses, and thieves tend to commit their crimes in "sprees" (Hochstetler 2002) with increasing desperation. Many offenders, like the one quoted below, are aware that eventually they will be arrested if they continue:

> When I was straight, I'd think about getting caught. I could get this and that [penalties] . . . And then I would think, well, I know this is going to end one day, you know. But you get so far out there and get so far off into it that it really don't matter. But you think about that. . . . I knew eventually I would get caught.
>
> When I got caught—and they caught me right at the house—it's kind of like, you feel good, because you're glad it's over, you know. I mean, a weight being lifted off your head. And you say, well, I don't have to worry about this shit no more, because they've caught me. And it's over.
>
> —(Shover 1996, p.78)

CONTEMPORARY RESPONSES TO STREET-LEVEL PROPERTY CRIME

As we discussed earlier, street-level property crime rates have dropped dramatically in the United States over the last 30 years. Sociologists and criminologists point to a number of factors that provide partial explanations for this drop in street crime. One factor in reduced crime is that the US population has become older, with a higher proportion of Americans over 30 today than three decades ago. Since street crime is primarily committed by the young, the US population is to a significant degree "aging out" of these types of crime. A second factor, especially for robbery, is that we have moved toward becoming a cashless society. With the rise of credit and debit cards, fewer Americans carry significant amounts of cash with them than in the past. This is particularly the case with more affluent Americans, as recognized by some street criminals who have told researchers that they avoid trying to rob wealthier-looking people because they seldom carry much money on them (Wright and Decker 1997).

Yet, another set of factors that some scholars feel help explain reductions in street crime are associated with J. Q. Wilson and George Kelling's *broken windows* theory of crime, which contends that signs of a lack of order and caring in neighborhoods (as exemplified by broken, unrepaired windows) creates an environment in which criminal activities tend to flourish. Maintaining and monitoring urban environments in a well-ordered condition, they propose, may prevent escalation into more serious crime. Drawing on Wilson and Kelling's broken windows theory, New York City, Boston, Los Angeles, and many other cities implemented policies in the 1990s to clean up at least portions of their communities. In the 1990s, New York City mayor Rudy Giuliani called upon the NYC police to implement a "zero-tolerance" policy toward graffiti, panhandling, prostitution, and other public order crimes. By sending a message of community attention to public order, city governments around the country have sought to create community environments that do not encourage more serious criminal activity. The effectiveness of such policies has been questioned by many scholars who argue that this approach to reducing crime tends to focus on relatively minor crimes rather than serious criminal activity and that it contains an implicit bias against minority neighborhoods (e.g., Sampson and Raudenbush 2004).

Other changes related to public and private surveillance and security practices in the United States over the last 30 years have undoubtedly reduced the opportunity for some forms of property crime. Shoplifting security has become a major business with heavy investment in in-store closed circuit television, radio-frequency detection tags, and loss prevention officers to monitor shoppers. The massive increase in gated residential communities (e.g., Blakely and Snyder 1997) and home security systems has also played some role in reducing opportunities for burglary.

Finally, some criminologists argue that street crime is lower today than several decades ago in large part because we have massively increased the number of street criminals who are confined in jails and prisons—and thus reduced the number of criminals on the streets. In the late 1970s, US states and the federal government began implementing "get tough on crime" policies that increased jail and prison sentences for a wide variety of criminal activities. In the 1990s, many states also passed three-strikes laws that mandated longer prison sentences for offenders who were convicted of three or more serious criminal offenses. As longer prison terms and three-strikes laws took effect, the number of convicted felons held in US prisons rose, from under 200,000 in 1975 to over 1.5 million in 2013. In addition, US jails today hold nearly 750,000 inmates who are either awaiting court hearings or serving time for criminal convictions.

While the US criminal justice system has clearly gotten tougher on crime in general over the last several decades, street-level property crime and drug offenses have been the focus of greatest attention. The rates of incarceration for poor and minority young men have increased most dramatically. Criminologists who study the impact of social class and race on criminal justice processing have documented the unequal treatment of the poor and minorities in the criminal justice system. At every stage of the process, from arrest to sentencing, lower-class and minority offenders are treated more harshly than more affluent citizens. First, they are more likely to be arrested for a crime than are white and more affluent offenders. When arrested, they are more likely to be refused the opportunity—or financially unable—to make bail and thus be released until court hearings. Their cases are more likely to be handled by overburdened public defenders and they are more likely to be convicted of the crimes for which they have been charged. If convicted, lower-class and minority offenders tend to receive longer prison sentences for comparable crimes. And once in prison, they serve longer prison terms than their more affluent and white counterparts.

These social class and racial disparities in treatment of street crime offenders have long raised concern among many criminologists and at least some policy-makers. They serve as one stark indicator of the impact of inequality on the lives of American citizens. As long as certain portions of the population are privileged in terms of resources *vis-à-vis* the criminal justice system, the impact of get-tough policies toward crime will fall disproportionately on less privileged groups in society. This is evident when we look at the social class and racial composition of the US prison population, which is 60 per cent African-American and Hispanic, twice as high as their percentage of the total US population.

Beyond the social justice issues raised by the disparities in treatment for crime, the impact of the "race to incarcerate," as Marc Mauer (2006) terms our current policies, has several other unintended consequences. Looking at state-level prison data, Pew researchers found that property crime offenders who were released in 2009 served almost half a year longer in custody than similar offenders released in 1990. While it is clear that incarcerating a convicted burglar makes it impossible for him to burglarize for the length of his jail or prison sentence, the costs of putting them behind bars for long periods of time may outweigh the benefits. For one thing, there is the sheer cost of incarceration. According to research by the Pew Center on the States, the average monthly cost nationwide for incarcerating an offender in prison in 2009 was $2,593 (Pew Research Center 2012). This means states were paying on average an additional $15,000 to incarcerate nonviolent property offenders (robbery offenders are considered violent crime offenders and not included)—on top of the $56,000 that their incarceration would have cost if prison time had remained the same as in 1990. To put these figures in some perspective, the average victim losses for property crimes in 2014 was $2,251 for burglary, $941 for larceny-theft, and $6,537 for motor vehicle theft (FBI 2015). The enormous price of imprisonment is taking a heavy toll on state budgets and many states are considering reducing the use of jail and prison terms for nonviolent property offenders in favor of less expensive alternatives, such as closely supervised probation (Pew Research Center 2012).

In addition to paying for incarcerating offenders, there are other costs associated with using prisons as a way of dealing with property crime. Young men who end up in prison for large chunks of their late teens and twenties often leave young families behind that they are unable to help support while in prison. These men also lose a critical period for building work skills and histories. Further, little provision has been made for when they get out. It can be extremely difficult for convicted felons to compete for jobs after they are released from prison (Pager 2003). This is all the more sobering since ex-prisoners who find stable jobs are far less likely to return to committing crimes.

In short, not all street-level property crime offenders are identified and arrested. Those who are arrested and convicted are far more likely to be poor and minority young men. Street-level property or financial crime convictions most often result in prison sentences—far more, we will see, than is the case for white-collar crimes. Convictions for "property crimes of the poor," including most robbery, burglary, and auto theft, result in prison sentences for over 80 per cent of the convicted offenders (Reiman and Leighton 2013). Yet, while prison sentences serve as a harsh punishment for those convicted of street-level property crimes, Devah Pager has voiced the concern of many criminologists that "In our frenzy of locking people up, our 'crime control' policies may in fact exacerbate the very conditions that lead to crime in the first place" (2003, p.961).

CLAIMS-MAKER PROFILE

Dolfinette Martin

Dolfinette Martin was 24 when she was arrested for shoplifting $300 worth of clothes at a New Orleans Macy's in 1994. The case against her was ultimately dropped, but since she was not able to post bail Martin remained in the jail for 60 days in spite of the fact that she was five months pregnant. In 2003, Martin was arrested again for shoplifting and served 15 months in prison. Her shoplifting was spurred in large part by heavy drug use. "I wasn't just addicted to drugs," she recalls, "I had become addicted to shoplifting too." Less than a year after her release from prison, she was arrested on shoplifting charges once more. Since she was on parole, she received a hard time sentence of seven years in prison.

Dolfinette's life turned around after a friend invited her to go to a prison church service. She was reluctant at first, but kept going back. "It wasn't until I truly developed a relationship with God that I was no longer empty. I knew then that my mission in life, my purpose, was to reach others just like me."

After spending 10 years in and out of jails and prisons, Martin works today as an Administrative Assistant with the Vera Institute's New Orleans Pretrial Services (NOPTS) where she advocates for the rights of those detained and awaiting prosecution. The NOPTS website recognizes her as "a voice for the thousands of incarcerated women who sometimes seem forgotten, highlighting the effects that mass incarceration has on families of color."

"I wholeheartedly believe" Martin says, "that if I would have had an organization like NOPTS to help me on the journey to recovery, employment, and education, I would not have made a lot of the negative choices I made."

Black defendants sitting in jail awaiting trial are far overrepresented across the country, but especially in New Orleans Parish, which has been called the "jail capital of America" (Mock 2015). Dolfinette Martin has found purpose in life through commitment to advocating for pretrial jail inmates' rights. "I am grateful every day," she says, "to be right where I am" (Martin 2015).

STIGMA MANAGEMENT AND RESISTANCE

Street-level thieves typically report feeling little or no guilt when carrying out their crimes. Most of the convicted robbers interviewed by Wright and Decker (1997) claimed that they needed the money and could not afford to feel sorry for their victims. Many of them invoked techniques of neutralization to claim that their crimes were not all that bad. Those who robbed other lawbreakers, such as drug dealers and men-seeking prostitutes, often engaged in "denying the victim," arguing that their victims deserved no sympathy. Others argued that getting robbed was just a fact of life on the streets and could easily happen to them. "It's like this," one robber said, "you never know, somebody probably do me like that. That's why we don't feel guilty. It might happen to us" (1997, p.126). Another told Wright and Decker, "I just don't feel sorry for my victims. I been robbed before and I feel like, if somebody rob me, they ain't gonna feel sorry when they rob me, so I don't feel sorry for nobody" (1997, p.126). Some accounted for their lack of guilty feelings by talking about the values they were raised with, as did one who explained, "My father always told me never to feel no pity for anybody. So I don't feel no pity for nobody" (1997, p.128).

Other offenders reported feelings of guilt after the fact if a victim had been hurt, but in the moment of their offenses they avoided facing such emotions. As we have also seen, most street-level property criminals do not think much about the potential negative consequences they themselves might face for their actions if they get caught. And among those who get arrested and convicted, there is little or no expectation that they will be shown sympathy or understanding. In contrast to the white-collar criminals discussed in the next chapter, street thieves tend to accept—at least on the surface—the stigma and punishment that are directed toward them as consequences of their criminal acts. However, the experience of prison—a topic that can only be touched on in this chapter—often takes a deep psychological toll. As Neal Shover explains:

> Enduring extremely harsh or brutal treatment can reassure some prisoners even as it kindles dangerous emotions. I refer specifically to embitterment, anger, and the desire to wreak revenge. This reaction can crystallize and strengthen a conception of oneself as a person who has been treated unfairly by authorities.
>
> —Shover (1996, p.181).

The prison experience often builds a toughness and resentment, while the challenge of putting together a life after prison looms as a struggle against the odds, especially for young minority men with limited education and work skills. Many young men move back in with family members as they attempt to find legal ways to support themselves after release from prison. They frequently start out optimistic about their ability to improve their lives, but become demoralized when they cannot find opportunities to earn a legal living (Trimbur 2009). After struggling for a period of time without success, many reengage with the criminal economy as a way to survive. Yet those who manage to find employment and some stability after prison often reevaluate their participation in such criminal activity as they get older. In part this is a matter of realizing that they will be sentenced more severely if they are convicted again. Their expectations of the potential outcome of criminal activity changes and their perception of the risks of criminal behavior loom larger. As a 46-year-old convicted thief explained:

> If I go out there and commit a crime now, I got to think about this: Hey, man, I ain't got to get away with it. See what I'm saying? I have—man, it would be just my luck that I would get busted. Now I done fucked up everything I done tried to work hard for; man, you know, to get my little family together.
>
> —Shover (1985, p.123)

Still others street thieves fail to find or take advantage of opportunities to create more stable and pro-social personal lives. Many lose their lives to drugs and violence on the streets of urban America. Yet, others end up re-offending and cycling through long prison terms. And many struggle to eke out a life as "urban outcasts" (Wacquant 2008) in big city ghettoes across the country.

BLURRED BOUNDARIES II: A COLLEGE EDUCATION FOR PRISONERS?

For over two decades the US state and federal criminal justice systems have emphasized a tough on crime approach to street crime that has included mandatory minimum sentences for many crimes, three-strikes laws that require a life sentence after three felony convictions, and various other policies that result in long prison sentences and the elimination of many programs to help prisoners reenter their communities after release from prison. As part of the tough on crime approach, the 1994 Violent Crime Control and Law Enforcement Act eliminated Pell educational grant funding for "any individual who is incarcerated in any Federal or State penal institution." Many tough on crime proponents argued that public funds should not be used to provide lawbreakers with educations benefits. If taxpayers' money had to be spent, they asserted, it should be directed to having more police on the streets and more prisons to house the criminals they catch. In New York, the number of college programs in state prisons dropped from 70 in the early 1990s to just four in 2004, while the number of college degrees awarded to inmates fell by more than 85 per cent.

Today, over 20 years since President Bill Clinton signed the Violent Crime Control and Law Enforcement Act into law, the United States has the highest incarceration rate of any country in the world and federal and state budgets are challenged by the cost of running America's prison complex. Incarcerated offenders experience long prison sentences and when they are released, they face major challenges finding ways to live meaningful and productive lives.

Some lawmakers and policy analysts have begun to reconsider the value of providing college education to prison inmates. Maryland Congresswoman Donna Edwards and several other members of the House of Representatives introduced the Restoring Education and Learning Act in the spring of 2015 and the Obama Administration has proposed a US Department of Education plan that would provide new education grants under the "Second Chance Pell" program (*New York Times* Editorial Board 2016). Several studies, including those by the Vera Institute of Justice (2016) and the UCLA Department of Policy Studies (Bazos and Hausman 2004), suggest that investing in prisoner education is both more humane and cost-effective than punitive incarceration. In their multifaceted analysis, UCLA professors Audrey Bazos and Jessica

Hausman estimated that "a one million dollar investment in incarceration will prevent about 350 crimes, while that same investment in [correctional] education will prevent more than 600 crimes." The bottom line, they argue, is that "correctional education is almost twice as cost effective as incarceration" (2004, p.2). The Rand Corporation has also found considerable value in correctional education programs, reporting that "in general, inmates who participate in an education program are forty-three percent less likely than other inmates to return to prison within three years of release" (Davis et al. 2013).

However, in some quarters there is vocal opposition to offering college education to criminal offenders. In 2014, when New York Governor Andrew Cuomo proposed spending one million dollars on college classes in prisons (out of a $2.8 billion Department of Corrections budget), he was forced to rescind his proposal under a torrent of opposition from legislators who objected to "rewarding lawbreakers" by offering them college classes. In response to Cuomo's proposal one prominent politician spoke about how he and his wife were saving to pay for their children to go to college. "Maybe we should sit down our 10-year-old son," he commented, "and explain how to rob a bank" (Gonchar 2016). A less caustic, but equally opposed state senator explained her position with a statement that, "College is so expensive, I think it sends the wrong message to people who follow the law and play by the rules" (Morris 2014).

Ultimately two different, but interrelated, arguments are made in support of providing education for incarcerated street crime offenders. One argument is that offenders should be offered a chance to improve their lives by pursuing education and job training that will enable them to live more fulfilling and law-abiding lives upon their release. The other argument is that society is better served—that the costs of crime are lower and safety of law-abiding citizens is higher—when incarcerated offenders are given educational opportunities. In the years ahead, Americans will continue to debate how best to address the costs and ethics of our criminal justice system.

What kinds of educational opportunities—if any—do you think incarcerated offenders should be offered? If you do believe they should be given educational opportunities, how would you respond to critics who say criminals don't deserve that?

SUMMARY

- Street-level property crime includes such acts as robbery, burglary, car theft, and shoplifting.
- The majority of those arrested, convicted, and incarcerated for street-level property crimes are young lower-class males, largely from African-American and Hispanic descent.

- 10–15 per cent of US citizens are victims of street-level property crimes each year.
- Most property crimes involve larceny-theft (nonviolent theft, including shoplifting). Burglary accounts for nearly a quarter of reported property crime, while motor vehicle theft accounts for about 10 per cent. Robbery is the least common property crime.
- The UCR data we have on street crime are among the most accurate statistics we have on any type of deviance.
- Many criminologists conduct interviews with incarcerated offenders, while a few criminologists interview active offenders.
- Modern western societies extend the right to own property to every citizen and have laws against the taking another's possessions without their approval.
- There are three main social responses to individuals who are identified as thieves, including demanding restitution or repayment, punishing offenders, and seeking to reform them into law abiding citizens.
- In colonial America, what counted as property crime was defined largely by race. Land was taken from Native Americans by legitimized national force and black slaves had few property rights and were considered property of their white masters.
- As business expanded in the United States following the Civil War, train commerce and banks presented opportunities for daring robberies that became part of national lore.
- The American public became increasingly concerned with street crime after World War II.
- By the early 1980s, street-level property crime was declining in the United States. Today, street-level property crime in the United States is about one-third the rate it was in the late 1970s.
- Merton's anomie theory argues that in societies where financial success is highly valued those who do not have legitimate ways to make much money may turn to crime as an alternative.
- Most street-level property crime is spur-of-the-moment activity with very little planning.
- Many persistent thieves are involved in a party lifestyle with heavy drug and alcohol use.
- Over time, often punctuated by prison terms, aging thieves tend to find crime less appealing.
- Mass incarceration of street offenders over the past 30 years has removed many young, especially African-American, men from the streets, increased the length of time that offenders spend in jail and prisons, and created few opportunities for successful reentry into life outside of prison.
- Educational programs for incarcerated property offenders can increase employment opportunities when they are released, but such programs are rare within the US criminal justice system.

KEYWORDS

anomie theory (Merton): Robert Merton's adaptation of the concept of anomie to explain some kinds of crime as resulting from a lack of legitimate ways to achieve socially valued goals, exemplified in street-level property crime among members of the underclass.

broken windows theory: A theory of crime which contends that signs of a lack of order and caring in neighborhoods creates an environment in which criminal activities tend to flourish.

burglary: The crime of breaking and entering a building illegally, typically with the intent of stealing property from the premises.

corporal punishment: Physical punishment, such as whipping or branding, for criminal activity.

felony: Serious criminal acts typically punishable by jail or prison sentences.

larceny-theft: Illegally taking the property of another without use or threat of violence.

life as party: The lifestyle orientation of persistent thieves, focused on drugs, alcohol, sexual conquests, in which the need for money to support their lifestyle motivates them to engage in criminal activity.

misdemeanor: A criminal offense that is defined as less serious than a felony and punished less severely.

motor vehicle theft: The criminal act of stealing or attempting to steal a motor vehicle.

reform: Criminal justice corrections practices focused on changing bad attitudes and behaviors of criminals.

retribution: Punishment inflicted as revenge for a criminal offense.

restitution: Court-mandated payment or service to crime victims as repayment for harm or loss of stolen property.

robbery: The illegal taking of another person's property in their presence and by the use of violence or intimidation.

street crime: Crimes such as robbery, theft, street prostitution, and inner-city drug dealing that occur in public places and are associated primarily with lower- and working-class populations.

white-collar crime: Illegal and harmful actions of elite members of society, such as business men and government officials, carried out for economic gain in the context of legitimate organizational or occupational activity.

three-strikes laws: Laws that require courts to impose harsher sentences, such as longer prison terms, to offenders who are convicted of three or more serious criminal offenses.

CHAPTER 8

White-Collar Crime

Crime in the suites (Bill Varie/Alamy Stock Photo).

CONTENTS

LEARNING OBJECTIVES

After reading this chapter, you will be able to:

- Describe the most common types of white-collar crime recognized in the United States today
- Explain the challenges and strategies for studying white-collar crime
- Identify different historical definitions, causal explanations, and responses to white-collar crime
- Apply anomie theory to white-collar crime
- Analyze the interactional contexts in which white-collar crimes most often occur
- Explain the ways in which white-collar offenders manage the stigma of white-collar crime
- Assess the arguments for and against pardoning philanthropic white-collar offenders

BLURRED BOUNDARIES I: TWO WHITE-COLLAR CRIMES

The business career of Bernard Lawrence "Bernie" Madoff in many ways exemplified the American Dream of financial success—at least until late in 2008. After marrying his high school sweetheart and graduating from college in 1960, Madoff used money he had earned from a summer lifeguarding job and a loan from his father-in-law to start an investment firm, Bernard L. Madoff Investment Securities. His father-in-law, a retired certified public accountant, helped Madoff attract clients. Madoff's early success in investment grew in part through using computer technology to disseminate stock quotes, which led to the creation of the NASDAQ (National Association of Securities Dealers Automated Quotations) where Madoff would later serve as chairman of the board. As his reputation grew, Madoff became famous in investment circles and by the 1980s his firm was handling nearly 5 per cent of the trading on the New York Stock Exchange. His clients included a range of social luminaries including movie producer Steven Spielberg, actor Kevin Bacon, and the Holocaust survivor and humanitarian Elie Wiesel.

As his company grew, Bernie Madoff employed many of his family members, including his sons who worked as investment traders. He and members of his family served widely in financial organizations, including those that oversaw regulation of the securities industry. Madoff and his brother, Peter, sat on the Board of Directors of the Securities Industry and Financial Markets Association (SIFMA).

Madoff and his family lived an upscale life with private jets at their command, a 55-foot yacht at their mansion in Palm Beach, Florida, another ocean side mansion in Montauk, New York, and a fashionable Upper East Side apartment in Manhattan. Madoff's American Express card charges for January 2008 illustrated the family's lavish spending, with a single-month bill of over $100,000 that included charges for designer clothes in Paris, limousine services, and a host of expenses for a Jackson Hole ski vacation.

But by December of 2008 Bernie Madoff's fame was no longer that of an investment genius, but rather that of the perpetrator of the largest financial fraud in US history. He was arrested on charges of securities fraud and pled guilty to money laundering, theft from employee benefit plans, perjury, and false filings with the Securities Exchange Commission. Most of the billions of dollars his clients had invested with him were nowhere to be found—either spent on lavish lifestyle, lost on investments, or siphoned away. After pleading guilty, the 71-year-old Madoff was sentenced to 150 years in prison.

The story of Bernie Madoff's use of his power and privilege to steal the money of those who trusted him stands as a clear example of white-collar crime. But not all white-collar crime is as obvious and convincing. Consider the following case brought by hemophiliacs against US drug companies and their executives.

In the late 1990s, many US pharmaceutical company executives had reason to worry that they could be brought up on criminal charges for selling blood products that led to HIV infection of many Americans. Over the preceding decade, thousands of hemophiliacs had become infected with HIV from blood products. Several US drug companies produced and sold potentially infected products without notifying hemophiliacs of the enormous risks they faced every time they used the medications. Around the world, many of those in charge of protecting the blood supply were held accountable for similar acts. In France, a former Prime Minister was charged with manslaughter in relation to contamination of that country's blood supply. In Japan, drug company executives and a prominent physician were sentenced to prison terms for not having protected citizens who relied on them to insure the safety of the blood supply. The tragedy in the United States was especially severe. In Japan, an estimated 1,800 people had been infected, and in France about 4,000. In the United States, it was estimated that contaminated blood products infected 6,000–10,000 hemophiliacs. A "Committee of Ten Thousand," named after the potential 10,000 infected US hemophiliacs, pursued legal action against the drug companies. Their case against the companies included evidence that the companies had collected blood from prison populations that were at much higher risk of infection than the general population and had failed to recall products that were known to have great risk of contamination. The drug companies refused to release information that could have helped show what they had done. Nonetheless, the damage was done and by the early 1990s medical experts estimated that as many as 80 per cent of all US hemophiliacs who had received Factor VIII blood products between 1980 and 1985 would die of AIDS-related disease (Perey 1991). While not admitting responsibility, the drug companies finally reached a settlement in 1997 for $660 million with victims and their families, but no American companies or CEOs were convicted of any wrongful doing.

Was the devastation of America's hemophiliac community a case of corporate crime and a miscarriage of justice? Many members of the Committee of Ten Thousand who lost their loved ones clearly held the drug companies and their executives responsible, but judgments about the criminality of this tragedy are complicated. Unlike the case against Bernie Madoff, who confessed to his crime, the case against the pharmaceutical companies is laced with complex medical, technological, and legal issues, making it difficult to ever determine whether this was a case of illegal corporate actions or legal business behavior that led to tragic results.

While some of the white-collar crime discussed in this chapter is crystal clear like Madoff's crimes, much of white-collar crime occurs at the blurred boundaries of legal and business life, making it hard to see and understand, even though the costs are enormous.

CURRENT CONSTRUCTIONS OF WHITE-COLLAR CRIMES IN THE UNITED STATES

When we talk about property theft, we tend to think primarily about street crimes like those examined in the previous chapter. Yet, most scholars agree that the costs of street-level property crimes pale in comparison to the costs of white-collar crimes committed by socially privileged thieves in the course of their business and financial dealings. While street crimes and "suite" crimes (so called because they often take place in corporate boardrooms or business suites) both involve acquiring other people's money or goods by illegal means, these kinds of property crimes differ greatly in terms of offender characteristics and the ways in which crimes are committed—and treated.

Types of White-Collar Crime

At the start of the twentieth century, a prominent sociologist of the time, Edward A. Ross, developed the term "criminaloid" to refer to businessmen whose desire for wealth and profit led them to exploit their workers and the general public. The criminaloid, Ross wrote, was a man "who picks pockets with a railway rebate, murders with an adulterant instead of a bludgeon, and cheats with a company prospectus instead of a deck of cards" (1907, p.7). Such criminals, he observed, were often rewarded for their crimes against their fellow men even though their actions threatened the very foundations of justice. Thirty years later, criminologist Edwin Sutherland proposed the term "white-collar criminal" to similarly describe "crime in the upper or white-collar class, composed of respectable or at least respected business and professional men" (1940, p.1). Sutherland argued that white-collar crime had a long history in the United States and, like Ross before him, he pointed out the staggering costs of such crime.

The definition of white-collar crime used in this chapter comes from David Friedrichs' book, *Trusted Criminals* (2010). White-collar crime, says Friedrichs, involves "the illegal and harmful actions of elites and respectable members of society carried out for economic gain in the context of legitimate organizational or occupational activity" (2010, p.6). White-collar crime can be an act of an individual (such as much of Bernie Madoff's investment fraud) or it can involve collective activity over a span of time. Among the most common types of white-collar crimes are investment scams, insurance fraud, tax evasion, and environmental crimes.

Investment scams involve stealing people's money by offering fake or overstated opportunities to invest at incredible rates of profit. Rather than actually investing the money, those in charge of the investments steal some or all of the money, as did Bernie Madoff. One of the most common types of investment scams is a *Ponzi scheme*, named after an early twentieth-century con man,

Charles Ponzi, but more associated today with Madoff. Ponzi schemes involve offering investors exceptionally high returns on their investments, but they are a scam because the high returns investors make are creamed off of the money invested by people coming after them. As long as continually more investors kept coming to Madoff with their money, he was able to keep investors believing in his promises, even as he siphoned off money for himself and his relatives. When the economy tightened and investors became anxious, federal regulators began to take a close look at Madoff's accounts and saw that he had kept fake records and lost tens of billions of dollars of investors' money. Given the complexity of financial and accounting transactions, few white-collar criminals commit investment scams alone—but often who was aware, or should have been aware, of the criminal activity is difficult, if not impossible, for investigators and the courts to decide.

The massive healthcare industry in the United States has also been the site of significant white-collar crime, revealed perhaps most strikingly in high-profile cases of Medicare *insurance fraud*. Medicare is the federal program that provides health insurance to older Americans, with nearly 45 million Americans on Medicare and annual expenditures of over $600 billion in recent years. Given the enormous amount of money involved and the intricacies of healthcare and billing, Medicare has presented exceptional opportunities for some physicians and other healthcare providers to submit false claims, such as billing for services that were not provided or conducting unnecessary services and tests. In July 2016, the federal government charged several healthcare service providers in Miami for filing false claims of nearly a billion dollars for nursing home services over a fourteen year period (Weaver 2016). While it is impossible to know the full extent of Medicare fraud, several observers have suggested that it may account for as much as one out of every seven dollars spent by the Medicare program.

The costs of Medicare fraud are shouldered by American taxpayers—the people who fund the Medicare and other government programs and services. But a significant number of individuals and businesses engage in *tax evasion* to avoid paying the amount of taxes that they are legally required to pay. Tax evasion is by no means limited to the wealthy, but the amounts that stand to be gained by ordinary workers who cheat on their taxes are miniscule compared to the savings that large corporations can achieve by misstating corporate earnings or costs. So, for instance, businesses may use "shell companies" in the Cayman Islands or Bermuda to hide their profits or engage in transfer pricing schemes, such as selling their corporate logo to a subsidiary in a low tax country and then paying a high price to rent it back, thus shifting their profits out of the United States. Through sophisticated accounting and bookkeeping practices, many companies find ways to make large profits and avoid paying taxes—and even to receive government rebates. In stark contrast to street-level theft, where it is typically easy to recognize if a crime has been committed, white-collar and corporate tax evasion is often so complex that even experts may disagree about whether or not a company has illegally cooked its books.

A fourth important category of white-collar offenses involves *environmental crimes*. Environmental crimes can be broadly defined as illegal acts which directly harm the environment, such as unauthorized disposal of hazardous material or discharge of pollutants into the air, water, or ground. The first significant environmental protection law was enacted by the US Congress in 1899 when the Rivers and Harbors Act made it illegal to dump waste into waterways without a permit from the Army Corps of Engineers. But there was little governmental concern with environmental pollution and damage to ecosystems before several dramatic events highlighting environmental damage in the 1960s and 1970s. One such event occurred in 1969 when the Cuyahoga River near Cleveland caught fire because of volatile wastes that were being emptied into it. When *Time* magazine's cover profiled a photo of the flames on the river, public and governmental concern rose and ultimately led to the creation of the Environmental Protection Agency (EPA) and the passage of laws to govern the creation and disposal of hundreds of toxic chemicals.

Each of the types of white-collar crime described above illustrates financially motivated illegal behavior by business people and/or government officials. The personal, physical, and financial damage done by white-collar crimes is immense. Environmental harm, associated with pollution of the air, land, and water, injure and kill more people than street crime on an annual and daily basis. Banking fraud and insider trading erode young people's opportunities to afford buying homes and senior citizen's retirement security. The losses associated with white-collar crime are so enormous, scholars have argued, "that they are difficult to estimate in any accurate manner, so large as to make the losses to street crime seem paltry" (Burns et al. 2008, p.xix).

Statistical Snapshot

Despite the huge costs of white-collar crime, unlike street crime, we have very limited concrete data on its prevalence. Efforts to collect information on financial crimes by CEOs and other powerful elites from corporate and governmental offices are fragmented at best—and at worst, officially distorted. In many cases, the best data we have are those derived from journalistic and legislative investigations into major scandals—such as the financial debacles associated with Madoff Investments and Enron. But such cases are only the tip of the iceberg. No central clearing house exists for collecting and analyzing data related to white-collar crime. Compared to the statistical snapshots we can compile for other types of deviance examined in this book, in the case of white-collar crime, we have a statistical black box. The lack of accessible data presents unique challenges for researchers seeking to understand white-collar crime.

CHALLENGES IN RESEARCHING WHITE-COLLAR CRIME

Social scientists have bountiful quantitative and qualitative data to address the extent and nature of street-level property crime. In contrast, there is little support for research on white-collar crime. The number of government and nonprofit funding sources for street crime and juvenile delinquency research is huge in comparison to funding opportunities to study corporate crimes. Additionally, corporate offenders have the ability to keep their activities secret from investigators' prying eyes. Of all the categories of deviance discussed in this book, none presents more difficulty for study than "elite deviance."

Counting Crime in the Suites

There are several reasons for the shortcomings of official data on white-collar crime and criminals. For one thing, while people usually recognize a street crime when it occurs, white-collar crimes are far more difficult to see when they happen. Unlike many street crimes, individuals victimized by environmental crimes may not know that they have been victimized or may be unable to identify the source of their injuries. Fraudulent practices by corporations, such as insurance fraud and tax evasion, may ultimately cost large numbers of citizens, but these crimes are far beyond the skills of most of us to recognize. Further, many people feel uncertain about who to go to for reporting white-collar crimes. While we all know that we can go to the police to report the theft of our car, it can be far more difficult to figure out who we should report what we believe is intentional double-billing of hospital charges or suspected illegal toxic waste disposal by a factory.

In fact, we may not know if what we have seen is a crime or not or who is responsible for it. A significant amount of white-collar crime involves the concerted acts of many people in businesses or government acting across time and space—so there is no one person who committed the crime, nor one specific place and time at which the crime was committed. Without a single agency or set of agencies focused on responding to white-collar crime, there is no standardized set of data that can be used to generate a white-collar crime counterpart to the *Uniform Crime Reports* that the FBI compiles for street crimes. The *UCR* data do include certain types of "occupational crime," but they collect only low-level occupational crimes like embezzlement of corporate funds by an individual, rather than more complex (and lucrative) elite crimes like price-fixing and insider trading. James Coleman has argued that most of what gets counted as white-collar crime in the *UCR* statistics would not be counted under most traditional definitions of white-collar crime (2006, p.9). Finally, while virtually all of us agree about what constitutes a street crime like robbery, white-collar crime often involves gray areas, including such things as controversial business practices or of changing regulations regarding toxic chemicals or potentially harmful medications. At times, it may be clear that an individual or group of people has suffered harm, as in the case of HIV-infected hemophiliacs, but far less clear whether that injury is legally a crime.

The foregoing issues make it difficult to get good data regarding the extent of white-collar crime in American society. But the investigation—and social control—of elite deviance is also obstructed by the fact that the well-connected individuals and groups who commit white-collar crimes use their power and influence to define their actions as acceptable and to protect themselves from detection and prosecution. Businesses and government elites have many sophisticated legal and social safeguards to avoid punishment for questionable behavior. Elite wrongdoers often have deep pockets out of which to pay for the best attorneys. In the years since Enron executive Jeffrey Skilling was charged with—and convicted of—insider trading and securities fraud, for instance, he has paid tens of millions of dollars to his personal defense team and kept his case on almost constant appeal. White-collar criminals are also often able to hide evidence of their wrongdoing, as in the case of CEOs of cigarette manufacturing companies who maneuvered to withhold evidence that their companies promoted the development of cigarette additives that would increase their addictive quality (Glantz and Balbach 2000).

Sociologists and other social scientists studying white-collar crime are faced with the daunting task of collecting and analyzing large amounts of data from a variety of sources to get anything close to a full picture of even one major case of white-collar crime. Often criminologists studying white-collar crime collect their data from government reports, Congressional hearings, and investigative media accounts. But as Coleman notes, "it is clear that the funding for such efforts is so small and the investigators themselves are so compromised that only a small percentage of the offenses ever comes to light" (2006, p.9). Further, there is little support for research on white-collar crime.

Given the challenges in collecting data, the aggregate impact of white-collar offending is impossible to measure with any degree of precision, but most scholars estimate that the costs of these crimes far exceed those of conventional street crimes. How can so many criminologists claim that white-collar crime is our most serious crime problem? The answer, says Coleman, is simple. "The crimes we know about are so huge, and their consequences so devastating, that they dwarf any known street crime" (2006, p.8). Rosoff et al. (2014) estimate that white-collar crimes cost Americans $250 billion per year, about 14 times the estimated yearly costs of robbery, burglary, assault, and other street crimes. Even a single white-collar crime or a cluster of related offenses can take a staggering toll. The Enron scandal, for instance, cost nearly 20,000 employees over two billion dollars in retirement funds and resulted in tens of billions of dollars in losses to creditors (McLean and Elkind 2004).

Getting Close

Just as researchers find it more difficult to locate and count white-collar crimes than street crimes, they also find it harder to get access to white-collar criminals themselves to learn about their views and the contexts in which they commit their illegal acts. By virtue of their elite status and the resources they control, white-collar criminals have many ways to protect themselves that lower-class street offenders do not have. It is one thing (however challenging) to gain access to the settings in which street criminals work and interact, and quite another to get into corporate boardrooms and elite country clubs where upper-level business and governmental elites socialize and conduct business, including the business associated with white-collar crime.

In addition, gaining admission to elite settings does not lead automatically to open access to information about potential white-collar crime. Business people and government officials are often careful about sharing sensitive information—especially with outsiders who are interested in the "inside story." It can be difficult to get access to elite corporate and governmental settings when the research focus is on issues related to deviance and corporate ethics. Not only do business elites fear bad publicity, but they are also often extremely busy and unwilling to take the time to talk to prying outsiders. As Peter Yeager and Kathy Kram observe, "The organizational resistance to research by outsiders is rooted in the bureaucratic instinct to protect against intrusion into potentially sensitive matters and the unproductive use of valuable managerial time" (1990, p.130).

In the past, like deviance scholars investigating other topics, some social science researchers in business settings relied on covert observation. In his classic 1950s study of business management, Melville Dalton did not even attempt to propose his research to top management. "I have seen other researchers do this," he explained, "and have watched higher managers set the scene and limit the inquiry" (1959, p.275). Instead, Dalton covertly conducted his study as an employee in two companies, at times even getting other employees to steer conversations in directions with managers as he secretly took notes on what they said and did.

While some journalists today still engage in covert observation, social science researchers are required to openly identify themselves to those they are studying. Still, in doing so, they find it useful to frame their research in terms that are nonthreatening and relevant to business interests. In his study of corporate ethics, Robert Jackall decided to explain his research to business executives as a study of "public relations" and of corporate managers' perceptions of "how their values and ethics appear in the public eye" (1988, p.15). Similarly, Peter Yeager and Kathy Kram (1990) carefully framed the focus of their study of corporate decision-making to minimize how threatening it might feel to business elites.

Finally, access into corporate settings and governmental agencies is often multilayered, requiring researchers to build relationships with personnel at many different levels in order to see the bigger picture. In contrast to most street crime, much of white-collar crime is *organizational crime* committed by a set of people in and across organizations and over a protracted period of time. Researching such activities takes enormous time and energy, and may become particularly complicated when workers at different levels of an organization, or across different agencies, are in conflict with each other. Gaining access to one organization, or part of an organization, may limit access to other levels and groups, as when researchers gain valuable access to one key *whistleblower*, or informant, only to find themselves shut out from communication with officers and gatekeepers in the organization.

Given the many challenges in researching white-collar crime, as well as the limited funding that is available for researching such deviance, many white-collar crime researchers rely largely on governmental investigations and hearings in which business elites are interviewed. At least Congress can demand an appearance and testimony from even the rich and powerful, although it is common for CEOs to invoke their Fifth Amendment right to remain silent when brought before Congressional investigators. In short, those who are socially powerful and privileged are often able to hide their financial crimes from view, even from the most probing of sociological researchers.

CROSS-CULTURAL CONSTRUCTIONS OF WHITE-COLLAR CRIME

Property crime extends back in history as far as human cultures have conceived of the notion of property as something that could be owned by individuals. Most historical human cultures specify some property rights and by virtue of this also identify some kinds of taking of goods or money as a form of theft. In small societies with minimal wealth and belongings, most theft was limited to property crimes relatively similar to those discussed in the previous chapter. In larger and wealthier societies, there are far more complex and profitable ways to rob people of their money and belongings. Consistent with the social constructionist approach to crime and deviance, we must keep in mind that no activity can be considered robbery or criminal theft until it has been defined as a crime. Across much of human history privileged and powerful individuals and social classes have exploited less powerful people without their actions being considered criminal. Rights of property ownership, access to government funds and support, and favorable tax laws often have been negotiated by elites to privilege themselves and their families. Still, several kinds of exploitation have been defined as crimes of privilege in many societies.

Different Definitions

White-collar crime is based on the offender's privileged social status or access to material resources and information. Many societies have defined several kinds of privilege-based exploitation as morally reprehensible and illegal.

Hoarding or monopolizing of precious resources, such as food, in order to be able to sell them at inflated and unfair prices has been condemned as immoral at least as far back as early Talmudic scriptures (Sharfman 2007). In Shakespeare's play, *Coriolanus*, the citizens of Rome lash out against the ruling elite who are hoarding food supplies—a drama made all the more disturbing today since historians have recently suggested that Shakespeare himself may have been involved in illegally hoarding grain during the disastrous plague years of the late 1500s (Lee 2013).

Fraud, or falsification of information related to financial transactions, has also been morally condemned in both religious texts and laws. One of the earliest recognized legal documents, the Code of Hammurabi (from approximately 1750 BC), records ancient Babylonian laws against tampering with weights and measurements for food and other commodities. Another form of fraud, insurance scams, came into being shortly after the Greeks developed an early form of maritime insurance called "bottomry" to insure against ships sinking at sea with their cargo. Taking advantage of being at sea and away from watchful eyes, several unscrupulous Greek shippers faked sinking boats in order to illegally collect the insurance and then sell their goods at other ports (Trenerry 2009). Fraud can take an almost endless variety of forms, from claims of miracle cures with "snake oil" medications (common in the United States in the early 1900s) to art forgery in which famous works of art are replicated and sold as originals. The emergence of Internet business and personal financial transactions over the past quarter century has opened extensive opportunities for online "identity fraud."

The questionable use of public resources has often led to charges of criminal behavior too. Kings, emperors, and other absolute rulers may have been in positions to legally take advantage of their nation's wealth and use it in any way they desired, including ways that we would consider immoral or illegal today. But less absolute rulers and government officials have often been labeled as criminals for misappropriation of public funds. In the fourth-century BC, Aristotle complained about theft of funds by road commissioners and the architect of the Parthenon itself had to flee Athens to escape charges of embezzlement (von Fritz and Kapp 1950). In the war-plagued years of medieval China, military officials were accused of using the armies and supplies they commanded for private construction projects (De Heer 1986). Human history is filled with examples of powerful people directing public resources to their own advantage in illegal and deceitful ways. While a wide variety of laws and policies in the United States today are designed to protect public funds, news of politicians and government officials abusing the public trust are common themes in investigative journalism.

What is perceived as a white-collar or elite crime has varied from one culture to another. Today in the United States we do not allow one class of people to own other people as property, as was legal until the passage of the 13th Amendment in 1865. But it is also important to recognize that some financial activities that we accept today have been considered crimes in other cultures. Perhaps the best example of this is the practice of *usury*, or the loaning of money with a requirement that the person taking the loan repay it with interest. Philosophers as far back as Aristotle have viewed usury as immoral and both the *Bible* and the *Qur'an* have passages in them that forbid the loaning of money for interest. Throughout much of Christian history theologians and church leaders have defined lending for gain as a sin. During the Reformation, Martin Luther proclaimed vehemently that anyone who charged interest was a thief and murderer, and in 1745 Pope Benedict XIV issued a papal decree that renewed the Church's position that usury was a sin (Jones 2010). In France, the ban on usury continued until the French Revolution (McManners 1998) and today the practice of lending for interest (without risk to the lender) continues to be viewed as immoral in many Muslim societies.

In contrast to Islamic and earlier Christian views, lending for interest is widely practiced throughout western societies today. In the United States, interest-bearing credit is fundamental to home and car ownership, and even education, with two-thirds of graduating college students holding an average $24,000 in student loans (Mitchell 2012). Yet, in other times and cultures, the loaning of such funds for profit would be viewed as criminal and immoral.

Different "Causes"

Many of the explanations for why socially privileged and powerful individuals engage in white-collar property crime are similar to explanations for street crimes like robbery and burglary. Demonic explanations focus on greed. Greed is listed as one of the seven Roman Catholic deadly sins and cautionary tales throughout European history have warned of the consequences of giving into temptation. Washington Irving's (1865) classic early American tale, "The Devil and Tom Walker," tells the story of a miserly farmer in the American colonies who becomes a greedy loan shark at the Satan's urging, only to lose his soul to the devil in the end.

At the heart of the demonic view of property crime is a belief that temptation can lure people to pursue short-term pleasure at the expense of long-term good. As the *New Testament* counsels, "Lay not up for yourselves treasures upon earth, where moth and rust doth corrupt . . . But lay up for yourselves treasures in heaven . . . For where your treasure is, there will your heart be also" (Matthew 6:19–20). Jesus warned that the combination of temptation and opportunity presented huge moral challenges to the privileged and powerful. "It is easier," Jesus is quoted in the Gospel of Mark, "for a camel to go through the eye of a needle, than for a rich man to enter into the kingdom of God" (Mark 10:25).

From a social science perspective, psychologists and sociologists propose personality and cultural causes for white-collar crime. Numerous psychological studies of personality profiles of white-collar criminals have found that those who engage in such activities exhibit high levels of egotism and low levels of self-control (Ragatz and Fremouw 2010). Sociologists look more at socialization in upper-class families and social life, where competitiveness and a sense of entitlement may lead to expectations and opportunities that encourage pushing the boundaries of acceptable behavior (Shover and Hochstetler 2006).

In contrast to negative views of privileged property crime as based in evil greed, others have viewed greed as an essential part of human nature and necessary for human progress. In an often-vilified 1986 commencement speech at the University of California, Berkeley, wealthy stock-trader (and soon thereafter, convicted white-collar criminal) Ivan Boesky told graduating students and their families, "Greed is all right. I want you to know that. I think greed is healthy. You can be greedy and still feel good about yourself" (*Chicago Tribune* 1986).

The Renaissance Italian philosopher, Niccolò Machiavelli, made an even stronger argument in his political treatise, *The Prince*, that privilege and power should have no relation to morals and that a capable and ambitious ruler should use any means at his disposal to maintain and increase his power. "A savvy Prince, never lacks legitimate reasons to break his promise," Machiavelli wrote (2005, p.78). While a successful ruler should appear merciful and kind, he must rule by fear and deceit—thus elevating immoral and exploitive behavior to the essence of political authority. As the saying goes, "might makes right."

Yet, while it is clear that greed, power, and privilege continue to play central roles in social life today as well as in the past, Machiavelli's view contrasts deeply with the principle, expounded in the US Declaration of Independence and other documents of democratic revolutions throughout the world, that "all men (and women) are created equal." The tension between the rights of all and the privileges of elites is a key feature across cultures in defining what constitutes property crimes and how those who commit them are treated.

Different Responses

Societal reactions to white-collar crime tend to be dramatically different from the harsh punishments inflicted on street criminals. Often the powerful and privileged members of a society feel—quite accurately, based on their experience—that they are largely above the law. For one thing, even though their actions may harm many people—as in the case of tobacco companies' hiding the harmful effects of smoking (Kluger 1996) or reckless speculation by banks that cost investors billions of dollars (Calavita et al. 1997)—their activities often are not specifically illegal. Many types of white-collar crime are largely defined by *civil law* or regulatory policies rather than criminal law. Even when crimes clearly appear to have been committed, wealthy and powerful individuals and corporations can marshal immense legal resources to challenge both criminal allegations and interpretations of the law. Facing such strong and well-funded defenses by white-collar criminals, prosecutors often decide to settle for more modest penalties and no admission of guilt on the part of elite offenders and their companies. Given the great rewards and low risks of detection and prosecution, criminologist John Braithwaite has argued, the real question should be, "Why do so many business people adopt the economically 'irrational' course of obeying the law?" (1985, p.6)

However, just as with other kinds of deviance, different cultures and societies respond differently to white-collar crime. As we saw in the blurred boundaries section at the start of this chapter, both Japanese and French courts prosecuted officials in charge of approving tainted blood products more severely than US courts. Similarly, while in the United States the 2008 banking financial crisis led to banks being offered loans from the federal government, the small country of Iceland reacted to the collapse of its banking system that same year by establishing a well-staffed Special Prosecutor's Office to identify bankers and others who had engaged in fraud, insider trading, breach of trust, and related financial crimes, leading to arrests and prison time for a number of offenders.

At times, the financial crimes and abuses committed by elite offenders can produce extreme reactions, including playing major roles in national revolutions. In Nicaragua in the 1970s, Pedro Chamorro, a reporter for the newspaper *La Prensa*, wrote a series of articles exposing the dictator, Anastasio Somoza Debayle's ownership of blood plasma centers where political prisoners were forced to donate blood that was sold by the dictator's company. When the reporter was assassinated on the streets of Managua, 30,000 people followed the procession to his burial site. Widespread rioting broke out in the city and the Somoza family's plasma centers were burned down in protest (Anderson 1988). Financial corruption was a major factor in other revolutions during the twentieth century as well, including the toppling of the Shah of Iran in the late 1970s and of the Philippines ruler, Ferdinand Marcos, in 1986. Such epic cases of corruption and revolution illustrate the far extremes of elite deviance and white-collar crime across the globe.

HISTORY OF WHITE-COLLAR CRIME IN THE UNITED STATES

While it is uncomfortable for many of us to acknowledge it, property crime, or at least financial exploitation, among the socially powerful and elite has characterized American history since the first Europeans arrived in the New World. As Robert Merton observed, "The history of great American fortunes is threaded with strains toward institutionally dubious innovation" (1968, p.185). The opportunity to exploit the people and lands of the New World for their riches was a key motivation of European royalty and financiers who bankrolled exploration and business ventures in the Americas from the start. While, technically, much of the brutal exploitation of the New World was not crime—since there were no laws regarding treatment of the natives in faraway lands, the looting of civilizations that occurred at the hands of European soldiers and explorers would be considered crimes against humanity by most of us today. In the early 1500s, for instance, the Spanish monarchy embarked on aggressive foreign policies that could only be sustained by gold from the New World. King Ferdinand, in a famous quote, called upon those Spaniards who sailed to the New World, "Get gold, humanely if you can; but at all hazards, get gold!" (Edwards 2004, p.66). Conquistadores like Hernando Cortes, who marshaled the looting of the Aztecs, and Francisco Pizarro, whose forces overthrew the Incas, quickly found that bloody force was the easiest way to rob the New World people of their riches.

Rise of the Robber Barons

The early North American colonies and the fledgling United States, up through the Civil War, was a land of few protections from shady business practices, as well as a land where slavery, genocide, and the usurping of lands and goods from Native Americans were common and acceptable, at least in many white social circles. It was an era populated by both small-scale con artists and powerful businessmen who became legends in their own day by building massive fortunes through often ruthless practices. John Jacob Astor provides a good example. Astor immigrated to the American colonies from Germany in 1784 with $200 to his name, intending to make wooden flutes in his new country. But the ship bringing him to the America was forced to harbor in Chesapeake Bay because of bad weather and he was introduced to the fur trade industry. By the time he died in 1848 he had amassed a fortune of $20 million. Astor's business techniques were often questioned but were almost always successful. "While openly advocating plying the Northwest Indians with liquor in order to make them more amenable to doing business, he was also a renowned philanthropist who actively sought to put forward a kinder image of himself" (Geisst 2004, p.19).

The latter observation—of Astor's philanthropy—captures a common aspect of the lives and actions of powerful white-collar deviants. While ruthless in business, many of them have been generous contributors to philanthropic causes. This was perhaps most dramatically the case with major industrialists, railroad moguls, and bankers of the late 1800s and early 1900s. Widely criticized for harsh treatment of workers and ruthless manipulation and bribery of government officials, these businessmen established monopolies that enabled them to control entire industries and to reap enormous and questionable profits. Excoriated in the press as *robber barons* who hoarded the country's wealth to themselves, these ruthless businessmen also often became major philanthropists. The names of many of these turn-of-the-century captains of industry, including steel magnate Andrew Carnegie, and railroad moguls, Leland Stanford and Cornelius Vanderbilt, are today associated primarily with the universities they founded with what many at the time felt were ill-gotten gains. John D. Rockefeller, considered by many to have been the wealthiest man in human history, created his financial empire in the oil industry through secret deals with the railroads, price-fixing, harsh labor practices, and running his competitors into bankruptcy so that he could buy their businesses at auction. By the 1880s, his company, Standard Oil, had a monopoly hold on the US oil industry and was characterized in *New York World* newspaper as "the most cruel, impudent, pitiless, and grasping monopoly that ever fastened upon a country" (quoted in Segall 2001, p.60). But at the same time, Rockefeller used much of his wealth to support education and healthcare. He gave $80 million to help develop the University of Chicago; funded Spelman College, one of the first colleges for African-American women; and provided key financial support for medical research universities including Johns Hopkins and the Rockefeller Institute (now Rockefeller University). By the end of his life, Rockefeller had reputedly donated half of his billion dollar financial estate to educational, health, and charity causes. As historian Ron Chernow has written, "What makes Rockefeller problematic—and why he continues to inspire ambivalent reactions—is that his good side was every bit as good as his bad side was bad" (1998, p.19).

Progressive Era and Regulatory Control

Despite public and media complaints against the early American robber barons, these industrial and financial moguls pursued business and banking in a society that did little to regulate business activities. As a key scholar of American finance has observed, "One of the great puzzles of American history is just how long Wall Street and its dominant personalities were allowed to remain totally independent from any meaningful source of outside interference despite growing concern over their power and influence" (Geisst 2004, p.5). But at the start of the twentieth century the federal government began to take more interest in setting policies to control big business.

The regulation of US business in the early 1900s was spurred by a combination of public concern and governmental action referred to as the Progressive Movement. Many regulations focused on major public health abuses. Laws to monitor fraudulent and unsafe medical products were among the first to be passed, including the Biologics Control Act of 1902. Public concern over unregulated food production was widespread after a Spanish-American War general proclaimed that spoiled meat sold to the Army by meatpacking companies had killed more troops than had been killed by the enemy in the war (Demaris 1974). Shortly thereafter, Upton Sinclair's 1906 novel, *The Jungle*, vividly portrayed the unsanitary and brutal conditions prevalent in Chicago meatpacking plants of the day. After a federal investigation, in 1906 President Teddy Roosevelt signed into law the Federal Meat Inspection Act to regulate the sanitary processing of meat products. Beyond public health issues, the federal government also moved into the regulation of business and finance. The Federal Trade Commission was created in 1914 to police anticompetitive business practices such as monopolies. In the aftermath of the stock market crash of 1929, the Securities Exchange Commission was established to protect investors.

The legislation against white-collar crime has been primarily monitored and enforced through administrative regulations and civil law rather than criminal law, often leading to a perception that corporate violations of the law are not really crimes. This view was challenged by criminologist Edwin Sutherland in his book, *White Collar Crime*, published in 1949. Sutherland examined the 70 largest US manufacturing, mining, and mercantile corporations, and the legal decisions made against them. He found that each of these businesses had legal decisions against them with an average of 14 decisions against each corporation. But only 16 per cent of the decisions against them were from criminal courts. Most common violations were restraint-of-trade, infringement of patents, unfair labor practices, and fraudulent advertising. Sutherland was outraged by the fraud, profiteering, and tax evasion of many prominent companies during World War II. He considered white-collar crime a kind of organized crime, noting that, like other organized crime offenders, businessmen caught violating the law seldom suffered loss of status among their peers. In fact, the culture of the business world was generally contemptuous of laws that tried to regulate their conduct.

Sutherland's damning portrayal of white collar disregard for the law was censored to delete the names of the businesses he studied when it was first published in 1949. In the heady pro-business years following World War II, the book did not gain public attention. But Sutherland's study surged in recognition in the 1960s and 1970s as critiques of American business resurfaced. The preeminent consumer advocate of those years, Ralph Nader, drew inspiration from what he called Sutherland's "courageous work of criminological scholarship" (quoted on dust jacket of Sutherland 1983). Nader and his colleagues published numerous exposés of corporate America's focus on profit-maximizing over public safety. In the mid-1960s, sociologists and criminologists began to focus significantly more attention on white-collar crime.

The 1970s witnessed a new wave of state action against white-collar crime as part of a broader social movement responding to disillusionment with political and business leaders, including protest over the Vietnam War and the Watergate crimes of the Nixon administration. During this era concern for the environment became a major social and public health issue, leading to creation of agencies to regulate business impact on the environment. The EPA was founded in 1970, growing out of public environmental concern. President Barack Obama's administration was supportive of the EPA's mission and by the end of the Obama presidency in 2017, the EPA employed nearly 20,000 people to monitor air and water quality, mining, and hazardous waste disposal. The functioning of the EPA illustrates the complex and politicized nature of regulating business and policing white-collar crime. The agency's regulations and policies fluctuate over time as businesses and political groups vie for dominance in defining environmental laws and their enforcement. President Donald Trump has expressed hostility for EPA regulations, appointing a new head of the agency who has sued the agency over a dozen times and proposing a 30 percent cut in the EPA budget. When the law changes significantly from one presidential administration to the next, it is easy to see how white-collar crime may be seen by many people as less serious than other kinds of crime, even though its human and environmental consequences may be far more extensive.

White-Collar Crime in the United States Today

Over the past three decades a series of high-profile scandals among US financiers has dramatically illustrated the huge profits in, and national costs of, white-collar crime. In the late 1980s and early 1990s, Wall Street financiers including Ivan Boesky and Michael Milken made hundreds of millions of dollars by illegally trading on insider information related to business deals. Milken, known on Wall Street as the "junk bond king," made a billion dollars in four years at a Wall Street investment banking firm that went bankrupt following his indictment on 98 counts of racketeering and insider trading (Kornbluth 1992). In 1991, Milken took a plea bargain, accepting guilt for a set of lesser charges for which he served 22 months in prison and paid $600 million in fines and restitution. A decade later, Jeffrey Skilling, the CEO of the huge energy company, Enron Corporation, was charged with insider trading after selling his stock in Enron shortly before the public learned of the company's massive accounting fraud that ultimately cost billions of dollars to shareholders and employees (McLean and Elkind 2004). Within a year of Skilling's conviction, WorldCom CEO, "Bernie" Ebbers, was convicted of fraud and conspiracy as a result of MCI WorldCom's false financial reporting, and subsequent investor losses of over $100 billion (Jeter 2004). Between 2001 and 2005, researchers have estimated that just five large corporations (Enron, WorldCom, Qwest, Tyco, and Global Crossing) committed financial frauds resulting in losses of approximately $460 billion (Rezaee 2005).

So, where do we stand in the United States in terms of white-collar crime today? Some scholars argue that the laws against white-collar crime have become so weak that it is basically condoned as acceptable behavior (Snider

CLAIMS-MAKER PROFILE

Elizabeth Warren

Elizabeth Warren is a US Senator from Massachusetts and the most well-known advocate of banking reform and consumer fraud protection in the country. Senator Warren's father worked as a janitor and maintenance worker, and after he suffered a heart attack when Elizabeth was 12, her mother took a job as a Sears catalog-order clerk. At the age of 13, Warren began waitressing at her aunt's Mexican restaurant. An excellent student, she graduated from high school at 16 and entered law school several years later on her first child's second birthday. She earned a law degree at Rutgers University and began researching the impact of bankruptcy on financially distressed companies, women, the elderly and the working poor.

Warren had a distinguished academic career, including 20 years as the Leo Gottlieb Professor of Law at Harvard, where she taught courses on commercial law and bankruptcy and wrote several books on the economic plight of American families. In 2008, she was appointed to a Congressional Oversight Panel to monitor distribution of Troubled Asset Relief Program in the aftermath of the financial crisis of 2007–2008. She has been a vocal critic of lax enforcement of white-collar crime. Her efforts to create stronger oversight of corporate finance led *Time Magazine* to refer to her as a "New Sheriff of Wall Street."

In a recent report, "Rigged Justice 2016: How Weak Enforcement Let's Corporate Offenders off Easy," Warren (2016) criticizes federal regulators for failing to impose meaningful accountability on white-collar crime. While there are regulations and penalties in place to prosecute corporate offenders, Warren argues, "Federal regulators regularly let big corporations and their highly paid executives off the hook when they break the law." At a congressional banking committee hearing in March 2013 she asked Treasury Department officials to justify why no criminal charges were brought against HSBC bank when the bank was found to have laundered huge sums for major drug cartels. After Treasury officials skirted answering her question, she stated in frustration:

> If you're caught with an ounce of cocaine, the chances are good you're going to go to jail . . . But evidently, if you launder nearly a billion dollars for drug cartels and violate our international sanctions, your company pays a fine and you go home and sleep in your own bed at night. That is just not right.

2000). Others point to national opinion polls that show Americans supporting stronger penalties against white-collar criminals (Cullen et al. 2009). In contrast to our solid data on street-level property crime, our data on white-collar crime are so limited and flawed that we cannot state with certainty whether such crimes have decreased or risen. But it is clear that several major changes in American financial markets, including increasing complexity and lack of visibility of financial transactions in the Internet age, the increasing gap between control and ownership of companies, and the deregulation of financial markets, provide new opportunities for business elites to profit illegally at the expense of other Americans.

MERTON'S SOCIAL STRUCTURE AND ANOMIE

As discussed in previous chapters, Robert Merton proposed anomie theory to explain how cultural norms and values can motivate individuals to engage in criminal behavior—and financially motivated crime in particular. Lacking legitimate opportunities to achieve the goal of financial success, poor young men, according to Merton, may "innovate" and turn to street crime as a way to find such opportunities. Merton argued that such innovation is common among members of the lower class because they face strong pressures to be financially successful, but they have few legitimate ways get there.

While Merton focused his analysis of financially motivated crime as innovation primarily on the lower class, he did acknowledge that more affluent Americans feel the pressure (and have opportunities) to pursue financial gain through illegitimate means. Other sociologists have argued strongly that Merton's concept of innovation offers a particularly valuable approach to understanding white-collar crime. Nikos Passas (1990) has argued that societies based on capitalistic principles have cultural and structural contradictions that promote widespread corporate deviance. The dominant goal in capitalist businesses is to maximize profit. By virtue of the competitive structure of capitalist economies, businesses are always under pressure to improve their performance. Further, as corporations compete in a never-ending profit game, they face uncertainty about where the line between legitimate and illegitimate behavior is drawn—and pressure to push to the edge, or even beyond, legal boundaries. Thus, according to Passas, corporate crime is an inevitable byproduct of capitalistic economies. Similarly, Edward Gross (1980) argued that by virtue of the pressure to maximize profits in capitalistic corporations, those who rise to the top tend to be "organizational strainers," who are shrewd, ambitious, and morally flexible.

The career of Enron executive, Jeffrey Skilling, provides a good example of illegal white-collar innovation. After receiving an MBA from the Harvard Business School, Skilling went to work for an energy consulting company where his drive and ambition helped him become one of the youngest partners in the firm. Pushing questionable accounting and investment strategies, Skilling moved up through the business ranks and in 2000 became CEO of Enron Corporation, the largest wholesaler of gas and electricity in the United States. As a reward for growing the company, Skilling received $132 million in compensation.

But six months after becoming Enron CEO, Skilling resigned and quickly sold $60 million worth of Enron stocks. Later that year, Enron Corporation filed for bankruptcy and its stock, which had sold a year earlier for 90 dollars a share, dropped to less than a dollar per share. Quickly it became clear that Enron's revenues and assets had been grossly overstated and the Enron scandal became synonymous with accounting fraud.

Skilling, who had managed to sell most of his stock before the company's collapse, was arrested by the FBI on charges of *insider trading* (selling stocks with insider knowledge) and fraud (in exaggerating corporate earnings). Over the next two years, Skilling spent $40 million on his defense, but was convicted of counts of conspiracy, insider trading, making false statements to auditors, and engaging in securities fraud. He was sentenced to 24 years in prison (later reduced to 14) and fined $45 million.

Since "financial success" does not have a clear upper limit, the value that American society places on material riches can motivate even the wealthy and powerful to use questionable or illegal opportunities to get ahead—even further ahead than they already are. Skilling is hardly alone in his insider trading. A recent *Wall Street Journal* examination (Pulliam and Barry 2013) found widespread examples of senior executives selling large volumes of their company stocks for high prices—based on optimistic reports of their companies' futures—shortly before negative news and a drop in their stock's value. About three-quarters of the 2,389 corporate officers who sold between swings in company reports would have received less money if they had waited. While the *Journal* investigators could not say with certainty that individual corporate officers knew of the looming bad news about their companies, it seems highly unlikely that they made such overwhelmingly profitable decisions just by chance.

INTERACTIONAL CONTEXTS AND ETHNOGRAPHIC VOICES

All financial crimes involve some action or set of actions through which money or belongings are illegally taken from one or more people. However, the nature of the interaction between the perpetrators, the victims, and the criminal justice system varies significantly, depending on whether the property crime involved is street crime committed primarily by poor, young, and often minority males on the one hand, or elite property crime engaged in predominantly by affluent, well-educated, adult males on the other.

If "life as party" provides a social context in which street criminals decide to pursue street crime, the social world of affluent Americans provides a different set of social experiences and values from which white-collar offenders pursue more sophisticated and rewarding financial crimes. In their book, *Choosing White-Collar Crime*, Neal Shover and Andy Hochstetler provide insights into what they refer to as the *generative world* of white-collar crime. As they point out, studies of street crime "invariably highlight the importance of childhood pathologies. Poverty and dysfunctional families are pointed to repeatedly as problems" (2006, p.63). One can also make the case, they argue, for connecting white-collar crime with the childhood socialization of upper-class youth. As many studies have documented, the backgrounds of upper-middle and upper-class children, including those who later become white-collar criminals, are sharply different from those of poor and working-class children. Three key characteristics of their socialization include an expectation of *competitiveness*, a sense of *entitlement*, and *cultural capital*. These characteristics play a central part in creating "effective biographies" in which well-placed affluent American adults can find themselves open to engaging in questionable business practices.

As Annette Lareau has documented in her book, *Unequal Childhoods* (2003), competitiveness is fostered far more strongly in middle- and upper-class than in lower- and working-class homes. Middle- and upper-class children are far more likely to be pushed to compete and excel, and sent the message that their parents and others expect them to succeed. The normative expectation of competitive success, Shover and Hochstetler argue, produces an environment in which rules can come to be viewed as barriers to be overcome and used to advantage rather than followed.

The competitive ethos of affluent American childhoods occurs in the context of a broad sense of social entitlement. From childhoods of privilege, many of those who later pursue white-collar crime are used to being waited on, taken seriously, and giving orders rather than following them. For many white-collar offenders, a sense of entitlement over time develops into arrogance and a belief that they deserve to be treated with respect and deference. "The self-important, arrogant white-collar offender," Shover and Hochstetler note, "is a recurring figure in chronicles of white-collar crime" (p.66). The behavior of Kenneth Lay, who was Jeffrey Skilling's boss at Enron prior to the company's collapse, provides a good example:

> Betrayed a powerful sense of personal entitlement. Long after his annual compensation had climbed into the millions, Lay arranged to take out large personal loans from the company. He gave Enron jobs and contracts to his relatives. And Lay and his family used Enron's fleet of corporate jets as if they owned them. On one occasion, a secretary sought to arrange a flight for an executive on Enron business only to be told that members of the Lay family had reserved three of the company's planes.
>
> —McLean and Elkind (2004, pp.3–4)

Such arrogance and entitlement is buttressed by the enormous symbolic and material rewards that are available to the extremely privileged. The material and social success they achieve provides them with evidence of their importance. In terms of cultural capital, members of the upper class are typically recipients of the best educational credentials available in America.

Among other advantages their educations and credentials provide verbal skills that enable them to challenge arguments that their legal misdeeds are "really" criminal.

The upper-middle and upper class emphasis on competition and entitlement, along with the advantages conferred by their cultural capital and experiences, provides a set of values, identities, and behaviors that Shover and Hochstetler argue facilitate openness to playing loose with other people's rules, and, at times, their money. In a similar vein, James Coleman (2006) argues that white-collar crime occurs in the context of motivation for financial gain (a key feature of the competitive business world) and socially learned neutralizations of business crimes as deviant. Still, the majority of upper-class Americans do not engage in white-collar crime. Those who do commit such crimes, Coleman writes, must be in positions that provide them with the opportunity to gain access to other people's money and property without those people being in a position to protect themselves. As Sutherland wrote, white-collar crime "flourishes at points where powerful business and professional men come in contact with persons who are weak." And when they do, their social status and business connections may offer easy opportunities for huge profits at others' expense. "In this respect," Sutherland continued, "white-collar crime is similar to stealing candy from a baby" (1940, p.9).

Corporate crimes like embezzlement, insider trading, and fraud usually take place within the flow of everyday legitimate business activities and they are often easily hidden for long periods of time. As law professor and former bank regulator William Black has put it in the title of his 2005 book, "*The Best Way to Rob a Bank is to Own One*." With such insider access, Black argues, corporate executives have the opportunity to engage in *control fraud*, using their control of banks and corporations as a cover for financial crimes. Top company officers may use their power to pressure accountants they have hired—and could fire—to misstate earnings through "creative accounting" practices—as was the case with Skilling's and Lay's tactics at Enron. Top managers often have control over information that opens the opportunity for them to embezzle money, hide shortfalls and otherwise defraud investors, shareholders, or the public at large. One well documented type of control fraud involves *pump and dump* strategies in which company executives overstate or pump up the value of a company's income and assets, then sell or dump their stock shares in the company at inflated prices. Such strategies may be years in the making and fly under the radar of regulators by virtue of falsified financial statements. These crimes are often detected only when the company's overinflated value plummets, leaving everyone except the inside investors holding the now all but empty bag. Bernie Madoff, for instance, managed to bilk unsuspecting investors in his Ponzi scheme for over 20 years without being detected—indeed while being widely praised and admired by business leaders across the country.

CONTEMPORARY RESPONSES TO WHITE-COLLAR CRIME

One major difference between street crime and suite crime is that the latter is much more likely to evade detection. For one thing, victims of white-collar crimes are often unaware that they have been victims. While we are very likely to know it if a thief burglarizes our home, few of us would have the information and expertise to know if corporate executives have traded on insider information and damaged our retirement portfolios or engaged in price-fixing and illegally increased the cost of airfare or electricity. Given that few white-collar crimes, in comparison to street crimes, are identified directly by their victims, the reliance on trained law enforcement officials for finding and reporting elite financial crime is especially critical. However, the number of law enforcement officials focused on white-collar crime is far smaller than the number of police and other law enforcement officials directed toward street crime.

Few police officers are trained to monitor and respond to corporate and governmental deviance. Most of the work of policing or monitoring corporate wrongdoing is left to a variety of regulatory agencies, such as the Food and Drug Administration, the Securities Exchange Commission, the Environmental Protection Agency, and the Occupational Safety and Health Administration. Regulatory agencies often have a conflicted dual responsibility of both promoting the industries they oversee and policing them. The Federal Communications Commission (FCC) provides a good example. The FCC is the federal agency responsible for promoting strong communications companies and business practices across the United States. It is in charge of establishing policies and approving company mergers for television, radio, telephone, and Internet providers. It supports businesses with guidance on financial and technical issues and, at the same time, it is the agency responsible for insuring that companies do not overcharge their customers and that citizens' privacy rights are protected. The FCC and many other agencies in charge of monitoring businesses work within regulatory systems that are quite different from the criminal justice system. They have "inspectors" rather than "police," administrative courts rather than criminal courts, and an emphasis on gaining "compliance" from companies rather than on "punishing" offenders. Sutherland argued that the differences in monitoring and responding to corporate and elite deviance have little if anything to do with white-collar crime being less harmful to society. Rather, he wrote, corporate crimes were "administratively segregated and processed differently because the offenders, who are rich and powerful, demand and receive preferential treatment" (1983, p.6).

Preferential treatment, of course, is a matter of interpretation. What seems fair to one business, regulatory agency, or citizen group may seem unfair to others. But business officials have several advantages over the general citizenry in setting the terms for acceptable policies and regulations. Corporate officers have deeper knowledge, experience, and resources (either through their own experience or the experts who work in their field of business) to bring to regulatory deliberations. Additionally, businesses often have much to gain through changes in regulatory law that only slightly affect individuals. A modest increase in legally acceptable credit card interest rates may cost most individuals little more than a few dollars per month, but the credit card company may reap tens of millions in profits. By virtue of the benefits they stand to gain through changes in regulatory laws—as well as the resources at their command—businesses are motivated and able to engage in sustained efforts to influence regulatory policy in ways that citizens at large simply do not have the time, money, and knowledge to replicate.

Given their resources and long-term interest in limiting regulation, many industries have developed the expertise and political lobbying power to influence the agencies that set regulatory standards and consequences for violations in their industries (Frank and Lombness 1988). Through a process referred to as *regulatory capture*, current or former business employees may become the dominant rule-makers for the industries in which they have been employed, a situation that privileges corporate interests. Given the highly politicized nature of regulatory law, many white-collar offenders feel justified in pushing the edge of the law. Attorneys and accountants working for companies are often used to help find creative ways to get around regulations rather than to help businesses follow the rules. Further, as John Coffee has documented in his book, *Gatekeepers: The Professions and Corporate Governance* (2006), lawyers and accountants who work for companies involved in corporate fraud and other wrongdoings are often unwilling to report the misdeeds of their corporate clients.

For a variety of reasons, including difficulty identifying it, a lack of policing, and the social and legal privilege and resources of those who commit it, white-collar crime is rarely prosecuted. Erich Goode has argued that there are quite likely fewer arrests in comparison to actual violations for white-collar crime than there are for victimless crimes like drug sales and prostitution that have no complainant (2008, p.218). Further, there is an erratic fluctuation of prosecutorial fervor toward corporate crime. Major scandals often spur new regulation and increased scrutiny for a period of time. And businesses tighten up their practices when they feel more at risk of getting caught. Following the accounting fraud charges against executives at Enron and WorldCom in the late 1990s and early 2000s, a wave of corporations filed "earnings restatements," suggesting that many executives decided to clean up their books rather than risk being charged with accounting violations (Benson and Simpson 2015). Such business worries ebb and flow over time as prosecutorial fervor waxes and wanes with changes in presidential administrations and with the political fortunes of big business.

When a decision is made to take legal action against a white-collar violation, it is usually a company rather than an individual that is prosecuted. Corporations get fines, but often consider them part of the cost of doing business. The business as a whole, rather than the individual(s) who actually engaged in the violation, absorbs the financial penalty. When executives themselves are charged with criminal activity, they may deny participation in, or even knowledge of, wrongdoings. They often claim what Katz (1979) has called *concerted ignorance*, arguing that they did not have knowledge of the regulations or risks associated with their violations. Enron CEO Kenneth Lay asserted at his trial that he was not aware of the crimes committed by the Chief Financial Officer of the company. Further, he and other executives in the Enron case also argued that they did not commit a crime because they relied on the advice of lawyers and accountants (Coffee 2006). Lay's claims of ignorance were rejected by his jury, but such arguments have worked in many other white-collar crime cases and, as Benson and Simpson note, "the frequency with which it is invoked at trial suggests that in the upper reaches of many corporate hierarchies, concerted ignorance is standard practice (2015, p.130).

In those cases where individuals are charged with white-collar crimes, punishments tend to be significantly lighter than punishments for street crimes involving comparable amounts of money. Then senator and later Vice-President Joseph Biden described a glaring example of this difference in Congressional testimony, stating that:

> Under federal law, if. . .you steal a car out of my driveway and you drive it across [the state line] into Pennsylvania, [the sentence if convicted can be] ten years. Ten years, is federal guideline. But if you take a pension by violating the Employee Retirement Income Security Act, the federal system to safeguard pensions, [it is a] misdemeanor, maximum one year. The pension may be worth $1,800,000. My car may be worth $2,000.
>
> —Reiman and Leighton (2013, p.130)

Further, juries are often lenient toward white-collar criminals, unwilling to impose harsh sentences even when they are available. As Friedrichs notes regarding enforcement of white-collar environmental crimes, "there has been a systematic reluctance [in the U.S.] to imprison environmental offenders or to fine corporate environmental offenders more than a fraction (one to five percent) of the statutory maximum for these offenses" (2010, p.275). Occasionally a high-profile white-collar violator like several of those noted in this chapter receives a heavy sentence, but such punishments are largely symbolic given the large number of white-collar crimes that are never uncovered, let alone prosecuted.

The media also pay less attention to white-collar crime than street crime. While huge cases involving tens of billions of dollars, like the Savings and Loan Scandal of the 1980s, Enron in the late 1990s and early 2000s, and Bernie Madoff's Ponzi scheme conviction in 2009 get considerable coverage, most corporate crime does not have the straightforward sensationalistic appeal of street crime, even though the harm done by corporate crime is far greater. The advantages of social privilege are deeply evidenced in the American justice system. As Reiman and Leighton observe, when we look at "the kinds of crimes poor people almost

PUSHING YOUR BOUNDARIES

Whistleblower Program Response

Randall Watson is a 55-year-old investment advisor for a firm that provides services for university endowments (money donated to universities and invested to build funds for future goals). Over the past two years, Randall and his coworkers have been told to encourage universities to invest in a new fund, "First Five," that promises high returns on investments for the first five years. The company has provided bonuses to staff when new investments have exceeded benchmark goals. Recently Randall received an email in which his supervisor stated that while investments in First Five funds were failing to meet expectations, money from another fund was being "reassigned" to First Five in order to "ensure our bonuses continue to reflect our hard work." Randall believes this reassignment of funds is illegal and will hurt investors, but when he broached the subject with his supervisor he was told, "People higher up than us say it's okay. Who are we to turn down a bonus?"

After several sleepless nights, Randall is considering contacting the US Securities and Exchange Commission. He worries that if he blows the whistle, he will lose his job—and with a blot on his resume for company disloyalty, never find a position in his field again. On the other hand, he has heard of the SEC's whistleblower program that provides monetary incentives for individuals to come forward and report possible violations of the federal securities laws. Going to the SEC website, he finds a Frequently Asked Questions page that explains the program.

Log onto the FAQ page (https://www.sec.gov/about/offices/owb/owb-faq.shtml#P2_764) that Randall has located and read it. Based on the information there, do you think he will feel comfortable contacting the SEC with his concerns? How would you compare the act of reporting this criminal activity with the act of reporting a home burglary?

never have the opportunity to commit, such as antitrust violations, industrial safety violations, embezzlement, and large-scale tax evasion, the criminal justice system shows an increasingly benign and merciful face" (2013, p.123).

STIGMA MANAGEMENT AND RESISTANCE

As we saw in the previous chapter, street criminals seldom report feeling guilty when carrying out their crimes. However, when street offenders are arrested and convicted, they have little expectation that they will be shown sympathy or understanding. They tend to accept that what they did was a crime and that there are negative consequences for their criminal behavior. In contrast, white-collar offenders—even convicted ones—seldom see themselves as criminals. Unlike Bernie Madoff, who admitted that he knowingly committed criminal acts, most of those who are arrested for white-collar crime argue that what they did wasn't a crime and even if it was, they certainly didn't mean to commit a crime.

White-collar offenders support their assertions that they have not committed crimes in several ways. As Michael Benson (1985) notes, they *deny the guilty mind*, asserting that they did not intend to commit a crime or even understand that they had done so. They are nearly unanimous in denying the basic criminality of their actions, which they portray as consistent with broader business practices or so technical that they did not understand they had broken the law. Even though their actions have been defined by the criminal justice system as illegal, they often feel that the behavior they were convicted of should not be considered a crime—or at the very least, not a serious crime on par with street crimes that involve face-to-face confrontation and potential violence.

When white-collar offenders are arrested and subjected to prosecution, they tend to feel maligned by the media and the justice system. One white-collar criminal, interviewed by Mandeep Dhami in his study of convicted white-collar offenders, described his treatment in the press as "slanderous." Another told Dhami, "The local press were negative. The case was badly reported, sensational, and biased against me" (2007, p.65). They also voiced surprise that the judicial system would convict them of crimes. "I didn't expect to be convicted because the trial was so complex," one reported. Yet another recounted, "I was shocked with the judge's negative attitude. Sending a white-collar criminal to prison is a waste of time and money. . . . White-collar criminals are not a danger to other human beings" (2007, p.66).

In contrast to what they perceived as unfair negative treatment from the press and the justice system, the convicted white-collar offenders Dhami interviewed felt that their families, the prison staff, and other inmates viewed them positively. Most of them said their relationships with family members had actually been strengthened through the course of their criminal justice experience. And while they had bad memories of the jails and high security processing facilities they had been housed in during their trials and proceeding, they tended to feel well treated and respected at the minimum security prisons they were sentenced to after conviction. As one reported, "Staff are fine. Everyone is treated as human, rather than a convict. [In the higher security prison] the officers treated everyone like a criminal from day one" (2007, p.66).

In short, convicted white-collar offenders typically experience considerably less stigma and harsh punishment than street-level offenders. They tend to resist stigma by denying a guilty mind and arguing that their criminal activities have not actually harmed anyone. "There's no victim in white collar crime," one of Dhami's informants argued, explaining, "White collar crime isn't a danger to society. There was no visual damage, no one was hurt. It was mostly a financial matter" (2007, p.70). Of course, those whose well-being has been seriously damaged by such financial matters may have a different view about whether anyone was hurt by such crimes.

White-collar offenders' educations, verbal skills, and social capital enable them to frame their actions "through a sanitizing ideological prism, which gives them the appearance of not being criminal" (Simon and Eitzen 2012, p.298). They often buttress their claims of difference from "real criminals" by pointing to their broader social reputations and accomplishments, as illustrated in the case of Michael Milken in the following section.

BLURRED BOUNDARIES II: SHOULD MICHAEL MILKEN GET A PRESIDENTIAL PARDON?

In 1987, Michael Robert Milken made $550 million, more money than any US citizen had ever made in a single year (Eichenwald 1989). Hailed by some as a financial genius, and derisively known by others as the "Junk Bond King," Milken made his fortune through aggressive, complex, and sometimes illegal financial transactions. In 1989, a federal grand jury indicted Milken on 98 counts of racketeering and insider trading (Kornbluth 1992). In 1991, Michael Milken and his attorneys took a plea bargain, accepting guilt for a smaller number of charges for which he was sentenced to 10 years in prison and required to pay $600 million in fines and restitution. He was also permanently banned by the Securities and Exchange Commission from working in the US securities industry. At his sentencing, the judge admonished Milken:

> You were willing to commit only crimes that were unlikely to be detected. . . . When a man of your power in the financial world . . . repeatedly conspires to violate, and violates, securities and tax business in order to achieve more power and wealth for himself . . . a significant prison term is required.
>
> —Stewart (1992)

Milken's sentence was later reduced from 10 years to two, and with credit for good behavior, he served 22 months in prison. Despite the massive fines, penalties, and restitution Milken was required to pay, according to *Forbes Magazine* (2010), Milken is one of the 500 richest people in the world with a fortune of over two billion dollars. Still, even with his enormous wealth, Milken is a convicted felon.

Since the courts will not erase Michael Milken's conviction, he and his lawyers have turned to the President of the United States for a presidential pardon that would remove Milken's conviction from the criminal record. In 2008, Milken hired Washington, DC attorney Theodore B. Olson to push for his pardon with then President George W. Bush. The choice of Olson to make his case to President Bush was no accident. Olson served as solicitor general under President Bush and was his lawyer in the Supreme Court case that stopped the

Florida recount and assured his first presidential election. In the final months of Bush's second term, many prominent people in business, government, education, and medical research wrote letters supporting Milken's pardon.

Why would so many influential people support Michael Milken's appeal for a presidential pardon? One reason may be that Milken has long had friends and supporters in high places who feel he did not deserve to be convicted of a crime. But more importantly, at least in the arguments that have been made publicly for pardoning Milken, his supporters have pointed out that since his release from prison, Michael Milken has raised hundreds of millions of dollars for medical research. Following his diagnosis with prostate cancer in 1993, Milken has contributed millions of dollars personally to prostate cancer research and heads the Prostate Cancer Foundation. Beyond prostate cancer research, he has also championed and helped fund a wide range of other medical research and social causes. Given his charitable contributions, many influential people feel that he has earned the right to be pardoned for his criminal convictions. Andrew von Eschenbach, a former Commissioner of the US Food and Drug Administration, argues that Milken's philanthropy has transformed medical research, raised awareness of prostate cancer, and saved lives. "Forgiveness is something that's an important part of our culture," von Eschenbach told the *LA Times* reporters, adding "Here's a man who is really serving society" (Pfeifer and Petruno 2009).

Not everyone in high places has supported Milken's appeal for a pardon, and both Presidents Bill Clinton and George W. Bush denied his requests. But still, it is clear that Milken has voluntarily contributed huge sums of money to charitable causes that are providing improved medical treatment to people around the globe. The Michael Milken Foundation website states, "Mike (what everyone calls him) is now recognized for his three decades of driving medical research toward cures and improved treatments for all serious diseases" (www.mikemilken.com).

Given his undeniable philanthropic contributions, do you feel Michael Milken should receive a pardon for his white-collar crime conviction over two decades ago? Explain your reasoning for why you believe he should, or should not, be pardoned for his crimes.

SUMMARY

- White-collar crime committed by socially privileged thieves is far more costly to society than street-level property crime.
- The most common types of white-collar crime include investment scams, insider trading, insurance fraud, tax evasion, and environmental crimes.
- Research data on white-collar crime are negligible in comparison to the data we have on street crime.

- Social scientists find it difficult to access elite corporate and governmental settings in which white-collar crime may be planned.
- Demonic explanations of white-collar crime focus on greed, while psychological explanations identify high levels of egotism and low levels of self-control as motivations for white-collar crime.
- Many early American fortunes were amassed through ruthless expropriation of the peoples, lands, and riches of the New World.
- Much of the financial exploitation by early robber barons was not illegal since there were few laws to regulate financial practices.
- The first major laws to regulate corporate activities such as business monopolies, food safety, and stock market trading were enacted in the early 1900s.
- Few social scientists studied white-collar crime until the 1960s when the consumer advocacy movement spurred their interest.
- Merton's anomie theory provides insights into white-collar criminals who tend to be ambitious and morally flexible organizational strainers open to pushing the edge of the legal envelope.
- Given the limited data on white-collar crime, it is unclear whether such crimes have increased or decreased in recent decades, although changes in American financial markets have provided new opportunities for white-collar crime.
- The social world of elite Americans emphasizes competitiveness, entitlement, and interpretive license in following rules.
- Those who commit white-collar crimes must have access to other people's property without those people being in a position to protect themselves.
- Corporate crime takes place within the flow of legitimate business activities and is often easily hidden for long periods of time.
- White-collar offenders are far less likely to be caught than are street offenders.
- Most of the work of policing corporate wrongdoing is left to regulatory agencies that have dual responsibilities for both promoting the industries they oversee and policing them.
- When white-collar crime charges are filed, it is usually against corporations rather than individuals. Executives charged with criminal activity typically deny knowledge of wrongdoings.
- When individuals are convicted of white-collar crime, punishment tends to be much lighter than punishment for street crimes involving far smaller amounts of money.

KEYWORDS

civil law: A type of law focused on establishing responsibility and redressing harm through restitution and fines as opposed to punishment and incarceration of offenders.

compliance: Business adherence to regulations, such as abiding by federal food safety standards.

concerted ignorance: The practice among some business executives of avoiding direct knowledge of illegal activities or covering up their knowledge by claiming ignorance in order to avoid being charged with a crime.

control fraud: When a trusted person in a high position in a company uses their position and power to engage in fraud for their personal gain.

criminal law: A type of law focused on punishing offenders, often by incarceration in jail or prison.

denying the guilty mind: A common assertion by white-collar criminals that although their actions might have been technically illegal, they did not intend to commit a crime.

embezzlement: Illegally appropriating money or property from a company or employer.

environmental crime: Crimes, such as illegal toxic waste disposal, that damage the environment.

fraud: False claims and misrepresentation for financial gain.

generative world: The social contexts and biographical experiences in which individuals become open to participating in different kinds of behaviors, including white-collar crime.

hoarding: In white-collar crime this refers to privately collecting valuable resources (such as food or fuel) in sufficient quantity to profit by dictating the prices others must pay for them.

insider trading: Buying and selling of corporate stocks based on nonpublic "insider" information.

insurance fraud: Filing false insurance claims to receive insurance benefits.

organizational crime: White-collar crime committed by a set of people in and across organizations and over a protracted period of time.

Ponzi scheme: An investment scam in which fake investment profits are paid out to early investors with money put up by later ones until the scam is discovered.

Progressive Era: A period of social activism and political reform in the United States from the 1890s to the 1920s that focused on eliminating political and business corruption and improving the lives of US citizens and immigrants through science and philanthropy.

pump and dump: A corporate executive strategy of artificially pumping up the value of stocks or of a company and then selling one's stock shares or taking cut of the inflated profit before the bubble bursts.

regulatory capture: A situation in which businesses have dominant power in defining the regulations and penalties that apply to them.

regulatory law: Legal regulations created by administrative agencies, such as the Food and Drug Administration, to set official guidelines for businesses and penalties for violations.

robber baron: A derogatory term used widely in the Progressive Era to describe wealthy American businessmen of the 1800s and early 1900s who built their fortunes through ruthless pursuit of power.

securities fraud: Illegal misrepresentation of corporate stocks that encourages investors to buy or sell on the basis of false information.

suite crime: A term referring to white-collar crime as opposed to street crime, based on the location of many white-collar offenders in corporate offices and suites.

usury: The practice of loaning of money for interest, especially at exorbitant rates.

whistleblower: a person who blows the whistle or informs on a person or organization engaged in illegal activity.

SECTION

3

LIFESTYLE DEVIANCE

CHAPTER

9

Alcohol Abuse

Young woman using beer bong (REUTERS/Alamy Stock Photo).

CONTENTS

LEARNING OBJECTIVES

After reading this chapter, you will be able to:

- Describe the most common classifications of alcohol abuse recognized in the United States today
- Explain the challenges of, and strategies for, studying alcohol abuse
- Identify different historical definitions of, causal explanations for, and responses to alcohol abuse
- Apply social learning theory to alcohol abuse
- Analyze the interactional contexts in which alcohol abuse most often occurs
- Explain and give examples of punitive/treatment and contextual approaches to reducing drinking-related problems
- Assess complexities in developing policies to reduce drinking problems among university students

BLURRED BOUNDARIES I: TWO FACES OF PROBLEM DRINKING

Ronald Mooney has a problem with drunk driving. His latest drinking and driving arrest occurred after a police officer observed his pickup truck swerving off the road and into a strip mall. Officers found the bottle of vodka that he had been drinking under the driver's seat. After submitting to a Breathalyzer test, Mooney confirmed the officer's suspicions. He blew a 0.17 blood alcohol level, which is more than twice the legal limit. As it turned out, Ronald Mooney was no stranger to "driving under the influence." This was his ninth drunk-driving charge.

Mooney's latest arrest resulted in a conviction, permanent loss of his driving privileges, and a court-ordered symbolic flattening of his 1988 pickup truck in a county crushing machine. All of us would agree that something needs to be done to stop him from drinking and driving. Ron himself says that he is an alcoholic and needs help. "I'm okay until I have that first drink," he told the judge. "But if I have one, I can't stop." He looked like he was going to cry as he went on to say, "It's ruining my life. Hell, it already has."

When we think of alcoholics, images of people like Ron come to mind. Anti-drunk-driving activists, like the members of Mothers Against Drunk Driving (MADD), point to chronic drunk drivers like Mooney to make their case. He and others like him, they say, suffer from a serious illness and allowing them on the road puts all of us at risk of injury and death. Mooney clearly has a serious drinking problem.

But there are other cases of "problem drinking" that may spark disagreement among us. Consider the case of Meghan Bell. Is she, too, an alcoholic?

Meghan Bell woke up at 2:00 p.m. on Friday, 10 minutes before her last class was starting. Getting to class was the last thing on her mind. She was still wearing her clothes from the day before. Her head was pounding, she was thirsty, and she didn't know why her wrist was swollen and throbbing. As she swallowed a couple Advil, she recalled tripping off a sidewalk curb on her way home from a party late the night before. She remembered swearing at a guy she didn't know while her friends were laughing. But how she got home was anybody's guess.

Looking at her phone, Meghan saw a text message from her roommate. "Meg! You were crazy last night. Give me a call so I know you're okay. Meet me at the Broken Tap at 6:00—if you wake up by then."

Meghan didn't feel like going anywhere. She got a bag of frozen peas to put on her wrist and watched an afternoon soap opera until she felt awake enough to shower. She was feeling much better by the time she got out of the shower. Soon she was checking to see if she had enough money to meet her roommate for drinks at the bar. Later that evening over beer at the Broken Tap, she and her friends laughed about their antics the night before and promised to take care of each other if they got that drunk again.

To many people it seems clear that Meghan and her friends are problem drinkers. But not everyone sees it that way. Meghan and her friends view their drinking as a vital part of their lives as college students, and as a way to unwind, relax, and have fun. Millions of college students across the United States agree that college is a time to enjoy life—the "best four or five years of your life." Are Meghan and her friends deviants? The answer to this question, as we will see, depends on who you ask.

CURRENT CONSTRUCTIONS OF ALCOHOL ABUSE IN THE UNITED STATES

Alcohol abuse represents a major form of deviant behavior in American society today. Addiction specialists and other moral entrepreneurs have developed and publicized different (though often overlapping) kinds of problem drinkers. Among the most discussed categories of deviant drinkers today are the alcoholic, the college binge drinker, and the drunk driver.

Types of Alcohol Abusers

The term *alcoholic* is used today to refer to individuals who are believed to be physiologically and psychologically addicted to alcohol. If they do not receive help, treatment experts say, such individuals will progress through increasingly serious stages of alcoholism, from habitual heavy drinking to extended "benders" and ultimately to alcohol-induced illnesses and death. According to the worldwide self-help program, Alcoholics Anonymous, alcoholics suffer from an in-born vulnerability or "allergy" to alcohol. Any exposure to alcohol, the argument goes, will propel them into uncontrollable drinking. The only thing an alcoholic can control is whether or not to have that first drink. In many people's eyes, including his own, Ron Mooney fits the classic model of an alcoholic.

In contrast to an alcoholic, *binge drinkers* are viewed as reckless young people who lack the maturity to control their drinking behavior. While they do not depend on alcohol to negotiate the stresses of everyday life (as does an alcoholic), binge drinkers are prone to drink very heavily when the opportunity arises. They are episodic alcohol abusers who guzzle beer and hard liquor at fraternity parties and dormitories on the weekends. The binge drinker is seen as a partier who compartmentalizes work and play. He or she seldom parties without getting "wasted," and uses drinking games such as "flip cup" and drinking paraphernalia, like the "beer bong," to maximize and intensify their intoxication. For university health officials, Meghan, the student described above, exemplifies college binge drinker.

The third image, of the *drunk driver*, shifts attention away from the drinker's problems to focus on public harm. People have voiced concerns about drinking and driving ever since the early 1900s, but widespread condemnation of drunk drivers did not occur until the 1980s, when the group MADD (2016b) was created. Laws across the United States today classify anyone who is driving with a *blood alcohol content* (BAC) of .08 or higher as a drunk driver. While alcoholics and binge drinkers may drive when intoxicated, other drinkers do so too. Indeed, at the legal limit of .08, millions of otherwise "normal drinkers" violate the law each year.

Statistical Snapshot

In 2013, the American Psychiatric Association (APA 2013) revised its definition of alcohol abuse into a single diagnostic category of *alcohol use disorder* (AUD). The symptoms for alcohol abuse were modified in the new diagnosis and three levels of the disorder were established—mild, moderate, and severe. According to a study using the new criteria, 29.1 per cent of Americans (18 and older) have met the criteria for mild AUD—and nearly 14 per cent (35 million people) have met the criteria for severe AUD—at some point in their lives (Grant et al. 2015). The study reports that over eight million American adults have suffered from severe AUD in the past 12 months. Rates of problem drinking, researchers and public health officials suggest, are especially high among young adults—nearly twice as high as among the general adult population. Even more dramatically, many researchers have found that rates of college student binge drinking top 40 per cent—making alcohol abuse the most pervasive health problem on college campuses. Finally, approximately 1.1 million *DUI* arrests ("driving under the influence" of alcohol) were made in the United States in 2014—a significant number, but far lower than the estimated 121 million driving episodes by drivers with BAC above the legal limit (Centers for Disease Control and Prevention 2016). Young adults show higher rates for this

Table 9.1 Statistical Snapshot of Problem Drinking in the United States

Problem Drinking	Alcohol Abuse	Alcohol Dependence	College Binge Drinking	Drinking Driving	Drinking Driving Arrests Annually	Alcohol-Related Driving Fatalities
Adults	9.7 million	7.9 million	3.96 million	159 million drinking driving trips	1.5 million	17,602 in 2006
Adult rate	4.65%	3.8%	–	–	–	–
Young adult rate	6.95%	9.24%	44.4%	–	–	42% (drunk drivers 21–34)

SOURCES: NIAAA (2017), Wechsler et al. (2002), Quinlan et al. (2005), Hingson and Winter (2008).

kind of problem drinking too, with over 30 per cent of fatal accident drunk drivers being between 21 and 34 years old. Several statistics regarding American drinking problems are presented in *table 9.1.*

CHALLENGES IN RESEARCHING ALCOHOL ABUSE

Statistics on problem drinking are collected by many agencies and researchers. Like most statistical data, their numbers convey an impression of objectivity and certainty. And like other statistics, they are also based on research decisions regarding what counts as an example of a certain kind of behavior and how to find it. As with other categories of deviance, scholars who study alcohol abuse face a range of hurdles in their research.

Counting Alcohol Abuse

One key challenge for studying problem drinking is getting an accurate count of the people who experience alcohol-related problems. Researchers must define what alcohol abuse is and what the criteria are for counting individuals as alcohol abusers. In the years leading up to Prohibition, many moral entrepreneurs included any and all alcohol consumption as deviant behavior, but few people would support such an approach today. No scholar would be taken seriously if she or he claimed that all of the 60 per cent of American adults who drink alcohol are problem drinkers. So, what should be considered problem drinking—and why?

Researchers and treatment specialists typically define alcohol abuse as a mental illness. According to the APA alcohol abuse is indicated by some combination of the following symptoms: recurrent alcohol drinking that results in the failure to fulfill major obligations; recurrent drinking in hazardous situations; recurrent legal problems related to alcohol use; a craving for alcohol; and continued drinking despite personal problems exacerbated by alcohol use. While these symptoms give us some guidance in deciding whether or not an individual is an alcoholic, there are terms here that can be difficult to judge—such as what "recurrent" means. Some studies ask if the symptom has occurred in the last month. Others ask about the past year. Some ask if it has ever occurred (Grant et al. 2015). The wider the time window, the more problem drinking behavior will be identified.

In an effort to get around the difficulties of defining problem drinking, researchers often specify a certain number of drinks in one episode or how often a person drinks heavily to identify problem drinkers. Binge drinking is commonly defined as five drinks (a shot of hard liquor, a glass of wine, or a bottle of beer) in one episode for a man, and four for a woman. A "frequent binge drinker" is defined as a person who has engaged in three or more binge drinking episodes in the past two weeks. Measures like this are relatively easy to collect, but they assume that most people of the same gender respond similarly to equal quantities of alcohol—an assumption that many of us find inconsistent with our own observations.

One group of problem drinkers that would seem easy to count is drunk drivers. However, counting drunk drivers is more problematic than it first appears. Consider the issue of drunk-driving arrests. As table 9.1 shows, about 1.1 million arrests were made for drunk driving in 2014 in the United States. But given how widespread drinking and driving is in our culture, the number of drunk-driving arrests is a very poor indicator of the prevalence of the problem. Fluctuations in the number of DUI arrests have far more to do with policing than with drinking.

In summary, all counts of alcoholism and other forms of alcohol abuse are social constructions that depend on how drinking problems are defined and on the kinds of efforts and resources that are devoted to identifying "problem drinkers."

Getting Close

In order to gain a close familiarity with the subjective experiences of drinkers, qualitative researchers must spend time observing and talking with them. One common site for ethnographic research on drinking is in bars. Sherri Cavan's classic study of bar behavior (1966) is a good example. Cavan visited bars as if she was any other patron. Her fieldnotes recorded her observations and conversations in and around drinking establishments. Unlike survey researchers, "bar ethnographers" become familiar faces at the bars and get to know many drinkers on a first-name basis. Yet, other ethnographers have found it useful to work as a bartender (e.g., Kotarba 1970) or cocktail waitress (Mann and Spradley 1974) to gain access to a wide range of drinkers and their conversations.

Ethnographers who study drinking among minority and homeless populations frequently engage in "street-corner ethnographies," observing drinking in public settings such as parking lots, parks, and abandoned buildings. At least initially, these researchers may raise more suspicions than those who observe bar populations. While a generation apart in terms of research periods, ethnographers James Spradley (1970) and Thomas Vander Ven (1998) both faced the challenge of convincing hard-drinking street informants that they were not undercover law enforcement agents. Spradley gained trust by proving to be a reliable confidante who would not divulge information to the police and Vander Ven established trust on the corner by serving as a mediator between the often-drunk "corner men" and the police officers called to quell public disorder.

Several other ethnographic studies have focused on Alcoholic Anonymous meetings and talking with AA members. David Rudy (1986) spent 16 months regularly attending AA meetings, while Norman Denzin (1987a, 1987b) attended over 2,000 closed and open Alcoholics Anonymous meetings over a period of five years.

Anthropologist Michael Moffatt (1989) turned an ethnographic eye toward college undergraduate drinking when doing research in a Rutgers University dormitory. While university officials lamented student drinking and fought to control it, Moffatt documented how most dorm residents felt drinking was essential to their social lives. More recently, Thomas Vander Ven (2011) has conducted fieldwork in college bars and house parties and interviewed students. The drinking stories that students shared with him reveal the students' own understandings of their drinking experiences.

By going out to study the real-life contexts in which drinking takes place and seeking to understand the meanings that drinkers themselves attribute to their behavior, ethnographers expand our understanding of drinking in ways that go beyond the dominant negative perspective. Even when we do not accept drinkers' views, it is important for us to recognize the beliefs and feelings that guide their actions as well as the views of those who mobilize against them.

CROSS-CULTURAL CONSTRUCTIONS OF ALCOHOL ABUSE

All alcoholic drinks have the chemical ethanol (C_2H_5OH) as their base. Ethanol can be produced from a wide variety of starchy foods, including honey, sugar cane, grapes, grains, potatoes, apples, pears, and bananas. Alcoholic beverages have varied widely in their availability and potency. The remarkable variation in cultural practices surrounding the use of alcohol led anthropologist Mac Marshall to observe that "The cross-cultural study of alcohol presents a classic natural experiment: a single species (*Homo sapiens*), a single drug substance (ethanol), and a great diversity of behavioral outcomes" (1979, p.1).

Different Definitions

Many cultures have viewed alcoholic beverages as gifts from their Gods. Greek mythology tells of Dionysus, one of Zeus' half-human children, who escaped the wrath of Zeus' wife, Hera, by going to Egypt, where he learned the art of cultivating grapes and wine. Dionysus returned to his homeland to share the ecstasy of intoxicating drink with the Greeks and, later, as the god Bacchus with the Romans. His gift has been widely accepted in western societies where, "Since the Greeks, the drinking of wine, both alone and in company, has been equated with happiness, life, blood, well-being, warmth, and virility" (Sournia 1990, pp.9–10). The Jews also believed in the divine origins of alcoholic drink, as reflected in Solomon's words in the book of Psalms, that God created wine "to gladden the heart of man" (*Psalms* 104:15).

Throughout the Middle Ages, Europeans viewed alcohol as healthful and medicinal. Swiss chemists in the thirteenth century referred to alcohol as *aqua vitae*, claiming it had incredible healing powers (O'Brien and Chafetz 1991, p.xiv). Among the many medicinal effects attributed to alcoholic drinks were the curing of jaundice, deafness, baldness, and failing memory. In France, Arnald of Villanova, an eminent medieval professor of medicine, captured the beliefs of his era when he wrote that alcoholic beverages "strengthen the body and prolong life." Villanova even praised periodic drunkenness as a means of purging the body of "noxious humors" (Babor 1986, p.35).

Not all cultures have embraced alcohol as a gift to humanity, however. Drinking is forbidden in the *Qur'an* and has long been viewed as a sin in Islamic societies. In other societies, alcohol consumption has been accepted, while drunkenness has been widely condemned. While drunkenness drew little more than humorous responses in medieval Europe, by the 1700s it was perceived by many as a serious vice. The growing European perception of heavy drinking as harmful was due to several changes in the drinking landscape. As peasant populations moved from the countryside into industrializing cities, the social consequences of drunkenness became more severe since city immigrants lacked the social support they had before. Second, new distillation processes in the 1700s increased the production of inexpensive and potent hard liquors like vodka and whiskey that got people drunk much faster than beer. Finally, the factories in the industrial cities required higher levels of self-control and dexterity from workers than they had to show when working as field laborers.

Different "Causes"

Just as cultures vary in identifying problem drinking, they also vary in their explanations for why people drink to excess. The most common explanations have focused on sinful temptation and moral laxity. Strong distilled liquors have been particularly singled out for their evil qualities, as captured in the terms "demon rum" and "kill devil rum" reputed to be so strong it could kill the devil himself (Curtis 2007). Explanations of problem drinking as immoral pleasure-seeking have also often been used to explain alcohol abuse among marginalized ethnic groups, as in the stereotype of moral inferiority of the Irish that prevailed during the years of heavy Irish immigration into the United States (Stivers 2000).

Medical explanations of alcohol abuse emerged as modern medicine gained a foothold. Benjamin Rush, a Revolutionary War physician and signer of the US Constitution, contended that while beer and wine produced health and cheerfulness, hard liquors caused intemperance, vice, disease, and death. Alcohol abuse, he argued, was not a matter of low morals, but a physiological effect of strong liquor on the body and mind. Rush's "Moral and Physical Thermometer" which graphed the reputed effects of alcoholic beverages was widely circulated in the United States and Europe. Medical explanations since Rush's time have focused on biological views of alcoholism as caused by inherited genetic vulnerabilities, and psychoanalytic explanations that see alcoholism as caused by mental disorders. Unlike moralistic explanations, medical approaches imply that problem drinking is caused by factors beyond an individual's control.

A third explanation for heavy drinking focuses on stressful social environments. An early example of this approach was provided by Friedrich Engels (1892) in *The Condition of the Working Class in England in 1844*. Engels, a close associate and frequent coauthor with Karl Marx, argued that capitalism's degrading conditions of life and labor for the working class led workers to drink to escape from the harsh reality of their lives. More recently, David Snow and the author of this textbook (Snow and Anderson 1993) have similarly argued that heavy drinking among today's homeless should be understood, at least in part, as a response to their demoralizing and difficult life circumstances.

Different Responses

Governmental and religious efforts to control drinking have a long and varied history. Many religions and societies have sought to restrict heavy drinking. The Code of Hammurabi of Babylonia, dating from around 1700 BC, included various restrictions on the sale and consumption of alcohol. Egyptian documents from the pre-Christian era, as well as writings in the Old Testament and from Greek philosophy call on people to drink in moderation. Some societies, including the United States (from 1919 to 1932) and many Muslim societies (including Saudi Arabia and Iran today), have prohibited the sale and/or consumption of alcoholic beverages. Yet, few societies have managed to sustain a complete prohibition of alcoholic beverages for any extended time. The futility of trying to abolish drinking was captured by Chinese scholars who proclaimed in the *Canon of History* that "to prohibit it and secure total abstinence from [alcoholic] drink is beyond the power even of the sages" (O'Brien and Chafetz 1991, p.xii).

Still, while alcohol has seldom been effectively abolished in societies for any length of time, the drinking of alcoholic beverages tends to be "hedged about with rules concerning who may and may not drink how much of what, in what contexts, in the company of whom, and so forth" (Heath 1987, p.46). Among the most common restrictions have been those forbidding young people, slaves, and colonized populations from drinking.

Many cultures have also prohibited or limited women's drinking (Heath 1987). Even in those societies where women are permitted to drink, it is often more acceptable for males to drink in public and to the point of intoxication (Gefou-Madianou 1992). A historical example of different expectations or double standards regarding male and female drinking is provided by the *jungfrauenbecher*, a jointed, two-part "maiden's cup" for drinking in seventeenth-century Germany that provided a large mug for the man and a tiny cup to hold a smaller measure considered appropriate for a woman (Tlusty 2001, p.134).

HISTORY OF PROBLEM DRINKING IN THE UNITED STATES

Drinking has been part of American history since the earliest colonial settlements. Early North American settlers were strongly attached to their alcoholic beverages. Pervasive negative views of drinking and drunkenness in the United States are of a more recent vintage.

Pioneer America

Colonial religious leaders shared the belief that alcoholic beverages were a divine gift. The Reverend Increase Mather (1673) of the Massachusetts Bay Colony wrote of rum as "the good creature of God," and most church fathers recommended the use of beer, cider, and wine, believing them to be "nutritious and healthful for body and mind, good medicine for many ailments" (Fingarette 1988, p.14).

When alcohol was available, the American settlers drank often and abundantly. Their drinking was not restricted to certain times of day, as it tends to be in the United States today. It was common for adults to have a glass of whiskey before breakfast and during the work day. Farmers took generous amounts of liquor to the fields and, as factories emerged, alcohol was often consumed at work on the shop floor. Nor was it unusual for children to drink. Youngsters were encouraged to partake of the dinner beer, and school children were allowed to take a sip of whiskey during the school day (Goode and Ben-Yehuda 2009, p.13). Between the late eighteenth and the early nineteenth centuries,

Americans drank more than double the average consumption today. "To put is starkly," Lender and Martin write, "American colonists were serious drinkers" (1987, p.14).

However, American colonists were not problem drinkers, at least not in the minds of their companions. As Harry Levine has noted, "During the colonial period most people were not concerned with drunkenness; it was neither especially troublesome nor stigmatized behavior" (1978, p.151). On the other hand, many colonists and pioneers were concerned about potential problem drinking among slaves and Native Americans. In 1685, a West Jersey law was enacted that outlawed the "selling or giving of rum, or any manner of strong liquors, either to negro or Indian, except the stimulant be given in relief of real physical distress" (Herd 1991, p.355). Soon all of the colonies imposed regulations to restrict the sale of liquor to Indian tribes (Lender and Martin 1987, p.24).

Within the social context of white American immigrants and pioneers, drinking and occasional drunkenness had an accepted place in work and play at least until the 1830s. However, as the country became more industrialized, attitudes toward alcohol began to shift.

The Road to Prohibition

Early seeds of concern about alcohol's effects were sown in 1784 by Benjamin Rush's tract, *An Inquiry into the Effects of Ardent Spirits on the Human Mind and Body.* Rush believed that hard liquor represented a threat to the new republic by undermining discipline and morality, but his ideas failed at first to find a substantial audience. By the 1830s, however, American attitudes toward drinking had turned more negative. As urbanization and industrialization increased in the United States, heavy drinking became a more visible problem. Most major American cities, like New York and Boston, developed pockets of impoverished urban squalor that public officials attributed to the effects of alcoholism. Blaming heavy drinking provided an easy scapegoat for those who wished to avoid confronting more structural and economic problems in American society. Additionally, concerns about alcohol were flamed by waves of anti-Irish sentiment as nearly two million impoverished Irish citizens immigrated to the United States from 1830 to 1860.

By the 1830s, the American temperance movement was in full swing, with membership in temperance organizations climbing to 1.5 million by 1835. In 1836, the national temperance convention endorsed total abstinence from alcohol, or "tee-totaling," as the movement's goal. As the movement grew, popular novels and plays known as "Temperance Tales" warned of the dire consequences of drinking (Lender and Martin, 1987, p.84). The success of the temperance movement led activists to call for legal prohibition. In 1846, Maine outlawed the manufacture and sale of distilled liquors, followed soon by prohibition of all alcohol. "Maine Laws" swept through other states and territories, leading some reformers to claim the arrival of a "Dry Millennium." But by the late 1850s, the looming crisis over slavery and the preservation of the Union overshadowed concern about prohibition.

In the years following the Civil War, the temperance movement regained momentum, framing itself as the "next emancipation," destined to free society from "enslavement to drink." The Women's Christian Temperance Union and other temperance groups proved very effective and by 1913 over half of the US population lived under some type of alcohol prohibition (Lender and Martin 1987, p.129). The final push to national prohibition was aided a few years later by anti-German sentiment accompanying the US entry into World War I. By 1919, under wartime legislation, Congress had dramatically curtailed the distilling and brewing of alcohol. And in January 1920, the *Eighteenth Amendment* to the Constitution went officially into effect. For the next 13 years, the manufacture and sale of alcoholic drinks was illegal in the United States.

The colorful history of the *Prohibition Era* can only be touched upon briefly here. The effects of the Eighteenth Amendment were more complicated than temperance advocates had envisioned. Outlawing the manufacture and sale of alcoholic beverages did lead to a drop in alcohol consumption, at least for the poorer urban segments of the population as the price for booze skyrocketed. But prohibition did not put an end to drinking. Many wealthy drinkers had stocked up with huge purchases prior to Prohibition. In New York, the affluent Yale Club procured enough alcohol to last its members through the entire 13-year stretch of Prohibition. Since the brewing of alcohol for personal use was not against the law, Prohibition also fostered small-scale family distilling at a level that had not been seen since the frontier days. Rural stills became an important source for illegal "moonshiners" who provided liquor to city "rum runners." Alcohol was smuggled into the United States from Europe, the Caribbean, and Canada, providing a boon to underworld organizations.

A huge gap in prohibition emerged in the area of law enforcement. There was an overly optimistic belief among temperance advocates that only modest enforcement would be needed to police the sale and manufacture of alcohol. Early estimates for adequate enforcement were under $10 million per year—a figure that rose to as high as $300 million per year by the middle of the Prohibition era. Prohibitionists seriously miscalculated the continuing demand for alcohol and the fortunes that stood to be made by violating the law. Even law enforcement agents proved vulnerable, as officials were widely paid off to look the other way.

Prohibitionists and the temperance movement also lost momentum after the enactment of the Eighteenth Amendment. In contrast, those segments of the American population that supported access to alcoholic beverages gained focus, especially as business leaders like John D. Rockefeller and the DuPont family threw their support behind the Association against the Prohibition Amendment. In 1933, the Eighteenth Amendment to the Constitution was repealed. Once again, the legal spigots for alcohol were open in the United States.

The Medicalization of Problem Drinking

While the Prohibition temperance movement drew support from Rush's concern with the effects of heavy drinking on society, it paid little attention to his description of alcoholism as a disease. In the decades following the repeal of Prohibition, however, the disease model of alcoholism grew to dominate American discourse about problem drinking. One of the pivotal organizations promoting the disease model was the Yale Research Center of Alcohol Studies, which developed in the late 1930s and early 1940s. Under the leadership of E. M. Jellinek, the Center pursued research on the physiological and psychological effects of alcohol, and conducted a summer school on alcohol studies to educate those who were working in the emerging field of alcohol treatment.

Jellinek (1960) developed a model of alcoholism as a disease that progressed through four stages from psychological to physiological addiction. In what he termed the prealcoholic phase, some individuals were especially prone to enjoy and find relief in drinking. In the second, prodromal phase, those individuals began to drink more heavily and developed a pattern of habitual drinking. They also began to experience frequent hangovers and loss of memory of what they did while drunk. In the crucial phase of alcoholism, the drinker experienced a loss of control over drinking, with a single drink leading to an inability to stop. They became alienated from their families and spent most of their time drinking alone or with other heavy drinkers. The final stage in Jellinek's model was the chronic phase of alcoholism, characterized by "benders" that lasted for days, the abandoning of family and work, and physical withdrawal symptom when they couldn't drink. If the alcoholic did not find a way to stop at this point, continued drinking would lead to illness, insanity, or death. Jellinek's writings became so successful that many came to refer to the new disease of alcoholism as "Jellinek's disease." His work was at the forefront of popularizing the disease conception of alcoholism and building the professional alcoholism treatment industry that exists in the United States today.

At the same time, as the field of professional alcohol treatment was developing, a grassroots movement emerged focused on self-help among those with drinking problems. Originating in 1935 in the work of Bill W. and Dr. Bob, two self-identified alcoholics who committed themselves to mutual support in quitting drinking, Alcoholics Anonymous over time became a major international movement. Today, there are more than 100,000 AA groups and two million members around the world practicing recovery based on AA's Twelve Step tradition (Alcoholics Anonymous 2016a).

The AA conception of alcoholism fits very well with Jellinek's disease model, which is not surprising since Jellinek developed his model by examining survey data on AA members (Rudy 1986, p.81). In the years since they were first developed, the popular success of the disease model of alcoholism and of the AA approach to drinking problems have reinforced each other's legitimacy. Whether or not the disease model of alcoholism is an accurate representation of biological processes and human behavior, it serves as the most influential paradigm for understanding and treating problem drinking in the United States today.

The Age of Ambivalence

American attitudes toward drinking are characterized by a chronic tension between considering excessive drinkers as victims of the disease of alcoholism, on the one hand, and holding them responsible for their behavior, on the other. This ambivalence was revealed in Raul Caetano's (1987) study of public opinions about alcoholism. Caetano found that a large number of those he surveyed held seemingly contradictory attitudes, believing that alcoholism is a disease *and* that alcoholics drink because they want to. Caetano's respondents also voiced concern over the potential stigma associated with alcoholism, saying that they would be reluctant to accept alcoholism treatment for themselves out of fear of being publicly identified as alcoholics. Americans' ambivalent feelings about drinking go even deeper. American culture often warns against excessive drinking, and certain activities, including driving while intoxicated, are treated as serious legal offenses. But at the same time, the American media frequently portray heavy drinking in a positive light, associated with excitement, sociability, and sexual encounters.

SOCIAL LEARNING THEORY AND ALCOHOL ABUSE

Scholars who see alcohol abuse through the lens of social learning theory focus on how drinking traditions are passed down through families, peer groups, and other contexts of social interaction. Social learning theory views the "problem drinker" as one who, by virtue of his or her social relationships and interactions, has learned pro-alcohol abuse values and has become socialized into deviant drinking rituals and behaviors.

Recognizing that the attitudes and definitions of drinking, in general, and problem drinking, in particular, vary widely across different social contexts, Ronald Akers (1992) has suggested that individuals' drinking patterns differ significantly based on the social norms of the groups with which they are affiliated. Some groups take a firm anti-drinking stance. These groups have what Akers refers to as *proscriptive norms* regarding alcohol. They prohibit drinking altogether and hold abstinence as their ideal. The Church of Jesus Christ of Latter Day Saints (Mormons) and Baptists are good examples. In stark contrast

PUSHING YOUR BOUNDARIES

Drinking Contexts Observations

In a famous article, "How to Ask for a Drink in Subanun," anthropologist Charles Frake (1964) discussed the social rituals associated with drinking of "gasi," a kind of rice beer, in the Philippines. Frake observed that behaviors associated with drinking can be very different depending on the contexts in which drinking occurs. This assignment asks you to relate this insight to your own observations.

Answer the following questions about two different drinking settings. If you do not drink and do not have experience with drinking activities, interview someone who does have such experience.

Think about two different kinds of settings in which you have seen people drinking. For instance, you could consider a student party, a wedding, or a cookout at your boss's house.

Describe each setting in terms of the following:

- Who drinks in that setting? Everybody or almost everybody? Only some people? What is their relationship with each other?
- What kinds of alcohol are consumed? Beer? Wine? Hard liquor? Special drinks?
- When does drinking occur? Is there a time of day that is considered the right time? Do certain kinds of activities have to stop (or start) before drinking can occur?
- Where does the drinking occur?
- Who pays? Are there formal or informal rules about who pays?
- Are there rituals or activities associated with this kind of drinking? Toasts? Games? Other rituals?
- How much drinking is considered appropriate? How much is too much?
- Finally, do you think one of these drinking contexts is more likely than the other to result in problematic behavior (e.g., violence, injury, arrest)? If so, why?

to such groups, there are other social contexts and groups, such as college "party schools," where drinking—even to the point of drunkenness—is permitted and often encouraged. Akers refers to such groups as providing *permissive norms* for drinking behavior. The norms of yet other groups fit somewhere in between these two poles of total rejection and permissiveness. The norms of many social groups are open to drinking alcohol, but clearly define when, where, and how much alcohol is acceptable. These groups have what Akers refers to as *prescriptive norms* that permit drinking within certain limits and situations. Jewish American and Japanese American cultures are good examples. Finally, some social groups lack unified normative guidelines regarding drinking. These groups have what Akers refers to as *ambivalent norms* regarding alcohol consumption, often giving contradictory and mixed messages about what is appropriate and inappropriate drinking behavior. Many observers would point to the US popular media as a good example of such normative messages—condemning drinking at one moment and showing it as fun and sexy the next.

Social learning theory can help us understand alcohol use and abuse. But social learning advocates admit that the theory is not a full explanation of problem drinking behavior. Perhaps the most commonly cited problem is the difficulty of establishing which came first: alcohol abuse or deviant associations. Do people become problem drinkers because they are pressured to drink by their peers, or do alcohol-abusing individuals simply seek out like-minded friends? The answer is that both dynamics occur, varying in their importance for different individuals. Critics of social learning theory argue that drinkers do not just learn norms and definitions that are favorable and unfavorable to drinking. They often play an active role in creating and sustaining those norms and definitions.

INTERACTIONAL CONTEXTS AND ETHNOGRAPHIC VOICES

There are many reasons why people like to drink and many ways in which drinking is incorporated into social life. The pleasurable physical and mental effects of intoxication go far to explain the allure of alcoholic beverages. Physiologically, alcohol depresses or slows down the body's central nervous system. Many people who drink alcohol experience the suppressant effects of drinking positively, with a reduction in anxiety, fear, and tension.

Drinking also plays a role for many individuals and groups in marking a shift from serious activity, such as work, to more relaxed and playful social time, as captured in the term "Happy Hour." In her study of San Francisco bars, Cavan (1966) referred to this aspect of drinking as *time out*. A major attraction of drinking lies in its association with fun and spontaneous activity as opposed to the controlled routines of daily labor.

There is also a common belief in America that alcohol reduces social inhibitions, making drinkers feel free to engage in behaviors that they would not otherwise feel comfortable pursuing. Whether because of its chemical properties or because of cultural expectations (or both), drinking is often perceived as providing "liquid courage," making many people feel freer in social interaction. Further, since we expect drinking to lower inhibitions, those who drink can use intoxication as a cover for behaviors that would otherwise be viewed as socially aggressive, emotionally risky, or even stupid. Part of the allure of drinking is that it allows one to violate social norms without being held fully responsible.

Another attraction of drinking is that it takes place in social contexts that frequently invoke feelings of social connection. Drinking contexts often reduce social hierarchy and highlight values of human similarity, intimacy, and sharing. Meeting friends for a drink after school or work stands in stark contrast to interactions in classes or on the job. Even a surprise encounter with one's boss at a bar or a party often leads to more personal and relaxed interaction than at work. These alluring features of drinking can help us grasp the interactional contexts and meanings of problem drinking among college binge drinkers, alcoholics, and drunk drivers.

College Binge Drinker

Binge drinking refers to a pattern of excessive drinking in which the expectation is to get drunk rather than drink in moderation. In many ways, residential college campuses provide an ideal setting for binge drinking behavior. College campuses draw large numbers of young people in their late teens and early twenties. For many students, their first year at college is also the first time in their lives that they have been out from under the watchful eyes of their parents. Unlike high school, college also offers a much less structured social environment with a potentially much greater amount of discretionary time. Further, when students arrive on many residential university campuses, they find a flourishing drinking culture that places significant pressure on them to participate.

Drinking has been common among US college students for generations, providing opportunities for socialization, celebration, and entertainment. For many students, drinking with their peers is one of their most valued social activities. When asked why they like to drink, college students offer the same explanations as do most other drinkers, including the pleasure of intoxication, the use of drinking as "time out," and the ways in which drinking greases the gears of social interaction. Common college drinking settings at parties and in bars are central to dating and romantic encounters. As one 18-year-old male student explained to Thomas Vander Ven, "You are less afraid of the consequences, of being too shy to talk to a girl . . . it brings your inhibitions down, strengthens your confidence" (2011, p.64). A female student voiced similar feelings about a recent experience, recounting, "I felt a lot more open and laid back. I wasn't afraid to talk to the guys as I usually am when I am sober" (2011, p.65).

Heavy drinking experiences also provide opportunities for social bonding with peers in settings laced with intoxication, a sense of adventure, and freedom from the rules of everyday life. As Vander Ven explains,

> Drinking can be fun because it allows people to express themselves more freely in a world full of other people who have temporarily developed that same free-spiritedness. This combination leads to absurd sequences of events where anything can happen, giving birth to war stories that can last a lifetime.
>
> —Vander Ven (2011, p.76).

Students often revel in the stories of crazy antics, such as a fraternity "tradition" retold by a student in Thomas Workman's ethnographic study:

> Riding the buffer naked. We have a powered floor buffer. And uh, it's kind of a house tradition. You could plug it in and you'd sit on it, on the motor, and you'd grab a hold of it, and see how long you could ride it, like a bullride. And then you'd have like a championship, and it was, you know, just a bunch of drunk guys in the basement, riding a buffer around, and you'd just ride it all over the floor.
>
> —Workman (2001, p.436)

The settings of heavy college drinking are fraught with dangers—from alcohol poisoning to accidents, fights, and rape. While many students discount the risks of drinking, college officials have expressed concerns about heavy drinking among college students for years. But only in the past 15 years or so has the label "college binge drinker" become widely used to describe a particular kind of alcohol abuse. The emergence of college binge drinking as a social problem has been closely associated with Henry Wechsler, who has directed high profile studies of college drinking. In *Dying to Drink: Confronting Binge Drinking on College Campuses*, Wechsler and Wuethrich (2002) describe college binge drinking as the "Number One public health problem for college students." According to their research, over half of college students are at least occasional binge drinkers, including more than 75 per cent of males living in fraternity houses. "Nearly one in three college students," Wechsler et al. write, "qualify for formal diagnosis of alcohol abuse" (2002, p.207). Describing college campuses as "party houses awash in a sea of alcohol," they call for a "national fight to attack college binge drinking" (Wechsler et al. 2002, p.217).

In response to such alarming reports, the US Congress passed resolutions urging college presidents to reduce student binge drinking and the US Surgeon General called for a 50 per cent reduction of college binge drinking by 2010. The Surgeon General's goal was far from met, as a Centers for Disease Control review of 2010 statistics found that more students were reporting binge drinking in 2009 than had done so 10 years earlier (National Center for Health Statistics 2012, pp.26–11).

The Alcoholic

The term alcoholic is a medical term that describes a certain pattern of dysfunctional heavy drinking, with the specific criteria for what counts as alcoholism varying over time. The term is also commonly used in popular culture. Since the term alcoholic is used by different groups in different contexts, it is not a completely unified construct, but the various uses of the term do have an underlying similarity. All suggest that alcoholic drinkers suffer a disease or addiction. The use of addiction as an explanation for heavy drinking emphasizes a loss of personal control as one develops increasing tolerance to alcohol and physical and psychological dependence on it. The terms addiction and alcoholism also imply a lasting condition. The addict, it is argued, can quit using, but is never really cured.

Active drinkers seldom use the label of alcoholic to describe their own behaviors. Heavy drinkers have many ways to explain their drinking that do not embrace the view that their drinking is an illness or addiction. But the term is often invoked by formerly heavy drinkers who have quit drinking or are trying to do so. In Alcoholics Anonymous, for instance, members often begin their participation in meetings by proclaiming, "My name is X and I'm an alcoholic. It's been X days (or months or years) since my last drink."

The alcoholic label clusters a set of drinking-related problems into one explanatory picture. Whether the disease explanation is a medical reality or a "myth" as Fingarette (1988) proclaims, many people develop problematic patterns of drinking behavior that today are likely to lead their being labeled by themselves as well as others as alcoholics.

Heavy drinking in and of itself does not necessarily lead to being labeled an alcoholic. To become identified as an alcoholic, one's drinking must also be defined as a problem. This occurs when drinking or the aftermath of drinking disrupts social relationships and role expectations. Most commonly, drinking is experienced as disruptive by people with whom one is involved in routine role expectations. When drinking impedes the performance of family and work expectations it can lead to interactional problems, such as confrontations with spouses and complaints from bosses. Of course, levels of tolerance for drinking vary from one family or workplace to another. Some heavy drinkers become skilled at hiding their drinking in times or places that would be problematic. At home, for instance, they may hide their alcohol in a closet or the garage and drink only when they are alone. Or they may become adept at drinking on the job without getting caught.

Others may also play a part in enabling one to be a heavy drinker while avoiding being labeled an alcoholic. Family members and friends may help minimize problems associated with drinking or cover them up. In a classic examination of wives' adaptation to husbands' problem drinking, Joan Jackson (1954) described how many wives were reluctant to label their husbands as alcoholics. As their husbands developed patterns of heavy drinking, the wives adjusted their expectations and developed ways to hide their problems from the broader community. They covered for their husbands by calling in sick for them when they missed work. Some coached their children on what to say and not to say about their fathers' behaviors. And most of them withdrew from broader social interaction by limiting the number of people they invited to their homes.

But the protective cocoon that facilitates heavy drinking may break down. At times drinking may simply create too much chaos to withstand. Ruptured relationships, job loss, health problems, arrest—any or all of these may push the drinker or their associates to define them as alcoholic. When family members or others seek to impose the label of alcoholic on a drinker against his or her wishes, a battle of wills often ensues. On the other hand, there are many cases where drinkers come to accept that they are alcoholics and need help for their problem drinking.

Often self-labeling as an alcoholic occurs at a low point in one's life that results in what Denzin has referred to as an "epiphanic moment," or decisive turning point in one's sense of self. As Denzin notes, both AA narratives and Hollywood movies about alcoholics are rich with stories of such experiences. In AA members use the term *hitting bottom* to refer to such low points: those moments of shame, despair, and realization that one is indeed an alcoholic.

Yet, just as tolerance for drinking varies dramatically among different families, work settings, and ethnic groups, the experience of hitting bottom varies among those who become self-identified alcoholics. In an ethnographic study of AA, David Rudy (1986) found distinct patterns of "low" and "high" bottom AA members. Low bottom AA members fit our image of long-term heavy drinkers who have suffered through humiliation and social loss before they have accepted the label of alcoholic. In contrast, "high bottom" AA members accept the alcoholic label and commit themselves to living in accordance with AA principles while they still appear to be functioning in their daily lives. As one high bottom AA member explains on an AA discussion forum, "I never lost a home-car-job, etc. However, I did lose my self, [and] . . . my interest in anything but getting and staying drunk enough to blackout or pass out."

The experience of becoming an alcoholic then is not simply a matter of developing patterns of heavy drinking, or even heavy drinking that creates visible problems in one's life. Rather, becoming an alcoholic also involves being defined by others and/or oneself as an individual who has lost the ability to control their drinking and its destructive consequences—and who is therefore a person who needs outside help if they are ever to overcome their addiction.

Drunk Drivers

In the United States, it is difficult to separate most activities from automobile driving. We live in the most car-oriented culture in the world and driving is a routine activity for most adults. Americans own over 200 million cars and light trucks and the average US citizen travels over 10,000 miles by car per year—by far the highest of any nation in the world (US Bureau of Transportation Statistics). Most of our cities are less densely built than in other countries, with extensive suburban sprawl. Even in our cities—let alone in less urbanized areas—unless we drink only in our homes, we are likely to find ourselves in a car after drinking. If we drink at a friend's home, at a party, or in a bar, transportation must be involved. And for most of us, that means driving or being driven home.

Over the past 30 years, MADD has been widely successful in publicizing drunk driving and advocating for tougher policing and stiffer penalties for those who drive while intoxicated. In recent years, the police and the highway patrol have arrested over one million "drunk drivers" per year on DUI charges. Still, DUI arrests are but the tip of the iceberg. Studies suggest that only one out of a hundred cases of drivers with blood alcohol levels above the legal limit results in arrest (Centers for Disease Control and Prevention 2016).

The biggest reason for drinking and driving is that driving is the most convenient—sometimes the only—available means of transportation. Further, the chances of getting in an accident or arrested are relatively low on any given occasion. But beyond the fact that most drinking drivers do not get caught, many of them do not feel that they are intoxicated enough that their driving will be impaired. And typically, drinking peers support drinking drivers in their beliefs that they will be okay. As Gusfield has observed, "Drinking and driving is a normal event in the lives of bar patrons" (1996, p.121). The normal barroom assumption is that a competent adult drinker can drink to a certain level of intoxication and still drive capably.

The pathway into drinking and driving is wide open and well travelled. As long as people in the United States rely on the personal automobile as their primary source of transportation, drinking and driving will continue to be a widespread problem. The only reason we do not have more DUI arrests than we do now is that we don't put more resources into catching those who drink and drive.

CONTEMPORARY RESPONSES TO PROBLEM DRINKING

Since World War II, an extensive alcoholism treatment industry has emerged in the United States, composed of a wide range of inpatient and outpatient programs staffed by medical professionals and paraprofessionals, including many who are themselves "recovering alcoholics." Alcoholics Anonymous (2016a) also provides a lifestyle and fellowship approach to managing alcohol abuse that is consistent with a disease model of alcoholism. At the same time, law enforcement takes a punitive approach, particularly to drinking and driving. The primary approach to alcohol-related problems in the United States involves a combination of punitive and treatment approaches focused on individual drinkers. In contrast, a contextual approach looks at ways that drinking settings and the broader environment can be modified to reduce the potential risks associated with drinking.

Punitive/Treatment Response

A good example of how the disease model and a punitive approach are combined in responding to those who become labeled "problem drinkers" comes from the experience of drivers convicted of DUI offenses. Typically those who are convicted of DUI violations receive court-ordered punishments including some combination of driver's license suspension, fines, probation, and community service. They are also required to participate in some kind of alcohol education program that presents information about the physiological effects of drinking and the risks associated with driving while intoxicated. When Joseph Gusfield (1996) observed a mandatory educational program for drivers convicted of DUI offenses, he found that the problem was posed almost exclusively as a problem of excessive drinking. Driving after drinking was described by instructors as abnormal and getting arrested for it was seen as a sign of alcohol abuse or alcoholism. But many DUI students were resistant to seeing their arrests as a sign that they had serious drinking problems. They tended to see themselves as just ordinary drinkers who were unlucky enough to have been arrested. Given the number of drinkers who drive without getting caught, the DUI students had evidence to back up their claims.

The combination of punitive and medical approaches appears to have limited impact on many who are convicted of drunk driving. When Philip Gonzales (1993) interviewed over 70 DUI offenders, he found that many of them did not view the drinking and driving that led to their arrest as all that bad. About one in five of those Gonzales interviewed expressed deep shame about their arrests, but most of those he interviewed fluctuated between feeling ashamed, on the one hand, and viewing their arrest as just an accident of being in the wrong place at the wrong time. Many young men even viewed their arrests as a normal event on the way to becoming a man. As one 23-year old explained to Gonzales, "My brothers had DWIs before, and so they laughed and said, 'It's about time you got one'" (1993, p.266).

While it is hard to know how deeply DUI educational programs influence their students' future driving and drinking behavior, it is clear that most people who drink and drive never get arrested and therefore never end up having to take the classes. And even though several powerful public groups like MADD continue to call upon law enforcement to increase surveillance and arrests of "drunk drivers," it is impossible for the police and highway patrol to come anywhere near being able to arrest all drivers whose driving is impaired by drinking. Arresting one out of a hundred "drunk drivers" is not a highly effective deterrent to drinking and driving—especially in a society that is so dependent on automobile transportation.

Contextual Responses

In contrast to punitive/treatment approaches, contextual responses seek to manage the environment in ways that reduce the problems associated with drinking before they occur. One contextual approach is to prohibit drinking. The minimum drinking age represents a form of prohibition, making it illegal today for US youth under the age of 21 to drink—the highest legal drinking age for any country in which drinking is legal. The rationale for this policy is that

CLAIMS-MAKER PROFILE

Candace Lightner and Mothers Against Drunk Driving

While walking to a church carnival on May 3, 1980, 13-year-old Cari Lightner was struck and killed by a chronic drunk driver who was free on bail for a hit-and-run drunk-driving accident only two days earlier. The day after Cari's funeral, her mother, Candace Lightner, started the group Mothers Against Drunk Drivers (MADD 2016a). Before starting MADD, Lightner had no experience in activism or politics. "I wasn't even registered to vote," she later told a *People* magazine reporter. "But I promised myself on the day of Cari's death that I would fight to make this needless homicide count for something positive in the years ahead," she later wrote (Martin 1994, p.75). She quit her job and used her savings to fund the new activist group. Lightner drew on the stories of people who had lost family and friends to drunk driving to personalize the impact of the problem and to push for changes to alcohol legislation. Her advocacy played a major role in President Reagan's creation of a Blue Ribbon Commission on Drunk and Drugged Driving in 1982, followed by new drunk-driving laws across the country and the passage of the National Minimum Drinking Age Act of 1984 that raised the legal drinking age across the United States from 18 to 21.

Lightner left MADD in 1985 following disputes with other leaders about the direction and policies of the organization. She has criticized MADD's approach as "neo-prohibitionist," arguing that it focuses too much on reducing drinking in general. "I didn't start MADD to deal with alcohol," she has said. "I started MADD to deal with the issue of drunk driving." Today, Lightner serves as president of We Save Lives, a nonprofit organization focused on public safety issues related to drugged, drunk, and distracted driving. MADD remains the largest nonprofit organization addressing drunk driving in the United States. It offers victim assistance and advocacy programs. "One day," its website states, "MADD hopes to put an end to drunk driving through the development of in-vehicle technology that automatically determines whether or not a driver is at or above the legal limit of 0.08 blood alcohol concentration and signals the car not to operate if the driver is impaired" (MADD 2016b).

young people lack the maturity to drink safely. Prohibiting those under the age of 21 from drinking is an attempt to minimize drinking among members of a particularly vulnerable segment of the population.

Another policy option for reducing alcohol consumption is to increase the price of alcoholic beverages, especially through higher taxes. Research supports the argument that higher prices tend to reduce drinking (e.g., Cook 2007). However, legislators have been reluctant to increase taxes on alcoholic beverages. In fact, when adjusted for inflation, taxes have gone down for alcohol over the past 50 years (Cook 2007).

Yet, a third policy that can lower consumption is to reduce the easy availability of alcoholic beverages. Today, regulations on where alcohol can be sold vary widely from state to state. Advocates of restricting where alcohol can be sold are particularly concerned with reducing the sale of alcohol at places closely associated with driving, such as gas stations and drive-through convenience stores (Ross 1992, p.100). Some have suggested that if beer is allowed to be sold at convenience stores and gas stations, it should at least be sold warm and in six-packs and not, as is often the case, made easily available as single drinks in iced barrels put on display during the peak of commuter traffic after work.

The foregoing social policies focus on controlling individuals' access to alcohol. A second set of contextual responses looks for ways to reduce the problems associated with drinking rather than reducing drinking itself. Treating drinking and driving as a transportation problem rather than a drinking problem is a good example. When drinking/driving is viewed as a transportation problem, new potential ways of dealing with the issue emerge. For one thing, such an approach emphasizes the importance of car and road safety in general. As Ralph Nader urged in a congressional hearing on auto safety, "Let us produce an automobile that will be safe on the assumption that it will be driven by fools and drunkards" (Gusfield 1996, pp.287–288).

Looking at drinking and driving as a transportation issue also suggests that urban planners should pay more attention to the relationship between drinking and driving. When drinking establishments are located in shopping malls and roadside strips, their locations encourage the use of automobiles to get to them. The more convenient it is to access bars without driving, the less likely people will be to drink and drive. Dense urban areas (e.g., New York and Washington, DC) tend to have less drunk driving, largely because driving is relatively unnecessary, expensive, and inconvenient (Ross 1992). In large and densely built cities, drinking establishments could be congregated in areas that are supported by mass transit, thus reducing drunk driving. In less densely populated areas, subsidized free ride programs could be encouraged, especially during peak heavy drinking times like Friday and Saturday evenings. While critics may complain about subsidizing transportation for heavy drinkers, the cost should be weighed against current costs of accidents, arrests, and incarceration.

The individualistic punitive/treatment approach is by far the dominant orientation to problem drinking in the United States even though many experts contend that such an approach is costly and inherently limited in its effectiveness. Despite their limited effectiveness, however, individualistically oriented policies do not face the political resistance that is confronted by policies that advocate changing America's urban landscape and its commitment to automobile transportation.

STIGMA MANAGEMENT AND RESISTANCE

Those who drink heavily must manage the potential stigma of being labeled as problem drinkers, whether as alcoholics, binge drinkers, or drunk drivers. The stigma management strategies that heavy drinkers use depend on their social contexts and their personal perceptions of their behavior.

In-Group Strategies

Given the popularity of drinking as an American pastime, it is not surprising that there is widespread cultural resistance to negative images of heavy drinking. Drinkers themselves often praise drinking and intoxication, glamorizing its pleasures in parties, pub crawls, and other social activities. Further, heavy drinkers provide each other with a reference group and mutual support for what others might consider excessive intoxication. In his study of a working-class bar, Joe Kotarba found that the men who drank there reserved the term "heavy drinker" to refer to "one who visits the tavern almost daily and consumes a minimum of five drinks per visit . . . A customer who only gets drunk every Saturday evening is not considered [by them] to be a heavy drinker" (1970, p.154).

In-group strategies to ward off stigma often involve reframing seemingly negative aspects of heavy drinking in a positive light. In his study of fraternity drinking, Workman (2001) describes how "puking stories" are often retold as humorous tales, and close encounters with the police are recounted as adventures. Among college drinkers, Vander Ven explains, "the drinking crisis is part of the fun, can be redefined in favorable ways, and serves a function by generating opportunities for emerging adults to rise to meet a challenge by taking care of one another" (2011, p.82). Similarly, Gonzales (1993) found that fellow drinkers often provided peer support when their friends were arrested for drunk driving, telling them that getting busted for drinking and driving was a rite of passage into manhood.

In addition to providing moral support for drinking, peers may also help each other avoid or manage many dangers associated with drinking. Homeless drinkers on the streets, for instance, often gather in loose groups, sometimes referred to as "bottle gangs" (Rooney 1961), to provide each other with protection from other homeless people, marauding teenagers looking to "roll bums," and the watchful eye of the police. College drinking buddies often provide similar support for drunk peers, by caring for them when they are drunk and helping them avoid confrontations with the police or dormitory RAs (Workman 2001; Vander Ven 2011).

Out-Group Strategies

While many heavy drinkers pay little attention to the possibility that they have drinking problems, many others manage their drinking in ways that demonstrate their awareness that others could perceive it as a problem. At home, for instance, they may hide their alcohol or drink only late at night when others are in bed. They may seek to hide the extent of their drinking from friends by drinking at different bars on different nights of the week (Reese and Katovich 1991). Or they may become particularly adept at drinking on the job without getting caught. As one heavy drinker explained to Norman Denzin, "Oh I was good at hiding it. I kept a constant buzz at work. I'd take a short drink before 8:00 in the morning. Kept a bottle in my desk at work, and I would pour vodka into my coffee cup. Nobody knew" (Denzin 1987b, p.92).

In hiding their drinking from family and friends, heavy drinkers try to avoid being labeled informally or officially as problem drinkers in order to escape the penalties and stigma that come with that label. But even when they are labeled as problem drinkers, they may deny that they have a drinking problem and look for excuses to explain their behavior. AA lore is rich with stories of alcoholics' "denial" or evasion of their drinking problems. From the AA perspective, such stories illustrate how the disease of alcoholism clouds the drinker's honest and rational thinking. But for the drinker who makes the excuse, it is an attempt to manage definitions of one's self and the meaning of one's behavior.

At times a battle of the wills develops among those who seek to impose a problem drinking label on an individual and the individual himself or herself. An example of stigma management by resisting being labeled a problem drinker is provided by Gusfield's research on the interactions of those who had been arrested for DUI with probation officers. Probation officers tried to convince DUI arrestees that they were alcoholics or on the way to becoming alcoholics—and thus in need of help. Arrestees reacted with "cover stories" that explained their DUIs as unusual situations that did not reflect their typical behavior. So, for instance, they might claim that extreme circumstances led to their having to drive under the influence. Or, they might attribute their erratic driving to factors other than alcohol, as did a woman who explained, "I know I was weaving on the road, but it was because I was driving my son's car and it was strange to me" (1996, p.225). Probation officers who regularly face such excuses tend to become cynical of defendants' claims.

While many heavy drinkers continue to resist seeing themselves as alcohol abusers even after they have experienced family and work conflicts or received DUI convictions, others come to view their behavior as problematic and seek to find ways to avoid repeating the problems that have come to plague their lives. For many, this leads to exploring the social world of Alcoholics Anonymous.

Alcoholics Anonymous and Identity Transformation

According to the Alcoholics Anonymous tradition, the first stage in becoming a recovering alcoholic is experienced when a drinker "hits bottom." Whether through self-realization or pressure from others, at this point a drinker may turn to AA for support and may be encouraged by AA members to make the first step: "Admitting we are powerless over alcohol—that our lives have become unmanageable" (Alcoholics Anonymous 2016b). Further, individuals are encouraged to take actions to demonstrate serious commitment to recovery, such as embracing the "90/90 Rule" of committing to attending 90 meetings in 90 days. Such commitment focuses their attention on AA and minimizes the pull of outside influences. New members are encouraged to develop a relationship with an AA sponsor who is asked to guide them in their attempts at maintaining sobriety. They are also encouraged to commit themselves to reading and discussing the *Twelve Steps and the Twelve Traditions* that outline the AA philosophy.

In the process of becoming affiliated with AA, new members are encouraged to see their past behavior as morally bankrupt. As Denzin puts it, they are asked to subscribe to the "thesis of bad faith," that "lying, self-deception, and denial were part of their daily existence" (1987, p.21). In contrast, as they spend time in AA, there is a stripping away of excuses. "Once the member has internalized the A.A. program and surrendered to alcoholism, there are no longer any excuses for drinking" (1987, p.131). Nonetheless, AA recognizes that members—especially new ones—may slip and drink. Slips early on are seen as almost inevitable and as an indication of the power of the addiction to alcohol. They are also seen as providing learning experiences, events to be shared with the group as one seeks to develop stronger commitment and identity as a recovering alcoholic. As Denzin explains, "Slips highlight the adage that any member can slip at any time" (1987, p.134) and serve to emphasize for the group as well as the individual the need for constant vigilance in the recovery process.

Over time, those who become stable members are often asked to share their stories of recovery with others, thus further solidifying their recovery narratives and identities. By virtue of their dramatic stories, those who reached the deepest levels of degradation and despair while drinking are often accorded the greatest recognition in sobriety. As Heath Hoffman explains:

> Members with a good story who embody "good A.A." can acquire celebrity-like status as they are asked to tell their recovery stories at local, regional or national A.A. meetings. Thus, in a somewhat strange twist of fate, the sordid trials and tribulations that members experienced during their active alcoholism enhance their status in sobriety
>
> —Hoffman (2006, p.677)

Alcoholics Anonymous is based on what Trice and Roman (1970) refer to as the "delabeling and relabeling" process of spiritual awakening and identity transformation—a process that is completed by doing the final, "twelfth-step" work, of "carrying this message to alcoholics and practicing these principles in all our efforts.".

AA has emerged as a major program for identity transformation for innumerable drinkers over the past 80 years. Still, the majority of those who start AA quit over time. Some gain control over their drinking and find they no longer need the social support provided by AA. Others who have been pressured to attend AA by insistent family members or the courts quit attending once family pressure is reduced or their legal issues have been resolved. But some former drinkers continue to attend AA for years, even decades, after they have quit drinking.

BLURRED BOUNDARIES II: CONTEXTUAL RESPONSES TO COLLEGE DRINKING

Many medical authorities and university officials consider heavy drinking to be the biggest public health problem on college campuses. Even those who have a generally permissive attitude toward college drinking acknowledge that there are many problems with heavy student drinking. The question is: what could or should be done about it?

Many people believe that the answer is quite simple: reduce opportunities for heavy drinking. If you cut down on the amount of drinking, they argue, you will naturally get rid of many drinking-related problems. Yet, other people argue that focusing only on reducing drinking is not an effective way to handle those problems. For one thing, they say, drinking has long been a part of college life and it is unrealistic to think that it can be dramatically curtailed by university policies. Instead, they argue that many of the problems we associate with drinking could be reduced more effectively by managing the environments in which students drink.

In *table 9.2* we see a number of recommended strategies for reducing drinking on the one hand, and for managing drinking contexts on the other. Which of these positions is right?

First, consider the policies directed toward reducing drinking. One policy that has been adopted fairly widely in college and university settings is to require that students receive alcohol-related education. Educational materials used in these programs tend to emphasize the risks of alcohol consumption. The hope is that, when students are more educated about the risks of drinking, they will drink less than they would have otherwise. A second policy focuses on the deterrent effects of closer surveillance and punishment. Tighter control of bars and residence halls, for instance, especially when connected to higher penalties for violations (e.g., underage drinking or public intoxication) could reduce the number of students who were willing to take such risks. A third set of "drinking reduction" strategies looks at limiting the availability of alcohol. One way of limiting alcohol consumption is to reduce the number of places that sell it—such as easily accessible "college bars." Another, less direct way to

Table 9.2 Strategies for Reducing Problem Drinking by College Students

Reducing Drinking	Managing Environment
Mandatory alcohol education	Food at events with alcohol
More policing	Safe ride programs
Harsher penalties (e.g., fines, suspension)	Medical amnesty
Higher prices (e.g., taxes)	Good Samaritan rules
Fewer "college bars"	Make drinking legal at 18
More Friday classes	

limit availability is to charge more for alcoholic beverages. When drinks cost more, students will not be able to afford to drink as much. Finally, some people argue that one of the major reasons that students drink is that they have so much free time. At many universities, students attend classes only three or four days per week. For many, the weekend and heavy weekend drinking starts on Thursday evening. More demanding courses, along with an increase in Friday classes, it is argued, would force students to spend more time on educational activities and thus cut down on the amount of time that they can easily spend drinking.

In contrast to the previous policies, another set of policies turns attention to the environments in which student activities—including, but not limited to drinking—occur. How can those environments be made less conducive to drinking problems? One environmental change could be to encourage (say, through "free pizza and pop" programs) that food and nonalcoholic beverages be served at drinking events. Another policy is to provide better safeguards to help those who have been drinking. Safe ride programs, such as those discussed earlier in this chapter, provide one kind of protection. Yet, another policy along this line involves "amnesty programs" that allow people with drinking-related problems to seek help without being punished. So, for instance, underage drinkers who seek medical help under such policies are not charged with drinking violations. The idea is that this will make them more likely to get help if they need it. "Good Samaritan" policies extend this kind of protection to other individuals as well, such as friends who take a sick drinking buddy to the emergency room for help. Finally, another—certainly more controversial—policy would be to lower the drinking age to 18 as a way to "decriminalize" drinking for the large numbers of college students in the 18–20 age range. If drinking were not illegal for these students, some argue, they would be able to develop more responsible drinking patterns.

Which (if any) of these policies do you think would be effective? Can you think of other policies that might be useful?

Before finishing your assessment of these policies, take a few minutes to consider whether the policies might have *unintended consequences*, as well as intended ones. It is not unusual for policies directed toward punishing deviants or criminals to have counterproductive results, often because the policies have unanticipated effects. For example, university officials have long been concerned about the high rate of heavy drinking in fraternities. Based on these concerns, many schools pushed to have drinking officially prohibited in fraternities. This policy reduced drinking in the fraternities, but much of the drinking that used to go on there appears to have simply shifted to drinking in off-campus housing. Many university police officers, as well as numerous students, now believe that this has made student drinking situations more dangerous and harder to control. At least in fraternities, they argue, the university had some clout. Further, when students are forced to drink off campus, the chances of drinking and driving may increase significantly (Martin 2004). In short, the unintended consequences of this policy may outweigh its benefits.

After considering both the potential positive and potential unintentional consequences of the policies in table 9.2, what would you recommend as the best policies to reduce the problems associated with college student drinking?

SUMMARY

- The most common images of alcohol abuse today are the alcoholic, the binge drinker, and the drunk driver.
- The number of people counted as alcohol abusers depends on the criteria used to identify them.
- Heavy drinkers describe their drinking in positive terms, focusing on freedom, social bonding, and the pleasure of intoxication.
- In preindustrial societies drinking and even drunkenness was often integrated into social life. As peasants moved to cities during the Industrial Revolution, the potential for alcohol to create problems increased and drunkenness became viewed as a vice.
- The most common views of the causes of intemperate drinking include sinfulness, biological vulnerability, and a desire for escape from life stresses.
- White colonists drank heavily while restricting alcohol to slaves and Native Americans. Negative public attitudes toward alcohol emerged in the United States in the mid-1800s and reached a crescendo with the passage of the Eighteenth Amendment in 1920. Prohibition lacked broad public support and the amendment was repealed in 1933.
- Alcohol abuse came to be viewed as the disease of "alcoholism" after World War II.
- Today, Americans hold ambivalent beliefs, embracing both medical and personal choice explanations for why people drink.

- Social learning theorists argue that different social groups vary in normative orientations toward alcohol and that this influences their members' drinking patterns.
- College students are often attracted to binge drinking as part of college life. College officials and public health experts consider binge drinking the number one health problem on college campus.
- Heavy drinkers have many ways of avoiding being labeled as problem drinkers, including techniques of neutralization and peer support for their drinking activities.
- Some drinkers renounce drinking and find a new lifestyle and personal identity through participation in Alcoholics Anonymous or other treatment programs.
- Societal responses to those who are identified and labeled as problem drinkers are primarily focused on punishment and treatment, but an alternative set of contextual policies focus on changing the environment within which drinking occurs.
- Policies directed toward reducing student binge drinking are directed toward reducing student alcohol consumption, on the one hand, and on making drinking settings safer, on the other. Effective policies must recognize unintended consequences that can undermine the goal of reducing problems associated with student drinking.

KEYWORDS

alcoholic: A term with multiple and sometimes conflicting definitions that is used to refer to individuals who are believed to be physiologically and psychologically dependent on or abuse alcohol.

alcohol use disorder: The American Psychiatric Association's revised designation of the mental disorder associated with alcohol abuse.

ambivalent norms: Social norms that are in conflict with each other (as in social groups that have norms stigmatizing drinking while glamorizing it at the same time).

binge drinker: A term used to refer to a pattern of heavy episodic drinking, often associated with drinking with the intention of becoming drunk.

blood alcohol content (BAC): A measure of the level of alcohol concentration in the blood. In the United States, a person with a blood alcohol level of 0.08 per cent or higher is defined as legally too intoxicated to drive an automobile.

drunk driver: An intoxicated driver, especially one whose blood alcohol level is over the legal limit of .08 per cent.

DUI: Acronym for "driving under the influence" of alcohol at a high enough level of intoxication to be arrested.

Eighteenth Amendment: The 1919 amendment to the US Constitution that prohibited the manufacture and sale of alcoholic beverages in the United States, thus ushering in the era of Prohibition. The amendment was repealed in 1933.

hitting bottom: A term used in Alcoholics Anonymous to refer to a point of despair in which an alcoholic decides that he or she must change their life and quit drinking.

medicalization of problem drinking: The shift in explanations of problem drinking from sin and moral failure to disease and physiological dependence, especially the changes associated with the rise of Jellinek's model of alcoholism beginning in the 1940s.

permissive norms: Social norms that accept and support specific kinds of behavior (as in social groups that permit, or even encourage, drinking).

prescriptive norms: Social norms that focus on how specific kinds of behavior should be conducted (as in social groups with clearly defined limits on appropriate drinking behavior).

Prohibition Era: The years during which the commercial production and sale of alcoholic beverages was illegal in the United States, from the passage of the Eighteenth Amendment in 1920 until its repeal in 1933.

proscriptive norms: Social norms that define certain kinds of behavior as totally unacceptable (as in social groups do not accept any drinking of alcohol).

time out: A term used by Cavan to refer to drinking occasions as relaxed and playful time that is marked off as separate from more serious work activities and family responsibilities.

CHAPTER

10

Drug Abuse

Man and drug paraphernalia (MBI/Alamy Stock Photo).

CONTENTS

LEARNING OBJECTIVES

After reading this chapter, you will be able to:

- Describe the most common types of drug abuse in the United States today
- Explain the challenges of, and strategies for, studying drug abuse
- Identify different historical definitions of, and causal explanations for, drug abuse
- Apply social learning theory to the "causes" of drug abuse
- Analyze the interactional contexts and personal experiences associated with "soft" and "hard" drug abuse
- Explain key differences between treatment of minority drug sellers and college and middle-class sellers of drugs
- Assess the arguments for and against legalizing and regulating recreational drugs

BLURRED BOUNDARIES I: TWO DRUG ABUSERS

Brandy Preston's sister turned her in to the police when she found out her 25-year-old sibling was strung out on methamphetamine. She hated to turn her in, she told a friend, "but she was ruining her life." It wasn't the first time that Brandy had been behind bars for drugs. A year earlier she spent a week in jail after she and her then-boyfriend were caught shoplifting and found in possession of three small bags of meth. Since it was her boyfriend who was holding the drugs, Brandy was released from jail. Later she confided to her sister that she had been using meth for months, lost her job, and couldn't support her two-year-old daughter. Brandy's sister agreed to care for the little girl and give Brandy a loan to get back on her feet.

But rather than cleaning up and getting her life together, Brandy spent the money on meth and disappeared for six months. When she showed up again, she had lost 20 pounds, her face was covered with acne, and several of her front teeth were beginning to visibly decay.

Brandy's sister rallied to support her again, giving her a place to stay and buying her some clothes so she could go on job interviews. When Brandy got a job as a video store clerk, her sister also fronted her money to get an apartment—on the promise that Brandy would start attending Twelve Step meetings. Things seemed to be going well for the next two months and when Brandy said, "My daughter needs to be with me," her sister let Brandy take the girl home.

But when Brandy's employer called to try to find out why she hadn't shown up for work for three days, her sister went to her apartment and found her high on meth and unaware that her daughter was unfed and hiding in the bedroom. Brandy's sister responded by calling the police and taking the little girl home with her.

Given her relatively clean criminal record, Brandy's case was remanded to a drug court, where the judge said he would give her a chance to turn her life around by going into a drug treatment program. "But," the judge warned her, "if you don't get yourself together now, I don't know if you will live long enough to get another chance."

Brandy Preston exemplifies our image of a drug addict. What began as occasional drug use has taken control of her life and damaged her body and her family. Virtually all of us would agree that her story is a case of drug abuse and that society should have policies to minimize the number of people who make such choices in their lives.

But not all illegal drug use is as harmful as Brandy's meth addiction. Some illegal drug use is even motivated by positive social values. Consider Tim Wheaton. Ever since junior high school, Tim has set his sights on becoming a doctor. His ambition and high school grades won him a scholarship at a major university where he is an honors student in the premed program. While high school classes were always a breeze, Tim quickly found his honors college biology and chemistry classes required studying harder than he had ever done before. Late one night during his first semester at college, one of his fraternity brothers offered him what he called "our study buddy, Adderall," a drug commonly prescribed for young people with Attention Deficit Hyperactivity Disorder (ADHD). Tim took the offer and found the drug helped him focus and prepare for his final exams. Since that first semester in college, Tim has depended on Adderall during midterms and finals. He buys the drug from a fraternity brother who is diagnosed as ADHD and sells his extra pills. Without Adderall, Tim is not sure he would be able to keep the high GPA that he hopes will earn him a spot in medical school.

Unlike Brandy, Tim does not use drugs recreationally. When a friend asked him why he takes Adderall, he explained, "I like getting A's." While Brandy's drug abuse has caused clear harm to her and her family, Tim's use of Adderall, at least in his view, has had the opposite effect. Aside from trouble going to sleep after taking Adderall, he has never experienced any health problems from it. His grades are top-notch and his parents proudly introduce him to their friends as "the future doctor in the family." Tim Wheaton is far from alone in looking to study drugs for a competitive edge. Researchers have found from 6 per cent to 11 per cent of college students have used another person's prescription drugs to help them study (McCabe 2005).

Most of us would not think twice to consider Brandy Preston a drug addict, but does it make sense to label Tim Wheaton's occasional use of study drugs as "drug abuse"? Some of us are likely to believe it is drug abuse, but others may be less certain. These examples raise the question of just how drug abuse should be defined. What kinds of use or levels of harm qualify for considering drug use "abusive"? Further, what do we know about who uses drugs and why? Are we more likely to label some people's use of drugs abusive than we are others? These are among the issues related to drug abuse in American society that are explored in this chapter.

CURRENT CONSTRUCTIONS OF DRUG ABUSE IN THE UNITED STATES

Drugs, in one form or another, have been used in human societies for millennia for various purposes, from easing pain to heightening the pleasures of sex, and even for invoking religious insights. We live in a society in which drugs are a primary means of medical care and a routine part of everyday life. In the United States, more than four billion prescriptions are filled for pharmaceutical drugs annually (Lindsley 2012) and several drugs—including alcohol, tobacco, and caffeine—are legal for purchase and consumption. However, many medical experts, lawmakers, and the public view some drugs as particularly dangerous, physically, mentally, and socially.

Types of Drug Use and Abuse

Erich Goode (2012) distinguishes four types of drug use in the United States, including legal recreational drug use, legal medical use, illegal medical or instrumental use, and illegal recreational use. Goode's drug use typology provides clarity for looking at issues of drug use and abuse.

Legal medical drug use serves a huge range of purposes. They are prescribed for illnesses and discomforts from bacterial infections to mental health problems, sexual dysfunction, and chronic illnesses such as arthritis and diabetes. The US Food and Drug Administration regulates legal medical drugs, setting guidelines for legally acceptable usage—with the exception of medical marijuana, which is not approved by the FDA, but currently legal for medicinal use in 28 states and the District of Columbia (National Conference of State Legislatures 2017). Most drugs in the modern medical arsenal are useful for treating certain medical conditions, but not particularly appealing for any other purpose. Few of us would have any interest in taking penicillin or another antibiotic if we did not have an infection to cure.

In the United States, there are three particular common *legal recreational drugs*: caffeine, alcohol, and tobacco. Each of these drugs is used for the pleasurable effects that their users experience. Over half of American adults drink coffee on a daily basis. Alcohol is the second most popular legal drug in the United States, with two-thirds of American adults consuming alcoholic beverages at least once a month. Tobacco products are used by fewer people, with only 19 per cent of American adults reporting that they smoke regularly (Centers for Disease Control and Prevention 2014a). The harmful health and social consequences of smoking are widely recognized, and restrictions on smoking have been strengthened over the past 25 years. Even so, tobacco remains a legal drug available for adult purchase and consumption throughout the United States. Finally, a fourth drug, marijuana, is legal for recreational use in eight states and the District of Columbia, although it remains an illegal recreational drug in the rest of the country.

Illegal medical or instrumental drug use involves the use of medical pharmaceuticals by individuals for whom they have not been prescribed. Painkillers like Percocet and OxyContin are classified by the FDA as drugs that are highly susceptible to abuse. Some individuals who are prescribed these medications for pain management develop a dependency on them and may seek them illegally if they cannot get a legal prescription. Other legal pharmaceuticals may also be used illegally for purposes that are not officially or medically approved. Tim Wheaton's use of Adderall as a study drug is a good example.

Finally, some drugs are appropriated for *illegal recreational drug use*. Some drugs that can be legally prescribed for medically approved use are also popular recreational drugs. Opioid pain medications are particularly recognized for such potential use. When legal medicinal drugs are used illegally, they may be taken in ways that heighten the drug's effects, such as crushing pills and snorting the powder in order to deliver more of the drug into the blood stream more quickly. However, much illicit drug use involves the use of drugs that are illegal and not FDA-approved, especially marijuana.

Statistical Snapshot

The most extensive statistics on drug abuse in the United States are collected by the Substance Abuse and Mental Health Services Administration (SAMHSA). Table 10.1 shows the 2010 national rates of use for a range of illegal drugs as measured by the SAMHSA National Survey on Drug Use and Health (NSDUH). By far the most commonly used illegal drug is marijuana (legal in eight states). Nearly half of Americans 12 years of age and older report having used marijuana at some time, including 16 per cent in the past year and nearly 7 per cent in the last month. The number of Americans illegally using other drugs is far lower. Among illegal drugs, cocaine is the second most widely used, with a lifetime prevalence of 14.5 per cent, although fewer than 2 per cent of Americans 12 and older reported using it in the preceding year. The illegal use of prescription medications, primarily illegal use of pain relievers such as OxyContin and antianxiety "tranquilizers" such as Valium and Xanax, is reported at higher rates than several of the most recognized and feared illegal drugs, such as heroin, crack, and methamphetamine.

CHALLENGES IN RESEARCHING DRUG ABUSE

Like research on other types of behaviors labeled as deviant and often classified as illegal, collecting data on illicit drug use presents researchers with several

Table 10.1 Statistical Snapshot of Illicit Drug Use

Illegal Drugs	Lifetime	Past Year	Past Month
Marijuana	48%	16%	6.9%
Cocaine	14.5%	1.8%	0.6%
Crack	3.5%	0.4%	0.2%
Heroin	1.8%	0.3%	0.4%
Methamphetamine	4.7%	0.2%	0.1
LSD	9.1%	0.4%	0.1%
PCP	2.5%	0.1%	0%
Ecstasy	6.2%	1%	0.2%
Illegal Use of Prescription Drugs			
Opioid pain relievers	14.2%	4.8%	1.9%
Tranquilizers	9.1%	2.3%	0.8%
Stimulants	8.3%	1.3%	0.5%
Sedatives	3.1%	0.2%	0.1%
Any illicit drug other than marijuana	28%	8.1%	3.6%

SOURCE: SAMHSA (2012).

challenges, including difficulties in gathering accurate data regarding drug use and in getting close to the personal experiences of drug users themselves.

Counting Illegal Drug Use

Law enforcement officials record drug dealing and abuse, but their records are based on crimes that have been reported or uncovered by law enforcement officers. Drug dealing and drug use are classic victimless crimes since drug users want dealers to sell them drugs and the user is not committing a crime against another person when they take the drug. There is no harmed individual willing to report the crime to the police. By virtue of this, arrests for drug use overwhelmingly result from policing activities. Since poor and minority urban neighborhoods are disproportionately subject to heavy policing for drug crimes, the rates of drug arrest, especially for African-American men, are dramatically higher than for white males. While African-Americans make up approximately 13 per cent of the total US population, they account for over half of drug offenders in state prisons (Beatty et al. 2007). Research with white drug dealers in suburban high schools (Jacques and Wright 2015) and affluent college campuses (Mohamed and Fritsvold 2010) find widespread drug use and sales with virtually no law enforcement activities—and thus, very low records of arrest.

If law enforcement statistics are not an accurate way to count drug use, what other options are available? The best data on drug use at the national level come from SAMHSA's NSDUH. The NSDUH survey involves self-report data from an age-stratified national sample of over 68,000 Americans 12 years of age and older. Given the large and varied sample, NSDUH researchers are able to estimate national levels of the use of many illicit drugs.

How accurately does the NSDUH survey capture drug use? The first question most of us would ask is whether or not people will report honestly to NSDUH researchers. The answer to this question, by and large, is that most respondents answer accurately if they believe that their answers are anonymous and they will not get into trouble for being truthful. While it is likely that some underreporting occurs in the NSDUH self-report survey, the broad picture presented by the data gives a fairly good approximation of national drug use—with just a few exceptions.

One exception involves relatively rare kinds of drug users. Despite widespread media attention to methamphetamine in recent years, "meth" is used by relatively few people across the country, with only one in 500 NSDUH respondents reporting methamphetamine use during a one-year period. Even with a sample size of over 68,000 people, the number of methamphetamine users in the NSDUH survey is less than 150, which is not enough for people to establish accurate patterns of drug abuse. Further, many heavy users of drugs like methamphetamine, crack, and heroin are either homeless or in prison and people in neither of these situations are sampled in the NSDUH survey. In short, the large-scale drug use data that we have are far better for assessing rates of more common types of illicit drug use, such as marijuana and opioid pain relievers, than for rarer "street" drugs.

Getting Close

Deviance ethnographers who seek to get close to the lived experience of illicit drug use also face challenges in gaining access to and understanding illicit drug users. The most basic problem is gaining access to drug users and the settings in which they live. The locations of heavy inner-city street drug users can often be identified easily through news media reports and police records. It is especially easy to identify and locate drug users who have been arrested and incarcerated, as did Kristin Carbone-Lopez et al. (2012) when they interviewed female methamphetamine users in a Missouri prison. It is far harder to gain access to more dispersed drug using populations, such as middle- and upper-class abusers who are scattered in private homes across the country. In her research on suburban women who used methamphetamine, Miriam Boeri (2013) posted fliers in stores, gas stations, coffee houses, and public places announcing: "Female Methamphetamine Users Needed for a University Research Study." The fliers offered $30 in cash for interviews and stated that no names would be collected in the research.

After locating drug users and/or sellers, deviance ethnographers face the challenge of getting them to share their lives, whether through interviews or by allowing researchers to observe them in their daily activities. There is a rich history of street ethnography of drug subcultures from Agar's *Ripping and Running* (1973) to more recent books like Bourgois and Schonberg's *Righteous Dopefiend* (2009) and Boeri's *Women on Ice* (2013), all of which demonstrate that deviance ethnographers who approach their subjects with respect and patience can often establish trust with their subjects (Sandberg and Copes 2013).

However, it can be difficult to communicate with individuals under the influence of drugs. In her interviews with drug dealers, Patricia Adler (1993) found that trying to get information from those who were high on marijuana was often ineffective because these people were "confused, sleepy, or involved in eating" (p.105). Even more challenging was Lisa Maher's (1997) ethnography with street prostitutes who often nodded off from the effects of heroin while she was interviewing them. While cocaine and amphetamines tend to make users alert, they can present other difficulties. As Terry Williams et al. explain:

> When people are smoking crack, they go through different states, one of which is paranoia. The crackhead may comment, "Why are you watching me?" . . . The easy solution is to move away and not watch. Above all else, don't confront or challenge them. . . . After a while, the person's paranoia will subside and the person is open to conversation again—with little or no recollection of his comments or threats while high.
>
> —Williams et al. (1992, p.369)

While deviance ethnographers have demonstrated an ability to protect themselves as they conduct fieldwork in drug use settings, they have proven less successful in protecting others in those settings. Deviance ethnographers studying street drug use in particular may find themselves witnessing violence and harm to those they study. Street-level drug research is often conducted in what Bourgois and Schonberg (2009) refer to as desperate "gray zones" of violence and suffering, and to study such settings is often to bear witness to violence that one does not have the resources to significantly alleviate.

Deviance ethnographers are further challenged by the dangers posed by police and other law enforcement agents. Given the penalties associated with drug arrests and convictions, drug researchers must assiduously protect the identities of their informants. "When doing fieldwork or interviews with drug users," James Inciardi writes, "I never want to know the names and addresses of my informants. When I ask questions, I ask in such a way that the data collected would be considered as no more than hearsay in a court of law" (Inciardi et al. 1993, p.150).

CROSS-CULTURAL CONSTRUCTIONS OF DRUG ABUSE

Humans have long known the pleasurable and medicinal effects of certain plants—as well as potential harmful effects. The ancient Greek word for what we call drugs was *pharmakon*, a word that can mean both "remedy" and "poison," since it was recognized that many drugs could heal or harm depending on the circumstances, individuals, and the ways in which they were used.

Different Definitions

The use of drugs dates back millennia. The chewing of stimulant areca nuts wrapped in betel leaf, known today as "betel nut," appears to have been widespread in Southeast Asia for 10,000 years (Escohotado 1999). Records of Sumerian culture show that the opium poppy was being cultivated in Mesopotamia by 3400 BC. Sumerian references to opium emphasize its pleasurable effects, calling the plant Hul Gil, or the "joy plant." Both Greek and Roman physicians used opium for a variety of medical purposes, including relief from pain, soothing of skin rashes, and treatment for gastrointestinal disorders (Scarborough 1995).

Many cultures have myths about medicinal and psychoactive plants being gifts from the gods. In Hindu legend, the god Shiva is said to have rested in the shade of the cannabis plant on a particularly hot day and in gratitude to have given the plant to mankind (Morningstar 1985). In Greek culture, Homer's *Iliad* tells how Helen of Troy (the daughter of the god Zeus and his human lover, Leda) provided the drug *nepenthe* from the opium poppy to war-weary soldiers during the Trojan War. Similar stories connecting drugs with the gods can be found in the legends of pre-European cultures in what became the Americas. Among the Incas, the coca plant was associated with the goddess of health and joy, Mama Kuka, originally as legends tell, a promiscuous woman who was cut in half by her lovers and whose body grew into the first coca plant (Schultes and Hoffman 1992).

On the other hand, many of the same drugs have also at times been the focus of policies seeking to outlaw them or highly restrict their use. Those who seek to ban drugs have focused on defining them as destructive and immoral forces that wreak havoc on both individuals and the broader society. In classical Greek society, the harmful effects of drugs were associated with untamed desire and overindulgence, captured in the myths of Dionysus, the god of intoxication. In the Middle Ages in Europe, various drugs were considered evil substances used by witches to commune with the devil. And with the rise of modern medicine, especially in the twentieth century, illicit drugs came to be viewed as chemical substances that caused rather than cured sickness.

Different "Causes"

The most vehement social reactions against the use of various psychoactive drugs occurred in Europe during the Middle Ages, when drugs that were commonly used by folk healers became identified as tonics used in Satanic rituals. For nearly 400 years Medieval Europe was swept up in waves of religious fervor focused on fear of "a world full of witches and supernatural powers, thanks to their alliance with Satan" (Escohotado 1999, p.38). The drugs proclaimed as satanic substances by priests and inquisitors included everything from homeopathic pain relievers to hallucinatory toad skins and visionary mushrooms. Religious authorities believed the demonic use of drugs—overwhelmingly by women—was motivated by carnal lust to have sex with the devil. The witches broom came into legend at this time, portrayed as a stick on which various drug ointments were placed, with riding the broom having clear sexual connotations.

In contrast to supernatural views, today drug abuse is most widely understood from a medical perspective as an illness or addiction. However, there is no single authoritative medical explanation for what causes drug abuse. The classic medical model of addiction focused on intense physical dependency on a drug that causes withdrawal symptoms, such as fever, muscle spasms, and vomiting if an abuser quit taking the drug. While some drugs (such as heroin and heavy alcohol use) can cause withdrawal symptoms, the physiological and psychoactive effects of drugs are much more varied than earlier medical authorities understood. Current medical approaches suggest that some individuals are more vulnerable, psychologically or physiologically, than others to excessive and harmful use of drugs. There is no doubt that many illicit drugs can have a destructive impact on health, but it is also clear that popular and political perceptions of the dangers of recreational drugs have often been exaggerated.

Different Responses

For most of human history, drug abuse has not been viewed as a major problem. Until modern times many people had little access to drugs (except alcohol) and their use was largely unregulated and of little public concern. In cultures where drug use has been viewed as a social problem, the responses to it have reflected views about the causes of drug abuse. When drug abuse is seen as a moral failing or evil, the most common responses are punitive. If the problem is viewed as a medical issue, the responses tend to focus on medical or psychological treatment.

Medieval Europe witnessed some of the most intense punitive response to drugs in human history. Inquisitors used the widespread belief in drug-induced witchcraft to bring men and women—but primarily women—up on charges of witchcraft. "If the accused is found with ointments on her body, subject her to torture," admonished one inquisitor in his *Instructions for Judges in the Matter of Sorcery* (Escohotado 1999, p.38). Over the course of four centuries, more than 200,000 witches were identified, tortured, and executed. The torture and killing of witches, however, was not uniformly applied. Wealthy and well-connected members of society were seldom accused and punished, while members of minority ethnicities, those who held unpopular religious beliefs, and lower social classes were overwhelmingly the focus of punishment.

When drug abuse is viewed as a medical problem—as physical addiction or psychological dependency—the logical implication is that the solution must address the medical or psychological conditions that either caused or were caused by drug abuse. A wide range of treatment programs have existed over the past century, offering many different approaches to treatment for drug abuse and addiction. In several cases, a new, supposedly less dangerous drug has been recommended to treat addiction to a more harmful one. Sigmund Freud was one of many respected physicians to recommend using cocaine to ween people from morphine addiction. Medical and psychological theories of drug abuse proliferated in the twentieth century, leading to a range of treatments designed to overcome physical addiction and psychological dependence on illicit and sometimes legal, but overprescribed medications.

Many countries have tried to address drug abuse by reducing the availability of drugs. Outlawing drugs can reduce their availability, although the profits that can be made from selling banned drugs make it alluring for entrepreneurs who are willing to break the law—just as was the case for illegal rum runners during Prohibition. Since many illegal drugs are transported into countries from beyond their borders, nations may also seek to reduce foreign production and importation. During the mid-1800s European and American businesses reaped huge profits from growing opium in India and Indonesia and smuggling it into Southern China. The Chinese government tried to force an end to the opium trade, leading to two Anglo-Chinese wars known as the First (1839–1842) and Second (1856–1860) "Opium Wars," in which the British and French militaries negotiated trade agreements that allowed, among other things, importing opium to China as a core piece of European commerce in Asia until the early 1900s.

HISTORY OF DRUG ABUSE IN THE UNITED STATES

When Europeans first arrived in the "New World," they found indigenous cultures that embraced the use of several psychoactive plants, including coca and peyote in Central and South America and tobacco in North America. The European countries from which the early colonists came had long histories of alcohol use, and tobacco quickly gained widespread appeal. Little attention was directed toward "drug problems" until the late 1800s. Since then, however, successive waves of moral panic have rocked the country as one after another drug has been proclaimed a major menace to society.

Unregulated Early America

During the 1700s and first half of the 1800s, the only drugs besides alcohol and tobacco widely available in North America were opium products. In the 1800s, opium was used freely to treat pain, insomnia, diarrhea, and other ailments with little medical oversight. In such a laissez-faire context, medicinal use could lead easily to excessive and harmful use. By the 1850s, large numbers of women in particular were addicted to opiates—most of them middle-aged and middle to upper class. From 1850 to 1920, there were twice as many addicted women as men (Inciardi et al. 1993, p.108).

Several popular beverages of this era also owed their success to drug ingredients. In 1887, an Atlanta pharmacist and patent medicine seller created a tonic containing caffeine and coca leaf extract, called Coca-Cola. Since there were no agencies like today's Food and Drug Administration to oversee and regulate food and drug products in the 1800s, the creators of medicines and tonics were not required to divulge the ingredients they used or to substantiate the health claims they made about their products. Despite containing cocaine, Coca-Cola was advertised as a "temperance beverage," a safe "soft drink" alternative to "hard" alcohol (Reinarman and Levine 1997, p.323).

At the end of the nineteenth century, virtually all known drugs were available in US drugstores and by mail. The Sears catalog even sold mail order hypodermic syringes for morphine users. There were many people who used opium, morphine, and heroin in unhealthy ways, but the situation seldom drew the attention of newspapers or magazines, let alone that of judges or law enforcement officers (Escohotado 1999, p.74). From the vantage point of the late 1800s it would have been hard to imagine that a century later the US government would proclaim a "war on drugs."

Road to Punitive Prohibition

The shift in public and political perceptions of drugs started with opium, which is ironic since several American businessmen made fortunes selling opium in China during the early 1800s. When the California Gold Rush of 1849 and the ensuing need for railroad construction crews drew tens of thousands of young Chinese men to America, they brought the habit of opium smoking with them. Smoking opium was not a crime at that time and the Chinese immigrants who labored in building the railroads and mining gold relied on the drug to blunt the suffering and monotony of lonely labor in foreign lands. But by the late 1880s, public concern began to rise. The US campaign against opium, like movements against many drugs since then, was deeply racialized, fanned in this case by lurid tales of Chinese men drugging white women into sexual slavery. Public and political sentiment against the "Yellow Peril" of Chinese men led to the 1882 Chinese Exclusion Act, one of the most restrictive immigration laws in US history. Over the next 30 years, the United States enacted ever stronger restrictions on opium and in 1914 the *Harrison Act* outlawed its importation and use.

When the Harrison Act became law, there were hundreds of thousands of middle-class Americans who were dependent on opium products they had previously purchased legally. At first, doctors and physicians continued to make the drugs available to many long time users, but the federal government organized undercover operations to catch physicians and pharmacists who continued to supply middle-class users. From 1920 to 1930, 80,000 medical practitioners were sent to prison, while the emerging American Medical Association (AMA) struggled to establish doctors' authority to prescribe opium-based medications.

The Harrison Act also outlawed cocaine, which had previously been praised for many medical uses, including as a cure for opiate addiction, a treatment for asthma, and as the official remedy of the Hay Fever Association (Lyman 2011). As with opium, racialized fears played a major role in outlawing cocaine. Politicians and the media claimed that the use of cocaine induced African-American men to rape white women. A 1914 article in the *Literary Digest* proclaimed that "most of the attacks upon white women in the South are a direct result of a cocaine-crazed Negro brain" (Goode 2012, p.285).

Enforcement and expansion of the Harrison Act dramatically reduced both legal and illegal opium and cocaine use. By the 1930s and 1940s, illicit opiate use had shifted to the use of heroin and had become a problem mostly among inner-city minorities. In 1933, Prohibition was repealed, but a new drug scare arose over marijuana. The charge against "killer weed" was championed by Harry J. Anslinger, who led the Federal Narcotics Bureau in its efforts against recreational drug use for 30 years. Spurred in large part by a need to justify new funding for the Narcotics Bureau, Anslinger threw himself and the agency behind the cause of demonizing and eliminating marijuana (Becker 1963).

Following the pattern of earlier anti-drug crusades, racial anxieties—in this case, against Mexicans—were key to mobilizing public support against marijuana. Anslinger told audiences that marijuana was the worst evil of all drugs. "It is almost impossible," he claimed, "to estimate the number of murders, suicides, thefts, muggings, extortion, and misdemeanors of manic insanity provoked by marijuana each year" (Escohotado 1999, p.88). By the 1950s, marijuana was relatively confined to some minority and bohemian social groups, but it surged in popularity in the 1960s as the baby boom generation moved into adolescence and early adulthood and rebelled against the sexual and social norms of their parents, including the use of recreational drugs. For the first time in modern America, popular culture also embraced the use of hallucinogenic drugs, such as mescaline and LSD, for both spiritual insight and sensual gratification. College campuses became hotbeds of protest and recreational drug use. While the use of psychedelic drugs has abated significantly since the 1960s, marijuana use has gained even broader popularity across the US population.

In 1970, Congress enacted a bill titled the Controlled Substances Act. The legislation categorized drugs into five "Schedules" of control, based on two criteria: (1) approved medical uses and (2) beliefs about potential for abuse.

Schedule I drugs are those that have no federally accepted medical use and a "high potential for abuse." Among the Schedule I drugs are heroin, LSD, peyote, and (most controversially) marijuana. Schedule II drugs are those that the federal government identifies as having some legitimate uses, but also a high potential for abuse—such as opioid painkillers and amphetamines. Schedule III drugs also have accepted medical uses but more moderate abuse potential, while Schedule IV and V drugs are classified as having even less potential for abuse. Throughout the twentieth century, the AMA championed physicians' authority to prescribe medications. At times physicians disagree with the classifications of certain kinds of drugs under the Controlled Substances Act, but federal and state laws stipulate the legality and prescription policies for all substances identified in the Act.

The War on Drugs

The late 1980s and early 1990s marked a high-water era of governmental legislation against drugs. Like earlier anti-drug campaigns, this one drew on racialized fears, in this case especially associated with what was portrayed as a deadly epidemic of crack cocaine among black Americans. In 1986, *Newsweek* magazine proclaimed that crack cocaine was "the biggest story" in America since Vietnam and Watergate, and *Time* magazine called crack the "Issue of the Year" (Reinarman and Levine 1997, p.20). As part of a renewed "war on drugs" (a term first used by President Richard Nixon in the 1970s), President George Herbert Bush appointed a "drug czar" to focus the fight against drugs. His appointed czar, William Bennett, announced, "Crack is responsible for the fact that vast patches of the American urban landscape are rapidly deteriorating" (White House 1989).

Crack is a smokeable form of cocaine that produces an intense and immediate high that lasts only a short time, leaving many users longing for more. While it never became an extensively used drug in the United States, crack was used quite widely in the late 1980s primarily by the same inner-city poor population that had used heroin (Reinarman and Levine 1997, pp.2–3).

From 1986 through the early 1990s, the US media and politicians presented a sensationalized portrait of crack-related violence, creating a drug scare based on exaggeration and misinformation. Two "myths" about crack cocaine—that it was "instantaneously addictive" and that it had reached "epidemic proportions"—bear cookie-cutter resemblance to stories told about other drugs before and after the "crack panic." A *Newsweek* cover story in 1986 quoted a supposed "drug expert," who claimed that crack produced "instantaneous addiction" and was "the most addictive drug known to man" (Reinarman and Levine 1997, p.12). Similar claims had been made about other drugs before and would be repeated later about methamphetamine by the *New York Times* and other newspapers in the early 2000s (Goode and Ben-Yehuda 2009, p.212).

A second drug panic myth claimed that crack was spreading at "epidemic proportions." *Newsweek* again served as an outlet for such stories, proclaiming that crack had become "an epidemic in America, as pervasive and dangerous in its way as the plagues of medieval times" (Reinarman and Levine 1997, p.89). The epidemic metaphor for the spread of drug use has regularly been invoked to refer to other drugs as well throughout the latter half of the twentieth century. "Epidemics" of heroin and LSD were proclaimed in the 1960s, while in the 1970s PCP was reported to be reaching epidemic proportions. And in the early 2000s, the threat of methamphetamine was being announced in newspaper headlines with titles like "Governor Warns Meth Epidemic Growing like Kudzu" (Chitwood et al., 2009). Such drug scare pronouncements distort perspective on both the actual dangers of the scare drug of the moment and the dangers of other drugs or other sources of social harm. In the same year that former US Attorney General Alberto Gonzales stated, "meth is now the most dangerous drug in America" (Chitwood et al. 2009, p.35), fewer than 1,000 Americans died from meth use, while over 450,000 died from tobacco-related cancers and cardiovascular disease (Centers for Disease Control and Prevention 2014b).

Crack had a serious impact on the well-being of urban underclass minorities, but the claims made about the drug far outstripped reality. The stories told in the media and by politicians created support for severe policies aimed to stem what was being described as a deadly drug epidemic. The first major law in the 1980s War on Drugs, the Anti-Drug Abuse Act of 1986, passed with overwhelming support from both Democrats and Republicans. Among the key features of the laws were increased punishments for drug offenses, including mandatory minimum sentences. With misinformation rampant and emotions running high, Congress enacted a mandatory minimum sentence of five years without parole for possession of five grams of crack, used primarily by the urban poor, while a similar minimum sentence for powder cocaine (the preference of more affluent white cocaine users) was set at possession of 500 grams—a 100 to 1 disparity that clearly penalized urban underclass minorities.

The Anti-Drug Abuse Act also implemented mandatory minimum sentences for other illegal drugs, including marijuana. As part of the broader 1980s movement to get "tough on crime," the Act played a major role in the massive increase in US prison and jail populations, which climbed from 500,000 in 1980 to 1,500,000 by 1994 and to over 2,200,00 in 2014 (Bureau of Justice Statistics 2016b). More people in the United States than ever before are now either in prison or on probation for drug-related offenses. But public attitudes today regarding illegal drugs are mixed, depending on the drug or drugs in question. Marijuana remains a federally illegal drug, but many states have *decriminalized* the drug (eliminating criminal penalties for possession), and as of 2017 eight states have legalized recreational use. In short, the use of illegal drugs—as well as efforts to curb drug abuse—remains central to social life in the United States.

SOCIAL LEARNING THEORY AND DRUG ABUSE

Social learning theory is widely used in the study of drug use and abuse. As with drinking, attitudes and behaviors associated with drug use vary among different social groups. Social learning theory asserts that deviant behaviors such as drug use are learned through social interaction. The theory states that deviant behavior involves learning how to commit deviant acts and the specific attitudes that make the behavior attractive. Taken broadly, social learning theory provides an analysis focused on gaining access to drugs, learning how to use them, how to experience drug effects as pleasurable, and how to manage the negative consequences of drug use.

No one is a born drug user. While many studies suggest that some individuals are more physiologically or psychologically vulnerable to developing abusive patterns of drug use, it would be next to impossible for an individual to become a serious drug user without social connections and interactions. Consider the most fundamental requirement for drug use: getting access to them. While many drugs that are now illegal in the United States could easily be bought over the counter at a drugstore in the late 1800s, most new users of illegal drugs like marijuana, cocaine, or heroin rely on more experienced friends to provide the drugs they first use. Of course, physical access is only one aspect of drug use. One must also be "open" psychologically to using the drug. Attitudes toward acceptable drug use are influenced significantly by friendship networks. Some social groups are supportive of drug use, offering access to the drugs themselves and providing definitions of drug use that focus on its pleasurable and fulfilling aspects.

Having access to drugs and a favorable attitude toward experimenting with them is often not enough to enable a person to become a drug user. Another aspect of a social learning involves learning from others how to use the substance. Smoking marijuana, for instance, requires learning how to inhale and hold the smoke in order to get THC, the psychoactive ingredient of "pot," into the bloodstream. But even that is not enough. As Howard Becker (1953) observed in his classic study, "Becoming a Marijuana User," a person who first tries marijuana does not necessarily experience its positive effects. Rather, users must learn to experience the marijuana "high"—and to feel it as pleasurable. This can be difficult since initial experiences with drugs ranging from alcohol and marijuana to heroin often involve some mix of such unpleasant sensations as mental disorientation, shortness of breath, pain, and nausea. More experienced drug users may serve as guides in managing the physical and mental effects of drugs in ways that minimize unpleasant feelings and maximize the pleasurable experience.

Yet, another challenge that continuing drug users face is how to get regular access to the drugs. For "weekend" middle-class marijuana or cocaine users, this may involve simply making connections with regular suppliers through one's social network. Heavy users of hard street drugs may find getting money to purchase drugs is more of a challenge for them than finding a supplier. Here again, social learning theory focuses attention on how others with whom one associates can provide role models and connections, in this case, at times teaching and encouraging illegal money-making activities such as shoplifting, burglary, prostitution, or selling drugs in order to buy drugs for personal use.

The most important takeaway message from social learning theory's approach to drug abuse is that the social contexts in which individuals are exposed to the use of various kinds of drugs has a powerful impact on individuals' experiences and behaviors in relation to the drugs. With this in mind, we turn now to a discussion of the interactional contexts associated with several kinds of illicit drugs.

INTERACTIONAL CONTEXTS AND ETHNOGRAPHIC VOICES

Drug stories in the media often portray drug abuse as an inevitable result of playing with highly addictive substances, such as "the worst substance known to man" or a drug that causes "instantaneous addiction." The view of drug use as rooted in the physiological and psychological effects of the drugs themselves has been referred to as *pharmaceutical determinism*—a belief that such drugs inevitably lead to harmful outcomes. Yet, decades of drug research have revealed variability in drug experiences. Norman Zinberg's (1984) book, *Drug, Set, and Setting,* developed the most widely used framework for understanding variation in drug use and abuse. According to Zinberg, drug experiences are based on three interrelated factors: a drug's pharmacological properties, the individual psychological and biographical "set" that a person brings to the drug experience, and the "setting," or physical and social environment in which drug use occurs.

Zinberg developed his theory by comparing heroin addiction in Britain with the experience of American addicts in the 1960s and 1970s. He also visited Vietnam to conduct research on heroin use among soldiers during the Vietnam War. His research showed that soldiers' heroin use was in part attributable to their social setting in a "destructive war environment" (1984, p.x). While the US Army rejected this finding, later research with returning veterans found that when they came back to the United States, most were able to overcome their addiction. The high rates of desistance from heroin use among returning soldiers challenged the prevailing assumption that saw addicts as "once a junkie, always a junkie." Zinberg's focus on drug, set, and setting mirrors social learning theory in recognizing the fundamental role that the social environment plays in illicit drug use. At the broadest level of sociological analysis, this includes not only the immediate set of peers with whom one shares drug experiences, but the broader social setting as well, including the various ways through which drugs are acquired. In the following discussion we use the drug, set, and setting approach to examine the interactional contexts in the United States today for using the "soft" recreational drug, marijuana versus "hard" street drugs including heroin, crack cocaine, and methamphetamine.

Marijuana

About half of Americans 12 years of age and older have at least tried marijuana, with one out of six having done so in the past year. Typically marijuana is used socially rather than alone and most users are introduced to the drug in their mid- to late teens. It is popular across social classes—used by inner-city minorities, middle-class college students, and retired senior citizens. Over the past 20 years it has been legalized for medical uses in 28 states and the District of Columbia and for recreational use in eight states, with several more states currently anticipating voting on legalization. Today, there are an estimated two million registered medical marijuana patients across the United States (Marijuana Policy Project 2016). The Pew Research Center reports that a majority of Americans now support legalizing marijuana, although there are significant differences based on age, geographic region, and political affiliation (Pew Research Center 2015c).

The social contexts in which marijuana is used recreationally are similar to the private settings and some public settings (e.g., rock concerts) where alcohol is consumed. Given the range of people who smoke marijuana today and its ambivalent legal status, the experiences of marijuana users vary dramatically. In states where marijuana is legal or in settings where there is little if any law enforcement monitoring, smoking weed has little long-term sociolegal consequence. But the policing of marijuana varies widely depending largely on socioeconomic neighborhoods or contexts. Inner-city minority youth are far more likely to be arrested for marijuana possession than are middle-class college students. As a result, the lives of many inner-city youth are deeply impacted as they develop criminal records for small-scale drug offenses. According to data from the NSDUH, the use of marijuana peaks around the age of 20 and tapers off dramatically among those over 30. At that point the differential treatment of minority and middle-class youth who used marijuana in their teens and twenties has a serious impact, as underclass minority youths are far more likely to face criminal records for marijuana arrests that limit their educational and employment opportunities.

Hard "Street" Drugs

In contrast to the widespread recreational use of marijuana, hard drugs like heroin, methamphetamine, and crack cocaine are used by relatively few Americans. While half of Americans 12 and older have tried marijuana in their lifetimes, and one out of six have used it in the past year, similar figures for hard street drugs are dramatically lower, as was shown in table 10.2. Further, hard street drugs like meth, crack, and heroin are used for the most part in very different settings from those that are typical for marijuana.

News reports of celebrity hard drug use, such as crack use by former Toronto mayor, Rob Ford, and the heroin-related death of Philip Seymour Hoffman in 2014, do not represent the majority of hard drug users, most of whom come from economically impoverished social classes. Methamphetamine users are largely low-income and marginally employed white Americans, while crack cocaine use, which emerged in the mid-1980s and was significantly declining by the mid-1990s, has been far heavier among urban underclass African-Americans and Hispanics. Heroin addiction is primarily a problem among poor urban populations.

The interactional contexts of hard drug use are consistent with social learning principles, as first-time users are initiated into using the drugs by friends and family members who already use the drugs and provide them with the drugs and definitions favorable to using them. Cocaine and amphetamines produce almost immediate powerful sensual feelings of euphoria, often referred to by users as "orgasmic" in intensity. Physiologically, the most immediate way to deliver psychoactive drugs is to smoke them, delivering the drug to the lungs and bloodstream in close proximity to the brain. The rush of smoking crack cocaine is more immediate and powerful than even intravenously injecting cocaine. The intense crack high is also very short-lived, typically lasting less than 10 minutes, leaving users longing for more. The combination of a powerful, immediate, short-lived, and inexpensive one-time high make crack a very potentially dangerous drug. Philippe Bourgois situates the heavy use of crack, as well as heroin, within the context of inner-city poverty. Smoking crack, he writes,

> offers the equivalent of a born-again metamorphosis. Instantaneously the user is transformed from an unemployed, depressed high school dropout, despised by the world—and secretly convinced that his failure is due to his own inherent stupidity and disorganization. There is a rush of heart-palpitating pleasure, followed by a jaw-gnashing crash and wide-eyed alertness that provides his life with purpose: Get more crack—fast!
>
> —Bourgois (1989, p.65)

Given the urge to replay the high one has just experienced, cocaine users in general—and crack users in particular—often engage in binges in which they use all the cocaine available to them in one long session, lasting up to a day or more at a time. One of the most pressing challenges that hard drug users face is generating money to buy more drugs. Crack houses have been grimly described by researchers as places where women were treated abusively, with, as Inciardi et al. reported, "some women living as virtual slaves of the crack house owner, providing sexual services to crack house customers on demand in return for 'room and board'—typically, a mattress, junk food, and ready access to crack" (1993, p.39).

In comparison, female heroin addicts observed by Bourgois and Schonberg (2009) in San Francisco encampments of homeless heroin users engaged in prostitution primarily with men who did not use heroin. These women had far more control over the sex work they engaged in and were far less abused by male drug users, partially because the male heroin addicts that they teamed up and shared drugs with were often impotent because of their drug use.

Several criminologists have applied the concept of *deviance careers* to analyzing hard drug use. Research on the deviance careers of hard drug users typically describes drug use in a set of potential career phases, although it is important to recognize that not all hard drug users escalate through all phases, just as not all business careers follow the same trajectory. Charles Faupel's (1991) typology of heroin users provides a description of drug use career phases broadly consistent with those identified by other drug researchers (e.g., Sterk 1999; Boeri et al. 2006).

Most hard drug users start as *occasional users*, trying the drugs because of curiosity and social encouragement from people they know who use the drugs. As they occasionally use drugs—even hard drugs—many individuals are able to maintain conventional lives, working regular jobs, taking care of their children, and meeting social obligations and responsibilities. Several studies (e.g., Zinberg 1984; Waldorf et al. 1991) have documented that significant numbers of hard drug users never move beyond a controlled drug use stage even if they use drugs for years. Hard drugs such as cocaine, heroin, and methamphetamine, however, have pharmacological effects that make it difficult for many people to control their use of them. As just noted, these drugs create a powerful euphoric rush that the user may want to repeat as quickly as possible. Second, these drugs quickly produce tolerance so that more of the drug is needed to get a similar rush or high the next time.

When these pharmacological effects occur in social settings supportive of heavier drug use, some users move into what Faupel calls the *stable addict* role. Unlike the occasional user, stable addicts focus daily routines around their illicit substance use and tend to move away from conventional employment into criminal activities to support their drug habits. The stable addict is highly focused on using drugs, but their money-making routines still impose some structure on their lives and play a role in moderating their drug use (e.g., Sterk 1999).

The third career step, Faupel refers to as the *freewheeling addict* stage. This stage of hard drug careers is marked by the loss of control over drug use. While there are many potential reasons why an individual may lose control of their drug use, one of the most common patterns Faupel found was that an individual came into a relatively large amount of money, most often through a large "score" in criminal activity. Suddenly having lots of money, it is easy for the user to fall into a lifestyle where their drug use escalates out of control. When the money and drugs run out, a freewheeling addict may return to hustling like they previously did in the stable addict role. Those who have burned bridges

PUSHING YOUR BOUNDARIES

Storylines of Drug Abuse

In an article titled, "Women's 'Storylines' of Methamphetamine Initiation in the Midwest," Kristin Carbone-Lopez et al. (2012) reported findings from their prison interviews with women who had become involved in using methamphetamine. The researchers found four main story lines that women used to describe the social contexts and motivations related to their starting and continuing to use meth. One takeaway message from their study is that not all drug abusers have the same pathways into drug abuse. Even focusing exclusively on methamphetamine users, Carbone-Lopez et al. found that some of the women began using when encouraged by their parents or siblings. Others spoke of beginning to use meth as a way to numb the pain of adolescent and family conflict, while yet others recounted using meth in a quest for freedom from parental control. Finally, some women said they were drawn into meth use for instrumental reasons, to get an energy-boost, to lose weight, or to strengthen a romantic relationship. Using stories you find on the Internet, in newspapers, and magazines, identify three distinctly different "story lines" of drug abuse. That is, look for different reasons that people give for their drug abuse and different kinds of social relationships that they had while using illegal drugs. Come to class ready to share and compare your findings with those of other students.

with friends or damaged their bodies as freewheeling addicts may move to the fourth, and most desperate phase of hard drug use, that of the *street junkie.* At this point the drug user is likely to have developed a high level of tolerance for drugs, to have lost their ability to engage in effective hustling, and to live a desperate hand-to-mouth life in search of a "fix."

Finally, at any point in their careers, hard drug users may quit using. Many stable addicts as well as freewheelers and street junkies are forced to quit when they are arrested and incarcerated for criminal activities. Some, especially female, users decide to quit when they perceive their drug use impacting their children's lives. Heavy long-term users, however, often find it difficult to not return to the drugs that have been so central to their past lives.

CONTEMPORARY RESPONSES TO DRUG ABUSE

Prior to the start of the twentieth century, there was no widespread perception in the United States that drugs, at least other than alcohol, were a danger to society. That perception changed dramatically with the social concerns and governmental actions that led to the passage of the Harrison Act and its enforcement and expansion in the following decades.

Punitive Prohibition and Reducing Supply

In many ways the entire twentieth century constituted multiple waves of a war on drugs in the United States. In 1967, a presidential commission on drug abuse appointed by President Lyndon Johnson succinctly captured the approach to drugs that has dominated US policy. "Since early in the twentieth century," the President's Commission reported:

> We have built our drug control policies around the twin judgments that drug abuse was an evil to be suppressed and that this could most effectively be done by the application of criminal enforcement and penal sanctions.
>
> —President's Commission on Law Enforcement and Administration of Justice (1967, p.11)

The approach to drug abuse described by this commission has been aptly referred to as *punitive prohibition* (Reinarman and Levine 1997). It is built on criminal justice institutions and practices, on policing, courts, and prisons. While it was the most popular approach to drug abuse throughout the twentieth century, punitive prohibition became especially dominant in the War on Drugs in the late 1980s. As part of the get-tough-on-crime agenda, the Anti-Drug Abuse Act of 1986 set stiffer penalties for drug possession and sales and mandated new minimum sentences for many drugs, including marijuana. The mandatory prison sentences for drug-related crimes quickly led to a dramatic rise in prison populations and for the last 15 years, drug offenders have made up over half of the federal prison inmate population (Bureau of Prisons 2014), with about half of imprisoned drug offenders incarcerated on marijuana charges.

Federal and state policies also impose additional penalties beyond prison time on those convicted of drug offenses, including denial of public benefits or licenses, that are not applicable to those convicted of other types of crime (Chin 2002). The Higher Education Act of 1998 made students convicted for drug-related offenses while receiving financial aid ineligible for federal education grants, loans, or work assistance for a specified time. No other class of offense, including violent crimes or sex crimes, results in automatic denial of federal financial aid.

Since poor inner-city neighborhoods are far more heavily policed for drug use than are more affluent neighborhoods, and since underclass minority youth are far less likely to have resources to fight for themselves in the criminal justice system, the penalties for drug possession and sale fall heavily on black youth, especially young black men. As with the case of differential treatment among poor and black offenders for property crimes, the drug using poor end up in prison far more often than similar drug users from more affluent social classes.

A second component of the war on drugs has focused on reducing the supply of drugs. This goal has been approached through three key strategies. One strategy involves trying to work with other countries, such as the Southeast Asian countries that have been major producers of opium, South American countries that produce large quantities of cocaine, and Mexico which is the source of the bulk of methamphetamine in the United States. A second strategy involves interdiction, or the effort to prevent illegal drugs from coming across US borders. A third tactic for reducing drug supplies is to target street dealers who provide drugs directly to other users.

Efforts to reduce international drug supplies prove challenging. For one thing, some powerful people in drug-producing countries, often including government officials, benefit enormously from drug smuggling. Second, reducing or eliminating production in one country can raise the potential profits to be made, and production often pops up in another country. Large-scale illegal drug producers and distributors often have considerable resources at their disposal to protect their investments and themselves. By far the majority of drug "suppliers" in US prisons and jails are small time street dealers. Furthermore, in recent years, over 80 per cent of all arrests for US drug crimes have been for simple possession of drugs rather than for more serious drug crimes like trafficking and manufacturing (Federal Bureau of Investigation 2014b).

No criminologists or politicians would argue that the war on drugs declared in the 1980s has been won. Many would argue that the war has been misguided and destructive, with punishments for low-level offenders that far outweigh their offenses. In recent years there has been an increased interest in reevaluating the war on drugs. The 100 to 1 disparity in the mandatory sentencing requirements for crack versus powder cocaine has been especially controversial given its racial implications. In 2010, President Obama signed into law the Fair Sentencing Act, significantly reducing the difference in sentencing for these two types of cocaine. He also used his power as President in other ways to reduce some of the worst injustices associated with the War on Drugs.

Drug Courts

The dual concerns of the costs of prisons and the effective treatment of offenders have also played key roles in the emergence of *drug courts*, a type of court that did not exist in the United States prior to 1989 but is now popular across the United States with over 2,000 courts scattered throughout all 50 states (King and Pasquarella 2009). As the war on drugs policies of the 1980s took effect and courts became crowded with drug cases, many judges argued that incarcerating drug offenders crowded prisons and did little to change drug users' illegal behavior.

Drug courts are based on the model of *therapeutic jurisprudence*, or the use of the judicial system to support therapeutic treatment to overcome the

CLAIMS-MAKER PROFILE

President Barack Obama

In his 1995 memoir, *Dreams from My Father*, 34-year Harvard Law School graduate, Barack Obama, recounted his search for identity and meaning as a young black man. He was forthright in admitting that in his high school and early college days he smoked marijuana and occasionally snorted cocaine when he could afford it. "Junkie. Pothead," he writes, "That's where I'd been headed: the final, fatal role of the young would-be black man. . . . I got high to push questions of who I was out of my mind" (2004, p.93). It is ironic that the first and only US president to openly admit having used illegal drugs was thrust into a major role in addressing the problems created by the American War on Drugs. In his second year in office, Obama signed the Fair Sentencing Act of 2010 that dramatically reduced the 100 to 1 federal sentencing disparity for crack as compared to powder cocaine and eliminated the five-year mandatory minimum sentence for simple possession of crack cocaine, a mandate that had disproportionately fallen on African-Americans.

In 2014, President Obama took another step toward humane treatment of drug users, initiating a clemency program to reduce prison sentences of nonviolent drug offenders who would have been given shorter sentences if they had been convicted of the same crime under current laws. To be eligible, prisoners had to have served at least a decade with good conduct in prison and have no history of violence. During his term in office, President Obama commuted the sentences of over 1,300 federal inmates, more than the previous 11 presidents combined (Lamarty 2016).

Many of those who have been released under the clemency program are required to participate in drug treatment. President Obama advocated for increased support for treatment programs, urging legislators to move beyond "just thinking in terms of criminalization or incarceration, which unfortunately has been our response to the disease of addiction. Only Congress can achieve the broader reforms needed to ensure our federal sentencing system operates more fairly and effectively" (White House 2016).

personal problems that are believed to be causing criminal behavior. Drug courts demand a therapeutically revised form of confession: "I am sick" instead of "I am guilty" (Nolan 2001, p.142). Participants are expected to accept that they have an addiction and need treatment. They are required to attend counseling or Twelve Step meetings, submit to drug tests, meet regularly with case workers, and attend court hearings where their progress is reviewed. Drug court participants tend to have lower rearrest rates than those who are convicted of drug offenses and sentenced to incarceration (Spohn et al. 2001;

Gottfredson et al. 2003), although the programs do not work unless there is close monitoring and real sanctions if participants do not follow the rules. Since judges can impose jail time as a sanction for failing to abide by the rules, some drug court clients with low-level criminal charges end up spending more time behind bars by virtue of participating in drug court than they would have if they had been convicted and sentenced in a criminal court.

Harm Reduction

Both punitive prohibition and therapeutic jurisprudence seek to eliminate drug abuse. An alternative public health approach known as *harm reduction* focuses on reducing the harm that is associated with drug use. Harm-reduction advocates take what they believe is a pragmatic approach toward public health in regard to drugs. We must face the fact, they argue, that drug use exists and is highly unlikely to ever be completely eliminated. We also know that some drug use practices are far more physically and socially damaging than others. If our goal is to minimize the damage done by drugs, harm-reduction advocates assert, we should direct more of our attention to promoting safer ways of using drugs rather focusing solely on eliminating them.

Harm-reduction policies focus on safety first, supporting educational campaigns about (relatively) safe and responsible drug use, especially to drug-prone populations, such as 20-something club partiers or urban underclass minorities. Public harm-reduction education seeks to inform drug users about what kinds of drug combinations to avoid, what kinds of situations and behaviors to avoid when under the influence, how to pace one's drug use, and practices that ensure safer drug use. A good example of a harm-reduction policy is the *needle exchange programs* that gained support in the 1980s as it became clear that a major pathway of infection with the AIDS virus was via needle-sharing among intravenous drug users. Since needle sharing was due in large part to legal restrictions against the purchasing or providing of needles and syringes to drug users, many public health experts argued for a policy of providing clean needles to drug users in order to reduce the number of new infections. Critics of needle exchange programs argued that providing needles to drug users was implicitly condoning illegal drug use and could lead to higher rates of drug addiction as free needles became widely available. AIDS activists and other public health proponents of needle exchange have at times broken the law by providing clean needles to drug users. This example highlights the challenge faced by harm-reduction advocates. While the policies they promote may have clear impact on public health, any policy that accepts drug abuse as inevitable is vulnerable to charges of being soft on crime, or worse, encouraging it. Most harm-reduction proponents, however, are acutely aware of the hazards of drug use and do not support the legalization of hard drugs.

STIGMA MANAGEMENT AND RESISTANCE

Over the course of the twentieth century, US drug laws increased in scope and severity. While public attitudes toward illegal drug use waxed and waned, with particularly open attitudes among youth in the 1960s and 1970s, in the early decades of the twenty-first century illicit drug use is widely considered by the public to be a significant social problem and many drug users face both stigmatization and criminal sanctions for using drugs. Like members of other groups that have been categorized as deviant, drug users engage in many actions to avoid stigmatization and punishment.

In-Group Stigma Management

Among their peers, drug users manage stigma through techniques of neutralization, mutual protection, and emotional support. Fellow drug users offer positive definitions of drug use and invoke techniques of neutralization to counter negative views of their behavior. With their peers, drug users tend to focus on the fun associated with drugs and engage in denial of injury, as in claiming that marijuana is less harmful than alcohol. Many heroin, cocaine, and poly-drug users (that is, those who use more than one drug at a time) claim that their use of drugs is not harmful, and trade information about what drugs work well together and which mixes are dangerous and should be avoided (Reith 2005; Kelly 2007). Drug users also manage stigma among themselves by condemning the condemners, as in citing the health hazards of legal drugs like alcohol and tobacco in comparison to marijuana. Some drug users also appeal to higher loyalties in support of their drug use, as in claiming their rights to use hallucinogenic drugs in religious rituals or to have control of their own well-being through the use of medical marijuana.

In addition to providing each other with rationalizations for the acceptability of using drugs, fellow drug users help each other manage stigma by offering safe places to use drugs (whether in one's home, dorm room, or a homeless encampment) and protecting each other from potential dangers. In his study of New York City party club subculture, anthropologist Brian Kelly (2007) found that the college age youth he interviewed relied heavily on their peers to help them manage the risks associated with partying under the influence of Ecstasy and "Special-K" (ketamine). Since the quality of the drugs that were available in the Manhattan nightclubs was often suspect, partiers shared their knowledge about good and bad drugs, as well as testing techniques to detect adulterated pills. Partiers also depended on each other for physical and emotional support on days when they were recovering from long nights of rave clubbing. Similarly, homeless heroin addicts studied by Bourgois and Schonberg (2009) relied heavily on each other for both physical and emotional support.

While the stigma management strategies just described involve mutually supportive interaction among drug users, there are also situations in which some drug users seek to manage the stigma of drug use by comparing themselves to other, more degraded kinds of drug users. In interviews with convicted street hustlers, criminologist Heith Copes et al. found the terms "junkie," "crackhead," and "clucker" frequently used as derisive terms for drug users who are perceived as having lost control of their drug use and self-respect. As one convicted hustler explained, "The reason that we call them cluckers is when they don't have the crack they be clucking. They be like how a chicken will do because they be so nervous" (2008, p.262). When putting down crackheads, these hustlers were quick to assert that they were different. Another hustler explained, "See people like us, we go big. Crackheads will go do what they gotta do like steal lawnmowers and shit like that. . . . [In contrast] Whatever we do, it's gonna be worth something, you dig?" (2008, p.262). As this hustler's comment illustrates, many street drug users—such as those in Faupel's "stable addict" role described earlier—focus with some pride on their "main hustle," whether it be carjacking, burglary, sex work, or dealing drugs, because they believe their ability to engage in those activities demonstrates that they have control of their life situations. As Bourgois observed in his study of drug dealers in East Harlem,

> One message the crack dealers communicated clearly to me is that they are not driven solely by economic exigency. Like most humans on earth, in addition to material subsistence, they are also searching for dignity and fulfillment.
>
> —Bourgois (1995, p.324)

Out-Group Stigma Management

Out-group stigma management activities are directed toward those who are not part of the drug using subculture or experience. The goals of out-group stigma management are to avoid detection as a deviant, to minimize the impact of deviant labeling, or, alternatively, to directly challenge the deviant label. Drug users who interact with nonusers often try to pass as normal or hide their drug use. For many teenage marijuana users, learning to interact with parents or teachers while high is a rite of passage, far easier than hiding alcohol intoxication. Adult drug users also often hide their drug use from family members and coworkers or supervisors—and for surprisingly long times. In their research on long-term baby-boom generation heroin and methamphetamine users, Boeri et al. (2006) found that 50 per cent of methamphetamine users and 20 per cent of heroin users had managed controlled use over decades-long drug careers, maintaining mainstream social roles, such as work and family membership without being discovered.

While a considerable number of drug users evade detection for years, drug users in some settings are particularly closely monitored by law enforcement.

Inner-city minority neighborhoods are often subject to intense police scrutiny, thus making drug users in those neighborhoods more likely to get caught than users in other settings. Numerous ethnographies of inner-city drug use have documented high levels of police surveillance and arrests. In contrast, the affluent college student drug users and suppliers that were studied by Mohamed and Fritsvold for their book, *Dorm Room Dealers*, never extensively interacted with law enforcement and did not perceive the police as a serious threat to their drug activities. As a female college drug dealer who at one point was selling over $10,000 of marijuana per week told them:

> I got the impression in college that you were protected by being in college to some extent . . . That obviously the authorities should be spending their time busting people that are not working toward a potentially better future. So I guess I always felt that there was a safety umbrella over folks in college.
>
> —Mohamed and Fritsvold (2010, p.141)

Despite a nonchalant attitude toward everyday drug transactions and a near total lack of security, the affluent white student dealers that Mohamed and Fritsvold studied were never arrested. Black youth, on the other hand, as Michael Tonry has noted, "are arrested and confined in numbers grossly out of line with their use or sale of drugs" (1995, p.49). And once arrested and convicted of drug offenses, black youths, especially black young men, face problems associated with the stigma of a criminal record when they are released from prison. As Lucia Trimbur (2009) has documented in her study of young black boxers at New York's Gleason's Gym, while many young men leave prison with a deep commitment to avoiding street drug culture, their lack of legitimate employment opportunities can ultimately push them back toward participation in the drug economy.

Yet, another possible way of managing the stigma associated with drug abuse is to quit using drugs and to cease actively engaging in the drug user role. A significant number of drug abusers "mature out" of their drug activities (Boeri et al. 2006), reducing drug use over time as they settle into conventional social roles and responsibilities. Yet, other hard drug users experience quitting drugs as more of a struggle. Overcoming physical addiction and dependency on drugs presents one set of challenges, but recovery also involves exiting a social role with which the user has come to identify.

Drug researchers Tammy Anderson and Lynn Bondi (1998) have drawn on Ebaugh's (1988) four stages of role exit as a useful framework for understanding the experiences of drug users as they seek recovery. The initial stage in exiting the drug user role occurs when an individual experiences first doubts about using drugs. Such feelings may arise for a variety of reasons: because of burnout, loss of a loved one due to drugs, getting arrested, or feeling a loss of control in one's life. Often first doubts include some degree of self-disgust or negative feeling about oneself and behaviors, such as self-concern about failing to be a good parent or worker. Once a drug user has experienced doubts about using drugs, they may begin seeking alternatives, looking for ways to move out of the drug user role. Many drug users seeking to quit turn to Twelve Step programs like Alcoholics Anonymous and Narcotics Anonymous which provide social support and a structured approach for achieving sobriety. It is not uncommon for drug users to spend months or even years with uncomfortable doubts about their drug use without giving up drugs completely. The fourth stage in recovery from drug using is the creation of the "ex" role, or developing an identity as a former or recovering drug user. Twelve Step programs provide a classic model for the "ex" role for substance abusers. Based on an understanding of drug abuse as rooted in a disease of addiction, Twelve Step programs assert that complete abstinence from drugs is the only path to recovery and that recovery is a lifelong process. The recovering-addict role manages the stigmatized identity of drug abuser by embracing abstinence and the "ex" role of recovering addict, as Twelve Step programs put it, "one day at a time."

Collective Action

Yet, another approach to managing the stigma of drug use involves publicly challenging the very assumption that drugs are bad. While few people today would try to make the case that hard drugs like heroin and methamphetamine are safe for recreational use, a widespread social movement to legalize marijuana has developed across the United States. One of the first grassroots pro-marijuana organizations was the National Organization for Reform of Marijuana Laws, commonly referred to by its acronym, NORML. Founded in 1970, NORML today has 135 chapters across the United States. Along with other pro-marijuana organizations like the Marijuana Majority and Students for Sensible Drug Policy, NORML advocates for changes in marijuana policies in several ways, including support for the legalization of medical marijuana, decriminalization of marijuana possession in states where it is classified as criminal behavior, and legalization of marijuana for adults. Pro-marijuana organizations fight against stigmatization of the drug in a variety of ways. The very names of these organizations project positive social images of marijuana use as normal, sensible, and favored by a majority of Americans. They build support at the grassroots level while recruiting high profile officials and celebrities as advisory board members and spokespeople. NORML's advisory board includes country music legend, Willie Nelson, and actor, Woody Harrelson, as well as a Nobel Prize-winning chemist and a former Seattle chief of police. The political success of the pro-marijuana movement over the past 20 years has been extensive. Despite continuing federal laws against marijuana, since 1996 28 states and the District of Columbia have legalized medical marijuana and more than two million Americans now have medical cards that allow them to purchase marijuana from licensed dispensaries. Eight states and the District of Columbia have legalized recreational use of marijuana by adults and several other states are in the process of voter referendums on legalization. The collective action of pro-marijuana groups has had a powerful impact in the United States, leading to striking inconsistencies across state borders and between the states and the federal government. In some states both medical and recreational marijuana use are legal, while a person taking marijuana to the state next door may face serious criminal prosecution, including jail or prison time and denial of federal benefits including student loans, food stamps, and public assistance. In one state, marijuana vendors can make a legitimate career out of selling the drug at a store or even a farmer's market. Indeed, in 2014 the US Department of Justice informed banks that they can legally provide loans to state-licensed marijuana businesses (*The Week* 2014, p.9). On the other hand, anyone convicted of selling marijuana in many states will be labeled a criminal and barred from ever working with children, in the medical field, and many other lines of employment. Such inconsistencies provide additional fodder for the pro-marijuana social movement which has gained momentum in recent years and shows no sign of abating.

BLURRED BOUNDARIES II: IS IT TIME TO LEGALIZE DRUGS?

Marijuana advocates in the United States promote legalizing marijuana by arguing that it has minimal harmful effects and many social and physical benefits. Few people would make that argument for street drugs like heroin, crack, and methamphetamine. But at a special session of the United Nations General Assembly in the spring of 2016, Kofi Anon, the former UN Secretary General, joined with leading medical researcher from Johns Hopkins University to promote legalizing hard drugs around the world. In a *Huffington Post* editorial titled, "It is Time to Legalize Drugs," Anon (2016) argued that we must accept that a drug-free world is an illusion. "It is time," Anon wrote, "to acknowledge that drugs are infinitely more dangerous if they are left solely in the hands of criminals who have no concerns about health and safety. Legal regulation protects health." Johns Hopkins University medical experts agreed, writing that:

> The enforcement of drug control policies undermines the well-being and health of the drug users and the communities the policies are meant to protect. . . . Further, mass incarceration of African-Americans and Hispanics for non-violent drug crimes has led to deterioration of families and communities.
>
> —Benham (2016)

Given our national history of punitive prohibition, many of us at first react with dismay to such arguments. But is it possible that they are right? Could legalizing and regulating hard drugs reduce the problems associated with drug abuse?

One argument proponents of legalization make is that if drugs were legal it would be possible to regulate their production. Many health problems associated with drug abuse come from the substances street drugs are often "cut" with before they are sold. Some relatively benign substances such as flour and saccharin are often added to drugs like cocaine and heroin to bulk up the product and deceive the buyer as to how much of the drug they are getting. At other times, street drugs are laced or cut with substances, such as mild anesthetics like lidocaine or stimulants such as caffeine, that increase their psychoactive effects. Given the unregulated production of illicit street drugs, there is no oversight of their purity or the sanitary contexts in which they are produced. If such drugs were under the regulatory power of the Food and Drug Administration, these health risks could be significantly reduced. The outlawing of drugs and drug paraphernalia also contributes to the spread of communicable diseases like Hepatitis C and HIV infection. A second argument is that legalizing drugs would enable state and federal governments to tax such products and use money that currently makes its way back to illegal drug producers and dealers. The states of Washington and Colorado, for instance, each collected over a hundred million dollars in taxes from recreational marijuana sales in 2015 (Ellison 2016; Illescas 2016).

Almost all of us are likely to agree that current laws against illicit drugs have glaring problems. But is legalizing drugs the best answer to those problems? And what issues should be considered in making such legal and medical decisions?

SUMMARY

- Drug use can be classified in four categories: legal medical use, legal recreational use, illegal medical use, and illegal recreational use.
- By far the most used illegal recreational drug is marijuana (legal now in eight states). Cocaine is the second, followed by illegal use of prescription painkillers and antianxiety medications.
- Far fewer people use hard illegal street drugs, such as heroin, crack cocaine, and methamphetamine.
- Researchers find that most people will self-report their drug use when asked anonymously.
- Deviance ethnographers have a record of establishing rapport with drug users, although some drug use settings create challenges for protecting themselves and their informants.
- Many societies have myths about psychoactive plants being gifts from the gods.
- Efforts to reduce or eliminate illicit drugs focus on punishing drug users or treating them for what is viewed as illness or addiction.
- In the nineteenth century virtually all drugs could be bought without prescriptions in the United States.
- Fears about opium-using Chinese laborers and "cocaine-crazed Negroes" played major roles in the 1914 enactment of the Harrison Act, the first major

US drug law. This was followed in the 1930s by a campaign against marijuana that drew on fears of Mexicans.
- Criminal justice prosecution of drug use became particularly intense during the "War on Drugs."
- Social learning theory explains that gaining access to drugs and learning to use and enjoy them requires associating with others who use the drugs.
- Personal drug experiences are based on three interrelated factors: a drug's pharmacological properties, the psychological set that a person brings to the drug experience, and the setting in which drug use occurs.
- Most hard drug users start as occasional users and are able to maintain conventional lives. Those who move beyond occasional use may progress to other patterns of drug abuse:
    - Stable addicts whose daily routines revolve around their illicit substance use.
    - Freewheeling addicts caught up in extended drug binges.
    - Street junkies who have burned through their resources and live hand-to-mouth while seeking drugs.
- Punitive incarceration and mandatory prison sentences for drug-related crimes have led to a massive increase in prison populations.
- Drug courts offer some convicted offenders the opportunity to avoid prison time if they pursue treatment for their drug abuse.
- Harm reduction offers a public health approach to drug abuse that focuses on promoting safer drug use.
- Drug users manage stigma by invoking techniques of neutralization and providing each other with protection and support. They often manage their interactions with nonusers by hiding their drug use and many "controlled" drug users evade discovery throughout their drug careers.
- Inner-city minority drug users are at far higher risk of arrest and prosecution than are more affluent white drug users.
- Some users make a commitment to quitting drug use, often turning to Narcotics Anonymous and other recovery programs for support.
- Marijuana advocates have become moral entrepreneurs in their own right, campaigning for the legalization of marijuana which has been legalized for medical use in 28 states and recreational use in eight, although it is still illegal under federal regulation.

KEYWORDS

addiction: A term used in two different ways in reference to drug use: (1) physiological dependence on a drug which produces withdrawal symptoms when the drug is not used; (2) a compulsive behavior in which an individual repeats unhealthy drug use without being able to control it.

decriminalization: The reduction or abolishing of criminal penalties for possession and/or use of a drug, as in the decriminalization of marijuana in several states in the United States.

drug courts: Courts established to divert drug offenders away from criminal prosecution and into drug treatment programs.

freewheeling addict: A hard drug user who has acquired resources for almost unlimited drug use, at least for a short time, in a stage of heavy drug use that often leads to destitution and movement into the street junkie role.

harm reduction: An approach to controlling drug abuse through a variety of policies, such as syringe exchange programs and healthcare for drug users, that focuses on minimizing the harmful effects of drug use rather than punishment of drug users.

Harrison Act: Federal legislation enacted in 1914 that dramatically restricted the availability of previously unregulated opium and coca products.

illegal medical or instrumental drug use: The use of pharmaceutical drugs without a prescription for medical (e.g. pain reduction) or instrumental (e.g., weight loss) purposes.

illegal recreational drug use: The use of illegal drugs for pleasure or recreational purposes.

instrumental drug use: The use of a drug for medical treatment or to achieve a particular goal, such as use of stimulants to study for an exam or steroids to build body mass and strength.

legal medical drug use: The use of pharmaceutical drugs with a prescription for approved medical purposes.

legal recreational drug use: The use of legal drugs (e.g., tobacco, alcohol, and marijuana in some states) for pleasure or recreational purposes.

legalization: The replacement of laws against certain drugs with the creation of policies to regulate the selling and use of drugs, as in the legalization of marijuana in several states.

needle exchange programs: A harm-reduction policy of providing clean needles and syringes to IV drug users in order to reduce the spread of infectious disease through needle sharing among users.

occasional user: An individual who uses drugs on a sporadic or occasional basis and whose life is not structured around drug-related activity.

opioid: Narcotic drugs derived from opium or synthetically produced drugs that produce similar pain-relieving effects.

pharmaceutical determinism: The belief that certain drugs are inherently dangerous and lead unequivocally to specific harmful outcomes.

punitive prohibition: The use of police and the criminal justice system as major drug control policies.

stable addict: A hard drug user whose daily routines are oriented toward their illicit substance use, but whose money-making strategies provide some structure to daily life and an identity beyond drug use.

street junkie: A hard drug user who has lost control of drug use and who lives a hand-to-mouth existence engulfed in the drug addict role.

therapeutic jurisprudence: The use of the judicial system to provide treatment to overcome the personal problems, such as drug addiction, that are believed to be causing criminal behavior.

CHAPTER

11 Sex Work

San Francisco North Beach Clubs (Christopher/Alamy Stock Photo).

CONTENTS

LEARNING OBJECTIVES

After reading this chapter, you will be able to:

- Describe the common types of sex work in the United States today
- Explain the challenges of, and strategies for, studying sex work
- Identify different historical definitions of, and causal explanations for, sex work
- Apply a combination of social learning and anomie theories to sex work
- Analyze the interactional contexts in which various forms of sex work occur
- Explain the risks of violent exploitation associated with the various contexts of sex work
- Describe the stigma management strategies used by sex workers
- Assess the arguments for and against John shaming programs targeting men who use prostitutes

BLURRED BOUNDARIES I: THE STREET PROSTITUTE AND THE *PLAYBOY* COLLEGE GIRL

Tina Pearl took a drag off her cigarette as she stood in light rain looking out at the evening traffic on Bissonnet Street in Houston. While a couple of other girls near her waved to passersby, Tina stood by the curb ready to be the first to get to next car that stopped. When a car pulled up, she tossed her cigarette and poked her head in the open car window. "Hey hon," she smiled. "Lookin' for something?" After a brief conversation, Tina jumped in the car and it sped off to the back of a nearby fast-food parking lot. There, Tina gave unprotected oral sex to a middle-aged man who she had never met before and would probably never meet again. The sex, which he paid for with 40 dollars in cash, lasted less than 10 minutes. When it was over, the man told her to get out of the car, leaving her in the parking lot. For a moment, Tina considered going into the fast-food restaurant to get something to eat, but even though she was hungry, she was more desperate to get some crack.

Within an hour Tina had managed to score two vials of crack, which she smoked quickly before heading back to the Bissonnet thoroughfare. At 21, Tina has been working the streets for three years, almost ever since she started using crack. She has been arrested several times. After each arrest, she returned to the area, in part to get drugs and in part because that was where she had grown up and felt at home.

Tina's life prospects are sobering. She quit high school before graduating and now has a criminal record for prostitution and drug possession. Aside from babysitting, she has never had a job except as a prostitute. Her time on the streets has not been easy. She has been beat up several times and between her drug use and sex work, she has developed other health problems. She has been treated several times for sexually transmitted diseases—which is not surprising, since many of the men she sells sex to resist using condoms. She refuses to get tested for HIV, fearing that she has acquired AIDS and not wanting to know for sure.

Often when Americans think of sex workers, images of street prostitutes like Tina come to mind. Such young and frequently drug-dependent women can be found plying what has been called the "oldest profession" in sketchy areas of major cities across the United States. While laws and police efforts to end street prostitution have never managed to eliminate it, street prostitutes like Tina are seen by most of us as deeply damaged women, victims of circumstances and bad judgment.

However, sex work includes a broad range of sexually explicit activities that go well beyond street prostitution. While most of us look with disgust and sympathy at urban street prostitutes, other kinds of commercial sexually oriented activities may strike many of us as more acceptable. For a decade, *Playboy* published an annual photo feature of "party school girls" from universities across the country. At many universities, the arrival of *Playboy* scouts and photographers was met by a crowd of young women seeking to be considered as possible "playmates." In one of its party school issues, *Playboy* featured 24-year-old San Diego State University gerontology student, Alison Waite, as its "Miss May" cover girl and centerfold. Following her photo shoots for *Playboy*, Ms. Waite built a successful media career as a TV correspondent and a sex and dating advice columnist.

Playboy and other men's magazines have featured hundreds of college coeds. A few go on to careers in pornography, but for many of these young women, posing nude for *Playboy* was their only experience being paid for sexually provocative photos. Is such activity immoral? Sex work occurs along a continuum from clearly exploitive and degrading to celebrity status. Where should we draw the line between the permissible and what should be outlawed or banned?

Several issues come to the foreground when we seriously examine sex work. One set of issues involves our views of sexual morality. What should the rights of individuals be to sell and pay for sexual pleasure? Should sharing of one's body, visually and physically, be restricted to erotic acts based on romantic intimacy, or is sex outside of love and marriage acceptable? Another set of issues involves the contexts of sex work and the consequences for individuals and society. The social experiences and personal impact of Tina Pearl's street prostitution are dramatically different from Alison Waite's *Playboy* photo shoots. Tina's sex work involves providing actual sex in unsafe conditions and interactions where she is constantly at risk of victimization. She receives a small amount of money for each act, often with more than a dozen men per day. The money she makes is quickly spent on drugs that damage her health and keep her in a vicious cycle of prostitution-drugs-arrest with little hope of better times. And given her customer's resistance to using condoms, she is both a victim of, and medium for, sexually transmitted diseases.

In contrast, Alison posed for *Playboy* with professional photographers in a clean and upbeat studio. She did not engage in actual sex—thus avoiding the possibility of sexually transmitted disease—and she was highly paid for her time, as *Playboy* playmates received tens of thousands of dollars for just a few days' work. Rather than facing dismal consequences, Alison's sex work opened doors for a well-paid public career.

As we examine sex work in this chapter, we will see that this category of deviance has varied far more across human history than most of us realize. Today, especially with the rise of the Internet and smartphones, the opportunities for, and varieties of, sex work continue to expand and challenge us to explore the blurred boundaries of social life.

CURRENT CONSTRUCTIONS OF SEX WORK AND PORNOGRAPHY IN THE UNITED STATES

Ronald Weitzer provides a social science definition of sex work. "Sex work," he writes, "refers to the individuals and organizations involved in sexual commerce, which includes prostitution, pornography, stripping, and erotic telephone or webcam enterprises" (2013, p.713). Each of these activities involves individuals, and often organizations, that provide sexually oriented services or materials to others who purchase them.

Types of Sex Work

Prostitution is the direct selling of sex. While most prostitution involves men paying female prostitutes, male prostitutes also sell sexual favors to women and homosexual and bisexual men. The most common varieties of prostitution today include street prostitution, massage parlors, and escort services. *Street prostitution* involves seeking customers in public settings such as street corners and bars. Prostitutes can legally work in *brothels* in the state of Nevada, or in what are often called *massage parlors* in cities where prostitution is illegal. Brothels and massage parlors hire a number of women who work inside, offering sex to customers in private settings. At the high-end of the prostitution industry are *escort services* that send women to hotels or other private locations. Escort services cater to affluent men and may charge several hundred dollars per hour. High-end escorts tend to have a smaller number of clients to whom they devote considerable time and emotional attention.

Stripping, often referred to as "exotic dancing," involves sexually provocative dancing, typically while taking off pieces of clothing until the dancer is naked or only scantily clad. Dancers in strip clubs make money through tips and selling dances to their customers. By virtue of their close proximity to sexually aroused men, some strippers find strip clubs provide opportunities for prostitution as well as dancing.

Pornography is sexually graphic images, especially in magazines and video, intended to be sexually arousing. Pornographic materials range from mild to extreme. Soft-core pornography, such as that shown in *Playboy* magazine, portrays women in sexually provocative and revealing poses, but not engaging in explicit sex. At the other end of the spectrum, hard-core pornography ranges from one-on-one explicit sex to more extreme acts, such as group sex and BDSM encounters. Federal laws define pornographic photos and videos of sex with minors as illegal and most states also restrict pornography depicting humans having sex with animals, although an illegal market for such materials manages at times to evade law enforcement.

Yet, another venue for sex work taps electronic media to provide live phone and video interactions. While not physically present with their customers, phone and video sex workers provide real-time interaction, playing out their customers' fantasies and desires, typically culminating in the caller's sexual climax. Like those involved in many other sex work encounters, phone and video sex workers may specialize in niche fantasy markets, acting out such roles as *dominatrix*, school girl, or attractive neighbor, often enacting fantasies that men are uncomfortable sharing with their marital partners.

Statistical Snapshot

It is impossible to get reliable big-picture data about sex work because it encompasses such a wide range of activities. Some illegal sex work, such as child pornography, has clear victims, and—at least when identified by law enforcement—is recorded in crime statistics. But most illegal sex work in the United States is victimless crime in which two or more adults consent and wish to keep their actions hidden from law enforcement. Even legal kinds of sex work, such as stripping and adult pornography, are widely stigmatized with both sex workers and their customers hiding much of their involvement.

Some statistics are available to give us a sense of the extent and nature of some aspects of sex work and its consumption. Americans spend over 13 billion dollars annually on legal X-rated magazines, videos, Internet pornography, telephone sex, and strip clubs (Weitzer 2010, p.1). There are approximately 3,800 strip clubs in the United States (Association of Club Executives 2014), with the attendance statistics suggesting that about one in 10 American adults visited a strip club annually (Weitzer 2009, p.2).

The General Social Survey reports 15–18 per cent of US men say they have paid for sex at least once in their lives, with 2–4 per cent saying they have done so in the past year (Weitzer 2009, p.2). The real number is undoubtedly higher. Researchers have estimated that about 10–20 per cent of US prostitution involves street prostitutes, while the rest is spread across massage parlors, bar prostitution, escort services, and brothels (Porter and Bonilla 2010, p.163).

Viewing pornography is much more common than paying directly for sex. Based on data from the General Social Survey, 34 per cent of men and 16 per cent of women report having watched a sexually explicit video in the past year (Weitzer 2013, p.717). Among young adults the percentage may be considerably greater, as suggested by Simon Lajeunesse's research on college men's exposure to Internet porn. "We started our research," he reports, "seeking men in their twenties who had never consumed pornography. We couldn't find any" (McCormack 2013).

Even though significant numbers of Americans are consumers of one or more varieties of sex work, the sex industry is widely regarded as immoral. Over 70 per cent of Americans say they feel that pornography is an important moral issue for the country. Surveys report that about 40 per cent of Americans feel that pornography should be banned, and almost 50 per cent believe that strip clubs should be illegal. In short, sex work presents a paradox: "a lucrative industry that employs a significant number of workers and attracts many customers but is regarded by many people as deviant and in need of stricter control" (Weitzer 2009, p.3).

CHALLENGES IN RESEARCHING SEX WORK

"In no other area of the social sciences," Weitzer observes, "has ideology colored knowledge production more than in the field of sex work" (2013, p.714). Funding for research in this field has been minimal, with most funding requiring that researchers examine sex work as a social problem.

Counting Sex Work

Researchers seeking to calculate the amount and nature of sex work are beset by several challenges. Some sex work is legal, some is criminal, and all of it is subject to stigmatization. The crime statistics for victimless crimes like prostitution are misleading since they are directly tied to the amount of police effort focused on the crime at any given time. Jumps in arrest rates for prostitution are mostly the result of increased police surveillance.

Crime statistics on prostitution are also biased in capturing women engaged in providing sex twice as often as their male customers. This is the only crime listed by Bureau of Justice Statistics for which more women are arrested than men. And yet, since prostitutes engage in paid sex with many men rather than just one, the number of men breaking the law by buying prostitutes' services undoubtedly exceeds the number of prostitutes.

Street-based sex work is easier to observe than indoor sex work, but getting accurate numbers of even street prostitutes, let alone their clients, is a major undertaking. Ric Curtis et al.'s research (2008) on underage sex workers in New York City (NYC) illustrates one way of collecting accurate data—and the contributions that such data can make to improving our understanding of sex work dynamics. Like many other people categorized as deviants, underage sex workers represent a hidden population. Most of the research on underage sex workers is based on interviews with the most easily located youth who are in detention facilities, group homes, or rehabilitation programs. As valuable as their stories are, they may not be representative of the broader underage sex worker population. Curtis and his colleagues adopted a "respondent-driven sampling technique" to get a more representative sample of minor sex workers on the streets. They began by distributing coupons that could be turned in for 20 dollars, along with offering respondents 10 dollars each for up to three other referrals. After a youth was interviewed, he or she was given three numbered coupons to give to other youth on the streets. When new youth agreed to be interviewed, they were also given numbered coupons to recruit others. Using this technique, Curtis and his coresearchers were able to chart the social network of underage NYC sex workers and to establish a representative sample for analysis. Their study revealed that many beliefs about this population were inaccurate. Contrary to assumptions that underage sex work was mostly engaged in by teenage girls who were managed by pimps, Curtis et al.'s study revealed that nearly half of underage sex workers were boys, and that only 10 per cent of all the youth worked with someone who served in a pimping role.

Getting Close

Deviance ethnographers find it relatively easy to negotiate access to some kinds of sex work. Strip clubs and settings where street prostitutes work are easy to gain access to in comparison to massage parlors and escort services. Getting access to settings, however, is only part of the challenge. Developing rapport with sex workers and getting them to talk about their experiences can be very demanding in terms of an ethnographer's time and energy.

In her study of drug-addicted street prostitutes (discussed in Chapter 10), Maher (1997) describes the challenges of following the homeless women she was studying as they engaged in sex work, watched out for the police, bought and consumed drugs, and sought shelter. Maher had to adapt her interviews to short time frames that fit into their hectic lives, especially since many of the women were heroin users who were often unable to focus due to drug use or withdrawal symptoms.

Like other deviance ethnographers, sex work ethnographers must make decisions about how close they will get to the experiences they study. Teela Sanders was asked by one of the prostitutes she was studying to watch her have sex with a client to see how business-like it really was. Sanders declined to watch, but later reflected, "Maybe I should not have been perturbed by Astrid's invitation but instead should have looked on the occasion as an opportunity to watch what I was asking them to describe" (2005, p.34).

While no researchers report engaging in prostitution in their research, some researchers have participated in other parts of the sex work industry. A few sociologists (e.g., Flowers 1998; Mattley 2005) participated as phone sex workers in the 1990s when phone sex was most common. A larger number of female scholars have blended work as exotic dancers with their academic interests. The discussion of exotic dancing in this chapter draws on the autoethnographic research conducted by Carol Ronai (1998, 1999), Katherine Frank (2002), Mindy Bradley-Engen (2009), and Danielle Egan (2006).

Several researchers have taken nondancing roles in strip clubs that gave them access to dancers and customers. Kim Price-Glynn (2010) found that a job as a cocktail waitress gave her the physical and social proximity to conduct her research. Mary Nell Trautner (2005) conducted fieldwork by presenting herself as a paying customer. Other researchers have relied primarily on interviews with dancers. Bernadette Barton (2006) considered dancing when she started her research, but was uncomfortable with what she saw as exploitive and unpredictable interactions with the male customers. She collected most of her data by interviewing dancers outside of the clubs, in coffee shops and other settings.

One glaring imbalance in sex work research involves the predominance of research directed toward sex workers compared to studying those who purchase or consume sex work. One reason for this imbalance stems from the different nature of consuming sex work as opposed to producing it. Many sex workers tend to work at least modestly routine schedules in specific locations, making them relatively easy to find. Their customers are more unpredictable. Further, today a considerable amount of sex work consumption, such as watching pornography, is done on the Internet in private homes. While this can create unique challenges, the Internet has also proven to be a valuable source of data for sex work researchers. Significant numbers of *johns*, or men-seeking prostitutes, use Internet sites like Craigslist and Backpage to locate sex workers. Online forums exist where men post information about how to find prostitutes, the sexual services available, costs, and potential threats of being robbed or arrested (Holt and Blevins 2007). Many out-call escorts also have their own websites with photos, information about the services they provide, and even customer reviews. And, of course, the Internet now provides easy access to thousands of porn sites. Sex work scholars as well as customers are able to learn more about the variety and extent of sex work through online research. Thomas Holt and Kristie Blevins (2007) have analyzed active Internet forums for johns in 10 US cities, while Sarah Earle and Keith Sharp (2008) have studied the accounts posted by over 2,500 men online regarding their experiences with legalized prostitutes in the United Kingdom. And in their best-selling book, *A Billion Wicked Thoughts* (2011), computational neuroscientists Ogi Ogas and

Sai Gaddam mined data from over a hundred million Internet users to examine preferences in Internet pornography.

CROSS-CULTURAL CONSTRUCTIONS OF SEX WORK

The selling of sex dates back to some of the earliest human civilizations and has often been referred to as the "oldest profession." In many societies the trading of sex for money has been acceptable for certain classes of women. In other times and societies prostitution and other sex work have been regarded as immoral and even illegal.

Different Definitions

Among the earliest documents describing prostitution are Sumerian texts describing religious rites in which temple priestesses served as sacred prostitutes. The purpose of sacred prostitution is not clear, although many scholars believe it reflected earlier fertility rituals. In any case, these prostitutes' earnings accounted for a substantial part of the temples' income. Other religions have endorsed temple-based prostitution, although they did not consider it a sacred duty. When the headquarters of the Catholic Church were moved to Avignon, France, in the fourteenth century, the pope sanctioned the creation of a church brothel where, as sex historian Reay Tannahill writes, "the girls spent part of their time in prayer and religious duties and the rest of the time servicing customers" (1982, p.279).

In contrast to the affiliation of prostitution with religious institutions, in ancient Greece one category of prostitutes—known as the *hetaerae*, or what later came to be called *courtesans*—were distinguished for intellectual and artistic talents as well as for their erotic skills. Ancient Greece was intensely patriarchal and the wives of male citizens were highly restricted. Greek men looked to their wives for procreation, but often to prostitutes for most of their sexual pleasure. As the Greek statesman, Demosthenes, wrote, "Man has the courtesan for erotic enjoyment, concubines for daily use, and wives of his own rank to bring up children and be faithful housewives" (Roberts 1992, p.21). The *hetaerae* were primarily freed slave women who did not face the social constraints that were experienced by Greek wives. Some of them were educated in the women-centered colleges in Greece. The poet Sappho is reputed to have run one such school on the island of Lesbos. The *hetaerae* were mistresses to the greatest poets, artists, and statesmen of Greek society, including the playwright, Sophocles, and the philosopher, Plato.

Worldly courtesans have been particularly visible in societies where most women are confined to narrow domestic roles. 2000 years after classical

Greece, Renaissance Europe witnessed a surge in courtesans. "Like the earlier Greek *hetaerae*," historian Nikki Roberts writes:

> the courtesans of Venice, Florence and Milan were educated, influential and talented beauties who specialized in catering to the sexual and social needs of men who had excluded their wives from fully participating in their lives.
>
> —Roberts (1992, p.101)

In contrast, prostitution has often been viewed as immoral. Public and religious leaders in many societies have outlawed prostitution. Yet, other leaders have viewed prostitution as a "necessary evil." Saint Augustine argued that prostitution was a necessary outlet for the lust of men. "Prostitution in the towns is like the cesspool in the palace," he explained. "Take away the cesspool and the palace will become an unclean and evil-smelling place" (Roberts 1992, p.74).

Different "Causes"

The most widely recognized motivation for sex work is the money or other material advantages it provides. Looking at prostitution in European history, Roberts argues, "From the women's point of view, prostitution largely represented the only path of upward mobility and, as often as not, survival; particularly for those whose livelihoods had been ruined by war, famine, plague—or taxes" (1992, p.98). Many of the popular picaresque novels of eighteenth-century Europe told stories of women who fell into prostitution and the criminal underworld. Typically, the storyteller began by recounting her birth and childhood in a respectable family, followed by the death of her parents and being thrust alone into a harsh world to live by her wits. While first resisting, she soon found that her body and quick wits were her most valuable resources for survival.

While picaresque novels portrayed prostitutes as part of an underworld of crime and deceit, the criminal anthropologist Cesare Lombroso viewed prostitutes as degenerate humans who lacked the physical and mental capacities of modern people. In his book, *The Female Offender*, Lombroso claimed that prostitutes were characterized by hairiness, large jaws, and cheekbones that represented a throwback to primitive humanity. "The primitive woman," Lombroso and Ferrero wrote, "was always a prostitute" (1895, p.42). Lombroso further asserted that civilized women lacked sexual urges, which were a specifically male attribute. The sexual promiscuity of prostitutes, he believed, was evidence of their more primitive biology since "virility was one of the special features of the savage woman" (1895, p.71).

Finally, in some historical periods sex workers have been understood as victims who are taken advantage of and pushed into a life of sex work and prostitution in societies that offer little protection and economic opportunity for poor young women and men. In the late 1800s and early decades of the twentieth century, many European and American journalists wrote of prostitution as the worst social problem in society, believing that it pointed to the breakdown of family and community as well as organized predation on vulnerable young women. More recently, several notable sex work scholars (e.g., Jody Miller 2002, 2011) have focused on global political and economic contexts that push many impoverished young females and males into the sex tourism industry in Third World countries such as Sri Lanka, India, and Thailand.

Different Responses

Almost always when sex work has been defined as immoral, it is sex workers, not their customers, who are sanctioned for their behavior. Since the majority of prostitutes have been women this means that women have borne the brunt of punishment.

Sex workers have been subjected to physical punishment, often in public settings. Across Europe in the Middle Ages sex workers were subjected to whippings, brandings, and public humiliation. A decree by the king of Spain in 596 AD called for prostitutes to be whipped 300 strokes and banished from their cities or villages (Mizuta and Mulvey-Roberts 1994). In the twelfth century, the Roman Emperor Barbarossa punished prostitutes traveling with the army by having their noses cut off in an attempt to make them less attractive (Hardaway 2003). Some Lutheran countries practiced shaving the heads and cutting of the ears of prostitutes, in order to both humiliate and identify them. Yet, other societies have invoked the death sentence for prostitution. In the Old Testament, death by stoning and burning was described as punishment for women who shamed their families through prostitution. In 1586, just a century after Pope Julius II approved the creation of a church-sponsored brothel in Rome, Pope Sixtus V declared that the death penalty would be imposed on prostitutes, although his proclamation was resisted through much of Europe (Ringdal 2004) where physical punishment and banishment were more common.

Beginning in the 1700s an era referred to as the Great Confinement swept across Europe. During this era prostitutes as well as a wide range of other indigents, orphans, criminals, and the mentally ill were often removed to workhouses where they were imprisoned and forced to labor. The imprisonment of prostitutes was often justified as providing girls and women with an opportunity to redeem themselves. Magdalene Homes were established in the Middle Ages under Pope Innocent III as work houses to redeem and convert former prostitutes. Named after Jesus' follower, Mary Magdalene, who has often been portrayed as a repentant prostitute, Magdalene Homes specialized in providing laundry services and came to be known as Magdalene Laundries. The last Magdalene Laundry was closed in Ireland in 1996 following investigation of human rights abuses.

Not all responses to sex work have focused on eliminating it. In societies where prostitution is legal, and many where it is not officially legal but is unofficially tolerated, sex work is segregated to locales away from "respectable" neighborhoods. Segregated "red light districts" have existed in cities around the world. One of the oldest continuously existing red light districts in the world, the De Wallen district in Amsterdam, developed in the fourteenth century AD to serve the interests of sailors and merchants. Today, the De Wallen district is a major site for international sex tourism, drawing hundreds of thousands of international visitors yearly.

HISTORY OF SEX WORK IN THE UNITED STATES

While prostitution is against the law in all but one US state today, it was legal in most states until 1910. In the 1800s, "the sex industry in the U.S. could more than match any of its old world predecessors" (Roberts 1992, p.209). American tolerance for sex work declined dramatically by the mid-twentieth century, while the rise of the Internet has had a major impact on sex work in the new millennium.

Antebellum America and the Wild West

In the antebellum period (prior to the Civil War), prostitution was looked down upon by members of respectable society, but efforts to suppress it were meager at best. Cities and the frontier teemed with single men, providing robust markets for sex workers, while masses of poor female immigrants turned to sex work for survival.

Prostitution in New Orleans dates back at least to 1721 when a group of French convicts, including several convicted prostitutes, were deported to the French colony. A huge population influx in the decades following the Louisiana Purchase in 1803 created a vast prostitution industry. By the 1850s, New Orleans had a reputation as "the prostitution capital of all America" (Schafer 2009, p.3)—in part because New Orleans allowed racial mixing of sex workers and clients. The extent of prostitution in New Orleans before the Civil War is captured in the words of one resident who wrote that in some sections of the city in the evening "it is not unusual to see the windows and doors of almost every house as far as the eye can recognize them, filled with these working girls" (Schafer 2009, p.155).

In the 1800s as waves of men moved west across North America to work in the logging, mining, and railroad industries, sex workers followed them. As the Union Pacific railway was being built, camps of prostitutes trailed railroad crews, entertaining them in tents and wagons. When the transcontinental railroad was completed many prostitutes settled in centers of the cattle trade, such as Dallas and Amarillo, where railroad workers often left their red train lanterns on the working girls' porches, giving rise to the term "red light district" to refer to neighborhoods inhabited by prostitutes (Rutter 2005, p.29).

Mining towns across the West also attracted large numbers of "working girls." Denver had a large brothel neighborhood and the high altitude mining town of Leadville was reputed to have one of the wildest red light districts in the West. Often there was some modest effort by businesses to maintain a veneer of respectability. The term "upstairs girls" referred to prostitutes who were commonly sequestered on the second and third floors above bars and hotels, outside the direct view of all but those who sought their services.

The Gilded Age of US Prostitution

In large American cities the sex trade was confined to certain parts of town. Segregation of sex work was part of cities' broader business plans. Wealthy landowners benefited from the sex trade and protected their interests. In 1857, a regulation was passed in New Orleans called the "Lorette Law," in reference to a street in Paris notorious for streetwalkers. This "Ordinance Concerning Lewd and Abandoned Women" followed the "upstairs girls" practice of not allowing "public women" to pursue their trade on the first floor of buildings in sections of the New Orleans that were considered respectable. The law was challenged and rewritten four times before the city fathers officially settled on a red light district that came to be known as Storyville, in honor of the city alderman, Sidney Story, who championed the legislation. In its heyday, Storyville stretched for 38 city blocks with brothels, saloons, and dance halls.

Historian Timothy Gilfoyle (1992) refers to the late 1800s and early 1900s as the Gilded Age of prostitution in America. Not only did many cities sport extensive red light districts, but luxury brothels known as "parlor houses" were common in major cities. By 1900, the Everleigh Club in Chicago had become the most famous brothel in the world. The brothel was a stone mansion with "silk couches, easy chairs, a grand piano, and statues of Greek goddesses peering through exotic palms" (Abbott 2007, p.xxi). The Everleigh's clients included major politicians, European royalty, business tycoons, financiers, and artists.

The situations of girls and women working in the sex trade varied enormously. At the high-end, prostitutes worked in a business controlled largely by women and resided in comfortable neighborhoods. In lower-tier brothels large numbers of young girls (the age of consent in many states was 12–14) were pushed into prostitution. In the South prior to the Civil War, female slaves could be forced to work in brothels (Schafer 2009, pp.22–23). Among the most exploited and abused of sex workers during this era were Chinese girls who were transported to California following the gold rush in the 1850s and cramped into small rooms that were little more than jail cells.

At the end of the nineteenth century, prostitution was a well-established institution in large cities and frontier towns across the country. While many people—including the luckier and more privileged prostitutes—prospered from legal sex work, there were serious human rights abuses and widespread sad-luck tales of women whose lives as prostitutes ended in poverty and venereal disease.

The Great Social Evil

In the late 1800s, a social movement led by religious leaders and health workers gained momentum to ban prostitution. While other reform groups focused primarily on abolishing alcohol, the Social Purity movement viewed prostitution as society's most critical concern. Josephine Butler, the major moral entrepreneur of the movement, identified prostitution the "Great Social Evil." The Social Purity movement was backed by physicians and nurses who recognized that prostitution was a vector for transmitting venereal diseases. Some health officials argued that public health could be promoted through regulations and testing of prostitutes, but for social purity activists, the only acceptable solution was eradicating sex work. Stark assertions about the dangers of prostitution were invoked. The Social Hygiene Association declared that nearly 10 per cent of pregnant women in the United States were infected with syphilis and that congenital syphilis caused 30 per cent of all blindness in New York (Rosen 1982, p.53).

The campaign against prostitution drew on atrocity tales. Lurid stories described naïve country girls who moved to the city and were entrapped in prostitution by pandering city men, often identified as Russian Jews. The number of women who social purity activists claimed were directly victimized by organized prostitution varied wildly, ranging from 250,000 to 1.6 million. To put these numbers in perspective, if the latter figure were correct, it would have meant that nearly one in six 16–40-year-old females in the United States was forced into prostitution—a clearly exaggerated estimate.

Still, the myth of white slavery found fertile ground in American anxieties during this era of rapid urbanization, industrialization, immigration, and changing social norms and roles for women. In 1910, Congress enacted the White Slave Traffic Act, called the "Mann Act," after the senator Horace Mann who sponsored it. The law made it a felony to transport across state lines "any woman or girl for the purposes of prostitution or debauchery." The Mann Act was more symbolic than real in its impact on prostitution since it focused on transporting women across state lines for immoral purposes rather than directly addressing sex work itself. But the Act signaled a change in attitudes toward prostitution. Over the coming decade laws were passed in almost all states to make prostitution illegal. Red light districts disappeared and the number of prostitutes and their customers dropped dramatically.

It is unlikely that prostitution would have decreased so much in the years leading up to and following World War I if there had not been other social dynamics that contributed to the shift away from sex work. One major reason for the decline in prostitution was that the number of transient men and women in major urban centers plunged as ever more restrictive immigration laws were enacted. The demand for prostitutes plummeted as the numbers of single males moving through cities declined. At the same time, financial pressures for women to resort to sex work also diminished as the urban economy transformed and women found more opportunities for a living wage. Between 1910 and 1920, the proportion of women in nonmanual jobs rose from 17 per cent to 30 per cent. The clerical trades, which had been almost exclusively male, opened to women who found employment as telephone operators, clerks, and bookkeepers. As steady and secure jobs at living wages became available, fewer women were drawn to sex work as a way to make ends meet.

The postwar era was also a time of changes in heterosexual behavior. Premarital sex between romantic partners increased in the years after World War I, facilitated by the creation of condoms and other contraceptive products, even though most contraceptives were illegal until the 1930s. Social relations and sexuality in marriage changed as well, with the Victorian model of authoritarian patriarchy giving way to "companionate marriage" that emphasized affection and emotional warmth. Sex in marriage, which had previously focused primarily on procreation, was increasingly viewed as an expression of love between husbands and wives. The greater acceptance of premarital sex, the stronger role of sex within marriage, and easier access to contraceptives combined to reduce the role of prostitution in American society. In their pathbreaking study of American sexual behavior, Alfred Kinsey et al. (1948) found that the reported frequency of American men having sex with prostitutes declined by one-half to two-thirds from 1926 to 1948.

But while prostitution receded dramatically by the mid-twentieth century, a smaller market remained for paid sex and the circumstances of women who worked as prostitutes worsened. Just as Prohibition shifted the manufacture and sale of alcohol from legal businesses to organized crime, the demise of brothels and open red light districts resulted in organized crime moving in to fill the demand for sexual vice. Women who engaged in prostitution became more dependent than in earlier times on male protection. Around the United States brothels came to be replaced by the "bookie system," so called because pimps and organized crime would "book" prostitutes in different houses and apartments and move them around from week to week (Gilfoyle 1992, p.310).

The Internet Era

Pornography historian, Joseph Slade, has proposed what he refers to as "Slade's Law" regarding technology and sex. "Whenever someone invents a new technology," Slade writes, "another person will invent a sexual use for it" (2000, p.9). The meteoric impact of videocassette and DVD technology on the private viewing of pornography exemplifies Slade's Law. While most viewing of pornography through the early 1970s was at X-rated movie theaters, the development of videocassette technology for home use made it possible to view pornographic videos in the privacy of one's home and X-rated movie theater attendance plummeted. The rise of the Internet has had an even more pronounced impact on sex work. Pornography showed up on the World Wide Web almost as soon as the Internet became available in the early 1990s. By the late 1990s, massive amounts of explicit sexual imagery were available at the click of a mouse. Over time the quantity and diversity of erotica on the Internet has expanded, with both paid and free websites offering an almost limitless supply. Accurate figures on the number of pornographic websites and the amount of time people spend viewing them are a matter of debate, but even conservative estimates suggest that nearly 15 per cent of Internet searches and 4 per cent of websites are devoted to sex (Ogas and Gaddam 2011).

Beyond pornography, the Internet has influenced the organization of prostitution. Sex workers have found the Web to be an excellent venue for advertising. Many escort services have websites with escort photos and descriptions. Several books and websites offer practical advice on how to set up an escort business, and in recent years it has become increasingly common for escorts to become independent entrepreneurs. There are also sites on the Internet where sex work customers post reviews of escorts and advice about how to locate sex workers, the prevailing rates for services, and the dangers of law enforcement.

While the Internet has become a major venue for sexual services, it has not completely replaced other venues. Strip clubs continue to be a popular form of male entertainment and street prostitution remains a component of the sex work industry in many impoverished urban neighborhoods.

MERTON'S ANOMIE AND SOCIAL LEARNING THEORIES

Two positivistic approaches to crime and deviance that we have used in previous chapters, anomie theory and social learning theory, can be helpful in analyzing why some individuals become sex workers in spite of its illicit, or at least stigmatized, status.

Merton's anomie theory is particularly useful in explaining the decision to engage in financially oriented crime and deviance. Many young women who work as escorts and exotic dancers today are drawn to sex work because it offers an opportunity to make far more money than other employment that is available to them in their late teens and twenties. As one dancer explained to Susan Dewey, "No man is ever gonna walk into a McDonald's where you're working in your stupid little uniform and hand you two hundred dollars just because he thinks you're pretty. You might as well just give up hope and die in a job like that because it's never gonna get any better" (2011, p.xiii). Many sex workers see their activities as a means to a bigger goal, whether to accumulate cash and then leave sex work, or to finance other long-term ambitions. A significant number of strippers—by Bernadette Barton's count, about one-third of all the strippers she met during her research—were dancing to support themselves while they worked on a college degree (2006, p.28).

Of course, not all young women (and even fewer young men) who confront low-wage employment turn to sex work to improve their economic fortunes. Research on the pathways into sex work documents the importance of social learning theory in explaining how most individuals become involved in sex work. Future sex workers are often introduced to it by friends. Runaway homeless young people often find themselves hanging out with other homeless youths who have turned to sex work for survival and who teach them the ropes (Curtis et al. 2008). Strip club dancers are frequently introduced to clubs by girlfriends (and sometimes boyfriends) who encourage them to "try it and see if you like it." Many strippers start working at strip bars in some other capacity, such as a cocktail waitress, where they get to know dancers, deejays, and customers. Spending time in the setting, they become more comfortable with the people and activities before they begin dancing (e.g., Barton 2006). More experienced sex workers teach novices the "tricks of the trade," including how to find and manage customers, and how to avoid law enforcement, as well as providing them with techniques of neutralization that make them feel more comfortable with their behavior.

INTERACTIONAL CONTEXTS AND ETHNOGRAPHIC VOICES

A sociological understanding of sex work must address the diverse contexts in which sex work occurs. One variation in sex work has to do with the different kinds of sex work. While prostitution and stripping share some similarities, they are different enough that they warrant separate examination. Even within prostitution and exotic dancing, there are differences in how they can be organized and the interactions that occur. These differences play a major role in the levels of victimization, job satisfaction, and self-esteem that sex workers experience.

Prostitution

Weitzer has developed a *polymorphous paradigm* of sex work based on different ways in which sex work is organized and experienced (2013, p.714). He has applied this paradigm primarily to prostitution, but it can be applied to other kinds of sex work as well. Table 11.1 lists five organizational types of prostitution, where sexual transactions take place, the relative price typically charged by sex workers, and the risks of exploitation and victimization. As the table

Table 11.1 Characteristics of Types of Prostitution

Type of Prostitution	Business Location	Price Charged	Risk of Exploitation	Risk of Violent Victimization
Street prostitution	Street contact, cars, alleys, parks	Low	High	Very high
Massage parlor worker	Massage parlor	Moderate	Moderate	Low
Brothel worker	Brothel	Moderate	Moderate	Very low
Escort services	Escort agency, private premises/hotels	High	Moderate	Low to moderate
Call Girl	Independent operator, private premises/hotels	High	Low to none	Low

SOURCE: Adapted from Weitzer (2009).

shows, the most significant differences in exploitation and victimization can be found in comparing street prostitution with prostitution that takes place in indoor and private settings.

Street Prostitution

Many US cities have streets with a reputation as locations where prostitutes are available. Police officers interviewed by McQuiller Williams (2014) reported that neighborhoods where street sex work occurred were frequently home to businesses, such as bars, strip clubs, motels, and parking facilities that profit from, and sometimes support, sex work. Street prostitutes need two kinds of locations for their work: places where they meet and negotiate with clients and places to accomplish the sex act itself.

Corners and intersections near traffic lights are common locations for soliciting johns since prostitutes can pretend to be waiting to cross the street or to catch a bus. As one street prostitute explains:

> The traffic lights make the tricks stop. Now you can just play it off like you going to their car to get directions or you're giving out directions. This don't raise no suspicions from the heat [police].
>
> —Williams (2014, pp.673–674)

After reaching agreement about the terms of the transaction, street sex workers need a location for completing the act. Street prostitutes spend very little time with their customers. As one street worker described her customers, "Usually, they're not even interested in talking to you. What they want is quick sex" (Bernstein 2007, p.46).

The places where they consummate the transaction are often chosen to maximize business and maintain their safety. "Dates" who the women know and trust may negotiate private locations, such as hotel rooms. With unknown customers many street prostitutes prefer public places because it feels safer than in private. The public area, however, needs to provide cover. "My spots for sex have to be hidden from public view," a prostitute explained to Williams, adding, "Places like stairways or alleys allow me and my tricks to avoid being seen" (2014, p.675).

Street sex workers also try to be within earshot of someone in case the transaction turns violent. They try to avoid getting into tricks' cars—and especially getting into vans, where they fear other unseen men may be hiding. If they use a car to consummate the transaction, public parking lots, especially those with attendants, may be used, often with a "user's fee" to the lot attendant.

Researchers estimate that about 10–20 per cent of prostitutes in the United States are street prostitutes (Porter and Bonilla 2010). They often experience abysmal working conditions. By virtue of their work and frequent drug use they face high risk of sexually transmitted diseases and violence. Almost all of the drug-using sex workers Maher interviewed reported having been raped and beaten. Neighborhood residents often harass them and the police are a threat rather than a source of protection. Street sex workers are often young, from abusive backgrounds, with little education, records of criminal arrest, and drug dependency. Between their troubled personal lives, limited social capital, and minimal protection, they face perilous circumstances on a daily basis.

Massage Parlors and Brothels

The majority of prostitution in the United States takes place in indoor settings that can be distinguished between settings that involve customers coming to prostitutes or those involving sex workers going to their customers. Prostitution is only legal in the state of Nevada, but indoor sex work in massage parlors is common in many cities.

Indoor prostitution typically involves longer and more varied sex than street prostitution. In many massage parlors and brothels, when a customer arrives he is provided with a lineup of the women who are currently at work. The women, usually wearing lingerie, introduce themselves, and the customer chooses one of the women with whom to "party." Large brothels in Nevada have bars where customers can interact with the women before deciding who to select. Some suburban Nevada brothels also offer customers a virtual lineup so they can make an online reservation for a particular sex worker and a specific kind of party, such as striptease, romantic bubble bath, or fantasy-themed bungalow (Brents et al. 2010).

Most brothel services involve a 30- to 60-minute combination of one or two sexual acts, most commonly a "half and half" combination of oral and vaginal sex. In comparison to street sex work, which involves very little interaction and very quick sex, brothel customers often expect some expression of emotional connection. Diana Prince, who interviewed 150 brothel workers in Nevada, found that most of them believed that "the average customer wants affection or love as well as sex" (1986, p.490).

Legal brothel workers have protections that are not available to streetwalkers or even massage parlor masseuses. First, they are not at risk of arrest. In fact, local law enforcement officers have responsibility for protecting them if troubles arise. They also have the advantage of working in contexts where safe sex, especially the use of condoms, is mandated by law and not a matter of personal negotiation. Brothel workers, and often massage parlor masseuses, benefit as well from others monitoring the length of time they are with customers. In case of lingering or slow sex, the "management" will intervene to demand that the customer either pay extra or leave.

Indoor sex workers come from a wider range of backgrounds than street prostitutes. Massage parlors run the gamut from relatively well-established and structured businesses to fly-by-night establishments, with a range of sex workers including former street prostitutes, immigrant women, and women supplementing their service sector wages. Many women who seek employment in Nevada brothels come from backgrounds in low-paying service sector employment. Others come from illegal sex work, mostly from women who started working as escorts and turn to brothel work because it does not involve the stresses of illegal sex work (Brents et al. 2010, p.165). Another group of brothel workers come to Nevada from previous sex work in strip clubs or the adult film industry. These women tend to have invested more resources (such as cosmetic body work) in their careers and to have more experience in sexual commerce. They tend to be career focused and high earners. Some high earning brothel sex workers are good at investing their income, although young women new to the industry who have never had much income often lack the skill and discipline to save. As one brothel prostitute recounted, "Some of us make good money and a lot of us just leave and spend it and come back with nothing" (Brents et al. 2010, p.173).

Escort Services

While massage parlor and brothel sex workers pursue their trade in locations where customers come to buy their services, escorts, or "call girls," go to their customers. In most large cities escort agencies advertise on the Internet. Escorts working with agencies are sent to a location to meet a customer after the agency has briefly screened the caller. The agency monitors the time the escort spends with the customer in case any problems might occur. When the escort completes the engagement she or he calls the agency to let them know. With the rise of the Internet and smartphones, many women who previously worked for escort services today find they can work independently and keep the profits to themselves (Venkatesh 2011). By listing on specialty websites, escorts can pitch advertisements towards clients who have an interest in specific physical characteristics (such as large women, older women, Asian women), or sexual services for which they offer expertise (such as tantric yoga sex, sadomasochism, erotic massage). Many sites are also linked to escorts' personal websites, which may feature customer reviews.

Escort services cater to upper-middle-class men. In recent years the news media have reported several prominent politicians and businessmen as regular escort customers. The services offered by escorts are more varied than those available in massage parlors or brothels. In addition to providing niche sexual fantasies, escorts are often expected to display romantic interest. As one regular sex work customer told Sanders, "I don't want to be sexually processed, for me it's like dating" (2008, p.97).

In their study of online postings of escort reviews, Earle and Sharp (2008) found that, while some men are interested in quick sex, many seek what has come to be called a *girlfriend experience*, or "GFE," that entails a romantically staged sexual encounter. As one man wrote in his review of an escort, "I suppose the best I can say is that it was more like making love than having sex . . . the nicest—in every sense—girl I've met for absolute ages" (2008, p.70). Escorts recognize customers' desires to feel emotional connection and many escorts feign intimate feelings. Other escorts develop more genuine emotional bonds with at least some of their clients. As an escort remarked to Maria Perez-y-Perez:

> To me they're friends and I've never talked about them as "johns" or "jobs." . . . I get as much pleasure from them as I like to think they get from me, and I'm not just talking about the sex but building a real rapport with them. . . . I treat them as I would a boyfriend.
>
> —Perez-y-Perez (2003, p.204)

In the context of paid sexual transactions, such rapport can involve the calling forth of feelings that Chapkis (1997) has described as the emotional labor of sex work. Bernstein (2007) refers to this authentic (if fleeting) emotional connection as "bounded authenticity," recognizing that such time-limited intense emotional interaction is a common feature of many commercial service relationships today. In paid sexual encounters the authentic feeling girlfriend experience can offer a brief but meaningful human connection that some men may find hard to achieve or sustain in other relationships. Some sex workers come to view their work as a form of therapy. Yet, others view it more as providing their clients with a paid fantasy in which men can experience a combination of emotional and sexual attention without the strains and responsibilities of a noncommercial relationship.

Dancing for Dollars

Erotic dancing is both similar to and different from prostitution. It is similar in that it provides sexually oriented services that are for the most part culturally

PUSHING YOUR BOUNDARIES

Reddit Sex Worker Discussion Analysis

Reddit is a massive social news aggregation and discussion website that offers members and visitors opportunities to ask questions and share information. While the content and quality of discussions vary, Reddit provides a venue for open exchanges among participants. One discussion strand is designated Sex Workers Only (https://www.reddit.com/r/SexWorkersOnly/). While anyone can read the posts and comments in the strand, it is identified as:

> A place for discussion, advice and solidarity. Made by and for people who work in the sex industry. Please refrain from posting and commenting if you are not a sex worker. CLIENTS/OPINIONS FROM CLIENTS ARE NOT WELCOME HERE! POSTS FROM NON-SEX WORKERS WILL BE DELETED.

The Sex Workers Only site contains questions asked by experienced sex workers or individuals who are seeking advice on becoming sex workers, providing a frank and up-close view of their everyday concerns. Log onto the discussion page and examine questions and comments that are posted there. Answer the following questions.

- What are four common concerns (that is, either the subject of several strands or questions that produced extensive comments) that sex workers discuss on this site? Describe the concern and provide quotes to illustrate.
- If a person considering becoming a sex worker were to look at this site for possible advice, what are four pieces of advice you think they would take away from it? Use quotes that describe the advice.
- Do the discussions on the site give you a different perspective on sex work than what you had before looking at it or do they reinforce what you already thought about sex work? Or a bit of both? Explain.

Come to class ready to compare your findings and responses with other students.

expected to be confined to intimate relationships. In American society, all people except young children are expected to keep certain parts of their bodies clothed in public. Like selling explicit sexual services, making certain parts of one's body available for public view for money transgresses American cultural norms. Further, most erotic dancing involves dancers simulating sexual movements in order to arouse their audiences. But unlike prostitution, erotic dancing for the most part does not lead to actual sex. It involves seduction and flirtation, but not consummation. "Strip tease," as erotic dancing is often called, suggests just this kind of flirtatious interaction. It is the challenge of providing titillation but not consummation that most clearly distinguishes the sex work in erotic dancing from prostitution.

Several strip club ethnographers have distinguished different types of clubs. Based on observations over three years as a dancer in nearly 40 strip clubs, Mindy Bradley-Engen has described three types of exotic dance clubs: hustle clubs, social clubs, and show clubs.

Hustle clubs emphasize lust and sexual gratification. These clubs employ large numbers of dancers who compete with each other to attract customers. Most of the money made by hustle club dancers comes from lap dances and other private or semiprivate interactions. The club atmosphere emphasizes sexual references by deejays who present the dancers as objects of sexual gratification. These clubs tend to tolerate sexual harassment, such as customers grabbing dancers as they walk through the bar. Since dancers depend largely on private dances and tips for their income, they find it profitable to present themselves as sexually open to potential customers. Dancers' descriptions of hustle clubs illustrate the depersonalized environment. As one hustle club dancer told Bradley-Engen, "I hate it so much. We're just T and A [tits and ass]. It's like a meat market" (2009, p.42). Hustle clubs tend to create an aggressive hostility between dancers as well as distrust with club management. While the money can be good, turnover rates are high and dancers who work in the clubs tend to become more hostile and emotionally hardened toward other dancers over time.

Social clubs provide a very different working environment. As the term "social club" suggests, these clubs tend to emphasize more supportive social interaction. Dancers in social clubs make their money in tips from dancing on stage. There are no lap dances as in hustle clubs. The dancer population in social clubs is small, often half a dozen dancers as opposed to 50 or more at large hustle clubs, and the turnover rate for dancers is far lower. These clubs tend to have a larger proportion of regular patrons who develop more respectful relationships with the dancers. The dancers also build supportive relationships with each other rather than the hostility common among dancers at hustle clubs. While the money that dancers make at social clubs is considerably less, the work is far less stressful. Indeed, Bradley-Engen herself found this club environment very satisfying. While she made less money at social clubs, she reports of one of them, "I danced there regularly for the next three years. I cried the night I finally left" (2009, p.71).

Show clubs or "gentlemen's clubs" as they are often called, are the high-end of the strip club continuum. Show clubs cater to affluent male tastes and social display. Show clubs advertise themselves as having the "best looking women in town." Dancers wear professional costumes from high-end lingerie stores and present hypersexualized ideals of the female body. Their dance routines emphasize physical grace as well as sexually provocative performance. The dancer–customer interaction at show clubs is tightly regulated. No touching is allowed by customers, and dancers are seldom permitted to talk to customers while not on stage or in a private dance. Show clubs are a costly form of entertainment with admission charges, high priced drinks, and expensive private dances. The clubs exude a kind of beauty pageant atmosphere. When they are doing well, dancers get a lot of self-esteem as well as money from their club engagements. As one show club dancer said to Bradley-Engen, "I get told how gorgeous I am all night. There's nothing wrong with that. And yeah, they have to pay me" (2009, p.64).

Despite their "ideal bodies," show club dancers work in an environment that fosters insecurity. They regularly compare themselves to their co-dancers and strive to be thinner, prettier, and sexier. In contrast to the aggressive interpersonal behavior in hustle clubs, dancers in show clubs do not project hostility on other dancers who are making money. They tend to admire popular dancers and try to emulate them. But with constant feelings of insecurity and comparison with other dancers, they often live on a treadmill of dieting, exercising, using weight loss drugs, and getting cosmetic surgery (Wesley 2003; Roach 2007).

Strip clubs offer patrons the opportunity to receive sexually charged attention from scantily clad or naked women. Dancers know that their income is tied to giving the men what they want—within limits. Shrewd dancers learn skills for keeping men interested and paying. As a dancer in Elizabeth Anne Wood's research explained:

> Every day you have to plot and scheme. You have to find that new way to try and make these men think you have an interest in them. . . . The key thing is to keep them interested enough to think they might have a chance, but not too much of a chance. . . . You've got to string it along.
>
> —Wood (2000, p.18)

With strip club "regulars" there is often a lot of personal conversation, as men talk about their accomplishments and frustrations in their personal lives and share their sexual desires. In these interactions, dancers and their customers may construct a fantasy intimacy. Some men seek to believe that the commercial relationship is something more, that they are boyfriends or lovers rather than customers. Most men at strip clubs, however, are occasional customers rather than regulars. And while they may want to feel some authenticity in their interactions with dancers, they are often willing to believe the dancer's interest in them. As a dancer explained to Catherine Roach, "Most men don't know or don't care to know if your interest is faked, as long as you're not too obvious about it" (2007, p.122).

Oppression and Empowerment Paradigms

The debate over oppression versus empowerment in sex work can be addressed more adequately when the foregoing range of sex work experiences is acknowledged. As Weitzer observes:

> Victimization, exploitation, choice, job satisfaction, self-esteem, and other dimensions of sex work should be treated as variables that differ between types of sex work, geographic locations, and other structural and organizational conditions.
>
> —Weitzer (2009, p.10)

Antipornography feminists frame sex work within an *oppression paradigm* that presents all sex work—all stripping, prostitution, and pornography—as exploitation and violence against women. It is obvious that some sex work exposes sex workers to serious risks of both short-term and long-term violence. But painting all sex work with a broad brush of oppression masks more than it reveals, as illustrated by the stark differences between the opportunities afforded Nevada brothel workers as opposed to Houston streetwalkers, or the experiences of a hustle club stripper versus an elite show club dancer.

While admitting that sex work can be exploitive and oppressive and that many sex workers are exposed to humiliation and violence, *sex-positive feminists* embrace an *empowerment paradigm*, arguing that sex work can offer women who engage in it an opportunity to make good money and assert control of their sexual interactions. The key to empowering sex workers, sex-positive feminists assert, is to provide better working conditions. The empowerment paradigm asserts the similarities of sex work to other kinds of service and emotion work (such as massage and counseling) and emphasizes the benefits to sex workers' quality of life when their work is legalized and their working conditions are protected.

CONTEMPORARY RESPONSES TO SEX WORK

Earlier in this chapter we discussed the range of social control approaches to sex work across history. In any given era we find some subset of the approaches being invoked. Today in the United States, three main strategies are used to control sex work and its customers. These include policing and arrest, rehabilitation programs, and legalization and regulation.

Policing Prostitution

Efforts to police prostitution are motivated primarily by citizen complaints. The majority of police efforts focus on street prostitution following public complaints about visible sex acts, traffic and noise, disruption of business, and the health concerns associated with discarded condoms and syringes. The Houston Police Department's 2013 "Bissonnet Initiative" offers an example of a police crackdown on street prostitution. Prostitutes were widely known to walk a block-long stretch of Bissonnet Street known as "the track" to look for johns. After responding to more than 1,000 complaints over a two-year period, police went undercover and arrested more than 100 prostitutes and clients (Stanton 2013). The district attorney's office also filed lawsuits against a fast-food restaurant where prostitutes relaxed in air-conditioning while waiting for customers and a motel that rented them rooms by the hour. Several businesses were required to install surveillance cameras, hire security officers, and add more lighting. But while the efforts of the police reduced prostitution in the immediate area, neighborhood residents observed that much of the activity just shifted a few blocks away to an area mall. This whack-a-mole approach to policing street prostitution is an ineffective way to control prostitution even in the short term. Nearly 80 per cent of those arrested for prostitution in large cities are not held for prosecution, and only half of those brought to trial are convicted. "In other words," Chapkis explains, "despite large investments of police time and resources in the entrapment and arrest of sex workers, very few are even temporarily removed from the streets" (1997, p.132). This leads many criminologists to question whether costs associated with policing, arrest, and temporary incarceration of prostitutes is a good use of law enforcement resources. Julie Pearl's observation 30 years ago continues to resonate today that "even the most vigorous police battles against prostitution yield Pyrrhic victories [in which the costs far exceed the benefits] at best" (1987, p.771).

Rehabilitation Programs

Many cities and some states have developed rehabilitation programs to help sex workers leave prostitution. Similar to substance abuse courts that offer arrestees a choice to participate in programs designed to deal with their underlying problems rather than spending time in jail or prison, prostitution diversion programs offer prostitutes counseling and other resources to help them leave prostitution. In 2013, New York created specialized courts to handle prostitution cases (Rashbaum 2013). The courts refer defendants to services like drug treatment, domestic abuse shelters, immigration assistance and healthcare, as well as some job training, in an effort to keep them from returning to the sex trade. While the programs are designed to rescue sex workers from lives of crime, drug addiction, and violence, critics have observed that the support is an inadequate alternative to sex work income, especially since many minority and underclass women turn to sex work only occasionally as a means to supplement their income.

An alternative response to street prostitution focuses on reducing the demand side of the sex industry. In the last 20 years, programs called *john schools*, designed to educate men who are arrested for soliciting prostitutes, have grown in popularity. In some cities arrested johns are required to participate in classes focused on the abuse histories of prostitutes, the risks of sexually transmitted diseases, and negative effects of prostitution on families and communities (Monto 1998). Other communities offer arrestees a chance to have legal actions dropped if they attend classes. As with other criminal justice approaches to prostitution, the overwhelming majority of those caught and directed to john schools are arrested while pursuing street prostitutes.

Legalization and Regulation

While the preceding responses focus on illegal sex work, a vast amount of sex work is legal. Strip clubs and the viewing of pornography are legal across the country. Legalization also entails regulation. Strip clubs are regulated by local ordinances regarding the degree of nudity and acceptable level of contact with customers. Where businesses are involved, laws also regulate business licensing, occupational safety regulations, building zoning, taxation, and worker registration and mandatory medical examinations in operations that allow sexual contact (including legal prostitution in Nevada and pornographic video production).

STIGMA MANAGEMENT AND RESISTANCE

Even when sex work is legalized, it remains highly stigmatized in most of American society. To one degree or another most sex workers turn to stigma management to cope with the discrimination they fear or experience. Stigma management strategies vary according to the activities sex workers are engaged in and how those activities are organized, although some patterns are common across the sex work industry.

Techniques of Neutralization

Like other violators of social norms, sex workers turn to techniques of neutralization to justify their activities. Sex workers invoke "denial of injury" by arguing that unlike real criminals, they hurt no one. As one strip club dancer put it, "Every day there's people out there murdering, robbing, and raping people. We come in here behind closed doors and shake our tits for guys who pay to see us do it. What possible harm can come from that?" (Thompson et al. 2003, p.562). In addition to claiming that their activities cause no harm, they often use "appeals to higher loyalty," making the case that their reasons for participating in sex work justify their actions. One common appeal to higher loyalty involves claiming sex work as a means to provide family support, as in a dancer's statement that, "I have three children. Times are tough and jobs are hard to find. I'm not proud of what I do, but it supports me and my kids" (Thompson et al. 2003, p.564). Many sex workers also invoke a temporal neutralization, asserting that is acceptable to engage in sex work because they "are only doing it for a while."

All the college student strippers studied by Trautner and Collett (2010) viewed their dancing as a temporary employment they would quit once they received their degrees and moved into other careers.

Living in the Closet

Sex workers often protect themselves from disapproval by hiding their activities. As one escort explained to Juline Koken, "I have an ad on a website, you know a few photographs and then my face is kind of blurred out just enough so that people won't recognize me on the street" (2012, p.221). Many sex workers are particularly concerned about family members learning of their activities. Most are neither completely "out" nor completely "closeted" about their involvement with sex work, but rather "make selective judgments about with whom they will share information, when to disclose this information, and how to 'spin' their involvement with sex work" (Koken 2012, p.221). About half of the dancers interviewed by Thompson and his colleagues said that both of their parents knew, but several others said that they had told their mothers, but not their fathers. As one topless dancer told them, "My mother knows and is really supportive of me, but if my dad ever found out, he would die—or kill me" (Thompson et al. 2003, p.560). Many who disclose their involvement in sex work to friends, boyfriends, and family members are met with bad reactions. In an effort to maintain relationships that are threatened by their disclosure, some women come out and then go back into the closet, pretending to have quit their involvement in sex work.

Stigma Management with Customers

Since many forms of sex work involve interaction with customers, sex workers must manage potential interactional affronts. Some prostitutes and dancers speak of tactics for distancing themselves from their experiences with customers. The use of recreational drugs can provide a psychological buffer that allows them to "zone out" from their interactions. Sex workers also often develop verbal responses to keep their customers in line, as when a dancer learns to reply to a bar patron who says, "Come home with me," with the verbal zinger, "Get a permission slip from your wife and I will" (Spivey 2005, p.424).

Sex workers may also protect themselves in interactions with clients by setting clear limits on what they will and will not do. A massage parlor worker explained to Sanders, "Even if I have done the same client a million times, they still get the same *spiel*: I don't kiss, don't do anal and you can only kiss and touch on top" (2005, p.326). Many sex workers deal with the experiences of sex work by developing what Sanders refers to as a "manufactured identity" that they keep separate from their personal lives. As another informant told her:

> It is, like, coming into an acting role as soon as you come through the door. I am, like, that person and not who I really am when I am sitting at home. It is like being an actress for the day and when you go home you are not like that.
>
> —Sanders (2005, p.330)

The creation of a "sex worker self" as opposed to one's "real self" provides psychological and social separation that many sex workers find enhances their ability to engage in sex work while limiting the degree to which that work impacts the rest of their lives.

Mutual Support

Sex workers often turn to each other for support, finding that others who do the same kind of work are more accepting. One dancer explained, "You really can't understand this business unless you've been in it. These girls are my friends 'cause they know what it's like to do this" (Thompson et al. 2003, p.560). Strip club dressing rooms often provide a supportive environment away from the pressures of the dance stage and bar where dancers can let their hair down and relax with other dancers. "We don't compete in the dressing room," one dancer told Spivey, adding:

> Those of us who've worked here a while know it's a lot easier to . . . help each other out and feel good with each other than feel like shit alone. So you see all of us who've been here even four months or so . . . We keep each other right.
>
> —Spivey (2005, p.429)

Yet, another dancer asserted, "We're always supportive, even for girls who don't do as well. We'll always clap and whistle and try to make them feel good" (Price-Glynn 2010, p.135). But not all dancers recount such positive interactions with their peers. As Bradley-Engen and other dance club ethnographers report, the nature of relationships among dancers is strikingly different from one club to another. In hustle clubs, for instance, competition and cutthroat interactions among dancers are more common.

Coming Out of the Closet and Collective Action

In contrast to those who seek to avoid stigma by keeping their activities secret outside their work, some sex workers view their activities in a positive way and embrace their sex worker identities. Sex workers who publicly embrace their identity assert that their work provides positive benefits for society. "I feel that the services that I provide to some very lonely people are very valuable," says an escort (Koken et al. 2012, p.225). Consistent with this comment is a focus on sex work as "work," comparable to other service and helping professions. With a focus on "work" instead of "sex," the critical issues become those of working conditions rather than sexual morality. Over the past four decades there have

CLAIMS-MAKER PROFILE

Audacia Ray and the Red Umbrella Project

Audacia Ray came from a "good family" and had a "normal" childhood, went to college at the New School and Columbia University—and became a prostitute in her twenties. As she explained to a British interviewer, "I had one other friend doing it but I had never considered it. She made it sound easy and something I could do." For nearly a decade Audacia sold sex through Craigslist. "It's not the best job in the world, but it's not the worst," she says. "It took me a while to figure out what I was comfortable with and what my boundaries were" (James 2013).

In 2004, Audacia Ray founded a sex worker zine, *$pread Magazine*. Shortly after "retiring" from sex work, she published *Naked on the Internet: Hookups, Downloads, and Cashing in on Internet Sexploration* (2007), a book that draws upon her firsthand experience as well as that of other sex workers. She is also an active blogger—considered "NYC's Best Sex Blogger" by *The Village Voice*, which writes:

> No New Yorker scribbles about sex better than Audacia Ray, the brains and beauty behind [the blog] Waking Vixen. The adjunct professor of sexuality at Rutgers University and program officer of the International Women's Health Coalition lends her wise, engaging voice to porn-star literary events, interviews with children of sex workers, and more. Her topics are thoughtful and often lewd, but her insight makes them truly provocative.
>
> —*The Village Voice* (2010)

Ray's approach to sex worker advocacy combines both artistic expression and activism. She started a literary journal, *Prose and Lore*, devoted to sex workers and created the Red Umbrella Project (RedUP) that offers sex workers opportunities to share their stories at public readings. Ray recently produced the documentary video, *The Red Umbrella Diaries*, in which seven sex workers share their life stories, describing how isolating sex work can be when it is criminalized, judged, and stigmatized.

In their fight to make sex work safer for both sex workers and their customers, Ray and RedUP have recently advocated for a ban on the use of condoms as evidence of prostitution in legal cases. "Banning the use of condoms as evidence is not a matter of condoning the sex trade," the RedUP website states, "it is a common sense measure to ensure that people can protect themselves and each other from STDs, including HIV, as well as unwanted pregnancies."

been several grassroots efforts to mobilize sex workers in collective action to improve their working conditions. One of the most notable efforts was the prostitutes' rights organization, Call Off Your Old Tired Ethics, more commonly referred to by its acronym, COYOTE. Founded in California in 1973 by former prostitute, Margo St. James, COYOTE advocated for the repeal of prostitution laws, the recognition of prostitution as a valuable service occupation, and the protection of prostitutes' rights as legitimate workers (Jenness 1993). Following in the footsteps of COYOTE, in the 1990s through the mid-2000s, the San Francisco-based Exotic Dancers Alliance brought dancers and other sex workers together to fight for labor rights on the behalf of Bay Area sex workers (Barton 2006).

One of the most active sex worker organizations in the United States today is the Red Umbrella Project (RedUP) in NYC. Like COYOTE, the RedUP was founded by a former sex worker. In 2010, Audacia Ray created RedUP to advocate for sex workers and give them a public voice. RedUP runs peer-advocacy workshops for sex workers and lobbies for policies to reduce discrimination and violence toward sex workers. The organization also encourages creative writing and art projects by sex workers. Until recently, it sponsored a public reading series at a former Brooklyn massage parlor-turned cocktail lounge where sex workers shared stories from their memoirs (RedUP 2015).

Sex worker advocacy organizations offer social support and provide sex workers with opportunities to paint a different picture of sex work in American society—one that rejects the image of sex workers as deviants and seeks to redefine morality and frame their stigmatization as an act of oppression and a social problem that itself demands redress.

BLURRED BOUNDARIES II: THE JOHN SHAMING DEBATE

Recognizing that efforts to eliminate prostitution by arresting prostitutes are seldom successful, many cities are trying instead to reduce the number of men who look for paid sex. *John shaming* has developed as one popular, if controversial, tactic in the battle to stamp out prostitution. John shaming takes several forms, all of which involve publicly revealing the identities of men who have been arrested for soliciting prostitutes. In some cities the police department publishes the names of arrested johns on Facebook or releases the names to the news media. In other cities arrestees' names and mug shots are shown on television on what has been called "John TV" or posted on highway billboards. Former Chicago Mayor, Richard Daly, Jr., explained the message his city's john shaming policies intended to send: "We're telling everyone who sets foot in Chicago, if you solicit a prostitute, you will be arrested. And when you are arrested, people will know. Your spouse, children, friends, neighbors and employers will know" (Conroy 2006).

The first task in john shaming is for police to catch men negotiating sex for money. Police typically have female officers wired with hidden microphones and disguised as prostitutes hang out at popular sex work locations. The female officers interact with men on the streets and when a man offers to pay for sex, uniform police officers move in to arrest him. Another tactic, called a "reverse sting," involves placing escort ads in the dating or services sections of websites like Craigslist and Backpage. When men respond to the ads, the escort agrees to meet them at a hotel where police have arranged to arrest them as soon as they verbally agree to pay for sex. In many cities the names of men arrested for seeking prostitutes are released before they convicted of the offense, while other cities release only the names of convicted johns. The amount of information about the men also varies, with some cities publishing only their names, while others publish their mug shots and even their addresses.

Advocates of john shaming argue that it is an effective and gender fair way to reduce prostitution, punishing male consumers rather than the female providers. Reducing the demand side of sex work, they argue, gets at the root of the problem. It is also inexpensive to put john shaming policies into practice. When San Bernadino County launched its "Stop the John" web page, it cost practically nothing to set up and took off quickly, with 20,000 hits the first week (Foxhall 2014). While there is no solid research on the effectiveness of john shaming on reducing illegal sex work, about 850 US cities are using some form of it (Shively 2016).

Critics of john shaming tactics argue that it can have damaging long-term consequences. The practice of releasing arrestees' identities before they have been convicted or pled guilty strikes many critics as especially unwarranted. Even if the charges are dropped, the damage has been done. Journalist Suzy Khimm observes, "The internet has vastly expanded the potential audience for public ridicule and turned the enforcement of social norms into a collective pastime, while Google's enduring memory can allow that infamy to continue without end" (2016).

Shaming campaigns can also be messy and unpredictable. When Richmond, California, launched its program in 2014, the police were surprised when commenters on their Facebook page began adding other personal details about the men, including their workplaces, home addresses, schools they attended, and even graduation years (Foxhall 2014). Johns' wives, children, and employers can all quickly become victims of the public ridicule and harassment intended for the offender.

The most fundamental and overarching concern of law enforcement, public officials, scholars, and activists focusing on sex work is to reduce violence against women. Should john shaming be an acceptable tactic for reducing prostitution? How would you respond to city officials if you were asked to support john shaming policies in your community? Would you support such policies being used across the board for all men who are arrested for soliciting prostitutes, only for convicted johns, repeat offenders, or not at all? How would you weigh the potential lasting penalty of public shaming for johns and their families? Does john shaming serve the public good, or does it bring out the worst in public response?

SUMMARY

- Sex work refers to paid sexually oriented activities including prostitution, pornography, telephone sex, and exotic dancing.
- Significant numbers of Americans are consumers of one or more kinds of sex work, but it is regarded as immoral by large numbers of US adults.
- It is impossible to get accurate big-picture data about sex work because it encompasses such a wide range of legal and illegal activities. Further, most illegal sex work is a victimless crime that both parties wish to commit and neither is likely to report.
- In societies where prostitution is viewed as immoral and illegal, prostitutes are viewed as fallen sinful women or, more recently, as victims of entrapment and abuse.
- Illegal sex workers have been subjected to public humiliation, physical punishment, imprisonment, and even execution.
- Legal sex work is typically restricted to certain locales within a city.
- Prostitution was common in the United States until the early 1900s. The situations of girls and women working in the sex trade varied enormously.
- Prostitution and other forms of sex work declined dramatically by World War II in conjunction with shifts in sexual mores, including rising rates of premarital sex and use of contraceptives.
- Technological changes, especially the Internet, have led to the privatization of sex work and pornography.
- Merton's anomie theory and social learning theory together provide a useful approach to understanding sex work.
- Weitzer's polymorphous paradigm of sex work illustrates how the risks of sex worker victimization differ depending on the contexts.
- Exotic dancers provide customers with sexually charged interaction and attention. The interactions between dancers and patrons vary across different types of strip clubs.
- Three main strategies are used to control sex work in the United States: policing, prostitute rehabilitation programs, and regulation of legal sex work.
- Many cities have developed programs focused on men who are arrested for soliciting prostitutes, including:
    - John schools that allow johns to avoid prosecution if they attend classes on the harm associated with prostitution.

- ◦ Publishing the names and mug shots of men arrested for soliciting prostitutes.

- Sex workers often invoke techniques of neutralization to characterize their activities as acceptable.
- Many sex workers selectively disclose their activities to others whom they feel will be understanding.
- Some sex workers seek to redefine sex work as a positive contribution to society and engage in collective action to advocate for better working conditions for sex workers.

KEYWORDS

brothel: A house of prostitution.
courtesan: A paid mistress of a wealthy and powerful man.
empowerment paradigm (of sex work): A view of sex work as potentially empowering for sex workers.
escort: A prostitute who works on an out-call basis, meeting men in hotels or other private settings.
girlfriend experience (GFE): Prostitution that enacts romantic involvement similar to that of authentic romantic interactions.
hustle club: A type of strip club characterized by coarse sexual explicitness and relaxed attitudes toward physical contact between dancers and customers.
john: A man who has sex with a prostitute.
john school: A court-mandated or diversion program in which men who have been arrested for soliciting prostitutes attend classes on the harm and risks of paid sex.
massage parlor: A euphemistic term for brothels in US cities where prostitution is illegal.
oppression paradigm (of sex work): A position that views all sex work as demeaning violence against women.
polymorphous paradigm: An empirically based model of the different ways in which sex work is organized and the risk of victimization associated with different organizational types.
pornography: Sexually graphic images in print, photos, video, and other media that are intended to be sexually arousing.
sex-positive feminism: A feminist perspective that takes issue with antipornography feminists, viewing sexual freedom (including enjoyment of pornography) as essential to women's empowerment.
show club: A type of strip club with luxurious settings and hypersexualized models that caters to affluent men.
social club: A type of strip club characterized by regular clientele and a relatively small number of regular dancers with less aggressively sexualized interaction than hustle clubs and far less business clientele than show clubs.
Social Purity Movement: A social movement focused on eradicating prostitution that ran parallel to other prohibition movements in the late 1800s and early 1900s.
street prostitution: Prostitution involving solicitation of prostitutes and customers in public places.

SECTION

4

STATUS DEVIANCE

CHAPTER

12 Mental Illness

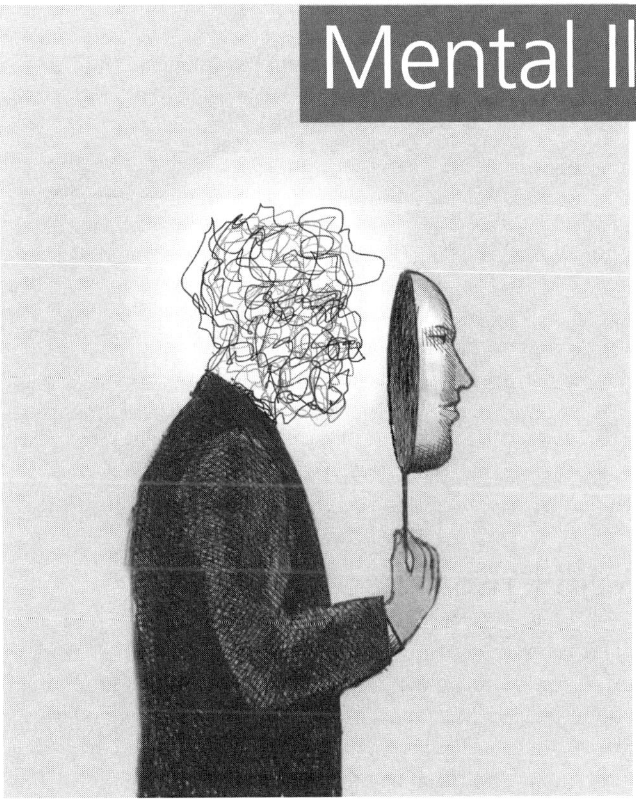

One artist's representation of mental disorder (Gary Waters/Alamy Stock Photo).

CONTENTS

LEARNING OBJECTIVES

After reading this chapter, you will be able to:

- Describe the most common types of mental illnesses diagnosed in the United States today
- Explain the challenges of, and strategies for, studying mental illness
- Identify different historical definitions of and explanations for mental illnesses
- Apply social stress theory to mental disorders
- Analyze the interactional contexts in which the mentally ill are identified and treated
- Explain the criminalization of mental illness and the goals of mental health courts
- Assess challenges in seeking effective treatment for ADHD children

BLURRED BOUNDARIES I: TWO FACES OF MENTAL ILLNESS

Jorge Herrera was a well-recognized figure on the streets near the University of Texas. He was a small man, but he often frightened those who came near him when his body shook in violent spasms and he shouted a string of words that no one understood. Jorge's dirty clothes often reeked, and his long, scraggly black hair and beard were often as covered with grime as his clothes. While the homelessness researcher had seen him many times, it took a while before the researcher gathered the nerve to talk to him. That hot, spring afternoon, Jorge sat against the wall of a drugstore near the university. He was in bad shape: his body twisted in periodic spasms and mucus covered his long mustache. He told the researcher that he had been very sick from eating bad food, but that he did not need to go to the hospital. As he muttered, he kept nodding off in the hot sun, then waking to scratch his ankles, which were covered with sores.

When the research team was later given access to police and medical records of the homeless in Austin (Snow et al. 1986a), they learned that Jorge had first been admitted to the Austin State Hospital for psychiatric problems at the age of 23 and had been on and off the streets for over 20 years. He ran away from the hospital and was sent back several times. Police records showed that he had been arrested occasionally over the past 15 years for strange behavior, including screaming that he was being chased by ghosts.

When most of us think of mental illness, we are likely to include images of people like Jorge, whose delusional ideas and odd behaviors are in striking contrast with what we consider normal and appropriate. A ranting homeless man, a schizophrenic in the midst of hallucinations, or a depressed individual in the act of attempting suicide—these are cases that we almost all would consider examples of mental disorder. But history is rich with conflicts over just where the boundary between psychiatric problems and normality lies. We are likely to disagree among ourselves at the edge of today's blurred boundaries of mental health and illness. Consider, for example, the case of Jessica.

Psychologist David Wodrich (2000) tells the story of meeting a 10-year-old girl named Jessica, whose mother brought her to Phoenix Children's Hospital for a psychological assessment. Jessica's mother explained, "I am not certain that my daughter really has a problem, but . . . she doesn't pay attention to what she is doing. It takes her forever to clean her room or to help out with the dishes. . . . As frustrating as home is, we could tolerate it if school were not a problem . . . but she is almost failing. The school psychologist . . . felt like she might have a hyperactivity-type problem" (pp.105–106).

Jessica's teacher and babysitters also described her as inattentive and disorganized. But while several adults were concerned about her disorganization and school performance, many who knew her (including her mother, her tutor, and her pediatrician) doubted that she suffered from *Attention Deficit Hyperactivity Disorder* (ADHD, for short).

In his evaluation, Dr. Wodrich found Jessica exhibited some ADHD symptoms such as failure to play close attention to details in school work, difficulty sustaining attention in tasks or play activities, and fidgety behavior. Yet, Jessica said that she did not feel hyperactive or have trouble slowing down and thinking. What she did feel, she told him, was "boredom, especially at school."

Is Jessica mentally ill? Or is she simply an active child who gets bored easily? What about the other 14 million American adults and children that official statistics suggest may be victims of ADHD? While most Americans would quickly agree about delusional bag ladies and hallucinating schizophrenics, many of us are skeptical of diagnosing our children as ADHD and using psychiatric medications to treat them. But many other Americans are true believers.

The controversy over ADHD as a psychiatric disorder has implications for understanding the social constructions and blurred boundaries of mental illness more generally. The official categories of mental illness are based on some degree of consensus (sometimes in the midst of considerable disagreement) among medical experts, public health officials, and different groups in the general population. In this sense, mental illness as a recognized category of deviance is socially constructed. The names of illnesses, the identification of symptoms, and treatments for them are developed or created by human beings. And, as we will see, the social constructions of mental illness have differed widely across time and cultures.

CURRENT CONSTRUCTIONS OF MENTAL ILLNESS IN THE UNITED STATES

The past 50 years in the United States has witnessed major changes in several deviance categories, but few have changed as dramatically as the category of mental illness. Most societies have identified only one or two types of mental illness. Even just a little over a century ago, the German psychiatrist, Emil Kraepelin (1896) distinguished only between schizophrenia and mood disorders. But by the 1950s, US psychiatrists had categorized nearly a hundred different mental illness diagnoses, which were described in the American Psychiatric Association's (APA) first *Diagnostic Statistical Manual*, or *DSM-I*, a small book that has since gone through five revisions. With each new edition, the number of mental illness categories has climbed. The current edition, *DSM-5* (APA 2013), is nearly 1,000 pages in length and includes more than 360 classifications of mental illness. This growth in the number of official mental illness diagnoses reflects increasing sophistication in identifying and classifying different symptoms of mental disorder. It also reflects the medicalization of deviance, with the inclusion of ever more human behavior under the rubric of "mental illness."

Statistical Snapshot

As the statistical snapshot in table 12.1 indicates, anxiety disorders are the most commonly identified mental illness in the United States, with over 84 million adults and children estimated to experience them during their lifetimes. Mood disorders, including depression and bipolar disorders, are the second most common diagnoses, with an estimate of nearly 60 million lifetime cases. The third largest category of mental illness (excluding the category of alcohol abuse and dependence covered in Chapter 9) is attention deficit disorders, which are estimated to affect about 25 million Americans, including over 20 million adults in spite of the popular assumption that ADHD is primarily a childhood disorder. In contrast to these more common categories of mental illness, several other disorders such as schizophrenia, and Alzheimer's disease are classified as major psychotic disorders, characterized by auditory and visual hallucinations, delusional thinking, and impaired insight. Schizophrenia tends to emerge in late adolescence and early adulthood, while Alzheimer's is a mental illness that is by far most common among adults in their mid-sixties or older. Psychotic disorders such as schizophrenia and Alzheimer's are much less common than the other mental illnesses in table 12.1, but they also pose especially challenging treatment. In sum, based on the figures below, mental illness is far and away the most common category of deviance in the United States today.

Table 12.1 Snapshot of Estimated Major Mental Illnesses Annually in the United States

Adult Mental Disorders	Anxiety Disorders	Mood Disorders	ADHD	Schizophrenia	Alzheimer's
Adults (in (millions)	72	52	20.2	2.7	5.4
Adult rate	28.8%	20.8%	8.1%	1.1%	2.1%
Children disorders (13–18 yrs.)	Anxiety disorders	Mood disorders	ADHD	–	–
Children (in millions)	12.5	7	4.5	–	–
Children rate	25%	14%	9%	–	–

SOURCE: National Institute of Mental Health (2016).

CHALLENGES IN RESEARCHING MENTAL ILLNESS

As we have noted throughout this book, researchers studying deviance face several daunting challenges. Studying mental illnesses and those who suffer from them presents some unique twists on many of the same challenges that researchers confront in other categories of deviance.

Counting Mentally Illness

Consider first, the issue of identifying and counting those who are mentally ill. Medical epidemiologists tackle this problem in a seemingly straightforward manner. Based on the current official classifications of mental disorders, such as those in the *DSM-5*, researchers develop screening criteria (lists of symptoms) and conduct surveys and face-to-face interviews to identify individuals who show a high enough number of symptoms to be classified as mentally ill. Such an approach makes sense. It provides relatively clear and standardized criteria for assessing an individual's mental health. But two particular problems can hinder the ability of researchers to accurately and comparably capture all of the appropriate people while not accidentally including inappropriate ones. These problems are the failure to find "hidden" cases, on the one hand, and a lack of contextual sensitivity, on the other.

To accurately estimate the number of people who are mentally ill, researchers must be able to adequately sample the general or specific (e.g., teenagers or senior citizens) population under study. If some cases are hidden from their view, the result will be an undercount. Hidden cases happen for a number of reasons. First, a researcher may miss an individual who is socially isolated. Second, family and/or friends may help an individual keep their mental disorder from public view. Family members may fear financial repercussions, as when a parent may lose a job or be hospitalized, and they may worry that the whole

PUSHING YOUR BOUNDARIES

Online Tests for Mental Illness

You can find many "self-tests" for various kinds of mental illnesses by doing an Internet search. Locate two self-tests for a particular kind of disorder (e.g., depression, anxiety disorders, ADHD). Take the tests and evaluate them by answering the following questions:

1. How many questions did the tests ask? Did one of the tests feel more thorough than the other? If so, explain how.
2. What kinds of symptoms did the tests seem to focus on? Do you feel that some of the questions could depend on a person's situation rather than their psychological health?
3. When you complete the test, does the site provide a statement about (a) whether or not you have the illness or (b) should see a doctor? What does the site recommend that you do?
4. Are there any advertisements on the website? If so, what are the advertisements for? Could the advertisers benefit in any way from increased numbers of people diagnosed with this illness? Does the website highlight a particular treatment or medication for the illness in the test?

Come to class prepared to share and compare your findings with other students.

family will be stigmatized by public revelation. As a result, some mentally ill individuals are likely to be hidden from view and left uncounted.

While hidden cases can result in an undercount, it is also possible for researchers to overcount the number of people experiencing mental illness. Human behaviors must be understood in the social and cultural contexts in which they occur. Viewed outside of their contexts, many behaviors seem inexplicable and bizarre. What we might take as a very probable sign of mental disorder in one social setting may be a normal and functional behavior in another. Criteria for judging mental illness must be context sensitive. Research on rates of mental illness among the homeless provides an example of how applying criteria that are contextually insensitive can lead to dramatically higher estimates of mental disorder on the streets than will more contextually situated criteria.

In the 1980s, David Snow and his colleagues conducted a fieldstudy of homelessness in Austin, Texas. At the time of their research, several studies had concluded that the overwhelming majority of the homeless—some studies suggested as high as 90 per cent—suffered from mental illness. Snow and his colleagues questioned the way in which many researchers identified the homeless as mentally ill. What they found particularly troublesome was the lack of recognition given to the social context of homelessness. Many of the communications and behaviors that researchers interpreted as symptoms of mental impairment, Snow et al. (1986a) argued, could better be understood as responses to the difficult nature of life on the streets. While an unkempt appearance, depressed mood, or sleeping and eating difficulties might well suggest mental illness for a comfortably housed middle-class person, they represent normal and understandable responses to the stressful and disorienting context of street life.

But if common symptoms represent inadequate measures for identifying mental illness in different settings, how might we more satisfactorily identify the mentally ill in such contexts? Snow and his colleagues suggested "triangulating" or using multiple kinds of measures rather than just one measure or rating scale to assess mental impairment. The logic of triangulation is that looking at a phenomenon from different angles will provide a better overall picture or understanding. Thus, Snow and his colleagues identified three possible indicators of mental illness: (1) history of mental health treatment, (2) whether their peers thought they were mentally ill, and (3) whether they exhibited seriously out-of-touch behavior. Snow and his colleagues were particularly attentive to whether other homeless individuals expressed belief that certain of their peers were "crazy" or "mentally ill." Using a broader and more context-sensitive set of indicators of mental illness, these researchers found rates of mental illness among the homeless to be far lower than earlier studies.

Getting Close

As is the case with other deviance categories, researchers studying mental illness may find it difficult to gain entrée into settings or to find appropriate individuals. While there are many people who suffer from mental illness, they are scattered through the general population. From a research perspective, one advantage of the mental hospital era was that so many of the "mentally ill" were available in one place. In the 1950s, Erving Goffman explored mental illness at St. Elizabeth's Hospital for the Mentally Ill in Washington, DC, which then housed over 7,000 patients. Some more recent researchers, like Nancy Herman, have continued to do research in mental hospitals, but have also expanded their studies to incorporate experiences after patients are released. Since most of the mentally ill spend far less time in mental hospitals today, researchers spend more time with them in community settings. Sue Estroff (1981) spent several years with seriously mentally ill clients in community-based treatment programs and Jennifer Huff (1995) got to know a similar group of people by spending time at a community-based drop-in center.

As important as such studies are, however, they only capture a certain range of individuals who have mental illness experiences. Many who are diagnosed as mentally ill have almost no contact with others who share similar experiences.

Scholars who seek to reach these more isolated (and sometimes secretive) individuals tend to rely on other strategies. David Karp has recruited depressed individuals and those who care for them from a wide variety of sources, including friends he knew who suffered from depression, referrals from friends, and participants in face-to-face and online support groups for people struggling with depressive and bipolar disorders. Over time, using these methods, Karp recruited more than 150 interviewees from a variety of backgrounds, providing the data for three valuable sociological studies on different aspects of depression (Karp 1996, 2001, 2006).

CROSS-CULTURAL CONSTRUCTIONS OF MENTAL ILLNESS

Mental illness is a prime example of a deviance category that has been viewed quite differently across different times and cultures. While virtually every society has some term or terms to identify those who seem mentally abnormal, there is striking variation in terms of the different "illnesses," causes believed to be responsible for those illnesses, and treatments to cure them.

Different Definitions

In a classic article titled, "Anthropology and the Abnormal," Ruth Benedict (1934) observed that the sorts of behaviors western psychiatry defines as abnormal—such as paranoia, seizures, and hallucinations—are often considered normal in other cultures. The Shasta Indians in California and the native people of Siberia studied by early anthropologists viewed seizures as signs of supernatural powers that marked individuals for leadership. Similarly, in many cultures, including several Native American tribes, it has been considered natural for the bereaved to hallucinate and talk with dead relatives (Kleinman 1987). On the opposite end of the spectrum, personality traits like cheerfulness and easy sociability—traits that we value so much today—would have been considered signs of craziness by the Dobuans of Melanesia (Benedict 1934).

Some types of mental illness are based on a very narrow range of symptoms, such as the culturally specific disorder known as *koro* among Malayasians, an illness characterized by intense fear among men that one's penis and testicles (or among women, that one's vulva and breasts) are shrinking and will soon disappear (Yap 1965). The Bena Bena peoples of New Guinea believed that adult men could be attacked by ghosts, causing them to fall into daylong episodes of highly aggressive behavior during which they would rush about, threatening their clanspeople with clubs and arrows—and after which they would return to normal, with no memory of their aberrant actions (Langness 1965). While such illnesses strike us as bizarre, we should recognize that many of the hundreds of kinds of mental illnesses we identify today, including attention deficit disorder and the eating disorder, anorexia nervosa, would seem similarly strange to most humans throughout the course of history.

Different "Causes"

Not only do different societies recognize different behaviors as signs of mental illness, but they also hold a wide variety of beliefs about the causes of mental illness. The most common belief has been that madness is a result of supernatural possession. Sometimes madness has been viewed as a gift from God, endowing the "touched" person with special talents, such as the ability to prophesy or to heal the sick. The ancient Hebrews, for instance, recorded the prophet Ezekial's bizarre behaviors, such as shaving his head with a sword and lying on one side of his body for 390 days as signs of divine inspiration (*Ezekial*, Chapters 4 and 5). More commonly, madness has been believed to be inflicted by God (or "the gods") as punishment for sin (Conrad and Schneider 1992) or caused by evil spirits, as in the witchcraft beliefs that dominated Europe in the Middle Ages.

Biological explanations that link mental illness to bodily dysfunctions have also been common historically. In early Greek society, Hippocrates argued that mental illness was a result of an imbalance in the body's four essential fluids: black bile, yellow bile, blood, and phlegm. Too much black bile, he wrote, caused depression, while an excess of yellow bile produced anxiety and manic behavior. Modern-day psychiatry discounts Hippocrates' notion of four essential bodily fluids, but it shares with him a focus on biological explanation for mental disorders.

Other theories of mental illness have focused on a lack of social or moral development. Many of these theories, such as Freudian psychoanalysis, focus on childhood trauma and thwarted psychosocial development. Others focus on the dangers of strong passions, especially of sexual urges. Some, like the Roman physician, Galen, believed in the importance of sexual release to keep the body and mind in balance, but many others have believed that giving in to "inappropriate" sexual urges (particularly masturbation) caused mental disorder, a view reflected in lunatic asylum records in Victorian England (Showalter 1987) and post-Civil War US mental hospitals that often listed "masturbation" as the cause of patients' insanity.

Finally, in several cultures we find counterculture ideologies that either glorify mental illness as unrecognized genius or assert its nonexistence. The view of mental illness as genius is captured in the writings of British counterculture psychiatrist R. D. Laing, whose best-selling book, *Politics of Experience* (1967), argued that far from being a form of mental pathology, schizophrenia is a special mode of insight in an insane world. While not glorifying abnormal behaviors in the way that Laing did, Thomas Szaz has been an influential US critic of psychiatry, arguing that it is nothing more than state-orchestrated medical social control—or as he terms it, "pharmacracy" (2001). Szaz's publications over nearly half a century, beginning with *The Myth of Mental Illness* (1961), have attracted a significant following, including support from the Church of Scientology and its most famous follower, the actor Tom Cruise.

Different Treatments

Treatments for mental illness have varied as widely as beliefs about its causes. Roughly paralleling ideas about what causes mental disorder, the three most common treatment approaches have focused on religious, physical, and socioemotional cures. Adherents of many religions believe in the power of divine healing through prayer and religious ritual. The specific practices invoked vary according to the nature of religious beliefs and may range from simple prayers to elaborate community ceremonies, such as the *goot* ceremony practiced in traditional Korean society, involving dancing, drums, and dramatic role-playing by the ceremony's participants (Kim and Rhi 1976).

The physical treatment of mental illness has never before been as dominant as it is today, but various kinds of medical interventions have been common for millennia. Following Hippocrates' claims that mental illness was caused by an imbalance of bodily fluids, Greek physicians employed purgatives, vomitives, and blood-letting to rebalance the body. In AD 4, a Roman physician is even recorded to have used an electric eel to administer an early form of "shock therapy" to treat the emperor Augustus. The use of medicinal drugs also has a long history, from early Ayurvedic herbal remedies in India to Hippocrates' recommendations for St. John's Wort (still a common "natural" remedy today) to treat "nervous unrest."

Not all treatments of the mentally ill have been concerned with helping them. Far from it. As stigmatized deviants, the mentally ill have often been segregated from the general population. In Europe, the social exclusion of the mentally ill reached its peak during the seventeenth and eighteenth centuries—a period referred to by Foucault (1965) as "the Great Confinement." During this era, those labeled as mentally ill were often confined to public institutions such as workhouses or prisons that held a wide mix of social undesirables, including vagrants, orphans, the physically disabled, and criminals. During this period, as social historian Roy Porter so aptly put it, the guiding principle was "out of mind, out of sight" (1988, p.23)—but not completely so. At times, the hospitalized mentally ill were offered as amusement to visitors, as in the case of London's Bethlehem Hospital for the insane, that admitted as many as 90,000 spectators to view their human oddities at a penny per visitor in 1815 (Cockerham 2013, p.17).

While the incarceration of the mentally ill seldom produced positive results, it was not seen at the time as particularly cruel. Even if their confinement was in brutal conditions, it was argued that the mad had little sense of suffering. As Foucault observes, "It was common knowledge until the end of the 18th century that the insane could support the miseries of existence indefinitely. There was no need to protect them. They had no need to be covered or warm" (Foucault 1965, p.74).

A final common type of treatment for mental illness has involved socioemotional remedies that focus on modifying the ill person's social environment or emotional states believed to cause or reflect mental disorder. A good example of mental health treatment through the management of emotion was Aristotle's belief in the importance of "catharsis," or the dramatic purging of strong emotions. According to Aristotle, Greek dramatic plays served a mental health function by enabling audiences to experience an emotional cleansing. Another major socioemotional approach to mental illness has focused on removing individuals from social environments believed to cause their distress. In the nineteenth century, many mental health reformers in Europe and the United States advocated what the French physician Philippe Pinel called *traitement moral*, or "moral therapy," that emphasized the curative powers of removing the mentally ill from stress and bad influences. Pinel and those he influenced were reacting in significant part to the brutal conditions of the Great Confinement in which the mentally ill had been imprisoned. Pinel became an icon of the Enlightenment and the French Revolution when he released from their chains mental patients at Bicetre Hospital and the Paris Asylum for insane women.

HISTORY OF MENTAL ILLNESS IN THE UNITED STATES

In the early years of North American colonial expansion, white colonists had little to offer those who suffered from mental illnesses. The stresses of migration, social isolation, and harsh living conditions on the "frontier" often took a heavy toll on the mental health of early white settlers, indentured servants, and slaves, but those who suffered from mental illnesses had only folk remedies, prayer, and personal fortitude to help them through their emotional struggles. As cities grew and expanded, the treatment of the mentally ill in the United States largely paralleled the Western European experience.

Era of the Asylum

By the middle of the nineteenth century, many of the mentally disturbed in the United States were held in jails and prisons. Concern over their treatment gave rise to the first great "moral entrepreneur" of American mental health, Dorothea Dix. A devout Unitarian and New England schoolteacher, Dix became outraged when she saw mentally ill women confined with criminals in a Massachusetts' jail in 1841. Over the next two years, she visited every jail in the state, and subsequently devoted her life to traveling around the country inspecting mental institutions and demanding increased governmental support. Dix is credited with helping establish 32 state mental hospitals. Over the following century, the number of state mental hospitals continued to grow, reaching a total of 265 hospitals that housed nearly 560,000 patients by 1955. Throughout this period, mental hospitals (frequently poorly funded and understaffed) were challenged to provide custodial care, along with some semblance of treatment, for expanding numbers of troubled and disabled people. Not surprisingly, many patients faced neglect and abuse at the hands of hospital staff.

The gathering of large numbers of the mentally ill in asylums made it easy for doctors to experiment with different kinds of treatment. Based on a now disconfirmed belief that epilepsy and schizophrenia were never found in the same individual, asylum doctors from the 1930s to the 1950s administered insulin to induce diabetic convulsions and coma (similar to epileptic symptoms) in schizophrenics—a practice that has since been discontinued. *Electroconvulsive treatment*, commonly referred to as "shock therapy," was also used widely, at first for schizophrenia and later primarily for long-term depression, for which it continues to be used today. The most highly publicized treatment for severe mental illness during this period was the *lobotomy*, "undoubtedly the most radical therapeutic procedure ever developed in psychiatry" (Grob 1994, p.182). Championed in the United States by a maverick psychiatric crusader, Walter Freeman, who invented the quick and simple "ice pick" technique of transorbital lobotomy, this form of brain surgery was conducted on roughly 40,000 American patients between 1939 and 1955. Freeman himself performed over 3,500 lobotomies during his career, including 228 surgeries in just one 12-day trip to West Virginia in 1952.

The lobotomy proved, by-and-large, to be a psychiatric flash-in-the-pan, highly popular for a short period of time, but ultimately falling into disrepute. The sensational positive press it received during Freeman's heyday was soon eclipsed by negative reports, including news of failed surgeries—some on children as young as four years of age (El-Hai 2005). While lobotomies frequently reduced violent behavior of troublesome patients, they also dramatically blunted patients' abilities to experience emotions. Today, lobotomies are outlawed in many countries around the world, especially as a treatment for children.

In 1952, the first *antipsychotic drug*, chlorpromazine (best known in the United States under the trade name Thorazine), was created. In 1954, chlorpromazine was approved for psychiatric treatment, and became an immediate success. The use of Thorazine spread like wildfire with almost all patients in many mental hospitals being treated with it. Smith, Kline, and French, the drug's manufacturer, made a fortune and soon other companies wanted a piece of the action. As is all too often the case, caution was cast to the wind in the face of *pharmacological optimism*, or the belief that a medication could provide a magic bullet for treating mental illnesses. The calming effects of Thorazine were obvious from the start, but only later were its serious side effects detected, including *tardive dyskinesia*, an irreversible neurological disorder caused by long-term use of the drug. Today, Thorazine has been replaced by newer antipsychotic medications with better side-effect profiles for the treatment of schizophrenia. Meanwhile, psychopharmacology became less dominant in US mental health discourse during the turbulent social era of the 1960s and 1970s—although it reemerged as an even more powerful force in the 1990s.

Deinstitutionalization Era

From the 1950s through the 1970s a number of forces converged that led to a massive reduction of mental hospital patients across the United States. First, the pharmaceutical optimism resulting from the success of Thorazine in reducing psychotic symptoms led to widespread hope that many mental patients would be able to move out of mental hospitals and live on their own. This hope was reinforced by concerns about the dilapidated condition of most mental asylums following their neglect during World War II—a problem made all the worse by the ever-expanding asylum population. Asylums had long been plagued by patient numbers that made anything more than custodial care difficult, if not impossible. As the civil rights movement grew during the 1960s, public-interest attorneys moved beyond the rights of racial minorities to concern with the rights of other marginalized populations. Mental hospital patients, who previously had virtually no access to legal services, were among the groups that civil rights lawyers came to represent, challenging vague and arbitrary commitment statutes, and supporting patients' rights for due process and treatment in "least restrictive" settings.

At the same time, a broader social movement emerged that was also critical of mental hospital care. The movement coalesced around ideas from a variety of sources, including novels like Ken Kesey's *One Flew Over the Cuckoo's Nest* (1962), and the writings of prominent academics, including Thomas Szaz, Michel Foucault, and David Rothman. One of the most influential sociological critiques came in Erving Goffman's book, *Asylums*, where Goffman drew striking parallels between mental hospitals and other "total institutions," such as prisons and military boot camps that were characterized by "abasements, degradations, humiliations, and profanations of the self" (1961, p.14). Human rights attorneys drew upon Goffman's work to substantiate their claims that mental hospitals were overcrowded and inhumane environments where mistreatment, rather than healing, was the rule.

The combination of pharmaceutical confidence among physicians along with financial, legal, and moral concerns regarding mental hospitals set the stage for mental healthcare reform. In 1963, Congress passed the Community Mental Health Centers (CMHC) Act, calling for reductions in mental hospitalization and the funding of less restrictive mental health services. After President Kennedy signed the CMHC Act into law, the numbers of hospitalized mental patients dropped dramatically, from 560,000 in 1955 to 337,000 in 1970 to 54,000 in 1997. While President Kennedy and the Congress enthusiastically endorsed the Act, massive underfunding hampered its goals. The assassination of President Kennedy robbed the Act of one of its most enthusiastic supporters, and despite his interest in Great Society social programs, President Johnson's administration was hamstrung by the escalating cost of the Vietnam War. In subsequent years, Presidents Nixon, Reagan, and Bush, Sr. made deep cuts in federal expenditures supporting community mental health services. The number of hospitalized mental patients declined precipitously, but community services on which they had been expected to depend were poorly supported. As a result, abuse and neglect in mental hospitals has often been traded for abuse and neglect on the streets and in social service ghettoes for the poor and disabled (Torrey 1988; Grob 1991).

Antidepressant Era

Today, in the United States, there are a range of beliefs and practices regarding mental illness, but the biological psychiatric model is far and away the dominant perspective. The 1990s witnessed expansive growth in the development and approval of new psychiatric drugs. Prescriptions for antidepressants and attention deficit medications soared, leading to what medical historian David Healy (1998) has referred to as the "Antidepressant Era." New diagnoses and more inclusive criteria for mental illness were developed—particularly in diagnoses that seemed to offer large markets for prescription drug sales (Horwitz 2002). Meanwhile, less profitable mental healthcare and support services for the most seriously mentally ill languished. It is against this social backdrop of new diagnoses, prescription drugs, and deinstitutionalization that we must seek to understand the experiences of the mentally ill in America today.

SOCIAL STRESS THEORY

We have argued throughout this book that unidimensional theories of deviance causation do not live up to the promise with which they were originally offered. The reason for this is that so many potential factors can influence the deviance process. Mental illness provides an excellent example. As Allan Horwitz and Teresa Scheid have explained, "Mental disorders exist at the intersection of genetic and biological influences, individual life experiences, and social context" (1999, p.11).

Social stress theory offers a good example of the kind of multifaceted theory that is needed to understand the many possible (and interactive) causes of mental disorders, as well as the factors that may help protect against mental illness. Social stress theory argues that high levels of stress deplete individuals' physical, psychological, and personal resources, and increase the likelihood of physical and mental illness. The social stress approach to mental illness incorporates both medical and sociological concepts. While psychiatrists and psychologists are more likely to emphasize medical aspects of the model and sociologists tend to emphasize the social dimensions, the theory incorporates both.

From the medical angle, stress theory examines how some people may be more biologically or psychologically vulnerable to developing mental disorders than others. Such vulnerability, it is argued, may be due to genetic predispositions or biochemical abnormalities. Stress will have a more severe impact on those who are more physically or psychologically vulnerable.

While not discounting that some people are more vulnerable to stress than others, those who focus primarily on sociological factors emphasize that stress and the resources for coping with it are unevenly distributed in society. Some life event stressors, such as the death of a loved one or a serious injury, can happen to any of us. But many chronic stresses, including barriers to achieving life goals, exposure to crime, exploitation, violence, and overcrowding, are more chronic and severe among marginalized, impoverished, and less powerful social groups. In addition, marginalized social groups tend to have fewer financial and social resources to cope with stressful life events. Social stress theorists argue that the uneven distribution of stress and the resources for handling it explains the higher rates of mental illness in lower social classes. They also believe that stress plays an important role even among those from higher social classes who become mentally ill. A major key to understanding how social forces contribute to mental illness, they argue, lies in examining the mix of stresses in people's lives and their resources for managing them.

As social stress research accumulates, the theory continues to be refined, providing a more nuanced view of the relationship between stress and mental illness. Three particular qualifications to the stress hypothesis are relevant to understanding mental illness careers. First, stress contributes less to mental illnesses that have strong genetic components (e.g., schizophrenia). In these cases, the causes of mental illness appear to be much more related to individual abnormalities than to stress (Horwitz 2002). Second, while stress increases the likelihood of both physical and mental illnesses, it does not determine specific outcomes. In some social group stress leads more commonly to physical illnesses than to mental illnesses (Lin and Ensel 1989), and among men stress is more associated with substance abuse disorders, while among women it is more associated with depression (Thoits 1995). Such differences reflect culturally patterned behaviors and expectations more broadly and highlight the role of culture in channeling the expression of mental illness symptoms.

INTERACTIONAL CONTEXTS AND ETHNOGRAPHIC VOICES

In exploring the experiences of those who become labeled as mentally ill, we will focus our attention primarily on those who are diagnosed in two of the

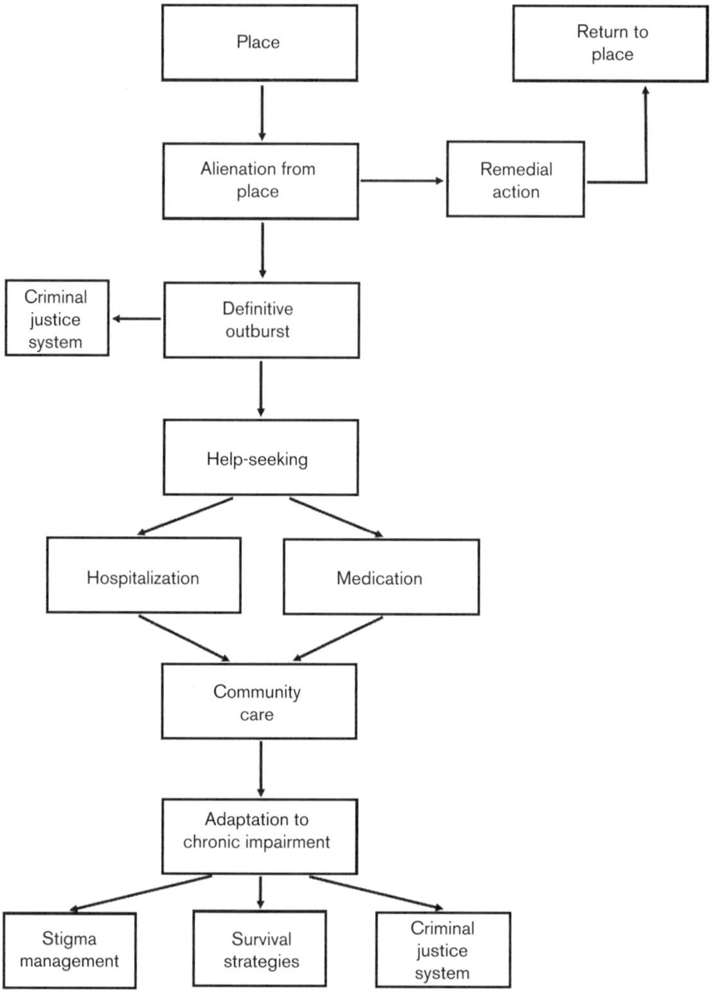

Figure 12.1 Career model of mental illness (adapted and expanded from Aneshensel 1999).

most well-known categories of mental disorder: depression and schizophrenia. Depression (of varying degrees) is so widespread that it has a reputation as "the common cold" of mental illness. Schizophrenia, while far less common, is a particularly vexing illness that presents major social policy challenges in American mental healthcare and the criminal justice system.

Drawing on the concept of deviance careers, figure 12.1 shows common pathways in the experiences of individuals who come to be labeled as mentally ill.

Alienation from Place

For practical purposes it is useful to begin our discussion with an individual who is relatively comfortable and stable within a basic social context that, drawing upon Goffman (1971), we can refer to as "place." Place refers to contexts within which we live our lives, such as our families, work organizations, and schools. Within these organizational contexts we tend to "know our place," meaning that we understand our position within the set of relationships, roles, and identities in the organization, as well as the expectations for what constitutes appropriate behavior. Given the established roles and expectations embedded in our sense of place, Cockerham notes, place provides not only "opportunities for interaction but also the general social conditions in which harmonious interaction is possible" (2013, p.224). The path to becoming labeled mentally ill begins with some perceived *alienation from place.* As Cockerham explains, alienation from place is not the same thing as acting insane. Rather,

> Alienation is the initial step in the experience of becoming mentally ill . . . a mental condition in which a person senses a psychological barrier between himself or herself and the social situation or 'place' in which he or she is located. These troublesome feelings or interpersonal difficulties are accompanied by undesirable emotional effects.
>
> —Cockerham (2013, p.224)

Many who experience alienation from place are able to regain their composure and sense of place, either by taking some remedial action (such as talking through their discomfort with a family member) or by simply waiting until the alienating feelings go away. Individuals often attempt to resolve their alienation from place by blaming situational factors, as did David Karp who writes, "I thought for sure my depression was rooted in situational demands and that once I got tenure it would go away" (1996, p.6). Similarly, family members, coworkers, and friends often respond to "out of place" behaviors with attempts to explain them away. But ultimately, family, coworkers, or friends may find themselves unable to cope when they are confronted with seriously troubling behavior.

Definitive Outburst

Sometimes psychologically or emotionally troubled individuals engage in behaviors that are so disturbing that it becomes impossible to sustain a sense that things are really normal. Such events constitute unmanageable emergencies for those around them, as in emergencies associated with suicide attempts or hallucinations. In such circumstances, those who are dealing with the individual may come to define the person's disruptive and inexplicable behavior as a sign of mental illness. Cockerham (2013, pp.237–240) refers to such situations as *definitive outbursts.*

Examples of definitive outbursts include individuals who actively respond to voices in their heads, who respond nonsensically to questions from other people, who show up bizarrely dressed and disoriented in public places, or who engage in self-injuring behaviors. Such events represent what Anselm Strauss (1962) referred to as "turning points," or critical incidents that force a person (and/or significant others) to see things in a new light—in this case, to view the individual as psychologically disturbed.

Help-Seeking

Whether an individual self-identifies or is identified by others as suffering from mental health difficulties, such recognition typically leads to reaching out for some form of help. Often those who are emotionally or mentally distraught turn to family members and friends for support and advice (Thoits 1995). As their difficulties continue without being resolved, they are likely to look to the mental healthcare system.

Those who seek mental healthcare often find initial help-seeking confusing. They may turn to a variety of sources for assistance, such as psychiatrists, mental health counselors, Twelve Step support groups, and church pastors. In the process, they may find themselves diagnosed with a bewildering flurry of explanations for their problems. As one young woman in Karp's research explained to him, "I kept going to doctor after doctor, getting like all these new terms put on me . . . My family was dysfunctional and I was an alcoholic with an eating disorder and bulimia and depression and it was just all these labels. 'Oh my God!'" (Karp 1996 p.65)

Yet, many experience considerable relief when they receive an explanation that feels convincing. Medical tests offer particularly compelling evidence for some that they are biologically ill. A 30-year-old male salesman told Karp:

> "They gave me a blood test that measures the level of something in the blood, in the brain. And they pronounced me, they said, 'Mr. Smith, you're depressed.' And I said, 'Thank God,' You know? It was a breakthrough . . . It was the beginning of being able to sort out a lifetime of feelings, events. It was the chance for a new beginning."
>
> —Karp (1996, p.65)

Further, many feel some relief when given a game plan for dealing with their problems. Today, medical diagnoses of mental illness almost always result in prescriptions for medication. But rather than being a sign that the end of one's illness is at hand, the start of medication is often only the beginning of a new series of challenges.

The Medication Experience

Most people seeking help for psychological troubles turn first to general physicians rather than psychiatrists. Whether one sees a psychiatrist or a family physician, the mentioning of emotional or psychological problems is likely to be met by suggestions for medication. Prescribing medication is a standard part of physicians' jobs and hundreds of drugs are now available to treat various kinds of mental disorders. But while doctors are often quick to prescribe drugs, patients are often disturbed by the prospect of taking them. Taking psychopharmacological drugs is far different for many people from taking an antibiotic for an infection or a vaccine to protect against a virus.

Depression and Medication

People who have just begun to seek help for emotional or psychological problems tend to be leery of using medication. But over time, Karp observes, most people with long-term depression move through a set of stages in relation to antidepressant medication: (1) desperation and resistance; (2) trial commitment and experimentation; (3) engagement; and finally (4) marriage to medications.

The first stage develops in conjunction with one's growing awareness of having some kind of psychological problem. This stage is marked by ambivalent feelings—of *desperation* for help on the one hand, and *resistance* to the idea of taking medication on the other. Resistance to medication is frequently increased by the doctors' unwillingness to talk with patients about their feelings, even though it is patients' bad feelings that pushed them into seeking help. As one young woman put it:

> This doctor sounded like a used car salesman for antidepressants. He was just like so gung-ho. "Oh yeh, you're the typical depressed person, here's the drug that will cure you. Let me know if you go home and just want to kill yourself or something. We'll try something different." I just really hated him.
>
> —Karp (1996, p.89)

Such bad experiences notwithstanding, most of those Karp has interviewed finally acceded out of desperation to their doctors' advice to at least try out antidepressants.

The second stage of adaptation to taking antidepressants involves what Karp refers to as *trial commitment and experimentation*. Many who are initially reluctant to take medication become more open to them when physicians suggest they "just try it out and see if it helps." The majority of people do not find a drug that works well on the first try. Most end up experimenting with various medications—including some that worsen their depression and cause other unpleasant side effects (such as insomnia, constipation, nausea, and headaches). Doctors respond by shifting them from one medication to another or prescribing additional medications to counter side effects.

Some of those who Karp interviewed never do find a medication that works for them. But many do find relief—at times such tremendous relief that they describe it as a miracle. As one young woman recounted, "All I can tell you is, 'Oh my God, you know when you're on the right medication.' It was the most incredible thing. And I would say that I had a spiritual experience" (1996, p.95).

Such experiences turn skeptics into true believers in the power of medication to cure depression. But antidepressants often lose some or all of their effectiveness over time. Individuals who hail their medication as a miracle face deep disappointment when their meds stop working or fail to work as well. In the end, most come to realize that their drugs are going to work imperfectly.

In the third stage of adaptation to antidepressant medication, which Karp refers to as *engagement*, the depressed person no longer questions whether or not they should take medication. Individuals now focus on the question, "How can I make the medication work best for me?" They may learn with their physicians how to combine medications in "drug cocktails" that produce the most satisfactory results, at least for the time being.

The final stage of the antidepressant medication process, Karp refers to as *marriage to medication*, in which patients become wedded to a medical version of mental illness that solidifies their relationship to medication. They believe that their drugs are essential to their day-to-day functioning and they integrate them into their daily routines. At this point, taking psychiatric medications becomes "emotionally equivalent to taking vitamin pills or brushing one's teeth before bedtime" (Karp 2006, p.92)

For some, reaching this stage of adaptation is highly positive. Yet, others feel ambivalent, thankful for the help drugs provide, but frustrated with the drugs' unpredictability as well as the dependency they have developed. In the end, Karp concludes, antidepressants are at best a mixed bag for most of the people who use them. "Right now," he writes, "pills remain blunt and unpredictable instruments. Psychiatry's unbridled enthusiasm for and commitment to medications far exceed their actual effectiveness" (2006, p.225).

Schizophrenia and Medication

As with antidepressants, antipsychotic medications used to treat schizophrenia work better for some individuals than others and patients must often go through a period of experimenting with different drugs before they find one that helps. Further, antipsychotic medications have side effects that are typically more severe than those for antidepressants.

When Estroff asked the subjects in her study about their medication experiences with Prolixin, the dominant antipsychotic medication at the time of her study, they generally agreed that the drug reduced their symptoms. But most of them found the side effects difficult to live with—and at times unbearable. In addition to common relatively minor problems like dry mouth, constipation, blurred vision, and drowsiness, many also experienced more serious side effects including *akasthisia* and tardive dyskinesia.

Akasthisia, which was called the "Prolixin Stomp" by patients in Estroff's study, is a general restlessness accompanied by jitters. Tardive dyskinesia, which is particularly common among long-term users of older antipsychotics (like Thorazine and Prolixin), is a nervous system disorder characterized by involuntary lip-smacking, chewing motions, and constant twisting of body and limbs.

One of the most compelling issues Estroff raises in relation to antipsychotic medication has to do with their impact on interpersonal relationships. "At a fundamental level, in order to develop and maintain an intimate relationship, one has to share time and space with another. A person literally has to sit still long enough to make emotional connections" (1981, p.113). Under the influence of their medications, even though they are largely free from psychotic symptoms, many of the clients found it extremely difficult to sit still long enough to facilitate those kinds of connections. Further, they were often embarrassed and depressed by the visible side effects of the drugs—tremors, drooling, head-bobbing, etc.—and avoided potentially painful interaction.

In the three decades since the publication of Estroff's *Making It Crazy*, a new generation of antipsychotic medications, referred to broadly as "atypical antipsychotics," have been developed. Drug manufacturers promote the new medications as having fewer side effects, claiming that the atypicals should be the preferred treatment for schizophrenia. However, some studies question the greater efficacy and improved side-effect profiles of the atypical antipsychotics (Vendantam 2006). Further, as the new antipsychotics have become more widely prescribed, concerns have grown about side effects particular to these drugs, especially their tendency to produce weight gain (some commonly in the magnitude of 50 pounds or more in long-term users) that may lead to diabetes and heart disease.

Ultimately, antipsychotic medications, like their antidepression counterparts, are a mixed bag for most of the people who use them. They do not cure schizophrenia, although they do reduce many of its most visible symptoms. But in the process they visit new burdens on those who suffer from schizophrenia, and in some ways contribute to their isolation from those around them.

Hospitalization

For a century following the Civil War, hospitalization of those experiencing psychiatric troubles was considered the front line of defense. Today, the huge old mental hospitals sit empty and abandoned, or are turned into research parks, condominiums, and shopping malls. Those who in the past would have been committed to mental hospitals are diverted in other directions. Large numbers of elderly who were cared for in the old asylums now reside in nursing homes. Meanwhile, the mentally ill tend to be hospitalized only briefly during periods of severe symptoms or following suicide attempts, and released once they are stabilized.

Virtually all who become inpatients are first committed to psychiatric hospital care at a time of crisis. Some recognize that they are having psychological problems and seek help themselves. Those who are seriously questioning their sanity may see hospitalization as a positive step toward the alleviation of their problems. But most people experiencing mental difficulties are very reluctant to consider entering a hospital.

Frequently other family members are the ones who feel the situation is severe enough to require hospitalization. Those whose psychiatric symptoms have become a serious stress in family life often find family members suggesting or demanding that they seek help. As one told Nancy Herman, "My wife told me if I wouldn't go see the doctor then she was going to leave me. She said that she'd take the kids and get as far away from me as possible" (2001, p.435). In managing crisis, family members often face the difficult task of getting an unwilling "ill person" committed to the hospital. Frequently they are stunned at how difficult it is today to get someone committed to a mental hospital against their will. A mother recalling her experience seeking hospitalization for her son, explained to Karp:

> He was in his dorm and he was obviously psychotic. I said [to the psychiatrist], "My son is talking to a closet. . . . Is there any way that we can intervene at this point without waiting until he becomes totally [self-destructive]?" He says, "No, just wait until he is in total crisis and bring him to an emergency room."
>
> —Karp (2001, p.193)

In their efforts to explore options, caregivers like the mother quoted here may consult with professionals, and even possibly make arrangements for hospitalization behind the troubled family member's back, a tactic that is likely to lead to bitter feelings when the patient learns of what feels like a conspiracy against them (Goffman 1961).

Other patients who do not view themselves as impaired are apprehended by the police and taken to a mental hospital, frequently not comprehending what they have done to warrant such treatment. But even those who recognize that they are having problems and who want to receive help can find it very disturbing to be committed to a hospital. While a few find entering the hospital an enormous relief from their struggles, more often, hospitalization is described by patients as a devastating experience that leaves them feeling like "damaged goods."

Those who are caring for a disturbed person may feel relief once they have been able to place the person in hospital care. Admission to the hospital feels like a victory, and those new to medical care for a mentally ill person are likely to believe that professionals can solve the problem. But as Karp writes, "Hospitalization they soon discover is just the beginning of an institutional journey for which they are ill prepared" (2001, p.205).

One of the first problems typically experienced by hospitalized mental patients and their families is the extreme difficulty of getting to speak with the hospital experts—especially, the psychiatrists—about the patient's situation. Virtually all studies of mental hospitals find that face time with psychiatrists is almost nonexistent. Under current "managed care" practices, highly paid hospital staff, like psychiatrists, are held to very tight patient schedules. Much of the decision about a patient's hospitalization is not based on issues of appropriate medical care, but rather on issues of insurance coverage. Karp notes how insurance "horror stories" (e.g., of individuals being released while still in a psychotic state) are disturbingly common.

CONTEMPORARY RESPONSES TO MENTAL ILLNESS

The short hospitalization typical today emphasizes reducing patients' symptoms with medication and releasing them back into the community, where they are expected to pursue outpatient care on their own. Recognizing the limited ability of their loved ones to manage such tasks by themselves, many families step in to try to help. Those without close family, or who have become alienated from their families, are left on their own or with the help of mental health caseworkers to navigate the confusing world of "community care."

Community Care?

Today, most chronically mentally ill individuals live in community settings, perhaps punctuated with short episodes of hospitalization. The obstacles that chronically mentally ill individuals and their caregivers (e.g., families) face in their communities are immense. Few of the programs that were envisioned in the CMHC Act of 1963 were ever developed, leaving a fragmented and overburdened system of mental health services. Further, the chronically mentally ill in the United States lack some very basic social and material needs, as well as medical services. They find themselves with few (if any) valued social roles, a dearth of caring personal relationships, little sense of personal agency or effectiveness, and few regular activities that provide structure to their daily lives. In such circumstances, Estroff (1981) has argued that all too often "community care" ends up replicating some of the worst aspects of the old asylums.

One of the most consistent findings of sociologists studying mental hospitals in the age of the asylum was the sinister effects of long-term mental hospitalization. Study after study (especially Goffman 1961; Rosenhan 1973) found that large mental hospitals fostered patient adaptation to the hospital environment and the sick patient role, leaving them ill-prepared to return to more normal life outside. In mental hospitals, patients were often treated as objects to be managed rather than as people. Staff rarely interacted with them except to enforce hospital routines. Patients were also subjected to intentional and unintentional humiliation and constant surveillance and, from the 1950s on, kept heavily medicated with powerful tranquilizers.

In *Making It Crazy*, Estroff reported that, "within the framework of a community treatment program, an examination of the clients' experiences of self in relation to others reveals distressing repetitions of hospital patterns" (1981, p.175). Specifically, community care often produces dependence, social isolation, and sick role engulfment that are strikingly similar to mental hospitalization. In its current form, community mental healthcare for the seriously mentally ill tends to trap them in poverty, fragmented and confusing services, and governmental support that puts up barriers to their attempts to become independent. They adapt by learning to "make it crazy"—to accept, however begrudgingly, the Catch-22s that they face, to live with diminished expectations, and to go through the motions, however perfunctorily, of the daily routines available to them.

Criminalization of Mental Illness

Given that mental illness is often publicly identified through disruptive behaviors and interactions, it is inevitable that the criminal justice system and the mental healthcare system intersect with each other. But as public mental hospitals across the country massively reduced their size and shifted the care of the mentally ill to insufficiently funded and disorganized community care, the police and criminal justice system assumed a greater role in managing the mentally ill population. Mental illness (at least major psychotic illnesses like schizophrenia and bipolar disorder) has become criminalized, many scholars argue, and America's jails and prisons have become the "new asylum" (Morrissey and Goldman 1986; Torrey et al. 1992; Lamb and Weinberger 1998).

The term "criminalization of mental illness" is used broadly to refer to how current social policies toward the chronically mentally ill put them in jeopardy of arrest and incarceration. In order to understand the nature and extent of the criminalization of mental illness in the United States, we need to know the number and proportion of jail and prison inmates who were mentally ill in the past as compared to today. Unfortunately, we have very little data on earlier times. A few local studies were done in various cities, but perhaps the first roughly accurate national "guestimate" comes from E. Fuller Torrey (1988) who projected that in 1987 about 9 per cent of US prisoners (or about 67,000 people) suffered from serious mental disorders (not including alcohol and drug problems). While we may assume that this percentage is higher than during the heyday of large mental hospitals in the 1950s, we have no solid statistics on which to base this claim. Even if we did, it would be hard to compare statistics since the criteria used to identify people as mentally ill have changed over time. Two studies from the US Bureau of Justice Statistics (*table 12.2*) illustrate how much the use of different criteria for counting people as mentally ill can change the reported rates of mental illness.

Table 12.2 Rates of Mentally Ill Jail and Prison Inmates in Two BJS Reports

Year		State Prisons	Federal Prisons	US Jails	Total
1999	Number	179,000	8,100	96,700	283,800
	Per cent	16%	7%	16%	16%
2006	Number	705,600	70,200	479,000	1,245,800
	Per cent	56%	45%	64%	57%

SOURCES: Bureau of Justice Statistics (1999, 2006).

The first study, published in 1999, found about 280,000 "mentally ill offenders" in US prisons and jails—approximately 16 per cent of a total prison and jail population of 1.8 million inmates (Bureau of Justice Statistics 1999). Just seven years later, a new report (Bureau of Justice Statistics 2006) presented findings that mentally ill inmates comprised nearly 57 per cent of the jail and prison population, with the number of mentally ill inmates then estimated at 1.25 million. Juxtaposed with each other, the reports give the impression of an astounding increase in the incarceration of the mentally ill. But closer examination reveals that the huge increase in numbers of mentally ill inmates is due primarily to different criteria for identifying them. The 1999 study classified inmates as mentally ill if they: (1) reported a current mental or emotional condition, or (2) reported an overnight stay in a mental hospital or treatment program. In contrast, the 2006 study classified inmates as mentally ill if they reported either of the preceding criteria OR if they exhibited such "classic" *DSM* symptoms of mental illness as insomnia, decreased appetite, diminished ability to concentrate, persistent irritability, and feelings of worthlessness.

It is hardly surprising that the majority of jail and prison inmates in this study were classified as depressed! But, just as Snow et al. (1986a) found problems with using conventional criteria to identify mental illness among the homeless, it is unreasonable to consider decreased appetite, irritability, or trouble sleeping as signs of mental illness in a jail or prison environment. Further, the very different criteria in the two studies for counting inmates as mentally ill make it impossible to compare the data and assess whether or not there has been a change in the rate of mentally ill in US prisons and jails.

If this kind of discrepancy can exist between studies within a single agency, then we must expect and be ready to discern such differences in other reports if we are going to be able to draw reasonable conclusions from them. Fortunately, Virginia Hiday (1999) has conducted a rigorous review of sociological research on this topic. Her review provides a more accurate assessment of the interrelated issues of the criminalization of mental illness and the degree of danger posed by the mentally ill.

In her review, Hiday notes that mentally ill individuals can end up in jails and prisons for two different kinds of activities. First, they may commit a crime as a result of their illness and be arrested and sent to jail rather than placed (some would argue, more appropriately) in a mental hospital. The other possibility is that a mentally ill person may be arrested for activities that stem from their impoverished living conditions rather than their illnesses. Both of these situations occur, although Hiday's review suggests that the second is more common, including large numbers of arrests for survival-oriented behaviors such as shoplifting and failure to pay for restaurant meals. But even the arrests directly related to psychiatric symptoms are typically for minor public disorder offenses such as disturbing the peace or loitering. In contrast, Hiday observes, "[F]ew of the mentally ill (either absolutely or proportionately) are arrested for the violent crimes the public most fears: murder, rape, aggravated assault, and arson" (1999, p.516).

In summary, while the experience of the mentally ill with the criminal justice system does appear to be far greater today than in the era of extensive mental hospitalization, the bulk of contact between the chronically mentally ill and the criminal justice system seems to have less to do with their mental illness than with a ghettoized existence that increases the likelihood that they will turn to illicit survival strategies or be arrested for disorderly public behavior. Only a small proportion of the mentally ill pose threats of serious violence, in contrast to the media emphasis on dangerous and delusional madmen.

Mental Health Courts

The presence of significant numbers of mentally ill individuals in US jails and prisons causes a wide variety of problems. Some of the mentally ill pose especially difficult disciplinary problems. Unlike mental asylums, corrections facilities are not designed to provide mental healthcare, which helps explain why half of the incarcerated mentally ill receive no treatment. The presence of large numbers of mentally ill individuals in the corrections population places extraordinary demands on jails and prisons and increases the cost of running them.

One recent legal response to the problems associated with mentally ill individuals in the criminal justice system has been the creation of *mental health courts* (often referred to as MHCs). Like other "problem-solving courts," MHCs are based on principles of *therapeutic jurisprudence*. The underlying assumption of MHCs is that mental illness has played a significant role in an individual's illegal activities and that if a person accepts and follows treatment for their mental illness, their criminal justice involvement will decline if not disappear. MHCs offer some offenders who have been diagnosed with mental illness the opportunity to avoid jail or prison time if they agree to participate in a program to address their mental health problems. In most

CLAIMS-MAKER PROFILE

Mental Health Court Judge Stephanie Rhoades

Judge Stephanie Rhoades has spent two decades working with mentally ill offenders in the Anchorage District Court. She has been a role model and advocate for mental health courts (MHCs) across the United States. Judge Rhoades had both personal and professional motivations for seeking to develop courts that are responsive to the needs of the mentally ill. She explains:

> I came upon the issue of criminalization of the mentally ill at the intersection of two experiences; one personal and the other professional. First, my youngest brother has mental health disorders and I serve as his family case manager. Second, about five years into my judicial career, I began to see a continued pattern of people with my brother's characteristics recycling through the jail on nuisance crimes. I was shocked to learn that individuals with mental illness comprised nearly half of Alaska corrections' population. I knew that if my brother were to be arrested, he would need me to explain to the powers-that-be that he really needed help and not jail. He would need me to get him out and keep him from going back. I wanted a program to provide a surrogate "good sister" to offenders who didn't have one. (Trawver and Rhoades 2013, p.177)

At first the prosecuting attorneys Judge Rhoades worked with resisted being part of an MHC treatment team, preferring their usual adversarial trial approach. Some ridiculed the MHC, nicknaming it "clapping court," because participants' successes were sometimes met with applause in the courtroom. But positive encouragement is a key component of the courts. "The relationship between the judge and the participant has always been a cornerstone of MHC practice," Judge Rhoades says. "The judge-participant relationship relies on catching participants in success and not failure. The judge walks the path along-side the participant, reflecting back to the participant even small successes so that he or she can gain the confidence to maintain a commitment to treatment, and to change."

When Judge Rhoades began the Anchorage Mental Health Court, it was one of only four MHCs in the United States. Today, there are over 300 mental health courts across the country.

cases, participants in MHCs must plead guilty to the offense with which they are charged, but their convictions and sentences are put on hold while they participate in activities mandated by the court. MHCs use a team approach that provides participants with case management, medications, substance abuse treatment (when needed), and counseling. Like drug courts, MHCs take a carrot and stick approach, offering incentives for good behavior as well as sanctions for failing to follow treatment guidelines. In addition to holding criminal charges in abeyance while the client is in the program, those who "graduate" from MHCs may have their criminal charges expunged from their records.

MHCs have expanded dramatically over the past 15 years, with over 300 such courts currently in operation across the United States (Council of State Governments 2016). While the first courts focused solely on misdemeanor offenders, many MHCs now accept some felony offenders as well (Redlich et al. 2006). Research on MHCs suggests that the courts reduce future involvement in the criminal justice system. However, the courts have also been criticized on several counts, including the requirement that participants plead guilty to charges in order to participate, the mandate for taking medications, and the longer time that MHC participants are under court supervision when compared to offenders who are processed through regular courts.

MHCs and other jail diversion programs can only be successful insofar as they address the causes of their clients' criminal behaviors. The assumption underlying MHCs is that the crimes committed by the mentally ill stem from untreated mental illness. And yet, as Nancy Wolff notes, "Like persons without mental illness, offending behaviors by persons with mental illness may be motivated by a host of socioeconomic and historical factors" (2003, p.155). To date there is no major research establishing that mental disorder is in fact the principal cause of crime that leads to the arrest and incarceration of the mentally ill. The impoverished living conditions of large numbers of the chronically mentally ill are closely associated with the majority of their arrests (Hiday 1999). If MHCs are to prove successful in reducing the criminal justice involvement of the mentally ill, their success will be based in part on improving the consistency and quality of community care for the mentally ill.

STIGMA MANAGEMENT AND RESISTANCE

In addition to experiencing their own psychological challenges, those who are labeled mentally ill face stigmatization and various kinds of social control in the broader society. They are often feared, avoided, and made the butt of jokes. Indeed, some scholars (e.g., Kaufmann 1999) argue—and many who are labeled mentally ill agree—that social mistreatment and rejection of the mentally ill based on stigmatizing stereotypes is more detrimental to their quality of life than are their illnesses. We conclude the discussion of mental illness careers by examining the stigma management practices used by the mentally ill today to challenge the impact of negative images and perceptions.

In-Group Stigma Management

In-group stigma management strategies among the mentally ill may occur in many face-to-face or virtual settings in which they find themselves in each others' presence. Three kinds of settings in particular provide rich opportunities for in-group stigma management: informal gatherings, formal face-to-face peer-support groups, and Internet settings.

Nancy Herman (1987) has documented the spontaneous peer support among chronically mentally ill residents in cheap hotels, rooming houses, and homeless shelters. Finding themselves sharing daily routines and spaces, over time the individuals Herman studied came to realize that they had many similar experiences—poverty, abandonment by family and friends, and stigmatization. As they developed closer relationships, they became informal social support groups for each other, sharing survival strategies, social expectations, and a self-protective ideology that countered conventional stereotypes of the mentally ill. As one of her informants explained:

> Every day, after I get kicked out of the boarding home, I go up town to a bench in front of the shopping center and meet a few "regulars" . . . We usually hang around four or five hours watching the people go by, cracking jokes, and rolling our smokes. The day goes by quick when you got someone to share it with.
>
> —Herman (1987, p.239)

Members of these groups often advised each other on how to handle common problems. Old-timers in the groups taught newcomers what social service and religious agencies could be counted on for free meals, clothing, and other handouts. Such social networks develop in large part to fill in the social and material gaps in marginalized lives of mentally ill individuals living in cheap board and care facilities.

In addition to this spontaneous casual support, the past 25 years have seen a dramatic growth in formal peer-support programs. Many have modeled themselves after Twelve Step programs, like AA. In addition to the practical and informational support that these programs provide, they are particularly rich environments for in-group encouragement. Schizophrenics Anonymous, for instance, pursues the goal of "helping to restore dignity" to schizophrenics by "offering fellowship, positive support, and companionship" (National Schizophrenia Foundation 2006). Other Twelve Step groups for the mentally ill include Depressed Anonymous, Obsessive Compulsive Anonymous, and Social Phobics Anonymous, among others.

The Internet also provides a variety of chat rooms and social support sites devoted to different kinds of mental illnesses. Many of these sites are often sponsored or monitored by mental health practitioners, but others offer peer-based chat groups and newsgroups. Even a cursory web search reveals an enormous amount of communication among the mentally ill. The "Depression Chat Rooms" website, for instance, offers blogs on which people can share their experiences and provide peer support. "Our primary objective," the website states, "is to connect people that have issues regarding depression and anxiety" (Depression Chat Rooms 2016).

Out-Group Strategies

Since mental illness is not usually immediately obvious to others, the most widespread stigma management strategy among the mentally ill is concealment of their illness and efforts to pass as "normal." An ex-hospital patient explained to Herman, "I decided from the moment that my treatment ended I would tell as few people as possible about my stay in the psychiatric hospital. . . . To this day, I've only confided in my friend Paul and a neighbor who had a similar illness a while back" (1993, p.308). As this quote suggests, those who conceal their history of mental illness also use a second strategy of *selective disclosure* of their deviant identity to a small number of people, primarily to family members and close acquaintances who are likely to be sympathetic. Disclosure to sympathetic others often provides emotional relief, as expressed by a 52-year-old woman in Herman's research:

> Keeping it inside of you all bottled up is no good. One day, I walked down the street to a neighbor of mine and she invited me in to have tea. I knew what had happened to her years ago. I let out all my anxieties and fears to her that afternoon. I told her everything and she was so sympathetic. She knew exactly what I was going through. Once I let it all out, I felt so much better.
>
> —Herman (1993, p.311)

At other times, they may reveal their mental illness histories to people with whom they are developing new friendships. The strategy of *preventive disclosure* allows those experiencing mental illness to reveal their potential stigma and to test the waters early in new relationships. As a 40-year-old man explained, "For me, it is best to inform people right off the bat about my mental illness. Why? Because you don't waste a lot of time developing relationships and then get rejected later" (1993, p.313).

Finally, those who disclose their mental illness histories often try to use a fourth strategy of *normalization*, doing their best to present themselves as normal in spite of their deviance. They downplay their deviant identity and emphasize their ability to fit in with "normal" others. As a 59-year-old former mental hospital patient stated:

> The third time I got out of the hospital, I tried to fit right in. I told some of my buddies and a couple of others about my sickness. It was easier to get it out in the open. But what I tried to show them was that I could do the same things they could, some of them even better. I beat them at pool, at darts, and I could outdrink them. . . . The key to success is being up front and making them believe you're just as normal as them.
>
> —Herman (1993, p.318)

Efforts at normalization, however, often achieve only partial success, as the mentally ill find themselves accepted as normal in some situations (e.g., work settings), but not in others (e.g., as romantic partners).

Collective Action

There have long been challenges to mainstream views toward mental illness—several of which we have discussed in this chapter. Spring-boarding from the civil rights movement, the "antipsychiatry" movement of the 1960s and 1970s became a base of collective action for many deinstitutionalized mental patients. The antipsychiatry movement defined itself largely in terms of reaction to psychiatric treatment, often invoking the term "psychiatric survivors" to reflect the mistreatment of the mentally ill by the mental health system. Rejecting the treatment they received, ex-patients in the antipsychiatry movement have advocated for greater patient choice in their own care, as described in Judi Chamberlin's (1978) book, *On our Own: Patient-Controlled Alternatives to the Mental Health System*, considered by many as the "Bible" of the patients' rights movement.

During roughly the same period that marked the rise of the antipsychiatry movement, other advocacy groups also emerged that were much more open to conventional mental health treatment. Some were created by former mental patients, while others were created by caretakers of mentally ill relatives. Today, there is an incredible range of groups which, taken together, form the "consumer/survivor/ex-patient"—or more simply, the "c/s/x"—movement (Morrison 2005). These groups provide opportunities for political activism among the mentally ill. They can be broadly categorized as either radical antipsychiatry groups or mainstream medically oriented groups. MindFreedom provides a good example of the former, while StigmaBusters exemplifies the second.

MindFreedom is an umbrella organization for antipsychiatry groups from around the world. Its stated purpose is "to win campaigns for human rights of people diagnosed with psychiatric disabilities" (MindFreedom 2016). The organization sponsors protests against mainstream mental healthcare professionals. Members regularly picket the annual conference of the APA. Another of MindFreedom's major activities is its annual Mad Pride celebrations, held on July 14, Bastille Day, which marks the anniversary of the storming of the Bastille Prison by Paris citizens in 1789, a key symbolic event in the French Revolution—and one in which psychiatric prisoners were among the freed. Mad Pride celebrations have included street theater, camp-ins at state capitols, music, and guest speakers—many of whom identify themselves as psychiatric survivors.

In contrast to MindFreedom, StigmaBusters is a program sponsored by National Alliance for the Mentally Ill (NAMI), a large grassroots organization comprised mostly of family members/caretakers and mental health professionals, but also including many mentally ill individuals. The StigmaBusters program offers various activities for members to become involved in "fighting inaccurate and hurtful representations of mental illness" (NAMI 2016). One program, Stigma Alert, relies on members to report and write letters of protest regarding demeaning portrayals of the mentally ill in the media and other venues. In one campaign, for instance, StigmaBusters protested an online retailer's marketing of an "Obsessive Compulsive Action Figure" as making fun of mental illness (NAMI 2006). Another of its programs supports amateur acting groups, often comprised of former mental patients, who develop theater performances with humorous and dramatic skits from the players' experiences as clients of the mental healthcare system and other aspects of their daily lives, with the goal of reducing misunderstanding and prejudice.

BLURRED BOUNDARIES II: A HYPER CHILD OF YOUR OWN

This final section of the chapter asks you to think about how you would approach caring for a child of your own who school officials told you needs to be tested for ADHD. It is quite possible that you or someone close to you will face this challenge in the years ahead. In fact, many students who read this book have experienced this issue firsthand, either personally or with a family member diagnosed as ADHD.

Imagine yourself as a parent of an active, sometimes stubborn and forgetful sixth grade child. One day you get a call from a school counselor. The counselor tells you that your child has been disrupting class, failing to pay attention to the teacher, and having trouble staying in their seat. During the past week, your child has also been involved in two scuffles during recess that had to be broken up by the assistant principal. These problems, the counselor says, may indicate that your child is suffering from ADHD, adding that it would be wise to get a medical opinion on the matter before your child's problems become worse.

What would you do? To whom would you turn for advice and assistance? What kinds of things would you worry about and what considerations would be most influential in your decisions about how to respond to your child's "problem"?

If you are like most of us, part of your decision would depend on your own experiences with your child at home. If your family life was not disrupted by your child's behavior, you might be quite surprised to hear of troubles at school and feel that the problem was more in the school environment than in your child's brain. On the other hand, if you were consistently frustrated with your child's behavior at home, you might find it a relief to hear that others had noticed the problem and were suggesting a possible solution.

If, following the advice of a school official, you took your child in for a medical evaluation, you might find a physician who wanted to do a fairly complete behavioral assessment. But many physicians decide to prescribe ADHD medication based on quick and superficial examinations. It could be upsetting to you as a parent just how quickly the doctor decided to put your child on drugs.

You might be hesitant to follow his or her orders, although most parents who are advised to put their children on medication end up doing so, even if with some reservations.

Once your son or daughter began taking medication, there would be several possibilities. Your child might be among the 40 per cent of children who respond favorably to medication, in which case you are likely to gladly embrace the medical diagnosis. But what if your child was among the 30 per cent of children who had some improvement, but also suffered side effects such as insomnia or heart arrhythmia? Your doctor might suggest shifting to a new medication or using a second drug to reduce the side effects of the first. The medication that at first seemed like a godsend would now seem more complicated.

You would face even more difficult choices if your child was among the 30 per cent of children for whom stimulant medication does not seem to work. In this case, the physician might recommend another drug, such as the nonstimulant medication Strattera, or an antidepressant. Or you might look for other approaches to dealing with your child's problems.

Today, many parents try to learn more by seeking information on the Internet. But a simple Google search for "ADHD" will pull up thousands of sites and a bewildering array of overlapping and conflicting claims and experts, many of whom warn readers against the dangers of remedies other than their own.

In your search for the best solution, you might also seek advice from other parents. A major support group, Children and Adults with Attention Deficit Disorder, or CHADD, has chapters in most large cities and is eager to provide both information and encouragement. While it is more difficult to find community-based groups with a critical attitude toward ADHD, the Internet offers chat groups and email contacts with people who share an aversion to the idea that ADHD is a real illness, and especially to the use of ADHD drugs on children. These groups will welcome you and give you compelling arguments for why you must avoid doing what CHADD and your doctor advise. Groups on both sides of this issue seem to be honest, caring, and knowledgeable in their own ways, but their suggestions often contradict each other.

In the end, you as a parent have to decide, and—as is always the case with deviance at the blurred boundary—it is easy to see how different people could make very different decisions. Given the importance of your decision for your child, how do you think you would proceed?

SUMMARY

- Nearly 50 million Americans suffer from anxiety disorders and nearly 30 million struggle with mood disorders annually. The numbers experiencing more extreme psychoses are smaller, but especially challenging to address.

- Getting accurate estimates of mental illness requires uncovering hidden cases and avoiding overcounting. The use of multiple methods to identify cases of mental illness is one strategy for more accurate evaluation.
- Drop-in centers, support groups, and Internet sites offer researchers some opportunities to access specific segments of the overall population of people experiencing mental illness.
- The most common explanations for mental illness across history have been demonic possession, emotional trauma, and biological dysfunction.
- Religious rituals, medical treatment, and psychiatric counseling have been used to treat mental disorders.
- Large numbers of mental patients were housed in mental hospitals in the United States from the post-Civil War era until the early 1980s.
- The deinstitutionalization movement decried inhumane conditions in mental asylums and advocated community treatment, but community services for the chronically mentally ill have not been well developed and many of those with serious mental illnesses today find themselves on the streets and caught up in the criminal justice system.
- Social stress theory asserts that when stresses exceed the coping ability of individuals, people are at heightened risk of mental illness. Some people are more vulnerable to stress-related mental illness than others by virtue of their physical constitution and coping resources.
- Deviance careers of the mentally ill frequently involve progression from initial feelings of social alienation to labeling by oneself and/or others as a person who suffers from mental illness.
- Doctors usually treat mental illnesses with medications, often prescribing several different drugs before finding ones that effectively address patients' symptoms.
- Inpatient mental hospital care is expensive and difficult to access, especially if the patient resists being hospitalized.
- Those who experience mental illness use various strategies to manage stigma, including in-group activities with their peers, out-group stigma management with "normals," and activism aimed toward promoting more positive conceptions of the mentally ill.

KEYWORDS

akasthisia: A generalized restlessness and jitters caused by taking the antipsychotic medication Prolixin. Referred to by patients in Estroff's study as the "Prolixin Stomp."

alienation from place: The first stage in mental illness careers, marked by a sense of estrangement from one's social surroundings and undesirable emotional feelings.

antipsychotic drug: Medication used to treat several major mental illnesses (especially schizophrenia and bipolar disorders) characterized by psychotic symptoms.

attention deficit hyperactivity disorder (ADHD): A controversial widely diagnosed mental disorder often first identified in childhood, characterized by fidgety overactive behavior and an inability to focus attention.
criminalization of mental illness: Social policies that treat mental illness symptoms or survival strategies of the seriously mentally as crimes to be processed through the criminal justice system.
definitive outburst: A disruptive and unexplainable act by a troubled individual that leads to others defining them as mentally ill.
deinstitutionalization: The movement of the mentally ill out of large mental hospitals as those hospitals were massively reduced in size (or closed), especially from 1960 to 1990.
electroconvulsive therapy: The administration of electric current to the brain to induce seizure activity, used in the treatment of certain mental illnesses (esp. depression).
lobotomy: Surgery on the brain's prefrontal cortex that was used to treat mental illness symptoms, mostly in the 1940s and 1950s.
medicalization of deviance: The framing of various kinds of deviance as medical illnesses that can be cured or controlled by medical treatment (e.g., surgery, psychological counseling, and medication).
mental health courts: Problem-solving courts created to address the treatment needs of mentally ill offenders by diverting them from jails and prisons as long as they abide by mental health and behavioral treatment goals.
mood disorders: Mental illnesses characterized by depression or mood swings between manic and depressive emotional states (the latter referred to as bipolar disorder).
pharmaceutical optimism: A belief in the ability of modern medicine to cure most mental problems with medications.
preventive disclosure: A stigma management strategy in which "mentally ill" individuals reveal their psychiatric history to people with whom they hope to build relationships, thus allowing them to see whether the other person will accept them.
selective disclosure: A stigma management strategy in which "mentally ill" individuals reveal their psychiatric history to a few other people, especially close friends and family.
social stress theory: A positivistic approach that focuses attention on social stress as a major cause of mental illness and on various social psychological factors that may reduce the impact of stress.
tardive dyskinesia: An irreversible neurological disorder caused by long-term use of older "typical" antipsychotic medications and characterized by lip-smacking, drooling, and bodily contortions.
therapeutic jurisprudence: The use of the judicial system to provide treatment to overcome the personal problems, such as mental illness, that are believed to be causing criminal behavior.
total institution: An organization (like a prison or traditional large mental hospital) that enforces total subordination of prisoners or clients and restricts inmate interaction with noninmates.

CHAPTER

13

Obesity and Eating Disorders

Young woman checking for body fat (Cultural Creative/Alamy Stock Photo).

CONTENTS

LEARNING OBJECTIVES

After reading this chapter, you will be able to:

- Describe the medical classifications of obesity and eating disorders in the United States today
- Explain the challenges of, and strategies for, studying body weight-related deviance
- Identify different historical definitions of, and causal explanations for, fat bodies and eating disorders
- Apply and evaluate self-control theory's explanation of the causes of obesity
- Analyze the interactional contexts and experiences in which weight-related deviance occurs
- Describe the main approaches to obesity in America today
- Assess the case for antidiscrimination laws to protect "fat" people in the workplace

BLURRED BOUNDARIES I: TWO "FAT" PEOPLE

Thomas Blake has always been large and heavy. In grade school, he endured insults from boys on the playground, where he was given the nickname "the great white whale." In junior high and high school, his size turned to some advantage as he served as a solid lineman on the football team. His performance as an offensive tackle during his last two years of high school led to a college scholarship, but a knee injury in his freshman year took him off the football field for the rest of his college career. He studied hard, but living mostly on fast food, he gained 60 pounds by the time he earned his degree. After college, Tom started a diet and resolved to get more exercise, but that summer he herniated a disc in his back while working in a warehouse. He battled depression and sat at home, watching television and playing video games while eating cheap but filling food packed with "empty calories."

Tom ultimately landed a good job and has progressed in an accounting career, but he has continued to pack on weight. Now in his early thirties, he weighs over 300 pounds. He has a host of physical problems associated with his weight and is at a high risk of developing Type 2 diabetes. In addition to his physical health, Tom struggles with depression, anxiety, and lack of a social life—all issues that he associates with his weight problems. Feeling trapped in a vicious cycle, he sometimes mounts a major effort to lose weight—having lost 60 pounds at one point while participating in Weight Watchers—but has not had the ability to keep it off. Recently he has considered bariatric surgery as a way to shed weight. The doctor he consulted suggested a "vertical sleeve gastrectomy" that removes three-fourths of the stomach, turning it into more of a sleeve like the intestines than a pouch. With less stomach to digest food, the doctor says, he could lose 50–80 per cent of his "excess weight." Tom's insurance will cover the surgery, but he is scared to go through with it, especially after reading about its potential side effects.

Several factors play into Tom's obesity. His parents and siblings are large as well, suggesting the role of genetics in his body size. He also has a mismatch between his daily caloric consumption and physical activity. His knee and back problems, which were brought on in part from his excessive weight, have made it even more difficult to get physical activity and his free time is often spent eating while surfing on the Internet or playing video games.

Tom is an individual that most of us (including himself) would consider problematically obese. But the fear of being overweight is a major preoccupation of other Americans that many of us would not consider "fat." Linda Williams is a 13-year-old girl who is on a diet with four friends who have vowed to lose weight. Linda is five feet one inch tall and weighs 110 pounds, giving her a body mass index (BMI) under 21, which is well within the healthy range for girls her age according to the Centers for Disease Control (CDC). Guidelines from the CDC, however, are less influential among Linda's junior high peers than the images of young models they see in the movies and online. "Fat talk" is a common theme among girls in her class. And looking in the mirror, Linda sees that she is not among the slimmest girls in the school.

Linda and her friends have adopted as their motto a quote from fashion model Kate Moss: "Nothing tastes as good as skinny feels." While they make exercise plans, their primary efforts to lose weight focus on restricting their eating—a matter that they take very seriously. They are far from the only students who do so. In one survey of junior high school students, over half of girls reported some form of dieting or cutting back on food intake as an attempt to control their weight (Esch and Zullig 2008).

Do Linda and her girlfriends—and the millions of other adolescent girls on diets across America—really have weight problems that warrant dieting? Or are they victims of a pervasive "cult of thinness" that idealizes slender bodies that few women can achieve without obsessive bodywork and potential harm to their health? Linda and her girlfriends' focus on dieting raises other issues as well. Are they learning healthy practices or are they in the early stages of cycling through diet weight loss followed by gaining back the weight, by far the most common pattern among dieters? In short, is it healthy for Linda and her girlfriends to pursue their dieting or is the cult of thinness a problem of misplaced values in American culture that leads to increased rates of eating disorders, unhealthy life consequences, and unfair discrimination against heavier men—and especially women?

Both Tom Blake and Linda Williams see themselves as "fat." Their stories highlight the complex and overlapping issues of cultural ideals, health, self-perception, and discrimination that lie at the core of body image deviance.

CURRENT CONSTRUCTIONS OF OBESITY AND EATING DISORDERS IN THE UNITED STATES

The US CDC and the National Institutes of Health (NIH) are the official federal agencies tasked with collecting data to understand health-related problems and promote healthy behavior. Their websites describe two types of weight-related deviance: obesity and eating disorders.

Types of Obesity and Eating Disorders

The CDC and the NIH focus considerable attention on problems associated with heavy body weight, which they break into the categories of overweight and obesity. For adults, overweight and obesity ranges are determined by using weight and height to calculate a number called the *body mass index*, or BMI. The CDC website provides a BMI Calculator where adults can enter their height and weight to calculate a BMI number. A BMI of 25.0 to 29.9 is considered "overweight," while a score of 30 or higher classifies an individual as "obese." For youth between the ages of two and 19, the CDC provides another calculator that compares them with their peers. Youth are considered in the healthy weight range if their BMI falls between the 5th to 85th percentiles of their comparison group. At five feet one inch tall and a weight of 110 pounds, Linda Williams has a BMI of 20.8, placing her at the 71st percentile of girls her age and height—well within the healthy weight range. On the other hand, at six feet one and 300 pounds, Tom Blake has a BMI of 39.6, far above the 30.0 BMI that is used as a threshold for identifying obese individuals.

The CDC and NIH, as well as the broader medical community, also recognize that some Americans engage in unhealthy behaviors in attempts to control their body size. Eating disorders are widely identified in the medical literature as a problem among adolescent girls and young women. *Anorexia nervosa* is characterized by severe food restriction and a compulsion to lose weight. A second eating disorder, *bulimia nervosa*, involves binge eating followed by purging to rid oneself of the food and calories—most commonly through induced vomiting or taking laxatives. Anorexia and bulimia are more prevalent among females than males, but a significant number of males, especially young male endurance athletes, develop eating disorders as well.

Statistical Snapshot

Official statistics regarding weight problems in the United States are usually reported in two categories: the number of people who are overweight—measured for adults as those with a BMI between 25 and 29.9—and those with a BMI of 30 or higher who are classified as obese. As shown in *table 13.1*, according to the CDC, two-thirds of US adults and one-third of youth fall at least in the overweight category. More than one-third of adults and one-sixth of youth are categorized as obese. According to the CDC, not only are most American adults overweight or obese, but the problem has grown over the last three decades, with twice as many adults and three times as many children and adolescents categorized as overweight or obese today as was the case in the

Table 13.1 US Overweight and Obesity Statistics

BMI	Under-Normal (%)	Overweight (%)	Obese (%)	Total Obese or Overweight (%)
2–19	68.2	14.8	17	31.8
20 and over	31.2	33.9	35.1	69
Female	33.5	30	36.5	66.5
Male	28.4	37.9	33.7	71.6
White	31.5	35.1	33.4	68.5
African-American	23.7	28.5	47.8	76.3
Hispanic	22.9	35.1	42	77.1
Asian	61.8	27.3	10.9	38.2

SOURCE: Ogden et al. (2014).

early 1980s (Health and Human Services 2015)—although rates of obesity have remained stable over the past 10 years and even dropped a bit for children (Ogden 2014). The prevalence of Americans with a "weight problem" remains near historic highs and the United States consistently ranks as the first or second "fattest" nation in the world.

Rates of overweight and obese adult Americans differ by age, race/ethnicity, and gender. Obesity is higher among middle-aged than among younger adults or older ones. In terms of race and ethnicity, African-American adults have the highest obesity rate (nearly 48 per cent), followed by Hispanics (42 per cent), and non-Hispanic whites (33 per cent). In contrast, Asian ethnic groups have a significantly lower obesity rate at slightly over 10 per cent (Ogden 2014).

Overweight and obesity are associated with a range of health risks, including heart disease, stroke, Type 2 diabetes, high blood pressure, and asthma. The CDC estimates the medical cost of obesity in the United States at around $150 billion dollars per year (Centers for Disease Control and Prevention 2016b). In addition to medical costs, the widespread concern of Americans with weight loss is demonstrated by the fact that Americans spend more than 60 billion dollars per year on weight-loss products and services (Kwan and Graves 2013).

In contrast to obesity, eating disorders are relatively rare. In a large national health survey in the mid-2000s only nine in 1,000 respondents reported suffering from anorexia at some point in their lives. Bulimia nervosa, characterized by a binge-eating/purging cycle, was only slightly more common, with a lifetime prevalence of ten in 1,000 respondents, or 1 per cent of the population (Hudson et al. 2007). Anorexia and bulimia are two to three times more common among females than males, and tend to develop primarily between early adolescence and young adulthood.

CHALLENGES IN RESEARCHING OBESITY AND EATING DISORDERS

Researchers face challenges in studying body image deviance at both ends of the spectrum. Counting obesity and its health impact is not as straightforward as it first appears, and those who experience eating disorders are often secretive about their behavior.

Counting Obesity and Eating Disorders

The CDC and NIH provide statistics on the number of obese Americans, as measured by BMI, which is easy to calculate. However, many medical experts believe that it is not an accurate measure of health and well-being. For one thing, not all individuals have the same body build and composition. The bodies of many athletes have considerably more muscle mass for their weight than the broader population. There are also clear differences across racial and ethnic groups. White populations with predominantly Western European ancestors have more slender bodies than many other groups. Pacific Islanders and African-Americans typically have larger body frames than Caucasians and also tend to have more muscle mass at a given BMI (Bhanoo 2009; Bialik 2013).

A second problem with BMI as a measure of health is that the causal connection between body fat (for which the BMI serves as a proxy) and poor health and mortality is far less absolute than is often claimed. In the 1940s, the Metropolitan Life Insurance Company began charting death rates of policy holders based on BMI and found that higher body weight was correlated with earlier death. This quickly became simplified to suggest that body fat causes death. But, as we have discussed before, correlation is not causation. Many researchers believe that BMI is mistaken for other factors, such as diet, exercise, and family history that play a more direct role in mortality. Also, many illnesses (including life-threatening ones, such as heart disease) often lead to obesity rather than being caused by it.

Eating disorders pose other problems in data collections. Those who are likely to be classified as suffering from them are often highly secretive about their behavior. The data that exist tend to be medical records of individuals who have been medically diagnosed with an eating disorder or self-report data from surveys ranging from local surveys of high school or college students (e.g., Stice et al. 2004) to national health surveys (e.g., Hudson et al. 2007). Given the findings that eating disorders are more common among junior high school through college age females, many surveys of anorexia, bulimia, and binge-eating focus solely on adolescent to early adult females. As a result, the rates and experiences of eating disorders among males are far less understood.

Getting Close

Deviant insiders' views of their status and experience seldom parallel the assumptions of those who label them that way. Recognizing this, Joan Chrisler argues, "We need to study fat women's lived experience in order to understand the positive aspects of their lives rather than assuming that the negative aspects are all there is" (2012, p.614). Only through getting close and listening to those who experience body image deviance can we learn the meanings that their experiences hold for them.

The sheer extensiveness of social activities related to weight management makes a wide range of settings relevant to researchers. Mimi Nichter (2000) and her team spent three years studying middle school and high school girls' talk and behavior surrounding body weight and dieting. Debra Gimlin (2002) conducted fieldwork in a beauty salon, aerobics classes, a plastic surgery clinic, and social events sponsored by the National Association for the Advancement of Fat Acceptance (NAAFA). Daniel Martin (2000) did a comparative ethnography of three weight-focused organizations: Weight Watchers, Overeaters Anonymous, and NAAFA. Several ethnographers, including Helen Gremillion (2003) and Robin Vogler (1993) have conducted participant observation in residential eating disorder programs. Others, including Karen Dias (2003) and Jeanine Gailey (2009), have studied controversial *pro-ana* websites—sites where anorexic individuals provide encouragement and advice to each other on how to avoid detection and push their bodies to the limits of thinness.

When ethnographers participate in settings or subcultures associated with fat stigma or eating disorders, they work to fit into the settings in ways that show their respect for others' identities and experiences. To research Weight Watchers and Overeaters Anonymous, Daniel Martin put on 25 pounds in an attempt to physically and mentally better understand the experiences of people struggling with weight problems. While studying eating disorders among male endurance athletes, Michael Atkinson participated in triathlon training, including restricting his food intake. During his first year of research, he intentionally lost 70 pounds (one-third of his body weight) and restricted his caloric intake to that common among athletes in the sport to get closer to their experience (2011, p.233). Recognizing that such extreme weight loss posed potential health risks, Atkinson consulted sports nutritionists and endurance coaches to monitor the changes in his body (2011, p.233).

Other researchers also acknowledge that they have opened themselves up to risk while researching eating disorders. April Chatham-Carpenter (2010) reports that even though she had been in therapy and considered herself cured of her disordered eating, when she began writing about her past anorexic experiences she found herself drawn back to self-destructive behavior. Jeanine Gailey experienced similar concerns while studying online postings at pro-ana websites. She recounts, "I had to limit how much time I spent viewing and reading their blogs, comments, and posts because I too found myself becoming increasingly fixated on my own eating and exercising habits" (2009, p.97).

CROSS-CULTURAL CONSTRUCTIONS OF OBESITY AND EATING DISORDERS

Across human history, different cultures have perceived certain types of bodies as attractive and others as unattractive. The variety of body ideals, the moral imputations attached to them, and the ways in which the ideals have been pursued reflect the physical environments and cultural beliefs in different societies.

Different Definitions

"Generally speaking," anthropologist Rebecca Popenoe writes, "fat bodies are appreciated where food is hard to come by, and thin ones are admired in places where food is abundant" (2005, p.17). Since food abundance has been rare across human history, it is not surprising that most human societies have shown a preference for plumper women. The inverse correlation between cultural conceptions of ideal bodies, especially women's bodies, and plumpness reflects the fact that body size often served as a marker of social status. In patriarchal societies with scarce food resources, a heavy woman has served as a symbol of male prosperity—the ability of a husband or father to provide a surplus of resources. Further, a large woman has also portrayed the potential for nurturing abundance. The depictions of earth goddesses in many cultures show a woman with a short, round body, large breasts, and rolls of fat around her waist. A thin woman in such cultures is often viewed as having not matured to full womanhood.

The emergence of cultures that idealize slimness is relatively recent. In Europe in the seventeenth century, the Flemish painter, Peter Paul Rubens, was famous for his portrayals of full-figured women—thus the term "Rubenesque" to refer to curvy female sexiness and beauty. In the late 1800s, however, some European and US physicians began to claim that "civilized populations" no longer viewed corpulence as a sign of status. The American physician, Leonard Williams, argued that savage tribes preferred women who were fat while in England and the United States women fought their tendency to gain weight because they knew that fat women were "repulsive sights degrading alike to their sex and civilization" (Williams 1926, p.4). The association of fat with uncivilized populations was supported by the criminal anthropology of Cesare Lombroso who argued that heaviness was a sign of primitive and criminalistics bodies, especially in women. The primitive woman, according to Lombroso and Ferrero, was "always a prostitute" (1895, p.542) and female criminals, they wrote, "are shorter than normal women; and in proportion to their stature, prostitutes and female murderers weigh more than honest women" (1895, p.126).

By the early 1900s, some members of the medical community were redefining heaviness as a sickness. Life insurance companies began to study the correlation between higher than normal weight and life expectancy. In 1942, Metropolitan Life Insurance published a report concluding, "The longer the belt line, the shorter the life line" (Schwartz 1986, p.159). Over the course of the twentieth century the perception of heaviness as an illness gained momentum.

The act of self-starvation, today associated with eating disorders, has also been defined differently in other societies. In Medieval and Renaissance Europe, some young women were admired for their prolonged fasting to achieve spiritual grace, an activity that doctors of the seventeenth century referred to as *anorexia mirabilis*, or miraculous loss of appetite. The most noted of the miraculous "fasting maids" was the Italian, Catherine of Siena, who engaged in extreme fasting throughout her adult life and died at the age of 33. The fasting maids' self-starvation was not focused on achieving an ideal body. It was focused on attaining divine communion. Many fasting maids were considered holy miracles during their lives—and beyond. Catherine of Siena was canonized as St. Catherine in 1461 and five centuries later Pope John Paul II designated her as one of the patron saints of Europe.

In contrast, the medical diagnosis of anorexia as a mental disorder was first proposed in the 1870s by British physician, Sir William Gull. The diagnosis became more common in the United States, beginning about 1920, with a surge in diagnosing the illness in the 1970s and 1980s (Brumberg 2000). The prevalence of anorexia increased in the United States and Western Europe at the same time that these societies were embracing ever thinner ideals for women's bodies, leading many scholars (e.g., Brumberg 2000; Hesse-Biber 2007) to conclude that the cultural idealization of thinness plays a major role in promoting eating disorders.

Different "Causes"

The first denunciations of fat as a sign of moral failing arose in the early Christian separation of the mind or spirit and the body. The Apostle Paul embraced an ascetic philosophy that viewed all pleasures of the flesh as impediments to spiritual attainment. In his epistle to the Philippians, he admonished those "Whose God is their belly, and who mind earthly things" (*Philippians* 3:19). Gluttony was classified as one of the seven deadly sins by the early Catholic Church. For St. Thomas Aquinas as for the Apostle Paul, gluttony was a serious sin because it represented the pleasures of the flesh over spiritual goals. Both Paul and St. Thomas Aquinas saw little distinction between inordinate sexual gratification on the one hand and "concupiscence in eating" on the other. The perception of overindulgent eating as a sin has resurfaced several times in western societies. In the early 1800s, the temperance movement leader Sylvester Graham, one of the first diet advocates in the United States, pronounced that "GLUTTONY and not starvation is the greatest cause of all evil" (Schwartz 1986, p.25).

As modern medicine expanded its reach over the twentieth century, obesity came to be viewed as a sickness rather than a moral failing. During the heyday of psychoanalysis in the 1950s and 1960s, obesity was seen as caused by mental and emotional problems that led people to overeat to compensate for feelings of inferiority and social isolation. More recent biological explanations of obesity focus on pituitary and thyroid disorders and on potential "fat genes" that genetically predispose individuals to be overweight.

In terms of eating disorders, the closest parallel to the self-starvation of anorexia nervosa today is the anorexia mirabilis of young Catholic women in Europe. The fasting maidens took Paul's ascetic religious philosophy to its extreme limit. Their suffering and privations were viewed by themselves and others of their times as caused by their deep spiritual devotion. In contrast, the self-starvation associated with anorexia nervosa today is viewed as a mental and behavioral disorder caused by some combination of biological predisposition, stress, and environmental factors.

Different Responses

Humans have been very creative in modifying their bodies to fit cultural ideals. Various methods have been used to create or contour the body to fit cultural ideals. For nearly a thousand years corsets were used by women in Europe to compress their midsections into an hourglass model with thin waists and lifted breasts. Girdles and, more recently, panty hose have been used to compress and shift weight in the hips and stomach areas without the major constriction of a corset. These physical constraints have allowed people, especially women, to shape their bodies in line with cultural ideals of their times.

Whatever their physical discomforts, one advantage of corsets and girdles is that they do not require much expenditure of energy on the part of the person wearing them. In the early 1900s, inventors created several mechanical devices that similarly offered to recontour the body without much effort. George Burwell's 1892 "Boston bon-contour obesity belt" claimed to reduce fat by zapping wearers with electrically charged magnetic discs. The "Gardner Reducing Machine" professed to pummel fat off the user with large rollers that vibrated around one's midsection. The widely praised "Bergonié chair" offered to stimulate muscles into passive exercise through electrical stimulation. "All this," an admirer writing for the *British Journal of Medicine* wrote, "without the intervention of the will, and almost no sensation, the patient being occupied during the treatment with his own thoughts or with the book he is reading"

(Humphris 1912, p.493). Popular interest in such contraptions faded by the start of World War II.

The most pervasive approach to weight control today is dieting, with thousands of diets marketed over the years as ways to slim down. Sixteenth-century Venice physician Luigi Cornaro was the first major diet advocate in Europe. Plagued by gout and stomach problems, at the age of 40 Cornaro committed himself to a life of temperate eating—of 12 ounces of food and 14 ounces of drink per day. Finding his health improved, he sought to bring his dieting plan to other Italians. "Every man," he wrote in 1558, "might become his own physician if he would only keep a strict watch over his appetite, which indeed ought to be every one's Chief Business and Concern" (Schwartz 1986, p.9). The practice of dieting was slow to gain followers. Influenced by the writings of Cornaro, in 1733 the British physician George Cheyne proclaimed, "The thinner my diet, the easier, more cheerful, and lightsome I find myself" (Schwartz 1986, p.13). It was not until the mid-1800s, however, that dieting became more widely practiced by members of the general population.

Various drugs have also served in the fight against fat. Greek physicians used laxatives and purgatives to treat corpulence. Prior to the era of regulated medical drugs the popular "Russell's Anti-Corpulent Medication" in the late 1800s was primarily citric acid, while "Every Woman's Flesh Reducer" added Epsom salts, camphor, alum, and soda (Schwartz 1986, pp.106–110). Tobacco has an especially long history as an appetite suppressant, in use since pre-Columbian times in the Americas, and featuring prominently in Lucky Strike cigarette advertising in their 1920s campaign calling on female smokers to "Reach for a Lucky Instead of a Sweet" (Brandt 2007).

Finally, physical exercise has long been embraced as a way to care for the body, from training for competition in public games in classical Greece to yoga in India and martial arts in ancient China. Throughout much of human history, exercise has been particularly associated with military training of men, reaching crescendos in heavily militaristic cultures, including the Roman Empire and Nazi Germany. The use of exercise as a means for countering obesity gained momentum in the late 1800s and early 1900s when obesity began to be defined as a health problem and a moral weakness.

HISTORY OF OBESITY AND EATING DISORDERS IN THE UNITED STATES

In the early years of European conquest of North America, new immigrants eked out a meager living as they moved across the continent, dislocating and often fighting with Native American inhabitants. The lives of pioneer families and displaced Native Americans were characterized by slim pickings and little chance to put on extra weight. As the nation's food supply grew more abundant over time, American views of obesity shifted dramatically.

Colonial America

Colonial Americans did not worry about being fat or eating too much. They were far more concerned with getting enough to eat and not starving to death. They worried about not having enough meat on their bones to survive when illness or food scarcity hit. When early English colonists arrived on the coast of what is now Virginia, they soon realized they were too late to plant crops. They struggled through what they would later call the "Starving Time" that took the lives of most of the first arrivals. Colonists traded and often fought with Native Americans as they appropriated land for their own needs. Most worked hard on skimpy fare and had little extra weight on their bones. For them, as for most humans over the course of history, fat was fine—if hard to come by. The perception of fat held by colonial Americans continued well into the nineteenth century, as captured in the words of a prominent Civil War physician who proclaimed, "plumpness, roundness, and size . . . are rightly believed to indicate well-balanced health" (Stearns 1997, p.9). In addition to health benefits, plumpness conveyed a sense of prosperity. In the world of business, "fat cats" were portly entrepreneurs who helped harness the "fat of the land." In 1866, the girth-celebrating Fat Man's Club of Connecticut was founded. Women too were expected to avoid thinness and to maintain a matronly size, reflecting their role in domestic life. While they cooked and cared for the family, they were warned against wasting their energy in more vigorous physical activities. Any but the most modest exercise was considered potentially damaging to women's reproductive abilities (Dworkin and Wachs 2009).

But all this was about to change. By 1903 when the Fat Man's Club of Connecticut closed its doors for good, middle-class Americans had begun to embrace a campaign against body fat—a change that would span the following century and continues to the present.

Rise of the Antifat Campaign

Between 1890 and 1910, middle-class America began its battle against body fat. The fight began as a spiritual project, not a medical one. The mobilization of public hostility toward fat and obesity had been presaged in the mid-1800s by Sylvester Graham, a Presbyterian minister and early temperance reformer who crusaded against gluttony and sexual excess, urging a return to a "simple" diet of mild, natural foods. Best known today as the creator of the "graham cracker," Graham was known in his time as a dietary reformer who called upon women to cook meals without spices, strong flavors, and anything that would excite the senses. For Graham and his followers, excesses in food and sex were forms of self-pollution and unnatural stimulation. Graham admonished women, as wives and mothers, to cook bland meals that would help their family members avoid overstimulation. Men, angry at the thought of their wives being told to do away with spices, coffee, and alcohol, often protested his lectures and threatened to tar and feather him.

By the 1890s, popular advocates for dietary restraint railed against the plump body that had been admired by earlier Americans. The prolific cookbook writer, Sarah Tyler Rorer, was a major voice in the campaign against fat from the 1890s until World War I. Rorer wrote 54 cookbooks while training thousands of young women at her Philadelphia Cooking School. She was among the first writers to condemn fat as a medical illness—one that had dire consequences. "An excess of flesh," she wrote,

> is to be looked upon as one of the most objectionable forms of disease, and must be treated as such. The disease of obesity—for it certainly is a disease—creeps on slowly until the whole machinery is overtaxed, joints will swell, feet will begin to shuffle, and the mind will become inactive. . . . The end comes quickly.
>
> —Schwartz (1986, p.96)

From the start of World War I in 1914 to the stock market crash of 1929, the United States saw a wave of weight-reducing diets geared to the new science of "calorie-counting." Dr. Robert Rose wrote *Eat Your Way to Health* in 1916, referring to calorie-counting as "a scientific system of weight control" while calling obesity "criminal negligence" (Schwartz 1986, p.175). Lulu Peters (1924) gained fame as America's best loved woman physician with her newspaper columns decrying obesity and her popular diet books, including a 1924 book subtitled *Diet for Children (and Adults) and the Kalorie Kids.* Pocket-sized calorie counters were sold in drugstores, while restaurant chains began publishing caloric values on their menus. As diet historian Hillel Schwartz observes, by the mid-1920s, "There could be no escaping the calorie" (1986, p.177).

Fat historian, Peter Stearns, refers to the years from the 1920s through the 1960s as a "misogynist era" in which the US antifat campaign was directed aggressively toward women. Magazines and books presented advice and expectations for women to watch their weight. In part, this campaign reflected cultural expectations associated with women's freedom for a life beyond the home. As Brumberg observes, in the 1920s,

> A woman with a slender body distinguished herself from the plump Victorian matron and her old-fashion ideals of nurturance, service, and self-sacrifice. The body of the "new woman" was a sign of modernity that marked her for more than traditional motherhood and domesticity.
>
> —Brumberg (2000, p.245)

As girls and women gained legal rights and cultural freedom in the 1920s, they were also confronted with new pressures to be thin. The iconic models of female freedom in the 1920s, the suffragette and the flapper, both embraced a boyish thinness that also became a necessary component of "boy-catching" and marriageability (Sobal and Maurer 1999).

The era also marked the stigmatization of heavier women, as expressed in an advertisement for the diet tablet Marmola. The ad proclaimed, "This is the day of the slender figure, and fat women are simply not tolerated either in business or social affairs" (Farrell 2011, p.112). The cultural idealization of thin female bodies became progressively more stringent over the following decades. In 1921, the first Miss America stood five feet one inch tall, with a 25 inch waist and a weight of 108 pounds. By the 1980s, Miss America winners averaged at least five inches taller with three inch smaller waists and only slightly heavier weights (Stearns 1997, p.72).

Fat in the Feminist Era

While feminists fought to gain workplace rights and equality in the 1960s and 1970s, cases of anorexia and bulimia escalated. In 1973, psychoanalyst Hilde Bruch published her influential book, *Eating Disorders: Obesity, Anorexia Nervosa, and the Person Within,* where she argued that eating disorders arise from dysfunctional childhoods in which permissive and/or smothering mothers overfeed their children to show affection and encourage dependency. In contrast to Bruch's "mother-blaming" explanation of eating disorders, Susie Orbach wrote in her book, *Fat is a Feminist Issue* (1978), that women's compulsive eating represented a coping mechanism as women battled sexual objectification, gender inequality, and damaging cultural stereotypes. Orbach called for women to claim comfort and pride at any body size. She continued, "As more women reject the stereotype of driven slimness and exhibit a pleasure in women's physical variety, individual women can draw on that collective strength to build acceptance and confidence" (1978, p.206). Calls for "size acceptance," however, gained far less popularity in the following decade than did the women's fitness movement, exemplified by the phenomenal growth of the Jazzercise franchise and Jane Fonda workout videos. The women's fitness industry has continued to expand over the decades since Fonda's workouts hit the market.

Looking back at the twentieth century, we can see a hundred-year war on fat, with recommended weights and fashion ideals becoming ever thinner. Metropolitan Life Insurance charts of recommended weights moved steadily lower over time, dropping 8 per cent from 1942 to 1959 alone (Stearns 1997, p.111). Female models, movie stars, and children's dolls became slimmer over the course of the century, while the media ideals for men grew more fat-free and muscular. The increasing gap between normal Americans' bodies and media cultural ideals has led some scholars to argue that we are experiencing what Dworkin and Wachs (2009) refer to as "body panic." Along the way, many of the strategies we have seen in other chapters for creating a moral panic have been invoked in the war against fat.

One common strategy for framing moral panics is to describe them as serious threats to public well-being. In 1994, C. Everett Koop, who had served as Surgeon General under Ronald Reagan, proclaimed obesity a "public health crisis." Three years later in 1997, the CDC declared obesity a disease—and announced that it had reached epidemic proportions. The announcement of the "obesity epidemic" was made more emphatic by new statistics on the extent of obesity in America. When the NIH lowered the cutoff for overweight from a BMI of 27.8 in men and 27.3 in women to a BMI of 25 for both, the number of Americans classified as overweight increased by 29 million overnight—even though their weight was the same as the day before.

A second common strategy in moral panics involves exaggerating the consequences of the problem. Reports of enormous health costs of obesity are often published with little fact finding to establish their accuracy. Even medical journals and governmental health agencies have made serious factual blunders in reporting the numbers of illnesses and deaths caused by obesity. In 2004, researchers from the CDC published a report in the *Journal of the American Medical Association* that estimated obesity was killing 400,000 Americans. When a congressional inquiry was initiated to examine the problem, the CDC was forced to amend its report to a far less impressive 26,000 Americans dying each year from weighing too much (Oliver 2006, pp.3–4). Obesity scholar Glenn Gaesser writes that "few of the [medical research] data support any of the numerous hypotheses about overweight as a primary cause of any of the major diseases for which it is routinely blamed (with the exception of osteoarthritis)." Nonetheless, he observes, "These hypotheses are constantly being presented to us as facts" (Gaesser 2002, p.57).

While obesity is portrayed in the media as a rampant epidemic among both men and women, the impact of body weight ideals is far more consequential for women than men. The ideal for women is both more challenging to reach and more consequential if they fail to approximate it. Many studies have documented that media depictions of ideal female bodies are more extreme than those of male bodies. In one study, titled "Ken and Barbie at Life Size," researchers compared the best-selling Ken and Barbie dolls with actual human adult bodies. They found that Barbie's measurements were attainable by about one in 100,000 women, while Ken's body was attainable by about one in 50 men (Norton et al. 1996). In addition, failing to approximate cultural body ideals has far more impact on women's lives.

Several studies have found that heavier women face steep financial discrimination. One study using data from the Health and Retirement Study of men and women in their fifties found that "overweight" and "obese" women have a lower net worth at retirement-age than do their nonfat counterparts (Fonda et al. 2004), while men do not experience similar consequences for being heavy. Weight-related financial costs in the job market begin as women move from the "thin" category into the "average weight." To put this in concrete financial

PUSHING YOUR BOUNDARIES

Online Weight-Loss Products Survey

In a culture where we are bombarded with messages that most Americans are overweight and would be more healthy and attractive if they lost weight, many turn to the Internet for guidance and suggestions about how to take off pounds. What advice and products do they find on the Internet to help them? Do a search on the Internet, using three different search terms such as "weight loss," "diet pills," and "take off pounds" in order to sample for diversity. Look for descriptions or advertisements for three different approaches to weight loss. Record the following information for each of the three approaches.

- What is this approach to weight loss?
- How does the site say the approach works? What does the product do to "take off pounds"?
- How long does the site say it will take before results are seen?
- What is the cost for the program or products?
- Are there claims made or implied about this product through testimonials, success stories, or endorsements? How do they make you feel that you can trust their program or product?
- Finally, how would you rate the potential health benefits of this product, program, or procedure in terms of promoting a healthy lifestyle?

terms, "all else equal, a woman who is average weight earns $389,300 less across a 25-year career than a woman who is 25 pounds below average weight" (Judge and Cable 2011, p.109).

Not surprisingly, given the emphasis on thinness in the United States today, about 75 per cent of women in the country consider themselves to be "too fat" (Boskind-White 2000). American women's dissatisfaction with their bodies has become what Judith Rodin et al. (1985) refer to as "normative discontent," meaning it is normal for a woman to struggle to feel positively about the size and shape of her body. Approximately 50 per cent of women are on a diet at any given time (Gremillion 2003), in spite of the fact that the overwhelming majority of dieters regain any weight they lose.

CALORIES IN-CALORIES OUT AND SELF-CONTROL THEORY

The prevailing approach to understanding obesity in American healthcare is the "Calories In-Calories Out" model, demonstrated in the graphic below. The CDC website states, "*Caloric balance* is like a scale. To remain in balance

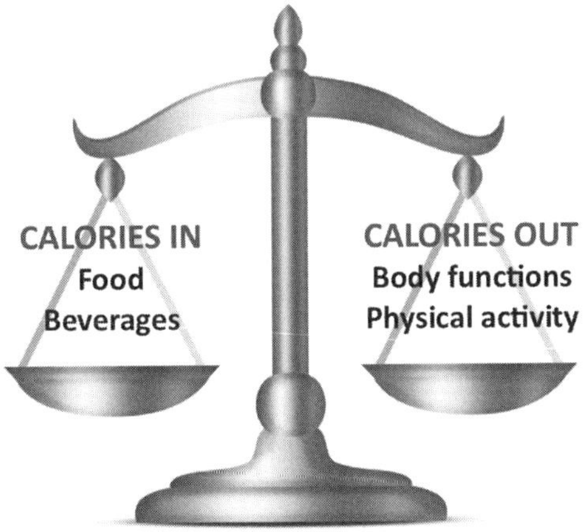

Figure 13.1 Calories in-calories out scale (adapted from Centers for Disease Control and Prevention 2016b).

and maintain your body weight, the calories consumed (from foods) must be balanced by the calories used (in normal body functions, daily activities, and exercise)" (Centers for Disease Control and Prevention 2015). The NIH website explains, "A lack of energy balance most often causes overweight and obesity":

- The same amount of energy IN and energy OUT over time = weight stays the same
- More energy IN than energy OUT over time = weight gain
- More energy OUT than energy IN over time = weight loss (NIH 2015)

As an explanation, this only moves the question to a different level. If caloric imbalance causes obesity, what causes caloric imbalance? Recent research with children has tested self-control theory as an explanation. Self-control theory is based on the proposition that "the common element in crime, deviant behavior, sin, and accident is low self-control," or the inability of some people "to avoid acts whose long-term costs exceed their momentary advantages" (Gottfredson and Hirschi 1990, p.3).

One study using self-control theory (Francis and Susman 2009) collected data on 1,000 children who participated in tasks requiring self-control. In the first task they were left alone in a room with a bunch of toys and told not to touch the one that was their favorite. In the second task, researchers looked at the same kids two years later. This time, they were tested on whether they could resist temptation for favorite snack foods. Researchers found that children who scored lower on both of these tasks were 30 per cent heavier than high self-control peers by the time they were 12. Another study by Allison Miller et al. (2012) reached similar conclusions. These studies suggest that self-control even at a very early age can predict obesity later in life, and anything that can be done to improve self-control could prove valuable in the fight against obesity.

Self-control approaches to obesity focus on the actions of individuals. The US Health and Human Services website agrees, stating that "change starts with the individual choices we as Americans make each day for ourselves and those around us" (Health and Human Services 2015). When we turn to children, Gottfredson and Hirschi argue that low self-control is largely the result of ineffective parenting. Self-control approaches to childhood obesity emphasize strategies parents can use to help their kids develop the ability to delay gratification. The ability to monitor and control one's behavior is considered critical to reducing undisciplined eating and weight gain. Gottfredson and Hirschi would argue that such training will reduce the propensity for deviance in other arenas of the child's—and later the adult's—life as well.

However, other obesity research scholars challenge the seemingly intuitive finding that self-controlled eating patterns lead to better weight management. In several studies, Eric Stice and his coresearchers have found that people who try to control their eating with diets actually increase their chances of gaining weight, not losing it. In one four-year study of weight-related behaviors of 500 adolescent girls, they reported, "One of the most striking findings was that participants with elevated dietary restraint scores showed an increased risk for obesity onset, which replicates the results from previous studies with adolescents and adults" (Stice et al. 2005, p.199). In short, this research suggests the possibility that "weight-control behaviors paradoxically increase risk for obesity onset" (Stice et al. 2005, p.200). If that is the case, efforts to manage weight through dietary self-control may in fact be counterproductive, a claim made by "intuitive eating" advocates discussed later in this chapter.

Whether or not self-control theory can be useful in reducing obesity in America, it is a positivistic theoretical approach, as opposed to critical or interpretive perspectives. It does not address the reasons behind, or the potential negative health impact of, ever-thinner and fat-free beauty ideals. Nor does it speak to broader issues of cultural norms and values or to the impact of fat stigma on the lives of heavier people. Yet, these issues are critical in the interactional contexts in which obesity, fat stigma, and eating disorders are lived experiences.

INTERACTIONAL CONTEXTS AND ETHNOGRAPHIC VOICES

As obesity has become viewed as a major health and social problem in the United States, our bodies have become sites of social conflict not only for physical well-being, but for mental health, social desirability, and even spirituality. In her book, *Fat-Talk Nation*, Susan Greenhalgh (2015) argues that the "war on fat" has created a nation in which people are "unhappy at every size," from high to normal and even low BMIs. Greenhalgh notes that body dissatisfaction and concern are episodic for some individuals, while for others they are a fairly constant focus of attention and dissatisfaction, even though those worries often do not lead to successfully achieving more ideal bodies.

Researchers studying body-weight attitudes, perceptions, and behaviors find that anxiety about body weight is especially common among more educated and employed white women in comparison to African-American and Hispanic women, particularly those with less education. In their study of weight perception, Rahman and Berenson (2010) found that white women who fit CDC categories of overweight or normal weight were more likely to perceive themselves as overweight than African-American women who fit the same categories. White women were also more likely to engage in healthy eating and exercise activities—as well as unhealthy weight control activities.

Certain social contexts are particularly intense sites for weight anxiety. Many of the 245 college students studied by Greenhalgh (2015) describe adolescence as an especially body-sensitive time in which their weight concerns first emerged, largely in response to social comparisons and humiliating interactions with their peers. College years are also often a critical time for body anxieties. In her book, *Perfect Girls, Starving Daughters*, Courtney Martin (2008) describes college as a "boot camp for body obsession." Young college women's concerns are buttressed by cautionary tales of the "freshman 15," an urban myth that most female college students put on 15 pounds during their first year in college (Karuso 2013). While research has found that most female college students have a small weight gain (less than five pounds) during their freshman year, and that more than a third of them actually lose weight that year, the freshman 15 myth circulates widely in college newspapers and student conversations. As one student explained to researchers, "Everyone in my apartment talks about it all the time . . . it's like the curse . . . you try to avoid" (Smith-Jackson and Reel 2012, p.17). For many young women, the primary motivation for avoiding weight gain is to attract romantic partners. As another student put it, "The main reason is for guys . . . As freshmen girls, you want guys to notice you and you want to be the center of attention and the one that everybody likes, and you think that would bring you happiness" (Smith-Jackson and Reel 2012, p.17). The desire to be perceived as physically attractive often trumps health concerns as the major motivation for trying to lose weight. Many weight-loss books and videos available today frame the issue of weight loss just as Susan Powter did 20 years ago in her best-selling weight-loss book, *Stop the Insanity*:

> Forget your health . . . I didn't lose 133 pounds to have a healthy heart. My motivation was to look better than my ex-husband's girlfriend, and my motivation now is to look and feel the way I want to look and feel. Getting healthy is a side effect. . . . Do it for your thighs. Do it to feel sexy and pretty.
>
> —Powter (1993, p.15)

Dieting and Fitness Programs

If one were to believe the weight-loss industry's publicity and advertising, there are a wide variety of highly effective weight-loss programs in the United States from diets to cleansing laxatives, exercise programs, medications, and cosmetic or bariatric surgeries. Many of these programs proclaim quick results, as captured in advertisements that lure customers with claims of "Flab to Fab in 30 Days" and "Size 22 to Size 10 in No Time Flat."

Several weight-loss programs promise personal transformation as well, as in Body-*for*-LIFE's statement that the program's "overarching goal is simple: To enable you to unlock your true potential and become the person you've always wanted to be" (Body-*for*-LIFE 2015).

Media stories portray the personal efforts to lose weight as grueling physical and moral accomplishments, epitomized in the struggles shown in the reality TV series, "Biggest Loser." The plot line of the show is always the same:

> A miserable fat person engages in a weight loss effort and, if successful, emerges thinner, stronger both mentally and physically, and therefore ready to enjoy social advantages never previously experienced.
>
> —Brown (2014, p.64)

Many people who take on personal weight-loss goals feel an initial sense of accomplishment and hopefulness in their commitment and determination even though the challenges of achieving the body ideals of what Greenhalgh (2015) refers to as the "thin fit biocitizen" promoted in the media are more than all but the most disciplined individuals can maintain on a consistent basis. The challenges are particularly intense for young working mothers who experience not only the pressures of the "first shift" (work), and the "second shift" (family care), but also a "third shift" of fitness practices (Dworkin and Wachs 2004).

Many weight-loss programs, especially those that promise quick results, emphasize dieting far more than exercise. A significant number of products claim to cleanse the body of harmful impurities while promoting weight loss. The draw of quick weight loss often lures people into using unhealthy products. Many of the students in Greenhalgh's study used diet pills—prescription, and more commonly over-the-counter supplements, to spur weight loss. "For many if not most," Greenhalgh found, "the prospect of losing weight . . . silences any nagging thoughts that they may not be totally safe" (2015, p.185). One diet pill user explained:

> Those extra few pounds were gone in two weeks and I felt good. Being able to walk around freely with just a bikini was refreshing. . . . Even though I hadn't done the healthiest thing to get there, I didn't care. If it meant looking good and fitting in with girls much smaller than I was, then I was willing to do it.
>
> —Greenhalgh (2015, p.185)

Some students find that stimulant ADHD medications like Adderall help them manage their weight by suppressing their appetites (Vecitis 2012). Yet, others find that illegal drugs such as amphetamines and cocaine can serve a similar purpose. As one of Greenhalgh's students wrote:

> One of my friends once tried coke for a few weeks to see how much weight she could lose in a month. My other friend who was recently arrested for possession of cocaine is going through Narcotics Anonymous. Her biggest fear is that she's going to gain weight.
>
> —Greenhalgh (2015, p.186)

Facing Failure

Most weight-losers' sense of accomplishment fades over time as early success slips away and pounds return. For nearly a century diet programs have been recognized as failing to provide long-term weight loss. In a diet book published in 1928, Dr. Robert Rose estimated 75 per cent of those who used diets failed. In the 1930s, another diet doctor wrote "if you are able to reduce fifty percent of your patients to ideal weight and keep them there for a year, you may consider yourself eminently successful" (Schwartz 1986, p.227). In the 1940s, Yale researchers found 80 per cent failure rates among dieters. More recently the dismal success of long-term dieting has been captured by fat activist Marilyn Wann's succinct (perhaps only slightly overstated) observation: "Percentage of dieters who regain the weight within three years: 90. Percentage of Americans who believe in miracles: 70" (Wann 1998, p.114).

There are several reasons why most dieters are unsuccessful in long-term weight loss. Many dieters do a poor job of staying on their restricted eating regimens. Nichter (2000) found that, while 60 per cent of girls in a survey she conducted reported having been on a diet, the diets were hit-and-miss affairs, with almost three-quarters of them reporting a diet that lasted less than two weeks. Yo-yo dieting, a pattern of episodic dieting interspersed with periods of less restricted eating, is particularly conducive to weight gain. Dieting induces hormonal and physiological changes that make the weight-reducing body different from a nondieting similar sized body. Dieting reduces the body's production of the appetite suppressing hormone leptin as well as slowing the rate at which the body burns calories. Thus, Greenhalgh argues, "it is quite possible to diet up to obesity" (2015, p.240).

Consistent physical activity can also be a challenge for many people. Commercial gyms, as well as community and employee wellness centers, have expanded significantly over the past several decades, but most Americans have relatively sedentary jobs and working adults spend an average of nearly an hour a day commuting to and from work (Ingraham 2016). Parents of young children, especially mothers, face the second shift of childcare responsibilities when they return from work and fit exercise in after that, if at all.

For a variety of reasons, then, despite the fact that Americans spend 60 billion dollars a year on weight loss and fitness, most prospective weight losers are disappointed with the results and many experience self-blame and despair like that expressed by Jessica, a student in Greenhalgh's research who wrote:

> I'm pretty sure I should lose weight, but when I try it almost never works. When it does work, I end up gaining the weight back in a couple of months . . . I have always been jealous of anorexics for having so much self-control and being able to achieve a thin body. What has stopped me from being anorexic has been my love of food. What has stopped me from being bulimic is the grossness. I hate the taste of throw-up. So for now I am stuck in this fat body, at least until I can save up enough money for liposuction or therapy to help me accept my body the way it is.
>
> —Greenhalgh (2015, p.80)

The Costs of Weight Obsession

While Jessica's actions stopped short of anorexia, bulimia, or other physically harmful behavior, Greenhalgh's student autoethnographies were full of stories of harmful effects of excessive weight loss, such as fatigue, weakness, and depression that were treated by students as ordinary costs of being thin and attractive. Yet, others described more serious side effects from weight-loss activities. One student, Travis, purchased a new dietary supplement called "Recreate" that was advertised as helping to "recreate your body in a whole new way." He developed a cluster of health problems from insomnia to vomiting and headaches on days he didn't take the pills. Finally, he recounts:

> I decided to go to my doctor. It turned out the reason I had all those problems was the pills had a monstrous amount of caffeine in them . . . My doctor told me my kidneys and adrenal glands could fail in months, and I could even develop heart problems.
>
> —Greenhalgh (2015, p.197)

Travis stopped taking the supplement and avoided more serious health consequences, but a significant number of people, especially young women, become so obsessed with weight loss that they risk serious bodily injury. The unhealthy eating patterns of anorexia offer perhaps the ultimate example of extreme damage. Historian Joan Brumberg observes that:

> Anorexia nervosa constitutes a modern credo of self-denial that has much to tell us about the situation of young women and about contemporary values. The disease starkly illustrates the predicament of the privileged but vulnerable adolescent female in a rapidly changing society that elevates thinness to the highest moral plane.
>
> —Brumberg (1989, p.7)

Brumberg and other feminist scholars argue that anorexia differs only (or primarily) in degree from normal dieting and exercise routines in pursuit of bodily ideals. Anorexia represents a quest for a perfection "that links personal salvation to the achievement of an external body configuration rather than a spiritual state" (1989, p.7). Jeanine Gailey's (2009) examination of recurring themes on "pro-ana" websites—Internet sites created by anorexics to connect with others who share their interest in anorexic behaviors and identities—reveals the discipline and control that these young women embrace in pursuit of physical perfection. Successful anorexia is portrayed on these websites as maintaining one's lowest goal weight while avoiding hospitalization, death, or therapy. The postings by these anorexic women describe how they push their bodies to extremes.

The largest theme on pro-ana websites is the tension between control and loss of control. The women repeatedly discussed trying to find a way to gain control over their chaotic lives. One young woman wrote, "This is everything I can control. The rest of my life is out of my hands. I can stay strong and reach my goals for perfection. Don't try and stop me. I'll only work harder." Another woman introduced herself on her profile page by writing, "The word is control. That's my ultimate—to have control" (Gailey 2009, p.100).

Young women who participate in the pro-ana subculture believe that people who succeed at anorexia are special and possess superior control and discipline. "Nothing splendid had ever been achieved," one woman writes, "except by those who dared believe that something inside of them was superior to circumstance." Another young woman tells people who view her page, "Anorexia is not a disease. Anorexia is not a game. Anorexia is a skill, perfected only by a few. The chosen, the pure, the flawless" (Gailey 2009, p.102).

While anorexia is most common among young women, Michael Atkinson (2011) has found that many male athletes in endurance sports intentionally lose 15–20 per cent of body weight during the competition season. Atkinson refers to this athletic focus as "thinnergy" in which being at razor thinness is believed to provide the best body for sport performance. Like the young women on pro-ana websites, emaciating male athletes focus on self-discipline and control. Such efforts require consistent Foucauldian self-surveillance. "When I watch friends eat out at a dinner," a young athlete reports, "it makes me nauseous. Every spoon or fork full of food they shovel in, and, I'm like doing mental calculations of calories in my head" (2011, p.240). Like their female anorexic counterparts, these male athletes do not view their emaciating behavior as an illness, but rather see it as the apex of personal achievement.

CONTEMPORARY RESPONSES TO OBESITY

Obesity is consistently ranked by public health officials as one of the most serious health problems in the United States today. In addition to health officials' warnings, the media constantly present images of thin girls and women, as well as lean fit men, as cultural ideals. Advertising by the weight-loss and fitness industries pervades magazines, television, and the Internet. Societal responses to the "obesity epidemic" and "fat Americans" can be found at all levels, from questionable commercial enterprises to the medical establishment and governmental agencies.

Weight-Loss and Fitness Industry

From the earliest days of America's "war on fat," there have been businesses seeking to profit from the elusive goal of losing weight. The weight-loss and fitness industry today offers thousands of diets and supplemental products to facilitate weight loss. While some diets and products are based on sound medical principles, Sondra Solovay observes, "The growth of the diet industry has resulted in decades of absurd cure-all claims reminiscent of the snake-oil sales of the nineteenth century" (2000, p.172). Officially, dietary supplements, like prescription drugs, are regulated by the FDA, but unlike doctor prescribed weight-loss medication, dietary supplements do not need testing and preapproval before marketing. Under the US Dietary Supplement Act, the FDA cannot ban a supplement without proving that the product does not do what it claims. Lacking adequate resources to test all dietary supplements, the FDA focuses mainly on those that are known to cause physical harm. As an FDA official explains, "There are so many hoaxes out there, we just concentrate on the dangerous ones" (Solovay 2000, p.174).

Commercial gyms and fitness programs offer a wide range of services geared primarily toward middle- and upper-class populations. Recently personal fitness devices and apps have also been developed for tracking daily activity. Fitness tracking devices can monitor heart rate, caloric intake, blood pressure, skin temperature, sleep patterns, caffeine intake, and a host of other measurements. Many devices offer daily comparisons of one's activities to those of other users. Never before in history have people had such extensive ability to track their every movement in pursuit of health and fitness.

Fitness apps represent a new form of what Michel Foucault (1988) termed *technologies of the self*, or practices that enable individuals to monitor and mold their bodies and minds toward an idealized self. Foucault argued that in modern societies individuals are less controlled by external forces than in the past. Rather people today embrace self-discipline, internalizing cultural values and expectations and engaging in self-surveillance. Weight-loss apps and fitness trackers enable second-to-second self-monitoring. Recently *PC Magazine* reported its 25 best "exercise apps" for smartphones, explaining:

> Mobile apps make ideal fitness companions. Because our smartphones and apps are always with us, they become constant reminders to check your progress, stay the course, and keep your willpower strong.
>
> —Duffy (2016)

These devices can instill a sense of capability and accountability for personal health outcomes, but critics argue that their constant feedback may also increase the pressure to pursue cultural ideals rather than personal health and well-being. As Rachel Sanders explains:

> In a context pervaded by themes of fat panic, bodily deficiency, and the societal imperatives of personal health and normative femininity, digital self-tracking devices may engage women in ever more intense, intricate, and extensive regimes of self-discipline and self-perfection.
>
> —Sanders (2016, p.15)

Medical Drugs

As obesity has been increasingly defined as a health problem, a range of medical interventions have been created to help Americans lose weight. Time and again, weight-loss medications have been announced as major advances, only to be found to have major negative health effects. In the 1950s and 1960s, amphetamines were widely prescribed to facilitate weight loss, but were pulled under tighter control by the FDA in the mid-1960s (Rasmussen 2008). Since then a number of other medications have been created by pharmaceutical companies to facilitate weight loss. In a review of weight-loss medications, John Rodgers et al. report that "the history of anti-obesity drug development is far from glorious, with transient magic bullets and only a handful of agents currently licensed for clinical use" (2010, p.4). Pharmaceutical companies have battled with "false starts, failures in clinical development, and withdrawals due to adverse effects that were not fully appreciated at the time of launch" (Rodgers et al. 2012, p.621). In the 1990s, one popular weight-loss prescription called "fen-phen" was linked to fatal pulmonary hypertension and cardiac problems and pulled off the market after a flurry of lawsuits that cost Wyeth Pharmaceuticals over 13 billion dollars (Avorn 2005). In 2012, the FDA approved the first two new weight-loss drugs in 13 years. In 2014, a new injectable weight-loss drug was approved by the FDA and other injectable medications, touted by some as "obesity vaccines" are currently being pursued in the hope of stemming the tide of obesity—and reaping enormous profits in the process.

Surgery

Over the past three decades the medical field has expanded surgical operations for weight reduction. The most common procedure is liposuction, a cosmetic surgery that is used to remove fat from the body—most commonly from the abdomen, thighs, buttocks, neck, and arms. In 2016, more than 400,000 liposuction procedures were done in the United States (American Society for Aesthetic Plastic Surgery 2017). Some weight is lost with liposuction, but the process is a cosmetic surgery not a method of permanent weight loss, and without increased exercise the weight is typically regained (Reynolds 2012).

In contrast to liposuction, *bariatric surgery* does produce weight loss. The surgery involves removing or restricting a portion of the stomach so that less food may be processed at any given time. The American Society for Metabolic and Bariatric Surgery (ASMBS) presents the procedures as major medical advances in the treatment of weight loss and associated health problems. The ASMBS website explains:

> With one operation, a person can be potentially cured of numerous medical diseases including diabetes, hypertension, high cholesterol, sleep apnea, chronic headaches . . . liver disease, and arthritis. Bariatric surgery is the only proven method that results in durable weight loss.
>
> —ASMBS (2014)

In recent years US medical insurance has increasingly covered bariatric surgery for adults with a high BMI and weight-associated health problems such as Type 2 diabetes, leading to a rise in the number of operations performed. The surgery is often followed by significant weight loss over the following year, but also often presents various medical complications, including gastric dumping, leakage, and nutritional deficiencies. The considerable risk of complications, estimated at 40 per cent of bariatric surgeries (Encinosa et al. 2006), means that such surgery is seldom if ever a relatively simple way to control body weight.

Social Policy and Government Regulation

Since the declaration of the obesity epidemic, numerous government agencies have developed programs promoting change in individual behavior. Losing weight has been presented as a responsibility of engaged citizens, as captured in former Health and Human Services Secretary Tommy G. Thompson's proclamation that, "To fight the epidemic, all Americans should lose 10 pounds as a patriotic gesture" (Rosenblatt 2001). This characteristic American focus on individual choice and change has been challenged by numerous journalists, researchers, and activists who emphasize the contexts within which individuals make their choices about eating and physical activity. They believe that obesity needs to be viewed as an interrelated set of cultural, social, economic, and environmental issues. We live, they argue, in an *obesogenic society*, or a social and economic environment that creates fat people. In order to combat obesity, they say, we need social policies directed toward eliminating foods and lifestyles that promote it.

Fast-food franchises have come under especially heavy attack by critics of obesogenic economic policies. Eric Schlosser's book, *Fast Food Nation: The Dark Side of the All-American Meal*, and Morgan Spurlock's documentary film, *Super Size Me*, have reached wide public audiences and put pressure on the fast-food industry to offer healthier food choices. The emerging *food justice movement* has also criticized the dearth of healthy food availability in low-income neighborhoods that lack supermarkets but abound in fast-food restaurants (Gottlieb and Joshi 2010). In 2012, the US Department of Agriculture responded to pressure from health advocates including first lady, Michelle Obama, by changing regulations for school lunches to require more whole grains, vegetables, and fruits, and less fat and sodium, and to establish calorie limits.

The push to limit marketing of unhealthy foods has butted up against food industry groups' calls to "let consumers decide what they want." In 2012, when New York Mayor Michael Bloomberg proposed banning the sale of sodas and other sugary drinks over 16 ounces in New York restaurants and food carts, he and his supporters were accused of pushing to create a *nanny state*, in which the government determines what is good for people like a nanny makes choices for children. In response, those who seek to regulate the food and beverage industry argue that not regulating commercial businesses ultimately limits healthy food choices as businesses focus on maximizing profits, which often accrue to empty calorie sugar and fat laden foodstuffs (e.g., Guthman 2011). The New York Court of Appeals ruled in 2014 that city of New York had exceeded its authority in implementing the large drink ban.

STIGMA MANAGEMENT AND RESISTANCE

Most people who perceive themselves as fat would prefer to eliminate the stigma of obesity from their lives. Their attempts at destigmatization include the range of weight-reduction strategies discussed in this chapter, from dieting and exercise to legal and illegal weight-loss drugs and surgery. The hoped-for transformation from obese to "thin fit biocitizen" (Greenhalgh 2015) is an example of "purification" in which a stigmatized identity is purged and replaced by a morally and socially valued one. Some "fat" individuals and groups, on the other hand, take more confrontational approaches, challenging mainstream ideas about health and obesity and fighting against weight-based discrimination.

Weight-Loss Support Groups

Several organizations provide support for those who seek to eliminate the stigma of fat from their lives. Two of the most notable are Overeaters Anonymous and Weight Watchers. While both Weight Watchers and OA view fat bodies as a problem that individuals should strive to overcome, their approaches to helping people are very different.

Overeaters Anonymous is a free support group that offers a Twelve Step approach to recovering from the "incurable disease" of compulsive overeating. OA asks members to commit to the Twelve Steps first developed by Alcoholics

Anonymous, including admitting to being powerless (in this case, over compulsive overeating) and "coming to believe that a power higher than ourselves could restore us to sanity." In OA meetings, members often share stories of past traumas that they feel played a role in their becoming compulsive overeaters and that reveal the depth to which they had sunk (in bingeing, stealing food, and other shameful behaviors) before "hitting bottom." Overeaters Anonymous offers members the opportunity of spiritual and emotional redemption from compulsive overeating through OA fellowship and turning one's life over to a higher power.

In contrast to OA, Weight Watchers is a commercial weight-loss program that invokes a calories in-calories out approach to weight loss. The official purpose of Weight Watchers is to help clients lose weight, not to achieve a deeper emotional and spiritual recovery. Success in Weight Watchers is focused on managing one's body through controlling eating and exercise and building relationships and routines that optimize weight loss. The program is focused on developing good techniques for managing food consumption. Clients are instructed to keep a food diary and participate in weekly weigh-ins. Weight Watchers emphasizes portion control of foods to manage calorie intake and offers its own line of food products, especially frozen meals that list a number of "points" used to calculate daily caloric intake. Weekly weigh-ins provide feedback on progress toward weight loss. Members who reach their weight goal and maintain it for six weeks are given free lifetime memberships as long as they remain no more than two pound above that weight—an inspirational goal, but one that many are unable to achieve on a consistent basis.

Challenging Frames

In contrast, fat activists and some health advocates challenge the idealization of thinness and claims of an obesity epidemic. Two major "challenging frames" (Saguy 2013) contest claims of the mainstream "war on fat." One of these challenging frames is the Healthy at Every Size (HAES) movement that seeks to promote healthy bodies rather than thin ones. The movement has been championed by nutritionist Linda Bacon, whose book, *Healthy at Every Size* (2008), lays out the argument and guidelines of the movement. The cover of her book proclaims:

> Fat isn't the problem. Dieting is the problem. A society that rejects anyone whose body shape or size doesn't match an impossible ideal is the problem. A medical establishment that equates "thin" with "healthy" is the problem.

HAES advocates argue that far too much emphasis is put into trying to uncover the causes of fat. While they acknowledge the role of biology, they argue that a focus on genetics and the search for the "fat gene" wrongly implies that fat—and a range of different body sizes—is a problem rather than a natural state of some bodies. Bacon and others contend that human bodies have natural weight set points to which they gravitate unless messed with by unhealthy weight-loss practices. "You don't have to worry about your weight," Bacon writes, "just trust yourself and everything is going to be okay. Your body can take good care of you." (2008, p.68). The HAES approach emphasizes stress reduction and enjoyable physical activity rather than grueling workouts. HAES also promotes *intuitive eating* (Tribole and Resch 2012) that relies on trusting and responding to body cues rather than seeking to control them. "You were born with all the wisdom you need for eating intuitively," Tribole and Resch counsel, arguing that rejecting your body's innate food sense is unhealthy and counterproductive.

The HAES movement challenges mainstream approaches as themselves creating a health epidemic rather than helping solve one. But as Saguy observes, "The healthy at every size frame does not assert that fat is beautiful or that fat is necessarily healthy. Rather it makes a weaker claim: that one *can* be fat and healthy, just as one can be thin and unhealthy. It neutralizes, without inverting the stigma associated with fatness" (2013, p.52).

Activists associated with the *fat acceptance movement*, on the other hand, challenge body size stigma and the cult of thinness as issues of social injustice. Discrimination based on body size and shape, they argue, is far more damaging—physically and socially—to America than the "obesity epidemic" (e.g., Kirkland 2008; LeBesco 2010).

The beginnings of the fat rights movement hark back to the late 1960s. The first collective action efforts to confront *sizeism* took an *assimilationist* approach, seeking to "aid fat Americans" through championing their rights to be treated like other citizens. In the early 1970s, some fat activists took a more confrontational *liberationist* approach. A group of radical lesbian feminists in Los Angeles broke from NAAFA and started the Fat Underground, which openly attacked the medical and diet industries through disruptive performances and protests at weight-loss clinics. The *Fat Liberation Manifesto* written by Judy Freespirit and Aldabaran in 2009 explicitly identifies the diet industry as the enemy of fat liberation:

> WE single out as our special enemies the so-called "reducing" industries. These include diet clubs, reducing salons, fat farms, diet doctors, diet books, diet foods and food supplements, surgical procedures, appetite suppressants, drugs and gadgetry such as wraps and "reducing machines."
>
> WE demand that they take responsibility for their false claims and acknowledge that their products are harmful to the public health.
>
> —Freespirit and Aldabaran (2009)

As Greta Rensenbrink notes, the fat feminist movement of the late 1970s and early 1980s "created a radical fat feminist identity politics that challenged the larger culture to redefine fat from a sign of sickness and failure to a sign of power, beauty, and resistance" (2010, p.213). This appreciation of fat is captured in fat activist Marilyn Wann's 1998 book, *Fat!So?*, where she playfully celebrates

CLAIMS-MAKER PROFILE

Fat Activist Marilyn Wann

On October 26, 1993, Marilyn Wann had a "really bad day." That day, she recounts:

> First, the guy I was dating said he was embarrassed to introduce me to friends because I was fat (ouch!). Then Blue Cross of California decided not to give me health insurance because of my weight (double ouch!) . . . All my life I had done everything I could to make sure people accepted me, perhaps even liked me, despite my fat.

But that day she realized that in both private and public life, "Being fat outweighed everything else about me."

The day after her "really bad day" Marilyn Wann started a magazine as a way of speaking up. As she considered what to call the magazine, she thought about being called Fatso as a child, "how painful and damning the word felt then. But I was fat, I am fat . . . I knew at that moment I simply had to publish *FAT!SO?*, the 'zine for people who don't apologize for their size' (1998, p.11).

Wann quickly gained an enthusiastic audience and soon she turned the 'zine into a book with the same title. Wann celebrates her weight, swimming with the fat synchronized water ballet troupe, Padded Lilies, and dancing with the Phat Fly Girls, a hip-hop dance ensemble. She has served on the board of the National Association to Advance Fat Acceptance and helped organize support for San Francisco's passage of a height/weight antidiscrimination ordinance.

Wann regularly visits high schools and college campuses to encourage students to "embrace the F-word" and celebrate their bodies. A person can be fit and healthy at any size, she claims. "The only thing that anyone can diagnose, with any certainty, by looking at a fat person," she writes, "is their own level of stereotype and prejudice toward fat people" (Wann 2009).

the fat body as a source of beauty and pride, promising readers, "You too can be flabulous" (1998, p.184). The fat activism movement challenges "the erasure of fat people in our culture while constructing new, positive identities and embodied practices for the fat community" (Greenhalgh 2015, p.11).

BLURRED BOUNDARIES II: BANNING WEIGHT DISCRIMINATION IN THE WORKPLACE

In her book, *Tipping the Scales of Justice: Fighting Weight-Based Discrimination*, Sondra Solovay asserts that "discrimination against fat people is the civil rights hurdle of the new millennium" (2000, p.29). In the United States today, many social groups are protected against discrimination based on statuses such as race, gender, age, physical disability, and religion. But size is not a protected category. Should it be? Should weight-based discrimination in the workplace be made illegal?

Solovay presents three principles behind antidiscrimination law:

1. It is wrong, generally, to discriminate against a person for a characteristic they cannot control.
2. Capable people should not be prevented from contributing to the economy and society.
3. It is wrong to discriminate when the result is an impingement on basic rights, freedoms, or human dignity. (2000, p.27)

These principles have been fundamental to outlawing other kinds of discrimination, but should they be applied to body size and weight? Research clearly suggests that heavier individuals, especially women, face employment biases that have significant impact on their lifetime earnings. Since the law has been invoked to prevent prejudicial treatment of other groups, why should we allow weight to remain an unprotected category?

If weight should be a category that is protected from workplace discrimination, how should that be achieved? Some advocates for antidiscrimination policies argue that obesity should be covered under the Americans with Disabilities Act. Obesity is an illness, they claim, and, like other disabled people, heavy individuals should be accommodated in the workplace. Fat activists oppose the very notion of considering overweight and obesity in and of themselves as disabilities. They contend that employment decisions for heavy individuals should be based on their ability to do the job, not on their size.

Do you feel that body size should be allowed to be considered when hiring or promoting employees? Are there certain occupations that you feel should be allowed to use weight in and of itself as a criterion for employment and promotion? If so, how do you see this as different from discriminating on the basis of categories that are currently protected from workplace discrimination?

SUMMARY

- The CDC has proclaimed that the United States is experiencing an obesity epidemic, with two-thirds of adults and one-third of youth overweight or obese.
- American beauty norms emphasize thinness and many young women engage in unhealthy eating behaviors to achieve extreme thinness.
- Obesity is typically measured as BMI by height to weight calculations. BMI is simple to calculate, but a problematic measure since body types vary from person to person and across racial and ethnic groups.

- Data on eating disorders come mostly from self-report data from anonymous surveys.
- Ethnographers study body image deviance in a host of settings, from schools and weight-loss clinics to gyms and the Internet.
- Plump bodies tend to be appreciated in societies where food is hard to come by, while thin bodies are admired in cultures where food is abundant.
- In the nineteenth century, as food became abundant in industrial societies, fat bodies came to be stigmatized and associated with "uncivilized" racial and ethnic groups.
- Dieting is the primary approach to weight control, although few dieters successfully manage their weight over time.
- Weight-related stigma is directed primarily toward females.
- The last two decades have witnessed increasingly intense moral panic over an obesity crisis.
- Some research supports self-control theory as an explanation of childhood obesity, finding that children with low self-control overeat and develop weight problems. Other researchers find that people who try to control their eating with diets increase their chances of gaining weight.
- Dissatisfaction with one's body has become normative in American society. Social contexts such as high school and college are particularly intense sites for body weight anxiety.
- Diet and fitness routines, as well as diet supplements, offer technologies of the self to pursue ideal bodies, albeit often without long-term success.
- Some activists argue we live in an obesogenic society and that governmental policies are needed to reduce unhealthy food and lifestyles that promote obesity.
- Some health advocates dispute the idealization of thinness and claims of an obesity epidemic. Fat activists challenge body size stigma and the cult of thinness as issues of social justice, advocating for workplace antidiscrimination laws to protect heavy individuals.

KEYWORDS

anorexia mirabilis: Self-starvation, or "miraculous loss of appetite," by young women (especially in Medieval Europe) seeking spiritual perfection.

anorexia nervosa: An eating disorder characterized by self-starvation and excessive weight loss.

assimilationist approach: A collective action approach used by some stigmatized groups that is focused on pursuing equal rights for stigmatized individuals, but not for broader social change.

body mass index (BMI): A measure of body mass that is calculated as body weight (in kilograms) divided by the square of the body height (in meters).

bariatric surgery: A surgical operation designed to achieve weight loss by reducing the size of the stomach and/or by gastrointestinal rerouting.

bulimia nervosa: An eating disorder characterized by binge eating followed by purging.

fat acceptance movement: A social movement that seeks to eliminate weight based discrimination and promote the acceptance of heavy people.

food justice movement: A social movement focused on issues of social justice in relation to food production (e.g., small grower, organic, and locavore production) and access to healthy food.

liberationist approach: A collective action approach that emphasizes broad social change in perception of body weight, including embracing fat as a sign of power, beauty, and resistance—and criticizing the weight-loss industry as damaging to personal health and social equality.

nanny state: A term used pejoratively to describe a government that legislates policies that are overprotective and interfere with personal choice.

obesogenic society: A society in which environmental conditions, accessibility of certain food types, and cultural values promote obesity.

pro-ana websites: Internet websites created by individuals supporting anorexic and bulimic behaviors.

technologies of the self: Physical and mental practices used by individuals to monitor and mold their bodies and minds toward an idealized self that meets broader cultural expectations.

CHAPTER

14

LGBTQ Identities

Lesbian wedding photo (Frank Chmura/Alamy Stock Photo).

CONTENTS

LEARNING OBJECTIVES

After reading this chapter, you will be able to:

- Describe the most common classifications of sexual identity and orientation in the United States today
- Explain the challenges of, and strategies for, researching LGBTQ identities and sexual orientations
- Identify different historical definitions of, and causal explanations for, LGBTQ orientations and sexual behavior
- Describe the historical emergence of the LGBTQ community in the United States.
- Explain the limitations of positivistic theory in examining LGBTQ orientations
- Analyze the interactional contexts and challenges in which individuals experience same-sex attraction in the United States today
- Assess ambiguities and gendered cultural perceptions of LGBTQ orientation in US culture today

BLURRED BOUNDARIES I: TWO STORIES OF SAME-SEX ATTRACTION

Sam Wilson married his college sweetheart shortly after graduating 16 years ago. They have been blessed with two children and a comfortable life in suburban St. Louis, where Sam works as a design engineer for a medical instruments company. Despite being married, however, Sam finds himself drawn to sexual encounters with other men. From his late teens on, Sam has had occasional anonymous sex with men he has met in parks, rest stops, sex video arcades, and at gay bathhouses while on business trips out of town. He has seldom known the names of his male sex partners and only a few times had sex with the same man more than a couple times. Sam has kept this side of his life in the closet, secret from his wife, family, and friends. Several times men he has had sex with have told him that he should "come out" as gay rather than feeling like he has to keep his attraction to men a secret. But Sam cannot imagine coming out as gay. Aside from episodic sexual attraction to men, he feels happy in his marriage and cannot see himself in an intimate relationship with another man.

Sam hides his sexual activities with men and often feels disgusted with himself after the encounters, especially when he has unprotected sex. He worries that he may have exposed himself to AIDS or other STDs. Once he was treated for chlamydia and avoided having sex with his wife for a month. At times he vows to stop having sex with men. After his chlamydia infection, he avoided sex with a man for almost a year. Even more than fear of STDs, Sam worries that someone he knows might see him and tell people. Perhaps this fear of being exposed plays a part in his public self-presentation as antigay, denouncing gay marriage and laughing at gay jokes. Most of the time he blocks his sex with men out of his mind—until he finds himself feeling the desire to have another sexual encounter.

Sam Wilson is one of many American men (and some women) who struggle with a discrepancy between their beliefs about heterosexual morality on the one hand and homosexual feelings and behaviors on the other. This side of his life is so hidden and secret that his family and friends would be shocked, and many of them appalled, perhaps as much with his secrecy and infidelity as with the homosexual activities. Many of the married men that Sam encounters in his anonymous sex experiences share his secrecy in their behavior and struggle with fear of being discovered. They fear their personal and social lives would be destroyed if their secrets were known.

Sam's sexual promiscuity strikes many, perhaps most, of us as disturbing, but what is it about his actions that disturbs us? For many, the biggest issue is his chronic infidelity, while for others a bigger issue is that his nonmarital sex is exclusively with other men. Sam has never had sex with another woman since he married his wife 15 years ago, but he has seldom gone more than a month without sex with another man. While his actions are not illegal, he and many of his sexual partners keep this side of their life "in the closet," hidden from view.

Over the past 15 years, however, the social landscape of sexuality and sexual identity has undergone an extensive transformation, creating many opportunities for open, accepting, and more equitable social lives for gay, lesbian, bisexual, transgendered, and questioning/queer (LGBTQ) individuals in the United States. Consider Wilhelmina and Tracy Emerson and their family.

Wilhelmina and Tracy are a married lesbian couple in their late thirties, living in San Francisco, one of the most LGBTQ friendly cities in the United States. "Mina" and Tracy have been together for 12 years and were legally married in 2008 when California made same-sex marriage legal. They consider themselves lucky to have been married before November of 2008 when the state passed Proposition Eight, a constitutional amendment (overturned in 2013) barring same-sex marriage. They also feel fortunate to be able to take advantage of many other rights that have only recently been extended to same-sex couples. In addition to a marriage license that officially recognizes their commitment to a family relationship with each other, they live in a state that provides them with rights to have children and to raise and care for them together. They also have other key rights, only recently granted to same-sex couples that enhance their ability to function as a family and that have long been fundamental rights of heterosexual couples, including the rights to own property together, to make medical and legal choices together, to receive medical benefits from each other's employers, and to inherit each other's property. Until recently, however, if "Mina" and Tracy had moved to another state, they might well have found their marriage not legally recognized. And even today in many states and communities they would face major legal and social barriers to their ability to function and be accepted as a family.

These biographical sketches of Sam Wilson, on the one hand, and Wilhelmina and Tracy Emerson, on the other, represent very different experiences with same-sex attraction and behavior. Despite his sexual attraction to men, Sam Wilson is outspoken in his opposition to same-sex marriage and often disgusted with his own behavior. Wilhelmina and Tracy embrace their same-sex attraction openly with their family, friends, and community. The two moms attend school events together with their children and look forward to taking the kids every June to watch the San Francisco LGBT Pride Parade. In the last 50 years, the LGBTQ category of "deviance" has witnessed the most dramatic transformation in American culture of any category of deviance examined in this book, moving from being perceived and treated as illegal and as a psychiatric disorder to being viewed by most Americans as an acceptable and even positive identity. In this chapter, we explore the remarkable transformation of perceptions and treatment of LGBTQ issues in the United States and the many issues that remain contested and in flux today.

CURRENT CONSTRUCTIONS OF LGBTQ IDENTITIES IN THE UNITED STATES

There are a range of different gender identities and sexual orientations captured under the LGBTQ umbrella. Same-sex erotic attraction and gender variation have been documented widely across human history and understood in a variety of ways. Four characteristics are typically considered today as identifying an individual in the most common LGBTQ constructions—as well as in the heterosexual category from which LGBTQ identities and behaviors are typically (albeit less than satisfactorily) distinguished: (1) sexual attraction, (2) sexual behavior, (3) sexual identity, and (4) gender identity (Sell 1997).

Today, in the United States and other western societies, the most commonly identified LGBTQ constructions are those of gay men, lesbian women, bisexuals, and transgendered individuals. Categorizing individuals within these constructions is problematic for two reasons. First, individual's sexual behaviors may not dovetail with their sexual identities. Sam Wilson in the first vignette above does not identify himself as gay—or even bisexual—even though he has a long history of sexual attraction and activity with other men. As Steven Seidman has observed, homosexuality is not necessarily self-defining or a core identity. "Some individuals may fashion an identity based on their homosexuality; others view it as simply a desire or behavior" (2002, p.211). Second, both sexual and gender identities are not necessarily fixed phenomena. An individual's feelings of sexual attraction and gender can vary over time, meaning that both heterosexual and LGBTQ identities and behaviors are not necessarily fixed and absolute within a given individual. In recent years, LGBT activists have added "Q" to the LGBT acronym to acknowledge that not all sexual orientations and identities are captured in LGBT categories. The "Q" in LGBTQ stands for both "queer" and "questioning." It is meant to recognize that some people find themselves uncomfortable with pigeonholing in specific existing categories of sexual identity.

The term "gay" is primarily used to refer to males whose sex lives and sexual identities are oriented toward other males. While gay is sometimes used as an umbrella term for both male and female homosexuals, the term "lesbian" refers specifically to women whose sex lives and sexual identities are oriented toward other females. The term bisexual is meant to encompass males and females who are sexually attracted to both males and females.

Transgender identity stands separate from sexual orientation and identity, referring to a subjective feeling of being a different gender than what one was assigned at birth. Transgendered individuals are not defined by their sexual orientation. Indeed, sexual orientation of transgendered individuals (in relation to their preferred gender identity) may be heterosexual, homosexual, bisexual, or queer/questioning.

Table 14.1 Research Estimates of LGB Identified Adults in the United States

Date	Study	Gay/Lesbian	Bisexual	Total LGB
2010	General Social Survey	1.4%	1.6%	3%
2010	National Survey of Family Growth	1.5%	2.6%	4.1%
2011	Williams Institute	1.7%	1.8%	3.5%
2014	Gallup	N/A	N/A	5.6%
2013	National Health Interview Survey	1.4%	2.3%	3.7%
2014	NHIS	1.6	0.6%	2.2%

SOURCES: Gates (2014), Gates and Newport (2012), Ward et al. (2014).

Statistical Snapshot

Statistical findings on the percentage of adult US citizens who identify as gay, lesbian, and bisexual vary significantly, as shown in *table 14.1*. Estimates range from a low of 2.2 per cent to a high of 5.6 per cent of the adult US population identifying as gay, lesbian, or bisexual. Overall, the numbers of males and females identifying as homosexual or bisexual are roughly the same, although most research finds that significantly more males identify as homosexual, while more females identify as bisexual (e.g., Gates 2011). The percentage of American adults who identify as LGBTQ differs between younger and older populations. The most extensive national survey of the distribution of the LGBTQ population in the United States (Gates and Newport 2012) reports that among adults between the ages of 18 and 29, 6.4 per cent of respondents identified as LGBTQ in comparison to 3.2 per cent of those 30 to 49 years old and only 2.6 per cent of those between 50 and 64 years of age. Among young adults there is also a significant gender difference with considerably more young women than young men identifying as LGBTQ. According to this study, approximately 3.5 per cent of adults in the United States identify as lesbian, gay, or bisexual, and an estimated 0.3% of adults are transgender. By this estimate, in the United States there are around eight million people who identify as gay, lesbian, or bisexual, and nearly 700,000 people who identify as transgender.

The figures reported here provide at best a fuzzy estimate of the numbers of Americans who are LGBTQ identified or who experience some degree of same sex erotic attraction. These figures are far lower than what the American public tends to guess. In recent years surveys have shown that the American public estimates somewhere around 25 per cent of the adult population is LGBTQ identified (Newport 2012). This public overestimation of the LGBTQ population is perhaps due in large part to the high visibility of LGBTQ issues in the media today and the dramatic changes in attitudes and laws taking place in American society today.

CHALLENGES IN LGBTQ RESEARCH

Researchers seeking to get good estimates of the number of LGBTQ individuals and their experiences in the United States have historically confronted a variety of challenges, including a lack of research funding, stigmatization of sex-related research, and questions about how to define and identify LGBTQ populations. The cultural shift toward LGBTQ acceptance in recent years has improved opportunities for LGBTQ research, enabling social scientists to address research challenges more successfully.

Counting LGBTQ Identities and Sexual Behavior

Throughout the twentieth century government and private funding for sexuality research faced low priority, suspicion, and at times outright hostility. While the American public showed appreciation for the findings of sexuality researchers, scholars struggled to finance their studies. In recent years, government and private funding for LGBTQ-related research has increased. Federal agencies like the Centers for Disease Control and the National Institutes of Health now regularly issue "requests for proposals" related to LGBTQ health issues; major private research organizations including the National Opinion Research Center, the Pew Research Center, and the Gallup polling agency support LGBTQ research; and several prestigious MacArthur Foundation Fellowships have been awarded to LGBTQ scholars, artists, and activists.

But even when researchers are able to get funding to study LGBTQ issues, they must address various research challenges. First among these is the definitional challenge. There are various ways to define and measure lesbian, gay, bisexual, and transgender identities. Sexual orientation can be addressed by asking an individual specifically about their sexual identity or by asking about their behaviors and sexual attractions. Far more people in surveys report some same-sex sexual experiences and/or attraction than identify themselves as LGBTQ. While 4.1 per cent of respondents in the 2010 National Survey of Family Growth identified themselves as lesbian, gay, or bisexual, nearly 9 per cent reported engaging in at least some same-sex erotic behaviors and 11 per cent reported same-sex attraction (Gates 2011, p.5).

While mainstream American society has become much more accepting of LGBTQ identities and behaviors over the past three decades, fear of stigma still influences the willingness of many people to identify as LGBTQ. Survey methods based on face-to-face interviews tend to produce low estimates of the size of the LGBTQ community because some people are unwilling to identify as LGBTQ in personal interaction with the researcher. Studies that allow respondents to complete questions anonymously on the Internet tend to report higher rates of LGBTQ identity (Gates 2011, p.2).

Recognizing that LGBTQ attraction is subject to underreporting, some researchers have used unobtrusive measures to try to get a better picture of same-sex erotic behavior and identities. Google data analyst, Seth Stephens-Davidowitz (2013) has analyzed Internet data including Facebook profiles, Craigslist personal ads, and Google pornography searches. His findings show that there are far more openly gay men in states with more tolerant attitudes, but that the rates of gay male pornography searches are remarkably similar from state to state, leading him to conclude that there are significantly more closeted gay men in less tolerant states.

Getting Close

Ethnographers who seek to gain contextual understandings of the meanings and experiences of sexual behavior and identities face challenges given the shifting landscape of stigmatization of LGBTQ identities and the ambiguity related to sexual behavior and identity. The most controversial deviance ethnography ever written in the United States is Laud Humphreys' *Tearoom Trade* (1970), a study of the mismatch between sexual behavior and social identity of men who frequented public restrooms for anonymous sex in the late 1960s. Humphreys pretended to be one of the men engaged in "cruising" the restrooms for sex. He observed sexual interactions, taking notes on the activities and roles of those involved. But his research went even further. As he observed the action at public restrooms, he also secretly collected the license plate numbers of cars driven by men who came to the restrooms. Working with a law enforcement friend, Humphreys got the home addresses of these men and went to their homes disguised as a survey researcher to gather personal information. When his findings were published, they received widespread attention. Over half of the men he had observed having sex outwardly identified as heterosexual, many of them from socially "respectable" backgrounds with wives who were not aware of their homosexual dalliances. Humphreys' study provided breakthrough insights regarding same-sex activities among publicly heterosexual men, but it also served as a rallying point for critics who opposed covert research. If the men he studied had been publicly identified, many would have lost their jobs and their marriages because of the information Humphreys collected without their knowledge. Today, no university human subjects review board would approve similar research.

The current social landscape for LGBTQ issues and activities is dramatically different from the late 1960s when Humphreys conducted his study. Across the United States, LGBTQ activities and identities are tremendously less stigmatized than in the 1950s and 1960s, although there remains considerable geographical and ideological variation. Further, LGBTQ participation openly spans the range of social institutions, including family life, politics, religion, and entertainment. Consequently, the range of social sites for LGBTQ ethnographies has both expanded and become far more open and accessible.

Many, but by no means all, ethnographers studying LGBTQ culture today are themselves LGBTQ identified. Autoethnographic research by LGBTQ identified scholars covers a wide swath of social life. Several LGBTQ autoethnographers, such as Tony Adams (2011), have chronicled their experiences becoming aware of and public about their LGBTQ identities. Peter Hennen (2008) has provided a rich account of his participation in middle-aged gay "bear" and "leather" communities. Others have studied and written about their experiences as LGBTQ parents (Dozier 2014), social activists (Young and McKibban 2014), drag performers (Hobson 2013), and as counselors for LGBTQ youth (Speciale et al. 2015).

Like other ethnographers, LGBTQ researchers who are not themselves insiders can still nurture rich and informative ethnographic relationships, even in contexts where LGBTQ identity still remains stigmatized. Tanya Erzen (2006) and Michelle Wolkomir (2006) have studied church-based support groups for gay and ex-gay men. Like other ethnographers, they have cultivated research relationships based on respectful treatment of those they study to gain their confidence.

CROSS-CULTURAL LGBTQ CONSTRUCTIONS

Human history is replete with records of same-sex love and sexuality, as well as transgender or "third gender" individuals, although a broad historical perspective cautions us against viewing sexuality in the past as similar to the way we view it today. As Jane Ward has explained, "People have long engaged in same-sex activity, but the sense that these sexual behaviors constitute an identity or personage is a quite modern idea" (2015, p.54).

Different Definitions

What counts as sex and sexual identity depends very much on the time and place in question. A good example is provided by Gilbert Herdt's (1982) research with the Sambia people in Papua New Guinea. In traditional Sambian culture, a critical ritual of initiation into manhood involved boys performing oral sex on older, but yet unmarried men. The semen from the older men was believed to be critical to the boys' abilities to become adult men. The younger males were inseminated by older bachelors who were once semen recipients themselves. But Herdt argues that the modern conception of homosexuality does not fit these acts. The intent of the act—becoming a man rather than giving sexual pleasure—he contends, separates it from sex. From a different perspective, girls and women in the Lesotho, Africa, kiss and even engage in what we would consider oral sex, but insist that this is not sex because there is no penis (Rupp 2009).

Even in cultures that have viewed same-sex erotic activities as sexual in nature, our current understandings of homosexuality seldom fit with their views. It is well known that powerful men in ancient Greece and Rome took young male lovers. Many writers and scholars over the last century have drawn upon the example of Greek homosexuality to make the case for the long history of homosexual attraction and identity. However, culturally knowledgeable scholars argue that Greek same-sex activities differed from homosexuality as we understand it today. Ancient Greek and Roman worlds based their sexual categorization not on differences in gender but on an active–passive dichotomy. "The fact that a man had sex with other men was usually incidental. The key question was exactly what he did with them" (Berkowitz 2012, p.121).

When European military adventurers, traders, and missionaries traveled into the Americas they found cultures that allowed and even celebrated sexual and gender presentations different from the rigid homophobic cultures in their home countries. French traders referred to such individuals as "berdaches," a term used in France for younger partners in male homosexual relationships. While European explorers and missionaries voiced disgust, the Native Americans often looked upon such individuals as having unique gifts and incorporated them positively into their cultures. Among the Mojave, Two-Spirit Initiation ceremonies allowed for a child around the age of 10 to switch gender identity and "allowed for homoerotic relations so long as they were between people in different gender roles" (Herdt 1997, pp.123–25).

While sex between men was largely accepted as natural in Greece and Rome so long as it conformed to societal gender norms, as Christianity gained influence, homosexuality came under attack. The Apostle Paul laid the groundwork for negative views toward homosexuality. Paul's writings against homosexuality can best be understood in the context of his distrust of physical pleasure as barrier to spiritual life. Paul viewed all pleasures of the flesh as impediments to spiritual attainment. While food and sex were necessary, he believed it was sinful to take pleasure in them for their own sake. Since homosexuality could never produce children, it was especially condemned. As Christianity gained influence in coming centuries, laws against homosexuality began to emerge, culminating in the edicts of the Byzantine emperor Justinian around 530 CE. Justinian believed that the earthquakes that shook Constantinople during his reign were God's punishment for male–male sex in the city. For the following 1500 years in Europe and in the Americas after the conquest, homosexual acts were officially associated with heresy and pathology.

Different "Causes"

Just as different cultures have viewed same-sex erotic acts in different ways, they have also taken different views regarding the "causes" of same-sex attraction. In some cultures, such as classical Greece and Rome, same-sex attraction was viewed as just a natural form of sexual pleasure based on the same sexual urges as other sexuality. Among many cultures in the preconquest Americas, homosexuality and transgender identity were viewed in a context that did not separate sexuality and gender into the heterosexual/homosexual binary that developed in Europe.

Across European and American history the most common view of homosexuality as deviance has been that it is caused by immoral temptation, consistent with Paul's condemnation of the pleasures of the flesh. In the Middle Ages throughout Europe lesbians were commonly viewed as devil worshipping witches (Crompton 1981), while popular British eighteenth-century pamphlets such as the widely read "Satan's Harvest Home" claimed that moral degeneracy of the Catholic Church (in contrast to the manly and virtuous Church of England) was the cause of homosexuality.

Biological explanations of homosexuality and transgender can be traced back as far as classical Greece where a class of "unmanly effeminate men" referred to as *kinaidos* were considered both deviant and biologically inferior to other, masculine men. Medical explanations of homosexuality gained prominence in the late 1800s and early 1900s. In 1886, the German psychiatrist, Richard von Krafft-Ebing, published his treatise on sexual psychiatric disorders, *Psychopathia Sexualis*. Homosexuality, he contended, could be caused by biological anomalies during pregnancy that produced a "sexual inversion of the brain." Many sexologists in the early 1900s argued that such sexual inversion was caused by "urning" in which a female mind was trapped in a male body (or vice versa). These works influenced the thinking of other psychiatrists throughout the twentieth century as homosexuality was viewed as product of unhealthy development toward natural adult heterosexuality. Psychotherapists frequently cited poor parenting by overprotective mothers and emotionally distant fathers as leading to a child's abnormal sexual orientation. But as the philosopher Michel Foucault has observed, psychiatrists' association of homosexuality with an individual's mind did something more radical than simply explain homosexual acts. By connecting homosexuality to the individual's psyche, psychiatrists made homosexuality a defining feature of an individual's identity. The homosexual was identified as a unique kind of being, an "invert" as sexologists termed it. "The homosexual," Foucault writes, "was now a species" (1978, p.43). The official classification of homosexuality as a mental illness continued in the United States until the American Psychiatric Association (APA) removed homosexuality from the *Diagnostic and Statistical Manual* list of mental illnesses in 1973.

Less morally laden biological explanations for the "cause" of homosexuality have consistently gained influence since its removal from the *DSM*. A variety of genetic and hormonal factors have been proposed as playing a role in sexual orientation, although no single biological determinant of same-sex attraction has been uncovered. Biological explanations for sexual and gender orientation have been accepted by many self-identified homosexuals and transgendered individuals who feel that their experiences resonate with the argument that they were "born this way" rather than having made a personal choice about sexual attraction. However, critics of this view argue that much of the research on the biological underpinnings of homosexuality is based on flawed science and unsupported assumptions (e.g., Walters 2014). Ultimately, questions about the "causes" of nonheterosexual erotic attraction and gender identities remain unanswered and perhaps, some would argue, far less important or consequential than contextual social issues related to sex, gender, and social power.

Different Responses

Societies where same-sex erotic activities have been accepted are characterized by little public response and even periodic celebrations of sexual diversity. But in cultures where LGBTQ acts and identities are stigmatized or illegal, a wide range of social control responses have existed to monitor and enforce the boundaries of acceptable sexuality and gender identity.

The Catholic Church condemned homosexuality, but laws against it developed slowly across Europe during the Middle Ages. Male–male sexual relations were not subject to any secular legal proscriptions in Britain before 1534, but then became a capital offense. European laws on executing "sodomites" drew their inspiration from earlier Justinian edicts as well as the call for execution of homosexuals in *Leviticus* 20:13: "If any man lyeth with mankind, as he lyeth with a woman, both of them have committed abomination; they both shall surely be put to death."

By far the majority of policing and punishment for homosexual acts in Europe focused on male homosexuality, reflecting the male dominance of European culture. Throughout much of Europe in the Middle Ages "it was an open question whether or not female-female sex without penetration or at least without a woman taking on the male role, was sex at all" (Berkowitz 2012, p.164). At times women having sex with women were not punished unless they simulated heterosexual acts using an "artificial instrument" (Berkowitz 2012, p.164).

When military explorers traveled to the New World, they reacted with extreme hostility toward the sexual and gender conduct of the native populations. In 1513, Spanish conquistador, Vasco Nunez de Balboa, had vicious mastiffs tear apart 40 Indigenous male natives who were dressed as women (Bronski 2011, p.5). Over the next hundred years many Indigenous natives were condemned to slaughter by conquistadors and European clergy for not conforming to European norms of gender and sexuality (Mogul et al. 2011).

As Europeans settled in North America, many communities or colonies invoked Old World laws. Jamestown and other southern colonies adopted the English "buggery" statute of 1533, which called for death for 'the horrible, detestable sins of Sodomie" (Rupp 1999, p.28). But few were prosecuted and even fewer executed.

While homosexual acts have been illegal in Europe and the United States as well as other societies, there have often been accommodations made to tolerate or accept the behaviors in segregated spaces. Homosexuality was declared a capital offense in England in the 1520s, but by the 1600s there were numerous clubs and taverns known as "molly-houses" where middle- and lower-class men with homosexual interests could socialize in sheltered meeting spots (Greenberg 1997, p.185). Molly-houses were episodically raided by law enforcement, but they persisted over time because they provided a relatively safe space out of the public eye.

Finally, medical diagnoses of homosexuality as mental illness at the start of the twentieth century suggested a new approach to homosexuality. In place of moral denunciation and punishment, doctors offered medical treatment for newly identified disease. Proposed cures ranged from psychotherapy to invasive medical treatments including castrations, electroshock therapy, and lobotomies (Scot 2013). One company, Farall Instruments, promoted its electroshock products with claims that "The effectiveness of paired visual stimulus and shock in converting homosexuals to heterosexuals is well documented" (Scot 2013). In extreme treatments, the shock device was attached to the genitals. For many patients there was undoubtedly little difference between punishment for a crime and treatment for an illness.

LGBTQ HISTORY IN THE UNITED STATES

Early LGBTQ history of the United States is shrouded by a veil of silence, but by the mid-twentieth-century lesbian and gay culture had gained public visibility and momentum. The second half of the twentieth century marked a tumultuous period of LGBTQ activism, conservative backlash, and devastation of the AIDS epidemic. The LGBTQ landscape in the United States today is far more culturally and legally supportive than just 20 years ago, although many challenges remain.

Early American Secrecy

The topics of homosexuality and transgender were almost never openly discussed in the early United States where homosexual acts were often referred to as "unnatural" and "unmentionable." Most evidence of homosexuality during this era is in poetry, stories, and diaries. In the era of long sailing voyages, sailors were well known to have sex with fellow sailors and "life-at-sea tales" recounted romantic relationships among the sailors and between officers and their cabin boys, usually eliding reference to actual sex. But as one old sailor explained in his diary in the early 1850s, "What can a feller do? Three years at sea and hardly a chance to have a woman. I tell you . . . a feller must do so" (Bronski 2011, p.61).

For most of the nineteenth century homosexuality was cloaked and indistinguishable (because unspoken) from other forms of male friendship, but by the 1880s it became more visible and acknowledged (Martin 1989, p.181). The most famous American poet of the nineteenth century, Walt Whitman, embraced sensual same-sex love in his poetry, invoking the term "adhesive love," which he borrowed from phrenology where it was used to describe male same-sex attraction. As his reputation and popularity increased, his poetry provided inspiration to many homosexual men, including the Irish playwright, Oscar Wilde, who was sentenced to two years of hard labor in prison following his conviction for "gross indecency with men" in the late 1890s. Yet, despite the strong homoerotic imagery in his poetry, when Whitman was asked publicly about the homosexual eroticism in his poetry and his life, he vehemently denied it—a clear reflection of the stigmatized status of homosexuality at the time.

1890s to World War II

By the late 1800s, a homosexual subculture had emerged in many large urban centers in the United States as gays and lesbians created ways of identifying each other and meeting. From the late 1800s into the early 1920s, historian George Chauncey writes, "Restaurants, speakeasies, and even bathhouses patronized by gay men were able to flourish so long as they kept out of public view" (1994, p.356). In the 1920s and 1930s, antigay laws were enacted that threatened to close down businesses that catered to gay clientele, but the tightening regulation of homosexuality was soon challenged by World War II.

The Army officially considered "homosexual proclivities" a disqualifying condition for military service at the start of World War II, but the realities of the war and the desperate need for servicemen and women trumped other concerns. Despite the official ban against homosexuality in the military, very few gays were actually rejected. Out of 18 million men examined for service, fewer than 5,000 were officially nixed for being homosexual (Bérubé 1991, p.33). As millions of men found themselves free from the confines of home life and surrounded almost exclusively by other men, World War II created a new erotic situation more open to homosexual activity and identity. LGBTQ historian, John D'Emilio, observes that "World War II created something of a nationwide coming out experience" (1983, p.24).

The War also offered lesbians more opportunities at home. The need for women in the workforce meant that more women could earn a living and have money to spend in the bars. In working-class industrial cities like Buffalo, New York, women's dress codes changed during the war. Butch lesbians who had previously only been able to wear pants in the privacy of their own homes were now free to present a more masculinized persona in public. Meanwhile, at least some young women whose male partners were serving in the military sought out romantic relationships with other women in the bars that were at the center of lesbian social life. As one lesbian recounted to Kennedy and Davis years later, when groups of straight women would show up at the bar, she and her friends would wisecrack, "Here come the war brides" (1993, p.39).

The Cold War on Homosexuals

As the war drew toward an end, the military instituted purges of gays and lesbians from its ranks through a system of dishonorable discharges known as "blue discharges" because they were printed on blue paper. In the end, the war had complex consequences for service members' perceptions of homosexuality, making them more aware of gay life and identity, but also raising worries of exposure and punishment (Rupp 1999, p.140).

The dangers of exposure and punishment increased dramatically in the postwar 1950s. Ironically, this wave of punishment for homosexuality followed the publication of Kinsey's *Sexual Behavior in the Human Male* (1948) that reported far higher numbers of men had same-sex experiences than had ever been imagined. As D'Emilio observes, "by revealing that millions of Americans exhibited erotic interest in their own sex, the report implicitly encouraged those still struggling in isolation against their sexual preferences to accept their sexual inclinations" (1983, p.37).

In contrast to the encouraging message of the Kinsey report, in 1950 the US Senate launched a series of investigations into "homosexual perversion" in government jobs. According to the Senate's report, homosexuals lacked "the emotional stability of normal persons" and were at risk of blackmail by foreign spies. FBI director, J. Edgar Hoover (believed by many today to have had a clandestine long-term relationship with his deputy Clyde Tolson), agreed. "The present apathy of the public toward perverts, generally regarded as harmless," Hoover stated, "should be changed to one of suspicious scrutiny. The harmless pervert of today can be and often is the loathsome mutilator and murderer of tomorrow" (Bronski 2011, p.124). President Eisenhower responded to such concerns by issuing an executive order to dismiss all homosexuals from government service (D'Emilio 1983, p.46).

In the 1950s and early 1960s across the United States, homosexuals were publicly denounced, along with communists, as the arch villains of national public safety. Many states passed laws against gay bars and increased arrests of gays and lesbians. Historian Allan Bérubé refers to this era as a "war on homosexuals" characterized by bar raids, police brutality, imprisonment, loss of employment, and suicides. In *Sexual Behavior in the Human Female*, their companion volume to the 1948 report on male sexuality in America, Kinsey et al. noted the severe ostracism and criminalization of homosexuality in the

US postwar years, observing that, "There appears to be no other major culture in the world in which homosexual relationships are so severely stigmatized" (1953, p.479).

Era of Collective Action and Conservative Responses

The Cold War hostility and police harassment of gays and lesbians reduced opportunity for open public life. It also spurred the founding of the first gay and lesbian organizations in the United States. In 1951, the Mattachine Society was founded by Harry Hay and others in Los Angeles who were concerned with the use of criminal law to arrest gay men and close gay bars. The Daughters of Bilitis was founded four years later in San Francisco to provide social opportunities besides lesbian bars that similarly exposed women to risk of arrest. The Mattachine Society and the Daughters of Bilitis pursued an *assimilationist* political agenda, emphasizing their underlying conformity to mainstream values and culture. They sought the opportunity to become accepted members of mainstream culture rather than to oppose it.

In 1969, a more confrontational gay movement burst onto the scene in response to a brutal police raid on the Stonewall Inn, a drag-queen bar in Greenwich Village. For three nights, more than 2,000 gays, lesbians, and allies fought police in the streets of lower Manhattan. Influenced by the antiwar and Black Power movements around them, gays formed the Gay Liberation Front. Asserting "gay power," activists demanded public respect and an end to antigay legislation and police harassment. While assimilationist groups like the Mattachine Society and the Daughters of Bilitis argued that homosexuals could find safety by promoting privacy, gay *liberationist* groups asserted that safety and liberation could only be achieved by challenging and changing the public sphere (Bronski 2011, p.208).

Gay rights activists protested at the 1970 national convention of the American Psychiatric Association (APA) in San Francisco, storming the stage during a presentation on aversion therapy to cure homosexuals (Polikoff 2008, p.37). Two years later an official gay group was formed within the APA and in 1973 the APA removed homosexuality from the list of mental illnesses in its *Diagnostic Statistical Manual*. The media began to take a more positive approach toward LGBTQ issues in the early 1970s as well, with magazine articles in *Life*, *Time*, and even *Playboy*. Peter Fisher's biographical look at gay sexuality, *The Gay Mystique* (1972), and Sidney Abbot and Barbara Love's "liberated view of lesbianism," *Sappho Was a Right-On Woman* (1972), marked a growing insiders' literature on gay and lesbian experiences.

The four decades since then have been tumultuous and at times devastating for the LGBTQ community. Various backlash campaigns were mobilized against gay rights from the 1970s through the 1990s. In 1977 after passage of a Dade County, Florida law prohibiting discrimination based on sexual orientation,

Anita Bryant, a singer and spokesperson for the Florida orange industry, championed a "Save the Children" campaign that called for repealing the antidiscrimination ordinance and banning child adoption by gay men and lesbians, which Bryant referred to as "human garbage" (Polikoff 2008, p.40). The LGBTQ community faced a legal blow in the mid-1980s when the US Supreme Court ruled 5–4 upholding a Georgia sodomy law criminalizing oral and anal sex between consenting adults. Calling homosexual acts "an offense of deeper malignity than rape," Chief Justice Warren Burger concluded, "To hold that the act of homosexual sodomy is somehow protected as a fundamental right would be to cast aside millennia of moral teaching" (Ghaziani 2008, p.88).

Despite conservative forces, gay and lesbian culture expanded from the 1970s through the 1990s. Beginning in the early 1980s, gay and bisexual men in the United States were devastated by the AIDS epidemic. AIDS was initially detected in the US gay male population, where the HIV virus that causes the illness spread rapidly. Moral Majority leaders quickly jumped onto the HIV/AIDS epidemic as an indictment of homosexuality. Televangelist Jerry Falwell proclaimed, "AIDS is not just God's punishment for homosexuals. It is God's punishment for the society that tolerates homosexuals" (Bronski 2011, p.226). In the 1980s, AIDS received little medical attention, while infections and deaths in the United States rose at a staggering rate (Bronski 2011, p.230).

In the face of governmental indifference, the gay and lesbian community mobilized to confront the crisis. In New York City, gay activists called on the gay community to demand healthcare and protection for AIDS victims, leading to the creation of the AIDS Coalition to Unleash Power, or ACT UP. ACT UP took to the streets with acts of civil disobedience. In 1988, ACT UP staged a protest so large that they shut down the offices of the Food and Drug Administration (FDA) for a day, demanding that the FDA respond more quickly to the medication needs of HIV victims.

The inauguration of President Bill Clinton in 1993 brought high hopes for gay and lesbian Americans. Clinton had expressed support for gay and lesbian rights, but soon confronted political and cultural resistance. One of the first LGBTQ battles Clinton faced was pushing for lesbian and gay military service. Despite the fact that many gays and lesbians had served honorably in service, the Joint Chiefs of Staff threatened to resign *en masse* if Clinton forced open inclusion of gays in the military (Faderman 2015, p.499). In the end, Clinton's administration settled for an awkward silence called "Don't Ask, Don't Tell" (DADT) that prohibited military personnel from discriminating against closeted homosexual and bisexual service members, but also barred openly homosexual or bisexual individuals from military service.

The "DADT" strategy of allowing LGBTQ individuals a right to military service as long as they passed as heterosexual "implied that gays and lesbians suffered no harm because they could hide" (Canaday 2009, p.256). That argument ran counter to the experiences of gays and lesbians seeking to care for their partners and share family life, especially for gay men in the thick of the AIDS epidemic. As gay partners found themselves barred from hospital visitation and denied the right to make medical decisions for their loved ones, the right to marry became an important issue for the LGBTQ community (Polikoff 2008, p.51). Conservative political forces mounted a preemptive attack against "gay marriage" when Congress passed the *Defense of Marriage Act* in 1996. The law defined marriage for federal purposes as "the union of one man and one woman," eliminating same-sex couples from eligibility for governmental spousal insurance benefits, social security survivor benefits, immigration rights, and the filing of joint tax returns. Twenty-five states banned same-sex marriage following the passage of DOMA in 1996 and by 2010 40 states had laws defining marriage as a right only for heterosexual couples.

A Post-Gay Era?

But legislation and legal battles over LGBTQ rights continued to seesaw. In 2003, the US Supreme Court struck down sodomy laws in Texas, ruling that individuals have a protected right to engage in consensual private sexual activity. The decision overturned the Court's 1986 ruling that had supported Georgia's sodomy law and it invalidated similar laws in 13 other states. In 2010, the US Senate repealed the "DADT" law, opening the pathway for homosexuals to serve in the military. And in 2015, the Supreme Court played a role in gay rights issues nationally when it ruled that the US constitution guarantees the right for same-sex couples to marry. Justice Anthony Kennedy stated in the majority opinion, "The Court, in this decision, holds same-sex couples may exercise the fundamental right to marry in all States." While legal battles will continue to be waged over LGBTQ rights for the foreseeable future, looking back over the past century, the LGBTQ rights movement stands as second only to the African-American Civil Rights movement as a major legal transformation in American society.

So, how can we best describe the social context of LGBTQ life today in the United States? Some observers contend that we have entered what can be called the *post-gay era* in American culture in which open communities and support for LGBTQ life no longer separate members of the LGBTQ community from other Americans. Those who make this argument point to the ability of gays and lesbians today to live openly "beyond the closet" (Ghaziani 2014; Seidman 2002).

The focus of most LGBTQ politics has changed as well, from ACT UP confrontational activism during the AIDS epidemic to current gay politics focused on family issues such as marriage, adoption, employment, and housing discrimination. As Amin Ghaziani (2011) observes, gay activism has turned from an "us versus them" approach to an inclusive "us and them" approach that builds bridges with mainstream society rather than opposing it. The focus on gay inclusion in family and workers' human rights is strengthened by the perception in the mainstream public and gay rights organizations that sexual

PUSHING YOUR BOUNDARIES

Surveying Generational LGBT Attitudes

Researchers have suggested that there are generational differences today between older and younger Americans' attitudes toward homosexuality. In this exercise you are asked to collect some data that could shed light on this hypothesis. Using a Likert Scale with ratings from 1—Strongly Agree—to 5—Strongly Disagree, ask five people over the age of 55 and another five under the age of 30 to respond to the following 10 statements.

1. I would be comfortable with my children (or grandchildren) staying overnight at the home of a child whose parents are lesbian or gay.
2. I would be comfortable working with a transgendered coworker.
3. I believe that same-sex marriage should be legal.
4. I believe that lesbians and gays should have the same rights for adoption as heterosexuals.
5. I would be comfortable with a family member who is openly lesbian or gay.
6. I have a close friend or friends who identify as gay or lesbian.
7. I would be comfortable with gay or lesbian neighbors.
8. I believe that gays and lesbians should be allowed to serve in the military.
9. I would be comfortable with my adolescent children having gay and lesbian friends.
10. I believe transgendered individuals should be able to use a public restroom of their choice.

Share your results with other class members to get a bigger picture. Do your data support the hypothesis of generational differences in attitudes? Do your data suggest that the United States is moving toward a post-gay era?

orientation is biologically determined rather than a matter of choice—as captured in Lady Gaga's popular gay anthem, "Born This Way."

While many LGBTQ individuals and organizations celebrate the in-roads made in recent years, others point out the uneven limits of liberation in the post-gay era. The mainstream gay agenda, they argue, has served the interests of affluent white gays and lesbians more than other members of the queer community, particularly minorities, for whom issues like gay marriage can be less important than citizenship rights and economic security (Alimahomed 2010). Further, the focus on same-sex marriage in the last decade has reduced the vision of what it "means to be gay" to monogamous coupling that parallels the heterosexual nuclear family rather than embracing a more expansive paradigm of sexuality. As LGBTQ scholar Steven Seidman writes, "Gay life today is defined by a contradiction: many individuals can choose to live beyond the closet but they must still live and participate in a world where most institutions maintain heterosexual domination" (Seidman 2002, p.6).

THE LIMITS OF POSITIVISTIC APPROACHES

In this book we have examined a wide range of stigmatized behaviors and identities. In each case we have looked at how a particular positivistic theory or set of theories would address the "cause" or "causes" of that particular kind of deviance. While no single positivistic theory fully explains any kind of deviance, many positivistic approaches help illuminate why people engage in various criminalized or stigmatized behaviors, from murder to drug abuse to anorexic patterns of eating. However, LGBTQ sexuality and gender identities bring us to the limits of positivistic theories. Today, no deviance scholars apply positivistic theories to sexual orientation and gender identity. Obviously, some people and groups continue to believe that LGBTQ behaviors and identities are caused by abnormal biology or psychological problems. But most LGBTQ scholars today view sexual orientation and gender identity as a diverse and normal range of human variability.

Positivistic approaches to deviance do not fit LGBTQ behaviors and identities for two reasons. First, and most obviously, American society has moved toward a post-gay era in which LGBTQ behaviors and identities are simply no longer considered deviant. Deviance scholar Erich Goode has gone so far as to argue that "within a generation homosexuality will probably no longer be discussed by sociologists as a form of deviance" (2015, p.243). Second, positivistic theories do a poor job of explaining variation in sexual behavior and gender identity. Today, only fringe scholars pursue the once-prevalent assertions that anything other than straight heterosexuality or clear male/female gender identity is a result of poor parenting, traumatic childhood experiences, deviant socialization, or a lack of self-control. The most commonly accepted popular explanation for sexual attraction and gender identity today is a belief that LGBTQ individuals are "born that way." However, even the biological explanation lacks a solid empirical foundation. No "gay gene" or set of genes has been definitively identified. And while many LGBTQ individuals and groups feel that a biological explanation for same-sex attraction provides strong justification for protecting LGBTQ human rights, others argue that it should not matter whether sexual orientation is innate or a choice—that people should have a fundamental right to define, experiment with, and even redefine their own sexual orientations.

In the following sections of this chapter we look at people today doing just that—engaging in same-sex activities and defining or resisting defining themselves as gays, lesbians, bisexuals, and transgendered.

INTERACTIONAL CONTEXTS AND ETHNOGRAPHIC VOICES

Deviance ethnographers and textbook writers in the past have primarily examined homosexuality as a stigmatized behavior and identity that acknowledges mainstream public disapproval and even criminal sanctions. In his classic analysis of stigma management, Erving Goffman (1963) drew on homosexual secrecy and passing as key characteristics of gay culture and identity. In the 50 years since *Stigma* was published, American attitudes toward, and treatment of, LGBTQ-identified individuals have changed dramatically. The issues and experiences faced by gay, lesbian, bisexual, and transgendered individuals have shifted as well.

Straight Gay Sex Today

Deviance researchers studying homosexuality in the 1960s discovered what many gay and lesbian insiders had long known: that a significant number of straight-identified people at least occasionally engage in homosexual activity. As Jane Ward observes, "straight-identified people . . . have engaged in homosexual activity since the modern invention of heterosexual identity itself" (2015, p.51). That does not mean that they see themselves as closet homosexuals. In a classic 1961 study of adolescent boys who engaged in paid sex with men, Albert Reiss found that, despite their routine participation in oral sex, the boys he studied did not define themselves as homosexuals. One of the boys explained, "No matter how many queers a guy goes with, if he goes for money, that don't make him queer" (1961, pp.103–104). The boys also defined themselves as straight because they said they only allowed men to perform oral sex on them, but did not perform sex on the men. Whether or not they were honest about all of their sexual activities, it was clear that these street youth defined themselves as heterosexual. When Laud Humphreys published *Tearoom Trade* in 1970, he provided even more evidence of straight-identified men in same-sex encounters. More than half of the men he witnessed having sex in public restrooms were involved in heterosexual relationships and only 14 per cent considered themselves homosexual and part of the gay community (Humphreys 1970). "Many men," Humphreys wrote, "married and unmarried, those with heterosexual identities and those whose self-image is a homosexual one, seek impersonal sex, shunning involvement, desiring kicks without commitment" (1970, p.2).

When Humphreys' book was published, many readers perceived it more as an exposé of lurid homosexual liaisons than as sociological research. Exposés of straight-identified men engaging in same-sex encounters have periodically been published for over a century in the United States. During the heyday of homophobia in the 1950s, a series of articles in the *Idaho State Journal* alleged a sex scandal in Boise involving young men in sexual acts with a "ring" of adult homosexual men. In an editorial titled, "Crush the Monster," the editors referred to homosexuality as a "moral perversion" and a "cancerous growth." *Time* magazine quickly picked up the story and gave it national attention in an article titled, "Idaho Underworld." The ensuing moral panic led to an 18-month criminal investigation in which over a thousand people were interviewed, resulting in sentencing from probation to life in prison for 15 Boise residents (Gerassi 1966). Whatever the real motivation for the Boise investigation, it used alleged homosexuality (then both a crime and a mental illness) as a way to attack members of the community.

More recently, African-American writer J.L. King's 2004 book, *On the Down Low: A Journey into the Lives of Straight Black Men Who Sleep with Men*, appeared on *The New York Times* best seller list for more than 30 consecutive weeks. The book, which was called by some a "long-overdue wake up call," discusses "down low" behaviors of black men and warning signs that African-American women should be on the lookout for. The publicity given to King's book, including an appearance on Oprah, has been criticized by many scholars (e.g., Robinson and Vidal-Ortiz 2013) for giving an impression that secretive same-sex activity is particularly common among black men, which is highly unlikely, as suggested by the homosexual scandals associated with such high-profile white Americans as former Senator Larry Craig, former Speaker of the House of Representatives Denny Hastert, and evangelical Christian pastor Ted Haggard.

For deviance ethnographers, the broader observation is that same-sex erotic activity can be defined by participants in a variety of ways, some of which disavow homosexual meaning—and even emphasize heterosexual identity. In her research, LGBTQ ethnographer Jane Ward collected and analyzed 234 men-seeking-men ads in the "Casual Encounters" section of Craigslist in Los Angeles. She found that the authors of the ads typically identified themselves as white, straight, in their twenties and thirties, and seeking sex with men, but then proceeding to offer numerous hetero-authenticating details, including homophobic disavowals of gay men, misogynistic references to violence against women, and invoking hetero-masculine props (such as beer, sports, and straight porn) for their sexual encounters. These ads suggest that being straight or gay is not about the biological sex of participants, but about "how the sex is done" (2015, p.128). Ward concludes:

> The line straight people draw between "actually gay" and "merely joking/getting off" is only minimally about sex acts. Instead, it is the circumstances of our sex acts . . . that have long sustained the hetero/homo binary and have, in many cases, trumped the raw facts about same-sex bodies engaged in sexual touching.
>
> —Ward (2015, p.193)

While the foregoing discussion focuses on male sexual behaviors and identities, similar interpretive license in defining sexuality has been observed among women. Based on her broad historical research on female same-sex erotic activity, Leila Rupp writes, "I am convinced that what we often find historically and cross-culturally is that sex was so defined by the participation of a penis that what women might do with their bodies did not count as sex (2012, p.850). Put simply, "If sex without a penis is not sex, then women might have the opportunity to do a lot of things with their bodies without having sex" (Rupp 2012, p.850).

But even when women have explicitly defined sexual encounters with other women, those acts carry less cultural assumption of homosexuality than is the case for men. The media attention to "girls kissing girls," captured in Katie Perry's popular hit song, "I Kissed a Girl," reflects a contemporary playfulness and openness to sexual experimentation for *heteroflexible* straight girls. In some college settings, girls making out with other girls has become a common party activity, raising questions among some observers about whether the girls are really attracted to each other or simply performing for the largely male audience. As Leila Rupp and Verta Taylor have found, the young women who participate have several explanations for why they do it. One common explanation involves the party setting atmosphere in which such sex play often occurs. As one college student explained:

> It's usually brought on by, I don't know, like shots or drinking, or people kind of saying something to like cheer it on or whatever. And it's usually done in order to turn guys on or to seek male attention in some way.
>
> —Rupp and Taylor (2010, p.30)

The emphasis on intoxication and male attention can suggest that nothing more sexually identifying than drunk playfulness is involved. As another girl put it, "It's just like it's okay because we're both drunk and we're friends. It's not like we identify as lesbian in any way" (Rupp and Taylor 2010, p.30).

Most of the young women Rupp and Taylor interviewed did not think that making out with another woman implied anything about their sexual identity. As one told them, "A lot of the girls that, you know, just casually make out with their girlfriends, would consider themselves straight. I consider myself straight." Nonetheless, as Rupp and Taylor note, these young women's stories "make clear that experimentation in the heterosexual context of the hookup culture and college party scene provides a safe space for some women to explore non-heterosexual possibilities" (2010, p.30). Men do not, at least in contemporary America, experience the same kind of cultural freedom for public display of sexual fluidity. Although a significant number of men may identify as straight and still have sex with other men (e.g., Anderson 2008), few make out at parties for the attention of women.

Coming Out

While some straight-identified individuals engage in same-sex erotic activities, today many people embrace homosexual or bisexual identities. The term "coming out" is frequently used to refer to the social processes involved in an individual's developing a nonheterosexual identity and sharing that identity with others. LGBTQ ethnographers, Mary Anna Robertson (2014) and Nicholas Guittar (2014), provide insightful and complementary analyses of coming out processes. Based on her work with youth at an LGBTQ drop-in center, Robertson discusses four processes of sexual identity formation. The first process involves a youth feeling that their behavior, thoughts, or body "violate the norms of compulsory heterosexuality" (2014, p.389). Many of the youth she interviewed felt that they experienced themselves as different or others saw them as different as a child. One gay-identified young man recounted:

> I always knew there was something different about me. Like—and this is just the way it is, like, I'm not a weirdo—but when I was younger like . . . even when I was really young, . . . say we were watching Power Rangers, they [his brother and cousins] would always be checking out the girls, and I would be like oh, look at the guys. I mean I always knew something was different.
>
> —Robertson (2014, pp.391–392).

The feeling of being different does not come with a ready-made explanation for why they or others perceived them as different. The second process Robertson uncovered was the youths' search for an explanation for their difference, looking for words that could provide a description of what they felt and why. Most first learned the words to describe homosexuality and homosexuals in a negative, stigmatizing context. As one explained:

> I . . . probably like thirteen. And um . . . my family would like once in a while—they'd say like "He's so gay," or "He's a faggot." Stuff like that. I was like, "What do you mean?" [My brother says], "It's this nasty guy who sleeps with another guy." That's all he said . . . And I'm like oh my god. Okay. And I was like I wanted to dig more. So I was like, "Well, what's wrong with it?" And he was like, "Well, I don't know, they're just attracted to the same sex." And I was like oh shit, that's me.
>
> —Robertson (2014, p.394)

In a similar vein, Tony Adams (2011) writes of "learning the closet," a process of becoming aware of same-sex attraction and the feeling that many people view it as socially unacceptable and something that should be hidden—that revealing such attraction may lead to rejection and disapproval. Many people engage in self-acceptance but do not "come out," at least to a wide range of other people (Guittar 2014). For many, "coming out" is experienced as coming out at least initially only to oneself, or in largely anonymous contexts. An Internet survey of LGBTQ-identified youth by OutProud! found that 30 per cent of their respondents were "out" only on the Internet, not with friends and family (Savin-Williams 2005, p.65). Some LGBTQ-identified individuals learn to "live in the closet" (Adams 2011), becoming adept at hiding their sexual feelings even while believing that their feelings of same-sex attraction will not go away.

Support and social venues for LGBTQ affiliations have increased enormously over the past two decades (since the OutProud! Internet survey was conducted) and more youth today than in the past have opportunities to openly socialize with members of the LGBTQ community. A third process in forming a sexual identity for such youth involves opportunities to explore sexuality where they are introduced to other gay and bisexual individuals and begin to learn how to fit in with the LGBTQ community. Miguel, for instance, spoke of meeting another young man who provided a role model for him:

> I was not out, and he was. And he was like the perfect model of everything that I wanted to embrace . . . Me dating without having to worry about anybody judging me. And if they were judging me, I didn't care . . . And I was like, I want that so bad. I am here hiding myself . . . And he's living the life that I wish I had.
>
> —Robertson (2014, p.396)

A fourth process involves coming to define oneself within the categories that are available to describe sexual identity. Some youth resist placing labels on their sexuality, while others find that a clear sexual identity affirms their sense of self. Anthony, for instance, came to define being gay as the most important part of his identity. For him being gay was associated with a particular kind of personality and community:

> Gays, lesbians, bi's, and all of them . . . they're fun-loving people. So I've sort of taken myself as part of that community. I see myself as a fun-loving, happy person. So that being in my sexuality base is kind of like . . . it's grown on me. I kind of like how it feels. So for me being gay is really fun to me.
>
> —Robertson (2014, p.398)

Yet others oscillated across various terms to describe their emerging and changing sexual identities. Travon, a 16-year-old, black young man who preferred to identify as "queer," explained:

> When I originally came out I was bi, I came out only as bi. And then I realized I like guys better so I said I was gay. And then I started having reoccurring feelings for women so I went back to being bi and I was like this is too much work. [Now] I identify as queer, it covers it all and it also doesn't exclude people like trans people and stuff and, like, I felt that it was a lot cooler to include everybody.
>
> —Robertson (2014, p.399)

The experience of coming out has changed over the past several decades as mainstream attitudes toward gays, lesbians, and transgendered individuals have become increasingly positive and as LGBTQ culture and community have expanded. Even so, coming out is only meaningful in *heteronormative* contexts in which same-sex attraction and sexual identity are considered "different," even if not necessarily bad. As Guittar notes, "coming out is a function of oppression" (2014, p.3). In contrast to straight-identified individuals who feel no need to self-proclaim their sexual orientation to family, friends, and coworkers, LGBTQ individuals even today often feel a need to announce their sexual orientation and identity.

The experience of coming out varies. For some LGBT individuals it is a matter of revealing one's sexual orientation to specific significant others, such as parents and siblings. For others it becomes a more expansive project. As one young woman told Guittar, "To me coming out is just finally being able to be completely yourself in all facets of life. If you're coming out, then you're coming out and you just need to be out" (2014, p.34). Another explained, "Coming out means all the way out, to the fullest extent" (p.35). Still, the process of coming out can involve interactional strategies designed to reduce the impact of the announcement. Some try to lessen the intensity of coming out through what Guittar refers to as *queer apologetic* in which a person comes out as a bisexual rather than homosexual. One 20-year-old woman recounted telling her parents: "at first I told them I was bisexual because I thought that they'd be more accepting, but in reality I was just trying to ease them into it" (2014, p.51).

Coming out is not a one-time event, but rather a recurring process as people's social circles and acquaintances change over time. Lesbian psychology professor, Suzanne Johnson, has described the process as a revolving closet door. "I constantly rotate through varying degrees of revelation and exposure," she writes. "It's like having a continuously moving revolving door on a closet . . . It's always moving, it's never closed" (2008, p.66).

CONTEMPORARY RESPONSES TO LGBTQ ISSUES

Historically homosexuality has been treated in the United States as a crime, a sin, and an illness. Today, homosexuality and other LGBTQ categories are much more commonly viewed as acceptable behaviors and identities, albeit ones that still are perceived as deviant and stigmatized by significant sections of the US population. But while the postcloset culture of LGBTQ acceptance is uneven across the United States today, major changes over the past two decades have made it possible to live, as Jane Ward puts it, *respectably queer.* By this Ward means that LGBTQ individuals have opportunities to live openly as accepted community members, with the rights that other law abiding citizens have. But the cultural and legal challenges over LGBTQ citizenship rights remain lively and in certain arenas, tense and unresolved.

The right of LGBTQ individuals to marry and have children has been an intense arena of legal conflict in recent years. Three issues in particular have played major roles in pushing LGBTQ family rights. First, changes in sodomy laws opened the way for recognition of long-term active same-sex relationships that had previously been criminalized. Second, the AIDS epidemic pushed many gay partners to seek legal protection for caregiving decisions and inheritance rights. And third, as lesbians and gays came out of the closet in increasing numbers in the 1980s and 1990s, same-sex (especially lesbian) families became more common. Family law emerged as an important issue for lesbians who faced potential loss of their children because of their sexual orientation (Richman 2010, p.24).

Family law is one of the most discretionary areas of American jurisprudence, with judges often able to make custody and adoption decisions based on their personal beliefs about what is in the "best interest of the child" (Richman 2010, p.3). There has been wide inconsistency from one judge to another, and one state or geographic region to another, in how laws have been applied and court decisions made. Until recently—and still in some parts of the United States—the mere presence of a homosexual parent has been considered by judges to be a threat *per se* to children's well-being" (Richman 2010. p.8). The US Supreme Court's 2015 ruling to support gay marriage rights marks a major institutionalization of broader citizenship rights for members of the LGBTQ community.

Other laws have been enacted at federal and state levels to protect and support LGBTQ individuals in the workplace and in public. Antidiscrimination policies including federal legislation and laws in 20 states are designed to protect LGBTQ individuals from employment discrimination. In 2009, the federal government also expanded hate crime legislation to include violent acts committed against a person based on their perceived sexual orientation or gender identity. Today, 30 states also include sexual orientation in their hate crime laws, although only 17 include gender identity.

The broad movement toward expanded rights and recognition for LGBTQ individuals has also played out over the last 30 years in the debate over the rights of homosexuals to serve in the military. From the Revolutionary War until the early 1990s the military had restrictions banning military service by homosexuals, although little was done to enforce such restrictions during times of man (and woman) power shortages. The compromise policy of "DADT" prohibited military personnel from harassing closeted homosexual or bisexual personnel, but barred openly LGBTQ persons from military service. For 17 years, "DADT" was the official policy of the US military. Between 1993 and 2010, however, public attitudes and those of top military leaders toward LGBTQ individuals shifted dramatically, leading to sufficient public and political support for the repeal of DADT. Today, open lesbians, gays, and bisexuals are eligible for military service, and plans have been made to repeal the military's restrictions on service by transgendered individuals (Brydum 2015). In May 2016, Eric Fanning, an openly gay man, was confirmed by Congress to serve as Secretary of the US Army.

While public attitudes and federal laws have shifted toward recognizing LGBTQ rights to full citizenship, many of the largest US religious institutions have remained opposed to same-sex behaviors and relationships. The Roman Catholic Church, the Church of Jesus Christ of Latter-Day Saints, the National Baptist Convention (the largest historically black church), and evangelical

Pentecostal denominations like the Assemblies of God—as well as various Islamic religious groups—consider homosexual acts sinful and prohibit their clergy from marrying same-sex couples. Yet, other religious denominations, including the Episcopal Church, the Society of Friends (Quakers), the Presbyterian Church, and the United Church of Christ accept same-sex relationships, including marriage.

Religious institutions opposed to gay sexuality and relationships confront challenging familial issues beyond that of gay marriage. One such challenge involves how the church acknowledges and deals with same-sex attraction. Some religious groups, such as Jehovah's Witness, take the position that any same-sex feelings or attraction are evil and warrant banishment from the church (Lalich and McLaren 2010). Other religious faiths have come to acknowledge that same-sex attraction is a reality for some individuals. The Church of Jesus Christ of Latter-Day Saints (the LDS Church) makes its position clear on its official website:

> The experience of same-sex attraction is a complex reality for many people. The attraction itself is not a sin, but acting on it is.
>
> —Church of Jesus Christ of Latter-Day Saints (2016).

A second challenge for churches is how to deal with the children of same-sex families. The LDS Church received high-profile attention, and garnered considerable criticism even from within its ranks, when its leaders decided to bar children living with same-sex couples from church affiliation and baptism (Goodstein 2015).

Social responses to LGBTQ issues in the United States will undoubtedly continue to change in the coming years. If the current trajectory lasts, we will see the increasing normalization of LGBTQ identities and behaviors in the years ahead.

STIGMA MANAGEMENT AND RESISTANCE

The ways in which people who engage in same-sex erotic activities and/or embrace LGBTQ identities respond to stigma depend in large part on their personal experiences and social relationships. A significant number of American adults, perhaps especially men like the "tearoom trade" studied by Laud Humphreys (1970) and men "on the down low" reported by J. L. King (2004), hide their involvement in same-sex activities from virtually everyone except their largely anonymous same-sex partners. For LGBTQ individuals who move beyond secretive anonymous sexual liaisons, in-group social life with others who share their sexual orientations serves a vital role in providing social support and countering stigmatization. In the United States today, opportunities for LGBTQ social life are richer than ever in the past with a variety of subcultural face-to-face and online venues in which different subgroups of gays (from gym-toned youth to middle-aged bears) and lesbians (from upper-middle-class "Abercrombie lesbians" to black Christian lesbians) may find opportunities for social connections and support.

The most notable feature of stigma management among LGBTQ individuals over the last half century has been the shift to extensive collective action for LGBTQ rights and protection and efforts to build alliances with members of the straight community.

The first US gay and lesbian rights groups, the Mattachine Society and the Daughters of Bilitis, were explicitly assimilationist in their efforts to present gay men and lesbian women as the same as other Americans except for their sexual orientation. Some LGBTQ advocates, including many who consider themselves activists, have taken a more radical approach, arguing that "queer activism" must challenge the basic structure of heterosexual society. Most LGBTQ activism today, however, takes an assimilationist, "us and them" rather than an "us versus them" approach, emphasizing similarities between LGBTQ and straight citizens and seeking to building alliances.

Groups within the LGBTQ community have created strong alliances with non-LGBTQ individuals and groups beginning in the 1970s with the creation of Parents and Friends of Lesbians and Gays (PFLAG). PFLAG grew out of a few parents participation a gay liberation parade in New York City in 1972. The original logo of the organization, "I refuse to be a closet parent," connected familial support with the LGBTQ cause. As support grew, the organization drew in other family members and branched out to "friends" as well, building an extensive network that today includes over 400 chapters and 200,000 members across all 50 states. PFLAG describes its purpose as helping to create "a society in which all lesbian, gay, bisexual and transgender persons may . . . participate fully in all the rights, privileges and obligations of full citizenship in this country" (PFLAG 2016).

College campus LGBTQ Allies and Safe Zone programs have also developed across the country, building supportive communities of students, faculty, and staff. These programs provide a wide variety of educational and outreach activities to foster LGBTQ acceptance as well as physical and social security for LGBTQ youth. Still, there continue to be significant struggles for many LGBTQ youth who experience feelings of difference and social isolation. Many studies suggest that gay-identified and "questioning" adolescents experience far higher rates of depression and attempted suicide (e.g., Russell and Joyner 2001). But in many parts of the country LGBTQ youth and young adults have significantly more social support today than in the past. Curricula on LGBTQ sensitivity training are available in college teacher curricula and educational media. Thousands of high schools and middle schools across the country sponsor Gay Straight Alliance programs to promote social inclusiveness and understanding and the media regularly cover news stories about lesbian and gay couples at

CLAIMS-MAKER PROFILE

Jeanne Manford and PFLAG

"I have a homosexual son and I love him." Those words were written by Jeanne Manford in a letter to the editor of the *New York Post* in April 1972. A week earlier, she and her husband Jules got a call from a New York City hospital telling them that their gay activist son, Morty, had been beaten while distributing flyers at a political gathering. At that time homosexuality was illegal in much of the United States and designated as a mental disorder by the American Psychiatric Association. Nonetheless, Manford followed up her letter with radio and television interviews and marching in the 1972 New York Pride March, where she carried a sign that read, "Parents of Gays Unite in Support for Our Children."

"The young people were hugging me, kissing me, screaming, asking if I would talk to their parents," she later recalled, adding that "few were out to their parents for fear of rejection" (Trounson 2013).

Soon after the march, Jeanne Manford and her husband, Jules, began holding meetings for a group they called "Parents of Gays" at a local Methodist church. Over the next several years similar groups were created around the country, consolidating into Parents, Families, and Friends of Lesbians and Gays in 1980. Today that group, known as PFLAG, has chapters across the United States and provides opportunities for straight parents, family, and friends to support LGBTQ rights.

In 2013, President Obama awarded Jeanne Manford posthumously with the 2012 Presidential Citizens Medal for her work in cofounding PFLAG and her years of LGBTQ advocacy. Jeanne's gay son, Morty, went on to become assistant New York State attorney general before dying of AIDS in 1992 at the age of 41.

high school proms. These progressive changes have by no means eliminated LGBTQ stigma in adolescence. A homophobic peer culture continues to exist in many, if not most, American high schools (Pascoe 2007). But many high schools provide much greater social support than was the case for LGBTQ youth just a decade ago.

On college campuses many social science and humanities instructors ask LGBTQ student panels to speak in their classes. The students who participate on the panels share their personal stories as a form of social activism (Polletta 1998). In their efforts to build bridges between straight and LGBTQ students, panels typically highlight aspects of their LGBTQ experiences that are likely to find acceptance and understanding from straight students, such as emphasizing nonsexual aspects of LGBTQ identity and experiences and highlighting committed long-term relationships (Crawley and Broad 2004).

As the LGBTQ movement has grown, concerted collective action has become a major challenge because of the diversity of experiences and concerns across the LGBTQ population. While the challenge of diversity has at times led to splintering of the movement, it has also been a major strength because the movement has never had the opportunity to become static and formulaic. In his history of national gay rights marches Ghaziani describes the challenging but productive conflicts that national organizers have faced in drawing large LGBTQ crowds under a common umbrella. While the first national march in 1979 emphasized social commonality and assimilation under the banner, "we are everywhere," the second national march in 1987 was focused explicitly on gay people, especially gay men as a unique and threatened social group in the midst of a governmentally ignored AIDS epidemic. Over time the national gay rights marches have also broadened to explicitly include lesbians (in 1987), bisexuals (in 1993), and transgendered individuals and groups in the 2009 "National Equality March."

While the assimilationist goals of equal rights for LGBTQ individuals remain the most visible and pervasive social agenda related to LGBTQ issues today, liberationists voice concern for more fundamental changes, such as moving away from privileging the nuclear family and embracing broader issues of racial, economic, and gender equality. These broader social justice issues were captured in focus of the 2016 San Francisco Pride March which was subtitled "For Economic and Racial Justice" in a conscious effort to emphasize broader issues of social inequality in the march (SF Pride 2016).

From the liberationist perspective, gaining rights within an unjust society can only be one step. The long-term goal must be the creation of a society that embraces diversity and social justice. Liberationists go on to argue that our society would benefit from recognizing and valuing the very differences that those under the LGBTQ umbrella can bring to reimagining how we organize and experience social life. It is not enough, argue LGBTQ liberationist scholars like Suzanna Danuta Walters, to promote tolerance for lesbians and gays who were "born that way" and deserve rights to live like the rest of us. "Couldn't we imagine a stronger case," she writes:

> Shouldn't we argue, instead, that our progeny would/could grow up with more expansive and creative ways of living gender and sexuality? Shouldn't we argue that same-sex marriage might make us all think differently about the relation between domestic life and gender norms and push heterosexuals to examine their stubborn commitment to a gendered division of labor?
>
> —Walters (2014b)

At this point, LGBTQ advocates embrace the role of moral entrepreneurs themselves, critiquing contemporary heteronormative society and proposing that not only tolerating, but actually valuing, LGBTQ identities and experiences has the potential to enrich all of our lives.

BLURRED BOUNDARIES II: "GAY" OR "STRAIGHT"?

In an effort to examine how imputations of sexual identity are different for males and females, LGBTQ ethnographer Jane Ward presents students with a variety of situations and asks them to say whether the act implies that participants are "gay" or "straight." In this project, take Ward's classroom exercise to three males and three females, asking them to say whether they would identify the person involved as "gay" or "straight." Do not offer the option of choosing another response, but make a note when any of your informants hesitates or expresses uncertainty about whether the "gay" and "straight" categories fit a scenario.

1. Straight-identified college women who kiss each other at a party while men cheer them?
2. Straight-identified college men who kiss each other at a party while women cheer them?
3. Young boys who touch each other's penises while playing?
4. Men who have sex with men in prison but not when on the outside?
5. Two women who have lived together for 30 years and sleep in the same bed but do not identify as lesbians?
6. Two men who have lived together for 30 years and sleep in the same bed but do not identify as gay?
7. A young woman who has sex with two women in college, and then marries a man after she graduates?
8. A young man who, while being hazed in a fraternity, strips naked and puts his finger in other guys' anuses?

Make a chart for the responses you collect. Looking at the chart, how consistent or divided are the responses of those you survey on each scenario? Are there differences in responses based on whether similar questions are asked about a male or a female? Are there differences based on whether your respondents are male or female? How do your findings compare with those of other students in your class? What do the patterns shown in your charts suggest regarding how Americans classify female and male sexual orientations? Is there a gendered double standard? If so, what does it appear to be?

SUMMARY

- LGBTQ is an acronym for lesbians, gays, bisexuals, transgender, and gender/sexuality questioning individuals.
- Researchers confront difficulties in identifying the LGBTQ population. More respondents identify as LGBT in gay friendly communities and in anonymous online surveys.

- Some recent studies estimate that there are around eight million Americans who identify as gay, lesbian, or bisexual, and nearly 700,000 who identify as transgender. Many more people report some same-sex sexual experiences or attraction.
- Same-sex romance and sexuality have been common throughout history, although seldom viewed through the heterosexual/homosexual lens that we use today.
- When homosexuality has been singled out as deviant, it has been viewed as caused by sinful temptation, poor parenting, or abnormal biology.
- Social responses to deviant homosexuality have ranged from unofficial toleration to periodic crackdowns and the use of various psychiatric and medical treatments to cure homosexual urges.
- Little is openly recorded about early LGBTQ history in the United States.
- By the late 1800s, homosexual subculture emerged in many large urban centers, but it was eroded by tightening social control of gay sexuality in the early 1900s.
- World War II thrust millions of young men together in contexts in which many embraced same-sex erotic opportunities.
- After the war, the US government banned homosexuals from government service.
- The first gay and lesbian organizations in the United States emerged in response to Cold War hostility and police harassment of gays and lesbians.
- The APA declassified homosexuality as mental illnesses in 1973.
- Since the 1970s American attitudes toward LGBTQ people and issues have grown increasingly positive, but with periodic backlash campaigns against gay rights.
- In the 1980s, the AIDS epidemic devastated the gay male community and brought confrontational protests as the government dragged its feet in response to the needs of AIDS victims.
- In the 1990s, the federal government and several states enacted laws to prohibit same-sex marriage. In 2015, the US Supreme Court ruled that same-sex marriage is a legal right across the United States.
- Identifying as gay or lesbian typically emerges as a process of discovery in adolescence.
- The coming out process involves accepting and revealing one's same-sex attractions and sexual identity.
- Many of the largest US religions have remained opposed to same-sex behaviors and relationships.
- The LGBTQ community engages in extensive collective action to advocate for gay rights and to build alliances with members of the straight community.

KEYWORDS

assimilationist: An advocacy approach to LGBTQ rights that emphasizes pursuing equal rights for LGBTQ individuals as citizens, but not for broader social change.
gay bear culture: A gay subculture that is focused on larger, hairier men with an image of rugged masculinity and other men who are attracted to them.
coming out: The act of publicly revealing one's homosexual feelings and identity.
Defense of Marriage Act (DOMA): A federal law passed in 1996 that officially defined marriage as legal only for heterosexual couples. Ruled unconstitutional by the US Supreme Court in 2013.
heteroflexible: A term describing individuals who consider themselves straight but open to occasional same-sex eroticism.
heteronormativity: Attitudes and practices based on the assumption that heterosexuality is the normal and natural state of human sexuality.
liberationist: An advocacy approach to LGBTQ rights that emphasizes broad social change, including expansion of family rights beyond the nuclear family, increased support of gender diversity, and legal and social reform.
post-gay era: A term used by LGBTQ scholars to refer to the current era in LGBTQ history in the United States, purportedly characterized by broad acceptance of LGBTQ individuals as a nonstigmatized citizens.
queer apologetic: A claim of bisexuality made by a homosexual individual to lessen the stigma of being potentially identified as a homosexual.
respectably queer: A social status of being LGBTQ-identified while fitting into normative expectations of social respectability in the post-gay era.
sodomy: A catch-all term used to describe various kinds of nonprocreative heterosexual and homosexual acts, especially anal sex.
transgender: An umbrella term used to describe individuals who experience a subjective feeling of being a different gender from what they were assigned at birth.

References

Abbott, Karen. 2007. *Sin in the Second City*. New York: Random House.

Abrahamsen, David. 1960. *The Psychology of Crime*. New York: John Wiley.

Adams, Tony F. 2011. *Narrating the Closet: An Autoethnography of Same-Sex Attraction*. Walnut Creek, CA: Left Coast Press.

Adler, Patricia A. 1993. *Wheeling and Dealing: An Ethnography of an Upper-Level Drug Dealing and Smuggling Community*. 2nd ed. New York: Columbia University Press.

Adler, Patricia A., and Peter Adler. 1978. "Tiny-Dopers: A Case of Deviant Socialization." *Symbolic Interaction* 1: 90–105.

———. 2006. "The Deviance Society." *Deviant Behavior* 27: 129–148.

Agar, Michael. 1973. *Ripping and Running: A Formal Ethnography of Urban Heroin Addicts*. New York: Seminar.

Agnew, Robert. 2001. "Building on the Foundation of General Strain Theory: Specifying the Types of Strain Most Likely to Lead to Crime and Delinquency." *Journal of Research on Crime and Delinquency* 38: 319–361.

Akers, Ronald L. 1985. *Deviant Behavior: A Social Learning Approach*. 3rd ed. Belmont, CA: Wadsworth.

———. 1992. *Drugs, Alcohol, and Society: Social Structure, Process, and Policy*. Belmont, CA: Wadsworth Publishing.

———. 1998. *Social Learning and Social Structure: A General Theory of Crime and Deviance*. Boston: Northeastern University Press.

Alcoholics Anonymous. 2016a. "What is A.A.?" Accessed on August 8, 2016 at http://www.aa.org/pages/en_US/what-is-aa

———. 2016b. "Estimates of A.A. Groups and Members as of January 1, 2016." Accessed on August 4, 2016 at http://www.aa.org/assets/en_US/smf-53_en.pdf

Alimahomed, Sabrina. 2010. "Thinking Outside the Rainbow: Women of Color Redefining Queer Politics and Identity." *Social Identities* 16: 151–168.

Altheide, David L. 2014. *Media Edge: Media Logic and Social Reality*. New York: Peter Lang Publishing.

Altman, Lawrence K. 1990. "Scientists See Link between Alcoholism and a Specific Gene." *New York Times*. April 18: A1.

Americans for Legal Immigration. 2014. "Drugs, Crimes, and Gangs Immigrating to America!" Accessed on September 6, 2015 at http://www.alipac.us/modules.php?name=News&file=print&sid=611

American Society for Aesthetic Plastic Surgery. 2017. "Quick Facts: Highlights of the 2016 Stats." Accessed on April 6, 2017 at http://www.surgery.org/sites/default/files/2016-quick-facts.pdf

Anderson, Eric. 2008. "'Being Masculine is not about Who You Sleep with. . .:' Heterosexual Athletes Contesting Masculinity and the One-time Rule of Homosexuality." *Sex Roles* 58: 104–115.

Anderson, Leon. 2006. "Analytic Autoethnography." *Journal of Contemporary Ethnography* 35: 373–395.

Anderson, Tammy L., and Lynn Bondi. 1998. "Exiting the Drug-Addict Role: Variations by Race and Gender." *Symbolic Interaction* 21: 155–174.

Anderson, Thomas. 1988. *Politics in Central America: Guatemala, El Salvador, Honduras, and Nicaragua*. Westport, CT: Praeger Publishing.

Aneshensel, Carol S. 1999. "Mental Illness as a Career." Pp. 585–603 in *Handbook of the Sociology of Mental Health*, edited by Carol S. Aneshensel and Jo C. Phelan. New York: KluwerAcademic/Plenum Publisher.

Anon, Kofi. 2016. "Why It's Time to Legalize Drugs." *Huffington Post*. February 23. Accessed on July 27, 2016 at http://www.huffingtonpost.com/kofi-annan/why-its-time-to-legalize-drugs_b_9298502.html

APA (American Psychiatric Association). 2013. *Diagnostic and Statistical Manual of Mental Disorders-5*. Washington, DC: American Psychiatric Association.

Armstrong, Elizabeth A., Laura Hamilton, and Brian Sweeney. 2006. "Sexual Assault on Campus: A Multilevel, Integrative Approach to Party Rape." *Social Problems* 53: 483–499.

ASMBS (American Society for Metabolic and Bariatric Surgery). 2014. "New Procedure Estimates for Bariatric Surgery." Accessed on June 13, 2015 at http://connect.asmbs.org/may-2014-bariatric-surgery-growth.html

Association of Club Executives. 2014. Accessed on October 18, 2014 at http://aceofnewyork.org

Athens, Lonnie H. 2005. "Violent Encounters: Violent Engagements, Skirmishes, and Tiffs." *Journal of Contemporary Ethnography* 34: 631–678.

Atkinson, Michael. 2011. "Male Athletes and the Cult(ure) of Thinness in Sports." *Deviant Behavior* 32: 224–256.

Atkinson, Paul. 1997. "Narrative Turn or Blind Alley?" *Qualitative Health Research* 7: 325–344.

Auguet, Roland. 1994. *Cruelty and Civilization: The Roman Games*. New York: Routledge.

Avorn, Jerry. 2005. *Powerful Medicines: The Benefits, Risks, and Costs of Prescription Drugs*. New York: Alfred A. Knopf.

Babor, Thomas. 1986. *Alcohol: Customs and Rituals*. New York: Chelsea House Publishers.

Back, A. L., J. I. Wallace, H. E. Stark, and R. A. Pearlman. 1996. "Physician-assisted Suicide and Euthanasia in Washington State. Patient Requests and Physician Responses." *Journal of the American Medical Association* 245: 919–925.

Bacon, Linda. 2008. *Healthy at Every Size*. Dallas, TX: BenBella Books.

Baron, Beth. 2006. "Women, Honour, and the State: Evidence from Egypt." *Middle Eastern Studies* 42: 1–20.

Barshis, Victoria R. Garnier. 1983. "The Question of Marital Rape." *Women's Studies International Forum* 6: 383–393.

Bartlett, Jamie. 2015. *The Dark Net: Inside the Digital Underworld.* London: Melville House.
Barton, Bernadette. 2006. *Stripped.* New York: New York University Press.
Baumohl, Jim. 1992. "The 'Dope Fiend's Paradise' Revisited: Notes from Research in Progress on Drug Law Enforcement in San Francisco, 1875–1915." *Drinking and Drug Practices Surveyor* 24: 3–12.
Bazos, Audrey, and Jessica Hausman. 2004. "Correctional Education as a Crime Control Program." Los Angeles: UCLA School of Public Policy and Social Research.
Beatty, Phillip, Amanda Petteruti, and Jason Ziedenberg. 2007. *The Vortex: The Concentrated Racial Impact of Drug Imprisonment and the Characteristics of Punitive Counties.* Washington, DC: Justice Policy Institute.
Beccaria, Cesare. 1963 [1764]. *On Crimes and Punishment.* Indianapolis, IN: Bobbs-Merrill.
Becker, Howard. 1953. "Becoming a Marijuana User." *American Journal of Sociology* 59: 235–242.
———. 1963. *Outsiders: Studies in the Sociology of Deviance.* London: Free Press of Glencoe.
Beeghley, Leonard. 2003. *Homicide: A Sociological Explanation.* New York: Rowman and Littlefield.
Beier, A. L. 1985. *Masterless Men: The Vagrancy Problem in England, 1560–1640.* London: Methuen.
Benedict, Ruth. 1934. "Anthropology and the Abnormal." *Journal of General Psychology* 10: 59–80.
Benham, Barbara. 2016. "Experts Urge Decriminalization of Minor Drug Offenses." *Johns Hopkins Magazine* March 24. Accessed on July 27, 2016 at http://hub.jhu.edu/2016/03/24/war-on-drugs-undercuts-public-health/
Benford, Robert D., and David A. Snow. 2000. "Framing Processes and Social Movements: An Overview and Assessment." *Annual Review of Sociology* 26: 611–639.
Benson, Michael L. 1985. "Denying the Guilty Mind: Accounting for an Involvement in White Collar Crime." *Criminology* 23: 589–599.
Benson, Michael L., and Sally S. Simpson. 2015. *White-collar Crime: An Opportunity Perspective.* 2nd ed. New York: Routledge.
Bentham, Jeremy. 1948 [1780]. *The Principles of Morals and Legislation.* New York: Hefner.
Berkowitz, Eric. 2012. *Sex and Punishment: Four Thousand Years of Judging Desire.* Berkeley, CA: Publishers Group West.
Bernstein, Elizabeth. 2007. *Temporarily Yours: Intimacy, Authenticity, and the Commerce of Sex.* Chicago: University of Chicago Press.
Bérubé, Allan. 1991. *Coming Out Under Fire: The History of Gay Men and Women in World War Two.* New York: Plume.
Besom, Thomas. 2013. *Inka Human Sacrifice and Mountain Worship.* Albuquerque: University of New Mexico Press.
Best, Joel. 1987. "Rhetoric in Claims-Making." *Social Problems* 34: 101–121.
———. 1995. "Typification and Social Problems Construction." Pp. 1–16 in *Images of Issues: Typifying Contemporary Social Problems.* 2nd ed. edited by Joel Best. New York: Aldine de Gruyter.
———. 2004. *More Damned Lies and Statistics: How Numbers Confuse Public Issues.* Berkeley: University of California Press.
Best, Joel, and David F. Luckenbill. 1994. *Organizing Deviance.* 2nd ed. Englewood Cliffs, NJ: Prentice Hall.
Bhanoo, Sindya N. 2009. "Study Suggests BMI Scale is Weighted against African Americans." *The Washington Post.* April 14. Accessed on June 5, 2015 at http://www.washingtonpost.com/wp-dyn/content/article/2009/04/13/AR2009041301823.html
Bialik, Carl. 2013. "Island Where Obesity May Not be All It Seems." *Wall Street Journal.* April 12. Accessed on June 5, 2015 at http://www.wsj.com/articles/SB10001424127887324695104578417043182612254
Black, William K. 2005. *The Best Way to Rob a Bank is to Own One: How Corporate Executives and Politicians Looted the S&L Industry.* Austin: University of Texas Press.
Blakely, Edward, and Mary Gail Snyder. 1997. *Fortress America: Gated Communities in the United States.* Washington, DC: Brookings Institution Press.
Body-*for*-LIFE. 2015. Accessed on March 11, 2016 at http://bodyforlife.com/
Boeri, Miriam William. 2013. *Women on Ice: Methamphetamine Use among Suburban Women.* New Brunswick, NJ: Rutgers University Press.
Boeri, Miriam William, Claire E. Sterk, and Kirk W. Elifson. 2006. "Baby Boomer Drug Users: Career Phases, Identity, Self-Concept, and Social Control." *Sociological Inquiry* 76: 265–291.
Boskind-White, Marlene. 2000. *Bulimia/Anorexia: The Binge/Purge Cycle and Self-Starvation.* New York: W. W. Norton.
Boswell, A. Ayres and Joan Z. Spade. 1996. "Fraternities and Collegiate Rape Culture: Why Are Some Fraternities More Dangerous Places for Women?" *Gender and Society* 10: 133–147.
Bourgois, Philippe. 1989. "Just Another Night on Crack Street." *New York Times Magazine.* November 12. 52–53, 60–65.
———. 1995. *In Search of Respect: Selling Crack in El Barrio.* New York: Cambridge University Press.
Bourgois, Philippe, and Jeff Schonberg. 2009. *Righteous Dopefiend.* Berkley, CA: University of California Press.
Bradley, Mindy S. 2007. "Girlfriends, Wives, and Strippers: Managing Stigma in Exotic Dancer Romantic Relationships." *Deviant Behavior* 28: 379–406.
Bradley-Engen, Mindy S. 2009. *Naked Lives: Inside the Worlds of Exotic Dance.* Albany, New York: SUNY Press.
Brady Campaign. 2016. "About Brady." Accessed on March 10, 2016 at http://www.bradycampaign.org/about-brady
Braithwaite, John. 1985. "White Collar Crime." *Annual Review of Sociology* 11: 1–21.
Brandt, Allen M. 2007. *The Cigarette Century: The Rise, Fall, and Deadly Persistence of the Product that Defined America.* New York: Basic Books.
Brents, Barbara G., Crystal A. Jackson, and Kathryn Hausbeck. 2010. *The State of Sex: Tourism, Sex, and Sin in the New American Heartland.* New York: Routledge.
Broadhead, Robert S., and Kathryn J. Fox. 1990. "Takin' It to the Streets: AIDS Outreach as Ethnography." *Journal of Contemporary Ethnography* 19: 322–348.
Bromley, David G., Anson D. Shupe, and Joseph C. Ventimiglia. 1979. "Atrocity Tales, the Unification Church, and the Social Construction of Evil." *Journal of Communication* 29: 42–53.
Bronski, Michael. 2011. *A Queer History of the United States.* Boston: Beacon Press.
Brown, Sonya C. 2014. "Big Losers: The Rhetorical Vision of the Weight Loss Narrative." *Journal of Popular Culture* 47: 64–83.
Bruch, Hilda. 1973. *Eating Disorders: Obesity, Anorexia Nervosa, and the Person Within.* New York: Basic Books.
Brumberg, Joan Jacobs. 2000. *Fasting Girls: The History of Anorexia Nervosa.* New York: Vintage Books.
Bryant, Howard. 2005. *Juicing the Game: Drugs, Power, and the Fight for the Soul of Major League Baseball.* New York: Viking.

Brydum, Sunnivie. 2015. "U.S. Military's Transgender Ban Begins to Fall Monday." *Advocate*. July 30. Accessed on February 13, 2016 at http://www.advocate.com/transgender/2015/07/30/us-militarys-transgender-ban-begins-fall-monday

Bureau of Justice Statistics. 1999. "Mental Health and Treatment of Inmates and Probationers." Washington, DC: U.S. Department of Justice.

———. 2006. "Mental Health Problems of Prison and Jail Inmates." Washington, DC: U.S. Department of Justice.

———. 2014a. "Survey of Sexual Violence in Adult Correctional Facilities 2009–11." Accessed on August 12, 2016 at http://www.bjs.gov/content/pub/pdf/ssvacf0911st.pdf

———. 2014b. *Criminal Victimization in the United States, 2013 Statistical Tables*. Accessed on August 12, 2016 at http://www.bjs.gov/content/pub/pdf/cv14.pdf

———. 2016a. "Female Victims of Sexual Violence, 1994–2010." Accessed on August 12, 2016 at http://www.bjs.gov/content/pub/pdf/fvsv9410.pdf

———. 2016b. "Total Correctional Populations." Accessed on August 14, 2016 at http://www.bjs.gov/index.cfm?ty=kfdetail&iid=487

Bureau of Prisons. 2014. "Offenses." Accessed on June 17, 2014 at http://www.bop.gov/about/statistics/statistics_inmate_offenses.jsp

Burgess, Robert, and Ronald L. Akers. 1966. "A Differential Association-Reinforcement Theory of Criminal Behavior." *Social Problems* 14: 128–147.

Burkett, Eleanor, and Frank Bruni. 1993. *Gospel of Shame: Children, Sexual Abuse, and the Catholic Church*. New York: Viking.

Burns, Ronald G., Michael J. Lynch, and Paul Stretesky. 2008. *Environmental Law, Crime, and Justice*. New York: LFB Publishing.

Caetano, Raul. 1987. "Public Opinion about Alcoholism and Its Treatment." *Journal of Studies on Alcohol* 48: 153–160.

Calavita, Kitty, Henry N. Pontell, and Robert Tillman. 1997. *Big Money Crime: Fraud and Politics in the Savings and Loan Crisis*. Berkeley: University of California Press.

Cameron, Mary Owen. 1964. *The Booster and the Snitch: Department Store Shoplifting*. New York: Free Press.

Campbell, Rebecca. 2002. *Emotionally Involved: The Impact of Researching Rape*. New York: Routledge.

Canaday, Margot. 2009. *The Straight State: Sexuality and Citizenship in Twentieth-Century America*. Princeton, NJ: Princeton University Press.

Carbone-Lopez, Kristin, Jennifer Gatewood Owens, and Jody Miller. 2012. "Women's 'Storylines' of Methamphetamine Initiation in the Midwest." *Journal of Drug Issues* 42: 226–246.

Carrier, J. M. 1976. "Family Attitudes and Mexican Male Homosexuality." *Urban Life* 5: 359–375.

Catalano, Shannan, Erica Smith, Howard Snyder, and Michael Rand. 2009. "Female Victims of Violence." Washington, DC: Bureau of Justice Statistics.

Cavan, Sherri. 1966. *Liquor License: An Ethnography of Bar Behavior*. Chicago: Aldine.

CDC. 2014a. "Smoking and Tobacco Use Fact Sheet." Accessed on March 12, 2014 at http://www.cdc.gov/tobacco/data_statistics/fact_sheets/fast_facts/index.htm#use

———. 2014b. "Tobacco-Related Mortality." Accessed on May 16, 2014 at http://www.cdc.gov/tobacco/data_statistics/fact_sheets/health_effects/tobacco_related_mortality/

———. 2015. "Finding a Balance." Accessed on July 3, 2015 at http://www.cdc.gov/healthyweight/calories/

———. 2016a. "Impaired Driving: Get the Facts." Accessed on August 7, 2016 at http://www.cdc.gov/motorvehiclesafety/impaired_driving/impaired-drv_factsheet.html

———. 2016b. "Adult Obesity: Causes and Consequences." Accessed on September 20, 2016 at https://www.cdc.gov/obesity/adult/causes.html

Chamberlin, Judi. 1978. *On our Own: Patient-Controlled Alternatives to the Mental Health System*. New York: Hawthorn Books.

Chambliss, William. 1973. "The Saints and the Roughnecks." *Society* 11: 24–31.

Chapkis, Wendy. 1997. *Live Sex Acts*. New York: Routledge.

Chatham-Carpenter, A. 2010. "'Do Thyself No Harm': Protecting Ourselves as Autoethnographers." *Journal of Research Practice* 6. Accessed on December 30, 2011 at http://jrp.icaap.org/index.php/jrp/article/view/213/183

Chauncey, George. 1994. *Gay New York: Gender, Urban Culture, and the Making of the Gay Male World, 1890–1940*. New York: Basic Books.

Chernow, Ron. 1998. *Titan: The Life of John D. Rockefeller, Sr.* New York: Random House.

Chicago Tribune. 1986. "A $100 Million Idea: Use Greed for Good." Accessed on November 24, 2013 at http://articles.chicagotribune.com/1986-12-15/features/8604030634_1_ivan-boeskys-greed-fund

Chin, Gabriel J. 2002. "Race, the War on Drugs, and the Collateral Consequences of Criminal Conviction." *Journal of Gender, Race, and Justice* 6: 253–265.

Chitwood, Dale D., Sheigla Murphy, and Marsha Rosenbaum. 2009. "Reflections on the Meaning of Drug Epidemics." *Journal of Drug Issues* 39: 29–39.

Chrisler, Joan C. 2012. "'Why Can't You Control Yourself?' Fat Should Be a Feminist Issue" *Sex Roles* 66: 608–616.

Church of Jesus Christ of Latter-Day Saints. 2016. "Same Sex Attraction." Accessed on February 13, 2016 at https://www.lds.org/topics/same-gender-attraction?lang=eng

Clinard, Marshall B., and Robert F. Meier. 2008. *Sociology of Deviant Behavior*. 13th ed. Belmont, CA: Thomson/Wadsworth.

Cloward, Richard, and Lloyd E. Ohlin. 1960. *Delinquency and Opportunity: A Theory of Juvenile Gangs*. New York: Free Press.

CNN. 2007. "Heart Disease Often Misdiagnosed in Women." February 7. Accessed at www.cnn.com/2007/HEALTH/02/01/heart.women/index.html

Cocca, Carolyn. 2004. *Jailbait: The Politics of Statutory Rape Laws in the United States*. Albany, New York: SUNY Press.

Cockerham, William C. 2013. *Sociology of Mental Disorder*. 9th ed. New York: Routledge.

Coffee, John C. 2006. *Gatekeepers: The Professions and Corporate Governance*. New York: Oxford University Press.

Coffey, Amanda. 1999. *The Ethnographic Self*. London: Sage.

Cohen, Stanley. 1973. *Folk Devils and Moral Panics: The Creation of the Mods and Rockers*. London: Paladin.

Coleman, James W. 2006. *The Criminal Elite: The Sociology of White Collar Crime*. 6th ed. New York: Worth Publishers.

Collinson, Patrick. 1967. *The Elizabethan Puritan Movement*. Berkeley: University of California Press.

Colvin, Mark. 1997. *Penitentiaries, Reformatories, and Chain Gangs*. New York: St. Martin's Press.

Conrad, Peter, and Joseph W. Schneider. 1992. *Deviance and Medicalization: From Badness to Sickness*. Expanded ed. Philadelphia, PA: Temple University Press.

Conroy, John. 2006. "The Electronic Pillory." *Chicago Reader*. April 6. Accessed on April 6, 2017 at: http://www

.chicagoreader.com/chicago/the-electronic-pillory/Content?oid=921777
Cook, Philip J. 2007. *Paying the Tab: The Economics of Alcohol Policy*. Princeton: Princeton University Press.
Cook, Philip J. and Kristin A. Goss. 2014. *The Gun Debate: What Everyone Needs to Know*. New York: Oxford University Press.
Cooke, Robert. 1990. "Now You See 'Em, Now You Don't: Scientists Trying to Identify Single Genes among the 100,000 in Human Chromosomes Often Seem to Have One Cornered, Then Lose It." *Newsday* 6.
Cooley, Charles Horton. 1902. *Human Nature and the Social Order*. New York: Charles Scribner's.
Cooper, Alexia, and Erica L. Smith. 2011. "Homicide Trends in the United States, 1980–2008." Washington, DC: U.S. Department of Justice.
Copes, Heith, and Andy Hochstetler. 2003. "Situational Construction of Masculinity among Male Street Thieves." *Journal of Contemporary Ethnography* 32: 279–304.
Copes, Heith, Andy Hochstetler, and J. Patrick Williams. 2008. "'We Weren't Like No Regular Dope Fiends': Negotiating Hustler and Crackhead Identities." *Social Problems* 55: 254–270.
Corrigan, Rose. 2013. *Up against a Wall: Rape Reform and the Failure of Success*. New York: New York University Press.
Council of State Governments. 2016. "Mental Health Courts." Accessed on May 21, 2016 at https://csgjusticecenter.org/mental-health-court-project/
Crawley, Sara L., and K. L. Broad. 2004. "'Be Your (Real Lesbian) Self": Mobilizing Sexual Formula Stories through Personal (and Political) Storytelling." *Journal of Contemporary Ethnography*: 33: 39–71.
Cressey, Donald R. 1953. *Other People's Money: A Study in the Social Psychology of Embezzlement*. Glencoe, IL: Free Press.
———. 1960. "Epidemiology and Individual Conduct: A Case from Criminology." *Pacific Sociological Review* 3: 47–58.
Crompton, Louis. 1981. "The Myth of Lesbian Impunity Capital Laws from 1270 to 1791." *Journal of Homosexuality* 6: 11–25.
Cromwell, Paul, and James Olsen. 2004. *Breaking and Entering: An Ethnographic Analysis of Burglary*. Belmont, CA: Cengage.
Cullen, Francis, Jennifer L. Hartman, and Cheryl Leo Jonson. 2009. "Bad Guys: Why the Public Supports Punishing White-collar Offenders." *Crime, Law, and Social Change* 51: 31–44.
Curran, Daniel J., and Claire M. Renzetti. 1994. *Theories of Crime*. Boston: Allyn and Bacon.
Curtis, Ric, Karen Terry, Meredith Dank, Kirk Dombrowski, and Bilal Khan. 2008. "The Commercial Sexual Exploitation of Children in New York City: Volume 1." New York: Center for Court Innovation.
Curtis, Wayne. 2007. *And a Bottle of Rum: A History of the World in Ten Cocktails*. New York: Crown Publishing.
Daley, Matthew V. 2008. "Flawed Solution to the Sex Offenders Situation in the United States: The Legality of Chemical Castration for Sex Offenders." *Indiana Health Law Review* 5: 87–122.
Dalton, Melville. 1959. *Men Who Manage*. Boulder, CO: Westview Press.
Davis, Lois M., Robert Bozick, Jennifer L. Steele, Jessica Saunders, and Jeremy Miles. 2013. "Evaluating the Effectiveness of Correctional Education." Santa Monica, CA: Rand Corporation. Accessed on May 30, 2016 at http://www.rand.org/pubs/research_reports/RR266.html
Death Penalty Information Center. 2016. "Death Row Inmates by State and Year." Accessed on August 25, 2016 at http://www.deathpenaltyinfo.org/documents/FactSheet.pdf
De Heer, Philip. 1986. *The Care-taker Emperor*. Leiden, Netherlands: E. J. Brill.
Demaris, Ovid. 1974. *Dirty Business: The Corporate-Political Money-Power Game*. New York: Harper's Magazine Press.
D'Emilio, John. 1983. *Sexual Politics, Sexual Communities: The Making of a Homosexual Minority in the U.S. 1940–1970*. Chicago: University of Chicago Press.
Denzin, Norman K. 1987a. *The Alcoholic Self*. Newbury Park, CA: Sage
———. 1987b. *The Recovering Alcoholic*. Newbury Park, CA: Sage.
Depression Chat Rooms. 2016. "Welcome to Depression Chat Rooms." Accessed on May 21, 2016 at http://www.depression-chat-rooms.org/
Dewey, Susan. 2011. *Neon Wasteland*. Berkeley: University of California Press.
Dhami, Mandeep K. 2007. "White-Collar Prisoners' Perceptions of Audience Reaction." *Deviant Behavior* 28: 57–77.
Dias, Karen. 2003. "The Ana Sanctuary: Women's Pro-Anorexia Narratives in Cyberspace." *Journal of International Women's Studies* 4: 31–45.
Dickson, Donald. 1968. "Bureaucracy and Morality." *Social Problems* 16: 143–156.
Douglas, Jack D. 1972. "Observing Deviance." Pp. 3–34 in *Research on Deviance*, edited by Jack D. Douglas. New York: Random House.
Douglas, Jack D., and Frances C. Waksler. 1982. *The Sociology of Deviance: An Introduction*. Boston: Little, Brown, and Co.
Douglass, Frederick. 1950. *The Life and Writings of Frederick Douglass*, edited by Philip S. Foner. New York: International Publishers.
Dozier, Raine. 2014. "Guy–Moms Unite! Mothering Outside the Box." In *Queering Motherhood: Narrative and Theoretical Perspectives*, edited by Margaret F. Gibson. Bradford, Ontario: Demeter Press.
Duffy, Jill. 2016. "The Best Fitness Trackers for 2016." *PC Magazine*. Accessed on March 7, 2016 at http://www.pcmag.com/article2/0,2817,2404445,00.asp
Durkheim, Emile. 1897/1966. *Suicide*. New York: Free Press.
———. 1938. *The Rules of Sociological Method*. New York: The Free Press.
Dworkin, Shari, and Faye Linda Wachs. 2004. "Getting Your Body Back: Post-Industrial Fit Motherhood and the Merger of the Second and Third Shifts." *Gender and Society* 18: 610–624.
———. 2009. *Body Panic: Gender, Health, and the Selling of Fitness*. New York: New York University Press.
Earle, Sarah, and Keith Sharp. 2008. "Intimacy, Pleasure, and the Men Who Pay for Sex." Pp. 63–79 in *Sex as Crime*, edited by Gayle Letherby, Kate Williams, Philip Birch, and Maureen Cain. Portland, OR: Willan Publishing.
Ebaugh, Helen R. 1988. *Becoming an Ex: The Process of Role Exit*. Chicago: University of Chicago Press.
Edwards, Bob, and John D. McCarthy. 2004. "Resources and Social Movement Mobilization." Pp. 116–152 in *The Blackwell Companion to Social Movements*, edited by David A. Snow, Sarah A. Soule, and Hanspeter Kriesi. Malden, MA: Blackwell Publishing.
Edwards, John. 2004. *Ferdinand and Isabella*. New York: Pearson/Longman.
Egan, Danielle. 2006. *Dancing for Dollars and Paying for Love*. New York: Palgrave Macmillan.
Eichenwald, Kurt. 1989. "Wages Even Wall St. Can't Stomach." *New York Times*. Accessed on November 3, 2013 at http://www

.nytimes.com/1989/04/03/business/wages-even-wall-st-can-t-stomach.html

El-Hai, Jack. 2005. *The Lobotomist: A Maverick Medical Genius and His Tragic Quest to Rid the World of Mental Illness.* Hoboken, NJ: John Wiley and Sons.

Ellison, Jake. 2016. "Washington's Total Recreational Marijuana Sales Pass $1 Billion." *Seattle PI.* Accessed on August 14, 2016 at http://www.seattlepi.com/local/marijuana/article/Washington-total-marijuana-sales-pass-1-billion-8346916.php

Emerson, Robert M. and Melvin Pollner. 2001. "Constructing Participant/Observation Relations." Pp. 239–259 in *Contemporary Field Research: A Collection of Readings,* edited by R. M. Emerson. 2nd ed. Prospect Heights, IL: Waveland Press.

Encinosa, W. E., D. M. Bernard, C. C. Chen, and C. A. Steiner. 2006. "Healthcare Utilization and Outcomes after Bariatric Surgery." *Medical Care* 44: 706–712.

Engels, Friederich. 1892. *The Condition of the Working Class in England in 1844.* London: Sonnenschein and Co.

Erzen, Tanya. 2006. *Straight to Jesus: Sexual and Christian Conversions in the Ex-Gay Movement.* Berkeley: University of California Press.

Esch, Laura, and Keith Zullig. 2008. "Middle School Students' Weight Perceptions, Dieting Behaviors, and Life Satisfaction." *American Journal of Health Education* 39: 345–352.

Escohotado, Antonio. 1999. *A Brief History of Drugs: From the Stone Age to the Stoned Age.* Rochester, VT: Park Street Press.

Estroff, Sue E. 1981. *Making It Crazy: An Ethnography of Psychiatric Clients in an American Community.* Berkeley: University of California Press.

Faderman, Lillian. 2015. *The Gay Revolution: The Story of the Struggle.* New York: Simon and Schuster.

Farrell, Amy Erdman. 2011. *Fat Shame: Stigma and the Fat Body in American Culture.* New York: New York University Press.

Faupel, Charles E. 1991. *Shooting Dope: Career Patterns of Hard-Core Heroin Users.* Gainesville: University of Florida Press.

Federal Bureau of Investigation. 2014a. Uniform Crime Reports. Accessed on June 30, 2016 at https://www.fbi.gov/about-us/cjis/ucr/crime-in-the-u.s/2014

———. 2014b. "Arrests for Drug Abuse Violations Percent Distribution by Region, 2012." Accessed on June 11, 2014 at http://www.fbi.gov/about-us/cjis/ucr/crime-in-the-u.s/2012/crime-in-the-u.s.-2012/persons-arrested/arrest_table_arrests_for_drug_abuse_violations_percent_distribution_by_regions_2012.xls

———. 2015a. "Crime in the United States 2014." Accessed on August 27, 2016 at https://ucr.fbi.gov/crime-in-the-u.s/2014/crime-in-the-u.s.-2014/offenses-known-to-law-enforcement/expanded-homicide

———. 2015b. "Offenses Cleared 2014." Accessed on August 15, 2016 at https://ucr.fbi.gov/crime-in-the-u.s/2014/crime-in-the-u.s.-2014/offenses-known-to-law-enforcement/clearances/main/clearances.pdf

———. 2015c. "Rape." Accessed on April 5, 2017 at https://ucr.fbi.gov/crime-in-the-u.s/2015/crime-in-the-u.s.-2015/offenses-known-to-law-enforcement/rape

———. 2016. "2015 Crime in the United States." Accessed on April 7, 2017 at https://ucr.fbi.gov/crime-in-the-u.s/2015/crime-in-the-u.s.-2015

Felson, Marcus. 2002. *Crime and Everyday Life,* 3rd ed. Thousand Oaks, CA: Sage.

———. 2006. *Crime and Nature.* Thousand Oaks, CA: Sage.

Felson, Richard B. and Henry J. Steadman. 1983. "Situational Factors in Disputes Leading to Criminal Violence." *Criminology* 21: 59–74.

Fingarette, Herbert. 1988. *Heavy Drinking: The Myth of Alcoholism as a Disease.* Berkeley: University of California Press.

Fisher, Bonnie, Francis Cullen, and Michael Turner. 2000. "The Sexual Victimization of College Women." Washington, DC: National Institute of Justice.

Flowers, Amy. 1998. *The Fantasy Factory.* Philadelphia: University of Pennsylvania Press.

Fonda, Stephanie J., Nancy Fultz, Kristi Rahrig Jenkins, Laura M. Wheeler, and Linda A. Wray. 2004. "Relationship of Body Mass and Net Worth for Retirement-aged Men and Women." *Research on Aging* 26: 153–176.

Forbes Magazine. 2010. The World's Billionaires: #488 Michael Milken. Accessed on November 3, 2013 at http://www.forbes.com/lists/2010/10/billionaires-2010_Michael-Milken_SSM6.html

Foucault, Michel. 1965. *Madness and Civilization: A History of Insanity in the Age of Reason.* New York: Pantheon.

———. 1978. *The History of Sexuality Volume 1: An Introduction.* New York: Pantheon.

———. 1988. "Technologies of the Self." Pp. 16–49 in *Technologies of the Self: A Seminar with Michel Foucault,* edited by Luther Martin, Huck Gutman, and Patrick H. Hutton. Amherst, MA: University of Massachusetts Press.

Fox, James Alan, and Jack Levin. 1999. "Serial Murder: Popular Myths and Empirical Realities." Pp. 165–175 in *Homicide: A Sourcebook of Social Research,* edited by M. Dwayne Smith and Margaret A. Zahn. Thousand Oaks, CA: Sage.

Foxhall, Emily. 2014. "Orange County Prostitution Fight Puts New Focus on Shaming of Johns." *Los Angeles Times.* November 20. Accessed at http://www.latimes.com/local/orangecounty/la-me-john-shaming-20141120-story.html

Frake, Charles O. 1964. "How to Ask for a Drink in Subanun." *American Anthropologist* 66: 127–132.

Francis, Lori A., and E. J. Susman. 2009. "Self-regulation and Weight Gain in Children from Three to Twelve Years." *Archives of Pediatrics and Adolescent Medicine* 163: 297–302.

Frank, Katherine. 2002. *G-Strings and Sympathy.* Durham, NC: Duke University Press.

Frank, Nancy and Michael Lombness. 1988. *Controlling Corporate Illegality.* Cincinnati, OH: Anderson.

Freedman, Estelle B. 1981. *Their Sisters' Keepers.* Ann Arbor: University of Michigan Press.

Freespirit, Judy, and Aldebaran. 2009. "Fat Liberation Manifesto, November 1973." Pp. 341–342 in *The Fat Studies Reader,* edited by Esther Rothblum and Sondra Solovay. New York: New York University Press.

Friedrichs, David O. 2010. *Trusted Criminals: White Collar Crime in Contemporary Society.* 4th ed. Belmont, CA: Wadsworth/Cengage.

Frohmann, Lisa. 1991. "Discrediting Victims' Allegations of Sexual Assault: Prosecutorial Accounts of Case Rejections." *Social Problems* 38: 213–226.

Gaesser, Glenn A. 2002. *Big Fat Lies: The Truth about Your Weight and Your Health.* Carlsbad, CA: Gurze Books.

Gailey, Jeanine. 2009. "'Starving is the Most Fun a Girl Can Have': The Pro-Ana Subculture as Edgework." *Critical Criminology* 17: 93–108.

Gallup. 2011. "For First Time, Majority of Americans Favor Legal Gay Marriage." Accessed on January 24, 2016 at http://www.gallup.com/poll/147662/First-Time-Majority-Americans-Favor-Legal-Gay-Marriage.aspx

Gamson, Joshua. 1998. *Freaks Talk Back: Tabloid Talk Shows and Sexual Nonconformity*. Chicago: University of Chicago Press.
Garfinkel, Harold, and Egon Bittner. 1967. "Good Organizational Reasons for 'Bad' Clinic Records." Pp. 186–207 in *Studies in Ethnomethodology*, edited by Harold Garkfinkel. Englewood Cliffs, NJ: Prentice Hall.
Garland, David. 1985. "The Criminal and His Science: A Critical Account of the Formation of Criminology at the End of the Nineteenth Century." *British Journal of Criminology* 25: 109–137.
Gates, Gary J. 2014. "LGBT Demographics: Comparisons among Population-based Surveys." Williams Institute, UCLA School of Law.
———. 2011. "How Many People are Lesbian, Gay, Bisexual, and Transgender?" Berkeley, CA: University of California Williams Institute. Accessed on August 29, 2016 at http://williamsinstitute.law.ucla.edu/wp-content/uploads/Gates-How-Many-People-LGBT-Apr-2011.pdf
Gates, Gary, and Frank Newport. 2012. "Special Report: 3.4% of U.S. Adults Identify as LGBT." Princeton, NJ: Gallup. Accessed on January 11, 2016 at http://www.gallup.com/poll/158066/special-report-adults-identify-lgbt.aspx
Gefou-Madianou, Dimitra. 1992. "Introduction: Alcohol Commensality, Identity Transformations and Transcendence." Pp. 1–34 in *Alcohol, Gender, and Culture*, edited by Dimitra Gefou-Madianou. New York: Routledge.
Geisst, Charles R. 2004. *Wall Street: A History from Its Beginnings to the Fall of Enron*. Revised ed. New York: Oxford University Press.
Gerassi, John. 1966. *The Boys of Boise: Furor, Vice and Folly in an American City*. Seattle, WA: University of Washington Press.
Ghaziani, Amin. 2008. *The Dividends of Dissent: How Conflict and Culture Work in Lesbian and Gay Marches in Washington*. Chicago: University of Chicago Press.
———. 2011. "Post-Gay Collective Identity Construction." *Social Problems* 58: 99–125.
———. 2014. *There Goes the Gayborhood?* Princeton, NJ: Princeton University Press.
Gilfoyle, Timothy J. 1992. *City of Eros: New York City, Prostitution, and the Commercialization of Sex, 1820–1920*. New York: W. W. Norton.
Gimlin, Debra L. 2002. *Body Work: Beauty and Self-Image in American Culture*. Berkeley: University of California Press.
Glantz, Stanton A., and Edith D. Balbach. 2000. *Tobacco Wars: Inside the California Battles*. Berkeley: University of California Press.
Goffman, Erving. 1961. *Asylums: Essays on the Social Situation of Mental Patients and Other Inmates*. Garden City, NY: Doubleday.
———. 1963. *Stigma: Notes on the Management of Spoiled Identity*. New York: Simon and Schuster.
———. 1971. *Relations in Public*. New York: Harper and Row.
Gonchar, Michael. 2016. "Should Prisoners Be Given the Opportunity to Get an Education?" *New York Times*. Accessed on May 30, 2016 at http://learning.blogs.nytimes.com/2016/03/01/student-question-should-prisoners-be-given-the-opportunity-to-get-an-education/
Gonzales, Philip B. 1993. "Shame, Peer, and Oscillating Frames in DWI Conviction: Extending Goffman's Sociological Landscape." *Symbolic Interaction* 16: 257–271.
Goode, Erich. 1999. "Sex with Informants as Deviant Behavior: An Account an Commentary." *Deviant Behavior* 20: 301–324.
———. 2005. *Deviant Behavior*. 7th ed. New York: Prentice-Hall.
———. 2008. *Deviant Behavior*. 9th ed. New York: Prentice-Hall.
———. 2012. *Drugs in American Society*. 8th ed. Boston: McGraw-Hill.
———. 2015. *Deviant Behavior*.11th ed. New York: Routledge.
Goode, Erich, and Nachman Ben-Yehuda. 2009. *Moral Panics: The Social Construction of Deviance*. 2nd ed. Oxford, UK: Blackwell Publishing.
Goodstein, Laurie. 2015. "New Policy on Gay Couples and Their Children Roils Mormon Church." *New York Times*. November 13, 2015. Accessed on February 13, 2016 at http://www.nytimes.com/2015/11/14/us/mormons-set-to-quit-church-over-policy-on-gay-couples-and-their-children.html?_r=0
Gopnik, Adam. 2015. "The Outside Game: How the Sociologist Howard Becker Studies the Conventions of the Unconventional." *The New Yorker*. January 12. Accessed on December 2, 2016 at http://www.newyorker.com/magazine/2015/01/12/outside-game
Goss, Kristen A. 2006. *Disarmed: The Missing Movement for Gun Control in America*. Princeton, NJ: Princeton University Press.
Gottfredson, Michael, and Travis Hirschi. 1990. *A General Theory of Crime*. Stanford, CA: Stanford University Press.
Gottfredson, Denise C., Stacy S. Najaka, and Brook Kearly. 2003. "Effectiveness of Drug Treatment Courts: Evidence from a Randomized Trial." *Criminology and Public Policy* 2: 171–196.
Gottleib, Robert, and Anupama Joshi. 2010. *Food Justice*. Cambridge, MA: MIT Press.
Gould, Stephen Jay. 1981. *The Mismeasure of Man*. New York: W. W. Norton.
Grant, Bridget F., Rise B. Goldstein, Tulshi D. Saha, S. Patricia Chou, Jeesun Jung, Haitao Zhang, Roger P. Pickering, W. June Ruan, Sharon M. Smith, Boji Huang, and Deborah S. Hasin. 2015. "Epidemiology of DSM-5 Alcohol Use Disorder: Results From the National Epidemiologic Survey on Alcohol and Related Conditions." *JAMA Psychiatry* 72: 757–766. doi:10.1001/jamapsychiatry.2015.0584.
Greenberg, David F. 1997. "Transformations of Homosexuality-Based Classifications. Pp. 179–193 in *The Gender/Sexuality Reader Culture: History, Political Economy*, edited by Roger N. Lancaster and Micaela di Leonardo. New York: Routledge.
Greenhalgh, Susan. 2015. *Fat-Talk Nation*. Ithaca, NY: Cornell University Press.
Gremillion, Helen. 2003. *Feeding Anorexia: Gender and Power at a Treatment Center*. Durham, NC: Duke University Press.
Grob, Gerald N. 1991. *From Asylum to Community: Mental Health Policy in Modern America*. Princeton, NJ: Princeton University Press.
———. 1994. *The Mad among Us: A History of the Care of America's Mentally Ill*. New York: Free Press.
Gross, Edward. 1980. "Organization Structure and Organizational Crime." Pp. 52–76 in *White-Collar Crime: Theory and Research*, edited by Gilbert Geis and Ezra Stotland. Beverly Hills, CA: Sage.
Guittar, Nicholas A. 2014. *Coming Out: The New Dynamics*. Boulder, CO: Lynne Rienner Publishers.
Gusfield, Joseph R. 1996. *Contested Meanings: The Construction of Alcohol Problems*. Madison: University of Wisconsin Press.
Guthman, Julie. 2011. *Weighing In: Obesity, Food Justice, and the Limits of Capitalism*. Berkeley: University of California Press.
Hamer, Dean, and Peter Copeland. 1994. *The Science of Desire: The Search for the Gay Gene and the Biology of Behavior*. New York: Simon and Schuster.

Hanawalt, Barbara. 1979. *Crime and Conflict in English Communities, 1300–1348*. Cambridge, MA: Harvard University Press.

Hardaway, Robert M. 2003. *No Price Too High: Victimless Crimes and the Ninth Amendment*. West Port, CT: Praeger.

Healy, David. 1998. *The Anti-Depressant Era*. Cambridge, MA: Harvard University Press.

———. 2002. *The Creation of Psychopharmacology*. Cambridge, MA: Harvard University Press.

Health and Human Services. 2015. *The Surgeon General's Vision for a Healthy and Fit Nation: Fact Sheet*. Accessed on May 17, 2015 at http://www.surgeongeneral.gov/priorities/healthy-fit-nation/obesityvision_factsheet.html

Heath, Dwight. 1987. "A Decade of Development in the Anthropological Study of Alcohol Use, 1970–1980." Pp. 16–69 in *Constructive Drinking: Perspectives on Drink from Anthropology*, edited by Mary Douglas. Boston: Cambridge University Press.

Hennen, Peter. 2005. "Bear Bodies, Bear Masculinity: Recuperation, Resistance, or Retreat?" *Gender and Society* 19: 25–43.

———. 2008. *Faeries, Bears, and Leathermen: Men in Community Queering the Masculine*. Chicago: University of Chicago Press.

Herd, Denise. 1991. "The Paradox of Temperance: Blacks and the Alcohol Question in Nineteenth-Century America." Pp. 354–375 in *Drinking: Behavior and Beliefs in Modern History*, edited by Susanna Barrows and Robin Broom. Berkeley: University of California Press.

Herdt, Gilbert H. 1982. *Rituals of Manhood: Male Initiation in Papua New Guinea*. Berkeley: University of California Press.

———. 1997. *Same Sex, Different Cultures: Gays and Lesbians across Cultures*. Boulder, CO: Westview Press.

Herman, Nancy J. 1987. "The 'Mixed Nutters' and 'Looney Tuners': The Emergence, Development, Nature, and Functions of Two Informal, Deviant Subcultures of Chronic Ex-psychiatric Patients." *Deviant Behavior* 8: 232–258.

———. 1993. "Return to Sender: Reintegrative Stigma-management Strategies of Ex-psychiatric Patients." *Journal of Contemporary Ethnography* 22: 295–330.

———. 2001. "Creating Crazies/Making Mentals: The Pre-patient Phase in the Moral Career of the Psychiatric Patient." Pp. 427–439 in *Deviance: A Symbolic Interactionist Approach*, edited by Nancy J. Herman. Dix Hills, NY: General Hall.

Hesse-Biber, Sharlene. 2007. *The Cult of Thinness*. 2nd ed. New York: Oxford University Press.

Hiday, Virginia. 1999. "Mental Illness and the Criminal Justice System." Pp. 508–525 in *A Handbook for the Study of Mental Health*, edited by Allan V. Horwitz and Teresa L. Scheid. New York: Cambridge University Press.

Hilgartner, Stephen, and Charles L. Bosk. 1988. "The Rise and Fall of Social Problems: A Public Arenas Model." *American Journal of Sociology* 94: 53–78.

Hine, Christine. 2000. *Virtual Ethnography*. London: Sage.

Hingson, Ralph, and Michael Winter. 2008. "Epidemiology and Consequences of Drinking and Driving." Accessed on April 17, 2017 at http://pubs.niaaa.nih.gov/publications/arh27-1/63-78.htm

Hirschi, Travis. 1969. *Causes of Delinquency*. Berkeley: University of California Press.

Hobbes, Thomas. 1991 (orig. 1651). *Leviathan*, edited by Richard Tuck. New York: Cambridge University Press.

Hobson, Kathryn. 2013. "Performative Tensions in Female Drag Performances." *Kaleidoscope* 12: 35–51.

Hochstetler, Andy. 2002. "Sprees and Runs: Opportunity Construction and Criminal Episodes." *Deviant Behavior* 23: 45–73.

Hochstetler, Andy, and Heith Copes. 2003. "Managing Fear to Commit Felony Theft." Pp. 87–98 in *In Their Own Words: Criminals on Crime*. 3rd ed., edited by Paul Cromwell. Los Angeles: Roxbury.

Hochstetler, Andy, and Heith Copes. 2006. "Managing Fear to Commit Felony Theft." Pp. 102–112 in *In Their Own Words: Criminals on Crime*. 4th ed., edited by Paul Cromwell. Oxford, UK: Oxford University Press.

Hoffman, Heath C. 2006. "Criticism as Deviance and Social Control in Alcoholics Anonymous." *Journal of Contemporary Ethnography* 35: 669–695.

Holt, Thomas J., and Kristie R. Blevins. 2007. "Examining Sex Work from the Client's Perspective: Assessing Johns Using On-line Data." *Deviant Behavior* 28: 333–354.

Horwitz, Allan V. 2002. *Creating Mental Illness*. Chicago: University of Chicago Press.

Horwitz, Allan V., and Teresa L. Scheid. 1999. "Approaches to Mental Health and Illness: Conflicting Definitions and Emphases." Pp. 1–11 in *A Handbook for the Study of Mental Health*, edited by Allan V. Horwitz and Teresa L. Scheid. New York: Cambridge University Press.

Hudson, James I., Eva Hiripi, Harrison G. Pope, Jr., and Ronald C. Kessler. 2007. "The Prevalence and Correlates of Eating Disorders in the National Comorbidity Survey Replication." *Biological Psychiatry* 61: 348–358.

Huff, Jennifer. 1995. "Gender and Peer Support among Members of a Psychosocial Rehabilitation Center." MA thesis, Ohio University.

Hughes, Everett C. 1945. "Dilemmas and Contradictions of Status." *American Journal of Sociology* 50: 353–359.

Hughes, P. H., N. Brandenburg, and D. C. Baldwin. 1992. "Prevalence of Substance Abuse among U.S. Physicians." *Journal of the American Medical Association* 267: 2333–2339.

Humphreys, Laud. 1970. *Tearoom Trade: Impersonal Sex in Public Places*. Chicago: Aldine.

Humphris, Francis H. 1912. "Electricity in the Treatment of Obesity." *British Medical Journal* 2: 493–494.

Hunt, April. 2016. "Robert Agnew: Pioneering Work on the Causes of Crime." March 10, 2016. Emory Report. Accessed on April 7, 2017 at http://college.emory.edu/main/php/news-modal.php?sid=eb3a36190ae7232f41816600c4490857

Ikegami, Eiko. 1995. *The Taming of the Samurai: Honorific Individualism and the Making of Modern Japan*. Cambridge, MA: Harvard University Press.

Illescas, Carlos. 2016. "Marijuana Sales Tax Revenue Huge Boon for Colorado Cities." *Denver Post*. Accessed on August 14, 2016 at http://www.denverpost.com/2016/05/26/marijuana-sales-tax-revenue-huge-boon-for-colorado-cities/

Inciardi, James A., Dorothy Lockwood, and Anne E. Pottieger. 1993. *Women and Crack-Cocaine*. New York: MacMillan Publishing Company.

Ingraham, Christopher. 2016. "The Astonishing Human Potential Wasted on Commutes." *Washington Post*. Accessed on September 17, 2016 at www.washingtonpost.com/news/wonk/wp/2016/02/25/how-much-of-your-life-youre-wasting-on-your-commute/

Irving, Washington. 1865. *Tales of a Traveller*. New York: Putnam.

Jackall, Robert. 1988. *Moral Mazes: The World of Corporate Managers*. New York: Oxford University Press.

Jackson, Joan. 1954. "The Adjustment of the Family to the Crisis of Alcoholism." *Quarterly Journal of Studies on Alcohol* 4: 562–586.

Jacobs, Bruce A. 1992. "Undercover Deception: Reconsidering Presentations of Self." *Journal of Contemporary Ethnography* 21: 200–225.

Jacques, Scott, and Richard Wright. 2015. *Code of the Suburb: Inside the World of Young Middle-Class Drug Dealers*. Chicago: University of Chicago Press.

James, Susan Donaldson. 2013. "Sex Workers Tell Tricks of the Trade." July 12, 2013. *ABC News*. Accessed on April 7, 2017 at http://abcnews.go.com/Health/sex-workers-tricks-trade-memoir-class/story?id=19643868

Jellinek, Elvin M. 1960. *The Disease Concept of Alcoholism*. New Brunswick, NJ: Hillhouse Press.

Jenkins, Philip. 1994. *Using Murder: The Social Construction of Serial Homicide*. New York: Walter de Gruyter.

Jenkins, Philip. 1998. *Moral Panic: Changing Concepts of the Child Molester in Modern America*. New Haven, CT: Yale University Press.

Jenness, Valerie. 1993. *Making It Work: The Prostitutes' Rights Movement in Perspective*. New York: Aldine.

Jeter, Lynne W. 2004. *Disconnected: Deceit and Betrayal at WorldCom*. Hoboken, NJ: John Wiley & Sons.

Joey. 1973. *Killer: Autobiography of a Hit Man*. New York: Pocket Books.

Johnson, John M. 1995. "Horror Stories and the Construction of Child Abuse." Pp. 17–32 in *Images of Issues: Typifying Contemporary Social Problems*. 2nd ed., edited by Joel Best. New York: Aldine de Gruyter.

Johnson, Suzanne. 2008. "My Revolving Closet Door." *Journal of Lesbian Studies* 12: 59–67.

Jones, Norman. 2010. "Usury." *EH.Net Encyclopedia*. Accessed on October 1, 2011 at https://eh.net/encyclopedia/usury/

Judge, Timothy A., and Daniel M. Cable. 2011. "When It Comes to Pay, Do the Thin Win? The Effect of Weight on Pay for Men and Women." *Journal of Applied Psychology* 96: 95–112.

Jurik, Nancy C. and Russ Winn. 1990. "Gender and Homicide: A Comparison of Men and Women Who Kill." *Violence and Victims* 5: 227–242.

Kalab, Kathleen. 1987. "Student Vocabularies of Motive: Accounts for Absence." *Symbolic Interaction* 10: 7183.

Karp, David A. 1996. *Speaking of Sadness*. New York: Oxford University Press.

———. 2001. *The Burden of Sympathy: How Families Cope with Mental Illness*. New York: Oxford University Press.

———. 2006. *Is It Me or My Meds?* Cambridge, MA: Harvard University Press.

Karuso, Sylvia R. 2013. "College Weight Gain: Debunking the Myth of the 'Freshman 15.'" *Psychology Today*. September 10. Accessed on March 9, 2016 at https://www.psychologytoday.com/blog/the-gravity-weight/201309/college-weight-gain-debunking-the-myth-the-freshman-15

Katz, Jack. 1979. "Concerted Ignorance: The Social Construction of Cover-up." *Urban Life* 8: 295–316.

———. 1988. *Seductions of Crime: Moral and Sensual Attractions of Doing Evil*. New York: Basic Books.

———. 1991. "The Motivation of the Persistent Robber." Pp. 277–305 in *Crime and Justice: A Review of Research*, edited by M. Tonry. Chicago: University of Chicago Press.

Kaufmann, Caroline L. 1999. "An Introduction to the Mental Health Consumer Movement." Pp. 493–507 in *A Handbook for the Study of Mental Health*, edited by Allan V. Horwitz and Teresa L. Scheid. New York: Cambridge University Press.

Kelly, Brian. 2007. "Club Drug Use and Risk Management among 'Bridge and Tunnel' Youth." *Journal of Drug Issues* 37: 425–444.

Kennedy, Elizabeth L., and Madeline D. Davis. 1993. *Boots of Leather, Slippers of Gold: The History of a Lesbian Community*. New York: Routledge.

Kesey, Ken. 1962. *One Flew Over the Cuckoo's Nest*. New York: New American Library.

Khimm, Suzy. 2016. "The Shame Game." *New Republic*. March 9. Accessed on October 1, 2016 at https://newrepublic.com/article/130803/shame-game

Kim, K. I., and B. Y. Rhi. 1976. "A Review of Korean Cultural Psychiatry." *Transcultural Psychiatric Research Review* 10: 101–114.

Kimble, Matthew, Andrada D. Neacsiu, William F. Flack, and Jessica Horner. 2008. "Risk of Unwanted Sex for College Women: Evidence for a Red Zone." *American Journal of College Health* 57: 331–337.

King, J. L. 2004. *On the Down Low: A Journey into the Lives of "Straight" Black Men Who Sleep with Men*. New York: Broadway Books.

King, Ryan S., and Jill Pasquarella. 2009. "Drug Courts: A Review of the Evidence." Washington, DC: The Sentencing Project.

Kingsworth, Rodney, Randall MacIntosh, and Jennifer Wentworth. 1999. "Sexual Assault: The Role of Prior Relationship and Victim Characteristics in Case Processing." *Justice Quarterly* 16: 276–302.

Kinsey, Alfred, Wardell B. Pomeroy, and Clyde E. Martin. 1948. *Sexual Behavior in the Human Male*. Philadelphia: W.B. Saunders Co.

———. 1953. *Sexual Behavior in the Human Female*. Philadelphia: W.B. Saunders Co.

Kirkland, Anna. 2008. *Fat Rights: Dilemmas of Difference and Personhood*. New York: New York University Press.

Kitsuse, John I. 1962. "Societal Reaction to Deviant Behavior: Problems of Theory and Method." *Social Problems* 9: 247–256.

———. 1980. "Coming Out All Over: Deviants and the Politics of Social Problems." *Social Problems* 28: 1–13.

Kitsuse, John I., and Aaron V. Cicourel. 1963. "A Note on the Uses of Official Statistics." *Social Problems* 11: 131–139.

Kitsuse, John I., and Malcom Spector. 1975. "Social Problems and Deviance: Some Parallel Issues." *Social Problems* 22: 584–594.

Kleinman, A. 1987. "Anthropology and Psychiatry: The Role of Culture in Cross-Cultural Research on Illness." *British Journal of Psychiatry* 151: 447–454.

Klockars, Carl B. 1974. *The Professional Fence*. New York: The Free Press.

Kluger, Richard. 1996. *Ashes to Ashes: America's Hundred-Year Cigarette War, the Public Health, and the Unabashed Triumph of Philip Morris*. New York: Alfred A. Knopf.

Koken, Juline A. 2012. "Independent Female Escort's Strategies for Coping with Sex Work Related Stigma." *Sexuality and Culture* 16: 209–229.

Konradi, Amanda. 2007. *Taking the Stand: Rape Survivors and the Prosecution of Rapists*. Westport, CT: Praeger.

Kornbluth, Jesse. 1992. *Highly Confident: The Crime and Punishment of Michael Milken*. New York City: William Morrow and Sons.

Kotarba, Joseph A. 1970. "One More for the Road: The Subversion of Labeling within the Tavern Subculture." Pp. 152–160 in *The Sociology of Deviance*, edited by Jack D. Douglas. Boston: Allyn and Bacon.

Kraepelin, Emil. 1896. *Psychiatrie: Ein Lehrbuch fur Studierende und Artze*. 5th ed. Leipzig: Johann Ambrosius Barth.

Krouse, Mary Beth. 1999. "Feminist Discursive Pivoting: Charting the Politics of AIDS." *Humanity and Society* 23: 32–48.

Kwan, Samantha, and Jennifer Graves. 2013. *Framing Fat: Competing Constructions in Contemporary Culture*. New Brunswick, NJ: Rutgers University Press.

LaFree, Gary. 1999. "Homicide: Cross-National Perspectives." Pp. 115–139 in *Studying and Preventing Homicide*, edited by M. Dwayne Smith and Margaret A. Zahn. Thousand Oaks, CA: Sage.

Lalich, Janja and Karla McLaren. 2010. "Inside and Outcast: Multifaceted Stigma and Redemption in the Lives of Gay and Lesbian Jehovah's Witnesses." *Journal of Homosexuality* 57: 1303–1333.

Lane, Roger. 1997. *Murder in America: A History*. Columbus, OH: Ohio State University Press.

Laing, R. D. 1967. *The Politics of Experience*. New York: Pantheon.

Lamarty, Jamiles. 2016. "Barack Obama Commutes Sentences of a Record 153 Federal Prisoners in One Day." *The Guardian*. Accessed on December 21, 2016 at https://www.theguardian.com/us-news/2016/dec/19/barack-obama-commutes-sentences-presidential-pardons

Lamb, H. Richard, and Linda E. Weinberger. 1998. "Persons with Severe Mental Illness in Jails and Prisons: A Review." *Psychiatric Service* 49: 483–492.

Langness, L. L. 1965. "Hysterical Psychosis in the New Guinea Highlands: A Bena Bena Example." *Psychiatry* 28: 258–277.

Lareau, Annette. 2003. *Unequal Childhoods: Class, Race, and Family Life*. Berkeley: University of California Press.

LeBesco, Kathleen. 2010. "Fat Panic and the New Morality." Pp. 90–97 in *Against Health*, edited by Jonathan Metzl and Anna Kirkland. New York: New York University Press.

Ledbetter, Sheri. 2014. "What Americans Fear Most—New Poll from Chapman University." Accessed on August 21, 2016 at https://blogs.chapman.edu/press-room/2014/10/20/what-americans-fear-most-new-poll-from-chapman-university/

Lee, Alexander. 2013. "'Making a Famine Where Abundance Lies': Shakespeare the Hoarder." *History Today*. Accessed at http://www.historytoday.com/blog/2013/04/%E2%80%9Cmaking-famine-where-abundance-lies%E2%80%9D-shakespeare-hoarder

Lee, Matthew R. 2011. "Reconsidering Culture and Homicide." *Homicide Studies* 15: 319–340.

Lemelle, Anthrony J., Jr. 2003. "Linking the Structure of African American Criminalization to the Spread of AIDS." *Journal of Contemporary Criminal Justice* 19: 270–292.

Lemert, Edwin M. 1951. *Social Pathology: A Systematic Approach to the Theory of Sociopathic Behavior*. New York: McGraw-Hill.

Lender, Mark E., and James K. Martin. 1987. *Drinking in America: A History*. New York: Free Press.

Levi, Ken. 1981. "Becoming a Hit Man: Neutralization in a Very Deviant Career." *Urban Life* 10: 47–63.

Levine, Harry Gene. 1978. "The Discovery of Addiction: Changing Conceptions of Habitual Drunkenness in America." *Journal of Studies on Alcohol* 39: 143–174.

Liebow, Elliot. 1993. *Tell Them Who I Am: The Lives of Homeless Women*. New York: Free Press.

Lin, Nan, and Walter M. Ensel. 1989. "Life Stress and Health: Stressors and Resources." *American Sociological Review* 54: 382–399.

Lindsley, Craig W. 2012. "The Top Prescription Drugs of 2011 in the United States: Antipsychotics and Antidepressants Once Again Lead CNS Therapeutics." *ACS Chemical Neuroscience* 3(8): 630. DOI: 10.1021/cn3000923.

Lofland, Lyn H. 1973. *A World of Strangers: Order and Action in Urban Public Space*. New York: Basic Books.

Lombroso, Cesare. 2006 (original, 1876) *Criminal Man*, translated by Mary Gibson, and Nicole Hahn Rafter. Durham, NC: Duke University Press.

Lombroso, Cesare, and William Ferrero. 1895. *The Female Offender*. New York: D. Appleton and Company.

Loseke, Donileen R. 1992. *The Battered Woman and Shelters: The Social Construction of Wife Abuse*. Albany, NY: SUNY Press.

Loseke, Donileen. 2007. "The Study of Identity as Cultural, Institutional, Organizational, and Personal Narratives: Theoretical and Empirical Integrations." *The Sociological Quarterly* 48: 661–688.

Lott, John R., Jr. 2010. *More Guns, Less Crime: Understanding Crime and Gun Control Laws*. 3rd ed. Chicago: University of Chicago Press.

Luckenbill, David F. 1977. "Criminal Homicide as a Situated Transaction." *Social Problems* 25: 176–186.

Lyman, Michael D. 2011. *Drugs in Society: Causes, Concepts, and Control*. 6th ed. Burlington, MA: Anderson Publishing.

Lyng, Stephen. 1990. "Edgework: A Social Psychological Analysis of Voluntary Risk Taking," *American Journal of Sociology* 95: 851–886.

Lyons, Christopher J. and Becky Pettit. 2011. "Compounded Disadvantage: Race, Incarceration, and Wage Growth." *Social Problems* 58: 257–280.

Machiavelli, Niccolò. 2005. *The Prince*, edited and translated by Peter Bondanella. New York: Oxford University Press.

MADD (Mothers Against Drunk Driving). 2016a. "Cari Lightner and Laura Lamb's Story." Accessed on April 2, 2016 at www.madd.org/about-us/history/

———. 2016b. "Understanding .08." Accessed on October 29, 2016 at http://www.madd.org/drunk-driving/about/understanding-08.html

Madigan, Lee and Nancy Gamble. 1991. *The Second Rape: Society's Continued Betrayal of the Victim*. New York: Lexington Books.

Maher, Lisa. 1997. *Sexed Work: Gender, Race, and Resistance in a Brooklyn Drug Market*. New York: Clarendon Press.

Malamuth, Neil M., Christopher L. Heavey, and Daniel Linz. 1992. "Predicting Men's Antisocial Behavior against Women." Pp. 63–97 in *Sexual Aggression: Issues in Etiology and Assessment, Treatment, and Policy*, edited by Gordon C. Nagayama Hall, Richard Hirschman, John R. Graham, and Maira S. Zaragoza. New York: Hemisphere.

Mankoff, Milton. 1971. "Societal Reaction and Career Deviance: A Critical Analysis." *The Sociological Quarterly* 12: 204–218.

Marijuana Policy Project. 2016. "Medical Marijuana Patient Numbers." Accessed on August 14, 2016 at https://www.mpp.org/issues/medical-marijuana/state-by-state-medical-marijuana-laws/medical-marijuana-patient-numbers/

Marshall, Mac. 1979. *Beliefs, Behaviors and Alcoholic Beverages: A Cross-Cultural Survey*. Ann Arbor: University of Michigan Press.

Martin, Courtney. 2008. *Perfect Girls, Starving Daughters*. New York: Berkley Books.

Martin, Dan. 2004. "DUIs up Due to 'Dry' Campus Drinking Policy." *DU Clarion*. February 5. Accessed on June 7, 2008 at http://duclarion.com/2004/02/duis-up-due-to-dry-campus-drinking-policies-4/

Martin, Daniel D. 2000. "Organizational Approaches to Shame: Avowal, Management, and Contestation." *The Sociological Quarterly* 41: 125–150.

Martin, Dolfinette. 2015. "How Pretrial Services Empower the Underprivileged." Accessed on November 8, 2016 at https://www.vera.org/blog/justice-in-katrinas-wake/how-pretrial-services-empowers-the-underprivileged

Martin, Mike W. 1994. *Virtuous Giving: Philanthropy, Voluntary Service, and Caring.* Bloomington, IN: University of Indiana Press.

Martin, Patricia Yancey. 2005. *Rape Work: Victims, Gender, and Emotions in Organization and Community Context.* New York: Routledge.

Martin, Patricia Yancey and Marlene R. Powell. 1994. "Accounting for the 'Second Assault': Legal Organizations' Framing of Rape Victims." *Law and Social Inquiry* 19: 853–890.

Martin, Robert K. 1989. "Knights-Errant and Gothic Seducers: The Representation of Male Friendship in Mid-Nineteenth Century America." Pp. 170–182 in *Hidden from History: Reclaiming the Gay and Lesbian Past*, edited by Martin Duberman, Martha Ficinus, and George Chauncey, Jr. New York: New American Library.

Massey, Douglas S. 1995. "Getting Away with Murder: Segregation and Violent Crime in Urban America." *University of Pennsylvania Law Review* 143: 1203–1232.

Mather, Increase. 1673. *Wo To Drunkards.* Cambridge, MA. Printed by Marmaduke Johnson.

Matsueda, Ross. 1989. "The Dynamics of Moral Beliefs and Minor Delinquency." *Social Forces* 68: 428–457.

Mattley, Christine. 2005. "Aural Sex: The Politics and Moral Dilemmas of Studying the Social Construction of Fantasy." Pp. 141–156 in *The Handbook of Fieldwork*, edited by Richard T. Wright and Dick Hobbs. Thousand Oaks, CA: Sage Publications.

Matza, David. 1969. *Becoming Deviant.* Englewood Cliffs, NJ: Prentice-Hall.

Maugh, R.H. 1988. "Study Ties Schizophrenia to Genetic Flaw." *Los Angeles Times.* February 26. A1.

Maume, David J. 1989. "Inequality and Metropolitan Rape Rates: A Routine Activity Approach." *Justice Quarterly* 6: 513–527.

Mauer, Marc. 2006. *Race to Incarcerate.* Revised ed. New York: New Press.

Mayhew, Henry. 1861. *London Labour and the London Poor.* London: Charles Griffin and Co.

Mazerolle, Paul. 1998. "Gender, General Strain, and Delinquency: Empirical Examination." *Justice Quarterly* 15: 65–91.

McCabe, S. E., J. R. Knight, C. J. Teter, and H. Wechsler. 2005. "Non-medical Use of Prescription Stimulants among U.S. College Students: Prevalence and Correlates from a National Survey." *Addiction* 100: 96–109.

McCall, Andrew. 2004. *The Medieval Underworld.* Gloucestershite, UK. Sutton Publishing.

McCormack, David. 2013. "Porn Study Had to be Scrapped After Researchers Failed to Find ANY 20-Something Males Who Hadn't Watched It." Mail Online.com. Accessed on October 29, 2014 at http://www.dailymail.co.uk/news/article-2261377/Porn-study-scrapped-researchers-failed-ANY-20-males-hadn-t-watched-it.html

McLean, Bethany, and Peter Elkind. 2004. *The Smartest Guys in the Room: The Amazing Rise and Scandalous Fall of Enron.* New York: Penguin.

McManners, John. 1998. *Church and Society in Eighteenth Century France.* Oxford, UK: Oxford University Press.

McQuiller Williams, Laverne. 2014. "Sex in the City: Why and How Street Workers Select Their Locations for Business." *Journal of Contemporary Ethnography* 43: 659–694.

Mead, George Herbert. 1934. *Mind, Self, and Society.* Chicago: University of Chicago Press.

———. 1938. *The Philosophy of the Act.* Chicago: University of Chicago Press.

Meier, Diane E., Carol-Ann Emmons, Sylvan Wallenstein, Timothy Quill, R. Sean Morrison, and Christine K. Cassel. 1998. "A National Survey of Physician Assisted Suicide in the United States." *New England Journal of Medicine* 338: 1193–201.

Merton, Robert K. 1938. "Social Structure and Anomie." *American Sociological Review* 3: 672–682.

Merton, Robert K. 1968. *Social Theory and Social Structure.* New York: Free Press.

Messner, Michael. 2015. "A Recipe for Sexual Assault." *The Atlantic.* Accessed on July 5, 2015 at http://www.theatlantic.com

Messner, Steven F. and Richard Rosenfeld. 2007. *Crime and the American Dream.* 4th ed. Belmont, CA: Thomson/Wadsworth.

Miethe, Terance D. and Wendy C. Regoeczi. 2004. *Rethinking Homicide: Exploring the Structure and Process Underlying Deadly Situations.* New York: Cambridge University Press.

Miller, Allison L., Mildred Horodynski, Holly Brophy Herb, Karen Peterson, Dawn Contreras, Niko Kaciroti, Julie Staples-Watson, and Julie Lumeng. 2012. "Enhancing Self-regulation as a Strategy for Obesity Prevention in Head Start Preschoolers: The Growing Healthy Study." *BMC Public Health* 12: 1040.

Miller, Jody. 2002. "Violence and Coercion in Sri Lanka's Commercial Sex Industry: Intersections of Gender, Sexuality, Culture and the Law." *Violence Against Women* 8: 1045–1074.

———. 2011. "Beach Boys or Sexually Exploited Children? Competing Narratives of Sex Tourism and their Impact on Young Men in Sri Lanka's Sex Industry." *Crime, Law and Social Change* 56: 485–508.

Milner, Larry S. 2000. *Hardness of Heart/Hardness of Life: The Stain of Human Infanticide.* New York: University Press of America.

Milner, Christina, and R. Milner. 1973. *Black Players: The Secret World of Black Pimps.* New York: Bantam Books.

MindFreedom. 2016. "Who We Are." Accessed on May 22, 2016 at http://www.mindfreedom.org/who-we-are

Mitchell, Josh. 2012. "Student Debt Rises by 8% as College Tuitions Climb." June 1, 2012, *The Wall Street Journal*, A5.

Mizuta, Tamae, and Marie Mulvey-Roberts. 1994. *Perspectives on the History of British Feminism.* London: Taylor and Francis.

Mock, Brenton. 2015. "How New Orleans Stopped Making Jailing a Business." *The Atlantic.* Accessed on November 8, 2016 at http://www.citylab.com/crime/2015/06/how-new-orleans-stopped-making-jailing-a-business/396188/

Moffatt, Michael. 1989. *Coming of Age in New Jersey: College and American Culture.* New Brunswick, NJ: Rutgers University Press.

Mogul, Joey L., Andrea J. Ritchie, and Kay Whitlock, eds. 2011. *Queer (In)justice: The Criminalization of LGBT People in the United States.* Boston: Beacon Press.

Mohamed, A. Rafik, and Erik D. Fritsvold. 2010. *Dorm Room Dealers: Drugs and the Privileges of Race and Class.* New York: Lynne Reinner.

Monahan, Brian A., Joseph A. Marolla, and David G. Bromley. 2005. "Constructing Coercion: The Organization of Sexual Assault." *Journal of Contemporary Ethnography* 34: 284–316.

Monto, Martin. 1998. "Holding Men Accountable for Prostitution: The Unique Approach of the Sexual Exploitation Education Project. *Violence against Women* 4: 505–517.

Moore, Judith. 2005. *Fat Girl: A True Story.* New York: Hudson Street Press.

Morningstar, P. J. 1985. "Thandai and Chilam: Traditional Hindu Beliefs about the Proper Uses of Cannabis." *Journal of Psychoactive Drugs* 17: 141–165.
Morris, Caitlin. 2014. "Pros, Cons of College Inmate Program Weighed." *Saratogian*. February 20. Accessed on May 30, 2016 at http://www.saratogian.com/general-news/20140220/pros-cons-of-college-inmate-program-weighed
Morrissey, Joseph P., and Howard H. Goldman. 1986. "Care and Treatment of the Mentally Ill in the United States: Historical Developments and Reforms." *The Annals of the American Academy of Political and Social Science* 484: 12–27.
Morrison, Linda J. 2005. *Talking Back to Psychiatry: The Psychiatric Consumer/Survivor/Ex-Patient Movement*. New York: Routledge.
Mustaine, Elizabeth E. and Richard Tewksbury. 2002. "Sexual Assault of College Women: A Feminist Interpretation of a Routine Activities Analysis." *Criminal Justice Review* 27: 89–122.
Musto, David F. 1999. *The American Disease: Origins of Narcotic Control*. 3rd ed. New York: Oxford University Press.
NAMI (National Alliance for the Mentally Ill). 2006. "Fight Stigma: Become a Stigma Buster." Accessed on September 27, 2006 at http://www.nami.org/Content/NavigationMenu/Take_Action/Fight_Stigma/Fight_Stigma_StigmaBusters.htm
———. 2016. "Stigma Busters." Accessed on May 22, 2016 at http://www.namihelps.org/advocacy/stigmabusters.html
National Center for Health Statistics. 2012. *Healthy People 2010 Final Review*. Hyattsville, MD: Centers for Disease Control.
National Conference of State Legislatures. 2017. "State Medical Marijuana Laws." Accessed on April 5, 2017 at http://www.ncsl.org/research/health/state-medical-marijuana-laws.aspx
National Crime Victimization Survey. 2014. Washington, DC: Bureau of Justice Studies. Accessed on August 13, 2016 at http://www.bjs.gov/content/pub/pdf/cv13.pdf
National Institute of Drug Abuse. 2006. "Anabolic Steroid Abuse." Accessed on November 15, 2006 at http://www.nida.nih.gov/ResearchReports/Steroids/AnabolicSteroids.html
National Institute of Mental Health. 2016. *What is Prevalence?* Accessed on June 28, 2016 at http://www.nimh.nih.gov/health/statistics/prevalence
National Public Radio. 2007. "Virginia County Passes Law Targeting Illegal Immigrants." *Morning Edition*, July 11.
National Schizophrenia Foundation. 2006. "Schizophrenia Anonymous." Accessed on September 29, 2006 at http://www.nsfoundation.org/sa.htm
Newport, Frank. 2012. "Americans Greatly Overestimate Percent Gay, Lesbian in U.S." Accessed on January 14, 2016 at http://www.gallup.com/poll/183383/americans-greatly-overestimate-percent-gay-lesbian.aspx
New York Times Editorial Board. 2016. "A College Education for Prisoners." *New York Times*. February 16. Accessed on May 30, 2016 at http://www.nytimes.com/2016/02/16/opinion/a-college-education-for-prisoners.html?_r=0
NIAAA. 2017. "Alcohol Facts and Statistics." Accessed on April 7, 2017 at https://www.niaaa.nih.gov/alcohol-health/overview-alcohol-consumption/alcohol-facts-and-statistics
Nichter, Mimi. 2000. *Fat Talk: What Girls and Their Parents Say about Dieting*. Cambridge, MA: Harvard University Press.
NIH (National Institutes of Health). 2015. "What Causes Overweight and Obesity." Accessed on July 3, 2015 at http://www.nhlbi.nih.gov/health/health-topics/topics/obe/causes
Nolan, James L. 2001. *Reinventing Justice: The American Drug Court Movement*. Princeton, NJ: Princeton University Press.
Norton, Kevin L., Timothy S. Olds, Scott Olive, and Stephen Dank. 1996. "Ken and Barbie at Life Size." *Sex Roles* 34: 287–294.
Obama, Barrack. 2004. *Dreams of My Father: A Story of Race and Inheritance*. New York: Three Rivers Press.
O'Brien, Robert, and Morris Chafetz. 1991. *The Encyclopedia of Alcoholism*. 2nd ed. New York: Facts on File Press.
O'Connor, Patrick, and Anderson Spickard. 1997. "Physician Impairment by Substance Abuse." *Medical Clinics of North America* 81: 1037–1052.
O'Dell, Rob, and Anne Ryman. 2016. "'It Means Her Life Was Not in Vain': The Tragedy That Gave Birth to the Clery Act." *The Arizona Republic*. Accessed on November 8, 2016 at http://www.azcentral.com/story/news/local/arizona-investigations/2016/04/15/tragedy-that-gave-birth-to-clery-act/82811052/
Ogas, Ogi, and Sai Gaddam. 2011. *A Billion Wicked Thoughts: What the Internet Tells Us about Sexual Relations*. New York: Penguin.
Ogden, Cynthia L., Margaret D. Carroll, Brian K. Kit, and Katherine M. Flegal. 2014. "Prevalence of Childhood and Adult Obesity in the United States, 2011–2012." *Journal of the American Medical Association* 311: 806–814.
Oliver, J. Eric. 2006. *Fat Politics: The Real Story behind America's Obesity Epidemic*. New York: Oxford University Press.
Orbach, Susie. 1978. *Fat is a Feminist Issue: A Self-Help Guide for Compulsive Eaters*. New York: Paddington Press.
Pager, Devah. 2003. "The Mark of a Criminal Record." *American Journal of Sociology* 108: 937–975.
Park, Robert E. and Ernest Burgess, eds. 1925. *The City*. Chicago: University of Chicago Press.
Parsons, Sharon K., Peter L. Cruise, Walisa M. Davenport, and Vanessa Jones. 2006. "Religious Beliefs, Practices and Treatment Adherence among Individuals with HIV in the Southern United States." *AIDS Patient Care and STDs*. 20: 97–111.
Pascoe, C. J. 2007. *Dude, You're a Fag: Masculinity and Sexuality in High School*. Berkeley: University of California Press.
Passas, Nikos. 1990. "Anomie and Corporate Deviance." *Contemporary Crises* 14: 157–178.
Pearl, Julie. 1987. "The Highest Paying Customers: America's Cities and the Costs of Prostitution Control." *Hastings Law Journal* 38: 769–800.
Perey, Ron J. 1991. "Hemophiliacs, Transfusions, and AIDS." *Trial Diplomacy Journal* 14: 137–158.
Perez-y-Perez, Maria-Victoria. 2003. "Discipline, Autonomy and Ambiguity: Organisations, Markets and Work in the Sex Industry." PhD diss., University of Canterbury, Christchurch, New Zealand.
Peters, Lulu. 1924. *Diet for Children (and Adults) and the Kalorie Kids*. New York: Dodd, Mead, and Co.
Petit, C. 1993. "New Evidence of 'Gay Gene' in Some Men: Study Says Hereditary Trait is Passed along by Mother." *San Francisco Chronicle*. July 16: A1.
Pew Hispanic Center. 2015. "Five Facts about Illegal Immigration in the U.S." Accessed on September 6, 2015 at http://www.pewresearch.org/fact-tank/2015/07/24/5-facts-about-illegal-immigration-in-the-u-s/
Pew Research Center. 2012. *Time Served: The High Cost, Low Return of Longer Prison Terms*. Accessed on August 14, 2016 at http://www.pewtrusts.org/~/media/legacy/uploadedfiles/wwwpewtrustsorg/reports/sentencing_and_corrections/prisontimeservedpdf.pdf

———. 2015a. "Less Support for Death Penalty, Especially among Democrats." Accessed on August 26, 2016 at http://www.people-press.org/2015/04/16/less-support-for-death-penalty-especially-among-democrats/

———. 2015b. "Continued Bipartisan Support for Expanded Background Checks on Gun Sales." Accessed on August 26, 2016 at http://www.people-press.org/2015/08/13/continued-bipartisan-support-for-expanded-background-checks-on-gun-sales

———. 2015c. "In Debate over Legalizing Marijuana, Disagreement over Drug's Dangers." Accessed on July 27, 2016 at http://www.people-press.org/2015/04/14/in-debate-over-legalizing-marijuana-disagreement-over-drugs-dangers/#current-opinion-on-legalizing-marijuana

Pfeifer, Stuart, and Tom Petruno. 2009. "Michael Milken Is Still Seeking Redemption." *Los Angeles Times*. Accessed on June 17, 2012 at articles.latimes.com/2009/feb/03/business/fi-milken3

PFLAG. 2016. "About PFLAG." Accessed on February 19, 2016 at https://www.pflag.org/about

Plowman, Timothy. 1986. "Coca Chewing and the Botanical Origins of Coca in South America." Pp. 5–33 in *Coca and Cocaine: Effects on People and Policy in Latin America*, edited by Debra Pacini and Christine Franquemont. Cambridge, MA: Cultural Survival, Inc.

Polikoff, Nancy D. 2008. *Beyond Straight and Gay Marriage: Valuing All Families under the Law*. Boston: Beacon Press.

Polk, Kenneth. 1994. *When Men Kill: Scenarios of Masculine Violence*. New York: Cambridge University Press.

Polletta, Francesca. 1998. "Contending Stories: Narrative in Social Movements." *Qualitative Sociology* 21: 419–446.

Popenoe, Rebecca. 2005. "Ideal." Pp. 9–28 in *Fat: The Anthropology of an Obsession*, edited by Don Kulick and Anne Meneley. New York: Jeremy P. Tarcher.

Porter, Judith, and Louis Bonilla. 2010. "The Ecology of Street Prostitution." Pp. 163–186 in *Sex for Sale*, 2nd ed. edited by Ronald Weitzer. New York: Routledge.

Porter, Roy. 1986. "Rape—Does It Have a Historical Meaning?" Pp. 216–236 in *Rape*, edited by Sylvania Tomasell and Roy Porter. Oxford: Basic Blackwell.

———. 1988. *A Social History of Madness: The World through the Eyes of the Insane*. New York: E.P. Dutton.

Powter, Susan. 1993. *Stop the Insanity*. New York: Simon and Schuster.

President's Commission on Law Enforcement and Administration of Justice. 1967. *Task Force Report: Narcotics and Drug Abuse*. Washington, DC: U.S. Government Printing Office.

Price-Glynn, Kim. 2010. *Strip Club: Gender, Power, and Sex Work*. New York: New York University Press.

Prince, Diana. 1986. "A Psychological Study of Prostitutes in California and Nevada." PhD diss., San Diego, CA: U.S. International University.

Progrebin, Mark, Paul B. Stretesky, N. Prabha Unnithan, and Gerry Venor. 2006. "Retrospective Accounts of Violent Events by Gun Offenders." *Deviant Behavior* 27: 479–501.

Pryor, Douglas W. 1996. *Unspeakable Acts: Why Men Sexually Abuse Children*. New York: New York University Press.

Pulliam, Susan, and Rob Barry. 2013. "Executives Hit Stock-Sales Sweet Spot." *Wall Street Journal*. November 14, A1, A16.

Quinlan, Kyran P., Robert D. Brewer, Paul Siegel, David A. Sleet, Ali H. Mokdad, Ruth A. Shults, and Nicole Flowers. 2005. "Alcohol-impaired Driving among U.S. Adults, 1993–2002." *American Journal of Preventive Medicine* 28: 345–350.

Ragatz, Laurie, and William Fremouw. 2010. "A Critical Examination of Research on the Psychological Profiles of White Collar Criminals." *Journal of Forensic Psychology Practice* 10: 373–402.

Rahman, Mahbubur, and Abbey B. Berenson. 2010. "Self-perception of Weight and Its Association with Weight-related Behaviors in Young Reproductive-age Women." *Obstetrics & Gynecology* 116: 1274–1280.

Rashbaum, William K. 2013. "With Special Courts, State Aims to Steer Women Away From Sex Trade." *New York Times*. September 25. Accessed on February 16, 2015 at http://www.nytimes.com/2013/09/26/nyregion/special-courts-for-human-trafficking-and-prostitution-cases-are-planned-in-new-york.html?_r=0

Rasmussen, Nicholas. 2008. "America's First Amphetamine Epidemic 1929–1971: A Quantitative and Qualitative Retrospective with Implications for the Present." *American Journal of Public Health* 98: 974–985.

Ray, Melvin C., and Ronald L. Simons. 1987. "Convicted Murderers' Accounts of Their Crimes: A Study of Homicide in Small Communities." *Symbolic Interaction* 10: 57–70.

Redlich, Allison D., Henry J. Steadman, John Monahan, Pamela Clark Robbins, and John Petrila. 2006. "Patterns of Practice in Mental Health Courts: A National Survey." *Law and Human Behavior* 30: 347–362.

RedUP (Red Umbrella Project). 2015. "Prose and Lore: The RedUP Literary Journal." Accessed on March 15, 2015 at http://redumbrellaproject.org/

Reese, William, and Michael A. Katovich. 1991. "Untimely Acts: Extending the Interactionist's Conception of Deviance." *The Sociological Quarterly* 30: 159–184.

Reiman, Jeffrey and Paul Leighton. 2013. *The Rich Get Richer and the Poor Get Prison: Ideology, Class, and Criminal Justice*. 10th ed. New York: Routledge.

Reinarman, Craig. 2009. "The Social Construction of Drug Scares." Pp. 139–150 in *Constructions of Deviance*. 5th ed., edited by Patricia A. Adler and Peter Adler. Belmont, CA: Thomson/Wadsworth.

Reinarman, Craig, and Harry G. Levine, eds. 1997. *Crack in America: Demon Drugs and Social Justices*. Berkeley: University of California Press.

Reiss, Albert. 1961. "The Social Integration of Queers and Peers." *Social Problems* 9: 102–120.

Reith, Gerda. 2005. "On the Edge: Drugs and the Consumption of Risk in Late Modernity." Pp. 227–244 in *Edgework: The Sociology of Risk-Taking*, edited by Stephen Lyng. New York: Routledge.

Rensenbrink, Greta. 2010. "Fat's No Four-Letter Word: Fat Feminism and Identity Politics in the 1970s and 1980." Pp. 212–238 in *Historicizing Fat in Anglo-American Culture*, edited by Elena Levy-Navarro. Columbus, OH: Ohio State University Press.

Reynolds, Gretchen. 2012. "After Liposuction, Exercise Keeps the Fat Off." *New York Times*. June 13. Accessed on March 26, 2016 at http://well.blogs.nytimes.com/2012/06/13/after-liposuction-exercise-keeps-the-fat-off/?_r=0

Rezaee, Zabihollah. 2005. "Causes, Consequences, and Deterrence of Financial Statement Fraud." *Critical Perspectives on Accounting* 16: 277–298.

Richman, Kimberly D. 2010. *Courting Change: Queer Parents, Judges, and the Transformation of American Family Law*. New York: New York University Press.

Riedel, Marc. 2008. "Homicide Arrest Clearances: A Review of the Literature." *Sociology Compass* 2: 1145–1164.

Ringdal, Nils Johan. 2004. *Love for Sale: A World History of Prostitution*. New York: Grove Press.
Ripley's. 2006. "Orlando's Only Odditorium." Accessed on October 12, 2006 at http://www.ripleysorlando.com/info/
Roach, Catherine M. 2007. *Stripping, Sex, and Popular Culture*. New York: Berg.
Roberts, Nickie. 1992. *Whores in History*. London: HarperCollins.
Robertson, Mary Anna. 2014. "'How Do I Know I Am Gay?': Understanding Sexual Orientation, Identity and Behavior among Adolescents in an LGBT Youth Center." *Sexuality and Culture* 18: 385–404.
Robinson, Brandon Andrew, and Salvador Vidal-Ortiz. 2013. "Displacing the Dominant 'Down Low' Discourse: Deviance, Same-Sex Desire, and Craigslist.org." *Deviant Behavior* 34: 224–241.
Rodgers, R. John, P. Holch, and A. J. Tallett. 2010. "Behavioural Satiety Sequence (BSS): Separating Wheat from Chaff in the Behavioural Pharmacology of Appetite." *Pharmacological Biochemical Behavior* 97: 3–14.
Rodgers, R. John, Matthias H. Tschöp, and John P. H. Wilding. 2012. "Anti-obesity Drugs: Past, Present, and Future." *Disease Models and Mechanisms* 5: 621–626.
Rodin, Judith, Lisa Silberstein, and Ruth Striegel-Moore. 1985. "Women and Weight: A Normative Discontent." Pp. 267–308 in *Nebraska Symposium on Motivation, Psychology and Gender*, edited by T. B. Sonderegger. Lincoln, NB: University of Nebraska.
Ronai, Carol Rambo. 1998. "Sketching with Derrida: An Ethnography of a Researcher/Erotic Dancer." *Qualitative Inquiry* 4: 405–420.
———. 1999. "Wrestling with Derrida's Mimesis: The Next Night Sous Rature." *Qualitative Inquiry* 5: 114–129.
Rooney, James F. 1961. "Group Processes among Skid Row Winos: A Reevaluation of the Undersocialization Hypothesis." *Quarterly Journal of Studies on Alcohol* 22: 444–460.
Roper, W. G. 1996. "The Etiology of Male Homosexuality." *Medical Hypotheses* 46: 85–88.
Rosen, Ruth. 1982. *The Lost Sisterhood: Prostitution in America, 1900–1918*. Baltimore: Johns Hopkins Press.
Rosenblatt, Robert A. 2001. "Surgeon General Takes Stern Stance on Obesity." *Los Angeles Times*. December 14. Accessed on February 27, 2016 at http://articles.latimes.com/2001/dec/14/news/mn-14788
Rosenfeld, Richard, Steven F. Messner, and Eric P. Baumer. 2001. "Social Capital and Homicide." *Social Forces* 80: 283–309.
Rosenhan, David L. 1973. "On Being Sane in Insane Places." *Science* 179: 250–258.
Rosoff, Stephen M., Henry N. Pontell, and Robert H. Tillman. 2014. *Profit without Honor: White Collar Crime and the Looting America*. 6th ed. New York: Pearson.
Ross, Edward A. 1907. *Sin and Society: An Analysis of Later Day Iniquity*. New York: Harper and Row.
Ross, H. Laurence. 1992. *Confronting Drunk Driving: Social Policy for Saving Lives*. New Haven, CT: Yale University Press.
Rudy, David R. 1986. *Becoming Alcoholic: Alcoholics Anonymous and the Reality of Alcoholism*. Carbondale, IL: Southern Illinois University Press.
Rupp, Leila J. 1999. *A Desired Past: A Short History of Same-Sex Love in America*. Chicago: University of Chicago Press.
———. 2009. *Sapphistries: A Global History of Love between Women*. New York: New York University Press.
———. 2012. "Sexual Fluidity 'Before Sex.'" *Signs: Journal of Women in Culture and Society* 37: 849–856.
Rupp, Leila J. and Verta Taylor. 2003. *Drag Queens at the 801 Cabaret*. Chicago: University of Chicago Press.
Rupp, Leila J., and Verta Taylor. 2010. "Straight Girls Kissing." *Contexts* 9: 28–32.
Russell, Stephen R. and Kara Joyner. 2001. "Adolescent Sexual Orientation and Suicide Risk: Evidence from a National Study." *American Journal of Public Health* 19: 1276–1281.
Rutter, Michael. 2005. *Upstairs Girls: Prostitution in the American West*. Helena, MT: Farcountry Press.
Saguy, Abigail C. 2013. *What's Wrong with Fat?* New York: Oxford University Press.
Salgado, Gamini. 1972. *Cony-catchers and Bawdy Baskets: An Anthology of Elizabethan Low Life*. Harmondsworth: Penguin.
SAMHSA (Substance Abuse and Mental Health Services Administration). 2012. *Center for Behavioral Health Statistics and Quality, National Survey on Drug Use and Health, 2011 and 2012*. Accessed on December 28, 2013 at http://www.samhsa.gov/data/NSDUH/2012SummNatFindDetTables/DetTabs/NSDUH-DetTabsSect1peTabs1to46-2012.htm
Sampson, Robert J., and W. Byron Groves. 1989. "Community Structure and Crime: Testing Social Disorganization Theory." *American Journal of Sociology* 94: 774–802.
Sampson, Robert J., and Stephen W. Raudenbush. 2004. "Seeing Disorder: Neighborhood Stigma and the Social Construction of 'Broken Windows.'" *Social Psychology Quarterly* 67: 319–342.
Sanday, Peggy Reeves.1981. "The Socio-Cultural Context of Rape: A Cross-Cultural Study." *Journal of Social Issues* 37: 5–27.
Sandberg, Sveinung, and Heith Copes. 2013. "Speaking With Ethnographers: The Challenges of Researching Drug Dealers and Offenders." *Journal of Drug Issues* 43: 176–197.
Sanders, Rachel. 2016. "Self-tracking in the Digital Era: Biopower, Patriarchy, and the New Biometric Body Projects." *Body and Society* Online First at http://bod.sagepub.com.dist.lib.usu.edu/content/early/2016/07/18/1357034X16660366.full.pdf+html
Sanders, Teela. 2005. *Sex Work: A Risky Business*. Portland, OR: Willan Publishing.
———. 2008. *Paying for Pleasure: Men Who Buy Sex*. Portland, OR: Willan Publishing.
Sarasalo, Elina, Bo Bergman, and Janos Toth. 1997. "Kleptomania-Like Behaviour and Psychosocial Characteristics among Shoplifters." *Criminological Psychology* 2(1): 1–10.
Sarason, Irwin G., and Barbara R. Sarason. 2005. *Abnormal Psychology: The Problem of Maladaptive Behavior*. 11th ed. Upper Saddle River, NJ: Pearson/Prentice Hall.
Savin-Williams, Ritch C. 2005. *The New Gay Teenager*. Cambridge, MA: Harvard University Press.
Scarborough, John. 1995. "The Opium Poppy in Hellenistic and Roman Culture." Pp. 4–23 in *Drugs and Narcotics in History*, edited by Roy Porter and Mikulas Teich. Cambridge, UK: Cambridge University Press.
Schafer, Judith Kelleher. 2009. *Brothels, Depravity, and Abandoned Women: Illegal Sex in Antebellum New Orleans*. Baton Rouge, LA: Louisiana State University Press.
Schlosser, Eric. 2001. *Fast Food Nation: The Dark Side of the All-American Meal*. New York: Houghton Mifflin Co.
Schultes, Richard Evans, and Albert Hoffman. 1992. *Plants of the Gods: Their Sacred, Healing and Hallucinogenic Powers*. Rochester, VT: Healing Arts Press.
Schuman, Howard and Stanley Presser. 2013. "The Gun Control Paradox." *Contexts* 12: 68–19.

Schur, Edwin M. 1971. *Labeling Deviant Behavior: Its Sociological Implications*. New York: Harper and Row.

Schutz, Alfred. 1962. *Collected Papers of Alfred Schutz*, Vol. 1. The Hague, Netherlands: Martinus Nijhoff.

Schwartz, Hillel. 1986. *Never Satisfied: A Cultural History of Diets, Fantasies, and Fat*. New York: Free Press.

Scot, Jamie. 2013. "Shock the Gay Away: Secrets of Early Gay Aversion Therapy Revealed." *Huffington Post*. June 28. Accessed on February 21, 2016 at http://www.huffingtonpost.com/jamie-scot/shock-the-gay-away-secrets-of-early-gay-aversion-therapy-revealed_b_3497435.html

Scott, Marvin B. and Stanford M. Lyman. 1968. "Accounts." *American Sociological Review* 33: 46–62.

Scully, Diana. 1990. *Understanding Sexual Violence: A Study of Convicted Rapists*. Boston: Unwin Hyman.

Segall, Grant. 2001. *John D. Rockefeller: Anointed With Oil*. New York: Oxford University Press.

Seidman, Steven. 2002. *Beyond the Closet: The Transformation of Gay and Lesbian Life*. New York: Routledge.

Sell, Randal L. 1997. "Defining and Measuring Sexual Orientation: A Review." *Archives of Sexual Behavior* 26: 643–657.

Sellin, Thorstein. 1938. *Culture Conflict and Crime*. New York: Social Science Research Council.

SF Pride. 2016. *SF Pride Parade*. Accessed on January 10, 2016 at http://www.sfpride.org/parade/

Sharfman, Keith. 2007. "The Law and Economics of Hoarding." *Loyola Consumer Law Review* 19: 179–193.

Sharkey, Patrick. 2013. *Stuck in Place: Urban Neighborhoods and the End of Progress toward Racial Equality*. Chicago: University of Chicago Press.

Shaw, Clifford R., and Henry D. McKay. 1938. *Brothers in Crime*. Philadelphia: Albert Saifer.

———. 1942. *Juvenile Delinquency in Urban Areas*. Chicago: University of Chicago Press.

Shea, Christopher. 2009. "An Anthropologist Bridges Two Worlds." *Chronicle of Higher Education* 55(39): B1–B6. Accessed on December 8, 2106 at http://www.philippebourgois.net/Chronicle%20of%20Higher%20Education%202009.pdf

Sheldon, William Herbert. 1949. *Varieties of Delinquent Youth: An Introduction to Constitutional Psychiatry*. New York: Harper.

Shively, Michael. 2016. "Shaming." Demandforum.net. Accessed on October 3, 2016 at http://www.demandforum.net/shaming/

Shover, Neal. 1984. "The Official Construction of Deviant Identities." Pp. 66–74 in *The Sociology of Deviance*, edited by Jack D. Douglas. Boston: Allyn and Bacon.

———. 1985. *Aging Criminals*. Beverley Hills: Sage.

———. 1996. *Great Pretenders: Pursuits and Careers of Persistent Thieves*. Boulder, CO: Westview Press.

Shover, Neal, and Andy Hochstetler. 2006. *Choosing White-Collar Crime*. New York: Cambridge University Press.

Shover, Neal, and David Honaker. 1992. "The Socially Bounded Decision Making of Persistent Property Offenders." *Howard Journal of Criminal Justice* 31: 276–293.

Showalter, Elaine. 1987. *The Female Malady: Women, Madness, and English Culture, 1830–1980*. New York: Penguin Books.

Shteir, Rachel. 2011. *The Steal: A Cultural History of Shoplifting*. New York: Penguin Press.

Siegel, Larry J. 2007. *Criminology: Theories, Patterns, and Typologies*. Belmont, CA: Thomson/Wadsworth.

Simon, David R., and Stanley Eitzen. 2012. *Elite Deviance*. 10th ed. New York: Pearson.

Slade, Joseph W. 2000. *Pornography in America*. Santa Barbara, CA: ABC-CLIO, Inc.

Smith-Jackson, TeriSue, and Justin J. Reel. 2012. "Freshmen Women and the 'Freshman 15': Perspectives on the Prevalence and Causes of College Weight Gain." *American Journal of College Health* 60: 14–20.

Snider, Lauren. 2000. "The Sociology of Corporate Crime: An Obituary." *Theoretical Criminology* 4: 169–206.

Snow, David A. and Leon Anderson. 1993. *Down on Their Luck: A Study of Homeless Street People*. Berkeley, CA: University of California Press.

Snow, David A. and Robert D. Benford. 1988. "Ideology, Frame Resonance, and Participant Mobilization." *International Social Movements Research* 1: 197–218.

Snow, David A., E. Burke Rochford, Steven K. Worden, and Robert D. Benford. 1986a. "Frame Alignment Processes, Micromobilization, and Movement Participation." *American Sociological Review* 51: 464–481.

Snow, David A., Leon Anderson, and Susan Gonzalez-Baker. 1989. "Criminality and Homeless Men: An Empirical Assessment." *Social Problems* 36: 532–549.

Snow, David A., Leon Anderson, Susan Gonzalez-Baker, and Michael Martin. 1986b. "The Myth of Pervasive Mental Illness among the Homeless," *Social Problems* 33: 407–423.

Sobal, Jeffery, and Donna Maurer, eds. 1999. *Weighty Issues: Fatness and Thinness as Social Problems*. Hawthorne, New York: Aldine de Gruyter.

Solovay, Sondra. 2000. *Tipping the Scales of Justice: Fighting Weight-Based Discrimination*. Amherst, NY: Prometheus Books.

Sommerville, Dianne Miller. 2004. *Rape and Race in the Nineteenth Century South*. Chapel Hill: University of North Carolina Press.

Sournia, Jean-Charles. 1990. *A History of Alcoholism*. Cambridge, MA: Oxford University Press.

Speciale, Megan, Jennifer Gess, and Stacy Speedlin. 2015. "You Don't Look Like a Lesbian: A Coautoethnography of Intersectional Identities in Counselor Education." *Journal of LGBT Issues in Counseling* 9: 256–272.

Spector, Malcom, and John I. Kitsuse. 1977. *Constructing Social Problems*. Menlo Park, CA: Cummings.

Spivey, Sue E. 2005. "Distancing and Solidarity as Resistance to Sexual Objectification in a Nude Dancing Bar." *Deviant Behavior* 26: 417–437.

Spohn, Cassia, and David Holleran. 2001. "Prosecuting Sexual Assault: A Comparison of Charging Decisions in Sexual Assault Cases Involving Strangers, Acquaintances, and Intimate Partners." *Justice Quarterly* 18: 651–688.

Spohn, Cassia, R. K. Piper, Tom Martin, and Erica Davis Frenzel. (2001). "Drug Courts and Recidivism: The Results of an Evaluation Using Two Comparison Groups and Multiple Indicators of Recidivism." *Journal of Drug Issues* 31: 149–176.

Spradley, James P. 1970. *You Owe Yourself a Drunk: An Ethnography of Urban Nomads*. Boston: Little, Brown, and Company.

Spradley, James P., and Brenda J. Mann. 1974. *The Cocktail Waitress: Woman's Work in a Man's World*. New York: Wiley.

Stanton, Robert. 2013. "Burger King Faces Lawsuit over Prostitution Claims." *Beaumont Enterprise*. July 19. Accessed on February 16, 2015 at http://www.beaumontenterprise.com/news/houston-texas/houston/article/Burger-King-faces-lawsuit-over-prostitution-claims-4675636.php

Stark, Rodney. 1987. "Deviant Places: A Theory of the Ecology of Crime." *Criminology* 25: 893–909.

Stearns, Peter N. 1997. *Fat History: Bodies and Beauty in the Modern West*. New York: New York University Press.

Stephens-Davidowitz, Seth. 2013. "How Many American Men are Gay?" *New York Times*. Accessed on January 10, 2016 at

http://www.nytimes.com/2013/12/08/opinion/sunday/how-many-american-men-are-gay.html
Sterk, Claire E. 1999. *Fast Lives. Women Who Use Crack Cocaine.* Philadelphia, PA: Temple University Press.
Stewart, James B. 1992. *Den of Thieves.* New York: Simon and Schuster.
Stice, Eric, Melissa Fisher, and Erin Martinez. 2004. "Eating Disorder Diagnostic Scale: Additional Evidence of Reliability and Validity." *Psychological Assessment* 16: 60–71.
Stice, Eric, Katherine Presnell, Heather Shaw, and Paul Rhode. 2005. "Psychological and Behavioral Risk Factors for Obesity Onset in Adolescent Girls: A Prospective Study." *Journal of Consulting and Clinical Psychology* 73: 195–202.
Stivers, Richard. 2000. *Hair of the Dog: Irish Drinking and Its American Stereotype.* New York: Continuum.
Stockhammer, Morris, ed. 1965. *Thomas Aquinas Dictionary.* New York: Philosophical Library.
Strauss, Anselm L. 1962. "Transformations of Identity." Pp. 63–85 in *Human Behavior and Social Processes: An Interactionist Approach*, edited by Arnold M. Rose. London: Routledge & Kegan Paul.
Sudnow, David. 1965. "Normal Crimes: Sociological Features of the Penal Code in a Public Defender's Office." *Social Problems* 13: 255–276.
Sunday, Billy. 1920. "Booze Sermon." Accessed on April 20, 2007 at www.billysunday.org/sermons.
Surowlecki, James. 2015. "Taking on the N.R.A." *New Yorker.* October 19. Accessed on August 26, 2016 at http://www.newyorker.com/magazine/2015/10/19/taking-on-the-n-r-a
Sutherland, Edwin. 1940. "White-collar Criminality." *American Sociological Review* 5: 1–12.
———. 1949. *White Collar Crime.* New York: Holt, Rinehart, and Winston.
———. 1983. *White Collar Crime: The Uncut Version.* New Haven: Yale University Press.
Sutherland, Edwin H. 1937. *The Professional Thief.* Chicago: University of Chicago Press.
Sutherland, Edwin H., Donald R. Cressey, and David F. Luckenbill. 1992. *Principles of Criminology.* 11th ed. New York: Alta Mira Press.
Sykes, Gresham M. and David Matza. 1957. "Techniques of Neutralization: A Theory of Delinquency." *American Sociological Review* 22: 664–670.
Szaz, Thomas S. 1961. *The Myth of Mental Illness: Foundations of a Theory of Personal Conduct.* New York: Harper and Row.
———. 2001. *Pharmacracy: Medicine and Politics in America.* London: Praeger.
Tannahill, Reay. 1982. *Sex in History.* New York: Scarborough Books.
Tannenbaum, Frank. 1938. *Crime and Community.* New York: Ginn.
Terry, W. Clinton, III, and David F. Luckenbill. 1976. "Investigating Criminal Homicides: Police Work in Reporting and Solving Murders." Pp. 79–95 in *The Criminal Justice Process: A Reader*, edited by William B. Sanders and H. C. Daudistel. New York: Praeger.
Tewksbury, Richard, and Patricia Gagne. 2006. "Assumed and Presumed Identities: Problems of Self-Presentation in Field Research." Pp. 51–73 in *Research Methods: A Qualitative Reader*, edited by J. Mitchell Miller and Richard Tewksbury. Upper Saddle River, NJ: Pearson/Prentice Hall.
The Village Voice. 2010. "Audacia Ray—Best Sex Blogger." *The Village Voice.* Accessed on April 7, 2017 at http://www.villagevoice.com/best-of/2010/sports-and-recreation/best-sex-blogger-6449204
The Week. 2014. "Weed, Inc." May 30, 9.
Thompson, William E., Jackie L. Harred, and Barbara Burks. 2003. "Managing the Stigma of Topless Dancing: A Decade Later." *Deviant Behavior* 24: 551–570.
Thorne, Deborah, and Leon Anderson. 2006. "Managing the Stigma of Personal Bankruptcy." *Sociological Focus* 39: 77–97.
Thornhill, Randy, and Craig T. Palmer. 2000. *A Natural History of Rape: Biological Bases of Sexual Coercion.* Cambridge, MA: MIT Press.
Thoits, Peggy A. 1995. "Stress, Coping, and Social Support Processes? Where Are We? What Next?" *Journal of Health and Social Behavior* 35: 53–79.
Time Warner. 2009. "Fortune Survey: NRA Deemed Most Powerful Lobbyist by Lawmakers and their Staffers." Accessed on August 4, 2009 at http://www.timewarner.com/corp/newsroom/pr/0,20812,667546,00.html
Tlusty, B. Ann. 2001. *Bacchus and Civic Order: The Culture of Drink in Early Modern Germany.* Charlottesville: University of Virginia Press.
Tobach, Ethel, and Rachel Reed. 2003. "Understanding Rape." Pp.105–138 in *Evolution, Gender, and Rape*, edited by Cheryl Travis. Cambridge, MA: The M.I.T. Press.
Tonry, Michael. 1995. *Malign Neglect.* New York: Oxford University Press.
Torrey, E. Fuller. 1988. *Nowhere to Go: The Tragic Odyssey of the Homeless Mentally Ill.* New York: Harper and Row.
Torrey, E. Fuller, Joan Steiber, Jonathan Ezekial, Sydney M. Wolfe, Joshua Sharfstein, John H. Noble, and Laurie M. Flynn. 1992. *Criminalizing the Seriously Mentally Ill: The Abuse of Jails as Mental Hospitals.* Washington, DC: Public Citizens' Health Research Group and the National Alliance for the Mentally Ill.
Trautner, Mary Nell. 2005. "Doing Gender, Doing Class: The Performance of Sexuality in Exotic Dance Clubs." *Gender and Society* 19: 771–788.
Trautner, Mary Nell, and Jessica L. Collett. 2010. "Students Who Strip: The Benefits of Alternate Identities for Managing Stigma." *Symbolic Interaction* 33: 257–279.
Trawver, Kathi R., and Stephanie L. Rhoades. 2013. "Homesteading a Pioneer Mental Health Court: A Judicial Perspective from the Last Frontier." *American Behavioral Scientist* 57: 174–188.
Trenerry, Charles F. 2009. *The Origin and Early History of Insurance.* London, UK: Law Book Exchange, Ltd.
Tribole, Evelyn, and Elyse Resch. 2012. *Intuitive Eating.* 3rd ed. New York: St. Martin's Press.
Trice, Harrison M. and Paul Michael Roman. 1970. "Delabeling, Relabeling, and Alcoholics Anonymous." *Social Problems* 17: 538–546.
Trimbur, Lucia. 2009. "'Me and the Law is Not Friends': How Former Prisoners Make Sense of Reentry." *Qualitative Sociology* 32: 259–227.
Trounson, Rebecca. 2013. "Jeanne Manford Dies at 92; Co-founder of Group for Parents of Gays." *Los Angeles Times.* Accessed on November 10, 2016 at http://www.latimes.com/local/obituaries/la-me-jeanne-manford-20130110-story.html
Tunnell, Kenneth D. 1998. "Honesty, Secrecy, and Deception in the Sociology of Crime: Confessions and Reflections from Backstage." Pp. 206–220 in *Ethnography at the Edge: Crime, Deviance, and Field Research*, edited by Jeff Ferrell and Mark Hamm. Boston: Northeastern University Press.
———. 2006. *Living Off Crime.* 2nd ed. Boulder, CO: Rowman and Littlefield Publishers.
Tuck, Angela. 2013. "Genarlow Wilson's Journey from Prison to Morehouse." *The Atlanta Journal-Constitution.* Accessed on

June 29, 2016 at http://www.myajc.com/news/news/crime-law/genarlow-wilsons-journey-from-prison-to-morehouse/nXwB2/
Turner, Ralph H. 1972. "Deviance Avowal as Neutralization of Commitment." *Social Problems* 19: 308–321.
United Nations. 2012. *Crime and Criminal Justice Statistics*. Accessed on June 30, 2016 at https://www.unodc.org/unodc/en/data-and-analysis/statistics/crime.html
USA Today. 2007. "Record for Blind Skier: 100 MPH." Accessed on August 10, 2007 at http://blogs.usatoday.com/ondeadline/2006/04/blind_skier_set.html
Vander Ven, Thomas. 1998. "Fear of Victimization and the Interactional Construction of Harassment in a Latino Neighborhood." *Journal of Contemporary Ethnography* 27: 374–398.
———. 2011. *Getting Wasted; Why College Students Drink too Much and Party So Hard*. New York: New York University Press.
Vecitis, Katherine Sirles. 2012. "Drugs and Eating Disorders: Women's Instrumental Drug Use for Weight Control." Pp. 141–151 in *Drugs and the American Dream: An Anthology*, edited by Patricia A. Adler, Peter Adler, and Patrick K. O'Brien. West Sussex, UK: John Wiley and Sons.
Vendantam, Shankar. 2006. "Federal Study Finds No Benefit Over Older Cheaper Drugs." *Washington Post*. September 20.
Venkatesh, Sudhir. 2011. "How Tech Tools Transformed New York's Sex Trade." *Wired*. Accessed on October 18, 2014 at http://www.wired.com/2011/01/ff_sextrade/all/
Vera Institute of Justice. 2016. "Pathways from Prison to Postsecondary Education Project." Accessed on May 30, 2016 at http://archive.vera.org/project/pathways-prison-postsecondary-education-project
Vigarello, Georges. 2001. *A History of Rape: Sexual Violence in France from the 16th to the 20th Century*. Cambridge, UK: Polity Press.
Vogler, Robin Jane Marie. 1993. *The Medicalization of Eating: Social Control in an Eating Disorders Clinic*. Greenwich, CT: JAI Press.
von Fritz, Kurt, and Ernst Kapp. 1950. *Aristotle's Constitution of Athens and Related Texts*. New York: Hafner Publishing Co.
Wacquant, Loïc. 2008. *Urban Outcasts: A Comparative Sociology of Advanced Marginality*. Cambridge: Polity Press.
Wacquant, Loïc J. D. 1998. "Negative Social Capital: State Breakdown and Social Destitution in America's Urban Core." *Netherlands Journal of Housing and the Built Environment* 13: 25–40.
Waldorf, Dan, Craig Reinarman, and Sheigla Murphy. 1991. *Cocaine Changes: The Experience of Using and Quitting*. Philadelphia: Temple University Press.
Walters, Suzanna Danuta. 2014. *The Tolerance Trap: How God, Genes, and Good Intentions Are Sabotaging Gay Equality*. New York: New York University Press.
Wann, Marilyn. 1998. *FAT?SO! Because You Don't Have to Apologize for Your Size*. Berkeley, CA: Ten Speed Press.
Wann, Marilyn. 2009. "Foreward: Fat Studies: An Invitation of Revolution." Pp. xi–xxvi in *The Fat Studies Reader*, edited by Esther Rothblum and Sondra Solovay. New York: New York University Press.
Ward, Brian, James Dahlhamer, Adena Galinsky, and Sarah Joestl. 2014. "Sexual Orientation and Health among U.S. Adults: National Health Interview Survey, 2013." *National Health Statistics Reports* 77: 1–10.
Ward, Jane. 2015. *Not Gay: Sex between Straight White Men*. New York: New York University Press.
Warren, Elizabeth. 2016. "Rigged Justice 2016: How Weak Enforcement Let's Corporate Offenders off Easy." Washington, DC: U.S. Senate Office of Elizabeth Warren.
Waskul, Dennis, Mark Douglass, and Charles Edgley. 2000. "Cybersex: Outercourse and the Enselfment of the Body." *Symbolic Interaction* 23: 375–397.
Watford, Monique L. 2008. "Bereavement of Spousal Suicide: A Reflective Self-Exploration." *Qualitative Inquiry* 14: 335–359.
Weaver, Jay. 2016. "Feds Break up $1 Billion Medicare Scam in Miami — Biggest in U.S. History." *Miami Herald*, July 22. Accessed on April 6, 2017 at http://www.miamiherald.com/news/local/community/miami-dade/article91231277.html
Wechsler, Henry, Jae Eun Lee, Meichun Kuo, Mark Seibring, Toben Nelson, and Hang Lee. 2002. "Trends in College Binge Drinking During a Period of Increased Prevention Efforts." *Journal of American College Health* 50: 203–217.
Wechsler, Henry and Bernice Wuethrich. 2002. *Dying to Drink: Confronting Binge Drinking on College Campuses*. New York: Rodale.
Weiss, Karen G., and Lisa M. Dilks. 2016. "Intoxication and Crime Risk: Contextualizing the Effects of 'Party' Routines on Recurrent Physical and Sexual Attacks among College Students." *Criminal Justice Review* 41: 173–189.
Weiss, Rick. 2006. "Behavioral Genetics and the Media." Pp. 309–326 in *Wrestling with Behavioral Genetics: Science, Ethics, and Public Conversation*, edited by Erik Parens, Audrey Chapman, and Nancy Press. Baltimore: Johns Hopkins Press.
Weitzer, Ronald. 2009. "Sociology of Sex Work." *Annual Review of Sociology* 35: 213–234.
———. 2010. "Introduction." Pp. 1–11 in *Sex for Sale*, 2nd ed. edited by Ronald Weitzer. New York: Routledge.
———. 2013. "Researching Sex Work in the Twenty-First Century." *Contemporary Sociology* 42: 713–722.
Wesley, Jennifer K. 2003. "Exotic Dancing and the Negotiation of Identity." *Journal of Contemporary Ethnography* 32: 643–669.
White House. 1989. *National Drug Control Strategy*. Washington, DC: U.S. Government Printing Office.
———. 2016. "Commutations." Accessed on December 31, 2016 at www.whitehouse.gov/issues/clemency
Williams, Leonard Llewellyn Bulkeley. 1926. *Obesity*. London: Humphrey Milford.
Williams, Terry, Eloise Dunlap, Bruce D. Johnson, and Ansley Hamid. 1992. "Personal Safety in Dangerous Places." *Journal of Contemporary Ethnography* 21: 343–374.
Wilson, Robin. 2016. "'Yes' to Sex? How Students Deal with that Policy." *The Chronicle of Higher Education*, May 27: A10.
Wirth, Louis. 1938. "Urbanism as a Way of Life." *American Journal of Sociology* 44: 1–24.
Wodrich, David L. 2000. *Attention Deficit Hyperactivity Disorder: What Every Parent Wants to Know*, Revised ed. Baltimore: Paul H. Brooks Publishing.
Wolfthal, Diane. 1999. *Images of Rape: The "Heroic Tradition" and Its Alternatives*. New York: Cambridge University Press.
Wolff, Nancy. 2003. "Courting the Courts: Courts as Agents for Treatment and Justice." Pp. 143–198 in *Community-based Interventions for Criminal Offenders with Severe Mental Illness*, edited by W. H. Fisher. Boston, MA: JAI Press.
Wolfgang, Marvin E. 1958. *Patterns in Criminal Homicide*. Philadelphia: University of Pennsylvania Press.

Wolkomir, Michelle. 2006. *Be Not Deceived: The Sacred and Sexual Struggles of Gay and Ex-gay Christian Men*. New Brunswick, NJ: Rutgers University Press.

Wood, Elizabeth Anne. 2000. "Working in the Fantasy Factory: The Attention Hypothesis and the Enacting of Masculine Power in Strip Clubs." *Journal of Contemporary Ethnography* 29: 5–31.

Workman, Thomas A. 2001. "Finding the Meanings of College Drinking: An Analysis of Fraternity Drinking Stories." *Health Communication* 13: 427–447.

Wright, Richard T., and Scott H. Decker. 1994. *Burglars on the Job: Streetlife and Residential Break-Ins*. Boston: Northeastern University Press.

———. 1997. *Armed Robbers in Action: Stickups and Street Culture*. Boston: Northeastern University Press.

Wright, Richard, Scott H. Decker, Allison K. Redfern, and Dietrich L. Smith. 1992. "A Snowball's Chance in Hell: Doing Fieldwork with Active Residential Burglars." *Journal of Research in Crime and Delinquency* 29: 148–161.

Yap, P. M. 1965. "Koro: A Culture-Bound Depersonalization Syndrome." *British Journal of Psychiatry* 111: 69–79.

Yeager, Peter Cleary, and Kathy E. Kram. 1990. "Fielding Hot Topics in Cool Settings: The Study of Corporate Ethics." *Qualitative Sociology* 13: 127–148.

Young, Stephanie L., and Amie R. McKibban. 2014. "Creating Safe Places: A Collaborative Autoethnography on LGBT Social Activism." *Sexuality and Culture* 18: 361–384.

Zarinebaf, Fariba. 2010. *Crime and Punishment in Istanbul: 1700–1800*. Berkeley: University of California Press.

Zinberg, Norman E. 1984. *Drug, Set, and Setting: The Basis for Controlled Intoxicant Use*. New Haven, CT: Yale University Press.

Index

Note: The page locators with b, f, and t represents box, figure, and table, respectively.